THE BUILDINGS OF SCOTLAND

FOUNDING EDITORS:
NIKOLAUS PEVSNER
COLIN McWILLIAM

DUMFRIES AND GALLOWAY

JOHN GIFFORD

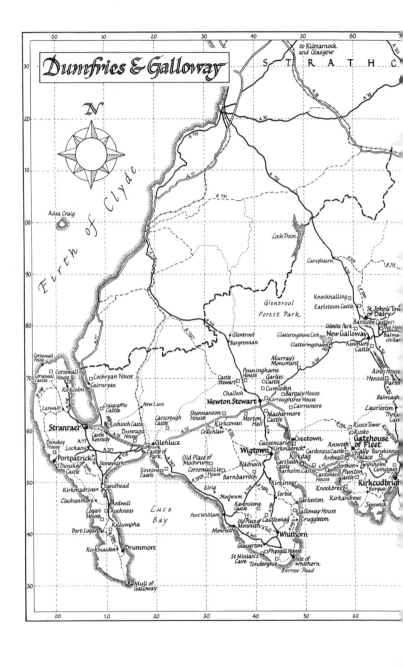

Dumfries & Galloway

STRATHC

to Kilmarnock
and Glasgow

N

Firth of Clyde

Ailsa Craig

Loch Doon

Carsphairn

Knocknalling
Earlstoun Castle

St John's Tow
of Dairy

Glentrool
Forest Park

Barscobe Castle
The Holm
Balma-
clellan

Glenlee Park

Glentrool
Bargrennan

Clatteringshaws Loch
Clatteringshaws

New Galloway

Kenmure
Castle

Corsewall
Point
Corsewall
House
Corsewall
Castle
Kirkcolm
Cairnryan
Lochryan House

Leswalt

New Luce

Craigcaffie
Castle

Castle
Stewart

Penninghame
House

Murray's
Monument

Garlies
Castle
Cumloden
Bargaly House
Kirroughtree House
Cairnsmore

Airds House
Henson
Parton

Balmagh

Stranraer

Lochinch Castle
Castle
Kennedy
Dunragit
House

Dunskey
House

Portpatrick

Dunskey
Castle

Stoneykirk

Castle of
Park

Glenluce

Carscreugh
Castle

Challoch

Shennanton
House

Newton Stewart

Kirkcowan

Craichlaw

Merton
Hall

Machermore
Castle

Laurieston
Threa
Cast

Rusco Tower
Rusko

Gatehouse
of Fleet

Cassencarie

Creetown

Anwoth

Cally
Palace

Barwhinn

Kirkmaden

Cardoness Castle
Carsluith
Castle
Kirkdale
Barholm Castle
Cardoness
House

Ardwall

Girthon
Plunton
Castle

Twynholm
Cumston

Kirkmadrine

Clachanmore

Logan
House

Sandhead

Antwell
Auchness

Killumpha

Port Logan

Drummore

Kirkmaiden

Mull of
Galloway

Luce
Bay

Wigtown
Kirkmabreck

Old Place of
Mochrum
Corsemailzie
House

Bladnoch

Barnbarroch

Elrig

Mochrum

Ravenstone
Castle

Port William

Kirkinner

Sorbie

Castlewigg
Galloway House
Cruggleton

Old Place of
Monreith

Garliestown

Monreith

Whithorn

Kirkandrews
Knockbrex

Knockbrex

Kirkcudbrigh

Sorque

Senwick

Glasserton

St Ninian's
Cave

Tonderghie

Physgill House
Isle of
Whithorn
Burrow Head

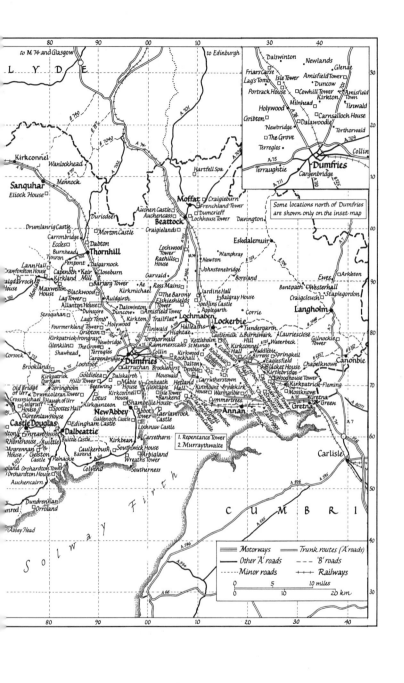

THE BUILDINGS OF SCOTLAND TRUST

The Buildings of Scotland Trust is a charitable trust, founded in
1991, which manages and finances the research programme
needed to sustain *The Buildings of Scotland* series. The trust is
sponsored by Historic Scotland (on behalf of the Secretary of
State for Scotland), the National Trust for Scotland, and the
Royal Commission on the Ancient and Historical Monuments of
Scotland. The Buildings of Scotland Trust is grateful for and
wishes to acknowledge the support of the many individuals, charitable trusts and foundations, companies and local authorities
who have given financial help to its work. Without that support it
would not be possible to look forward to the completion of the
research programme for the series. In particular the Trust wishes
to record its thanks to the National Trust for Scotland, which carried the financial responsibility for this work over a considerable
period before the new trust was set up.

The Trustees wish to acknowledge the generous support of
H.M. The Queen and H.R.H. The Prince of Wales.

Special thanks are due to the following major donors:
Binks Trust, Dulverton Trust
Dumfries and Galloway Regional Council,
Esmée Fairbairn Charitable Trust,
Marc Fitch Fund,
Gordon Fraser Charitable Trust,
A.S. and Miss M.I. Henderson Trust,
Historic Scotland, Leverhulme Trust,
MacRobert Trusts,
Merchants House of Glasgow,
Nancie Massey Charitable Trust,
National Trust for Scotland, Pilgrim Trust,
Radcliffe Trust, Joseph Rank Benevolent Trust,
Royal Bank of Scotland plc, Russell Trust,
Visit Scotland, James Wood Bequest Fund

A very special mention is required of the
Colin McWilliam Memorial Fund, which made a
large grant (the residue of the fund) towards the
costs of research for *Dumfries and Galloway*

Dumfries and and Galloway

BY

JOHN GIFFORD

THE BUILDINGS OF SCOTLAND

YALE UNIVERSITY PRESS

NEW HAVEN AND LONDON

IN ASSOCIATION WITH

THE BUILDINGS OF SCOTLAND TRUST

YALE UNIVERSITY PRESS
NEW HAVEN AND LONDON
302 Temple Street, New Haven CT 06511
23 Pond Street, London NW3 2PN
www.yale.edu/yup
www.yaleup.co.uk
www.pevsner.co.uk

Published by Penguin Books 1996
First published by Yale University Press 2002
2 4 6 8 10 9 7 5 3 1

ISBN 0 300 09671 2

Printed in China
through World Print
Set in Monotype Plantin

FOR

THE McWILLIAM FAMILY

MAP REFERENCES

The numbers printed in italic type in the margin against the place-names in the gazetteer indicate the position of the place in question on the index map (pages 2–3), which is divided into sections by the 10-kilometre reference lines of the National Grid. The reference given here omits the two initial letters (formerly numbers) which in a full grid reference refer to the 100-kilometre squares into which the country is divided. The first two numbers indicate the *western* boundary, and the last two the *southern* boundary, of the 10-kilometre square in which the place is situated. For example, Glenluce, reference 1050, will be found in the 10-kilometre square bounded by grid lines 10 (on the *west*) and 20, and 50 (on the *south*) and 60; Langholm, reference 3080, in the square bounded by grid lines 30 (on the *west*) and 40, and 80 (on the *south*) and 90.

CONTENTS

LIST OF TEXT FIGURES AND MAPS

ACCESS TO BUILDINGS

Many of the buildings described in this book are in public places, and in some obvious cases their interiors (at least the public sections of them) can be seen without formality. But it must be emphasized that the mention of buildings or lands does not imply any right of public access to them, or the existence of any arrangements for visiting them.

Some churches are open within regular hours, and it is usually possible to see the interiors of others by arrangement with the minister or church officer. Particulars of admission to Ancient Monuments and other buildings in the care of the Secretary of State for Scotland (free to the Friends of Historic Scotland) are available from Historic Scotland, Longmore House, Salisbury Place, Edinburgh EH9 1SH. Details of access to properties of the National Trust for Scotland are available from the Trust's head office at 5 Charlotte Square, Edinburgh EH2 4DU. Admission is free to members, on whose subscriptions and donations the Trust's work depends.

Three useful annual directories are *Historic Houses, Castles and Gardens Open to the Public* (British Leisure Publications), which includes many private houses, and the booklets listing gardens, houses and churches open to visitors under Scotland's Gardens Scheme, available from 31 Castle Terrace, Edinburgh EH1 2EL, and Scotland's Churches Scheme, available from Gifford Cottage, Main Street, Gifford, East Lothian, EH41 4QH, and many bookshops.

Tourist offices run by local Councils can advise the visitor on what properties in each area are open to the public and will usually give helpful directions as to how to get to them.

FOREWORD

The first volume of Sir Nikolaus Pevsner's The Buildings of England *was published in 1951, the last in 1974, when several of the earlier volumes had already been republished in revised editions. Not long before his completion of the English series Pevsner set out to launch equivalent series for Ireland, Scotland and Wales, entrusting the editorship of the Scottish series to Colin McWilliam, who himself wrote* Lothian, *the first volume, published in 1978, and was co-author of the next volume,* Edinburgh. Dumfries and Galloway *should also have been by Colin McWilliam. He had begun work on it in 1984, much helped by being given free accommodation at Drumlanrig Castle by the Duke of Buccleuch and Queensberry, and undeterred by having to teach his younger daughter to drive. However, his heavy teaching and many other commitments prevented him from achieving much before his death in 1989, by which time he had already asked me to collaborate on the volume. I have used such of his visiting notes and few draft descriptions as could be found as aids on my own visits to buildings and pointers as to how to approach their description. Clearly, however, the present book is very different from what Colin, either alone or in collaboration, would have produced; but he should be counted as its inspirer and its faults the consequence of my missing his polite but not always uncritical oversight of the series.*

At the beginning of the Buildings of Scotland *series Colin McWilliam stated its objectives as being 'to present all the buildings that merit attention on architectural grounds, to do it for the whole country, and to do it with all possible speed.' To those objectives must be added the aim that the volumes be thoroughly researched and their authors sceptical of information unsupported by documentation, even though this might mean upsetting some buildings' owners, who are endearingly eager to pass on family or local tradition. This desire for thorough research has meant some sacrifice of speed, although increasing familiarity with the available sources has seen progressively less time wasted in searching for information.*

Starting points for research have been provided by David Mac-Gibbon and Thomas Ross's two works, The Castellated and Domestic Architecture of Scotland *(5 vols., 1887–92) and* The Ecclesiastical Architecture of Scotland *(3 vols., 1896–7), and by the Royal Commission on the Ancient and Historical Monuments of Scotland's Inventories of* Wigtownshire *(1912),* Kirkcudbrightshire *(1914), and* Dumfriesshire *(1920); but none of these provides information on buildings constructed after 1707. For buildings of the C18 and later, quite a lot of information is provided by Historic Scotland's List of Buildings of Special Architectural or Historic Interest, but its compilers have been under at least as much pressure as any author of* The Buildings of Scotland *to produce lists quickly, with some unavoidable skimping on research and analysis. Moreover, the list omits a fairly large proportion of the buildings mentioned in the volumes of this series. For the series as a whole, I extracted some years ago all Scottish references from C19 and C20 architectural and building periodicals (The Builder, The Building News, The Architect etc.). The arrangement of these notes by individual buildings grouped within parishes was undertaken by me for Dumfriesshire, by Serena Hutton for the Stewartry, and by Ierne Grant for Wigtownshire. We also greatly supplemented these notes with information collected from such sources as the various* Statistical Accounts of Scotland, *C19 gazetteers (*The Ordnance Gazetteer of Scotland, *ed. Francis H. Groome, 5 vols., 1882–5, being the fullest), and a mass of local histories and guidebooks, some of this work being undertaken by Yvonne Hillyard and Simon Green. I also looked through manuscript sources, especially ecclesiastical and estate records now housed in the Scottish Record Office, whose staff have proved consistently helpful and forbearing. My gratitude is just as great to the staff of the National Library of Scotland, the Edinburgh Central Public Library (especially the Scottish and Fine Art Departments), and the Ewart Library in Dumfries. The National Monuments Record of Scotland has become almost a second home and its staff, past and present, especially Catherine Cruft and Ian Gow, have been midwives as much to this volume as to others in the series.*

Anne Riches combed the typescript in a search for omissions. Elizabeth Williamson provided a multitude of comments and suggestions from which the book has gained greatly in clarity. Other architectural historians have been generous in sharing their own discoveries and ideas, and I must particularly thank Howard Colvin, John Dunbar, Richard Fawcett, Aonghus MacKechnie, Colin Menzies, Anne Riches, Joe Rock, David Walker and Antony C. Wolffe. Morag Williams, the archivist of the Dumfries and Galloway Health Board, besides sharing her unrivalled knowledge of the history of the region's hospitals, was a magnificent guide to these buildings, gaining me access to parts which had not seen a visitor for most of this century. She was only one of many (priests, ministers, church officers, and the owners of country houses and other private buildings) who put themselves to considerable trouble to let me see over the buildings in their care and often provided valuable information and generous hospitality. Planning and architects' departments of the regional and district councils have supplied the names of architects and the dates of several recent buildings.

Many of the photographs in this volume were taken specially by the photographers of the Royal Commission on the Ancient and Historic Monuments of Scotland, whose ability to procure sunshine during a notoriously wet summer mystifies me. The cover photographs were taken by Martin Charles and Eddie Ryle-Hodges. The maps and town plans were specially drawn by Reg Piggott, and the plans of buildings by Richard Andrews. Stephany Ungless gallantly co-ordinated all this work and much more besides. Judith Wardman prepared the typescript for the printer and compiled the Index of Places. This is the fifth volume in the series on which she has worked. By rights she should be fed up with the whole enterprise but has appeared surprisingly encouraging, calming and unflappable.

The boundaries of the area covered by this volume are those of the region of Dumfries and Galloway formed in 1975 from the three former counties of Dumfriesshire, Stewartry or Kirkcudbrightshire, and Wigtownshire. All the entries for towns, villages and major rural buildings in the gazetteer are amalgamated into a single alphabetical run. More minor buildings (e.g. farms or cairns) have been placed in the entry for the nearest town or village but are also included in the Index of Places.

In Dumfries and Galloway, *as in the preceding volumes of* The Buildings of Scotland, *certain general policies have been adopted. The format remains that established by Sir Nikolaus Pevsner in* The Buildings of England, *but with some Scottish quirks. Almost all churches and public buildings are included as a matter of course, as are buildings, especially in towns and villages, which, whatever their architectural quality, are too conspicuous to be entirely ignored. With some minor buildings, such as late Georgian farmhouses, those which are in or immediately next to a village or town have been mentioned but isolated examples left out. The more important rural buildings such as castles and country houses have individual entries in the gazetteer. An entry in brackets shows that the building has not, for whatever reasons, been personally visited. There are bound to be mistakes and omissions in this volume. I shall be grateful to anyone who takes the trouble to tell me about them.*

The research and travelling costs for this series are necessarily high and for many years were underwritten by the National Trust for Scotland. The task has now been taken over by The Buildings of Scotland Trust, which is raising from public and private sources the funds necessary to see the series through to completion.

ACKNOWLEDGEMENTS FOR THE PLATES

We are grateful to the following for permission to reproduce photographs:

Historic Scotland: 6, 10, 11, 12, 13, 14, 15, 63, 64, 65, 74, 76, 77
RCAHMS: 1, 2, 3, 4, 5, 7, 8, 9, 16, 17, 18, 19, 20, 21, 22, 23, 24, 25, 26, 27, 28, 29, 30, 31, 32, 33, 34, 35, 36, 37, 38, 39, 40, 41, 42, 43, 44, 45, 46, 47, 48, 49, 50, 51, 52, 53, 54, 55, 56, 57, 58, 60, 61, 62, 66, 67, 68, 69, 70, 71, 72, 73, 75, 78, 79, 80, 81, 82, 83, 84, 85, 86, 87, 88, 89, 90, 91, 92, 93, 94, 95, 96, 97, 98, 99, 100, 101, 102, 103, 104, 105, 106, 107, 108, 109, 110, 111, 112, 113, 114, 115, 116, 117, 118, 119, 120, 121, 122, 123, 124, 125, 126, 127
Simon Reed and The Henry Moore Foundation: 59

The plates are indexed in the indexes of artists and places, and references to them are given by numbers in the margin of the text.

INTRODUCTION

TOPOGRAPHY AND BUILDING MATERIALS

The landscape of Dumfries and Galloway is arguably the most attractively varied in Scotland, juxtaposing a coastal plain with gentle hills, bare moorland and forest. This is a pastoral region largely cut off from the rest of Scotland to the N and E by the Southern Uplands, an almost continuous belt of high ground stretching from the North Sea to the Irish Channel and filling the northern part of the region. The highest peaks, about 800 metres high, are White Coom and Hart Fell near Moffat, Carserine near New Galloway, and Merrick near Newton Stewart. The hills are broken by the narrow valleys of the Ewes and Esk and the much broader dales of the Annan, Nith, Dee and Cree. The upper slopes are moorland or covered with forestry plantations. To the S of the hills, the land is generally rolling but with almost flat coastal strips, deeply indented by the natural harbours of bays and river mouths, along the Solway Firth.

The different ROCK FORMATIONS underlying the topography run in diagonal bands from NE to SW. The northern three-quarters is composed predominantly of Ordovician and Silurian stone, formed from the accumulation of muds, shales, silts, sands and pebbles laid down, three to four hundred million years ago, in the sea that then covered the greater part of Britain, and folded by intense mountain-building movements into hills later scoured by glaciers. Their effect is most dramatic at the Devil's Beeftub near Moffat and the Dalveen Pass N of Durisdeer. Along the region's SE side, from Langholm to Abbey Head near Kirkcudbright, is a belt of carboniferous rock made up of later deposits of sands, muds and limestone. More carboniferous rock, containing coal seams, occurs in the Nith Valley W of Thornhill and around Sanquhar and Kirkconnel. Studded in these broad bands are small pockets of igneous rock and, more importantly, massive intrusions of granite, most notable in the rugged outcrops between New Abbey and Dalbeattie, and at Cairnsmore of Fleet and Merrick to the N of Gatehouse of Fleet. As significant although not as noticeable as the granite are the large pockets of red-coloured Permian sandstone found in Annandale between Hightae and Moffat, in Nithsdale around Dumfries and Thornhill, and, in the W of the region, between Luce Bay and Loch Ryan. There is one sizeable deposit of Triassic sandstone between Annan and Gretna Green.

These rocks have produced BUILDING MATERIAL exploited for grander buildings from prehistoric times but more generally only since the C18. The hard and shiny greywacke (popularly, although not quite accurately, known as whinstone) was the most commonly used stone, often shaped into brick-like lumps, although its intractability makes it unsuitable for dressings. These are generally of granite or red sandstone, the most common materials for the grander buildings. Both were quarried on a large scale from the C18, the main quarries for granite being near Dalbeattie, and for sandstone at Locharbriggs near Dumfries; both of these supplied a large export trade to England and the rest of Scotland by the late C19. The brick clays in the region were exploited by the C17; one now vanished house in Annan was built of brick as early as 1666, another near Leswalt followed *c*.1680, and the large block added to Kirkconnell House in 1755–60 was an unashamed display of warm-coloured brickwork. Commercial brick and tile works were set up at Newton Stewart and near Drummore by the mid-C19. The lead seams at Wanlockhead were mined on a commercial scale from 1675, their product displayed with proprietorial pride by the rainwater goods and turret roofs of the Duke of Queensberry's Drumlanrig Castle.

Other building materials were largely imported; timber was brought from the Baltic by the C16, slates, principally from Lancashire, in the C18 and C19. In common with the rest of Scotland, Dumfries and Galloway has imported most of its building materials in the later C20, but the intensity of the region's love affair with the aluminium window is exceptional and thought by some prudish outsiders an embarrassing infatuation.

PREHISTORIC DUMFRIES AND GALLOWAY

The first humans reached Scotland from the S *c*.7000 B.C. They were hunter-gatherers, present only in tiny numbers and apparently peripatetic, occupying any one site only for short seasonal periods. Evidence of their presence in Dumfries and Galloway has been found at Luce Bay and Wigtown Bay. Excavation of one of these MESOLITHIC sites, probably occupied at the end of the fifth millennium B.C., the top of a low cliff at Low Clone on the E side of Luce Bay, produced over sixteen hundred flints, including such tools as scrapers, blades, awls and corers. In the centre of the site, which had been scooped out to form a boomerang-shaped hollow, were stakeholes for the structural framework of a not very substantial shelter.

From *c*.4000 B.C., perhaps encouraged by climatic warming, NEOLITHIC settlers arrived in Scotland. They seem to have cleared some of the heavily wooded land, presumably by slash-and-burn methods, to establish fixed settlement sites, preferably with good natural drainage and relatively light soil, on which to practise a mixed agriculture of crop-cultivation and livestock-raising; their food supplies were probably augmented to some extent by fishing and hunting.

The strongest evidence of their presence is provided by CHAM-BERED TOMBS, usually built on a hillside and each apparently providing some sort of religious focus or shrine (presumably associated with ancestor worship) for an individual family of farmers. In Dumfries and Galloway each tomb seems originally to have begun as a single chamber designed for communal inter-ments, its walls and roof formed of slabs and drystone walling, which was covered with earth and stones to form a round or oval cairn mound. A small number (the Bargrennan group), perhaps of the early third millennium B.C. and concentrated in an upland area of north Galloway, have quite long passages from the exterior to the chamber, e.g. the three sited near Glentrool or the Caves of Kilhern near New Luce. Each of these is isolated, suggesting that the family it served occupied a relatively large farm, probably devoted mainly to stock.

The tombs belonging to the region's other main type (the Clyde group), perhaps constructed from the fourth millennium, are sited on better land, generally on well-drained hillsides, their slopes facing S or SW, and had chambers entered directly from the outside. They were constructed in groups of two or more, suggesting some degree of communal co-operation between adjacent farmers on land suited to grow arable crops as well as to support livestock. The two long cairns at Mid Gleniron, near Glenluce, both developed in a similar way, the process clearest at the better-preserved Mid Gleniron I. That began with a chamber enclosed in a small oval cairn. A second similar chamber was then built to its N, the W and S sides of its cairn mound rather flattened in shape, apparently so as not to obstruct the approach to the entrance of the earlier tomb. A third stage, probably in the third millennium B.C., was the construction of another chamber at right angles to the other two, its E end intruding on the space between the earlier cairns. Probably as part of this third stage, all three chambers were covered by a large single mound, the N chamber was given a short entrance passage, and the mound's N front was made a U-plan forecourt faced with slabs and drystone walling, this area presumably intended for religious ritual. The same apparent enlargement of cairn mounds for new and more elab-orate ritual is shown by the two cairns at Cairnholy, near Kirkdale, 3 each begun as a single chamber and later extended with an ante-chamber and slab-fronted forecourt.

Further evidence of religious and presumably social develop-ment in the third and second millennia B.C. is provided by stone CEREMONIAL CIRCLES. The largest in Scotland is the Twelve Apostles, near Holywood, c. 88m. in diameter; the eleven (perhaps originally twelve) upright stones are so arranged that the tallest face each other. There may originally have been another stone in the centre, as there is in the circle of boulders at Glenquicken, near Creetown. The circle at Torhousekie, near Wigtown, is composed of squat granite boulders, their heights and spacing graded, the centre filled with a line of three more stones. Of

individual STANDING STONES, sometimes arranged in twos or
threes (e.g. at Laggangarn, near New Luce, or Drumtroddan,
near Port William), some probably marked Bronze Age burials,
whilst others may have denoted boundaries or meeting places:
the huge Lochmaben Stane, sited between the mouths of the
Kirtle Water and the River Sark near Gretna, perhaps indicated
an assembly point on the plain beside the Solway and near a
crossing of the River Esk.

If the significance of standing stones remains uncertain, even
more enigmatic are contemporary ROCK CARVINGS, incised cup
shapes, some surrounded by rings (cup-and-ring marks), and in
places with radial grooves joining the cups. At Drumtroddan,
near Port William, and Cauldside, near Anwoth, they are associated with standing stones or ceremonial circles, as may also
originally have been the 30m.-long group carved on an exposed
low rockface at High Banks, near Kirkcudbright.

From the later third millennium B.C. a new element in the
population or a change in its culture appears with the introduction
of bronze-working and the pottery known as Beaker ware. With
the BRONZE AGE a change took place in burial customs; interment in the communal mausolea or ossuaries provided by chambered tombs was replaced by the burial of individual bodies,
usually in a crouched position, inside a stone-slabbed cist, either
inserted in an existing cairn or covered by its own small round
cairn. Examples of both types have been found at Cauldside,
near Anwoth. In the second millennium B.C. cremation became
common, the ashes being buried in a pottery vessel, the site
sometimes marked by a cairn.

In the later Bronze Age (c. 900 B.C.–500 B.C.) metal-working
technology improved and the socketed axe-head was introduced,
together with bronze swords which could be used to slash as well
as stab, and sickles, knives, chisels, cauldrons and buckets. The
end of this period was marked by the arrival of immigrants,
perhaps in quite small numbers, who brought the Celtic language
and iron technology, although the use of iron did not become
widespread until the C I A.D.

The end of the Bronze Age and the beginning of the IRON
AGE seems to have been a period of ostentatious wealth but also
of considerable unrest, probably in part the consequence of a
society composed of slaves, farmers and craftsmen on the one
hand and a warlike aristocracy on the other. Bronze hoards were
buried and not recovered. Defensive structures were built, requir-
ing considerable amounts of labour. A few were crannogs, small
artificial islands formed of layers of timber and brushwood consolidated by stones and vertical wooden piles, sometimes linked
by causeways to the shores of their lochs. Others were hilltop
FORTS. One of the simplest, the fort on Burnswark Hill, was
defended in the late Bronze Age by a palisade and trench. A new
defence, probably erected at the beginning of the Iron Age, was
provided by an earth and stone rampart, its front originally revetted with timber but given a stone face soon after completion; a
stone-fronted outer rampart was built on one side at the same

time. The forts at Castle O'er, near Eskdalemuir, and Brieryshaw Hill, near Ewes, each had a pair of stone and earth ramparts with a ditch between. Other forts, e.g. those at Trusty's Hill, near Anwoth, or Tynron Doon, occupied promontory-like spurs and used ditches and ramparts to cut off the approach and a stone wall to enclose the summit; the CI rampart at Trusty's Hill is laced with timber. Other forts again (e.g. Kemp's Walk at Larbrax, near Leswalt, or Barsalloch Point, near Monreith) occupied coastal promontories and relied for defence on ditches and ramparts only across the approach. Three forts, all on sea-girt promontories in W Galloway, are of types more commonly associated with the Northern Isles, Caithness and Skye and Lochalsh. One, Castle Haven, near Kirkandrews, is a dun, its walls enclosing outer and inner D-plan areas; the outer wall is built of solid masonry, the inner mostly of two stonework skins with narrow galleries between. At Crammag Head, near Kirkmaiden, and Doon Castle, near Ardwell, the landward approaches were defended by a wall behind which stood the broch itself, a round enclosure surrounded by a thick stone wall. That at Doon Castle contains hollowed-out cells, above which probably rose a double-skinned wall containing galleries, as at Castle Haven. Inside each broch's circular enclosure there would originally have been a central hearth, surrounded by wooden structures built against the inner face of the enclosing wall.

Inside many of the hillforts, evidence survives of stances for round houses, which might have been numerous; the exceptionally large fort at Burnswark Hill is estimated to have had space for 150 houses, although it must be doubtful that it ever contained so many at one time. On quite a different scale were the numerous homesteads of farmers. One which has been excavated was at Boonies, near Bentpath.* This was a roughly oval enclosure of c. 0.07ha. surrounded by an earth bank (datable to the earlier CI A.D.), probably erected to contain livestock rather than as a defence. Most of the enclosure formed a yard at whose back was a space occupied originally by a single house but later by five, all circular and constructed of whole or split timbers set in support trenches and supported on each side by a packing of small stones.

THE ROMANS IN DUMFRIES AND GALLOWAY

BY DAVID J. BREEZE

In A.D. 68 Nero, the last of the family of Julius Caesar to reign as emperor, committed suicide. The ensuing civil war ('The Year of the Four Emperors') ended with the success of Titus Flavius Vespasianus, commander of the army of Judaea. The new

* This is one of several sites which have been excavated but are not included in the gazetteer because nothing is now visible there.

emperor, better known to history as Vespasian, had served in Britain after the Roman invasion of 43, and he decided on a new forward policy, presumably with the intention of completing the conquest of the island. The Brigantes of northern England were subdued in the early 70s and completion of the conquest of Wales followed.

Two tribes are known to have occupied the area now called Dumfries and Galloway. In the valleys of the Annan and the Nith lay the Selgovae, while further W were the Novantae. The names of places in the territories of these tribes, although we cannot locate them with any certainty, are known from information provided by a C2 geographer, Ptolemy, who probably acquired it as a result of Agricola's campaigns, although not at first hand.

In 79 (or, less probably, 80) the Roman army, under Gnaeus Iulius Agricola, the governor of Britain, reconnoitred as far N as the River Tay. In the process, according to the biography written twenty years later by Agricola's son-in-law, Tacitus, they were operating within the territory of 'new tribes'. These may have been newly conquered but may not have been 'hitherto unknown' (as were the tribes N of the Tay met two years later): a dendro-chronological date of 72 for a timber used in the construction of the Roman fort at Carlisle opens up the possibility that the governor of that time, Petillius Cerealis, had already campaigned in SW Scotland. Certainly the tribes between the Solway Firth and the Forth–Clyde isthmus do not appear to have offered serious resistance to the Roman advance, for Tacitus recorded that Agricola even had time to build forts that season. The following summer was spent consolidating control over the area over-run.

It is remarkable that it is only since 1945 that the framework of the military installations W of the Annan has appeared. Until the late 1930s the region was known only to possess two forts (Birrens, and Raeburnfoot, near Eskdalemuir), two camps (Gilnockie, near Canonbie, and Torwood, near Lockerbie), and the 'siege works' at Burnswark Hill. The fort at Birrens towards the S end of Annandale is the most famous fort in the region. It has been the subject of three series of excavations and was the first fort to be examined by the Society of Antiquaries of Scotland in its series of excavations which started in 1895. Further N in Annandale, a fort was discovered at Milton, near Beattock, in 1938. About the same time a fort was recognized at Carzield, near Kirkton, in Nithsdale. Through aerial reconnaissance since 1945 many new sites have been discovered, including forts at Dalswinton and Drumlanrig, both in Nithsdale, and, further W, at Glenlochar at the S end of Loch Ken and at Gatehouse of Fleet, and several fortlets and camps at Glenluce and at Girvan (Ayrshire).* The last two may relate to Agricola's unfulfilled proposal to invade Ireland in 81. No other camp is certainly associated with the

---

* Sites where nothing or very little is visible from the ground have not been included in the gazetteer.

movements of Agricola's army, although the very size (8.7ha.) of the earliest phase at Dalswinton suggests that it may have been a military base for operations in the area, perhaps against the Novantae.

These Agricolan marching camps, and those which were put up in later Roman invasions of Scotland, were erected by the army each time it halted while on campaign. A single rampart was formed from earth dug out of the surrounding ditch. Stakes stuck into the top of the rampart provided extra defence. The wide entrances, necessary for easy movement of the army, were protected by additional defence, normally in the form of a detached section of rampart and ditch. Excavation has suggested that temporary gates, perhaps made from hurdles, may have been placed in the entrances. Within these defences the soldiers camped in row upon row of tents, placed according to a set plan which facilitated both construction and discipline. Each tent was made of leather and resembled a Black's Niger.* It has been calculated that over thirty calf skins would have been required for a single tent. The army normally stayed no more than three nights in each camp while on campaign, for in that time it would have eaten all the food in the area and fouled its own water supply.

Each army group contained scouts to gather military intelligence and spy out the land ahead. Further information was obtained from merchants, local people and prisoners. This information was recorded and, it seems, filed for future use. Ptolemy was one of the geographers and mappers who made use of information gathered by Agricola's army, and several surviving documents record the information so carefully collected.

The framework of military control during this brief first period is reasonably clear. The main route N lay up the valley of Annandale, with a small fort at Birrens and a more substantial base at Milton, near Beattock.‡ From Birrens a second road led W to Dalswinton, Glenlochar, Gatehouse of Fleet and beyond. Probably another fort, as yet undiscovered, lay at or near Newton Stewart; a camp was discovered at Glenluce in 1992. There was a road N up Nithsdale from Dalswinton to Drumlanrig, where it forked, one branch crossing the Dalveen Pass to join the Annandale road near Crawford (Lanarkshire), the other heading NW to Irvine (Ayrshire), where it may have joined a road along the W coast, although evidence of this has not been found.

The first Roman occupation of southern Scotland was marked by fluidity. No fewer than four superimposed forts were constructed at Dalswinton and perhaps two at Glenlochar. This suggests that the disposition of the frontier units changed in response to expanding knowledge and the changing military situation as the army moved N.

The Roman army's success in defeating the Caledonians at the

---

* The standard style of tent made by Blacks of Greenock which was long familiar to those who served in the Boy Scouts.

‡ A 9.7km. stretch of this road is visible and walkable from the A701 near Moffat N to the Regional boundary, passing, on the l., the earthworks of a signal-station 0.5km. N of the A701 crossing at Auldhousehill Bridge, 6.2km. N of Moffat.

battle of Mons Graupius, probably somewhere in NE Scotland, in 83 or 84 was shortly afterwards negated by defeats on the Continent, leading to the withdrawal of troops from Britain and the abandonment of most forts N of the Cheviot Hills by 88 at the latest, although the forts at Milton (near Beattock), Dalswinton and Glenlochar seem to have survived for another fifteen or so years until the army relinquished all forts N of the Tyne–Solway isthmus.

During the reigns of two emperors, Trajan (98–117) and Hadrian (117–138), the Roman army consolidated the Tyne–Solway line as the northern frontier of the province of Britain. On this line Hadrian ordered the construction of the Wall which still bears his name. This barrier was not, however, the northernmost limit of Roman power or influence. Beyond the Wall, to the NW, were outpost forts. One of these was at Birrens, where the earlier station was buried beneath a new fort erected in the mid-120s. The purpose of these outpost forts is not entirely clear. They may have served as bases for soldiers patrolling outside the province. Alternatively, they may have been to protect outlying members of the Brigantes cut off from the rest of their tribe by the construction of Hadrian's Wall, a possibility given some support by the discovery at Birrens of a dedication of the later C2 to the goddess Brigantia.

The Emperor Hadrian died in July 138, and in the following year preparations were put in hand for a second major advance into Scotland. The reasons for this change in policy are unclear. It has been variously suggested that there was trouble in southern Scotland serious enough to require military intervention, that Hadrian's Wall was out of touch with the Caledonians, the main enemy in the N, or that the new emperor, Antoninus Pius, required a military triumph to help secure his position.

The northern advance resulted in the reoccupation of the land between Hadrian's Wall and the River Tay and the construction of the Antonine Wall from Bo'ness on the Firth of Forth to Old Kilpatrick on the River Clyde. Hadrian's Wall was abandoned. In SW Scotland a new fort was erected at Glenlochar on the site of the Agricolan fort abandoned forty years before, but no evidence has been found of bases further W. In Nithsdale, the fort at Drumlanrig was rebuilt but not that at Dalswinton, a new fort being placed instead at Carzield, near Kirkton, a few kilometres down the valley. In Annandale, the fort at Birrens was again rebuilt. A new fort was placed at Raeburnfoot, near Eskdalemuir, on the line of a new road running NE from Annandale towards Newstead (Borders).

A feature of this second Roman occupation was the construction of fortlets. Thus the day-long marching intervals between the forts were broken by the emplacement of fortlets apparently providing accommodation for no more than eighty men. One fortlet site has been totally excavated at Barburgh Mill, near Auldgirth; another is still well preserved at Durisdeer.

The regiments based at the forts formed part of the provincial army of Britain. The best evidence of these regiments has been found at Birrens. Here, in the mid-C2, was stationed the *cohors II Tungrorum milliaria equitata*. '*Milliaria*' indicates that the regiment was nominally a thousand strong, and '*equitata*' that some of the soldiers were mounted. In fact, its theoretical complement was 800 infantry and 240 cavalry, but surviving records suggest that the normal strength would probably have been less. It seems likely that this regiment and the others provided soldiers to man the fortlets. Originally raised in present-day Belgium, the unit at Birrens would have recruited locally from the time of its arrival in Britain and its members would be well used to the climate.

Individual forts were often built for single units, but those in Dumfries and Galloway exhibit variation; indeed every fort in the region was unusual. Birrens, for example, contained the normal complement of principal buildings (headquarters, commanding officer's house, and granaries) but the barracks followed a plan unique in Britain. Each barrack appears to have been formed of two thin buildings instead of the usual single block. It seems possible that the sleeping quarters and living rooms were separated, facing each other across a narrow street. The buildings' footings were of stone but their superstructure was of timber, the walls formed by wattles coated with clay daub and plastered. The cavalry fort at Carzield contained a mixture of stone and timber buildings, but within the region's other forts and fortlets the buildings were uniformly of timber. Both forts and fortlets had ramparts of turf or earth, probably surmounted by a timber breastwork. The C2 turf ramparts at Birrens were underpinned by a stone base.

The troops in these forts and fortlets were charged with the duties of protecting the province from external attack – most forts consequently being placed on roads leading N to the frontier – and of controlling the tribes of the frontier zone. The number of C2 fortlets, probably manned by soldiers outposted from the forts, suggests close surveillance over the local tribesmen as well as protection of traffic on the roads. Documents from elsewhere in the empire suggest that the soldiers may have been away from their parent unit for several years.

The advance ordered by the Emperor Antoninus Pius in 139 lasted little more than a generation before there was again a withdrawal to the Tyne–Solway line. Only the fort at Birrens survived, operating once more as an outpost of Hadrian's Wall. Precisely when it was abandoned is uncertain, but it cannot have survived the demise of the Emperor Septimius Severus' attempt to complete the conquest of the whole island of Britain in 208–11, an attempt which itself had no discernible effect on Dumfries and Galloway. Thereafter the tribesmen of SW Scotland may have been no more than passive observers of the campaigns of later Roman emperors attempting to exercise some influence or control over the more northerly tribes.

These tribesmen may have observed one other activity. Close to Birrens is Burnswark Hill, the site of an Iron Age hillfort long abandoned by the time the Romans arrived. On each side of the hill is a Roman camp. It was long thought that these were erected in anger, but it now seems that they were constructed as training camps where soldiers could exercise and practise, so that, in the words of Josephus, their exercises became bloodless battles and their battles bloody exercises. The existence of a Roman camp has long been known beside another Iron Age fort, that at Ward Law, near Caerlaverock. Recently it has been suggested that this too was a semi-permanent work, perhaps designed for use on manoeuvres.

The story of the Romans in Dumfries and Galloway is essentially military. We know practically nothing of the camp followers who must have accompanied the regiments N. We know very little of contact with the local tribes. Certainly some Roman goods found their way onto native farmsteads, but the agencies of contact elude us. A burial cremation in the Roman manner at Torrs Warren, near Glenluce, appears to have been that of a Roman traveller, perhaps a sailor.

The abandonment of the fort at Birrens towards the end of the C2 did not mark the end of Roman interest in the land N of Hadrian's Wall. Treaties with the northern tribes certainly existed at that time, and it may be presumed that Roman patrols kept the area N of the Wall under surveillance. In fact, a reference to events in 367 seems to suggest that it was in that year that the scouting system N of the Wall was abandoned. Only then, nearly three hundred years after the arrival of the Romans in Scotland, did Roman soldiers cease to operate in the region now known as Dumfries and Galloway.

EARLY MEDIEVAL DUMFRIES AND GALLOWAY

Rome's formal renunciation of responsibility for the defence of Britain in 410 may at first have had relatively little impact on Dumfries and Galloway. The area by then formed part of the kingdom of Rheged, its centre the Roman town of Carlisle, its rulers claiming descent from Magnus Maximus, who had attempted to become emperor in 383. The name of Rheged has survived in Dunragit ('fort of Rheged') near Glenluce. That the kingdom was at least partially Romanized and Christian in nature is attested by a few gravestones. One, discovered at Whithorn in 1880 and datable from its lettering to the C5, commemorates a man called Latinus and his daughter. Two more C5 pillar stones are now in the porch of Kirkmadrine Church, each carved with a circled cross forming the Christian Chi-rho monogram; one commemorates the 'chief priests' (presumably bishops or abbots) Viventius and Mavorius, evidence of some degree of religious organization.

Further evidence of the continuity of ecclesiastical life has been given by recent excavation at Whithorn, apparently a Christian centre by the early C5, when St Ninian was sent there as bishop.

There in the C5 was a metalled roadway leading from the coast towards the present Priory Church, the likeliest site of the original church, and an enclosure bounded by a bank of rubble including lumps of lime (probably waste building material) revetted with a wattle fence. Inside the enclosure were oblong bow-sided huts, probably of wattle construction, containing central hearths. Associated with this settlement were numerous sherds of imported Mediterranean pottery.

A settlement of markedly secular character has been excavated at Mote of Mark, a rocky crag overlooking Rough Firth, near Colvend. This seems to have been a major C6 stronghold of Rheged. The site was enclosed by a massive rampart, c.3m. in width and perhaps the same in height, constructed of earth and stones and with its front laced with timber. From the artefacts found inside it is clear that this was a manufacturing centre where a wide variety of iron tools was produced, glass worked, and ornaments cast in bronze, and perhaps silver and gold, including brooches and decorative mounts for caskets and harness trappings. Pottery and glass were imported from France and the Rhineland. All this testifies to a society whose chiefs were able and eager to indulge in conspicuous expenditure.

In the early C7 the timber in the rampart at Mote of Mark was set on fire, causing the surrounding granite to vitrify. Probably this was the result of an attack, perhaps launched by the Anglians, who were expanding into Dumfries and Galloway at this time. The British kingdom of Rheged was finally absorbed into Northumbria, and Anglian domination of the area and its largely British inhabitants was presumably well established by c.730, when an Anglian, Pecthelm, became Bishop at Whithorn. After this there seems to have been comprehensive redevelopment of the buildings in the area of that town S of the present medieval Priory Church, with the erection of a timber oratory and burial chapel (the two later combined as a church) and with wooden buildings laid out on a rectilinear grid to the S; the smaller of these were very similar to C8 buildings at the Northumbrian monastery of Hartlepool in County Durham.

The most important group of structures to have survived from the period of Northumbrian domination in the region is composed of STONE CROSSES. Probably the earliest, perhaps dating from the early C8, and incomparably the grandest, is the very tall Ruthwell Cross in Ruthwell Parish Church. The carving on the sides of its shaft resembles some of the decoration of the similar cross at Bewcastle (Cumbria), birds and beasts in spiralling foliage. The two main faces have panels containing scenes from the life of Our Lord, a depiction of the desert monks St Paul and St Antony, and emblems of the Evangelists. The quality of carving, probably by a sculptor from the Monkwearmouth or Jarrow workshops, and the rich iconographical scheme, together with the incised runes quoting a version of *The Dream of the Rood*, make this quite exceptional; but sculptured crosses were a prominent feature of Anglian art. Some, like the Ruthwell Cross or the cross shaft standing in a field near Burnhead, which is probably of the late C9 and is decorated with interlacing and animals, seem always to have stood alone; but at or near monastic sites crosses proliferated. Fragments of at least seven crosses of the C8 and C9, almost all richly carved, have been found at the former Hoddom Parish Church, the almost certain site of an Anglian monastery. About twenty-five crosses have been found at Whithorn, and about another twenty-five in the adjacent countryside; Whithorn seems to have had its own school of sculptors in the C10. Their distinctive form of cross was usually a monolith, its shaft decorated with interlacing and topped by a disc; on the front of the disc were carved the cross arms which extended to the edge of the circle. The centre of the cross was marked by a boss. Bosses were also often placed in the spaces between the arms, but at the cross now in Kirkinner Parish Church these spaces are pierced.

Scandinavian invasions and settlements of northern England, Ireland and the Western Isles in the C9 and C10 were accompanied or followed by some settlement in Dumfries and Galloway, as is clear from place-names ending in the Old Norse 'beck' (brook) or 'bie' (settlement), e.g. Waterbeck, Middlebie, Sorbie. But the extent of direct Norse settlement was surprisingly small. Perhaps of greater import was the domination of Galloway from this time by Gaelic-speaking immigrants, probably from the GAELIC-NORSE kingdoms of Ireland or the Western Isles. By the C11 they seem to have provided Galloway with its name, ruling family and the Gaelic language, which persisted in the area until the C13. The square timber houses with rounded corners and oblong hearths built at Whithorn in the C11 are most closely paralleled in the Irish-Norse towns of Dublin and Waterford. Norse taste intruded into the monuments of the region, most strikingly at the Kilmore Stone Cross in Kirkcolm Parish Churchyard; one of its faces is decorated with apparently Celtic carving of snakes under a cross decorated with a chalice and host, the other with a much cruder Norse representation of the triumph of the crucified Christ over a heathen god. More usually the influence was shown in the modification of Anglian designs, whose patterns became looser and less regular, as with the interlacing on the C11 cross base now in Kirkconnel Parish Church, or by the introduction of new motifs such as the spiralling dragon which confronts an Anglian leaf-scroll on the stone, probably also of the C11, re-used over a door at Wamphray Parish Church.

MEDIEVAL CHURCHES, MONASTERIES AND COLLEGES

Early C12 Scotland underwent an ecclesiastical reformation insti-gated by Queen Margaret, wife of Malcolm III, and largely carried out in the reign (1124–53) of her son David I. The three main strands of reform were the regularization of the diocesan episcopate, the establishment of a parochial system, and the foundation of religious houses belonging to the European orders which had arisen from the work of St Benedict. In 1123 David I, then 'prince of Cumbria', reconstituted the diocese of Glasgow to cover an area which included Dumfriesshire. Galloway to the W was a semi-independent principality ruled by its own lords, but here too the religious changes took place with at least as much vigour as elsewhere in Scotland.

Around 1128 the see of Whithorn or Galloway, in abeyance since the C8 or C9, was revived, probably at the instance of Fergus, lord of Galloway, who is credited with having endowed a priory of canons regular (perhaps Augustinians, but later followed by Premonstratensians) at its cathedral church at Whithorn, itself built or rebuilt at this time. Other monastic foundations by Fergus followed with his endowment of a (now vanished) Premonstratensian abbey at Soulseat, near Castle Kennedy, and an Augustinian priory (also disappeared) at St Mary's Isle. Perhaps also a foundation of Fergus, although more generally credited to David I, was the Cistercian house at Dundrennan. At about the same time Turgis de Rosdale, a major landowner in Eskdale, founded an Augustinian priory, a dependency of Jedburgh Abbey, at Canonbie. Probably also of the late C12, and certainly before 1255, was the foundation of the Premonstratensian Holywood Abbey in Nithsdale, probably by one of the lords of Nithsdale. Fergus' elder son, Uchtred, lord of Galloway (†1174), reputedly established a convent of Benedictine nuns at Lincluden, near Dumfries, and both Uchtred's son and grandson continued the work; Roland, lord of Galloway, founded the Cistercian abbey at Glenluce, c.1190, and Alan, lord of Galloway, the Premonstratensian Tongland Abbey, probably in 1218. The last of the major monastic foundations was undertaken by Alan's daughter, Devorgilla, lady of Galloway, in the 1270s with the establishment of the Cistercian Sweetheart Abbey (see New Abbey).

Of these religious houses substantial remains survive of the three Cistercian abbeys at Dundrennan, Glenluce and Sweetheart. Dundrennan and Sweetheart were directly comparable in size to the great abbey of the same order founded by David I at Melrose (Borders) in the 1130s. Each abbey seems to have housed between fifteen and twenty choir monks and, until the Cistercian reforms of the C15, a number of lay brothers. Unsurprisingly, in view of the Cistercian order's stress on uniformity, they have very similar plans; their churches comprised an aisled nave, a crossing and transepts, each with two E chapels (at Dundrennan an afterthought), and an unaisled presbytery. The nave and S transept formed the N side of a square cloister, its E range containing the chapter house and the choir monks' dormitory, from which a stair down into the S transept gave access to the church for the monastic night offices. On the S side of the cloister were the kitchen and monastic refectory. The W range (perhaps not built at Sweetheart) contained the lay brothers' quarters.

In accordance with Cistercian principles the architecture is severe Gothic, although at Dundrennan it is not without elegance, 10 if rather compromised by apparent afterthoughts during the

course of construction. Little remains of the abbey church at
Glenluce. The late C13 work at Sweetheart's church is ambitious –
the foiled circlets in the presbytery window heads are among the
earliest examples of bar tracery in Scotland – but the earthbound
detail of the late C14 completion of the church is disappointing.
The chapter houses at Dundrennan and Glenluce were both
rebuilt in later remodellings. At Dundrennan the mid-C13 W
wall is smartly panelled, its windows set in nailhead-enriched
overarches, the door given an elaborate cinquefoil head. Glenluce's late C15 chapter house is much more complete; the simi-
larity of the tracery in its windows to that of the chapter house at
Crossraguel Abbey (Ayrshire) suggests that the same masons may
have worked at both buildings. The vaulted interior is not without
ostentation; the clustered shafts of its central pier have capitals
carved with foliage, the ceiling bosses are elaborately ornamented,
and the abbot's stall is surmounted by a mitre.

The cathedral/priory church and monastic buildings at Whithorn were largely demolished after the Reformation, but the
church's plan and an outline of its development have been established. It began in the early or mid-C12, presumably at the recon-
stitution of the diocese, as a not very ambitious small cruciform,
but it was much enlarged in the early C13 for the Premonstratensian canons, providing a long unaisled nave, transepts,
each with an E chapel, an aisled choir of five bays and, projecting
at its E end, a sixth unaisled bay, probably containing the shrine of
St Ninian. In contrast to the Cistercian abbeys, whose presbyteries
had the function and atmosphere of private places of worship
reserved for the choir monks, Whithorn's choir was designed for
processions of pilgrims come to venerate the relics of the saint.
This public aspect was probably reinforced by the construction
of a Lady Chapel, almost certainly at the SE, c.1430. Whatever
architectural splendour there was has been almost entirely obliterated by the post-Reformation destruction of the church's E part
and the utilitarian remodelling of the nave as a parish church.
However, the present SW door of the nave, although made up
in the early C17 from two originally separate features, displays
strongly moulded C12 Romanesque decoration, a tantalizing
reminder that this was one of the main pilgrimage sites of medieval Scotland.

The late medieval fashion for votive masses and the endowment
of chantry chaplainries by particular families or trade guilds would
now pass unremarked in Dumfries and Galloway were it not for
one sumptuous building. That is Lincluden Collegiate Church
(now swallowed up in a Dumfries suburb), a former Benedictine
nunnery refounded in 1389 by Archibald ('the Grim'), third Earl
of Douglas, as a college of secular canons. The endowment
was augmented in 1429 by the Princess Margaret, Countess of
Douglas, daughter of King Robert III. Although work seems to
have continued through the C15 the choir's design must be of its
earlier years; one window is so similiar to early C15 work at
Melrose Abbey (Borders) and Paisley Abbey (Renfrewshire) that
common authorship is likely. The Lincluden choir exhibits a

magnificent display of curvilinear window tracery, remarkably unified in its diversity, a roof covered with late Gothic vaulting springing from heraldic corbels, and a richly sculpted stone pulpitum dividing it off from the nave. All this is a setting for the grandiloquent tomb of the Princess Margaret (†1450), the only 15 royal tomb surviving in Scotland; the blind arcading on the front of its sarcophagus frames a display of heraldry, and there is an elaborate superstructure formed by a canopy for the Princess's effigy.

The development of a regular parochial system from the C12 rarely produced PARISH CHURCHES of much elaboration. Some of the endowment of cathedral and monastic establishments and of collegiate churches came from grants of the parsonages (and sometimes also the vicarages) of parishes, with the consequent right to receive the tiends or tithes. By the Reformation three-quarters of the parsonages of parishes in Dumfries and Galloway had been appropriated in this manner. The parson of a parish was responsible for upkeep of the chancel of its church, the vicar and parishioners for the nave. Monasteries were more likely to spend their income, even if received from tiends, on their own houses than on the parish churches of which they were parsons.

Lay magnates were not necessarily much concerned with the parish churches in their domains. Often they enjoyed a close connexion with a monastery, whose church might serve as their burial place. Thus Alan, lord of Galloway, was buried in Dundrennan Abbey in 1234 and his daughter, Devorgilla, at Sweetheart Abbey, a monastery on which money was spent in the late C14 by Archibald, third Earl of Douglas and lord of Galloway. The Bruces, lords of Annandale from c.1124, were closely linked to Guisborough Abbey in Yorkshire, to whose use they appropriated the parsonages of four Annandale churches in the C12.

Parish churches were not necessarily neglected but they seem for the most part to have been built without undue expense or embellishment. Probably typical were the churches at Southwick, near Caulkerbush, and Senwick, both perhaps of the C12 or C13. They were plain rectangles, the chancel at Senwick perhaps marked off by a rood beam, that at Southwick perhaps by an arch. Better preserved but quite plain is the ruined Buittle Old Parish 7 Church: the nave is likely to have been built in the C12, with a couple of small round-arched windows in its N wall; the wider chancel is an addition, probably of the C13, but the only decoration is provided by the attached shafts of its pointed chancel arch. More expensive was the church built at Cruggleton, prob- 8 ably in the first half of the C12, where the S door has cushion-capitalled nook-shafts and the chancel arch is of two orders with reeded and cubical cushion capitals. One much grander parish church was that of Sanquhar, which contained the tombs of the Roses, lords of Sanquhar, and their successors in that barony, the Crichtons. It was still standing in 1684, when it was described as 'a considerable and large fabrick, consisting of a spacious church and a stately quire'. Other exceptions to the general pattern of utilitarian thrift must have been the now lost churches of some of the royal burghs. At the Reformation the parish church in Dum-

fries contained, besides the High Altar and Lady Altar, seven
other altars of which at least five had been endowed by local
families and one by the burgh's incorporation of tailors.

Very little in the way of medieval CHURCH FURNISHINGS has
survived. In the garden of the Selkirk Arms Hotel in Kirkcudbright
18 stands a font of the 1480s carved with the MacLellan coat of arms
and a jolly depiction of a bird holding a leashed fox. Now in
17 the porch of St Bride's Parish Church, Sanquhar, is the statue,
probably early C15, of a bishop (perhaps St Nicholas)
accompanied by a boy.

Except for the monument to the Princess Margaret in Lincluden Collegiate Church (*see* above) medieval TOMBS have survived only in battered form and small numbers. There are a
couple of arched tomb recesses at Dundrennan Abbey and one
at Sweetheart Abbey, where there are also fragments of the sarcophagus tomb of Devorgilla, probably an early C16 replacement.
Effigies from such tombs are also few. Dundrennan Abbey contains the mutilated figure of a knight, probably C13, and Sweetheart Abbey the torso of Devorgilla's effigy. Better preserved are
the figure of *c.*1500 of a knight resting his feet on a lion at
Mouswald Parish Church and the contemporary effigy of a priest
in St Bride's Parish Church, Sanquhar.

Rather more survives in the way of stone COFFIN LIDS and
16 GRAVESLABS. In Dundrennan Abbey a gorily pictorial slab, probably of the C13, depicts an abbot dead of a stab wound, his feet
resting on a small kilted figure, presumably his assailant, whose
intestines spill out from a wound in his side. Much less entertaining is the same abbey's coffin lid (probably C12) of Abbot
William, decorated with a cross and crozier. Another coffin lid at
Dundrennan, that of Abbot Giles, probably C14, is decorated
with an elaborate floriated and ringed cross. A similar cross is on
the fragment of a graveslab, perhaps dating from a little earlier,
in Lochmaben Parish Church; this slab also displays a pair of
shears. Built into the w gable of Torthorwald Parish Church is
another slab carved with a floriated cross, together with a sword
and shield and the date 1450. Of two late medieval slabs in
Sweetheart Abbey one shows a sword and shield, the other an
uprooted tree. Still crisp is the fragmentary relief of a priest carved
on a slab, probably of the early C16, now in Parton Parish Church.

POST-REFORMATION CHURCHES

At the Scottish Reformation of 1560 the religious orders were
suppressed and their lands granted to laymen. Deprived of their
function as the setting for conventual services, most abbey and
priory churches were abandoned, although the choir of Dundrennan Abbey and the nave of Whithorn Priory were adapted
for parochial worship, as was the refectory of Sweetheart Abbey.

Because reformed worship placed at least as much emphasis

on prayer, Scriptural readings and preaching as on the eucharistic sacrament,* it was important that the minister or reader should be as audible as possible to the congregation. For this the medieval parish churches were not especially well suited, but most continued in use until the C18, often probably with a pulpit erected in the middle of one long wall. The first POST-REFORMATION CHURCHES in Dumfries and Galloway were not much different in shape from their predecessors. Parton Old Parish Church of 1592 (or possibly 1534) and Anwoth Old Parish Church and the former Girthon Parish Church, both probably of the 1620s, were all long and relatively narrow low rectangles, Parton only *c*. 4.3m. broad but 19.8m. long, Anwoth *c*. 21.3m. by 5.6m., and Girthon *c*. 21.9m. by 7m. The dimensions are probably explained by their walls standing on medieval foundations; Girthon retains the medieval E gable. Anwoth's interior may have been conservatively arranged, with the pulpit and, conceivably, a holy table at the E end, where the S window has two lights instead of the others' one. Girthon, despite its awkwardly long shape, was clearly planned for reformed worship: the pulpit stands in the middle of the long S wall, a gallery fills the E end, and the main entrances are placed in the gables. Another church of the 1620s, Portpatrick Old Parish Church, was cruciform, the pulpit probably sited near the centre, the transeptal jambs perhaps containing the seats of local lairds.

The first church in the region built on what was to become a standard post-Reformation plan was Kirkmaiden Parish Church of 1638, a rubble-walled T, with the N 'aisle' or jamb containing the laird's gallery or pew of the McDoualls of Logan placed above their burial vault, and the pulpit standing in the centre of the long S wall. Another mid-C17 T-plan kirk was the (demolished) Dunscore Parish Church of 1649, its walls mortared with shell-lime, the roof joists and sarking of oak. All of these post-Reformation churches were probably equipped from the start with a bell or were provided with one soon after construction; this was a legal requirement by 1642. The bell at Parton was housed in a sturdy bellcote, apparently of 1635. At Portpatrick it hung in an earlier (probably C16) round tower. Another round belfry, perhaps of 1611, stands on the S side of the otherwise rebuilt Crossmichael Parish Church.

So far as church building in the region was concerned the second half of the C17 was a fallow period, and fewer than twenty new parish churches were constructed in the first half of the C18, doubtless partly because of a disinclination to spend money on the part of the heritors (landowners) who were responsible for their erection and maintenance. Most parishes still made do with patched and remodelled medieval buildings, although the earlier decades of the C18 saw a move towards a more fashionable roofing material than the previously widespread heather thatch, which

---

* Despite the wish of the first reformers for the Holy Communion to be celebrated at least monthly, and preferably weekly, the General Assembly of 1562 stipulated only that it was to be celebrated four times a year in urban parishes and twice a year in rural. In the event, celebrations were less frequent.

was presumably deemed unacceptable by 1732, when the Presbytery of Annan ordered that it should be replaced at Dornock Parish Church with slates. This alteration had already been undertaken a few years earlier at Kirkpatrick-Fleming and Hoddom Parish Churches. At Hoddom this was justified as an economy, 'in regard a thatched Church was expensive on the heretors'.

The new CHURCHES OF THE C18 were generally shorter and broader than those of the C17, only the now demolished Rerrick Parish Church at Dundrennan of 1743 (c. 21.3m. by 6m.) perpetuating the medieval tradition of the long narrow rectangle. Most were straightforward oblong boxes but made some not too expensive attempt to show that they were buildings of quality. Dalton Old Parish Church of 1704 was given V-jointed rustication at the rectangular window surrounds, a bullseye window in the E gable and a birdcage bellcote. The corners and W gable apex of Kirkconnel Parish Church, built in 1728, were crowned with urns, as were the corners of its ogee-roofed bellcote, whose panelled faces were decorated with the winged heart armorial device of the Duke of Queensberry, the principal heritor of the parish. At both Glasserton Parish Church of 1732 and Kirkgunzeon Parish Church of 1790 the windows were roundheaded and one gable was topped by a ball finial, the other by a birdcage bellcote. Several rural parish churches were T-plan. One of the smartest is the church at Kirkbean (probably by *William Craik*, 1776), which has a Venetian window in the gable of the jamb and, projecting from the long W side, a tower, exceptional enough in a rural church but made the more so by the Diocletian window in its upper stage. The jamb of Sorbie Old Parish Church (1755) contained a gallery for the Earl of Galloway, the principal heritor, with a retiring room behind.

The *beau idéal* of the nobleman's place of worship must be Durisdeer Parish Church, built for the third Duke of Queensberry in 1716–29, probably to a design by *James Smith*. The church itself is T-plan, but the jamb is balanced by a pre-existing mausoleum which Smith had added to the previous church in 1695–1708. As viewed from the E, the body of the church appeared as a piend-roofed centrepiece projecting from between ogee-roofed pavilions (the effect now marred by later reroofing of the church and jamb). Seen from the W, it displayed the ducal requirement for something far better appointed than Lord Galloway's modest retiring room at Sorbie, the Duke of Queensberry being provided with a two-storey block built at right angles across the end of the church, with a tower (formerly topped by a lead spire) rising through its roof.

Churches of the C18 in the royal burghs were expressions of civic dignity. The first was the New Church (now demolished) at the top of the High Street in Dumfries, designed by *Alexander McGill* and built in 1724–7, a big piend-roofed box with roundheaded windows, a steeple projecting from the centre of its S side, the battlemented tower's merlons triangular, the octagonal stone spire studded with lucarnes. In 1742–9 Dumfries replaced its medieval parish church with the present St Michael's and South

Church, whose general appearance is very like that of the New Church. The importance of its prominent site is emphasized by the W steeple, the stumpily pinnacled parapet of its tower squashed by the Gothic-survival spire. The same composition as at Dumfries' New Church was adopted for Annan's Old Parish 21 Church in 1789, but the language was, understandably, more firmly classical, the steeple's entrance placed in a Roman Doric aedicule under a Venetian window, and the belfry stage of the tower an octagon under the spire.

During the FIRST HALF OF THE C19 about half the region's parish churches were rebuilt. A few were very simple, like the humble Carsphairn Parish Church of *c.*1815 or the large but utilitarian box of Kelton Parish Church of 1805–6. Showing slightly more sense of style are the T-plan kirks of Kirkmichael (by *John McCracken*, 1813–15) and St Mungo (now a school) at Kettleholm (by *William McGowan*, 1841–2), each with round-arched windows and a birdcage bellcote, or the Tudor-windowed Twynholm Parish Church of 1818. But such simple bellcoted churches were exceptions. Most of the new parish churches were designed as landmarks, their presence usually proclaimed by a tower, their style unarchaeological Gothic.

The majority of early C19 parish churches seem to have been the work of local architects. The most prolific of these was *Walter Newall* of Dumfries. His parish churches (e.g. Borgue of 1814, Buittle of 1817–19, Anwoth of 1826–7, Parton of 1832–3, or Kirkpatrick Durham of 1849–50) are generally straightforward Perp or Tudor Gothic, the 'k' of 'Gothick' still in evidence, but a touch serious-minded. Each has an end tower with spiky pinnacles rising at the corners of its battlement. At the tower of Kirkmahoe Parish Church, Kirkton, of 1822–3, where Newall was both the designer and superintended the work, the pinnacles rise from diagonal buttresses; the E gable of this church is dressed rather more expensively than usual, with a pair of Tudor porches projecting under blind crosslet arrowslits and a quatrefoil. Expensive too, but in a classical manner, are the top stages Newall added in 1835–6 to the tower of Kirkbean Parish Church, the octagonal belfry cupola surmounted by a lantern.

Very similar to the generality of Newall's Gothic work was that of another Dumfries architect, *James Thomson*, whose parish churches at Lochmaben (1818–20), St Bride's, Sanquhar (1822– 27 4), and Dunscore (1823–4) are all Georgian Gothic boxes with hoodmoulded Y-traceried windows and spikily pinnacled end towers. At both Sanquhar and Dunscore Thomson returned the moulded eaves course across gables to suggest pediments. At Lochmaben he provided quatrefoils in the openings of the tower's bottom stage.

The New Galloway architect and contractor *William McCand-lish* designed three parish churches in a more adventurous mode, although their Gothic detail is just as innocent of scholarly intent as that of Newall or Thomson. Kells Parish Church, near New 23 Galloway, of 1822, is a T-plan made cruciform by the addition of a tower, its diagonal buttresses again topped by spiky pinnacles.

McCandlish used the same plan at Dalry Parish Church, St
24 John's Town of Dalry, in 1830–2 and Glencairn Parish Church,
Kirkland, in 1836–7, but at both churches the gable of the jamb
contains a gigantic arched recess, its back pierced by a huge
window. Glencairn Parish Church is made more muscular by
clasping buttresses at the corners of the body and the tower. Less
disciplined are the buttresses at Kirkcowan Parish Church (1834),
which almost elbow each other aside, those at the centre of the s
wall seeming to have captured a cross-finialled pedimented
outshot. Frivolous by comparison is the slim tower of Wamphray
Parish Church (by *William McGowan*, 1834), topped by a ball-
finialled birdcage bellcote, the idea of having a tower not to
contain the bells but to support the bellcote perhaps taken from
John McDonald's nearby Johnstone Parish Church at Johnstonebridge of 1818–19.

Several parish churches, especially the largest, were designed
26 by architects from outside the region. Eskdalemuir Parish Church
of 1826 seems to have been designed by *John Smallwood* of Dalkeith. Its pretensions are limited, but the tower is enjoyable, its
upward stages marked by a pointed door, a Gothick window, a
blind quatrefoil, and hoodmoulded belfry openings, all topped
by an octagonal spire. Smallwood was presumably appointed
because he was employed by the fifth Duke of Buccleuch, who
owned two-thirds of this moorland parish. For the far more
25 expensive Canonbie Church of 1821–2, whose parish was much
richer and wholly owned by the Duke, the architect was *William
Atkinson* of London. He had previously designed additions for
the Duke's seat of Bowhill (Borders) and his Chamberlain's house
at Dabton (q.v.). At Canonbie he produced a severe ashlar box,
with two tiers of windows (Tudor-arched below, four-centred
above) expressing the galleried interior. In the centre of the w
side is a big tower, its buttresses topped by turrets.

Another outside architect who received commissions through
the patronage of the Dukes of Buccleuch was *William Burn* of
Edinburgh. The first church he designed in Dumfries and Galloway was that of Keir, a parish half-owned by the Duke. He was
appointed in 1813, before he is known to have done any other
work for the Buccleuchs, and the result was a distinctly stolid
Tudorish box with a dumpy battlemented tower. By the 1830s
and 1840s, when he designed three more churches for parishes
controlled by the Duke (Tynron in 1835, Morton, at Thornhill,
in 1839, and Langholm in 1842), Burn was well established as his
architect, having worked on his houses at Dalkeith (Lothian),
Drumlanrig and Bowhill (Borders). Of the three churches,
Tynron was the cheapest – just as its parish was the poorest – and
the quirkiest: the skewputts and Gothic birdcage bellcote are all
carved with dragon gargoyles, and the join of the church to the
low vestry is announced by large Tudor chimneys. Morton Parish
Church at Thornhill is a simplified Romanesque box with a big
tower and a huge interior, its ceiling decorated with plaster ribs
29 and bosses to suggest vaulting. Langholm Parish Church is Gothic
of a Georgian-survival kind, its sturdy buttresses and large bird-

cage bellcote giving the outside a heavy presence. The interior is covered by a hammer-beam roof.

Two of Burn's other churches in Dumfries and Galloway (Monigaff Parish Church of 1834–6 and Penninghame St John of 1838–40, both in Newton Stewart) were for parishes whose chief landowner was the Earl of Galloway (for whom Burn was to design additions to Galloway House a few years later). Both are large and Gothic, with end towers. The flaming urn finials topping the pinnacles of the buttresses at Monigaff Church almost make it fun. Penninghame St John is thrifty and serious but has an octagonal spire for added vertical emphasis. Another of Burn's Gothic churches is at Portpatrick (1840–2), a parish whose chief landowners, the Hunter Blairs of Dunskey, had commissioned plans from him for rebuilding their house. It is hardly lighthearted, but the loop-traceried windows and the tall w tower enlivened by cannon spouts lift it well clear of the routine. Burn's only other church in the region, the parish church at Kirkcudbright (1835–8), is a big and bare cruciform, Tudor in feel though not in its Gothic detail, the steeple overpowering the domestic scale of the small burgh.

Another Edinburgh architect, *John Henderson*, produced two churches in Dumfries and Galloway. Kirkmabreck Parish Church at Creetown (1831–4) is an urbane version of the local architects' Perp preaching boxes, the verticality of its end tower attenuated by immensely tall windows and foliaged finials. For St Mary's 28 Church in Dumfries (1837–9) Henderson produced a high fire-screen Perp front topped by a bellcote. The suggestion of a nave and aisles behind this façade was echoed at Stranraer Old Parish Church of 1838–40, a building outclassed, however, by a much more prominently sited chapel of ease (now High Kirk) of 1841, whose heavily battlemented tower is a landmark from Loch Ryan. A tower of confidently unfussy Georgian Gothic appearance was added to Glasserton Parish Church in 1836–7 by another outside architect, *J. B. Papworth* of London, appointed presumably because he was working on the additions to the nearby Cally Palace.

OTHER DENOMINATIONS besides the established Church of Scotland built places of worship in the late C18 and early C19. There was a sizeable Roman Catholic population in the area just w of Dumfries, where the Maxwells of Terregles were the dominant landowners. The Episcopal Church, formed after 1690 from clergy and laity unable to accept the newly imposed Presbyterian order in the Church of Scotland, was predominantly Jacobite in political sympathy and had been persecuted for much of the C18; but it was resurgent after 1792, when the repeal of penal laws again allowed the erection of Episcopalian churches. Congregationalism, often allied to Baptist doctrine, was making an appearance at this time, but more significant in terms of numbers were the breakaway Presbyterian sects. The Cameronians (later Reformed Presbyterians) were the lineal descendants of the hardline Covenanters of the late C17, who had stood aloof from the 'uncovenanted', albeit Presbyterian, Church of Scotland established by William III. More numerous were the 'Seceders', whose concern for purity of doctrine and practice led to many denominational splits but who formed two main groups: congregations descended from a secession from the established Church in 1733 (Original Secession, later United Associate and United Secession) and the Relief Church, which began with a second secession in 1752.

In some towns these sectarian divisions had produced by 1840 a multiplicity of churches and meeting houses. In Dumfries, besides two parish churches and two chapels of ease belonging to the established Church of Scotland, there were a Roman Catholic chapel, an Episcopal church, a Methodist church, a Congregational church, a Reformed Presbyterian church, an Original Secession church, a United Associate church, and a Relief church, all serving a population of about 10,000. In the much smaller town of Annan, with a population of a little over 4,000, there were the Parish Church, an established chapel of ease, a Roman Catholic church, a Congregational church, a United Associate church and a Relief church. Stranraer, with fewer than 5,000 inhabitants, contained a parish church, a chapel of ease, one Reformed Presbyterian church, two United Associate churches, and one Relief church.

The churches of the Presbyterian sects were generally fairly humble meeting houses. The United Associate Church built at Gatehouse of Fleet in 1840 (now St Mary's Episcopal Church) is a broad Gothic box, neither large nor pretentious. The Reformed Presbyterian and Relief churches of the 1820s in Stranraer are both unadventurous, consoled cornices over the rectangular windows their principal extravagance. That town's Original Secession Church of 1843 is a little more extravagant, the pointed windows of its front enjoying hoodmoulds, the corners surmounted by ball-topped foliaged finials. More stylish, if only because of its shape, was the octagonal Reformed Presbyterian chapel of 1798 at Quarrelwood, near Duncow.

The Roman Catholics eschewed triumphalism. Their churches at Dumfries (St Andrew's, by *John McCracken*, 1811–13) and Dalbeattie (1814) are utilitarian. Even more assertive is St Mary's Church at New Abbey, designed by *Newall* in 1824 as a more conveniently sited replacement for the large but simply detailed brick-walled chapel which had been built in 1815 at Kirkconnell House. The New Abbey church is quite plain and hides behind the contemporary Tudor priest's house as if fearful of an anti-Popery demonstration. Very much smarter, and clearly intended for a prosperous clientèle, was the Episcopal church in Dumfries by *T. F. Hunt* of London (1817), suavely villa-like but with a giant pedimented Ionic portico. Surprisingly prosperous too, although less assertive, is that burgh's Italianate Congregational church of 1835.

In the 'Disruption' of 1843 over one-third of ministers of the established Church left its General Assembly and constituted themselves the Free Church of Scotland, claiming adherence to the true Presbyterian principles and Calvinist theology betrayed by the majority in the Church of Scotland. Four years later the United Secession and Relief churches came together as the United Presbyterian Church. These new groupings of the 1840s seriously challenged the hegemony of the established Church. Right from the start the Free Church set out to build a place of worship in every parish in Scotland; standard designs for cheap churches had been prepared even before the formal break of the 'Disruption'. One of these designs (by *Cousin & Gall* of Edinburgh) was adopted for the Free church built at Borgue in 1843, a very plain rubble-walled box. Slightly more ambitious were the contemporary Tongland and Twynholm Free Church at Ringford, with gablets over its roundheaded windows and a simple Gothic bellcote, and Stranraer Free Church (now Lewis Street Gospel Hall), which has a pagoda-like bellcote on the shaped centre gable of its neo-Jacobean front. Much more of an architectural challenge to the temples of the establishment were the Free churches of Maxwelltown in Dumfries (by *John Thomson*, 1843), Girthon and Anwoth in Gatehouse of Fleet (1844) and Annan (1847, now St Andrew's Greenknowe Erskine), all with end towers. Also with a tower but more muscular in its Gothic was Corsock Free Church (now Parish Church) of 1851–2. Its site was perhaps chosen to enable it to look down on the nearby and slightly earlier established chapel of ease, and its design by *William McCandlish* was more expensive than that of the generality of early rural Free churches, presumably because it was financed by the local laird, Alexander Murray Dunlop, the chief legal adviser to the Free Church.

The United Presbyterians already had places of worship, but a new self-confidence, perhaps due to the weakening of the Church of Scotland by the 'Disruption', can be seen in the large North United Presbyterian church built at Sanquhar in 1849, its gable front plentifully pinnacled and with a big Y-traceried window under an ogee hoodmould.

FROM THE 1860s, both the Free Church and the United Presbyterian Church put up much larger and more expensive buildings, the architecture generally, though not invariably, Gothic of an archaeological character. At Dumfries, the 1840s Maxwelltown Free Church, despite having a tower, was replaced by *James Barbour* in 1865–6 with a new church (now Maxwelltown West Church) on a more prominent site. Its tall bellcoted firescreen front is still Georgian in feel despite the correct Dec detail. Free churches of the 1840s were replaced at Lockerbie (1866–7), Kirkcudbright (1872–4), both by *John Honeyman* of Glasgow, Dalbeattie (by *Francis Armstrong*, 1880–1; now Park Baptist Church), Portpatrick (by *Richard Park*, 1886–7) and Moffat (by *David B. Burnie*, 1890–2; now St Mary United Free Church). All these new churches were large, Gothic, dignified with towers or steeples, and architecturally disappointing. Unusual in the area for its adoption of an Italianate style was the remodelling of Free St George's Church (now St George's Church) in Dumfries by *James Halliday* in 1892–3.

In 1860–1 the United Presbyterians built a conspicuously sited

box-like church designed by *James Barbour* at the rapidly growing
burgh of Dalbeattie, the centre of its front gable slightly advanced
under a bellcote. Like the Free Church, the United Presbyterians
also replaced existing churches with larger buildings, all Gothic
in manner, e.g. the North and South United Presbyterian Churches at Langholm (by *Robert Baldie* of Glasgow, 1867, and by
Michael Brodie of Hawick, 1883–4), and the United Presbyterian
churches at Waterbeck (by *James Barbour*, 1868–9), Castle
Douglas (by *James Barbour*, 1870), Lockerbie (now Holy Trinity
R.C.; by *Ford Mackenzie* of Wigan, 1874–5) and Newton Stewart
(by *Richard Park*, 1877–8); Waterbeck is the only one of these to
show a confident quality. At Stranraer, the Glaswegian *Alexander
C. Pettigrew's* West United Presbyterian (now St Ninian's)
Church of 1883–4 is engagingly inept in its determination to be
noticed. More conventional, employing without imagination a
Scots late Gothic, is the same town's Ivy Place (now St Andrew's)
Church by *John B. Wilson* of Glasgow, 1896–8, contemporary
with his similarly detailed United Presbyterian (now Virginhall)
Church at Thornhill. Another example of late Gothic used by a
Glasgow firm is at Whithorn, where the United Presbyterian
church was rebuilt in 1892 with a dumpy tower to a design by
Thomson & Sandilands.

After the large-scale rebuilding of parish churches in the earlier
C19, the established CHURCH OF SCOTLAND had little need to
replace existing churches, nor were the heritors generally eager
to spend money on such projects. A few churches did require
replacement. Wigtown Parish Church, largely rebuilt in 1730, was
in 1839 thought 'an old mean-looking edifice'; a new church, by
the London architect *Henry Roberts*, was built in 1851, still using
the Georgian T-plan but clothed in austere Gothic dress and with
a French pavilion roof on the tower. Penpont Parish Church
and Closeburn Parish Church, both of the C18, were rebuilt,
Penpont's design of 1867, by the Buccleuch estate architect
Charles Howitt, reminiscent of Burn's churches, Closeburn, of
1878, an ambitious example of *James Barbour's* uninspired Gothic.
Just as mechanical are Barbour's New Abbey Parish Church built
in 1875–7, allowing the removal of an C18 kirk from among the
ruins of Sweetheart Abbey, and Tundergarth Parish Church of
1899–1900, again replacing an C18 building. A couple of new
parish churches seem to have been built because a prominent
local landowner wanted something better. The erection of Inch
Parish Church at Castle Kennedy in 1858–61, designed by the
Edinburgh architect *J. Maitland Wardrop*, was a preliminary to
the building of Lochinch Castle, also by Wardrop, for the parish's
principal heritor, the Earl of Stair. A new St Mungo Parish Church
(*see* Kettleholm) was put up in 1875–7 on the edge of the park of
the recently completed Castlemilk, whose owner, Robert Jardine,
paid for its construction. Like Castlemilk it is by *David Bryce* of
Edinburgh, its powerful late Scots Gothic style an ecclesiastical
counterpart to the Scottish Baronial of the mansion house.

The C19 growth of the new burghs of Castle Douglas and
Dalbeattie necessitated the erection of parish churches. The one

at Castle Douglas (now in other use) developed haphazardly from 1869, acquiring an immensely tall tower in 1890; Dalbeattie Parish Church (by *Kinnear & Peddie* of Edinburgh, 1878–80), a plain Gothic cruciform, has a steeple that dominates the town. Moffat, an older burgh, developed greatly as a spa and holiday town after the railway arrived in 1847, and a new and much larger parish church (St Andrew) was constructed in the 1880s. Its austerely 34 Gothic design, by the Edinburgh architect *John Starforth*, provides a powerful build-up at the front from bowed stair towers to a battlemented tower whose single corner turret gives a wilful touch of asymmetry. Twenty years earlier Starforth had given Dumfries its new Greyfriars Church (replacing the C18 New Church), with 32 a steeple that presides over the N end of the High Street. Another large ecclesiastical edifice built in a growing C19 burgh is Lockerbie's Dryfesdale Parish Church of 1896–8; unfortunately, despite the example of Dumfries and Moffat in commissioning an inventive Edinburgh designer, this was the work of a local architect, *F. J. C. Carruthers*, who produced a boxy Gothic building, neither its height nor its steeple providing excitement.

After the foundation of the Aberdeen (later Scottish) Ecclesiological Society in 1886, many ministers and some parishioners of the Church of Scotland were influenced by the ideas of that organization, which advocated an internal arrangement of churches along High Presbyterian lines, with the communion table placed as the focal point, preferably in an apse or chancel, flanked by the pulpit and font. As a result, some churches acquired chancels (e.g. St Mary, Dumfries, in 1896). Others were remodelled, one of the more imaginative schemes being at Brydekirk Parish Church, a straightforward rectangular chapel of ease of 1835, where the space inside the end tower was used *c.* 1900 to form an apse. But the fullest expression of 'ecclesiological' principles could be achieved in new churches. By far the largest of these is the Crichton Memorial Church of 1890–7 at the 36, 37 Crichton Royal Hospital, Dumfries, officially undenominational but planned along the most developed 'ecclesiological' lines. This marvellously inventive late Gothic edifice, designed by the Edinburgh architect *Sydney Mitchell*, dominates the surrounding ward blocks like a cathedral in its close. In both spirit and plan it is far removed from the standard preaching box of the early C19, the aisled nave, transepts, crossing tower and semi-octagonal sanctuary almost dangerously reminiscent of the pre-Reformation Church.

Other late C19 and early C20 'ecclesiological' churches were more circumspect. Ardwell Church, by *P. MacGregor Chalmers* of Glasgow, 1900–2, is austere Gothic. Southwick Parish Church at 38 Caulkerbush, by *Kinnear & Peddie*, 1889–91, is a sturdy mixture of Early Christian (i.e. a simplified Romanesque evocative of the supposed purity of the pre-medieval Church) and Norman, although the shape of the crossing tower (though not its detail) is clearly derived from the C14 tower of St Monans Church in Fife. *J. M. Dick Peddie* used a purer Early Christian manner at Dalton Parish Church in 1894–5 and was followed by *P. MacGregor*

Chalmers at Colvend Parish Church in 1910–11 and Urr Parish Church, Haugh of Urr, in 1914–15.

The ROMAN CATHOLICS gradually enlarged their church at Dumfries, adding a tower in 1843, giving it a spire fifteen years later, and then, in 1871–2, extending the building with transepts and an apse-ended chancel designed by *George Goldie* of London. Goldie also provided the plain but sizeable Gothic Church of St John the Evangelist at Castle Douglas in 1867–8 and, in partnership with *Charles Child*, Our Lady and St Ninian at Newton Stewart in 1875–6. Just as austere was the chapel of the Convent of the Perpetual Adoration at Dumfries designed by *Pugin & Pugin* in 1880.

The EPISCOPALIANS put up little in the region, and the churches they did construct were mostly small and designed by English architects. The sturdily simple Gothic Church of St John the Evangelist at Annan, by *John Hodgson* of Carlisle, 1843, was a prototype for the two churches by *James Caird Macfarlane*, St John, Stranraer (demolished), and St Andrew, Newton Stewart, built in the 1890s. Also small, but both with towers intended to carry spires, are Christ Church, Dalbeattie, by *Francis Armstrong*, 1875, and the aggressively detailed rogue Gothic St Ninian, Castle Douglas, by *E. B. Lamb* of London, 1856–61. The village atmosphere of these churches is even stronger at the picturesque All Saints, Lockerbie, by *John Douglas* of Chester, 1901–3, and St Margaret of Scotland, New Galloway, by *W. H. Harrison* of London, 1904–8, which was given a lychgate in 1912. Much more expensive, and standing in open country, is All Saints, Challoch, designed by *W. G. Habershon & Pite* of London and built in 1871–2 as a private chapel for Edward J. Stopford Blair, owner of the nearby Penninghame House. It is a Geometric container for an elaborately finished Tractarian interior, the altar very much the focal point. Less exuberant internally, but just as Tractarian in its planning, is the Church of St John the Evangelist at Dumfries, by *Slater & Carpenter* of London, 1867–8, its steeple a centrepiece for the prosperous suburb in which it is placed.

The TWENTIETH CENTURY has brought some denominational unions. In 1900 the Free and United Presbyterian churches came together (except for a Free Church rump) as the United Free Church, which in turn joined (again minus a rump) with the Church of Scotland in 1929. Without formal unions, or even much in the way of conversation, denominations have come architecturally closer. During the First World War the munitions township of Gretna was provided with three places of worship, Church of Scotland (St Andrew), Episcopalian (All Saints) and Roman Catholic (St Ninian). Each is in a different style – St Andrew (by *C. M. Crickmer*, 1917) very simple, All Saints (by *Geoffrey Lucas*, 1917) Early Christian, and St Ninian (by *C. Evelyn Simmons*, 1918) Byzantine – but each is cruciform, with an aisled nave and the altar or communion table placed as a focus at the E end. There seems little reason why they should not be denominationally interchangeable. At the same time Crickmer also designed an Episcopal church, St John the Evangelist at the nearby Eastriggs, the pyramid roof on its S tower a powerful variant on that of his St Andrew, Gretna. All these churches were in the Arts and Crafts tradition, with simplicity and truth to materials to the fore. More consciously 'designed' was the Belgian *Charles J. Menart*'s chapel at St Joseph's College, Dumfries, erected as a war memorial in 1923, which has neo-Celtic touches diversifying its simplified Romanesque. The next year Menart enlarged St Joseph's Roman Catholic Church at Stranraer by adding a square E tower, its red-tiled roof a gentle Mediterranean reminder, the interior containing a new sanctuary. *J. M. Bowie*'s blocky late Gothic Middlebie Parish Church of 1929 was the only interwar Protestant church of any size.

Churches built in Dumfries and Galloway since the Second World War have been few. In 1951–3 *Ian G. Lindsay* provided Moffat with the Episcopal Church of St John the Evangelist; it is very simple, of harled brick, with a touch of neo-Georgian. Slightly more assertive, but disappointing, is the Roman Catholic Church of SS. Ninian, Martin and John at Whithorn by *Goodhart-Rendel, Broadbent & Curtis*, 1959–60. Less traditional is St Teresa's Roman Catholic Church, Dumfries, by *John Sutherland*, 1956–8, the huge broached spire an effective landmark in the encircling housing. Sutherland's St Andrew (R.C.), Dumfries, of 1963–4 shows the influence of the liturgical reforms associated with the Second Vatican Council, the seating for the congregation placed in an arc round the altar at the E corner, and the roof swept down from this clearstoreyed focus. Otherwise the late C20 has produced only a handful of cheap buildings intended to serve new housing estates, one (St Ninian (Episcopal), Carrick Road, Dumfries, by *Colin Morton* and *Charles Fotheringham*, 1967) later converted to a public house without evident loss of character.

The FURNISHINGS of a well-equipped Georgian church can be exemplified by Eskdalemuir Parish Church of 1826, which has galleries on three sides and a high pulpit placed in the centre of the long W wall. A rather grander version is Crossmichael Parish Church as remodelled in the 1820s, where the S corners of the body are occupied by lairds' pews, each with a pilaster-framed basket arch facing the pulpit.

GALLERIES, enabling the maximum number of people to be close to the pulpit, had been erected in churches since the early C17, if not before. By the time the medieval St Michael's Parish Church, Dumfries, was demolished in 1744, it contained a large W gallery (its front divided into the Magistrates' and Merchants' Lofts, its back being the Common Loft) and lofts for the trades of tailors, smiths, wrights, weavers, shoemakers, glovers and fleshers. In the C18 and C19 the churches of all except the most sparsely populated parishes contained at least one gallery. Generally they were simply finished, although there could be touches of sophistication such as the marbled cast-iron columns in Kirkcowan Parish Church of 1834. Sometimes one gallery was reserved for a local laird and his family, as at Durisdeer Parish Church, although the Duke of Queensberry's gallery of 1784 here is surprisingly unostentatious. In burgh churches part of a gallery might

be reserved for the town council. The smartest example of a
30 magistrates' pew is in the N gallery of Annan Old Parish Church
of 1789, the seats covered by a canopy carried on fluted piers, the
frieze decorated with acanthus leaves, the coved soffit with swags
and a rose. More restrained but still sumptuous are the magistrates' seats of 1868 in the S gallery of Greyfriars Church, Dumfries, their backs inlaid with rose designs.

PULPITS were regarded as essential in churches by the early
C17, although none now in Dumfries and Galloway pre-dates the
C18. The early C19 pulpit at Durisdeer Church is still equipped
with C18 wrought-iron brackets holding a baptismal basin and
hourglass. In St Michael's and South Church, Dumfries, the
Corinthian-pilastered back and urn-finialled sounding board of
the 1746 pulpit survive, although the body was replaced in 1869.
A well-finished pulpit of the 1820s, with a crown finial on its
sounding board, is in Dunscore Parish Church. Much smarter is
the pulpit of 1832 in Dalry Parish Church, St John's Town of
Dalry, its ogee-domed and crown-finialled sounding board
carried on clustered shafts. The big parish churches designed by
31 *William Burn* in the 1830s and 1840s at Kirkcudbright, Newton
Stewart (Penninghame St John) and Langholm have big Tudor-
or Jacobean-style pulpits, all canopied, the first with pinnacles,
the others with strapwork cresting on the sounding board. At
Greyfriars Church, Dumfries, the Gothic pulpit of 1868 is decorated with blind quatrefoils and coloured inlay. For ostentation
it is hard to beat the pulpit of 1898 in Dryfesdale Parish Church,
Lockerbie, its bowed marble body supported on sandstone shafts.
More restrained but quite exceptionally roomy is the 1860s pulpit
in Hoddom Church, Ecclefechan, a church originally belonging
to the United Presbyterians whose ministers traditionally required
space to roam whilst preaching.

A fair number of pulpits stand in front of ORGANS. The use of
instrumental music in Presbyterian worship was first permitted
in the Church of Scotland by its General Assembly of 1866, a
decision followed by the United Presbyterian and Free churches
soon afterwards. The first Presbyterian organ in Dumfries and
Galloway was introduced in 1873 to Greyfriars Church, Dumfries,
where it was given a lavishly inlaid case. Like other early examples,
e.g. at Penninghame St John, Newton Stewart, it was housed
relatively inconspicuously in a gallery, but pride in organs soon
became common. In 1905 the organ displaced the pulpit from the
apse of Dryfesdale Parish Church, Lockerbie, and the organ of
1912 in St Mary's United Free Church, Moffat, is so large as to
render all other furnishings insignificant. In 1912 the organ pipes
at Annan Old Parish Church were used to form a canopy over
the pulpit.

COMMUNION TABLES were rare until relatively late. Many
churches in the C18 and C19 made do with trestle tables set up
only for the infrequent celebrations of the Holy Communion.
Some had a more permanent arrangement. In Durisdeer Parish
Church the two rows of mid-C19 table seats in front of the pulpit
can be converted to communion pews. In the centre of Carsphairn

Parish Church is a long communion table, probably of the mid-C18, with a pew each side, now contrasting rather strangely with the new communion table introduced in the 1930s and placed in an apse in accordance with the 'ecclesiological' ideas which became influential from the 1880s. By the mid-C20 all churches had acquired permanent communion tables, many as First World War memorials. Two of the less routine examples are the late Gothic table of 1902 in Ardwell Church, its front carved with figures of saints, and the Art Nouveauish table of 1923 (by *J. Jeffrey Waddell & Young*) in Penpont Parish Church. These tables are freestanding, with seats for the ministers and elders behind. This seating could have something of the character of a reredos, as at Inch Parish Church, Castle Kennedy, of 1895–6 or the Crichton Memorial Church of 1897 at the Crichton Royal Hospital, Dumfries, whose stalls are topped by canopies.

Besides emphasis on the communion table as the focal point of a church, the 'ecclesiologists' advocated that the chancel arch, if one could be provided, should be flanked by a pulpit and font. In the new churches of the 1890s and early 1900s (e.g. Southwick Parish Church, Caulkerbush, Ardwell Church, and Colvend Parish Church) the font was of stone and in a simplified Romanesque style, the pulpit wooden and Perp or neo-Jacobean, the styles perhaps asserting the Church of Scotland's continuity with the first Christians in Scotland and its pride in the C16 Reformation which reintroduced preaching of the Word as an integral part of public worship. Almost all Presbyterian churches have been touched by 'ecclesiological' influence, often in uneasy conjunction with an earlier arrangement of furnishings.

The Episcopalians and Roman Catholics were, until the liturgical reforms of the later C20, much more certain of what they required in their churches. The altar was the focus of worship, standing in a sanctuary at the E end; the pulpit stood to one side nearby, often balanced by a lectern; and the font was placed at the W end. Most Roman Catholic and Episcopalian churches are small and quite simply furnished, but the altars of the chapel in the Convent of the Perpetual Adoration, Dumfries, and of St Mary (R.C.), New Abbey, have been dignified by large wooden REREDOSES (of 1884 and 1890), the latter framing a copy of the Sistine Madonna. Much more delicate is *J. Ninian Comper*'s beautifully coloured reredos of *c.*1920 in All Saints Episcopal 43 Church, Lockerbie; its framework, of Italian Renaissance inspiration, encloses carved and gilded alabaster figures under gilded Gothic tabernacle work. Two Episcopal churches (St John the Evangelist, Dumfries, and All Saints, Challoch) display the full panoply of furnishings available to Tractarian-minded Victorian congregations, with stone fonts (that at Dumfries a copy of Thorwaldsen's kneeling angel), lecterns, stone pulpits, chancel screens, choir stalls, altar rails, reredoses (one with mosaic work, the other's decoration painted) and encaustic tiles. Dec was the prevalent style, the work verging on the fussy. A later and calmer Episcopalian ensemble of most of these furnishings was provided by *Geoffrey Lucas* at All Saints (Episcopal) Church, Gretna, in

1917, but the idiom is now generally Arts and Crafts, although the tall font cover, topped by a pelican in piety, is in the late medieval manner, and the altar's riddel posts with gilded angels owe much to Comper.

Until the later C19, STAINED GLASS was distrusted by Presbyterians as likely to foster idolatry, although abstract decoration, such as was provided in the 1830s at Monigaff Parish Church, Newton Stewart, or the fleur-de-lis patterns at Johnstone United Presbyterian (now Hoddom) Church, Ecclefechan, of the 1860s, might escape censure. A pioneering installation of stained glass depicting people, of *c.*1850, is in the former United Associate (now St Mary's Episcopal) Church at Gatehouse of Fleet, where roundels in the windows contain portraits of heroes of the Old and New Testaments and the Reformation. However, as late as 1876, when the expensively Gothic St Mungo Parish Church, Kettleholm, was built and paid for by the magnate Robert Jardine, its windows, although all filled with stained glass by *James Ballantine & Son*, included only one figurative subject, that of the dove. Eleven years later, when St Andrew's Parish Church, Moffat, was opened, it had two stained-glass windows (both by *James Ballantine & Son*), one depicting the emblematic figures of Faith, Hope and Charity, the other Our Lord's command to St Peter to feed His sheep. From then until now, only the constraints of cash or taste have deterred congregations from filling church windows with stained glass.

The largest single purveyor of stained glass in the late C19 and early C20 was the Edinburgh firm of Ballantine (successively *James Ballantine & Son*, *A. Ballantine & Gardiner* and *James Ballantine II*), whose work was almost always competent but never inspired. For the Episcopal Church of St John the Evangelist, Dumfries, in 1868–1912, the English firm of *Clayton & Bell* provided glass designed both to complement the architecture and to provide a coherent iconography (scenes from the life of Our Lord in the end windows, Old Testament figures in the s nave aisle, New Testament scenes in the N, saints in the chancel). The same firm produced a window in 1906 for the Episcopal Church of St Margaret of Scotland, New Galloway, where other glass came from *James Powell & Sons* and *C. E. Kempe*. Kempe windows appear in another Episcopalian church, All Saints, Challoch, together with work of the 1870s by *C. A. Gibbs*. All Saints (Episcopal), Lockerbie, has characteristic works of *N. H. J. Westlake* (1910), *J. Ninian Comper* (*c.*1920) and *William Morris & Co.* (made *c.*1925, when that firm was in decline). Morris & Co. also supplied a window to New Abbey Parish Church in 1914. Another English firm, *Heaton, Butler & Bayne*, crossed the denominational divide with windows installed in Crossmichael Parish Church (1898), Inch Parish Church, Castle Kennedy (*c.*1900), Corsock Free (now Parish) Church (*c.*1905), and St Andrew's Episcopal Church, Newton Stewart (1910). The Birmingham firm of *Swaine, Bourne & Son* produced three windows for Tundergarth Parish Church in 1900–9 and *H. W. Lonsdale* one for Kirkmahoe Parish Church, Kirkton, in 1895. Tynron Parish Church has a lush window of 1893 by *Cottier & Co.*, a firm which originated in Scotland but had moved to London in 1870.

Much of the glass was by Scottish firms. Richer in feeling than the Ballantines' polite Edinburgh glass was that produced by Glasgow studios at the end of the C19 and the early C20. Examples of the darkly coloured work of the *Stephen Adam* firm and *Alfred A. Webster* are in St Andrew, Stranraer (1898), Kirkconnel Parish Church (1901 and 1914), Twynholm Parish Church (1906), St Michael's and South Church, Dumfries (1910), and Colvend Parish Church (1918). *William Meikle & Sons* are represented in the churches at Wanlockhead (1911) and Waterbeck (1917), *J. & W. Guthrie & Andrew Wells Ltd* by a dramatic window of 1918–19 in Portpatrick Parish Church.

The use of strong colours has been characteristic of Scottish stained glass since *c.* 1920. Expressionist windows of that time by *Douglas Strachan* are in the parish churches of Kirtlebridge and Buittle. Much better, with the emphasis on clear draughtsmanship, are windows by *Margaret Chilton* and *Marjorie Kemp*: examples from the 1940s and 1950s can be seen in the past and present parish churches of Castle Douglas and in Christ Church (Episcopal), Dalbeattie. Earlier (1926) and more enjoyable is their depiction of St John being bullied by an eagle in Colvend Parish Church. Also of the 1920s is an early work by *Gordon Webster* in Balmaclellan Parish Church, the realism stylized. Three more of Webster's strongly coloured windows (of 1938–55) are in Tinwald Parish Church and one (of 1961) in Greyfriars Episcopal Church, Kirkcudbright. More exuberant but sloppier are windows by *William Wilson*; there are examples at Ardwell Church, St Michael's and South Church, Dumfries, and St Teresa (R.C.), Dumfries, of the 1950s, and at the parish churches at Brydekirk and Kirkmahoe (*see* Kirkton) of the 1960s. Much paler but semi-abstract is the window by *Alexander Hollweg*, *c.* 1985, in Corsock Parish Church, a contrast to that church's rather earlier stylized light by *Brian Thomas*, whose window (of 1976) in the secular setting of Clatteringshaws Forest Wildlife Centre manages to be realistic without suggesting a picture postcard.

MAUSOLEA, MONUMENTS AND STATUES

In 1581 the reformed Church of Scotland forbade burial inside churches. For the majority of the population this can have had little import, but the greater landowners had expected interment within a church. One way of continuing to enjoy the benefit of resting inside what was effectively part of a church building was employed by Agnes, Lady Herries, when in 1588 she rebuilt the then redundant chancel of Terregles Parish Church as a mausoleum, whose external appearance was just like that of a late medieval apsidal-ended chancel. Another solution which satisfied the letter if not the spirit of the law was to add a JAMB or 'AISLE' on one side of a parish church. This was done at Kirkcudbright by the MacLellans of Bombie, probably in the late C16 (their 'aisle' now forms the chancel of Greyfriars Episcopal Church), and at Kirkmaiden Parish Church by the McDoualls of Logan in the 1630s or 1640s. These 'aisles', which seem to have contained seating to be used by the laird's family during services as well as a burial place for their bodies, both opened into the church. So too did the very grand 'aisle' built for the Dukes of Queensberry at Durisdeer Parish Church in 1695–1708 to a design by *James Smith*, its ogee-domed lead roof smartly up to date, its large Gothic window (since removed) a late survival of that style. The interior is exuberantly Baroque, the walls decorated with carved reliefs and the central hatch to the vault covered by a swaggering baldacchino derived from Bernini's over the high altar in St Peter's, Rome.

An alternative to the addition of an 'aisle' was the erection of a self-contained MAUSOLEUM or BURIAL ENCLOSURE in the churchyard, either abutting the church or freestanding. One of the earliest in Dumfries and Galloway is the Fergusson burial enclosure of 1675 in Glencairn Parish Churchyard, Kirkland, only its crude balustrade and ball finials making it more than a utilitarian walled rectangle. Not much more ambitious except for its rusticated quoins the early C18 Johnston Stewart mausoleum at Glasserton. But in 1742 Thomas Kirkpatrick of Closeburn provided his family with a very smart mausoleum in Closeburn Parish Churchyard, with ashlar walls articulated by rusticated pilasters, a large window in each bay, and an aediculed frame at the entrance. Inside he erected a frieze, its repeated warning '*Sic Transit Gloria Mundi*' interspersed with skulls and crossbones.

Less flamboyant was the Hannay Mausoleum of 1787 at Kirkdale Churchyard (possibly by *R. & J. Adam*), its front displaying an open pediment, its sides with pointed windows. Certainly by 51 *Robert Adam* is the Johnstone Mausoleum of 1790 in Westerkirk Parish Churchyard at Bentpath. It is a domed Greek cross, the limbs very shallow projections, the entrance marked by a pediment carried on coupled columns. These are fluted and, except for their Roman necks, Greek Doric, one of the very earliest revivals of that order, but columns of the same design had been used by Adam the year before at another mausoleum for the same family built at Alva (Clackmannanshire). Also in an Adam manner, but that of the decorator rather than the pioneer of the 53 Greek revival, is the early C19 Gillespie Mausoleum in Glencairn Parish Churchyard (*see* Kirkland), with urn-topped acanthus-capitalled pilasters at the corners and an urn on the domed roof.

A mausoleum which is also a public monument was erected in 54 1815–16 over the grave of Robert Burns in St Michael's and South Churchyard, Dumfries; *T. F. Hunt*'s design is an Ionic version of James Wyatt's mausoleum at Cobham Hall (Kent) of thirty years before, but with a domed attic instead of a pyramid top, which makes it a little too polite. More powerful is the Ægypto-Greek 52 mausoleum of Sir William Douglas near Kelton Parish Church, put up in 1821, the battered sides rising to a pagoda-like attic, and the Doric columns at the entrance placed between battered jambs. Powerful too, but Gothic, is *E. B. Lamb*'s mortuary chapel 55 or mausoleum of 1847 near Carnsalloch House, its buttresses exaggeratedly sturdy, the door topped by a pointed window with extravagant cusped loop tracery.

MONUMENTS, not necessarily directly connected with a burial lair, were erected in both churches and mausolea. The earliest of post-Reformation date to have survived is the graveslab of 1568 to Edward Maxwell in the chancel (or 'queir') of Terregles Parish Church, carved with the rumbustious relief portrait of a gentleman with a hat and sword, pointing to the placard on his breast inscribed 'IHS' (for 'Jesus'), presumably testifying his acceptance of the lordship of Christ. Also at Terregles is the wall monument of *c*. 1605 commemorating Sir Robert Maxwell of Spottes and his first wife. Its two panels are carved with reliefs of a kneeling man and woman and placed in a frame of baluster-like attached columns supporting an entablature whose ends are topped by pinnacles, the centre by a stone carved with an angel (the soul) in a tabernacle niche. The design of this monument breaks with medieval tradition since it makes no suggestion that it is itself a tomb. However, two other early C17 monuments, the Gordon 44 monument in Anwoth Old Parish Church and the MacLellan 45 of Bombie monument in Greyfriars Episcopal Church, Kirkcudbright, take the form of a sarcophagus. The Gordon monument is the simpler of the two; it is a tomb-chest decorated with reminders of death, coats of arms and inscriptions and topped by ball finials and a central heraldic disc. The MacLellan monument is medieval in form, a tomb-chest topped by a segmental-arched recess containing the effigy of a knight; but this recess is placed in a classical frame topped by an aedicule, which is, in turn, surmounted by a forward-leaning cherub.

The monument incorporating a sarcophagus was given flamboyantly Baroque form in the Queensberry Aisle of Durisdeer Parish Church in 1713 when *John van Nost* executed a huge commemoration of the second Duke of Queensberry and his wife, 48 their effigies resting (she lying, he reclining) on top of a double sarcophagus framed by a Corinthian aedicule backed by marble curtains hanging from a domed pelmet. Minor parts in the seeming drama are played by tearful cherubs, foliaged pendants, reminders of death and a large heraldic achievement.

The only other church or mausoleum monument in the region to rival the scale of the Queensberry monument is the relief in the Burns Mausoleum at St Michael's Church in Dumfries, showing the poet summoned from the plough by the poetic genius of Scotland. First carved in 1817–19 by *Peter Turnerelli*, but replaced by *Hermon Cawthra* in 1936, it is almost informal compared with the hieratic splendour of the earlier work. From the C18 the usual form for church monuments was a modest tablet, sometimes with an urn in relief. One of the more ambitious is that to Dr Walter Ross Munro of *c*. 1820 by *Henry Rouw* in Glencairn Parish Church (*see* Kirkland), adorned with the relief of a lady mourning over a sarcophagus; Dr Munro appears in a cloud above. The 1890s bronze in Dryfesdale Parish Church, Lockerbie, commemorating a cavalry officer, Lieutenant-Colonel Cecil Francis Johnstone Douglas, shows a horse as the chief, indeed only, mourner.

Probably because of lack of space and often height inside churches, large monuments were erected in churchyards. The earliest are in St Michael's and South Churchyard, Dumfries, where monuments to John Corsane †1629 and Francis Irving †1633 are built into the enclosing wall, both displaying classical detail. Also classical of a sort is the monument in Glencairn Parish Churchyard (*see* Kirkland) to Stephen Lawrie †1637. In Kirkcudbright Cemetery, however, the Ewart monument of 1644 is very similar to the slightly earlier MacLellan monument in the same burgh's Greyfriars Episcopal Church and, like it, is set in a classical frame but with the recess over the sarcophagus forming a pointed arch, whose profile is repeated on the inscription stone above. There is no evidence that the recess ever contained an effigy. More thoroughgoing classical intention is shown by the fluted pilasters and steep pediment of the monument to the Rev. Samuel Austin †1669 in Penpont Parish Churchyard, although its display of grisly reminders of death gives a touch of folk art that is seldom absent from churchyard monuments before the C19. More reminders of death occur on the back of the light-hearted aedicule commemorating Susanna Muir †1710 in St Michael's and South Churchyard, Dumfries, which has a crowd of angelic heads over the inscription tablet, and a pediment crowned by a cartouche and urns. The monument in the same churchyard to John Crosbie †1720 has carved tasselled curtains falling from an angel's mouth framing the central panel. Very much grander are the huge urn-finialled Corinthian aedicules to William Gordon of Greenlaw †1757 in Crossmichael Parish 49 Churchyard and to Patrick Heron and Patrick Heron jun., both †1761, in Monigaff Parish Churchyard at Newton Stewart, both celebrations of the importance of local landed families. Chaster but equally dominant memorials were provided by the urn-topped obelisks erected to Dr James Mounsey †1773 in Lochmaben Old Churchyard and to Captain James Finan †1796 at Kirkpatrick-Irongray. More delicate is the monument to James McKie †1816 in Monigaff Parish Churchyard, its marble relief of a cherub weeping beside an urn signed by *S. & T. Franceys* of Liverpool.

The region's late C17 and C18 HEADSTONES provide a magnificently vigorous display of folk art. Certain motifs recur, either locally, for example the vines on the C18 stones in a graveyard near Eskdalemuir, or generally: popular examples were reminders of death (skulls, crossbones, hourglasses and skeletons), almost always accompanied by an angel's head to represent the soul. One of the best displays of these grisly emblems is on the headstone to Robert Miller †1732 in Dalgarnock graveyard; its panelled pilasters and wavy top frame an angel's head above an array of reliefs including a pair of scissors, a corpse, bones and a hand holding a book. Several headstones display standing human figures, usually portraits of the deceased but occasionally of the bereaved. In

Durisdeer Parish Churchyard, the headstone to Marren Poirglas
†1739 shows a woman standing on crossed bones, but the same
graveyard's stone of 1685 to the children of the mason *William
Lukup* shows a mason, presumably Lukup himself, holding a skull.
In Wamphray Parish Churchyard the headstones to Margaret
Holladay †1740 and John Burges †1742 are decorated with the
figures of a woman holding bones and a man standing on a skull.
Charmingly cheerful is the headstone of *c.*1755 in Kirkpatrick-
Fleming Parish Churchyard to John and James Lam, both dead
in infancy, with the figures of two children standing above a pair
of coffins. In Kells Parish Churchyard, New Galloway, are a
couple of early C18 headstones carved with figures of Adam and
Eve, one (of 1706) with a coat of arms surmounting the Tree of
Knowledge. Other stones are carved with emblems of the dead
person's trade. The crowned hammer of the smiths is the most
common, but the stone in Girthon Churchyard to a gardener,
Robert Glover, †1776, bears reliefs of a rake, hoe and spade; and
in Kells Parish Churchyard, New Galloway, the headstone to 47
John Murray †1777, a gamekeeper, is carved with a grouse, dog,
gun, powder flask and fishing rod. A late example of a trade
emblem is the monument in Kirkmaiden Parish Churchyard to
James Scott, a lighthouse keeper's son, †1852, which takes the
form of a miniature lighthouse. Even later, and chargeable as
kitsch, is the monument in St Michael's Cemetery, Dumfries, to
William Ord Pinder, 'equestrian and circus proprietor', †1941,
topped by a sorrowful horse. But most C19 and C20 headstones
are sadly routine; the most satisfying single collection is perhaps
that in the graveyard at Wanlockhead, where every stone dating
from the 1790s to the 1880s bears an urn in low relief – a successful
example of the virtue of finding a winning formula and sticking
to it.

TABLE STONES commemorating Covenanting martyrs of the
late C17 are a notable feature of the region, which was a stronghold
of opposition to episcopacy. They were erected in the early C18
and usually carved with lengthy accounts of sufferings endured at
the hands of government soldiers. These idiosyncratically lettered
inscriptions were almost all recut in the late C18 or early C19.

COMMEMORATIVE ARCHITECTURAL MONUMENTS, usually
financed by public subscription, are prominently sited. In the
centre of Dumfries stands *Robert Adam*'s monument of 1780 to 56
the third Duke of Queensberry, a 6.4m.-high column topped by
a flaming urn. In 1835 two monuments were placed on hilltops:
one, on Whita Hill near Langholm, commemorating General Sir
John Malcolm, the other, Murray's Monument, to the orientalist
Dr Alexander Murray. Both are granite obelisks, Murray's Monument blunt-topped. Another obelisk (by *James Raeburn*) was
erected at Mount Kedar near Mouswald in 1846 in honour of Dr
Henry Duncan, founder of the savings bank movement. It is less
conspicuous but more inventive, with a battered base pierced by
segmental arches. A hill overlooking Wigtown was chosen in 1858
for the Covenanters Monument (by *James Maclaren*), its battered
plinth Ægypto-Greek in manner and carrying a tapered octagonal

shaft topped by a cinerary urn. The use of a tall base topped by a shaft reappears at *Richard Park*'s monument to the ninth Earl of Galloway in Newton Stewart (1874–5), but the style is heavy and mechanically detailed Gothic and the urn is replaced by a gabled spire crowned by a cross. Just as the 1830s obelisks used hills as their bases, hill and monument forming one huge object, so the bulk of Whirstone Hill near Ringford was made more conspicuous in 1928 by the erection of the granite pyramid which forms Neilson's Monument. The late C20, perhaps fearful of the public gesture, has relegated the monument to Lord Dowding at Moffat (by *D. Bruce Walker*, 1972) to the relative obscurity of a municipal park, and its overlapping ashlar walls are more an exploration of space than a triumphalist statement.

TOWERS were built as foci for civic pride or commemoration.
57 The strangest is *F. T. Pilkington*'s battily battlemented clock tower of 1871 in Gatehouse of Fleet, a whinstone and granite vertical affront to the burgh's carefully tended douce Georgian character. Much less assertive, although again of granite and battlemented, is the clock tower erected at Creetown to commemorate Queen Victoria's Diamond Jubilee of 1897. Smaller but stronger is Laurieston's Crockett Memorial Tower by *J. Jeffrey Waddell*, 1932, its sides battered, the top a dome.

STATUES are few, and some are inconspicuously sited, such as *David Dunbar*'s of Admiral Sir Pulteney Malcolm (1842) behind the Library at Langholm or *J. W. Dods*' of Edward Irving (1891–2) on the edge of Annan Old Parish Church's graveyard. Others have been given pride of place. Moffat's High Street is dominated
58 by *William Brodie*'s angry bronze ram atop the Colvin Fountain of 1875, just as the High Streets of Lochmaben and Dumfries are by *John Hutchison*'s sandstone portrayal of Robert the Bruce (1876–9) and *Mrs D. O. Hill*'s Carrara marble statue of Robert Burns (1882). A boost to the number if not the quality of statues was provided by the ending of the First World War. Many war memorial statues depict a soldier with head bowed and gun reversed, e.g. at Penpont (by *Kellock Brown*, 1920) or Canonbie (by *Thomas J. Clapperton*, 1921); but *Henry Price* provided a much more dramatic soldier, with arms outstretched in a gesture of crucifixion, at Maxwelltown, Dumfries, in 1920 and *G. H. Paulin* an allegorical statue of a swordsman defending a boy at Kirkcudbright in 1921. *James B. Dunn*'s War Memorial at Lockerbie (1921–2) seems eager to enjoy the peace, its bronze figure of Victory (by *Henry C. Fehr*) skipping into the future.

The late C20 has produced one work of haunting symbolism, *Jake Harvey*'s metal open-book monument to Hugh MacDiarmid on the slope of Whita Hill near Langholm; one good joke, *Robbie Coleman*'s fibreglass rhinoceros on top of a Dumfries bus shelter; and one superb collection of sculpture, assembled by Sir William Keswick on his moorland estate at Glenkiln, four works of the 1950s by *Henry Moore* ('Standing Figure', 'King
59 and Queen', 'Glenkiln Cross', and 'Two Piece Reclining Figure No. 1'), *Auguste Rodin*'s 'John the Baptist' and *Jacob Epstein*'s 'Visitation'.

MOTTES, CASTLES AND TOWER HOUSES

At the beginning of the C12 Dumfries and Galloway was divided into three principal lordships. That of Annandale was held directly by the Crown whilst the lordships of Nithsdale and Galloway were held by two native dynasties, each accepting the overlordship of the King of Scots but acting as quasi-independent princes. Immediately after his accession to the throne in 1124, David I, as part of his policy of introducing the feudal system to Scotland, granted the lordship of Annandale to Robert Bruce, an Anglo-Norman Yorkshire magnate and co-founder with David of Selkirk Abbey. Bruce held by knight service and presumably granted fiefs to the knights he imported.

This spectacular introduction of the feudal system to Annandale was followed, possibly under royal pressure, in Galloway, whose lords granted the fiefs of Colvend to Gospatrick fitz Orm, lord of Workington in Cumbria, *c.*1150, of Urr to Walter de Berkeley, a member of a Somerset family, *c.*1160, of Borgue to Hugh de Moreville, a Northamptonshire landowner, by the 1160s, after which it passed to Sir Ralph de Campania, and of Anwoth to David fitz Teri, lord of Over Denton in Cumbria, *c.*1170. The same process of infeudation took place in Nithsdale, where it was probably hastened after *c.*1165, when most of that lordship passed to the Crown (the Anglo-Norman family of de Ros, for example, having acquired the fief of Sanquhar by the late C12), and in Eskdale, which was entirely held by Anglo-Norman families.

That infeudation was part of royal policy and extensive seems clear from an English chronicler's account of a revolt against the Crown in 1174 by Uchtred and Gilbert, the lords of Galloway, who 'at once expelled from Galloway all the bailiffs and guards whom the King of Scotland had set over them and all the English whom they could they slew; and all the defences and castles which the King of Scotland had established in their land they besieged, captured and destroyed, and slew all whom they took within them.' The revolt was suppressed and infeudation resumed, together with the construction of 'castles', apparently with the acquiescence of the lords of Galloway. Indeed, during the fifteen years before his death in 1200, Roland, lord of Galloway, is said to have constructed 'castles and numerous defences'.

These 'castles' of the C12 infeudation of Dumfries and Galloway were MOTTES, more numerous here than in any other part of Scotland, spread across the whole region but clustered most thickly in the centre of the Stewartry and along the strategic valleys of the Nith and Annan. The motte castle typically consisted of a mound, its top crowned by a wooden tower forming the last point of defence; the base was often surrounded by a ditch. Some of the mounds, e.g. at Balmaclellan, Parton, St John's Town of Dalry, Barmagachan (near Kirkandrews), or Mote of Urr (near 60 Haugh of Urr), are largely artificial, constructed of earth dug

from the encircling ditch and shaped like truncated cones. Other
mottes were formed by heightening natural rock outcrops, as at
Boreland Mote, near Borgue, by scarping a hillock, as at Lochwood Tower or the motte beside Lincluden Collegiate Church,
Dumfries, or by cutting off part of a bank or ridge, as at Roberton,
near Kirkandrews, Lochmaben Old Castle or the motte at Innermessan, near Stranraer. The motte's purpose was primarily
defensive, although it was perhaps sometimes also intended to
overawe. It was always accompanied by a bailey or larger enclosure containing the stables, kitchens, stores and general living
accommodation. Many baileys may have been defended by no
more than a palisade. However, where a motte was formed by
cutting a ditch through a natural ridge, it was common to cut a
second ditch lower down the ridge; the space between these two
ditches would be occupied by the bailey, as at Lower Ingleston
(Kirkland), Boreland of Anwoth (Anwoth), or Lochrennie, near
Moniaive, this last unusual in having a bailey occupying a smaller
area than the motte. In some cases the motte stood inside the
bailey, usually at one end, e.g. at Dinning (Closeburn) or Mote
60 of Urr (Haugh of Urr), where the exceptionally large oblong
bailey is surrounded by a wide ditch and the motte at the E end
of the bailey is defended by a second ditch.

Relatively peaceful conditions obtained in Dumfries and Galloway for most of the C13, the authority of the Kings of Scots
having been strengthened after the suppression of a revolt in
Galloway following the death of Alan, lord of Galloway, in 1234.
One possible assertion or reinforcement of royal authority in the
early C13 was the grant of the lands of Caerlaverock at the mouth
of the Nith to John Maxwell, Chamberlain of Scotland. Here
Maxwell began the construction of a CASTLE OF ENCLOSURE,
the first Caerlaverock Castle ('Old Caerlaverock'). It occupied a
rectangular area surrounded by a rampart and moat from whose
inner sides rose the castle's enclosing stone walls, probably with
a projecting tower at each corner, one of these perhaps being
a keep containing the living quarters of the lord. The general
conception was not far from that of the motte inside a bailey, but
the stone enclosure walls provided much more substantial defence
than the earth ramparts or palisades of C12 baileys, and the keep's
function was primarily domestic. This first castle at Caerlaverock,
possibly abandoned before completion, was quickly followed by
61 a second and more ambitious castle, probably completed in the
1270s, whose site, a rocky outcrop in the generally marshy land,
was well defended by two moats with a rampart between. From
the inner moat rose the walls of the castle itself, its triangular
shape probably dictated by that of the outcrop. Projecting from
the two S corners were round towers. At the third corner was a
twin-towered gatehouse.

This combination of a stone-walled enclosure with projecting
corner towers and twin towers guarding the entrance makes Caerlaverock a close counterpart of the contemporary castles being
erected in Wales by Edward I, although it lacked, as did later
Scottish castles, the outer ring of stone-walled defences charac-

teristic of Edwardian castles. Before and after Edward I's invasion of Scotland in 1296, the beginning of the thirty-year Wars of Independence, castles of the same general type as Caerlaverock were built, for example at Kirkcudbright and Tibbers Castle, which was being built for Sir Richard Siward in 1298. Both were rectangular, with the entrance placed at the end of one wall so that a corner tower could double as one of the gatehouse towers. Also rectangular, with round corner towers and the entrance placed at the end of a wall, is Auchencass, again of the late C13, but here the second gatehouse tower was omitted. Probably of the early C14 is Morton Castle, its twin-towered gatehouse placed 62 at one corner of the front and containing the lord's lodging. Another castle of enclosure was the new Lochmaben Castle begun by Edward I c.1300. It was a rectangle, probably originally intended to have towers at the outer corners of the s front (the only side approachable by land) but with the entrance placed in the centre of this front and defended by its own gatehouse whose twin towers were replaced, probably during construction, by a boldly projecting barbican.

In the later C14, perhaps as a result of Scotland's continuing intermittent warfare with England, this front of Lochmaben Castle was radically altered and made U-plan by the construction of a new wall on the line of the barbican's face and, projecting from this wall's corners and carried by arches across the moat, narrow towers from which raking cross-fire could be provided. Roughly contemporary with this late C14 remodelling of Lochmaben Castle was the construction by the Crichtons of Sanquhar Castle, again apparently a rectangular castle of enclosure, probably with a tower at each corner, although only the SW keep survives. That castle was remodelled and largely rebuilt in the C15, when an L-plan gatehouse block containing the lord's living quarters was constructed in the centre of the N front; the jamb was a massive rounded tower projecting as a defence for the entrance. The dual use of the gatehouse as the chief defence for the castle and the lord's lodging was given its most formidable expression when the gatehouse at Caerlaverock Castle was remod- 63 elled in the C15 as a potent expression of baronial power designed to withstand attack from the courtyard behind as well as from the front.

The courtyard of a castle of enclosure contained domestic accommodation, including a kitchen, hall and sleeping quarters. These buildings must often have been of wooden construction, but two large stone-built halls survive at Morton Castle and Torthorwald Castle. Both are probably of the earlier C14 (the hall at Torthorwald later enlarged and given stone vaulting). The upper (hall) floor at Morton Castle was of wood, supported by a row of posts dividing the lower floor, perhaps the kitchen, into two aisles. Both these halls seem to have been separate from the lord's lodging, which at Morton was in the adjoining gatehouse but self-contained. This provision of a hall range adjoining but separate from a gatehouse/lord's lodging occurs again at Caerlaverock Castle, whose W hall range of c.1500 presents to the courtyard a muscular procession of mullioned and transomed windows and wallhead chimneys.

Many of the main elements of a castle of enclosure could be gathered together in compact form in a TOWER HOUSE, a single building combining defence and living accommodation. The earliest and largest in Dumfries and Galloway is the powerfully stark 64 Threave Castle, built *c.*1370 for Archibald ('the Grim'), third Earl of Douglas and lord of Galloway. The island site provided natural defence, apparently unsupplemented by walls, until the need for artillery defence in the mid-C15. The rubble-walled rectangular tower was designed to provide its own defence; the entrance, placed high up, was approached by a ladder and defended by machicolation at the third floor, where wooden hoardings on the other three sides allowed effective high-level defence. The interior contained storage, a well, a kitchen, a large hall (probably for the lord and his immediate retinue), two private rooms, and, at the top, a barrack room to house a garrison in time of war. Strongly defensive as this was, Threave was not without comfort; the large hall windows were provided with seats, and there was an adequate though not abundant provision of garderobes at the two principal floors.

An outer artillery defence was provided at Threave Castle just before the earldom of Douglas was forfeited in 1458. That forfeiture of the lands of an overmighty subject who also held the earldom of Wigtown and the lordships of Galloway and Annandale provided an opportunity for a number of local families to acquire land held by Crown charters. The C15 also saw the beginning of the break-up of monastic estates by disposing of them in 'feu ferm', i.e. in return for a lump sum and an annual money payment (whose value was quickly lessened by inflation). This growth in prosperity of a class of lairds was accompanied by the erection of tower houses. The predecessors of these lairds' towers may often have been of wood. If they were of stone, a clue to their appearance may be Fairgirth House, which seems to have been built as a monastic grange, perhaps in the early C16. It was originally of two unvaulted storeys, the lower a store, the upper a living room with a fireplace. Something similar seems to have comprised the earliest part of Kirkconnell House, which was begun *c.*1440, Elshieshields Tower, again probably begun in the C15, Spedlins Castle of *c.*1500, and Old Buittle Tower, built *c.*1535, its upper floor reached by a forestair.

Several of the C15 tower houses were little grander. Cumstoun Castle was a simple rectangle, the floors all of wood. The C15 NE tower at Lochnaw Castle showed more pretension, though on a tiny scale; the ground floor is a vaulted store, the upper rooms enjoy window seats, and the top is finished externally with timidly projecting angle rounds at three corners and a caphouse on the fourth. Closeburn Castle was constructed of three superimposed vaults, the lowest over a store, the second over the hall and taller, the third subdivided by two entresol floors. Much larger is 68 Comlongon Castle, probably built *c.*1450 for the Murrays of Cockpool. Externally it was unadorned except by heavy moulded corbels under the battlement, but the interior expresses both its owner's power and his artistic patronage. Some of the features (the internal well, the ground-floor vault divided by an entresol floor, the window seats in the upper rooms) could have been borrowed from Threave Castle, but the interior at Comlongon is exceptionally well finished. Unusually, although conveniently, the narrow first-floor kitchen is at one end of the hall. The ceiling beams of the hall are supported on corbels carved with a display of heraldry, and there is foliage decoration on the jambs of the 69 fireplace, which is surmounted by a relief of the royal arms flanked by corbels, probably lampstands, again carved with heraldry. Even more of a show-off piece is the hall's aumbry, whose foliaged cinquefoil head is skewed off-centre to give a sense of spiralling movement. As exceptional as the expense of Comlongon's decoration is the honeycombing of its walls to provide minor rooms, including a pit prison, this degree of honeycombing paralleled, together with the pit prison, only at the Castle of St John in 75 Stranraer of c.1510.

The most strikingly sited of the C15 tower houses is Cardoness 65 Castle, perched above the valley of the Fleet. It is another rubble-walled oblong but with cornices over the main windows and, inside, besides window seats, an ogee-arched hall aumbry and smart Gothic chimneypieces. These hints of luxury at Cardoness are accompanied by reminders of a still feudal and frequently violent society; the entrance lobby ceiling is pierced by a *meurtrière* hole, and the walls contain two prisons, one provided with a garderobe, the other only with a ventilation slit. A short distance to the N of Cardoness is its slightly younger and smaller sister, Rusco Tower of c.1500, very similar in concept and detail but 67 with the added refinement of a 'laird's lug' (a listening hole from a wall chamber into the hall). The most unusual of the C15 towers is Orchardton Tower of c.1460, a tapering drum, the upper rooms 66 circular, the hall decorated with a trefoil-headed aumbry.

Tower houses multiplied in the C16. Some were decidedly thrifty; Castle Stewart of c.1500 and the slightly later Drumcoltran Tower even had rounded corners to avoid the need for dressed masonry. About half the number in the region were simple rectangles, generally of three storeys and an attic. The wallhead is usually topped by a parapet projected on corbelling with rounded, sometimes barely projecting angle turrets, and perhaps a caphouse over the stair contained in the wall thickness of one corner. Ground-floor gunloops could add a hint of martial purpose. This standard type is exemplified by Hills Tower of c.1530, or the mid- 71 C16 Gilnockie Tower, but some of these features might be omitted. A wall-walk all round the tower was of fairly little practical value for defence, and at Craigcaffie Castle of the 1570s the walks are carried only across the gables, but the angle turrets, as if in compensation, are pierced with shotholes. Other houses, such as the diminutive Isle Tower (near Holywood) of 1587 or Fourmerkland Tower, probably of 1590, dispensed with the parapet altogether and provided turrets only at two diagonally opposed corners.

The general internal arrangement was standardized. On the ground floor, usually vaulted, was a store or kitchen, on the first floor a hall, and, on the floor or floors above, bedchambers, sometimes, as at Isle Tower (near Holywood), with closets in the turrets. This generally domestic character of the simpler C16 tower house was occasionally belied by the provision of a prison in the wall thickness, as at Bonshaw Tower of *c.*1545.

More accommodation could be obtained by making the tower house L-plan, although this was not generally done in Dumfries and Galloway before the mid-C16. In an L-plan house, the jamb contained the main stair to the first floor (and fairly often to floors above), but frequently a secondary stair was corbelled out in the inner angle to serve rooms on the upper floors of the main block and the jamb. The architectural effects of L-plan tower houses are surprisingly varied. For some the addition of the jamb appears little more than a sensible convenience. Drumcoltran Tower is unpretentiously dumpy, its corners rounded, its parapet corbels crudely moulded; only the panel of Latin platitudes over the door testifies to the owner's sophistication. Even less pretentious is Old Buittle Tower as remodelled in the 1590s, when it acquired its jamb and upper floors but no wall-walk and only two corner turrets. Also of the 1590s, but dispensing with turrets altogether,
73, 72 is Castle of Park. By contrast, Elshieshields Tower, enlarged and completely remodelled probably in 1567, although it does without a wall-walk and its turrets serve as closets, makes much of the jamb, which is a self-consciously tall and narrow tower rising above the main block. Corbelled out from one of the jamb's crowstepped gables is the stand for a beacon to be lit in the event of an English invasion, a feature found also at the mid-C16
70 Gilnockie Tower and Repentance Tower of 1565. Repentance Tower was a watchtower for the nearby and contemporary Hoddom Castle, which is a very much larger version of Elshieshields Tower. At Hoddom the jamb enjoys its own angle rounds (made into conical-roofed turrets in an early C17 heightening). The L-plan was developed to provide an exceptional amount of
76 accommodation at the dourly purposeful MacLellan's Castle in Kirkcudbright of 1581, where the inner angle is partly filled by an L-plan projection and a tower protrudes at the SE corner. Most remarkable of all the region's tower houses is the immensely tall
74 Amisfield Tower of 1600. Its round stair turret is corbelled out just above the ground at one corner of the square main block and crowned by a two-storey rectangular caphouse, which is straddled by a second and yet higher caphouse, the verticality and top-heaviness giving the spectator the delicious thrill of wondering whether it will overbalance.

At these C16 tower houses external ornamentation is generally restricted to roll-moulded openings and frames for heraldic panels, but some detail is more expensive. At Elshieshields Tower the panel frame is carved with nailhead ornament; at Craigcaffie Castle the surround of a second-floor window has dogtooth decoration. Dogtooth appears again at the main windows of Stapleton Tower, whose door's roll-and-hollow moulding is carved with low-relief foliage. Hints of classicism appeared from the 1580s. Two windows in the entrance front of MacLellan's Castle, Kirkcudbright, are pedimented, one decorated also with dogtooth ornament, the other (a dummy) with heraldry. Corniced windows in a near symmetrical arrangement were provided at the top floors added to Spedlins Castle in 1605. Interiors may show touches of luxury. The kitchen of MacLellan's Castle is exceptionally well equipped, with an oven in one side of the fireplace and a serving hatch. In the entrance lobbies of both Bonshaw Tower and Robgill Tower are stone pendants carved with the sacred IHS monogram. The first-floor hall of Elshieshields Tower contains an aumbry fronted by a pair of roundheaded arches sharing a central pendant. A very similar aumbry, painted with stylized flowers, is in the ground-floor hall added to Fairgirth House in the mid-C16. The hall chimneypiece of 1605 in Spedlins Castle, with its consoled jambs and procession of consoles along the frieze, is a remarkable intimation of full-blooded classicism breaking into the world of the tower-house laird.

COUNTRY HOUSES

The influence of the tower house, with its affirmation of lairdly status, continued into the C17, but there very quickly appeared houses, best described as lairds' houses, which dispensed with the paraphernalia of battlements and turrets and whose chief function was to provide comfortable accommodation. One of these EARLY SEVENTEENTH-CENTURY houses, Rockhall ('laitlie constructit' in 1610), was a straightforward T-shape, with the rounded stair jamb projecting from the E side. Another, the early C17 Old Place of Monreith, was an irregular cruciform, with a centrally placed E wing but an off-centre rounded stair tower on the w. A couple of circular shotholes in the stair tower seem principally for decoration, although perhaps useful for scaring off a burglar. The mid-C17 Barscobe Castle's lairdly status is proclaimed by steeply pedimented dormerheads instead of martial accoutrements.

Larger houses could be just as pacific. The early C17 Maxwelton House and the 1660s additions to Lochnaw Castle are straightforwardly domestic, stone dormerheads the main architectural feature at Lochnaw. That thoughts of defence had not been entirely abandoned seems clear from the gunloops puncturing the outer face of the w range built at Kenmure Castle *c.*1630. However, that range's courtyard front is a joyful if wacky demonstration of how rope-moulded stringcourses and carved stones can be used to enliven a façade.

At two houses of the early C17 classicism appears. Castle Kennedy of *c.*1600 (*see* Lochinch Castle) is a tall Y-shaped building, of four storeys and an attic, and well supplied with gunholes. To that extent it is in the tower-house tradition. But, unlike a tower house, it is rigorously symmetrical, with square full-height wings projecting from the corners of the main block's E gable to provide a U-plan entrance front and with taller square towers in the inner angles behind. Pedimented dormerheads over the top windows of the wings relieved the austerity. Much more exuberantly classical, and without parallel in Scotland at that date, were the ranges built along the E and S sides of the courtyard of Caerlaverock Castle *c.* 1630 by the first Earl of Nithsdale. Conceivably it was hoped that they would house Charles I on his progress into Scotland in 1633. That would explain the apparent planning of the now badly ruined S range, with a ground-floor great hall from whose E end a grand stair led to the floor above, which could have been filled by a state apartment. The E range, its front windows all smartly pedimented, is façade architecture, the show-off grandeur unrelated to the importance of the rooms behind, but providing a suitably magnificent approach to the S block.

The 1640s and 1650s, a period of civil war followed by military dictatorship, were not propitious for extravagant building works. Nor did the years immediately after the RESTORATION of 1660 produce a flood of projects. However, *c.* 1675 Robert Stewart of Ravenstone enlarged and remodelled his L-plan tower house, Ravenstone Castle, filling the inner angle to produce a nearly symmetrical rectangular building. Its S front rises into a pair of crowstepped gables which, a little disconcertingly, are of different widths because the main block of the tower house had been broader than the jamb was long. New windows, regularly spaced, were provided, the centre openings of the two top floors linked by an armorial panel. Quite different in scale and splendour from this economical remodelling was the rebuilding (except for a small part) of Drumlanrig Castle, *c.* 1675–97, for the third Earl (later the first Marquess and first Duke) of Queensberry, as a Baroque palace of European ambition. The general model for Drumlanrig is clearly the quadrangular George Heriot's Hospital (now School) in Edinburgh. It had been begun in 1628 but was not fully completed when work started at Drumlanrig; successive Master Masons to the Crown had been employed on its building, and for the design of its entrance tower advice had been sought from Sir William Bruce. But, if Drumlanrig's general composition is derived from Heriot's, both this and the detail seem to have been modified in the course of construction under the influence of the new royal Palace of Holyroodhouse in Edinburgh, from which seem to have been borrowed Vignola's Doric order for the pilasters along the front's terrace-loggia and the ducally coroneted cupola over the entrance (in place of Holyrood's crowned cupola). All Drumlanrig's own, and giving its Baroque a swagger not attempted at Holyroodhouse, is the façade's perron copied from a plate in Pierre Le Muet's *Manière de bien bastir*, although the terrace-loggia behind this perron is covered by remarkably old-fashioned groin vaulting and the façade above bears an applied order of giant but very skinny Corinthian pilasters squeezed between the windows. Whatever criticisms may be made, Drumlanrig's sheer bravura, aided by superb carving and the warm pink of its sandstone walling, carries the day.

The interior was arranged in accordance with the conventions apparently introduced to Scotland after the Restoration by Sir William Bruce. The ground and first floors of the s range were occupied by two identically planned apartments or suites of rooms (just as Bruce had provided in his remodelling of Thirlestane Castle (Borders) in 1670–82), the lower for the Duke, the upper, reached by a state stair, the state apartment and theoretically reserved for the King or his representative. In each apartment was an enfilade of dining room, drawing room and bedchamber, with a dressing room at right angles in the w range. The whole of the N side's first floor formed a gallery which by the early c18 was filled 'from End to End, the whole length of one Side of the Building, with the Family Pieces of the Duke's Ancestors, most of them at full Length, and in their Robes of State, or of Office, as their History directed.' Although long galleries had been common in England since the c16, they were a late c17 innovation in Scotland and appeared only at the grandest houses, such as Leslie House (Fife) of 1667–72 and the Palace of Holyroodhouse. Apparently the Duke of Queensberry was determined not to be outdone by these.

Drumlanrig is a one-off. Had lesser landowners built scaled-down versions they could hardly have escaped ridicule. One EARLY EIGHTEENTH-CENTURY house possibly influenced by the general composition of Drumlanrig's façade is the H-plan Lochryan House of 1701. Before it was altered in the early c19, its front may have appeared as a central range gripped by end towers, but Lochryan eschews expensive detail. Most new houses built in the region in the early c18 were straightforward astylar classical. Some were simple rectangular blocks, e.g. Dornock House or Gretna Hall (1710), the architectural display confined to moulded window surrounds and some emphasis on the entrance. But at the piend-roofed Denbie of 1706 the quoins and margins of the front windows are all rusticated. Smarter still is Ross Mains of 1728, with a piended platform roof, its front framed by rusticated pilaster strips at the corners and an eaves-course-cum-lintel-course, and the pedimented door surround linked to the window above. Much more vertical in emphasis was Logan House of 1702, its two-bay centrepiece advanced under a pediment, the door framed by a Corinthian aedicule. At the larger Greenlaw House (1741) the door's surrounding aedicule is Ionic, and here Venetian windows, their lights very widely spaced, appear at the full-height bows of the gables.

The smartest of these early c18 houses is Tinwald House, 81 designed in 1738 by *William Adam*, who had also been responsible for the very plain Craigdarroch House ten years before. At Tinwald Adam provided a neo-Palladian main block, the pedimented centrepiece rising above the outer bays' urn-topped balustrade, and with an imperial stair up to the door. A flashier but wackier version of Tinwald had been produced four years earlier by an unknown architect at Springkell; here the central pediment is carried on Ionic pilasters which rise the full height of the house, from the bottom of the basement to the eaves. Larger than these houses, but barrack-like, is Galloway House, designed and built by *John Baxter* in 1740–2, its tall main block linked by quadrants to low pavilions, and the centrepiece marked by giant Corinthian columns surmounted rather awkwardly by panelled pilasters under the pediment.

Probably all these houses contained a state apartment, that suite of show rooms (dining room, drawing room and bedchamber) supposedly for use only in the highly improbable event of a royal visit but considered necessary in any nobleman's or laird's house since soon after the Restoration. At Denbie the state apartment apparently occupied the first floor, whose panelled bedchamber is still largely intact, its chimneypiece having a pilastered two-tier mirrored overmantel under a panel intended for a painting. On the floor below, the family parlour or low dining room (now drawing room) is also panelled, with a similar but slightly less smart chimneypiece and overmantel and a china cupboard. At *William Adam*'s Craigdarroch House the plan form has also largely survived; the family rooms are on the ground floor, with the private dining room in the centre of the garden front, and the state apartment occupies two-thirds of the floor above. At Tinwald House Adam placed the state apartment on the ground floor, whose tall aproned windows denote a *piano nobile*.

William Adam's death in 1748 was accompanied by the demise of the state apartment. No house built in the LATER EIGH-TEENTH CENTURY incorporated this functionally useless and space-consuming suite of rooms. However, there was no such clear break in the external appearance of country houses. Some, like Ardwall of 1762 or Knockhill of 1777, were simple classical boxes, quite plain except for aediculed doorpieces. Others were just as straightforward but joined by low links to flanking pavilions, e.g. Southwick House of *c.* 1750, *James Playfair*'s Langholm Lodge of 1786–7, Glenae of 1789–90, or *John Adam*'s Moffat House of 1762–7, whose pavilions are boldly advanced at right angles to the main block. The centre might be marked by a pediment, as at *Robert Mylne*'s Cally Palace of 1763–5 or Barnbar-roch of 1780, where it is dignified by a pedimented attic with a Venetian window. Rather more richly detailed and still Baroque in feeling is the urn-topped Arbigland of 1755, where the pedimented centrepiece enjoys pilasters and swags under the first-floor windows, the outer windows of the *piano nobile* segmental pedi-ments and aprons, the pavilions semi-octagonal fronts. This was probably designed by its owner, *William Craik*, and he may also have been responsible for the elegant Mossknowe of 1767, whose tall and narrow pedimented main block is joined by recessed links to lower pavilions. Rammerscales, built only one year after Mossknowe, introduced a quite different type of medium-sized country house, marked by a neo-classical accent. It is an austerely detailed box, the entrance placed behind a screen of Roman Doric columns *in antis* and surmounted by a tripartite window, its centre light pedimented. Just as austere were Dalswinton House of *c*.1790, where only the corniced ground-floor windows and a portico (now missing) relieved the starkness, and Monreith House of 1790–4.

A handful of country houses showed more ambition. Carnsal- 84 loch House, built in 1754–9, is urbane Palladian, the main block's three first-floor Venetian windows, each overarched, forbidding any suggestion of movement. Just as smooth, but austerely detailed, is *Robert Adam*'s Kirkdale House of 1787. His con- 88 temporary Glasserton House, now demolished, was a showier piece of classicism, his Barholm near Creetown of 1788 (not built exactly to his design, and also now demolished) a neat villa with giant Ionic pilasters at the pedimented centrepiece and overarches framing the door and pedimented ground-floor windows. The largest and weirdest of the region's late C18 houses is Raehills 87 House of 1782, by *Alexander Stevens Jun.*; all its top parts and two of its fronts are in the castle style, but the neo-Egyptian colonnade embracing the long E façade and the overarched Venetian windows on another front make a dotty contrast to the battlement above.

The trade blockade during the French Revolutionary and Napoleonic Wars of 1793–1815 pushed up agricultural prices and rents, so that landowners, already beginning to enjoy benefits from the agricultural improvements of the C18, had sizeable amounts of spare cash to spend on their estates and houses. For their design they turned to English as well as Scottish architects. Classicism was still the most popular style in the EARLY NINETEENTH CENTURY but was turning towards the heavier manner of the Greek revival presaged by the design of Hill of Burns at Creetown (1811) and the front block added (almost certainly by *James Gillespie Graham*) to Argrennan House in 1818. A lighter classical hand, with a touch of the Italianate, was used by *William Atkinson* for Dabton in 1820 and by *Robert Lugar* for Glenlee Park in 1823. Much heavier and starker was *Robert Smirke*'s Kinmount House, 89 begun in 1812, a powerful example of his 'New Square' style of stripped classicism. A very much smaller and stodgier house in the same manner and, like Kinmount, planned round a central hall, is Craigielands of 1817, designed by the executant architect of Kinmount, *William Burn*. An imposing approach to the principal rooms was provided in *J. B. Papworth*'s 1830s Greek-revival additions to Cally Palace, the Doric porte cochère fronting a marble-clad entrance hall from which a grand stair rises to the *piano nobile*. More enjoyable is Warmanbie of *c*.1820, which carefully varies the architecture at each front; but the smartest early C19 villa is the single-storey Barwhinnock of *c*.1830, with 91,92 Venetian-windowed shallow bows flanking the broad portico which opens onto the grandiose stair hall. Barwhinnock's stair is a show-piece but one which leads only to bedrooms.

Classicism was not the only style used in the early C19. Gelston Castle of *c*.1805, probably designed by *Richard Crichton*, is a large and picturesquely battlemented toy fort. Much staider were *William Burn*'s castellated additions to Hoddom Castle in 1826–32 and Raehills House in 1829–34. More lighthearted was the w

tower-house wing added to Barjarg Tower in 1806–7. *Thomas Hamilton* produced an inventive Tudor-Gothic design for Cumstoun in 1828, its varied composition and treatment perhaps a
90 little studied, as were *Thomas Rickman*'s Tudor essays at The Grove and Terraughtie in 1825. More relaxed Tudor and Jacobean manorial dress was adopted for the additions to Lochnaw Castle (by *Archibald Elliot*, 1820–1) and Blackwood (1842) and for the new houses of Hensol (by *Robert Lugar*, 1822–4), The Barony (by *William Burn*, 1832–3) and Burnfoot Hall (*c.*1835).

The Tudor style of William Burn reappeared in 1874–5 at Craigcleuch but must by then have seemed very old-fashioned. From the 1850s it had been supplanted by the much more toughly detailed SCOTTISH BARONIAL, a style whose introduction was credited by contemporaries to Burn's one-time partner *David Bryce*. The development of Bryce's style from manorial to fullblooded Baronial can be seen at Capenoch, where his first addition, of 1847–8, was low-key, except for crowstepped gables and the use of his characteristic canted bay window corbelled to a square gable; his second addition, of 1854–7, strives to suggest
95 that it is a tower house. At Bryce's very much larger Castlemilk of 1864–70, the main entrance is placed in a huge round tower derived from the early C17 Aberdeenshire examples of Castle Fraser and Huntly Castle. Another early C17 tower, that of Winton House (Lothian), was the model for one at Bryce's now demolished Halleaths of 1866. Tauter and fiercer Baronial but employing some of the same motifs was used by Bryce's former pupil, *C. G. H. Kinnear* of *Peddie & Kinnear* (later *Kinnear & Peddie*), at Crawfordton House (1863–6), Threave House (1871–3) and Cardoness House (1889) and by Kinnear's former pupil *Walter F. Lyon* at Kirkwood in 1880. Rather more relaxed was the work of another Edinburgh firm, *Brown & Wardrop*, who, in
93 the 1860s, designed Lochinch Castle, Penninghame House, the additions (since removed) to Ardwell House and the martial upper floors added to an early C16 tower house at Craichlaw.

The Baronial style was not generally intended to deceive the visitor into thinking a Victorian house to be C16 or C17[*]; it was a dress evocative of Scottishness which was also capable of the asymmetry imposed by the internal planning of the Victorian country house. This planning, with its demarcation of different zones for different activities or social groups, is most clearly expressed at Castlemilk, which is composed of four differentiated blocks – for estate business, entertainment, family life and servants.

One house created in the late C19 and early C20 which cannot
97 be entirely acquitted of deception is Old Place of Mochrum, a courtyard complex incorporating two towers, one probably C15, the other early C17 in origin, but both very ruinous by 1873, when restoration work was begun on them by *Richard Park* for the third Marquess of Bute. Their resulting appearance was largely

---

[*] Although *Peddie & Forbes Smith* added a quite convincing 'tower house' to Cowhill Tower in 1913–14.

conjectural, and a hall block and two new ranges were built round the court, the two ranges of 1900–2 being in the best Arts and Crafts manner. The interiors (almost all by *R. W. Schultz*, 1903–8) form the most enjoyable Edwardian ensemble in Scotland, beautifully crafted but quite without pomposity. Edwardian interior work of a less inventive, generally C18 character but remarkably complete survives in *James Kennedy Hunter*'s Dunskey House of 1901–4 (whose exterior is stripped Scottish manorial); and *Reginald Blomfield* gave Murraythwaite two rooms in his scholarly late C17 and C18 manner in 1902.

Country houses are almost always closely accompanied by walled gardens – most apparently dating from the late C18 or early C19 – stables, a doocot and one or more lodges. The grandest PARKLAND SETTINGS are at Drumlanrig Castle and Lochinch Castle, both laid out in the early C18 and restored in the early C19. Drumlanrig's park is an afforestation of the surrounding hills to provide a contrast with the strict formality of the parterres beside the house; Lochinch Castle has a formal pattern of rides, terraces and banks extending N from the ruined Castle Kennedy along an isthmus between two lochs. At Drumlanrig are mid-C19 summerhouses, presumably designed as stopping places for a stroller in the policies. More dominant is the folly, probably of *c.*1790, at Cowhill Tower, a 'ruined' screen wall incorporating earlier carved stones, which engages the view from the house. More formal in their architecture, but less formally sited, are the battlemented Temple of 1778 at Cally Palace and the Gothic folly temple of *c.*1800 at Orchardton House.

DOOCOTS, for pigeons as a source of fresh meat in winter, were symbols of lairdly privilege. Few freestanding ones have survived in the region, but Denbie has an octagonal lantern-topped doocot of 1775 and Genoch Mains, near Stoneykirk, a conical-roofed circular one, perhaps of *c.*1800. Many other doocots were incorporated in stables. At Blackwood the doocot (whose potence is still in place) occupies a pyramid-roofed tower over the pend arch in the rustically smart main stable range. The dressing up of the most prominent front of a STABLES court, often built at the same time as the house, was general. At Terregles House the 1830s stables had three utilitarian ranges and one, the show-front, smartly adorned with pilasters and an entablature. The placing of a tower over the arched entrance to the courtyard was common. At Jardine Hall's stables of 1825, the lowest stage of the tower contained the pend arch, the second (clock) stage was dignified by columns in the cut-out corners, and the top was formed by a domed lantern. At the large stable courtyard of Lincluden House in College Road, Dumfries, by *Walter Newall*, 1821, the principal front is Tudor, with a big centre tower that is battlemented and contains a doocot. Less conscious of a show-front are the mid-C18 stables of Arbigland, which have corner towers, another tower in the centre of the W range, and an urn-finialled pediment above the flight holes of the doocot over the pend arch. Unusual in the uniform treatment of their four fronts are the 1750s stables at Carnsalloch House, where a two-storey Diocletian-windowed

pavilion rises through the roof, and each face of the main block
has a pedimented centrepiece, the design perhaps derived from
Chiswick House. The effect, appealing to cognoscenti, was
perhaps too restrained to impress the locals, but they could hardly
99 fail to be overawed by the flashy front of Gelston Castle's stables
of *c.* 1805, a castellated fantasy with an immensely tall octagonal
tower of ridiculously martial swagger.

LODGES are often plain, with perhaps a portico or hoodmoulded openings in the front. Smarter than usual are the late
C18 pair at the East Gate to Dalswinton House, the pedimented
centrepieces of their front gables containing overarched windows.
100 Barjarg Tower's early C19 lodge combines with an arched gateway
in an endearing Gothick display.

ROADS, RAILWAYS, HARBOURS AND
LIGHTHOUSES

Until the C19, ROADS capable of taking wheeled traffic were few.
An act of 1617 made labour on the upkeep of highways a statutory
obligation on the population of each parish, under the oversight
of Justices of the Peace, and stipulated that roads to market towns
and sea ports be 20 feet (6m.) broad, but it seems to have
been observed carelessly. Nor were communications markedly
improved by acts of 1669 and 1676 which tightened the regulations
and gave responsibility for roads and bridges to the Commissioners of Supply (local landowners charged with the value of
lands for taxation) as well as the Justices of the Peace. The
provision and maintenance of roads remained dependent on the
goodwill of local landowners.

One major government initiative which produced an effective
E–W route through the region was the construction of the military
road from Carlisle to Portpatrick in 1763–5. In 1776 the first
act was passed for the construction of three turnpike roads in
Dumfriesshire,* trustees being appointed for the task with the
power to levy tolls every six miles, and the Stewartry Turnpike
Act was passed in 1797. By the mid-C19 many turnpike roads had
been constructed, and the local roads were said to be of a good
standard. In the C20 roads have been upgraded for motor traffic,
the main A74 from Carlisle to Glasgow has become a dual carriageway, and the A715 from Carlisle to Stranraer now by-passes
the towns and villages along its route.

BRIDGES are the most conspicuous architectural artefacts of
the road system. The only substantial medieval bridge to have
survived, perhaps one of very few large bridges in the region
101 before the C18, is the rubble-built Old Bridge of *c.* 1430–2 at
Dumfries (replacing an earlier bridge reputedly constructed by

---

* From Gretna to Moffat, from Dumfries to Moffat, and from Annan to a junction
with the Carlisle–Langholm road.

Devorgilla, lady of Galloway, in the C13); it was originally of
nine arches, slightly humpbacked and narrow. Also rubble-built,
humpbacked and narrow is the Old Bridge of Urr, probably of
1580. The bridge at Sanquhar was rebuilt in 1661 (and again in
1855), Annan's first bridge was erected in 1700–5, Skipper's
Bridge near Langholm *c.*1700, and the Old Bridge of Dee at
Rhonehouse in the early C18; but most major bridges are of the
late C18 or early C19, and the ferry at Kirkcudbright was not
replaced by a bridge until 1868. The large late Georgian bridges
of the improved roads were expensive and often unafraid of
proclaiming the fact. The Nith Bridge, near Burnhead, of 1777–8
is humpbacked and relatively plain, except for pointed cutwaters
and pedestrian refuges, but, like almost all the larger new bridges,
it is of ashlar and not rubble. Much smarter is the Old Bridge at
Auldgirth, designed by the Edinburgh architect *David Henderson*
and built in 1781–2, whose bow-ended cutwaters are surmounted
by coupled pilasters carrying entablatures and topped by half-
domed refuges. *Robert Adam*'s design of 1788 for a bridge at
Kirkdale was simplified in execution and built in rubble masonry
rather than rusticated ashlar; but the use of rock-faced ashlar,
together with a battlemented parapet, makes a powerfully romantic impression at Tongland Bridge of 1804–8 (by *Thomas Telford*,
probably with advice from *Alexander Nasmyth*). Other early C19
bridges were plainer, the most effective in its landscape *John
Rennie*'s elegantly curved Ken Bridge, near New Galloway, of
1820–1. Designs did not change much for most of the C19:
Shillahill Bridge, near Lockerbie, by *George Cadell Bruce*, of 1867
is easily mistaken for a work of forty years before. Increased traffic
led to the widening of some bridges. At Langholm, the Townhead
Bridge of 1775 was given cantilevered steel footpaths with lattice-
sided parapets in 1880. In 1892–3 the same process, but in more
pompous form, was undertaken at Dumfries' New Bridge of
1791–4. Dumfries acquired an additional bridge over the Nith in
1925 (by *J. Boyd Brodie*), its concrete construction hidden by
polite ashlar facing. Not at all polite, and with no attempt to mask
its concrete, is the contemporary bow-truss Kirkcudbright Bridge
designed by *Blyth & Blyth* and *L. G. Mouchel & Partners*, 1924–
6. More recent road bridges have been self-effacing, but the New
Bridge of 1979 at Auldgirth, unable to hide, is close to elegance.

Pedestrian bridges seem to have been put up almost as much
for decoration as use. In the grounds of Langholm Lodge is the
Duchess Bridge, by *William Keir Jun.*, 1813, an elegant lattice-
girdered segmental span over the Esk. In the middle of Langholm
itself, the Esk is spanned by a suspension bridge (Boatford Bridge)
by *E. Hernulewicz & Co.*, *c.*1871, the cables suspended from cast-
and wrought-iron pylons. Pylons recur at *D. H. & F. Reid*'s
George V Bridge, Newton Stewart, of 1911, but at Dumfries'
suspension bridge (by *John Willet*, 1874–5) the cables hang from
pairs of tall Doric columns. Also in Dumfries, and unequivocally
late C20, is the single-mast cable-stayed bridge over the by-pass
designed by *Hugh Murray* of *Dumfries and Galloway Regional
Council* in 1988.

Until 1883 turnpike roads were partly funded by the collection
of tolls. TOLLHOUSES are consequently quite common, although
many have been badly altered. Not untypical is the early C19
tollhouse at Creebridge, Newton Stewart, its end a semi-octagon.
Also with semi-octagonal ends, but battlemented, are the contemporary tollhouses at each end of the burgh of Langholm.
Some roadside INNS, away from towns or large villages, were
built to serve travellers. In 1792 Gretna Hall, a laird's house at
Gretna Green, was converted to an inn and given Venetian-
windowed additions. The small inn at Auldgirth was remodelled
c. 1804 with Gothick windows and a central chimney decorated
121 with crosslet arrowslits. The inn (now Old Brig Rest Home) at
Beattock of 1822, probably designed by *Thomas Telford*, appears
to offer more solid comfort, its entrance dignified with recessed
Greek Doric columns, the Vanbrughian chimneys contributing
to the heaviness. Less serious is the Ken Bridge Hotel, near New
Galloway, of c. 1830, with hoodmoulded windows.

As early as 1836 a group of Glasgow businessmen had proposed
the construction of a RAILWAY network for SW Scotland. The
principal lines were to form a triangle, its corners marked by
Portpatrick (still the principal Scottish port for Ireland but already
threatened by the use of steamships on the longer Glasgow–
Belfast crossing), Glasgow and Dumfries, from where a line would
run to Carlisle. The N end of this network was begun in 1837 by
the Glasgow, Paisley, Kilmarnock & Ayr Railway Company, and
by 1843 its SW and SE points were Ayr and Kilmarnock. Then
in 1845–8 the Caledonian Railway, in disregard of the original
proposals, constructed a line from Carlisle to Edinburgh and
Glasgow which passed through Annandale via Lockerbie and
Beattock. In 1846–50 a rival and shorter line from Carlisle to
Glasgow was built by the Glasgow, Dumfries & Carlisle Railway
Company in accordance with the original scheme, passing
through Annan to Dumfries and then up Nithsdale to meet a S
extension of the Glasgow–Kilmarnock line at Closeburn. The S
side of the originally proposed triangle, the line from Dumfries to
Portpatrick, was built in 1857–62, the section from Dumfries to
Castle Douglas designed by *John Miller Jun.*, the rest by *B. & E.
Blyth*. In 1870 it was joined at Glenluce near its W end by a
continuation of the Glasgow–Ayr line. Another line from England
(the Solway Junction Railway), avoiding Carlisle and carried
across the Solway on a viaduct c. 1.8km. long to join the Caledonian Railway's Annandale line at Kirtlebridge, was opened in
1869.

Branch lines were also constructed. The first, in 1863, joined the
Caledonian Railway's mainline station of Lockerbie to Dumfries,
serving also the small burgh of Lochmaben and the quarries
of Locharbriggs. The next year, lines from Castle Douglas to
Kirkcudbright and from the Carlisle–Hawick railway (outwith the
SE border of Dumfries and Galloway) to Canonbie and Langholm opened. In 1877 came the grandly named Wigtownshire
Railway, a line from Newton Stewart to Wigtown and Whithorn,
with a spur to Garlieston, followed in 1881 by the Moffat Railway,

a short branch from Beattock to the spa town of Moffat. In 1901–2 a light railway was constructed from Elvanfoot, on the main Caledonian Railway line, to the lead-mining village of Wanlockhead. Another light railway was built in 1905, from Dumfries to Dunscore and Moniaive.

The Solway Junction Railway closed in 1921 and its viaduct was later demolished. Closure of the line to Wanlockhead followed in 1935; the branch line to Moffat closed in 1964, the line between Dumfries and Glenluce in 1965, and the line from Lockerbie to Dumfries in 1966.

The Caledonian Railway's line up Annandale passed through fairly easy country without the need for major viaducts. The line between Carlisle and Dumfries is similarly easy; the chief viaducts are the two built in 1848 at Annan. The line up Nithsdale is in more rugged country. For the Crawick Viaduct, near Sanquhar, *John Miller* provided six roundheaded arches, with channelled hammerdressed ashlar masonry; at the shorter viaduct at Mennock, he treated the two outer spans as triumphal arches. On the line from Dumfries to Portpatrick *B. & E. Blyth* provided several viaducts, that over Loch Ken, at Parton, with central spans of iron, the Big Water of Fleet Viaduct, N of Gatehouse of Fleet, with twenty segmental arches, the arches of the tall viaduct near Glenluce supported on trapezoid piers.

Until the development of the railway system the principal means of transporting goods was by water. Many of the HARBOURS were natural shelters provided by the mouths of rivers, where little more than the construction of quays was required to allow the loading and unloading of ships. Such simple quayed harbours were constructed at Annan, Glencaple, Kirkcudbright and Wigtown, probably from an early period. Rather more ambitious were the artificial harbours, protected by sea walls and piers, constructed at Port William in the 1790s, Port Logan in 1818–22 and Portpatrick in 1821–36. The piers at Portpatrick and Port Logan were both given lighthouses. Portpatrick now has a brick-built replacement of 1896, but Port Logan's is of the 1830s, very much smarter and enjoying the convenience of a nearby latrine. Much larger than these harbours, but drably utilitarian, is that at Stranraer, which has developed since the later C19 as the main Scottish ferry port for Ireland. 104

The first LIGHTHOUSE erected on the Solway was at Southerness; as built in 1748–9, it appears to have been a straightforward tapered rectangular tower. Subsequent alterations in c.1785 and 1842–3 have produced its present memorably gawky appearance. In 1786 Parliament passed 'An Act for erecting certain Light-houses in the Northern Parts of Great Britain', by which Commissioners of Northern Lighthouses became responsible (as they still are) for the erection and maintenance of lighthouses. Four were built by the Commissioners in Dumfries and Galloway: Corsewall Point (by *Robert Stevenson*, 1815–16), Mull of Galloway (again by *Robert Stevenson*, 1828–30), Little Ross, near Senwick (by *Thomas Stevenson*, 1843), and Loch Ryan, at Cairnryan (by *Alan Stevenson*, 1847). All are tapering round 103 towers with cupola lights and accompanied by flat-roofed keepers' houses.

PUBLIC AND COMMERCIAL BURGH
BUILDINGS

From the C12 until the late C17 the right to engage in foreign trade was restricted to the merchant burgesses of royal burghs. Foundation of these BURGHS in Scotland probably followed an initiative of David I as part of his revolutionary modernization of Scottish society in the mid-C12 and, just as knights were imported to Scotland at this time, so merchants, probably predominantly English, were encouraged to settle the new royal burghs. Some other medieval burghs were burghs of barony, i.e. they were dependent on a lord other than the king and, theoretically at least, were barred from foreign trade but entitled to house incorporations of craftsmen and to hold regular fairs. Royal burghs, together with royal castles, seem to have been established at Dumfries by the late C12, at Wigtown some time in the C13, and at Kirkcudbright by the early C14. Burghs of barony were founded at Annan and Lochmaben, the sites of the two main castles of the Bruces, lords of Annandale, in the C12 and C13; both became royal burghs after Robert Bruce's accession to the throne in 1306. Other medieval burghs of barony, again associated with castles, were established at Urr and Sanquhar, Urr apparently existing only for a short period in the C12 and perhaps C13, Sanquhar elevated to the status of a royal burgh in 1598. One medieval burgh of barony associated with a cathedral/priory was Whithorn, which also became a royal burgh in the C16. The late C16 burgh of barony at Stranraer, founded in 1595, became the region's last royal burgh in 1617.

A sizeable number of new burghs of barony were founded in the C17 and C18 – Portpatrick, Langholm, New Galloway, Moniaive, Thornhill, Newton Stewart, Gatehouse of Fleet, Castle Douglas and Creetown – and Maxwelltown (now part of Dumfries) became one as late as 1810. Two of these, Gatehouse of Fleet and Creetown, had begun as villages shortly before becoming burghs, but generally the creation of a burgh before the later C19 was not recognition of an existing urban or quasi-urban community but a legal action intended to enable the bringing of such a community into existence. These C17 and C18 burghs, usually laid out on a formal plan (e.g. the gridiron of Castle Douglas), were founded in the hope of attracting craftsmen and industry drawn by the burghs' legal privileges. Industrial success was very limited, the cotton mills at Gatehouse of Fleet and Castle Douglas flourishing for brief periods, the woollen mills at Langholm enjoying a longer prosperity. Most of the burghs of barony, if they became much more than villages in size, grew as market towns.

The same motive lay behind the foundation of new VILLAGES in the C18 and C19. With a few exceptions, these were intended to house not farm or estate workers but industrial workers, often weavers, as at Springfield (*see* Gretna Green), which was laid out in 1791, or fishermen, as at Garlieston when it was begun *c.* 1760. The layout plan of the village of Brydekirk, begun in 1800, shows two mills (one for the manufacture of woollens) and bleaching greens. In the event, Brydekirk was unsuccessful in attracting either industry or many inhabitants. Success was reserved for a handful, the most notable Lockerbie, begun *c.* 1730, and Dalbeattie, begun in 1781. In the later C19, both of these became police burghs, allowing them municipal government. A few new villages have been founded in the C20. Gretna and Eastriggs, both laid out by *Raymond Unwin* according to the 'garden-suburb' principles he had previously followed at Hampstead Garden Suburb in London, were begun during the First World War to house workers in munitions factories, Glentrool and Ae in the 1950s for forestry workers.

Symbols of burgh status were provided by MARKET CROSSES, usually finialled shafts without, despite the name, a cross. Langholm's cross, perhaps of the early C17, is crude, its finial a boulder incised with a cross, and Moniaive's cross of 1638 was little more sophisticated. But some crosses were more decorative. At Lochmaben the finial, probably of the late C16, is decorated with carved flowers and was crowned with a sundial in 1729. The earlier of the two crosses at Wigtown, dated 1738, again has a sundial, topped by a pineapple. The second cross at Wigtown, of 1816, is suavely Gothic. Showiest is the cross erected at Thornhill in 1714, the volutes of its fluted Ionic column joined by swags, its winged-horse finial a supporter of the coat of arms of the Duke of Queensberry, the burgh's feudal superior.

Until the C19, the principal building in many burghs, besides the parish church, was the TOLBOOTH, partly intended, as the name suggests, for the receipt of market tolls and other burgh revenues and consequently as a strongroom. The tolbooth also usually served as the town lock-up and debtors' jail and as the meeting place of the burgh court and the town council. In some burghs, e.g. Dumfries, Lochmaben, Sanquhar and Langholm, it was prominently sited in the middle of the broad main street. Often it was dignified by a steeple. The steeples at Kirkcudbright 106 (1642) and Whithorn (1708) both have conical spires; Dumfries' 107 tolbooth, the Midsteeple, built and probably designed by *Tobias* 105 *Bachop* in 1705–7, closely resembles Sir William Bruce's Stirling Town House of a few years before, with the steeple set at one corner of the main block and topped by an ogee-roofed concave-sided spire. A compact design was employed in 1722–3 at Loch- 109 maben Town Hall which consisted of a piend-roofed two-storey block, with the advanced centrepiece carried up as a domed and cupolaed belfry (replaced by a dumpy stone spire twenty years later). A similar design was used in 1735–7 by *William Adam* for Sanquhar Tolbooth, and another steeple rising in the centre of 108 the tolbooth's long front is at Stranraer Old Town Hall of 1777.

From the late C18, the growing use of imprisonment as a possibly reformative alternative to capital or corporal punishment or transportation for convicted criminals created a need for prisons that could provide more than the few lock-up cells of the tolbooths. JAILS were built in 1807 at Dumfries (since demolished) and in 1815 at Kirkcudbright, where a tall tower and octagonal caphouse make a commanding landmark from a distance. At Stranraer the top two floors of the C16 Castle of St John were fitted up with tunnel-vaulted cells in 1821–2. A General Board of Directors of Prisons in Scotland was established in 1839, and its architect, *Thomas Brown Jun.*, provided the new Wigtown Jail in 1846–8, looking like a large Tudor villa. The late C19 produced utilitarian new prisons behind the Stranraer Sheriff Court in 1871–4 and at Dumfries in 1883.

Legislation in 1860 established proper financing for the erection of SHERIFF COURTS. In 1862–3 *Brown & Wardrop*'s boldly sited
111 County Buildings and Town Hall at Wigtown, a combined sheriff court and hall, was built in a mixed French and Flemish medieval manner. The same architects' Stranraer Sheriff Court of 1871–4 is Tudor and much less prominent. *David Rhind* was responsible for two other sheriff courts in the region, dramatically tall and stark Baronial at Dumfries (1863–6), a very serious toy fort at Kirkcudbright (1866–8). After 1856–7 each county was obliged to have a police force, and POLICE STATIONS were constructed in burghs and some villages. One of the earlier, the Langholm Police Station of 1865, was designed by *Alexander Fraser* in the same sort of Scottish Jacobean manner as he employed for banks. Much more suggestive of the strong arm of a not very friendly law are *James Barbour*'s Baronial County Police Barracks in Dumfries (1876) and *James Barbour & Bowie*'s small but aggressive stations at Thornhill (1909) and Clarencefield (1911).

COUNTY COUNCILS were set up in 1889; both they and BURGH COUNCILS were replaced by district and regional authorities in 1975, in turn replaced by unitary authorities (a single council covering Dumfries and Galloway) in 1996. In 1912 *J. M. Dick Peddie* produced a large neo-Georgian building to house Dumfries County Council (later Dumfries and Galloway Regional Council Offices*), rather too conscious of the authority of local government bureaucracy. Friendlier, if only because smaller, are the Municipal Chambers at Dumfries by *James Carruthers*, 1931–2, their English Baroque tinged by Art Deco. Of more recent productions the best are the chunky Annandale and Eskdale District Council Chambers‡ of 1980 at Annan, by the District Council's architect, *Brian Page*.

TOWN AND VILLAGE HALLS, designed for large meetings but often including municipal offices, were produced in quantity during the C19. Some, like the various masonic halls or *Thomas Boyd*'s undemonstrative classical Trades Hall of 1804–6 in Dum-

* The building was transferred to the ownership of the new Dumfries and Galloway Council in 1996.
‡ The building was transferred to the ownership of the new Dumfries and Galloway Council in 1996.

fries, belonged to particular groups, but most were intended for the general public. Moffat Town Hall, built in 1827 as an assembly room (with baths behind, filled with the spa water), was quite simple (except for a Doric portico) until 1881, when *James Barbour* enlarged it in a sort of Jacobean classical manner. A working men's institute (the Proudfoot Institute) was built in the same town in the 1880s and enlarged and remodelled with free Baroque detail in the 1890s. In 1861–2 Dalbeattie celebrated its recent acquisition of burghal status with the erection of a modest town hall. Castle Douglas's Town Hall of 1862–3 is Italianate (by *James Barbour*), Kirkcudbright's of 1878–9 a tall Renaissance block (by *Peddie & Kinnear*), Thornhill's Parish Hall of 1893–4 jolly French Renaissance (by *James Barbour*), and Annan's Victoria Hall of 1882 Baronial. Much more dominant in Annan is the Town Hall of 1875–8, *Peter Smith*'s design again Baronial but with a big steeple. This may have provoked the much newer burgh of Lockerbie to commission its Town Hall in 1887 from the local architect *F. J. C. Carruthers*, who mixed Jacobean detail into a Baronial outline and topped the immensely tall corner steeple's spire with a cupola. The result is memorably unpleasant.

Some parish LIBRARIES were established in the late C18 and early C19. One of these, at Wanlockhead, was housed in a purpose-built but humble building (by *Charles Howitt*) in 1850. Rather more conscious of its importance is the gently ecclesiastical Westerkirk Parish Library built at Bentpath in 1860. After 1854 burghs were allowed to finance public libraries from the rates but were slow to take advantage of this opportunity to demonstrate civic pride in the literacy of their inhabitants. However, in 1875–8 Langholm erected a sizeable public library, *James Burnet*'s Jacobean style in the manner of twenty or thirty years before. Dumfries acquired the Ewart Library in 1900–4, *Alan B. Crombie*'s free Renaissance design a stodgy disappointment. Much more successful are two Jacobean libraries by *George Washington Browne*, low-key but confident at Castle Douglas (1902–4), larger and more urbane at Annan (1906).

Of THEATRES, only Dumfries' Theatre Royal is worth mention. It was built in 1790–2 but completely remodelled in an unassertive classical manner by *C. J. Phipps* in 1876. More striking as a civic building intended for edification and amusement is the Dumfries Museum and Camera Obscura, a windmill remodelled for use as an observatory by *Walter Newall*, 1836, the windows and door placed in neo-Egyptian surrounds.

One of the professed aims of the leaders of the Scottish reformation was to provide a school in each parish. This had been largely achieved by the C18, although the SCHOOL BUILDINGS provided by the heritors generally consisted of no more than a schoolroom and modest living accommodation for the master. A few schools were endowed. In 1723 John Wallace, a Glasgow merchant, left £1,400 for the building and endowment of a school (the Wallace Hall Academy) in his native parish of Closeburn, and the school (later much altered) was built to *William Lukup*'s design in 1724–9. The school itself was a single-storey piend-roofed rectangle, but the schoolmaster's house was unusually large, of two storeys and five bays. Perhaps the admission of boarders was envisaged from the start. Certainly they had been introduced by 1790, and in 1795 an austere three-storey block was put up to house them. Other endowed schools in pre-dominantly rural parishes were the Hutton Hall Academy at Bankend, founded in 1712 under the will of Dr John Hutton, physician to Queen Anne, and Borgue Academy, endowed in 1803 by William Rainy from a fortune made in the West Indies. In some towns endowed schools were prominent features. In Sanquhar the Crichton School of *c.* 1833, both its blocks enjoying Roman Doric porticoes, was founded with money left for chari-table purposes by Dr James Crichton, a native of the burgh. A similar bequest by William Johnston in 1845 gave Kirkcudbright the Italianate Johnston Primary School of 1847–8. Newton Stewart contained no fewer than three endowed schools by the 1860s. One, founded in the late C18 by Archibald McCreddie, a native of the parish, consisted of no more than a schoolroom and master's house, but the other two were much grander. Samuel Douglas' Free School designed by *John Henderson*, 1834, was powerfully neo-classical, the Ewart Institute by *Thomas Cook*, 1862–4, Gothic.

Burgh schools built by town councils could be expressions both of civic pride and of the quality of education to be found within. The Dumfries Academy was rebuilt in 1802–4 and Kirkcudbright Academy in 1815. These have both been replaced, but *Thomas Brown*'s former Annan Academy of 1820 still stands, a sober but well-finished astylar classical block.

By the mid-C19 schools in villages and small burghs were becoming architecturally more ambitious than their C18 pre-decessors. The Penninghame Parish (now St Ninian's) School of 1849, which has been engulfed in the late C19 spread of Newton Stewart, was Tudor in style, as were the schools at Penpont of 1844–5 and at Thornhill (now Wallace Hall Academy) by *Charles Howitt*, 1864–5. The Education Act of 1872 established a national system of school boards and laid down standards for school buildings, many of which were replaced soon after. Charac-teristically the new schools were single-storey, with economical Gothic detailing, e.g. the former Penninghame School, Newton Stewart, by *Richard Park*, 1876, or Moniaive School of 1883–4 by *James Barbour*. Rebuilding or replacement of the large burgh schools took place a little later. In the 1890s *F. J. C. Carruthers* designed new academies at Annan and Dumfries, the one Jaco-bean, the other in a much more forceful English Baroque. *Alan B. Crombie*'s Kirkcudbright Academy of 1901 is plain classical, a cupola topping its clock tower. Austerity, but with Jacobean touches and a big tower, is the keynote of *Charles Hay*'s St Joseph's College, Dumfries, of 1907. The new Moffat Academy of 1932–3 by the Dumfries County Architect *John R. Hill* is simplified neo-Georgian. Hill's large addition of 1936 to Dumfries Academy is Art Deco without the fun.

Many schools were replaced in the 1950s and 1960s, generally in the flat-roofed lightweight style associated with the Festival of Britain. More recent schools have been much chunkier in design. Portpatrick School (by *Dumfries and Galloway Regional Council*, 1979) is one of the more successful, Sanquhar Primary School (by *Dumfries and Galloway Regional Council*, 1981) the most ingenious. FURTHER EDUCATION BUILDINGS began in 1971 with the neatly packaged Dumfries and Galloway College of Technology (by the Dumfries County Architect *Alastair D. Macintyre*). More forceful post-Modern has appeared at Stranraer with the John Niven Further Education Centre of 1988–90 and, with considerable accomplishment, at the large agricultural college extensions to The Barony by *Peter Nelson* of Dumfries and Galloway Regional Council, 1984–91.

Such medieval HOSPITALS as there were in Scotland disappeared after the Reformation and new ones came only in the C18. An infirmary was founded at Dumfries in 1776 and a purpose-built hospital block erected for it in 1777–8. A new Dumfries and Galloway Royal Infirmary (now Dumfries and 110 Galloway Health Board Offices) was put up by *John Starforth* in 1869–73, its North Italian medieval style taking full advantage of the hilltop site. Much less conspicuous is that hospital's sensible replacement of 1970–4 by *Boswell, Mitchell & Johnston*. This is placed on the edge of the grounds of the region's largest institution, the Crichton Royal Hospital, a lunatic asylum begun in the 1830s. Its first building, Crichton Hall, was designed by 112 *William Burn* (closely following the plan of Watson & Pritchett's West Riding Lunatic Asylum of 1816–18 at Wakefield in Yorkshire) as a vast Elizabethan palace but on too large a scale to be completed at the time. When this block was extended to provide more accommodation for private patients by *W. L. Moffatt* in 1867–71, an Italianate style was adopted, although plain Georgian-survival had been considered appropriate for the Southern Counties' Asylum, a block for pauper patients, built in 1848–9 and now demolished. In the 1890s the hospital acquired its own muscularly detailed farm steading and a large church (*see* p. 45 above) designed by *Sydney Mitchell*, who also, from 1897, provided a group of big Jacobean villas, each intended to house a group of patients. Outside Dumfries, *Woodd & Ainslie* designed the Jacobean Thomas Hope Hospital at Langholm in 1894 and *Richard Park* the unambitious Garrick Hospital at Stranraer in 1897. ALMSHOUSES are few, but Moorhead's Hospital, its civic status marked by a cupola, was built in Dumfries in 1751–3, the bargeboarded and multi-gabled Atkinson Place in Kirkcudbright *c.*1870.

Some buildings straddled the dividing line between public and commercial character. POST OFFICES were constructed by the government in the C19 and C20. The large Dumfries Post Office of 1887–9 (now Procurator Fiscal's Office) is unassertive Scots Renaissance in manner, the Annan Post Office of 1898 Georgian-revival. Rather self-consciously Scottish is the crowstepped rubble gable of Langholm Post Office by *H. M. Office of Works*, 1935.

BANKS, although commercial enterprises, put up buildings in

the C19 of a public rather than private character. Those built before 1850 are classical. The Commercial Bank (now Old Bank) in Irish Street, Dumfries, of *c.* 1830 is distinguished by a Doric screen across its recessed centre. At the austere former Southern Bank of Scotland at Annan of *c.* 1845 there is a pedimented Roman Doric portico. A much more brutally classical portico is attached to the same town's former British Linen Bank of the same date. The rusticated ground floor of the Trustee Savings Bank in Church Crescent, Dumfries (by *John Gregan*, 1847) forms a plinth for Ionic columns at the outer bays, and the blind centre light of the central Venetian window frames a statue of Dr Henry Duncan, the Dumfriesshire minister who had founded the savings bank movement in 1810.

120

Banking activity increased greatly in the second half of the C19 and banks proliferated. Large villages and small burghs might have only one, its building probably villa-like, e.g. the Georgian-survival Bank of Scotland (originally City of Glasgow Bank) of 1858 at Port William, but in the larger burghs there was a rivalry among banks to parallel the rivalry of the churches. There was also stylistic warfare, Baronial or Jacobean edifices fighting it out with Italian palazzi. However, neither the banking companies nor their architects showed particular loyalty to any one style. In 1862 *Alexander Fraser* designed a tall palazzo to house the National Bank in Dumfries; the next year, at Langholm, he provided the same bank with an austere Scots Jacobean block. The Royal Bank of Scotland's offices at Dumfries (by *Peddie & Kinnear*, 1856) and Annan (by *Sydney Mitchell*, 1881) were both Italianate, but its building at Newton Stewart (by *James Thomson*, 1873) is bare Baronial. The Bank of Scotland at Moffat (by *Peddie & Kinnear*, 1874) is Baronial, but the Newton Stewart office of the same company was remodelled five years later by *Wardrop & Reid* in an Italianate manner. Also Italianate are *John Starforth*'s heavy Renaissance frontage at the British Linen Bank in Dumfries (1872), the lighter-hearted Union Bank (now Bank of Scotland), Dumfries, by *William Railton*, 1875–7, and *David Rhind*'s Commercial (now Royal) Bank of Scotland, Stranraer, of 1874.

In the C20 banks have amalgamated and found themselves over-supplied with branches. However, a few new banks have been built. Dumfries acquired the Burnetian Baroque Clydesdale Bank in Irish Street, *c.* 1914, and *H. O. Tarbolton*'s British Linen Bank (now Bank of Scotland), its English Baroque polite but old-fashioned for 1934. More recently, also in Dumfries, the Royal Bank of Scotland has erected a cleanly detailed sandwich of stone, glass and brick (by the *Rowand Anderson Partnership*, 1982), and the Trustee Savings Bank a busy post-Modern block (by *Sutherland, Dickie & Copland*, 1993).

Most of the COMMERCIAL BUILDINGS in the burghs of the region are straightforward C19 developments of shops under flats. The region's one large department store was built at Nos. 24–36 Buccleuch Street, Dumfries, in 1878–9, *James Barbour*'s French Renaissance style rather low-key, but with no shortage of carved detail. Much more exuberant is the late C19 block at Nos.

15–17 Well Street, Moffat, its determined Baronialism crowned by the statue of a knight. Two towns have undergone major alteration in the late C20. Since 1960 the centre of Stranraer has been very largely redeveloped in a utilitarian commercial manner. Perhaps fortunately, the lack of pedestrianization and volume of traffic in that town leave little opportunity to look at the buildings. In Dumfries the High Street's late C20 redevelopment has been followed by pedestrianization, the Olde Worlde street furniture not entirely at ease with the architecture. Some of this is developers' bread-and-butter, although the huge Loreburne Centre by *Scott, Brownrigg & Turner*, 1988–91, enthusiastically embraces variety to disguise its bulk. The outcome is less than happy.

HOTELS were built from the C18 as stopping places for travellers. By 1815 Gatehouse of Fleet had acquired a trio of such establishments, the straightforward Murray Arms Hotel of 1766, the Venetian-windowed Angel Hotel of *c*.1800, and the Masonic 117 Arms of 1812, with a tripartite door linked to the three-light window above by an heraldic panel. The construction of railways was accompanied by the advent of a new type of hotel, designed as much for holiday-makers as for travellers. One of the first of these, the Eskdale Hotel at Langholm (by *Habershon, Spalding & Brock*, 1865–7), whose Gothic windows and carved bargeboards give it the look of an overgrown rectory, aimed for a serious-minded clientèle and was a combined temperance hotel and working men's institute, containing a reading room and two halls. Apparently designed for a more plutocratic market is *James Barbour*'s Queensberry Hotel of 1869 at Dumfries, its elaborate front a promise of plush within. Much less exuberant are Dumfries' Station Hotel (by *Milwain*, 1896–7), an overgrown broad-eaved villa, and the bay-windowed and verandahed Ellangowan Hotel at Creetown (by *George W. Webb*, 1898); but *F. J. C. Carruthers*' Central Hotel of 1898 at Annan, conveniently near the railway station, is redolent of pompous jocularity. Respectable families whose holidays revolved round seaside golf were catered for at the Portpatrick Hotel (by *James Kennedy Hunter*, 1905, enlarged by *J. M. Dick Peddie*, 1906–7), the dullness of its architecture calculated to send visitors out in search of fresh air.

BURGH AND VILLAGE HOUSING

Before the building of metalled roads and railways in the C19, lairds often owned TOWN HOUSES in their local burghs, for occupation during the winter 'season' and as a base for business. A pair of C17 town houses survives at Nos. 66–72 High Street, Kirkcudbright, each unpretentiously rubble-built and with a pend arch to the close behind, but the front of No. 72 flaunts the frame for a (now missing) heraldic panel. A much larger and more comfortable town house in the same burgh is Broughton House (No. 10 High Street), built in the mid-C18 for the Murrays of

Broughton, its centre gablet suggestive of a pediment, the interior panelled. Perhaps a little earlier is No. 29 Irish Street in Dumfries, with a brick front marked off by rusticated quoins into a five-bay centrepiece and one-bay ends, most of the windows dignified with lugged and key-blocked architraves. Smarter still is the house at
115 No. 24 Nith Place, Dumfries, built for the burgh's Town Clerk in 1753, which has a bullseye window in its three-bay pediment, urns on the parapet, and a Corinthian aedicule framing the entrance. Grand early C18 panelling has survived (re-used) in No. 79 High Street, Dumfries, originally the town house of Richard Lowthian of Staffold.

Such houses continued to be built into the early C19, now generally for professional men, merchants of the town, or those retired from some relatively lucrative occupation. One late C18 example is the pedimented and Venetian-windowed Ivy House in London Road, Stranraer. The best-surviving collection is in the High Street at Kirkcudbright, which includes No. 8 of 1817, its door framed by Ionic columns, its rear wing battlemented; No.
118 117 of c.1790, with a double-bow front; and the adjoining battlemented No. 119 of the early C19. Two ashlar-fronted buildings in Dumfries show how austerely smart town houses had become by c.1830: No. 61 Irish Street displays Doric porticoes to front and back, No. 101 George Street (by *Walter Newall, c.*1832) has a pedimented Greek Doric portico and aproned windows.

The main streets of most towns were developed or redeveloped from the late C18 with TERRACED HOUSING, generally of two or three storeys. The architecture was seldom ambitious, although
116 a double house (Carlyle's Birthplace) of 1791 at Ecclefechan has a Venetian window above its pend arch, and at the block of Nos. 34–40 High Street, Gatehouse of Fleet, also with a central pend, every other window is Venetian. The terraced houses of c.1815 along the shore at Carsethorn give a display of naively decorative fanlights. Very much smarter, and much more unified than the generality of these developments, is the 'New Town' development
119 at Castle Street, George Street and Irving Street, Dumfries, laid out in 1806 by the Edinburgh architect *Robert Burn*, who largely controlled the elevational designs. Elsewhere there are fragments of unified schemes, such as the short terrace of c.1840 at Nos. 52–60 St Andrew Street, Castle Douglas, each house with a heavy pilastered doorpiece, the early C19 terraces at Terregles Street and Laurieknowe in the Maxwelltown area of Dumfries, or the slightly later Albany Place in Nunholm Road, Dumfries.

Workers were mostly housed in cottages, often originally thatched, but at Gatehouse of Fleet very plain brick-built two-storey terraces were provided in the late C18 and early C19 for those employed in the cotton mills. ESTATE HOUSING was not always so dourly utilitarian. In the mid-C19 village of Beattock the cottages are gently picturesque, with broad eaves and barge-boarded dormers. Even more picturesque and just a touch self-
123 conscious is the L-plan terrace making up the hamlet of Parton, a model settlement provided with its octagonal communal privy, laundry and, after 1908, hall.

Larger in scale and enjoyably wacky is Queensberry Terrace at Cummertrees, designed *c.* 1900 by *F. J. C. Carruthers* as the first stage in a projected summer resort whose success must always have been doubtful because it was cut off from its beach by a railway. A little E of Cummertrees, and much more serious, are the two townships of Eastriggs and Gretna laid out on 'garden-suburb' lines by *Raymond Unwin,* the simple neo-Georgian housing for munitions workers enlivened with only a few decorative touches.

Simplicity was also the keynote of most of the interwar local authority housing. Among the best is an early scheme by *W. F. Crombie* at Park Terrace, Dalbeattie, 1920, the houses built of granite, with steep piended roofs and bracketed cornices over the doors. The post-war period has produced a sizeable quantity of straightforward local authority housing, mostly pleasant but lacking punch, although the development of 1972 by the *University of Edinburgh Architectural Research Unit* in St Mary Street, Kirkcudbright, strikes a more assertive note. In Dumfries blocks of flats were built beside the River Nith in the 1960s, only four storeys high and far removed from the ethos of the maligned tower block, but unexciting. More effective is the long block of 1963–4 at Nos. 129A–153B St Michael's Street, Dumfries, with continuous balconies providing strong horizontal emphasis, checked towards the street by the stone-clad stair towers. The most recent developments have been post-Modern in manner; one of the more successful, at Nos. 81–83 Glasgow Street (St Andrew's Court), Dumfries, by *Crallan & Winstanley,* 1988–90, evocative of Georgian architecture but with a decided late C20 twist.

SUBURBAN VILLAS, each set in its own garden, or even a miniature park, were built from the C18. One of the earlier is No. 16 Bruce Street, Lochmaben, of 1786, the ashlar centrepiece of its garden front making a showy display, with a Venetian window flanked by Corinthian pilasters. The castellated style appeared in Stranraer *c.* 1820 at North West Castle (Hotel), Port Rodie, a tall villa with a battlemented double-bow front; but classicism remained the favourite architectural dress until the 1830s. It is idiosyncratic, with a bowed portico, skied pediment and eagle-topped angle pilasters, at Larkhill, Old Well Road, Moffat, of 1807, much smoother at *Walter Newall*'s Ionic-porticoed Lady-field West, Glencaple Road, Dumfries, of 1812, and his Sidmount 122 Cottage, Sidmount Avenue, Moffat, of 1832, which presents a boldly advanced pedimented centre towards the street and a verandah to the garden. The verandah was a hint of a shift in taste towards informality. In 1834 Chapelmount House was built at No. 16 Laurieknowe, Dumfries, a *cottage orné* with a pyramid-roofed tower, its elaborately carved bargeboards precursors for those of the slightly later Gracefield (now Arts Centre) at No. 28 Edinburgh Road, Dumfries.

Most of the smarter mid-C19 villas were Jacobethan, sometimes with stripped classical porticoes, as at Scaurbank, Port Street, Annan, or No. 30 Laurieknowe, Dumfries, the latter with a delicate ironwork verandah along two sides. The most elaborate, but on a tiny scale, is Lincoln Cottage, No. 15 Culderry Row, Garlieston, a suburban villa in concept if not in position, glorying in inventively patterned glazing, corbelled-out buttresses flanking the central gablet, and human-head label stops at the attic window. Late C19 villas are abundant but few are inspired. One exception is *J. J. Burnet*'s Kilneiss House of 1886 at Moniaive, where the half-timbering applied to the white-harled walls gives the relaxed appearance of an English cottage confidently expecting the garden to be filled with hollyhocks. Not at all relaxed but pompously sure of its importance is the free Renaissance Nunfield House, set back from Edinburgh Road in Dumfries. Some awareness of the Modern Movement was shown at Portpatrick by *A. Maclean Goudie*'s blocky flat-roofed Drummuie, Heugh Road, of 1936. Also blocky, but with a rounded stair tower to contrast with the angularity, is *John A. Copland*'s No. 1 Hill Street, Dumfries, of 1966. The more recent rediscovery of the pitched roof is celebrated by *Ian Ballantine*'s prominently sited House o' Hill at Portpatrick of 1974–5.

RURAL MANSES, FARMHOUSES AND STEADINGS

Until the late C18 the rural economy of Dumfries and Galloway was largely based on peasant agriculture. Cultivable land was worked by tenants grouped together in 'townships', each usually enclosed by a dyke to protect crops from cattle, the principal form of livestock, which were turned out to graze on the pasture beyond or taken to hill pasture further away. There was little security of tenure, and rents were paid in kind.

The most substantial building in any parish, besides the church and laird's houses, was the minister's MANSE. After 1663 there was a legal obligation on the heritors (landowners) of each parish to provide a 'competent' manse costing between £27 15s. 6d. and £83 6s. 8d. sterling.* By the beginning of the C18 it seems to have been agreed in Dumfries and Galloway that the standard manse should be a two-storey rectangle, *c.* 11m. by 4.5m. internally, containing two principal rooms on each floor, with a cellar under the stair and a first-floor closet. One of these early C18 manses survives, though roofless, at Tinwald, a rubble-built house of two storeys and five bays dating from 1720. Roof coverings varied. Kells Manse was ordered to be thatched with straw or bracken in 1720, Stoneykirk Manse with 'bent' (reedy grass) in 1703, and St Mungo Manse with the more durable heather in 1704. But the new manse of 1723 at Kirkpatrick-Irongray had a slate roof and slate seems to have become the norm about that time: slate roofs

---

* A legal decision of 1760 held that the upper limit did not apply to the rebuilding of a manse.

were provided at the new manses of Kirkmaiden in 1738 (its predecessor having been thatched with straw and turf) and Dunscore in 1740. Manses also got larger in the course of the C18. The manse built at Middlebie in 1746 was 12.2m. by 7m. internally, and Keir Manse of 1777 fractionally bigger. Dalton Manse, which had been built to the standard early C18 dimensions in the 1750s, was enlarged by one room in 1781.

A further general increase in the size and comfort of manses took place in the early C19. At Parton Manse, a drawing room and dining room were added in 1809. By 1828 Keir Manse contained three public rooms, six bedrooms and a basement, a complement of accommodation standard for the many manses which were rebuilt in the early C19. When Sanquhar Manse (now Sanquhar House) was built in 1822–4, a water closet was provided, but external adornment was, as usual, restricted to the doorpiece.

For most of the C18 and, in some parts of the region, well into the C19, the HOUSES OF THE TENANTS of communal 'township' farms were, at least in the eyes of later generations, primitive. Samuel Smith wrote of these farmers in his *General View of the Agriculture of Galloway* (1810):

Their houses were commonly wretched dirty hovels, built with stones and mud, thatched with fern and turf; without chimnies; filled with smoke; black with soot: having low doors, and small holes for windows, with wooden shutters; or, in place of these, often stopped with turf, straw, or fragments of old clothes.

The construction of one such house can be seen at the much-restored Cruck Cottage in Torthorwald, which probably dates from the later C18. At the base of the walls is a footing of large boulders. Resting on these are the lower ends of three pairs of curved oak crucks, joined at the top by collar beams and tenoned into the underside of a saddle supporting the ridge beam. The roof rafters were of hazel or birch, on which was laid a layer of turf topped by straw thatch. The oak crucks and the mud-mortared stone walls suggest that this house may have been a superior example. Others, according to C19 accounts, were built with a framework of saplings and had walls of dry-stone construction. Some animals, notably cows, might share the dwelling with humans. Separate farm offices could be of the same type of construction as the houses. A surviving example at Priorslynn, near Canonbie, again probably of the later C18, has oak crucks, but the walls above the stone base are, as was not uncommon, of clay mixed with pebbles and straw.

From the later C18 the region's agriculture was revolutionized. The 'township' farms were swept away and the land divided into individual holdings, their fields enclosed with dry-stone walls. The buildings on these new farms frequently formed a rectangular courtyard; an octagonal horsemill often projected behind one range, and the farmhouse was usually on the courtyard's s side, if it were not placed a little apart. These new farmhouses were generally of two storeys, built of lime-mortared rubble and with slated roofs. As at the contemporary manses, decoration was usually kept to a minimum, although that does not prevent a farmhouse like that of Boreland of Anwoth of 1771 from making a pleasant presence in the countryside. A few were smarter. Balgowan, near Ardwell, was rebuilt or remodelled in the early C19 with a bowed centrepiece containing a three-light first-floor window. Like the farmhouses, the accompanying steading buildings were straightforward, again usually built with lime-mortared rubble walls and slated roofs; the mud walls of a steading built in 1843 on the Lochinch estate, near Castle Kennedy, were very much the exception.

Occasionally a steading might be more than utilitarian. Doubtless because of its proximity to the contemporary Kirkdale House, the steading of Kirkdale Mains of c. 1790 was designed as a smartly detailed octagon. From the 1820s until the later C19, a remarkable collection of superior farmhouses and steadings was erected on the Nithsdale estate of the Dukes of Buccleuch and Queensberry. Some of the first (e.g. Alton and Sweetbit, near Carronbridge, of 1829–31) were designed by *Walter Newall*, slightly later ones (e.g. Burn, near Carronbridge, of 1834) by *William Burn*, whose Tudor manner was continued into the 1860s by the estate architect, *Charles Howitt*. A decorative farmhouse in a more lighthearted idiom is the early C19 battlemented Gothic house at Corncockle, near Lochmaben. Also battlemented, but a Brobdignagian fantasy, is the large steading built at Corseyard, near Kirkandrews, in 1911–14. Compared with that the industrial sheds added to farms in the later C20 are a quiet relief.

125

INDUSTRIAL BUILDINGS

The principal business of Dumfries and Galloway has traditionally been farming, and many of the region's industrial buildings served industries linked to agriculture. Directly linked were the CORNMILLS. Until 1799 tenants were thirled to a laird's mill, i.e. bound to take their grain there for milling. Even after the right to commute this feudal servitude was granted, some of these large water-powered mills continued in use. The Town Mills at Dumfries, built by *Andrew Meikle*, c. 1781, are rubble-walled and utilitarian. Rather more stylish architecturally, and still with its machinery, is the three-storey cornmill at New Abbey, probably of the late C18, one range with gables topped by ball finials, the other with a kiln vent topped by a salmon weathervane. The late C18 mill complex at Old Bridge of Urr includes a house for the miller.

WINDMILLS were built from the late C17, their round stone towers carrying a moveable wooden cap to which were attached the sails. The tower of a late C17 mill survives at Logan Mill, near Ardwell, and another, of c. 1700, at Mouswald Grange. It was not, however, until the later C18 that winders worked by fantails were introduced, allowing the top to move automatically to bring the sails to face the wind. This improved technology was exploited at two later windmills whose towers still stand, one at Cannee, near Kirkcudbright, probably of the late C18, the other a very large tower built in 1798 at Dumfries and now part of the Dumfries Museum and Camera Obscura.

The predominantly pastoral character of the region's agriculture has made AUCTION MARTS for the sale of livestock important. Several were built in the 1890s and early C20 (e.g. at Castle Douglas, Lockerbie, Newton Stewart and Thornhill), all sited close to railway stations and all octagonal in plan, making it easy to drive the livestock round in a circle. The roof of the Castle Douglas mart is broken by lucarne ventilators. At others the ventilator was formed by a cupola; Lockerbie's is crowned with an onion dome. CREAMERIES to process the abundant milk into dairy products are strategically sited through the region. The earliest (now disused) is at Bladnoch, a utilitarian red-brick building of 1899, much extended in 1907. More conscious of architecture is the Kirkcudbright creamery of 1934–5, its vertical windows and slender buttresses emphasizing its height. The region's only DISTILLERY (now disused) is at Bladnoch; it was founded in 1814, but its Georgian-survival buildings are mostly of 1878, the kiln topped by the usual pagoda-shaped ventilator.

In the late C18, attempts were made to found a cotton industry in several of the region's burghs. Mills were built at Langholm, Castle Douglas, Newton Stewart and Gatehouse of Fleet; only the last of these burghs supported the industry for any length of time, and even there it lasted only until c. 1850. The surviving water-powered COTTON MILLS of c. 1790 at Gatehouse of Fleet are large but plain rubble-built structures. More ornamental were the steam-powered WOOLLEN MILLS built in the later C19 at Dumfries and Langholm, Langholm's Waverley Mills (by *Thomas Aimers*, 1865–7) with a prominent stair tower, and Dumfries' Rosefield Mills (by *Alan B. Crombie*, 1885–9) a vast Venetian palazzo, boldly sited beside the Nith and formerly looking across the river to the rival Nithsdale Mills (built in 1857–9 but now demolished). FACTORIES are relatively few, mostly recently built and hidden away on industrial estates. One which is very prominent on the approach to Dumfries along the A701 is the Gates Factory, built as a car factory in 1913, its concrete frame a structural novelty but uncompromisingly stark.

COAL was mined at or near Canonbie, Sanquhar and Kirkconnel from the C18 to the C20, but the pits have closed, leaving little evidence of their existence visible. More survives of the defunct LEAD MINES at Wanlockhead, worked from the C17 to the C20; the most striking reminder is the late C19 water-powered beam engine used to pump out the Straitsteps seam.

The Galloway hydro-electric scheme, begun in 1931, included the construction of POWER STATIONS. Two of the principal ones (by *Sir Alexander Gibb & Partners*) were Tongland (1934) and 126 Earlstoun (1936), near St John's Town of Dalry. Their principal

buildings are tall rendered boxes with vertical windows and
sparing Art Deco touches. Another means of producing electricity
was introduced to the region in 1955–60 with the building of a
127 nuclear power station at Chapelcross, the squat tapering cooling
towers a sturdy counterpart to the lightweight concrete-and-glass
blocks behind.

DUMFRIES AND GALLOWAY

ABBOT'S TOWER
0.9km. NE of New Abbey

Reconstruction of a C16 tower house begun in 1990 by *Ian Begg*, with the owner, *Peter Kormylo*, acting as clerk of works and builder. Most of the W side had survived, together with the lower part of the other walls, enabling the shape and height to be established, although much of the rest is conjectural; the new work is built partly of solid masonry and partly of cavity walling faced in stone.

The house was L-plan, the jamb projecting at the NW corner, of four storeys, built of granite boulder rubble with red sandstone dressings. The top of the jamb is projected on continuous corbelling to form a caphouse. In the inner angle, a stair turret sitting on continuous corbelling above a squinch arch, both turret and arch provided in the 1990s. Also of the 1990s are the turrets at the SW and NE corners, the NE cutting across the crowstepped E gable, and the top floor's dormerheads. Slit windows at the ground floor, their moulded margins all renewed except for one at the N. Roll-moulded margins to the first-floor windows, again mostly renewed, but the W window's sides and the lintel of the N window to the jamb are C16.

Unvaulted interior. On the ground floor, a store lit by small windows. In the jamb, a spiral stair (renewed) to the first floor. Here the lower parts of the jambs of the door into the hall are C16. In the hall, an E fireplace provided in the 1990s, as was the aumbry to its N, the jambs re-used C16 work. The N wall's aumbry is C16, as are the garderobe in the SW corner and part of the jambs of the W window. On the second floor, a C16 fireplace in the W wall; to its S, part of a window with a stone seat. Another C16 fireplace at the top floor; remains of an aumbry to its N.

AE

Small upland village built by the Forestry Commission following a layout plan prepared in 1947 by *John A. W. Grant*. Harled two-storey pitched-roofed houses, gablets over the first-floor windows.

AIRDS HOUSE
1.3km. NW of Parton

Scots-accented picturesque large villa, by *Kinnear & Peddie*, 1884. Main block of two storeys and an attic, built of whin with pale sandstone dressings, the roofs covered with red tiles. Bargeboards and bracketed eaves. At the entrance (S) front, an Artisan Mannerist doorpiece and a canted bay window. W elevation with a pair of full-height canted bay windows topped by jerkin-headed gables. Lower service court to the E, now partly replaced by a conservatory.

ALLANTON HOUSE
1.7km. S of Auldgirth

Harled late Georgian laird's house, enlarged and remodelled as a mid-Victorian Baronial manor. The original main block was of two storeys and a basement. Three bays with a pedimented Roman Doric portico at the centre. The Victorian remodelling added crowsteps to the gables and neo-Jacobean pedimented dormerheads to the two l. first-floor windows. The r. bay was heightened with a crowstepped gable from which is corbelled out a battlemented two-storey rectangular bay window. Battlemented canted bay window at the W gable. At the house's E end, a square battlemented tower with an octagonal turret in the inner angle. Plain but substantial rear wings.

AMISFIELD TOWER
1.6km. NW of Amisfield Town

74 Architecturally the most ambitious of the tower houses of Dumfries and Galloway, built in 1600 for John Charteris of Amisfield and his wife, Agnes Maxwell, whose coats of arms, initials and the date are displayed on two panels on the S front. The general concept is straightforward enough. Almost square crowstepgabled main block, constructed of mixed whin and red sandstone (probably harled originally), the corners' quoins and other dressings of good-quality ashlar. Round turrets at three corners. Projecting from the fourth, a stair tower topped by a caphouse. Thus far the design is that of the standard Scottish tower house of the late C16 and early C17. But these elements are treated with a quirky and determined individuality. The main block's height of four storeys, an attic and a garret makes it exceptionally tall (*c.* 23.5m. to the apex), especially in relation to its ground-floor area of *c.* 8.7m. by 9.6m. The turrets are each of two storeys, not the usual one, and, instead of curving into the main walling at each face, at the E and W gables they end with straight-walled rectangular tails projected from the wall, like the turrets themselves, on in-and-out corbels above

SECOND FLOOR

1   Upper hall
2   Store
3   Hall

THIRD FLOOR

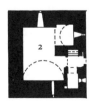

GROUND FLOOR

FIRST FLOOR

30 m

Amisfield Tower. Section and plans

continuous corbelling. These tails almost suggest that battlemented walks had been intended to cross the gables, but their
ends are too narrow to have contained more than their slit
windows. The stair tower is not the usual sturdy rectangle rising
from the ground but a circular rubble turret projected on
continuous corbelling from just above the base of the tower,
the refusal to provide a secure foundation making it a show-off
piece of constructional acrobatics. The jettied ashlar caphouse
above is not a device to finish this turret-tower with modest
emphasis but a crushingly large three-storey rectangle carried
well beyond the turret on corbelling from the main block's s
and E sides. Straddling the caphouse's N end, a second caphouse which extends across the apex of the tower house's E
gable.

Inventive and varied detail, especially smart at the s
(entrance) front. Wide-mouthed oval gunloops to the ground
floor; a double-keyhole gunloop in the E gable. Plain rounded
margins to the N and W sides' windows (the second-floor W
window built up) but the first- and second-floor s and E
windows have roll mouldings, the intervening hollow of each
filled with nailhead enrichment. More nailhead decoration on
the frames of the armorial panels which flank the tall second-
floor window of the s front. High up on this front and directly
above the entrance, a boldly projecting ashlar bretasche. It rises
to the eaves to support a pedimented dormer window whose
corner pilasters frame a battlemented moulded surround.
Under the eaves of the s front, delicate in-and-out corbelling
with nailhead enrichment. Stringcourse with the same detail
under the main caphouse's top floor. Plain cavetto cornice at
the N front. No parapet or battlement. At the caphouse's s
gable, rope moulding on the straight skews and chimney. Gableted dormerheads on the caphouse's E and W sides. In this
caphouse's NE inner angle, a rounded turret under the second
caphouse, this turret's stair lit by a crosslet and a quatrefoil
light.

The entrance door opens into a small tunnel-vaulted and
stone-flagged lobby, its E side open to the stair. On the w,
a step up to a low door into a tunnel-vaulted and rock-
floored guardroom. Gunholes in its w and s walls, a small
aumbry in the N. On the lobby's N side, a step down to a
door into a large tunnel-vaulted store, its floor cobbled. Two
gunholes in the E wall and one in the w. Their light is
supplemented by a couple of slit windows, placed high in the
E wall and low in the w. At the E end of the store's s side,
a recess covered by a two-thirds segment of a semicircular
vault, this space being under the stair; gunhole in its s wall.
The stair itself in the house's SE corner rises to the first floor
as a straight flight under an elliptical tunnel vault, its rising
line echoing that of the stair.

The stone-flagged first-floor hall is L-plan with a broad SW
jamb. Over the SE corner's entrance, a bowed projection made
by the stairwell of the turret stair to the upper floors. Wooden

ceiling, its beams supported by a mixture of corbels and wall sockets. In the centre of the hall's W wall, a fireplace with clustered shafts, their bases and capitals simple. Of the deep stone lintel, only the ends survive. In the fireplace's N ingo, a rectangular aumbry. In the S ingo, five round holes into a salt box, its main opening in the wall beside the fireplace. S of the fireplace, an elliptical-arched buffet recess. In each of the room's S, E and N walls, a decent-sized window. In the jamb's E wall, an aumbry checked for a door and with a projecting sill. Lamp recess at the E wall's S end beside the door. High up in the N wall's E end, a large cupboard lit by a small E window. It may have been designed as a safe or charter chest. At the N end of the E wall, a narrow door into a small close garderobe, which has a stepped sill at the double-keyhole gunloop that provides its light and ventilation.

Access to the floors above the hall is provided by the SE turret's comfortable and well-lit turnpike stair. Off it, at a mezzanine level above the stair to the first floor, a square chamber with a smallish S window and a peephole into the hall.

On the second floor, the upper hall, higher than the one below and with larger windows. It is rectangular except for the bowed intrusion of the stair wall into the SE corner. Wooden ceiling, the joists supported on corbels. Each wall has a window (the W blocked) in a segmental-arched embrasure, the N and W each with remains of a stone seat. At the W wall's S end, a large fireplace of the same type as in the hall below, its lintel intact. At the W end of the N wall, an aumbry. At the E wall's N end, a close garderobe, larger than the one below and with a rectangular E window. At the top of the upper hall's W wall, the surviving plaster is painted with a frieze of squat columns framing balls which flank roundels containing bulls' heads.

The third floor has contained a pair of bedchambers (the wooden partition wall now missing), each with a fireplace in the gable and a window in each outer wall. Stepped breasts to the gable windows. In one ingo of each, a door into a N turret. Off each of these two turrets, a close garderobe in the thickness of the N wall. The entrance to the SW turret is placed high in the W wall's S end and was presumably reached by a ladder or wooden steps. Similar arrangement in the main block's attic, whose floor is now missing. At this level, in the caphouse over the main turnpike stair, a rectangular room with a small S fireplace and windows to the E and S. Tighter turnpike to the floors above. In the garret of the main block, windows in the gables. On the upper floor of the main caphouse, another rectangular room provided with a S fireplace and small windows to the S, W and E. In the secondary N caphouse, a fireplace in the N gable.

The tower now sits in the SW corner of a GARDEN, its rubble walls perhaps early C19. – S of the tower, a double-pile MANSION HOUSE, its three-storey N block said to have

been built in 1631. Its exposed rear is now Georgianized but
has a blocked C17 segmental-headed archway. The piend-
roofed s block of two storeys and a high basement was added
in 1837. s front of five bays, the centre three advanced under
a pediment. Projecting from this centrepiece, a canted bay
window. Aprons under the windows, those of the *piano
nobile*'s outer bays corniced. Pedimented doorpiece at the E
gable.

w of the house and tower, early C19 U-plan STABLES, built
of painted rubble. Centre range composed of single-storey
piend-roofed wings flanking a two-storey block, its upper floor
a doocot. – At the end of the drive, a mid-C19 LODGE with
carved bargeboards.

AMISFIELD TOWN

0080

Not much more than a row of cottages, mostly mid-C19 and
rather altered.

SCHOOL. Mid-C19 but much enlarged in 1897. The adjoining
schoolhouse is of *c.* 1860.

AMISFIELD TOWER. *See* p. 90.
GLENAE. *See* p. 321.

ANNAN

1060

Small town near the mouth of the River Annan. It was founded
in the late C12 as a burgh of barony under the superiority of the
Bruces, lords of Annandale, who had a castle here. After the
accession of Robert Bruce to the throne in 1306, Annan was
regarded as a royal burgh.

By the mid-C16 the town consisted of one long street running
E from a ford across the river overlooked by the castle and then
parish church. The castle was demolished in the C17, a period of
decline for the town, whose councillors reported in 1692 'that
they have neither forraigne nor inland trade and that they hade
no wine nor brandie vented within ther toun these fyve years
bygone except one hogshead of each'. Despite the erection of a
bridge over the Annan in 1700–5, Daniel Defoe thought the burgh
in 1727 'in a State of Irrecoverable Decay', and Bishop Richard
Pococke, visiting in 1760, found it 'a small poor town' whose
inhabitants lived in 'thatched cabins'.

Development got under way after 1785, when a cotton-
spinning mill was established, and the first half of the C19
contributed improvements to the harbour at the mouth of the
Annan and the opening of a railway to Dumfries and Gretna.
However, cotton spinning ceased after a fire at the mill in 1878
and the town has never grown to be more than a local centre
overshadowed by its big brothers of Dumfries and, across the
border, Carlisle.

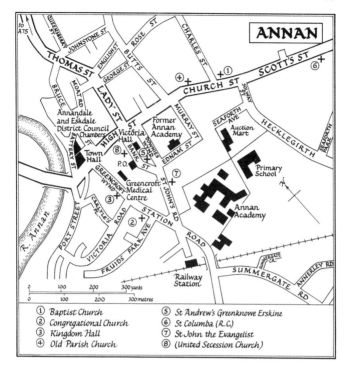

① Baptist Church
② Congregational Church
③ Kingdom Hall
④ Old Parish Church
⑤ St Andrew's Greenknowe Erskine
⑥ St Columba (R.C.)
⑦ St John the Evangelist
⑧ (United Secession Church)

CHURCHES

BAPTIST CHURCH, Church Street and Charles Street. Secularized. Minimal Gothic hall church of 1880.

CONGREGATIONAL CHURCH, Station Road. By *Johnstone Bros.* of Carlisle, 1901–3. Blocky Scots late Gothic on quite a large scale, of snecked and bullnosed red sandstone rubble.

KINGDOM HALL OF JEHOVAH'S WITNESSES, Greencroft Wynd. Built as a Congregational church in 1847 and now drydashed with painted dressings. Two tall storeys, the upper windows segmental-arched. Three bays with an anta-pilastered doorpiece at the advanced and gabled centre.

OLD PARISH CHURCH, Church Street. The body, a big rubble rectangle with rusticated quoins and a piended roof, was designed and built in 1789–90 by *James Beattie* and *John Oliver*, joiners, and *John Hannah*, mason, all of Annan. In the s front, tall round-arched windows with projecting keystones and imposts, containing intersecting wooden tracery. At the gables, rectangular windows (two converted from doors) lighting the area; round-arched windows to the gallery. In the centre of the s front, a steeple, its tower built in 1789–90, the spire added in 1798–1801. The tower's lowest stage has V-jointed rustication and a Roman Doric aedicular doorpiece with triglyphs on the frieze. In the front of the corniced second stage, a Venetian

window; blind round-arched windows at the sides. Low third
stage, corniced again, with an empty panel frame. The clock-
stage above is intaken and also corniced. Octagonal belfry
with round-arched openings and a corbelled cornice; above, an
octagonal spire topped by a weathercock. At the back of the
church, a large open-pedimented session house and flanking
porches, all added by *Hugh Ker* in 1873–4 and trying hard to
be in keeping.

Inside, a large ceiling rose which looks Georgian but has
been converted to a ventilator. – Deep galleries cutting across
the windows on the N, E and W sides, their panelled fronts of
1789, the fluted Corinthian columns replacements by *Hugh
Ker*, 1873–4. In the centre of the N gallery, the exceptionally
30   stylish MAGISTRATES' PEW of 1789, with fluted wooden piers
carrying a long rectangular canopy, its frieze decorated with
acanthus leaves. On the canopy's coved soffit, swags and a
central rose. – Plain PEWS of 1873–4. – Projecting from the
centre of the S wall, a low neo-Jacobean SCREEN of 1923. It
encloses the PULPIT provided in 1929. – Forming a canopy
over the pulpit is the cantilevered pipework of the ORGAN by
Ingram & Co., 1912. – STAINED GLASS. Flanking the pulpit,
two Renaissance-style windows (St Matthew and St John) of
1913. – On the N wall, a white marble Corinthian aedicule
MONUMENT to the Rev. James Alexander Crichton, with a
portrait bust in high relief, by *J. W. Dods*, 1910. – On the same
wall, a white marble TABLET to Christina Pringle † 1830, carved
with the high relief of a mourning lady.

HALL to the NW, by *J. B. Gladstone*, 1926–9.

GRAVEYARD. SE of the church, a white marble STATUE of
Edward Irving on a pinky Peterhead granite pedestal, by *J. W.
Dods*, 1891–2. – At the N end, an early C19 MAUSOLEUM.
Blind Gothic arches in the faces. Over the centre, a large
obelisk; there have been more obelisks on the corners.

ST ANDREW'S GREENKNOWE ERSKINE PARISH CHURCH,
Bank Street. Built as Annan Free Church in 1847. It is a
box, with tall Tudor-arched and hoodmoulded windows in the
droved ashlar gable. On this front, a pediment bisected by a
central tower; its bracketed cornice was formerly topped by a
balustrade.

ST COLUMBA (R.C.), Scott's Street. Built as a Congregational
chapel, *c.* 1795, and extended at both ends in a chunky late
Gothic manner for its present denominational use in 1905. At
the N (liturgical W) gable, a tabernacle niche containing a statue
of a dumpy St Columba. – HALL on the E added by *Sutherland,
Dickie & Partners*, *c.* 1964. – Contemporary wood-and-brick
covered link to the simple Tudor PRESBYTERY HOUSE, built
as a school in 1905.

ST JOHN THE EVANGELIST (Episcopal), St John's Road. Simple
Dec, by *John Hodgson* of Carlisle, 1843. Sturdily buttressed
nave and a lower chancel, its corners diagonally buttressed. NW
porch and SE vestry. Tall gableted W bellcote. Side windows,
each of two lights under a quatrefoil; their hoodmould stops

are carved with saints' heads. (Inside, STAINED GLASS E window of three lights (Scenes from the life of St John the Evangelist), by *Mayer & Co.*, 1892.)

UNITED SECESSION CHURCH, Bank Street. Disused. By *William Gregan*, 1834–5. Two-storey-and-basement rectangle covered by a piended platform roof. The three-bay ashlar-fronted E façade has anta pilasters at the corners and to mark off the pedimented centre bay containing the pilastered and round-arched entrance.

PUBLIC BUILDINGS

ANNAN ACADEMY, Station Road. By *F. J. C. Carruthers*, 1894–6. Low conglomeration with busy but not very forceful Jacobean detail, including shaped gables and ogee-roofed stone cupolas. In the centre of the front, a very tall tower. High up on each of its faces, a small roundheaded arcade under the moulded corbels which support the slightly projecting panelled stage above, its corners chamfered. At the corners of the parapet, ogee-roofed octagonal turrets linked by pedimented basket arches. Within the parapet, a battered slate-hung top stage under a lead ogee roof; tall lead finial. – To the NE, a contemporary detached single-storey PAVILION, its roof crowned by a lead-domed and wooden louvred octagonal cupola. – To the SE, another detached block, by *H. E. Clifford*, 1907, dour Tudor. – Extensive additions of 1964–9. – SWIMMING POOL by *Dumfries and Galloway Regional Council*, 1981–2.

Former ANNAN ACADEMY, Ednam Street. Now offices. Built in 1820 by *Hugh Ker*, following a design by the mason-architect *Thomas Brown*, and extended in 1895. Two-storey corniced front of droved ashlar, tied together by a moulded stringcourse. The early C19 building is of five bays, with slightly advanced ends, each topped by a rectangular stone block flanked by low obelisks. Sill course under the first-floor windows of the centrepiece. In its middle, a round-arched door in a pilastered and segmental-headed overarch; above, pilasters reaching to the cornice on which sits a corniced block inscribed 'ACADEMY' with the date 1820. The 1895 enlargement added two further bays at each end in tactful imitation of the original work.

ANNANDALE AND ESKDALE DISTRICT COUNCIL CHAMBERS,* High Street. By *Brian Page* of *Annandale and Eskdale District Council*, 1980. Pre-cast concrete frame faced with 'Forticrete' blockwork. Chunky but not without discipline, the metal roof partly jettied out as an oversailing attic.

GREENCROFT MEDICAL CENTRE, off Greencroft Wynd. By *Johnston & Wright*, 1989–91. A two-storey brick pavilion, its little ball finials hinting at classicism. – Beside it, an early C19 pavilion-roofed DOOCOT tower.

POST OFFICE, Bank Street. Opened in 1898. In a kind of Geor-

---

* The building was transferred to the ownership of the new Dumfries and Galloway Council in 1996.

gian-revival style. Two storeys and three bays, the ground floor of channelled ashlar, the outer windows bipartite. Advanced centre with a pilastered and segmental-pedimented doorpiece; on the parapet, the royal arms flanked by urns.

PUBLIC LIBRARY. *See* Victoria Hall, below.

RAILWAY STATION, off Station Road. Opened in 1848. The main office is a two-storey *cottage orné*, mixing together bracketed eaves, roundheaded lights and bay windows; Doric portico in the inner angle. The platform's M-roofed glazed awning is a late C19 addition.

RAILWAY VIADUCTS. Two viaducts, built in 1848. The longer is over the Annan, with five main arches and one smaller, all segmental-headed. Shorter viaduct over Port Street; four arches built on a skew.

TOWN HALL, High Street. By *Peter Smith* of Glasgow, 1875–8. The two-storey main block is plain Baronial with crowstepped gables and corbelled angle rounds; mullioned and transomed windows. Above the s gable's three-light first-floor window, a hoodmould and strapworked pediment. Boldly projecting from the E front, a four-stage tower. Round-arched entrance under a big rope moulding with knotted ends. Above the entrance, a corbelled balcony, cannon-spouts poking out from its angle rounds, all surmounted by heraldic beasts. At the tower's third stage, a huge but empty image niche. Pairs of narrow round-arched openings at the belfry; corbelled out from its corners, conical-roofed round turrets. Set within the belfry's corbelled balustrade, a slated and lucarned spire, each face held by a crowstepped gablet containing a clock face (the clock a replacement of 1901 by *William Potts & Sons*).

VICTORIA HALL AND PUBLIC LIBRARY, Bank Street. Built in two sections. The first, dated 1882, is the Victoria Hall at the N. Peaceful but determined Baronial in bullnosed masonry, with crowstepped gables and a fat tourelle. The Library, added by *George Washington Browne* in 1906, is smooth ashlar-faced Jacobean with a two-storey s porch and mullioned and transomed four-light windows, those at the Ionic pilastered first floor having round-arched lights. Central attic window framed by a pinnacled and segmental-pedimented aedicule rising above the shaped main gable.

DESCRIPTION

The BRIDGE over the River Annan at the W end of the town, by *Robert Stevenson*, 1824–6, is built of red Gallowbank sandstone ashlar and slopes slightly. Three segmental arches and low rounded cutwaters. Then the start of HIGH STREET. On the N, a small block of *c.* 1840, its gablet's stone finial composed of three tight scrolls. Beside it, THE BLUE BELL INN of *c.* 1800 with a corniced doorpiece. On the s, a late Georgian block with a bowed corner to Port Street. Across Port Street, the mid-C18 five-bay OLD GRAMMAR SCHOOL, of three storeys and a basement, the second-floor windows quite small. Rusticated quoins and scrolled skewputts; a consoled pediment over the door.

PORT STREET, running S, is a reminder of Annan's C19 industry and harbour. At its start, on the l., the sad remains of a mid-C19 MILL with an off-centre gablet over a tier of hoist doors. On the corner with Carlyle's Place, the two-storey ALBERT HALL of 1872. Round-arched openings in the broad gable front, a trefoil light at its top. Then Port Street jinks towards the river. On its r., a mid-C19 Georgian-survival terrace (Nos. 18–26) followed by SCAURBANK, a rather serious *cottage orné* of *c.*1840 set behind a front garden. L-plan with a stripped classical portico in the inner angle and a big Elizabethan gablet on the main block. Further out, on the l., No. 49 (BRAEHOUSE) of *c.*1800, a three-light window over its pilastered and pedimented doorpiece. Opposite, a mid-C19 BREWERY, the two- and three-storey front block L-shaped, the four-storey range behind of five bays, both straightforward industrial. After the railway viaduct (*see* Public Buildings, above), more mid-C19 WAREHOUSES on the r.: one of four storeys and five bays, with a central gablet over the hoist doors, another of three storeys and six bays. Opposite, the long two-storey mid-C19 WELLDALE MILL, two ranges (one of stores, the other of housing) joined by a screen wall pierced by a segmental arch. Finally, a small early C19 warehouse at the QUAY.

HIGH STREET resumes on the E side of Battery Street with a two-storey D-plan block of *c.*1840. Well-mannered classical detail with aproned ground-floor windows surmounted by a continuous cornice; console-pedimented doorpiece to Battery Street. Next, the bulk of the Town Hall (*see* Public Buildings, above); the short wynd on its E leads up to the OLD PARISH GRAVEYARD, the site of the parish church demolished in 1790. High Street now broadens into a triangle, most of the W side filled by the Town Hall. In front of it, the WAR MEMORIAL of 1921, a bronze soldier by *Henry Price*. On the N side, the ROYAL BANK OF SCOTLAND, insipid Italianate by *Sydney Mitchell*, 1881. On the W corner with Lady Street, an elaborate commercial block of *c.*1900, blowsy French Renaissance of a sort, with plenty of carved work. On the front, a pair of aedicular gablets, their Ionic pilasters narrowing to the bottom, their pediments carved with shell niches. They frame the second-floor windows' curvy broken pediments, again elaborately carved. At the corner, a two-storey oriel rising to a slated octagonal dome. To the E, the BUCK INN, neo-Jacobean of 1903, with a couple of roundels containing high-relief busts. A little further on is the ANNANDALE OBSERVER office of 1882, the front decorated with a niche containing a bust.

On High Street's S side, opposite the Town Hall, No. 23 of *c.*1860 has its front gable flanked by short strapwork balustrades; in the gable, a concave-sided pedimented aedicule. Then a generally rather undistinguished collection of late Georgian and Georgian survival, including the rendered late C18

QUEENSBERRY ARMS HOTEL, of three storeys and five bays, sill courses linking the upper windows. The Doric portico is a late Victorian embellishment. In the car park behind, a small but tall rubble-built lectern DOOCOT, dated 1690 on the door lintel. At the car park's SW corner, an early C19 Gothick GAZEBO. On High Street's W corner with Bank Street, the block by *T. Taylor Scott*, 1899–1900, is routine Jacobean, but its Artisan Mannerist gables and ogee-domed corner turret are
120 welcome. On the E corner, the old SOUTHERN BANK OF SCOTLAND (No. 73), *c.* 1845, an austere ashlar box of three storeys and a basement, five bays to High Street and three to Bank Street, the floors marked off by band courses. Pedimented portico with paired Roman Doric columns. Paired chimneystacks on the piended platform roof.

Not much of interest in the streets N of High Street. BUTTS STREET has the early C18 Nos. 6–8, two storeys and eight bays, the windows grouped 3/2/3, and, on the W side, No. 33, early C19 with an Ionic columned doorpiece. Quite a lot to the S of High Street. In GREENCROFT WYND, opposite the Kingdom Hall of Jehovah's Witnesses (*see* Churches, above), a pair of monkey-puzzle trees in the garden of the Victorian No. 11. After the set-back Greencroft Medical Centre (*see* Public Buildings), GREENCROFT, a mid-C18 villa with a segmental-arched and delicately rusticated fluted door surround. In STATION ROAD, the street's S continuation, the Congregational Church (*see* Churches), and, on the corner of Station Road and St John's Road, the V-plan CENTRAL HOTEL by *F. J. C. Carruthers*, 1898, dressed up with Jacobean shaped gables and corner towers. At the angle of the V, a semicircular Ionic portico topped by a balconied loggia, with Artisan Mannerist piers rising to its balustrade. For the railway station to the W and Annan Academy to the E, *see* Public Buildings, above.

ST JOHN'S ROAD provides a way back to the N. On its E side, No. 20, a late C19 villa with battlemented bay windows, has carved dragons on the ends of its rooftop. Otherwise, solid villas of the 1890s. For St John's Episcopal Church, *see* Churches, above. In EDNAM STREET, the former Annan Academy (*see* Public Buildings, above). On the SW corner of BANK STREET, the former BRITISH LINEN BANK of *c.* 1845, a very smart large double-pile villa, with two-light horizontally glazed windows, a band course and a brute classical portico; octagonal chimneystacks on the piended roofs. Attached to its N gable, No. 29 Bank Street, added as a single-storey banking hall, *c.* 1900, is Adam-revival of a sort, with rusticated masonry, a bowed E corner and overall balustrade; overarched Venetian windows flanking the pedimented tripartite door. For Bank Street's post office, public library and churches, *see* Churches and Public Buildings, above.

CHURCH STREET, continuing the line of High Street to the E, begins with the free Renaissance ARGYLE HOUSE of *c.* 1900, its round corner topped by a lead-domed octagonal turret.

Then late Georgian and Georgian survival, watched over by the Old Parish Church (*see* Churches, above). On the S, the early C19 Nos. 11 and 13, with anta-pilastered doorpieces, are followed by CUMBERLAND TERRACE, Georgian survival of 1852 with paired pilastered and corniced doorpieces. Round the corner, off Solway Street, SEAFORTH AVENUE has a row of houses of *c.*1900, with half-timbering in their bargeboarded gables, red-tiled roof-ridges and front conservatories.

At SCOTT'S STREET the tight-knit urban fabric collapses. In the garden of SEAFORTH COTTAGE on the r., a piend-roofed GAZEBO is dated 1834; Gothic ground-floor windows and bulls-eyes above. Contemporary No. 22 to the E, with a corniced and pilastered doorpiece. Pedimented porch at the late Georgian No. 34. Then St Columba's R.C. Church (*see* churches, above).

WARMANBIE. *See* p. 561.

ANWOTH 5050

Little more than the old and new parish churches standing near each other in well-wooded countryside.

OLD PARISH CHURCH. Roofless rubble-walled long rectangle 20 (*see* the Introduction, p. 37), built in 1627 but probably altered in 1710 if an inscribed stone inside refers to this building. Apparently of 1627 are the blocked door and rectangular windows in the S wall, its two W windows (one partly blocked) both with rounded margins. This S wall's E window, perhaps intended to light the communion table or pulpit, is of two lights, its concave-moulded jambs and mullion grooved for glazing. In each gable, a round-arched door under a rectangular window, both with chamfered margins and likely to be insertions of 1710 if the church was rearranged (probably with the pulpit moved to the centre of the S wall) at that time; another small window with chamfered margins near the N wall's E end. Sturdy gabled W bellcote; it could well be early C18.

Inside, in the blocked S doorway, a PANEL inscribed 'Rebuilt Anno 1710 by WM NS', bearing the arms of William Maxwell of Cardoness and his wife, Nicola Stewart. – In the centre of the church, a big sarcophagus MONUMENT commemorating 44 the mother and two wives of John Gordon, who, as his property grew, styled himself successively 'of Cullindoch', 'of Ardwall', and 'of Cardoness'. It must be of *c.* 1635. Splayed plinth carrying a tomb-chest enriched with alternating circles and diamonds set in squares. On the top, ball finials at the ends; at the centre, strapwork scrolls supporting a disc, its faces carved with the arms of Gordon and the initials I G for John Gordon and W G for his father, William. On the S end of the sarcophagus, high reliefs of a skeleton, crossbones, an hourglass and open book, and the tautologous 'MEMENTO MORI'. On the W face, three impaled coats of arms under the initials WGMM,

IGMC and IGCMC for John Gordon's parents, William Gordon of Cullindoch and Marion Mure, and himself and his two wives, Margaret McClellan and Christian MacCadam. To their r., an inscription to his second wife:

```
ZE.GAIZERS.ON.THIS.TROPHEE.OF.A.TOMBE.
SEND.OVT.ONE.GRONE.FOR.WANT.OF.HIR.WHOIS.LYFE
WYSE.BORNE.ON.EARTH.AND.NOW.IS.IN.EARTHIS.WOMBE
LIVED.LONG.A.VIRGINE.NOW.A.SPOTLES.WIFE.
CHURCH.KEEPIS.HIR.GODLIE.LIFE.THIS.TOMBE.HIR.CORPS
AND.EARTH.HIR.FAMOVS.NAME.
WHO.THEN.DOES.LOSE.HIR.HUSBAND.NO.SINCE.HEAVEN
HIR.SAVLE.DOES.GAINE.CHRISTEN MAKCADDAM.LADY
CARDYNES.DEPAIRTED.16.IVNVI.1628.ÆTATIS.SVÆ.33
```

On the E face, an inscription to Gordon's first wife:

```
DVMBE.SENSLES.STATVE.OF.SOME.PAINTED STONES
WHAT.MEANES.THY.BOAST.THY.CAPTIVE.IS.BOT.CLAY
THOW.GAINES.NOTHING.BOT.SOM.FEW.LIFLES.BONES.
HIR SOVLE.TRIVMPHIS.FOR.AY
THEN.GAZENG.FREINDIS DO.NOT.HIR.DEATH.DEPLORE
ZOW.LOSE.A.WHILES.SCHE.GAINES.FOR.EWERMORE
MARGRAT.MAKCLELLAN GOODWIFE.OF.ARDWEL.DEPAIRTED
THIS.LIFE.2.APPRILE.I[62-].ÆTATIS.SVA[E].31
```

On the N face, this commemoration of John Gordon's mother:

```
WALKING.WITH.GOD.IN.PVRITIE.OF.LIFE
IN.CHRIST.I.DIED.AND.ENDIT.AL.MY.STRYFE
FOR.IN.MY.SAVLE.CIRIST.HEIR.DID.DWEL.BY.GRACE
NOW.DWELIS.MY.SAVLE.IN.GLORIE.OF.HIS.FACE
THAIRFOIR.MY.BODIE.SAL.NOT.HEIR.REMAINE
BOT.TO.FVL.GLORIE.SAL.SVIRLIE.RYS.AGAINE
MARIOVNE.MVRE.GOOD.WIFE.OF.
CVLLINDACH.DEPAIRTED.THIS.LIFE
ANNO 1612
```

– Stuck in the ground to the NW, a rough SLAB incised with a bulbous cross, perhaps in the C12.

Immediately S of the church, a TABLE STONE, perhaps early C18, to the Covenanter John Bell †1685, with a weathered vengeful inscription. – To its E, HEADSTONE of John McKioum (?) †1723, carved with a plentiful display of reminders of death under an angel's head (the soul). – To its S, HEADSTONE of William Gourlay †1744, with a four-winged angel in high relief. – To the W, HEADSTONE to the four children †1757–63 of Robert McNish, three of their souls represented as angels' heads engaged in a display of aerial acrobatics above a skull and crossbones. – Just S of the W end of the church, a MAUSOLEUM rebuilt in 1878 by Sir William Maxwell of Cardoness with huge blocks of hammerdressed granite ashlar. Battered sides and entrance jambs. On the gable, a large cross above a coat of arms.

OLD SCHOOLHOUSE across the road, a charmingly unassuming rubble-built cottage of the earlier C19.

PARISH CHURCH. By *Walter Newall*, 1826–7. Tall harled rubble box, intersecting tracery in the hoodmoulded Tudor windows. Battlemented and pinnacled W tower of three diminishing

stages, each with a stringcourse. In the two lower stages, paired
lancet windows; triple lancets at the belfry. The interior was
transformed in 1905 by *James Barbour & Bowie*, who provided
an open kingpost-truss roof, w gallery, and new furnishings,
including a PULPIT complete with brass oil lamps. – Behind
it, a small ORGAN of 1924 by *The Positive Organ Co. (1922)
Ltd.* – On the e wall, a white marble MONUMENT by *W. Birnie
Rhind* to William Francis John Maxwell † 1915, carved with an
angel mourning over the inscription tablet and a relief portrait
bust at the base.

Harled MANSE, 0.2km. NE, built by *John Martin*, 1812, with
a bullseye window in the advanced and gabled centre.

RUTHERFORD MONUMENT, Boreland Hill, 0.4km. E. Tall
polished granite obelisk on a hammerdressed base, commemorating the C17 Presbyterian divine, Samuel Rutherford.
It was erected in 1842 by the mason, *John Stewart*, and rebuilt
in 1851 after being struck by lightning.

BORELAND OF ANWOTH, 0.9km. SE. Superior harled farmhouse of two storeys and three bays, dated 1771 above the door.
The flanking single-storey piend-roofed pavilions look late
Georgian but may be the additions built in 1861 to *John Graham*'s design.

Running into the marshy land immediately to the s, a sandy
promontory which was cut through, probably in the late C12,
to form a MOTTE AND BAILEY. 11m.-wide N ditch across the
approach to the bailey, an oblong area *c.* 73m. by 30m. At the
s end of the bailey, a 16m.-wide ditch dividing it from the
22m.-square motte.

CAIRNS AND STONE CIRCLES, Cauldside, 5.3km. NW. On
flattish land s of the Cauldside Burn, a round stony cairn,
c. 19m. in diameter, perhaps of the second millennium B.C., in
whose top has been placed a stone-slabbed cist. Immediately s
of the cairn, remains of a circle, *c.* 21m. in diameter, formed
of thin slabs, their tops mostly pointed. Small cairns to the
e. About 0.13km. N of the first cairn, foundations of another
large cairn containing a cist. Immediately to its s, two thin
slabs seem to be the remnants of another stone circle. On
the other side of the burn, *c.* 0.37km. N of the first cairn, a
whinstone boulder carved, probably in the second millennium
B.C., with two cups circled by rings, one quite simple, the
other more elaborate, its rings forming a spiral which is cut
through by a curved groove running from the cup to the
outer ring.

FORT, Trusty's Hill, 0.6km. E. C1 hilltop fort. The neck of the
rock promontory is defended by a ditch and bank. To the SW,
the roughly oval summit, *c.* 24m. by 15m., is enclosed by a
timber-laced stone rampart (now vitrified after a fire), *c.* 1.2m.
thick. Entrance on the s side. A rock beside it is carved with
Pictish symbols, perhaps the work of a raiding party, including
a water beast and a double disc crossed by a Z-shaped rod. In
front of the entrance, not very substantial outworks, probably
a refortification of the site in the C6 or C7.

ARDWALL. *See* p. 106.

ARDWALL. *See* p. 106.

1080   APPLEGARTH

Just the church, manse and a war memorial looking like the
market cross of a vanished village.

PARISH CHURCH. Tall white-painted T-plan kirk built in 1762–
3 by *Francis Patterson*, mason, and *James Bretton*, wright, but
much remodelled in 1884–5 by *F. J. C. Carruthers*. He raised
the walls by 1.2m., placed rose windows in the gables and
replaced the rectangular windows in the side walls with Gothic
lights whose hoodmoulds rest on foliaged corbels. He also
enlarged the existing N porch and added shallow porches at the
E and W. On the jamb's E side, the heavy forestair, its parapet
pierced by roundheaded arches, is of the 1880s, but it leads to
a basket-arched gallery door of 1762–3. The interior is of 1884–
5, with a busy open roof; gallery in the N jamb. – Two garishly
coloured STAINED GLASS windows flanking the pulpit (Our
Lord blessing a Knight; the Ascension) erected as a war memorial in 1920.

Attached to the church's SE corner is the BURIAL ENCLOS-
URE of the Jardines, probably late C17. Lugged architraved
door under a broken segmental pediment, its tympanum carved
with a cartouche under a star. Inside the enclosure, a large but
weathered red sandstone scroll-sided monument dated 1689.
Aedicular, the fluted pilasters now missing their capitals, the
segmental pediment broken by a cartouche. Inscription tablet
in a frame of drapery gripped by the teeth of a skull. – HEAD-
STONES. E of the church, Andrew Jardine †1777 and his wife,
Jean Atchison, the pilastered front carved with a high-relief
human figure, apparently female. – Beside it, John Jardine
†1769, heraldic. – Just N of the church, an C18 headstone
decorated with a skull and crossbones. – Also the fragment of
an C18 stone bearing the relief of two men holding hands. –
Small aedicular stone to Andrew Boyes †1710, its front carved
with a man being crowned by an angel.

JARDINE HALL. *See* p. 351.

JARDINE HALL. *See* p. 351.

9050   ARBIGLAND
                    1.9km. SE of Kirkbean

Georgian mansion house built in 1755 by the agricultural improver
William Craik of Arbigland, who may have designed it.* Piend-
roofed main block of two storeys above a basement whose
inferior status is denoted by small windows and a band course
marking it off from the floors above. Five bays, the three-
bay centrepiece slightly advanced and dignified by giant Ionic

---

* Craik prepared a sketch elevation and plan for Mossknowe in 1763 and is credited
with the design of Kirkbean Parish Church in 1776.

pilasters supporting a pediment. Stone swags under the first-floor windows, now almost hidden by a ground-floor addition of *c.* 1900 from which projects a contemporary parapeted porch whose console-pedimented door may be the 1750s door re-used.* In the outer bays, segmental-pedimented ground-floor windows with lugged architraves and polished red sandstone ashlar aprons reaching down to the band course below. At the first-floor windows, consoles under the sills of the lugged architraves. Rusticated quoins at the outer corners of the house. Overall cornice and parapet, with urns on its ends and at the centre pediment. On each side of this block there is a single-storey-and-basement link, with a round-arched ground-floor niche, to a semi-octagonal-fronted pavilion, whose rusticated quoins are flush with the main walling. On the apex of each pavilion's roof, a small urn.

The N (garden) elevation is a much plainer version of the entrance façade, the basement fully exposed. Again a three-bay pedimented centrepiece but without pilasters, the symmetry of this front now disturbed by an off-centre early C19 bow, whose polished ashlar makes a suave contrast to the rather rougher masonry of the C18 walling. Consoled sills to the ground- and first-floor windows, some of which have been enlarged; utilitarian but small late C19 additions.

Inside, much of the 1750s work survives. In the C18 entrance hall, doors with lugged architraves. Dining room to the W; its doorpieces have lugged and corniced architraves of *c.* 1755, and their fluted friezes' rosettes are of *c.* 1900, a possible date for the ceiling cornice, enriched with naturalistic grapes. C18 lugged surround to the chimneypiece. N stairwell squeezed in the W bay of the house's centrepiece, with a pair of roundheaded arches at the first floor. Library occupying the two E bays of the centrepiece behind the hall, its bow end and general character early C19. The drawing room fills the main block's E end. Panelled shutters carved with egg-and-dart enrichment. Plain C18 chimneypiece. Ceiling cornice with moulded mutules and rosettes on the flat. The walls were painted in the early C20 to imitate boarding. In the E pavilion, the Blue Room, the cornice of its C18 chimneypiece carved with egg-and-dart, its frieze with a shell and foliage design. On the first floor, a cove-ceilinged corridor, a plaster shell at one end.

Immediately W of the house, STABLES, perhaps built a little before the house itself. Four rubble-walled ranges enclosing a narrow courtyard entered from the E and W. At each outer corner and at the centre of the W range, a pavilion-roofed tower. In the centre of the E front, the roundheaded pend arch is surmounted by a row of flight holes (for a doocot) topped by a pediment, with urns at its apex and ends, and a blind bullseye window in the tympanum. Fronting the courtyard, round-arched C18 doors with projecting keystones and imposts.

---

* A view of the house before the addition of the porch shows a tall pedimented entrance approached by a perron.

E of the house, woodland GARDENS, probably begun in the
C18, bisected by the Broad Walk leading to the shore of the
Solway Firth. – S of the Broad Walk, a WALLED GARDEN of
1745. – To the N, overlooking the Solway, THE HOUSE-ON-
THE-SHORE, a rubble-walled version of a small Cotswold
manor house, designed by *Kathleen Blackett-Swiny*, 1936, as a
dower house for herself. – SW of the mansion house, a semicircular arrangement of classical GATEPIERS built *c.*1805 by
Allan Cunningham. They are rusticated and corniced with fluted
friezes; elegant urns on the stepped pedestal tops. To each side,
a late C19 carved stone falcon (the crest of the Blacketts, who
inherited Arbigland in 1872).

5050

ARDWALL
1km. S of Anwoth

The C18 mansion house of the McCullochs of Ardwall, enlarged
by the addition of flanking wings in 1895. The principal fact of
the building history is recorded on an incised plaque at the
back of the main block: 'Founded April 6th 1762'. It is a straightforward piend-roofed rectangle, harled with red sandstone
dressings. Two storeys over an exposed basement. Entrance
(N) front of five bays. Plain surrounds to the basement
windows. The ground-floor openings are taller and grander to
denote the *piano nobile.* Consoled sills to the moulded window
surrounds, the two inner ones with lugged architraves.
Concave-sided stone stair to the central door, which is framed
by a pedimented and Roman Doric columned aedicule; the
frieze metopes are carved with alternating rosettes and ox skulls.
First-floor windows all moulded and with consoled sills, except
for the centre window, which has a lugged architrave. The back
is again five-bay. In the centre, a round-arched door with
projecting keystone and imposts. The balustraded stone steps
up to it are probably of 1895. The stair window over the door
and the *piano nobile* windows seem to have been deepened in
the early C19. Late C19 dormer windows to front and back.

In 1895 *Thomas Leadbetter* enlarged the house to an H-plan
by the addition of a slightly lower wing each side, again
harled and with rusticated red sandstone quoins. The front
and back elevations of each wing are the same, with a
Venetian window at the *piano nobile* and a first-floor window
pushing up through the cornice into a pedimented stone
dormerhead; again, consoles under the sills. The result is less
tactful than was intended.

Inside the main block, an entrance hall with a modillioned
and rosetted cornice of the 1760s. On its S side, a pair of
roundheaded arches to the stairs down to the basement and up
to the first floor. The arches' central pier contains a built-in
clock (apparently there from the first). Just two ground-floor
rooms. The E (library) has a cornice with leafy modillions and
rosettes on the flat between. This is of the 1760s, but the marble

chimneypiece is early C19, presumably introduced when the
windows were lowered. Dining room at the W, its grey marble
chimneypiece and sideboard recess both early C19, the cornice
probably a replacement of *c.* 1950, when the adjoining wing was
reinstated after a fire.* In the E wing, a double drawing room
of 1895, its enriched ceiling a half-hearted evocation of late C18
work; Ionic pilasters at the Venetian windows. On the first
floor, two bedrooms with 1760s panelling and basket-arched
stone fireplaces.

To the W, a very plain STABLES AND COACHHOUSE courtyard built by *Peter McGaw* in 1811; just the suggestion of a
pediment over the rectangular pend opening for embellishment. – SE of the house, a rather small early medieval stone
SLAB incised with a cross. It came from Ardwall Island at the
mouth of the Fleet.

ARDWELL *1040*

Hamlet, a short row of white painted mid-C19 cottages its principal feature.

CHURCH, 0.9km. W. Big but austerely detailed Gothic cruciform, by *P. MacGregor Chalmers*, 1900–2, built of squared
and stugged snecked rubble, the slated roofs finished with
red-tiled ridges. Tall nave, with a sturdily buttressed and
parapeted baptistery projecting from its W end; bargeboarded
porch on the S side. Lower transepts and a rectangular
chancel. NW steeple, its bottom stage's W corners buttressed,
the S buttress formed by a projection of the S face's walling,
the N buttress taller and clasping; between the buttresses, a
segmental-arched entrance. Tall ashlar-faced belfry, with
nook-shafts at its two-light openings, their hoodmoulds
springing from a stringcourse. Spired octagonal corner pinnacles, each face panelled with a blind arch. Between them
rises the octagonal spire, alternate faces bearing tall gabled
and pointed-arched lucarnes.

Inside, an open wooden roof, its collar braces springing from
conical stone corbels. Walls faced with squared rubble. Pointed
stone chancel arch with clustered shafts. At the W end, two-
bay arcade to the baptistery, its broad pointed arches springing
from fat columns. Trefoil-headed aumbry in the baptistery's S
wall. – The FURNISHINGS are almost all of 1900–2. – Round
stone font. – Perp wooden pulpit on the chancel arch's N side. –
Late Gothic communion table, its front carved with figures of
SS. Peter, Andrew, John and Paul. – Laird's Pew in the S
transept. – STAINED GLASS two-light E window (Our Lord
stilling the Storm) by *William Wilson*, 1953, characteristically
colourful.

---

* This wing, originally containing a billiard room, was divided into smaller rooms
after the fire.

ARDWELL HOUSE

0.7km. SW

Harled laird's house with crowstepped gables and bellcast eaves. Most of the walling and the side elevations are of *c.*1720 but the front is of 1956 by *H. Anthony Wheeler*. He removed a large Baronial addition of 1869–72 (by *Brown & Wardrop*) whose general size and shape are now indicated by a terrace. The house is of two storeys over a high basement. Three-bay E front, with a concrete imperial stair to the broad segmental-arched door. Set into this front, two stones, both probably of *c.*1870, one carved with an owl, the other with a lion (the crests of MacTaggart and Stewart*). At the back of the house there survives a low SW service wing of 1869–72, crowstepped and rubble-built with a ground-floor loggia (the arches now infilled) and a large first-floor gablet.

Inside the house, the simple C18 stair survives. The rest is mainly of 1956. In the drawing room, a white marble chimneypiece, presumably of *c.*1870 but looking a little earlier. Female figures at the ends, a mythological scene on the frieze. The dining room's wooden chimneypiece must be of *c.*1870, with endearingly fierce dragons projecting diagonally from the corners and grotesque faces studding the frieze.

In woodland S of the house, a stone STATUE of an owl. It came from the Victorian addition and was one of two carved in 1871–2 by *John Rhind*. The other now stands outside the entrance to the WALLED GARDEN. This is perhaps of *c.*1800, the S wall partly faced externally with brickwork containing flues. In the centre of the garden, a rubble-walled ENCLOSURE of uncertain date and purpose, perhaps a pen for animals.

FARMS ETC.

ARDWELL MAINS, 0.6km. w. Rubble-built courtyard steading of the earlier C19. On one range, a clock-cupola of 1884 (the clock by *R. R. Child*), brought here from Southwick House (q.v.).

BALGOWAN, 2.3km. S. Smart piend-roofed farmhouse built of rendered rubble. In its present form it is early C19. Main block of two storeys and a basement, the centre bowed and with a three-light first-floor window; bay windows, probably C20, added at the outer bays. At the sides, lean-to links joining to single-storey pavilions. The basement, now cellarage but containing a former kitchen, seems to have been built as part of an earlier house. In the present entrance hall, an C18 stone carved with the coat of arms of the McDoualls of Logan.

CHAPEL ROSSAN, 0.6km. S. Harled early C19 Gothick L-plan house of two storeys, the jamb a broad-eaved semi-octagon. Y-tracery in the pointed windows and the door's fanlight; round chimneys.

---

* Sir Mark Stewart of Southwick had married the heiress of the MacTaggarts of Ardwell in 1866.

LOGAN MILL, 2km. SE. To the w of the farm steading, a rubble-built round TOWER, built in the late C17 as a windmill but converted to a meal mill in the early C19, when it acquired a battlement. – To its w, a gabled and bargeboarded COTTAGE of the earlier C19.

BROCH (DOON CASTLE), Ardwell Point, 4.3km. W. Broch, perhaps of the first century A.D., built overlooking the Irish Sea. The landward approach is defended by a wall and a natural gully spanned by a stone-fronted causeway. The broch itself is, as usual, circular, 9m. in diameter, the wall up to 4.6m. thick and 1.8m. high, its inner face built of large stone blocks. There have been at least two cells within its thickness. As well as the entrance from the main approach there is one on the seaward side.

AUCHNESS. See p. 112.

ARGRENNAN HOUSE 7050
2.5km. E of Ringford

Smart Georgian mansion house, the product of two stages of construction. The first, in the mid- or later C18, produced the present NE wing, originally a self-contained rubble-walled laird's house of two storeys above an exposed basement. Three-bay w (entrance) front with rusticated quoins and, originally, a centre door to the *piano nobile*, its presence marked by tall windows. At the back, a full-height central bow, with a Venetian window to both the basement and the *piano nobile*, that of the *piano nobile* with granite columns topped by rudimentary capitals.

A s block was added in 1818, its front almost identical to that of Mount Melville (Fife), which was designed in 1821 by *James Gillespie Graham*; he is likely to have been the architect here as well. Again of two storeys and a basement but much more urbane than the C18 house, built of squared whinstone with polished sandstone ashlar. Nine-bay front, each end advanced under a parapet which is one course higher than those of the links. Advanced and pedimented three-bay centre-piece from which projects a portico of paired Roman Doric columns, the ends of the parapet panelled, its centre carved with a blind balustrade. Sill courses linking the windows of the two main floors, those of the *piano nobile* dignified with cornices, consoled at the end bays. Narrow dummy lights flanking the central first-floor window. Bowed E gable, a cast-iron balcony under the tall ground-floor window. Behind this front block, a contemporary short jamb containing the principal stair. This covers the s third of the C18 house's w front, whose entrance door was presumably blocked at the same time. It was probably also in 1818 that the N and central *piano nobile* windows of the E elevation were lowered and acquired iron balconies.

Inside the C18 house, a geometric stone stair at the N end. In the centre, an E-facing bow-ended morning room, its large neo-classical chimneypiece probably a late C19 embellishment. Library to its s, the late C18 pine chimneypiece (possibly imported) with *rinceau* decoration on the frieze.

The front block of 1818 is much grander. Vaulted basement. In the groin-vaulted kitchen at the W end most of the original fittings (hot-plate, oven, stewing range etc.) survive. On the *piano nobile*, a central entrance hall with console-corniced door-pieces to l. and r. Ahead, a screen of Roman Doric fluted half-columns under a fanlight. This opens into the stair hall, to which the back of the screen presents attached piers instead of columns. A segmental arch marks the beginning of the stairwell itself. Stair with scrolly cast-iron balusters. At the first-floor landing, another columned screen. W of the entrance hall, a large dining room, with a sunburst plaster rose in the centre of the ceiling and a simple grey marble chimneypiece. E of the hall, an ante-room with double doors to the bow-ended drawing room; both have late C19 friezes under the Georgian cornices and fairly simple white marble chimneypieces.

WALLED GARDEN to the SE, probably early C19, the walls faced internally with brick (renewed in places). – E of the walled garden, the ROSE GARDEN (now planted with lavender); FOUNTAIN of 1831 in its centre. – To its s, a ROCKERY, also of *c*.1830, its low mounds not making the effort to suggest miniature Alps which later taste would have demanded. – LODGE to the W, an early C19 *cottage orné*, each of its hood-moulded windows containing two diamond-paned pointed lights. Semi-octagonal portico with shafts of clustered columns supporting the octagonal pavilion roof.

ARKLETON

3090

1km. NE of Ewes

Tall Baronial house, the architecture less than exciting. It is said to have been built in two stages. The first, in 1860 (the date over the N door), provided the three-storey crowstep-gabled W block, with a small gabled rectangular bartizan on its SW corner. The second stage, in 1884, produced the rest. A four-storey tower projects S from the W block's E side, with a round turret at the SW corner, a square bartizan with a cannon spout at the SE, and a battlement at the NE. Narrow three-storey E wing, the top floor jettied. Single-storey service court to the E.

Late C19 GARDEN to the NW, its rubble wall lined with brick. At its NW end, a polychrome brick gardener's cottage, with a bargeboarded porch. – E of the house, a single-storey crowstep-gabled STABLE COURTYARD, dated 1884.

AUCHENCAIRN

7050

A Y-plan village, its houses and cottages mostly C19 and looking decidedly prosperous.

FREE CHURCH. Secularized. Built in 1844; enlarged by *Francis Armstrong*, 1877. T-plan, with buttresses at the broad tail; pointed windows.

PARISH CHURCH. Simple Geometric of 1855. Tall nave with sturdy stepped buttresses; a lower short chancel, its E gable diagonally buttressed. SE vestry and NW porch. Walls all of grey granite except the bellcoted W gable, which is of bullnosed red sandstone ashlar.

Inside, a braced kingpost-truss roof, the ceiling diagonally boarded. Tall pointed chancel arch. – STAINED GLASS E window of three lights (Our Lord teaching), signed by *A. Ballantine & Gardiner*, 1903. – ORGAN by *H. G. Jones & Son*, 1956.

HALL. Early C20 and plain.

SCHOOL. Late C19. Shallow U-plan front with bracketed eaves and a gableted centre.

AUCHENCAIRN HOUSE, 2.3km. SE. Big and bare manorial mansion of *c.*1860 designed by *W. R. Corson* of Manchester for that city's former Lord Mayor, Ivie Mackie. The two-storey NE wing is earlier, a late C18 house, with the ends of its five-bay front slightly advanced. This wing was refronted and remodelled, either by Corson or a little earlier. Gabled ends with spiked ball finials at the top and pinnacled, turret-like embellishments at the corners. Ground-floor windows enlarged to two- and three-light. Corson's main block is, like the wing's front, of polished red sandstone ashlar. Corbelled eaves. Bay windows along the S front, roundheaded lights on the E side. At the SE corner, a square tower, its uncrenellated parapet projected on corbels. On its S face, an oriel window, again with a corbelled parapet. Sticking out from the tower's E face, a heavy Gothic porch squashed by a narrower but aggressive upper storey squatting on its parapet. Caphouse on the tower's NE corner. The result is more likely to produce than dispel nightmares. – Behind, a WALLED GARDEN, probably late C18 or early C19. – Late C19 granite-walled LODGE to the SE. Dottily tall, with a full display of Baronial features. Crow-stepped gables, corbelled battlement, canted corners brought to the square, and a conical-roofed round tower.

FARMS ETC.

BALCARY BAY HOTEL, 2.9km. SE. The core is a harled villa of *c.*1800, with a battlemented bow projecting from the E side. Major alterations and extensions since the early C20.

COLLIN HOUSE, 1.1km. N. Early C19 laird's house, built of pink-painted rubble. At the three-bay W front, a flight of steps oversailing the basement to the entrance. Over the door, a consoled cornice with rosettes on the frieze. Lower rendered wings have been added at the ends.

THE TOWER, 3.4km. SE. Victorian tower folly of a house, its battlements' merlons in the form of crowstepped gablets.

ORCHARDTON HOUSE. *See* p. 483.

AUCHENCASS
2km. NW of Beattock

Substantial remains of a late C13 castle of enclosure, probably
constructed for the Kirkpatricks, who held it in the first decade
of the C14.* The defences are all roughly square on plan, first
an outer rampart, probably intended to be palisaded, next a
ditch, then a mound (again probably palisaded) higher than
the rampart, and finally a stone-walled enclosure. On each of
its E, W and S sides (the N has been much disturbed), the outer
rampart broadens into an outward-projecting platform. Sunk
in the centre of the E platform, a badly ruined irregularly shaped
chamber from which a tunnel-vaulted underground passage,
perhaps a sally-port, runs S to the rampart's outer side; there
has been a guardroom at the passage's S end.

The approach to the central mound crossed the ditch,
probably by a drawbridge, near the N side's W end, in line
with an entrance into the enclosure itself. The enclosure is
formed by a curtain wall of good-quality coursed boulder
rubble. At each corner there has been a projecting round
tower; the one at the SW has been demolished, but the lower
parts of the ones at the NE and NW still stand, built of the
same boulder rubble as the main walls. More survives of the
SE tower, but its walling is thinner and built of much smaller
stones, so it is presumably a late medieval replacement; high
up in its outer face, a slit window. The inner faces of the
curtain wall originally rose for *c.* 1.5m. to a broad ledge or
walk, best seen at the SE corner, above which the masonry
is thinner. Roughly in the centre of the E wall, evidence of a
stair rising from this ledge, presumably to a parapet walk.
Under the stair, a room, probably a garderobe, its floor
containing a pit which drains into the ditch.

AUCHEN CASTLE
3km. NW of Beattock

Overgrown broad-eaved cottagey villa of 1849, with one large and
one small Italianate tower for vertical emphasis. The house
was altered and enlarged in 1869 after a fire; the S front was
remodelled, and a round Jacobean tower and stair turret were
added at the NE corner.

AUCHNESS
1.2km. SE of Ardwell

Small harled tower house poking defiantly through later additions.
The crowstep-gabled tower itself may be of *c.* 1600. Three
storeys and an attic with corner turrets, their battlements a late

---

* In 1306 Roger de Kirkpatrick, 'chevaler', was lord ('seigneur') of 'Haughencas'.

Georgian embellishment. Extending from the SW corner, a short stretch of crenellated wall which no longer makes sense but may have been part of a stair jamb. Plain two-storey S addition with a crowstepped gable; this is probably the extension built in 1843, but it looks a little earlier. On its S end, a single-storey wing with a centre gablet, again probably of the 1840s. Also likely to be of the 1840s is the W wing, which forms part of the N range of the attached courtyard steading. In the late C19 the original tower acquired a castellated bay window and battlemented two-storey porch.

AULDGIRTH   9080

Hamlet beside the A76. A small new village of local authority housing was built to the N in the 1950s.

DUNSCORE EAST CHURCH, 1.7km. SW. Originally Dunscore Free Church. By *James Gillison*, 1843–4, but reconstructed in 1899. Broad buttressed box of whinstone with red sandstone dressings. Round-arched windows; a big bullseye in the urnfinialled N gable. The S front's breadth is broken by a stepped buttress l. of the door and a squat battlemented tower on the r.; on top of the gable, a finial carved with the Burning Bush emblem of the Free Church.

BRIDGES. The red sandstone OLD BRIDGE over the Nith was 102 designed by *David Henderson* and built by *William Stewart* in 1781–2. Three segmental arches of ashlar. Bow-ended cutwaters of hammerdressed masonry, each surmounted by a pair of coupled pilasters carrying an entablature topped by a halfdome; this top part forms a refuge in which a pedestrian could crouch to escape the bridge's traffic. – Concrete NEW BRIDGE to the S by *Hugh Murray* of *Dumfries and Galloway Regional Council*, 1979, just missing elegance.

HALL. Built in 1886. Single-storey, of painted brick and looking just like a cottage.

PRIMARY SCHOOL. By the Dumfries County Architect, *A. A. Wilkie*, 1968. Podium of dark brown brick carrying a block faced with brick, drydash and weatherboarding, topped by a shallow monopitch roof.

DESCRIPTION. At the hamlet's N end, the piend-roofed early C19 AULDGIRTH INN, built of painted rubble; its appearance probably dates from *c*.1804, when it was said to have been 'lately repaired and augmented'. This is enjoyable, with small Gothick windows and a central chimneystack pierced by crosslet arrowslits. Then the Hall (*see* above) and a short terrace of harled C19 cottages, their windows now enlarged. At the S end, the Primary School (*see* above) and three late C20 houses.

ELLISLAND, 3.1km. SE. The house built here in 1788–9, during Robert Burns' short tenancy of the farm, was pulled down in 1812 and replaced by the present single-storey farmhouse. Quite plain, with walls of painted rubble and a slated roof.

Two ranges of farm offices, probably also of *c*.1812, to the W. Pyramid-roofed shed to the NE.

BLACKWOOD. *See* p. 129.
FRIARS CARSE. *See* p. 308.

1080

BALGRAY HOUSE
4.6km. N of Lockerbie

Lumpy sub-Italianate mansion of 1883–5, built of stugged red sandstone. Symmetrical at each face, with a big Ionic-pilastered porte-cochère in the middle of the E (entrance) front, a canted bay window at the S elevation, and broad open-pedimented centrepieces at the ends. Cornices over the small-paned ground-floor windows, pediments over the first-floor plate-glass windows. Parapet broken by the attic windows which rise from the main cornice to end in pediments.

6070

BALMACLELLAN

Small village, mostly of C19 vernacular cottages, watched over by the Parish Church, itself observed by a motte behind.

PARISH CHURCH. Harled T-plan kirk, the body built in 1753, the N 'aisle' added in 1833 by *William McCandlish*. He probably also provided the W bellcote, its sides formed by roundheaded arches, its roof a steep pyramid rising among obelisk corner finials. The long S wall's slightly advanced and gabled centre came in an alteration of 1886. So too did the projecting vestry, the corbelled eaves, and the narrow round-arched windows.

Interior of 1886. The kingpost-truss roof becomes elaborate at the centre, where the kingpost descends as a pendant through the intersection of the diagonal tie-beams. – STAINED GLASS W window (Christ as Lord of All), strongly coloured simplified realism, by *Gordon Webster*, 1928.

GRAVEYARD. SW of the church, a couple of early C18 head-stones carved with angels' heads (souls) above reminders of death. – To their S, a headstone to John and George Hope, also C18, with a crowned hammer (the emblem of the smiths). – To its SE, the ill-lettered headstone of James Ierland †1724, its front incised with a crude skull and crossbones. – Weathered early C18 TABLE STONE commemorating the Covenanting martyr Robert Grierson.

MOTTE. Small steep-sided round motte; diameter of the base *c*.42m., of the summit *c*.10m. Encircled by a ditch. It is clearly artificial and dates from the C12 or early C13.

GRENNAN MILL, 1.4km. NW. Small two-storey rubble-walled building of 1834, perhaps incorporating some earlier fabric. High-breast wheel. Most of the machinery survives inside.

IRONMACANNIE MILL, 3.7km. S. L-plan rubble-walled grain

mill, C19 in its present form. Iron overshot wheel at the E gable. Much of the machinery survives inside.

TROQUHAIN, 2.8km. E. Very plain and rather altered house of the earlier C19. In the garden, a SUNDIAL, its baluster shaft provided in 1855. The head, dated 1616, is cubical but with chamfered corners. Dials on the faces, carved human heads on the corners.

BARSCOBE CASTLE. *See* p. 124.

THE HOLM. *See* p. 346.

BALMAGHIE 7060

Just the church with a nearby manse.

PARISH CHURCH. Piend-roofed kirk of white-painted rubble, built in 1794. It is cruciform, with a N 'aisle' lengthened from one bay to two in 1894 by *Kinnear & Peddie,* who also added the W porch. The S limb is an octagonal belltower with bellcast eaves at its slated spire roof. The church's windows were given their present pointed form in 1913. Interior mostly of 1894 but with a late C20 boarded ceiling. – STAINED GLASS. In the S wall, two lights of 1904, with portrait roundels of St Andrew and St Peter. – Three-light N window (the Crucifixion) signed by *Arthur J. Dix,* 1893, and erected in 1895.

S of the church, a tall MONUMENT to the Rev. William McKie †1763, with fluted Ionic columns and a scrolly broken pediment topped by a short swagged column. – Nearby, an early C18 TABLE STONE commemorating two Covenanting martyrs, both named David Halliday. On it, the inscription:

BENEATH THIS STONE TWO DAVIDS HALLIDAYS
DOE LY WHOSE SOULS NOU SING THEIR MASTERS PRAISE
TO KNOU IF CURIOUS PASSENGERS DESYRE
FOR WHAT BY WHOME AND HOU THEY DID EXPYRE
THEY DID OPPOSE THIS NATIONS PERJUREY
NOR COULD THEY JOYN WITH LORDLY PRELACY
INDULGING FAVOURS FROM CHRIST'S ENEMIES
QUENCH'D NOT THEIR ZEAL THIS MONUMENT THEN CRYES
THESE WERE THE CAUSES NOT TO BE FORGOT
WHY THEY BY LAG SO WICKEDLY WERE SHOT
ONE NAME ONE CAUSE ONE GRAVE ONE HEAVEN DO TY
THEIR SOULS TO THAT ONE GOD ETERNALLY

CHAPEL, Glenlochar, 1.9km. S. Small Gothic chapel of *c.* 1840. Two-bay nave and a lower and narrower chancel, also of two bays. Clustered gableted buttresses at the W and E ends. More buttresses along the chancel sides. Nook-shafted and hood-moulded W door. Above it, a round panel containing a quatre-foil. Paired cusped lights to the nave. Single pointed windows at the chancel. – Pointed gateway in the surrounding ENCLOSURE WALL.

LIVINGSTON, 1.6km. NW. Mid-C18 laird's house. The harled front has five bays, with the centre three advanced under a ped-iment, an octagonal opening in its tympanum. A porch has been added, probably in the mid-C19, but the lugged architrave of its door looks like the C18 one re-used. Also of the C19, the widening of the ground-floor windows and the addition of a W wing.

0060   BANKEND

Small C19 village.

CAERLAVEROCK PARISH CHURCH, 0.7km. N. Rough ashlar, T-plan, built in 1781. Round-arched side windows, their keystones projecting slightly; bullseyes in the gables. Heavy bolection cornice. Tiny ball finials on the E and W gables; on the N jamb, a ball-finialled birdcage bellcote. Consoled pediment over the jamb door. In 1894 *James Barbour* added the piend-roofed porches and provided a new roof with a red tile cresting. The NE inner angle's lean-to vestry is a more recent addition. Interior recast in 1894.

Almost touching the church's SE corner is the plain BURIAL ENCLOSURE of the Kirkpatricks and Connells of Conheath; it is probably late C18. – To its SE, TABLE STONE to someone †1704, the weathered slab carved with a coat of arms at the top, a skull and crossbones at the bottom. – Some way S of the church, a pair of TABLE STONES. One, erected in 1722, commemorates the children of John Hutton; geometric decoration on the slab's sides and supports. – The other, to John Hutton †1704, has a vine-bordered slab, a skull at its bottom end. Roses and thistles on the sides; more thistles, together with panelled shields, on the lumpy baluster legs.

HUTTON HALL ACADEMY. Now in other use. The school was founded in 1712 with a bequest from Dr John Hutton, physician to Queen Anne, but the present building is by *James Barbour*, 1892. Prominently sited and sizeable; Jacobean in red sandstone ashlar.

BRIDGE. Built by *John Robieson*, 1812–13. Humpbacked single span of rough ashlar; flat-topped squat obelisks on the parapet ends.

CAERLAVEROCK CASTLE. *See* p. 140.
ISLE TOWER. *See* p. 350.

8050   BAREND

Sizeable collection of A-framed holiday log houses, most with balconies enjoying the view over the Solway Firth. It was developed from 1972 to a design by *Morris & Steedman*.

DRUMSTINCHALL, 2.1km. N. Modestly pretentious house of 1832 (the date over the door). Two storeys with an attic marked off by a band course. Anta-pilastered doorpiece flanked by canted bay windows, probably added later in the C19. The small attic windows are horizontally proportioned with curved sides. To the E, late C19 and C20 extensions of no great interest.

FAIRGIRTH HOUSE. *See* p. 307.

BARGALY HOUSE   4060

5.2km. E of Newton Stewart

Laird's house and its appurtenances. The complex was begun in 1691, when Andrew Heron, a younger son of Andrew Heron of Kirroughtree, took up residence here. In 1721 Sir John Clerk of Penicuik eulogized Heron's work:

This is the work of a gentleman of a small fortune, for I was told he had scarcely 500 m[ark]s a year, yet it shows what industry and frugality may doe. Hear I saw a little conveniente house upon the bancks of a small rivulet, which wanted no embellishments that any house in Britain has, save only those things that were not so nicely done. Here are gardens, orchards, parterrs, orangeries, waterworks, fishponds, bagnios, inclosures, arbures, wildernesses, woods, etc., with such a variety of fruit as I had not observed the like in any place of this country ... He had likeways a fine collection of various sorts of shrubs and evergreens.

The present small mansion house's piend-roofed main block is said to have been built for Heron in 1695–6 by 'on Mr *Hawkins* ane Ing[l]ishman'. Its general appearance, a piend-roofed two-storey three-bay harled box with sturdy chimneys at the ends, could be of the 1690s, but the detail is more suggestive of *c.*1800; perhaps it is the result of a remodelling. Granite strip quoins and a first-floor lintel course under the eaves cornice. Unmoulded margins to the windows. The door is framed by simplified Doric columns and entablature, again of granite. Each side of the centre block, a single-storey angled link to a pavilion. The W pavilion has a piended bellcast-eaved roof and is perhaps of the early C18; the E was raised to two storeys *c.*1900, its upper windows with gableted dormerheads. Set into the E pavilion's E gable, a moulded frame (harled over) enclosing a panel incised with a pious Latin inscription describing the house as only a place of sojourn in comparison with Heaven. Wing extending back from the centre of the main block. It may be partly C18 but was extended and recast with gableted dormerheads *c.*1900. Behind the W pavilion, a stable, probably C18 but heightened to two storeys in the early C20, the upper windows rising into dormerheads, their pediments alternately triangular and segmental. Low additions N of the E pavilion.

Immediately SW of the house, a late C17 or early C18 SUNDIAL bearing the initials of Andrew Heron and his first wife, Mary Graham, †1706. The square top is supported on a stone in the shape of a Greek cross, with pendants carved in the inner angles; a fluted half-globe below. C20 concrete pedestal. – SE of the house, a TOMB of 1729–30, restored in 1829 and again in 1929. The C18 design was by *Andrew Heron* but its present appearance, a stepped ashlar rectangle with crosses on the ends, looks more like work of 1829. However, it does incorporate C18 elements. On the centre, an urn. Set in each end, two panels, one bearing the coats of arms and initials of Andrew Heron and his second wife, Elizabeth Dunbar, flanking the words 'HOPE/FAITH/LOVE', the other inscribed 'we die hopeing/And our ashes/beleive life 1730'. Also in the end, a small stone carved with a crude skull in high relief. – To the NE, a second SUNDIAL, by *Adie* of Edinburgh, 1828, each face of its pedestal carved with a rosette; rather fussy top, small rosettes round the rim. – This sundial stands just outside the GARDEN, its rubble walls built by Heron in 1693; their internal facing of brick perhaps of the 1690s but probably C18. – In the centre of the garden's E wall, a pavilion-roofed APPLE STORE, probably of the early C18.

<h1 style="text-align:center">BARGRENNAN</h1>

3070

Just the church, set back from the road in a neat graveyard.

PARISH CHURCH. Unpretentious whin-rubble rectangle, built as a chapel of ease in 1838–9. Lattice glazing in the round-arched windows. Gabled bellcote on the S end from which projects a pair of sturdy stepped buttresses clasping a porch. Low piend-roofed N vestry, a later addition. Interior refurnished in 1909 by *P. MacGregor Chalmers*; simple neo-Jacobean PULPIT.

CAIRN (THE WHITE CAIRN). *See* Glentrool.

<h1 style="text-align:center">BARHOLM CASTLE</h1>

5050

1.3km. SE of Kirkdale

Roofless tower house on a steep hillside overlooking Wigtown Bay. The building history is far from clear, but there was a house at Barholm by 1541, when a charter was signed there, and it seems likely that the present building is largely of the early C16. It is a rubble-walled four-storey L-plan, the stair jamb projecting at the NE corner. The main block's masonry stands to the wallhead, now missing its parapet. Small S windows to the ground floor. At the first floor, two windows to the S and one to the N, all chamfered and corniced, the S front's W opening broader than the others and now lacking its sill. Chamfered second-floor openings in the S front. At the N, a moulded second-floor window with a small, almost square opening beside it. Top-floor window high in the W gable. In the stair jamb's N face, two windows. The lower is of two lights with the paired roundheaded arches springing from a central pendant, a feature found elsewhere in aumbries (e.g. at Elshieshields Tower, q.v.). The upper window has an ogee-headed arch. At the ground floor, in the inner angle, the door has a moulded segmental-headed arch under a rope moulding, the ends tied as knots, on which are carved a couple of human heads (one very worn) and a dragon who climbs down to get a good view of visitors. Above the door, an empty panel frame. The top of the jamb is jettied out as a flat-roofed caphouse, possibly an addition of the later C16 or early C17. In the inner angle, a round turret projected on continuous corbelling; it contains the stair from the third floor to the caphouse and was perhaps originally topped by a beacon.

All this seems fairly straightforward but in the E gable there is a first-floor door (now blocked) with, over it, the broken stonework of a projecting structure, perhaps a tall machicolation entered from the second-floor window immediately above. But if this first-floor doorway were the original main entrance, the stair jamb is presumably an addition. If so, was the ground floor entered, as it is now from the jamb, by a door at the E end of the main block's N wall, or was access to it originally by a ladder from the first floor, and its vault and present entrance inserted when the jamb was added? Also, if the jamb is an addition, the original access from the first floor to the second must have been by a ladder, although the probable machicolation implies that the house was of a status for which one might expect something more sophisticated. Other features, or the lack of them, are puzzling. There is no evidence of any gunloop, a standard embellishment of lairds' houses of the C16 or early C17. There have been wall-walks along the N and S sides, the N reached through a window, but they have not been carried across the gables and the S walk is interrupted by the big wallhead chimney containing the hall fireplace's flue.

Inside, on the main block's ground floor, a store covered by a rubble tunnel-vault. Two plain windows to the S. In the N wall, a couple of small and roughly constructed aumbries. Another small aumbry in the W side of this room's entrance. In the NE jamb, under the turnpike stair, a stone seat. Just before the stair reaches the first-floor hall, an aumbry; it is too small to rest a tray on, so was, perhaps, a lamp recess.

The first floor of the main block is occupied by the hall. S fireplace, the (broken) straight lintel supported by a corbel at each end. It is flanked by windows, the one at the E still with seats. At the E gable's N end, a window, which has also had stone seats. At this wall's S end, the blocked door to the outside. On the second floor, whose (missing) wooden floor was supported on wall scarcements, there have been two rooms, presumably bedchambers, each with a gable fireplace, both narrowed, perhaps in the C18. The E fireplace has a roll-and-hollow moulding on its earlier surround, but this surround is broader than the relieving arch above, suggesting that the fireplace opening may originally have been smaller, was then widened (perhaps in the late C16) and was later narrowed. In the N wall, a short passage from the stair with, at its W end, a pair of doors, one into each room. Opening off each room, a garderobe in the wall thickness, one at the house's SE corner, the other at the NW. The third-floor joists have been carried on moulded corbels in the gables. Again there seem to have been two rooms. In the caphouse over the jamb, a small segmental-vaulted room with a N fireplace.

Additions, perhaps of the C18, against the tower house's N and W sides have been removed.

BARJARG TOWER
                  2.5km. SE of Keir Mill

Sizeable mansion house, the product of at least five building
stages; the result is more unified than could reasonably have been
expected. The house was begun *c*.1600 by the erection of an
unpretentious L-plan tower house, built for the Maxwells or
perhaps for the Griersons, who acquired the estate in 1613. Probably in the late C17 this house acquired a S stair tower. In 1806–
7, after the estate had been acquired by the Rev. Dr Andrew
Hunter, a new block, possibly replacing an C18 extension, was
added to the tower house's W end. Apparently a little later in the
C19 the main (N) front was made roughly symmetrical by the
construction, at this new block's W end, of a second L-plan 'tower
house' with a wing behind. Then in 1914 *J. M. Bowie* of *James
Barbour & Bowie* remodelled both tower houses, made large
additions at the back and almost entirely revamped the interior.

The original TOWER HOUSE at the NE corner is, like the rest,
   built of thinly harled rubble. In its main part's N and S gables,
   narrow ground-floor windows. Blocked first-floor S window
   with a roll-and-hollow moulding. At each of the W front's upper
   floors, a window with a roll-and-hollow moulding, the top
   window enriched with dogtooth ornament. At the NE, NW and
   SE corners, round turrets on continuous corbelling. They were
   heightened and given conical roofs in 1914, when the tower
   acquired its present battlement and the castellated canted bay
   window which projects from the E front. In the SW jamb's N
   face, a roll-and-hollow moulded door in front of which has
   been hung an iron yett. The jamb's windows have been Georgianized. Battlement, again of 1914, with a bartizan and crowstep-gabled dormer window. Late C17 circular stair tower
   behind, its windows Georgian replacements, its conical roof
   dating from 1914.
      The MAIN BLOCK, built by *John Cook* in 1806–7, is of two
   storeys above a fully exposed basement. Tall windows to the
   ground-floor *piano nobile*. Five bays, the centre a projecting
   semi-octagon, its round-arched door a replacement of 1914.
   Hoodmoulded and mullioned windows at this centrepiece's
   top floor; at the sides of its basement and ground floor, hoodmoulded blind slits. Are these windows and hoodmoulds of
   1806–7 or are they alterations contemporary with the addition
   of the W 'tower house'?
      This crowstep-gabled W 'TOWER HOUSE' is, in general
   appearance, a careful balance to the original E tower. L-plan
   again. Corbelled turrets on the main part's front corners, also
   heightened and given conical roofs in 1914, when the SE jamb
   acquired a crowstepped dormer like that on the jamb of the E
   tower but, perhaps surprisingly, was not given a battlement. In
   the front of the main part, a large blind double-keyhole gunloop.
   The line of the turrets' continuous corbelling is carried across
   the fronts of both the main part and the jamb by chequer-set

horizontal stone blocks projecting inconsequentially from the wall. The rest of the detail (or lack of it) is by *Bowie*, who built up the main part's windows and replaced the jamb's early C19 door and segmental-arched windows with windows of plain Georgian type. On the jamb, above the basement window, a reset stone carved with the initials IG and GK (for John Grierson and Grizel Kirkpatrick) and the date 1680. It may have come from the late C17 stair tower behind the original house.

The back of the house is all of 1914, when Bowie added a tall SE WING, its first part, S of the C17 stair tower, plain except for a battlement. This forms a link to a broad crowstepped gable with angle rounds and a battlemented two-storey bay window. On this wing's S front, crowstepped dormerheads poking through broad eaves. The early C19 SW wing was largely rebuilt at the same time, again with crowstepped dormers and broad eaves. Across the back of the centre block was added a flat-roofed stack of corridors under a balustraded parapet. Also by Bowie is the balustraded screen wall on the S of the house's back court but at this wall's centre is a round two-storey conical-roofed building, its lower part a dairy, the upper floor said to have been used as an ice house; it looks early C19. More balustrades of 1914 edging the garden's terraces.

In the basement of the NE tower house's main part, a tunnel-vaulted store lit by narrow windows in the gables. In the E wall, what may have been a gunloop, its outer end blocked by the base of the bay window added in 1914. Turnpike stair with bottlenosed treads in the late C17 round tower to the S. The original first-floor hall was made a morning room in 1914, when Bowie added the bay window and inserted a Georgian-revival chimneypiece. Near the W wall's N end, a segmental-arched niche filling the embrasure of a blocked original window.

The central block's front door, approached by a flight of steps, opens, at an intermediate level between the basement and the *piano nobile*, into a circular entrance hall, its simple Gothick plaster ceiling a survival of 1806–7. From this, another flight of steps up to a short inner hall on the *piano nobile*. Groin-vaulted plaster ceiling, again of 1806–7, but the space is divided by a wooden screen of 1914 (apparently in the position of a Georgian predecessor), decorated with elaborate but small-scale carving in a Scots late Gothic manner. Almost certainly the main stair of 1806–7 rose originally at the S end of the inner hall but was removed in 1914, when a panelled corridor was built along the back of the centre block. Off this corridor's E end, in Bowie's SE addition, is the stair hall of 1914, lit from a rectangular cupola. Broad scale-and-platt stair rising to the first floor and descending to the basement. It is of gentle Jacobean character, the oak balustrades carved with fruit. At the basement, a screen, again in the late Gothic manner, gives access to the main basement rooms. Entered off the stair itself is a gentlemen's lavatory, the walls tiled in green, black and grey; lattice-decorated tiles on the floor. In the basement E of the

stair hall, a door into Bowie's oak-panelled music room. It is
of two-storey height, well lit from tall s windows and the bay
window on the E. On the N, a minstrels' gallery supported by
a fluted Ionic pier which is topped by a coat of arms separating
the gallery front's twin canted bays. On the room's W side, a
broad screen of widely spaced fluted Ionic columns *in antis*;
fireplace in the wall behind the screen.

The *piano nobile* of the central block has a room each side of
the inner hall, presumably entered from it before the alterations
of 1914 provided the s corridor. Both were remodelled by
Bowie. The W is the dining room. Simple compartmented
plaster ceiling and oak panelling. Neo-Tudor stone chimneypiece framed by broad Ionic oak pilasters; wooden overmantel carved with the arms of the Hunter-Arundells, the early
C 20 owners of Barjarg. In the drawing room E of the hall, the
walls are broken by pilasters decorated with plaster swags; the
panels between were probably intended to be covered with
fabric. Compartmented plaster ceiling with a big centre circle
and enriched with fruit and flowers. Georgian-revival chimneypiece of veined white marble inlaid with brass rosettes.

On the first floor of this block, another long corridor of 1914
at the back. It once formed a T with a passage bisecting the
block above the entrance and inner halls, but this N–S passage
was partitioned off as a room in the 1980s. The bedrooms have
early C 20 Arts and Crafts touches, e.g. at their chimneypieces.
At the house's SE corner, above the music room, a principal
suite of bedroom and dressing rooms. Its bathroom has the
same tiles as the gentlemen's lavatory. Huge early C 20 bath
and shower (by *Shanks* of Barrhead) still in place, the shower
equipped with water sprays at the sides as well as the top. In
the early C19 W 'tower house' is a broad turnpike stair, its flat-
topped newel decorated with a simple cornice.

100   Early C19 Gothick LODGE and GATEWAY at the SE entrance
to the park. Rectangular hoodmoulds over the lodge's pointed
door and windows; latticed glazing and crowstepped gables.
The gates are simple iron yetts, said to have come from the
former Dumfries Prison of 1802 (demolished in 1883). – The
drive is carried across a minor public road on a segmental-
arched BRIDGE of hammerdressed ashlar, presumably early
C19. – Second LODGE to the SW, mid-C19, with hoodmoulded
ground-floor openings, the windows containing latticed metal
glazing. The swept dormers over the first-floor windows look a
C 20 alteration.

3050   BARNBARROCH
                          2.4km. W of Kirkinner

Mansion house of the Vans Agnews of Sheuchan, built in 1780
but roofless since a fire in 1942. Two storeys, a basement and
attic, built of rubble with granite dressings. Entrance (N) front
with a projecting bow at each end. Pedimented attic centrepiece

containing a Venetian window, the top of the centre light filled with a stone shell. Porch fronted by a piered and pedimented portico added in 1806–8 as part of alterations by *J. C. Loudon.* s front of six bays, plain except for another centrepiece with Venetian windows and pedimented attic. Full-height w addition of 1806–8 with a ball-finialled overall balustrade; three-light ground-floor window to the s.

STABLES COURTYARD, probably late C18 but the front block remodelled or rebuilt in the earlier C19. This is of five bays, each marked off by stepped buttresses, diagonally set at the corners. The parapet rises into a bullseyed gablet over the broad centre. Hoodmoulds over the openings (one crudely enlarged).

THE BARONY

2.2km. SE of Kirkmichael

0080

Gentle Elizabethan manor house (formerly named Kirkmichael House), by *William Burn,* 1832–3, built of stugged red sandstone ashlar. Two-storey main block, with bay windows, mullioned and transomed openings, scroll-sided pedimented dormerheads, and diagonally set chimneys. Vertical emphasis is provided by slim conical-roofed round towers. Over the N front's entrance, a curvy strapworked pediment flanked by ball finials. To its l., an oval window under a scroll-sided pediment. Low office courtyard on the E, remodelled in the early C20.

The interior is for the most part plain. White marble Frenchy chimneypiece in the morning room at the SW. The dining room's chimneypiece, again of white marble, is blowsy neo-classical, its frieze carved with acanthus leaves and inverted palmettes; incised decoration on the jambs. Is this of the 1830s or a replacement following a fire early in the C20?

Attached to the house's SE corner, a courtyard of red-brick buildings serving the estate's present function as an agricultural college. They are by *Peter Nelson* of *Dumfries and Galloway Regional Council,* 1984–91. The E range's outer face picks up motifs from Burn (dormerheads and a bay window) and gives them a post-Modern twist. In the s range, a huge hall with stylized glass-fibre pediments over the entrances. In the N range, a pyramid-roofed hall topped by a cupola.

STONES. Against the house's s wall has been placed what looks like the entablature of a porch, perhaps of the early C18, its frieze carved with a pair of lions' heads which break up through the cornice. – Built into the N wall of the 1980s N range, a stone bearing the dates 1654 and 1761, those of the erection and rebuilding of the previous mansion house on the site. – In the 1980s courtyard, a dormerhead decorated with acanthus leaves flanking the coroneted letter C, presumably of *c.* 1702, when Sir Robert Dalzell of Glenae, then owner of the estate, inherited the earldom of Carnwath.

BARSCOBE CASTLE

6070

1.5km. NE of Balmaclellan

Mid-C17 laird's house restored by *Ian G. Lindsay & Partners*, 1971–87. It is a two-storey-and-attic rubble-walled L, the SW jamb taller than the main block. Above the roll-moulded door in the jamb's N face, a panel bearing two coats of arms, the initials WM and MG (for William MacLellan and his wife, Margaret or Mary Gordon) and the date 1648, probably the year of the building's completion. A second door, also roll-moulded, at the N end of the E side, has been formed by deepening a window opening. This side's central window looks a later insertion. Above, a big wallhead chimney flanked by steeply pedimented dormerheads, the one at the S carved with the initials and date 'W.^{C}MG/1648', the one at the N (formerly blank) with the date 1971 and the initials of Hugh Wontner, then the owner. Both the main block and the jamb have gables with straight skews interrupted by widely spaced steps. At the N end, there is a C19 addition; single storey and an attic, the catslide dormers provided by *Ian G. Lindsay & Partners*, who raised the roof pitch and opened up depressed arches in the gable (for a garage) and W wall (for a porch). Also in the gable, a couple of windows with roll-moulded surrounds, possibly re-used from the house's W gable when this addition was built.

The interior is unvaulted. There was a kitchen on the ground floor with a N fireplace; first-floor hall. Turnpike stair in the jamb.

A little to the S, a couple of unpretentious FARM BUILD-INGS, probably of the C19. In the E building's W front, a C17 dormer pediment carved with a pair of coats of arms. It may have come from the house's W side, where the roof construction provided for a dormer.

BARWHINNOCK

6050

1km. NW of Twynholm

91   Deliciously smart country house-villa of *c.*1830, built of whin with painted sandstone dressings and rusticated quoins. It is double-pile, both main blocks piend-roofed. Tall single-storey front (S) block of three bays. At each outer bay, a shallowly projecting bow pierced by an overarched Venetian window, its mullions treated as columns. Slightly advanced centre with a very broad Tuscan-columned portico in front of the tripartite anta-pilastered doorpiece. The back block is of the same height but two-storeyed; full-height canted bay at the centre of its N elevation. Across the ends of both the main blocks are placed lower recessed pavilions, each with a bowed end.

The interior is just as classy. In the centre of the front 92   block, a tall entrance hall divided in two by a broad elliptical arch. Starting just S of this arch, the flights of the horseshoe-shaped stair, its cast-iron balustrades decorated with acanthus leaf and eagles' head motifs and with plaques bearing a relief of a boy feeding an eagle (cf. Brooklands). Behind the stair, a bowed wall up to the height of the narrow landing. At the back of the landing, a screen of slender Greek Doric columns *in antis* opens into the corridor which runs the length of the back block's first floor. Over the stair a shallow round cupola.

W of the entrance hall, the dining room, its S end bowed. Cornice with anthemion decoration on the flat; rinceau frieze. Black marble chimneypiece, the ends of its broad panelled pilasters carved with stylized foliage. The drawing room, E of the hall, has both ends bowed. Tuscan-columned chimneypiece of white and veined grey marble, perhaps a touch severe for the room's function. At the back of the entrance hall, an arched doorway into the ground-floor corridor of the back block. On the corridor's N side, three pointed arches into the library; the centre opening is glazed but is likely to have been a door; the one on the r. is now a door but was probably originally a window, like the one on the l., which serves as a fanlight over a bookcase inside the room. The library has a white marble chimneypiece, severe except for foliaged consoles. The N end is a canted bay.

SW of the house, an oval GARDEN, also early C19, its walling of rubble except at the S end, where it is scooped up into a brick topknot. External brick facing at this end, where a glasshouse has stood outside the garden. – Also early C19 the LODGE to the S. Piend-roofed, the broad eaves supported on flat mutules. E porch with a deeply recessed door. Decorative neo-Tudor patterned glazing.

BEATTOCK   *oooo*

Small C19 and C20 one-street village running S from the BRIDGE over the Evan Water (a 1951 replacement for *Thomas Telford*'s bridge of 1819). Formerly on the main road from Dumfries to Edinburgh and Glasgow, it is now by-passed.

KIRKPATRICK-JUXTA PARISH CHURCH, 1.2km. S. Designed and built in 1798–1800 by *John McCracken*, mason in Dumfries, but thoroughly remodelled by *James Barbour*, 1875–7. The general shape (T-plan), the materials (whin rubble and red sandstone dressings), and the rusticated quoins are Georgian, the rest Victorian neo-Romanesque. Barbour provided new windows, including large roses in the E and W gables, heightened the gables (with his quoins dumped awkwardly on top of McCracken's), and added an E vestry, a bowed stair projection in the SW inner angle, a NE porch with chevron decoration and stilted blind arcading, and a slate-spired wooden bellcote.

The interior is all Barbour's. Pulpit in the centre of the long

N wall. Gallery with a boldly bracketed front across the ends of the main block and filling the s 'aisle'; it is carried on thin cast-iron columns which rise through it to support the collars of the open wooden roof.

HEADSTONES. Immediately SW of the church, William and John Reid †1835, aedicular with a scrolled broken pediment, the front carved with a large urn. – Near the graveyard's SE corner, John Imrie †1745, the front displaying an angel above a man holding a crowned hammer (the smiths' emblem) and with a skull beside him. – Just SE of the church, the smart MONUMENT erected in 1753 to William Johnston of Bearholm and formerly attached to a wall. It is an Ionic aedicule, a coat of arms carved on the pediment.

BEATTOCK OUTDOOR CENTRE, 1km. S. Built as a school, c.1875. Single-storey U-plan, of bullnosed red rubble. Mullioned and transomed windows. Tudor-Gothic porch filling the open centre, which is topped by a lead-spired octagonal bellcote.

DESCRIPTION. First on the entry from the N, but hidden behind its garden trees, is BEATTOCK HOUSE, a red sandstone villa of c.1870, the extravagantly carved bargeboards almost enjoyable. On the r. and directly facing the road is the OLD BRIG REST HOME, built as an inn in 1822 by the Commissioners for Highland Roads and Bridges, the estimate and probably the design being provided by *Thomas Telford*. Ponderous classical box, built of whin with painted sandstone dressings. In the centre of the five-bay front, a door framed by recessed Greek Doric columns and a heavy entablature; it is flanked by corniced and aproned ground-floor windows and surmounted by a window of three lights. More three-light windows in the gables' centre bays. The platform of the piended roof has heavy chimneystacks at its ends, each pierced by a roundheaded arch. To the SW, but well below because of the steep fall in the ground, contemporary STABLE OFFICES, with an elliptical-arched opening as their main feature. The village then develops a short street of mid-C19 broad-eaved cottages, mostly built of whin but many now painted or roughcast; good quantity of bargeboarded dormers. At the S end, straightforward HOUSING by the *Dumfriesshire County Architect's Department*, 1966.

ROMAN FORTLET, Milton, 1.6km. SE. The site is a ridge along which ran the Roman road through Annandale. Here lay a complex of forts and marching camps. The only structure now visible (but much reduced by ploughing) is a fortlet which was occupied in the mid-C2.

AUCHENCASS. *See* p. 112.
AUCHEN CASTLE. *See* p. 112.
CRAIGIELANDS. *See* p. 199.
LOCHHOUSE TOWER. *See* p. 408.
LOCHWOOD TOWER. *See* p. 423.

BEESWING 8060

Small village, the houses and cottages mostly C19; some C20 infill.

LOCHEND CHURCH. Built as a Free church in 1867–8; *James Barbour* was the architect. Gothic rectangle, the grey granite masonry set off by dressings of red sandstone. Angle-buttressed NW tower topped by a broached stone spire. – STAINED GLASS E window ('Blessed are the Peacemakers') of *c.*1950.

LOTUS. *See* p. 430.

BENTPATH 3090

Small upland village beside the Esk, the school, library and Telford Monument making a little detached group to the NW.

WESTERKIRK PARISH CHURCH. Gothic, by *James Burnet*, 1880–1. Buttressed snecked rubble rectangle, with hood-moulded lancet windows. At the S end, an angle-buttressed, battlemented and crocket-pinnacled tower.

GRAVEYARD to the E. In it, the JOHNSTONE MAUSOLEUM 51 of 1790, smartest classical by *Robert Adam* (*see* the Introduction, p. 52). It is a droved ashlar Greek cross with very short arms projecting from the domed square centre. At the S front, coupled fluted Greek Doric columns, but with simplified rosettes on their Roman Doric necks, topped by individual friezes decorated with ox skulls; above, a shallow pediment. This centrepiece is flanked by niches. At each of the other sides, an advanced centrepiece with broad piers from which springs a roundheaded overarch framing a niche (a window at the N). More ox skulls on the ends of the N and E sides' centrepieces. (Tunnel-vaulted interior. Along the walls, a Doric frieze, its metopes formerly carved with human skulls.) – Several C17 and C18 HEADSTONES decorated with reminders of death and angels' heads (souls). Two, N of the Mausoleum, are crisply well preserved. One is to the Rev. Hugh Scott †1680, with attached columns topped by outsize ball finials; above, an angel's head. The other commemorates members of the Mein family †1694–1720 (?), again with attached columns; an angel's head in the steep scrolled pediment.

N of the graveyard, THE WHITE HOUSE, built as Westerkirk Parish Manse in 1783 but much extended later, including additions by *R. B. Burnet*, 1910–11. On the front, a shallow bow, probably early C19; to its l., a small pediment truncated by a tall chimney.

BRIDGE. Narrow humpbacked two-span bridge built by *Andrew Coats* and *Robert Paisley* in 1734–7.

MONUMENT TO THOMAS TELFORD, 0.4km. NW. By *Curtis Gray*, 1928. Built of grey Creetown granite. A pair of seats flank a roughly dressed slab bearing a bronze relief portrait by *D. A. Francis*.

WESTERKIRK PARISH LIBRARY, 0.4km. NW. Built in 1860. Small but ecclesiastical-looking, with two-light Gothic windows and a Ruskinian Gothic chimney on the N gable.

WESTERKIRK SCHOOL, 0.4km. NW. Humble school and schoolhouse of the later C19.

WESTERHALL. *See* p. 562.

2070   BIRRENS
              0.9km. SE of Middlebie

The site of a fort on the Roman road up Annandale.

ROMAN FORT. The Roman Blatobulgium, this had the longest history of any Roman site in the region. A fortlet was placed here in the C1 but abandoned after a few years' occupation (*c.* 79–88). Then a fort was constructed in the 120s as an outpost of Hadrian's Wall. The ramparts were of turf but little is known of the buildings inside. This fort was in turn rebuilt *c.* 140 under Antoninus Pius, when the frontier of Roman Britain was moved N to the Antonine Wall (*see* the Introduction, pp. 28–9). The rampart was rebuilt on a stone base. Within lay the usual range of buildings (headquarters, commanding officer's house, granaries, barracks, and store-houses or stables). The barracks were of unusual plan, each consisting of two narrow buildings instead of the more normal wider single block. Inscriptions record the presence here of *cohors I Nervana Germanorum millaria equitata* and *cohors II Tungrorum millaria equitata* at different times in the C2. Both were nominally one-thousand-strong mixed infantry and cavalry regiments, and some of their men were probably outposted to the fortlets of Annandale. The fort was rebuilt in 158 following a fire and seems to have continued in occupation until the late C2.

The fort's earthworks are among the most impressive in Scotland. The earthen rampart, visible on all but the S front, protected an area of a little over 2ha. To the N lie six ditches crossed by the causeway leading out of the N gate. To the W lay a defended annexe (no longer visible); to the S and E were temporary camps (also no longer visible), testimony to the use of Birrens as a staging post for Roman armies on the move.

The inscriptions from Birrens are particularly fine, especially those of the *cohors II Tungrorum*. Most are now in the Museum of Antiquities in Edinburgh but some are in the Dumfries Museum. One altar was dedicated by Raetian tribesmen recruited when part of the regiment was serving in southern Germany between 147 and 153. Two inscriptions, presumably from Birrens, have recently been found re-used at the site of the Anglian monastery at Hoddom.

BLACKET HOUSE

2070

0.9km. E of Eaglesfield

Small Tudor country house by *Walter Newall, c.*1835. At the entrance (N) and garden (S) fronts, a broad projecting gabled bay at the E end. Steep gableted stone dormerheads over the first-floor windows. Low service court to the W.

Beside the house, remains of the L-plan rubble-built BLACKET TOWER, probably of *c.*1600. Only fragments survive of the main block. The crowstep-gabled stair jamb still stands. Chamfered margins to the windows. The top-floor room was converted to a doocot in the C19 and to a study *c.*1950. Extending from the tower's W side, a wall containing a door, its outer lintel carved with the date 1663, the inner with the date 1714, both displaying initials of members of the Bell family.

BLACKWOOD

9080

0.8km. NW of Auldgirth

Small mansion house, the product of development from the C18 to the C20. The earliest part, best seen from the back (N), comprises a three-storey harled house, dated 1750 on an ornamental rainwater head. Triple-pile, the E range a little longer than the others. At the W range's N end, an addition of *c.*1780, bellcast eaves to its pavilion roof. In the gable, a three-light first-floor window; sidelights to the door below. C20 verandah on the end. At the E range's N end, a single-storey billiard room extension of 1908–9.

A neo-Tudor front block was added in 1842, faced with droved red sandstone ashlar. Two storeys over a basement (concealed at the front). Four bays, the l. advanced as a broad gable from which projects a canted bay window of two storeys, its parapet decorated with strapwork; carved rosettes and quatrefoils on the band course between the ground and first floors. Porch in the inner angle, its parapet pierced with round-headed arcading and projected on modillions; anta pilasters at the corners. Hoodmoulds over the mullioned and transomed windows to the r. Over the upper-floor windows, steep triangular gablets with pinnacle finials on top and scrolls at the bottom. Large Tudor chimneystacks. In 1927 *W. F. Crombie* extended this front block W by three further bays, the new work almost a mirror image of the 1842 front but omitting the bay containing the porch. Commendably tactful in intention, but it removes the architectural zest. A cast-iron gargoyle rainwater head marks the join.

The C18 house's S entrance hall (now in the basement) survives. It is covered by a shallow segmental vault with applied ribs. To the E, a tunnel-vaulted room, the top of its round-arched door angled to fit into the line of the springing. At the back, a semicircular stair climbing round a spine wall. More tunnel-vaulting, of plastered brick, over the top-floor rooms. Inserted in the C18 house's SE corner, a stair of 1842. The 1840s rooms retain their C19 cornices but were otherwise remodelled in the 1920s.

STABLE COURT to the E, of whitewashed rubble, probably built in 1778, the date on the weathervane. Long two-storey W range facing the house, its S part's first-floor windows small octagons, its tall door roundheaded. The N part of this range is of the same height but single-storey, its door now built up. In the centre of the range, a tall roundheaded pend above which rises a pyramid-roofed tower, its second-floor windows octagonal, its top stage a DOOCOT. The doocot's interior is circular; sandstone-slabbed nesting boxes, the pine potence still in place. In the stables in the range's S part, brick partitions and tunnel-vaults over the stalls. More tunnel-vaulting at the floor above.

GARDEN N of the house, probably late C18, its wall of rubble except at the NE corner, where it is of brick. – N of this, remains of an OUTER WALL, also of rubble. In a rounded bastion at its NE corner, a square, rubble-built, battlemented and slit-windowed GARDEN HOUSE. It looks early C19.

At the end of the drive, an early C19 piend-roofed LODGE, white-painted with black trimmings. Busy rustication at the corners and openings. Octagonal first-floor front window. In each gable, a Venetian window; the arched top of its centre light is blind.

BLADNOCH

4050

Small village on the N bank of the River Bladnoch, the distillery at its W end, the creamery across the river.

BRIDGE. By *D. & T. Stevenson*, 1866. Gentle humpback of two segmental arches with low pointed cutwaters.

CREAMERY. Now disused. Utilitarian in red brick; opened in 1899 and much extended in 1907.

DISTILLERY. Now disused. Founded in 1814, but the buildings are mostly of 1878, with some C20 intrusions. Industrial Georgian-survival rubble ranges, those to the front single-storey, the rear blocks of two or three storeys. Pagoda ventilator on the kiln.

DESCRIPTION. The single street is one-sided. At the E end, single-storey mid-C19 cottages, their rubble walls often painted or rendered. A large club skewputt on No. 3. No. 18 rises to a second storey. The very low Nos. 23–24, formerly thatched, may be late C18. Then several two-storey houses, No. 31 with club skewputts. Behind No. 28, a mid-C19 former MILL, of painted brick with segmental-arched windows. The ashlar-fronted No. 33 near the W end is grander: Georgian-survival of *c.* 1840, with a channelled ground floor and Roman Doric piers at the doorpiece. Piended platform roof and octagonal chimneys.

BALDOON MAINS, 0.7km. SE. Large rubble-built STEADING of the 1840s. On its N side, remains of one rubble wall, probably C17, surviving from BALDOON CASTLE. To its N, a pair of mid- or late C17 GATEPIERS, their ashlar masonry decorated with carved latticework and crossed by bands of rock-faced rustication. Each is topped by a triangular finial with a scrolled inner face, the combination of the two finials giving the appearance of a broken pediment. They now mark the back drive to the single-storey and attic FARMHOUSE, built in 1842, its front originally of three bays with a Roman Doric portico but extended a little later to five bays and given cottagey stone dormers.

BONSHAW TOWER

2070

0.7km. SE of Kirtlebridge

A C16 tower house tenuously attached to a Georgian laird's house, sited close to the bank of the Kirtle Water. The TOWER HOUSE, built for the Irvings of Bonshaw c. 1565, is a plain rubble-walled rectangle. Uncrenellated parapet projected on a stringcourse surmounted by a row of moulded corbels. Between the corbels, roughly in the centre of the S, W and N sides and near the N end of the E front (over the entrance), are machicolation holes. Cannon spouts drain the wall-walk running all round the crow-step-gabled attic, whose S end is crowned with a chimney, its N with a bellcote. The roof's pitch has been lowered, probably in 1841, and its stone flags replaced by slates. In each face of the ground floor, a broad rectangular gunloop. Moulded slit windows to the stair in the NE corner. The first-floor windows, their mullions probably of 1841, are also moulded, the second-floor windows plain.

The tower house's entrance is hidden inside the flat-roofed and parapeted porch-passage of 1896 which joins the tower to the Georgian block. Over the moulded C16 door, the inscription 'SOLI.DEO.HONOR.ET.GLORIA'. Vestigial cornice and a small empty panel frame above. Gunloop to the r. Inside the door, a small vestibule in the thickness of the E wall, the stair entrance to its r., the door to the ground floor straight ahead. Hanging from the vestibule ceiling, a stone pendant, its boss carved with the IHS monogram. The ground-floor room is a tunnel-vaulted store, lit by gunloops and a small window high in the S gable. Stone slabbed floor incorporating a drain discharging outside at the S end of the W wall. In the wall thickness of the SW corner, a prison entered through a small door. It is windowless but has a ventilation hole in the vault.

The stair, mainly contained in the wall thickness at the NE corner but nudging into the room on each floor, is a comfortable turnpike. Just above the hall level, its N wall is pierced by a slop drain. In the first-floor hall, segmental-arched embrasures to the side windows, each with a cupboard in one ingo. Slit window in the N gable. At the S gable's W end, a square high-set window with steps up to it and provided with stone seats. It is placed beside the large but simply moulded and corniced fireplace. In the E wall, a large aumbry, its head a moulded ogee arch. Also in this wall, a corbel, presumably to support a joist of the floor above but redundant since that floor was replaced, perhaps in 1841. The second floor also seems always to have contained a single room. Small windows with deep sills, the embrasures segmental-arched. Small aumbries, unchecked for doors, in the E and W walls. Off-centre S fireplace, a small version of the one in the hall below but apparently an insertion,* probably of 1896, although there must have been a fireplace originally. In the NW corner's wall thickness, a well-appointed garderobe with a stone lavatory pedestal and a small window. The attic is lit by a small window high in the S gable.

The adjoining LAIRD'S HOUSE on the NE, detached until 1896, is a piend-roofed two-storey L-plan, built of coursed rubble. Three-bay S front, the pediment of its Roman Doric aediculed doorpiece inscribed with the date 1770 (presumably the year of the house's completion) and the names of W. Irvine and J. Douglas. Projecting from the W gable, a full-height bow, perhaps of 1770 though it may belong to the additions built in 1841 by *Peter Smith*, mason, and *James Scott*, joiner. Plain NW wing. Lower crowstepped extension on its N, probably of 1841; the crown glass in the windows suggests it cannot be much later. On the wing's E side, a lean-to Victorian addition.

The rooms inside the Georgian house have cornices and shutters of 1841. In the later C20 they were provided with imported chimneypieces of late C18 character but probably of late C19 or early C20 date. In the kitchen, a white marble chimneypiece carved with Empire garlands; it was moved here from the drawing room and is clearly the one supplied in 1841 by *John Kirkbride*, sculptor in Carlisle, at a cost of £12.

BORELAND

1090

Small and architecturally undistinguished village.

HUTTON AND CORRIE PARISH CHURCH. Harled kirk of 1710, the N 'aisle' added in 1764. Basket-arched windows with projecting imposts and keystones, perhaps all dating from 1799–1800, when new windows were inserted in the N wall. The two plain S windows flanking the pulpit may belong to the alterations of 1871, when *Alexander Crombie* added the E and N porches. Small W vestry of 1858. On the 'aisle', a red sandstone bellcote with an obelisk finial, presumably erected to satisfy the Presbytery's order of 1820 that a bellcote be provided.

Propped against the church's S wall, two GRAVESLABS dated 1681 and 1682, each decorated with a skull and crossbones. – Just to their S, the aedicular HEADSTONE of Peter (?) Graham

---

* No fireplace is shown in the plan of Bonshaw Tower published in David Mac-Gibbon and Thomas Ross, *The Castellated and Domestic Architecture of Scotland*, iii (1889), 400–1, and the present fireplace is backed by a blocked window.

†1755, its weathered front carved with the figure of a man, a skeleton and a crown; in the open pediment, an angel's head (the soul).

HEWK, 3.4km. SW. Small laird's house built in 1806. Two-storey piend-roofed main block of three bays. Central door recessed behind a distyle *in antis* Roman Doric screen. Tall ground-floor windows, the sills apparently lowered, perhaps in an early alteration. Lower back wing extended in the later C19.

BORGUE 6040

Small village, mostly of C19 cottages but with a broad-eaved late C19 Georgian-survival HOTEL.

FREE CHURCH. Secularized. Buttressed rubble-built box of 1843, its design a standard one produced for the Free Church of Scotland by *Cousin & Gall*, not especially ecclesiastical in appearance.

PARISH CHURCH. Begun by *Walter Newall*, 1814, as a rubble-walled cruciform, the E limb provided by a tower. This is of three slightly intaken stages, the hoodmoulded lancet openings paired at the second stage; battlement with pinnacled corners. The tower's E ground-floor window of two lights dates from alterations of 1897–8. At the same time the present lights were inserted in the church's original Tudor-arched and hood-moulded windows, the W 'aisle' was almost doubled in length, a porch was added to the main block's S end and a battlemented vestry to its N, all this new work executed in a Scots late medieval manner. Interior of the 1890s.

In the churchyard, the late C19 Gothic MAUSOLEUM of the Gordons of Earlston, backing against their ball-finialled late C18 BURIAL ENCLOSURE.

SCHOOL. Begun in 1803, but its present appearance dates substantially from major alterations by *James Barbour & Bowie*, 1911. – In the W boundary wall, a MONUMENT of 1900 to the poet William Nicholson, a block of Dalbeattie granite framing a bronze relief bust (after a portrait by *John Faed*) by *A. Macfarlane Shannon*.

BORGUE HOUSE, 0.3km. E. Broad-eaved Italianate-classical mid-C19 laird's house. To the N, the roofless BORGUE OLD HOUSE, its present form later C17 but probably incorporating an earlier building. Rubble-built Y-plan of two storeys and an attic, with two wings projecting S from the main block and a third, probably originally containing the stair, to the N. Moulded skewputts. Roll-moulded off-centre S door and flanking windows, but some other openings are chamfered. Large off-centre wallhead chimney on the main block's S front. Inside, there have been three rooms on each of the main block's two principal floors and one room in each wing. The ground floor's centre room has a chimneypiece with a deep stone lintel carried on a heavy corbel at each end; it can hardly be later than the beginning of the C17. Low S addition, perhaps C18, to the SW wing. – Big GARDEN, partly enclosed by rubble walls, probably late C18, to the E.

MOTTE, Boreland, 3.7km. NE. Made, probably in the late C12, by the artificial heightening of a rocky hillock to form a 6.5m.-high oval mound (its summit c. 36m. by 25m.) surrounded by a 12m.-wide ditch and counterscarp. Another rock outcrop to the SE may have been used as a bailey.

BROCKLEHIRST
1.9km. NW of Mouswald

0070

Big mid-C19 villa, mixing an Italianate tower and porch into a collection of cottagey gables dressed up with carved barge-boards. – Contemporary broad-eaved LODGE. At the gables, carved bargeboards; plain bargeboards on the inner angle's porch.

BROOKLANDS
3.7km. NE of Kirkpatrick Durham

8070

Two-storey piend-roofed villa of c. 1830, altered and doubled in size to the rear c. 1900. The original house is rubble-built with rusticated quoins. Entrance (S) front of three bays. At the slightly advanced centre, a boldly projecting porch fronted by a portico of two fluted Doric columns. The flanking ground-floor windows are now each of three lights, probably enlarged c. 1900. The back addition is tactful but dull, a full-height canted bay window on its E side. Inside, a cantilevered stair, its delicately foliaged cast-iron balusters decorated with low-relief plaques, each of a boy feeding an eagle (cf. Barwhinnock, q.v.). The drawing room and dining room retain some early C19 woodwork, but their friezes (a procession of *putti*, and cornucopia among foliage) and chimneypieces look like work of c. 1900.

Early C19 GARDEN to the NE, its rubble walls partly lined with brick. – LODGE at the SE entrance to the drive, again of c. 1830; the design is a simplified version of the 'Gothic Cottage' illustrated in J. B. Papworth's *Rural Residences* (1818; second edition, 1832). Square three-storey piend-roofed tower with gabled and crocket-pinnacled diagonal buttresses. On three faces of the top floor, blind crosslet 'arrowslits'. – Across the road, a crudely battlemented rubble SCREEN WALL, again of c. 1830. In its high centrepiece, tall 'arrowslits' and a (blocked) round-arched entrance.

BRYDEKIRK

1070

Planned village laid out as a gridiron in 1800 by Colonel Dirom of Mount Annan. Little more than the main street (Bridge Street) was developed according to his plan.

PARISH CHURCH. Built as a chapel of ease in 1835. Crowstep-gabled box (now roughcast), with broad lancet windows. E tower topped by merlons and corner pinnacles. The interior was recast and refurnished c. 1900, with an open roof, an apse formed in the tower, and a W gallery. – STAINED GLASS. In the apse, one brightly coloured light ('Suffer the Little Children') by *William Wilson*, 1962. – Circular W window ('Worship the Lord in the Beauty of Holiness') also of the later C20.

LUCE CHURCHYARD, 1.8km. N. Graveyard of a medieval parish united to Hoddom and Ecclefechan in 1609. A few C18 HEAD-STONES, two (of 1751 and 1785) decorated with emblems of death. – MAUSOLEUM of the Irvings of Luce. Corniced D-plan of rough ashlar. At the straight entrance (W) front, a flat-topped pediment containing a coat of arms and said* to have borne the date 1700, probably that of the mausoleum's erection.

BRIDGE, Bridge Street. Built by *Thomas Boyd* and *William Stewart*, 1798–1800. Humpbacked ashlar bridge of three segmental arches with triangular cutwaters.

SABBATH SCHOOL, Bridge Street. By *Johnstone* of Annan, 1891. Small Gothic hall, built of red sandstone ashlar.

DESCRIPTION. BRIDGE STREET, running downhill from the Parish Church to the bridge over the Annan, is lined with rows of single-storey cottages, some early C19 but altered, others C20. On the S side, next to the bridge, the two-storey harled BRIG INN of 1812.

CLEUGHHEAD, 0.8km. E. Single-storey red sandstone villa of c. 1840. The S front and the S end of the long E elevation form a piend-roofed square of three bays by three. At each elevation, an advanced and pedimented centrepiece, containing the entrance on the E, a canted bay window on the S. In the outer bays, aproned and wooden-mullioned shallowly projecting rectangular bay windows with horizontal glazing. Piend-roofed N wing of two long bays, its windows of the same type. Plain office court at the back. – Contemporary LODGE in the same manner at the entrance to the drive.

HODDOM CASTLE. *See* p. 342.
REPENTANCE TOWER. *See* p. 498.

BUITTLE   *8050*

Just the Parish Church, its medieval predecessor, and the former manse standing on a low hill.

PARISH CHURCH. Harled and buttressed Perp box, by *Walter Newall*, 1817–19. Hoodmoulded three-light windows. Spiky pinnacles on the corners. At the N end, a tower with diagonally set buttresses, their pinnacled tops rising above the battlement. Low S chancel added in 1902 by *James Barbour*; three stepped

---

* By George Irving, 'Parish of Luce (Hoddom)', *Transactions of the Dumfriesshire and Galloway Natural History and Antiquarian Society*, n.s., xvii (1900–5), 8.

lancets in the gable. Inside, over the body, a flat plaster ceiling of 1819 with very simple Jacobean panelled enrichment. Braced collar roof in the chancel. – FURNISHINGS of 1902. – STAINED GLASS. Three-light S window (the Horsemen of the Apocalypse, flanked by the Way of the Cross and the Annunciation), brightly coloured but disciplined, by *Douglas Strachan*, 1920.

7   In the churchyard, to the S, the roofless OLD PARISH CHURCH, substantially medieval but altered after the Reformation. Rubble-built nave and chancel, clearly of two builds, the narrower and lower nave apparently the earlier and perhaps dating from the C12. The chancel, its axis slightly N of the nave's, might be C13. In the nave's N wall, two small round-arched windows (now blocked), probably original. In its S wall, the blocked rectangular doorway at the E end and the window at the W must be post-Reformation insertions, perhaps of the C17. The basket-arched window beside the door also looks an insertion and may be C16. The W gable was rebuilt in 1743–5. On its apex, a sturdy gabled bellcote. Round-arched door and window above aligned with the chancel and so off-centre in the gable. At the W end of the chancel's N wall, a narrow pointed door, apparently medieval. So too seems to be the window to its E, round-arched with chamfered margins, a broad internal splay and semicircular rear-arch. In the chancel gable, three narrow and barely pointed lancet lights, all with segmental rear-arches, the tall centre light truncated by a rectangular door of 1743–5. The chancel's thinner S wall is, at least in part, a 1740s rebuild. Round-arched window opposite the one in the N wall, again with an internal splay and semicircular rear-arch but placed lower. Is this end of the wall medieval or has the window been re-used? Near the wall's W end and facing the N door, a round-arched door with chamfered margins just like that in the W gable and clearly also of 1743–5. Contemporary rectangular window to its W. Inside, a pointed chancel arch on attached shafts of pointed section with simply moulded caps and bases; it must date from the building of the chancel.

On the S wall of the Old Parish Church nave, the corniced top of a MONUMENT, perhaps of the C17. – Immediately W of this church, HEADSTONE to Mary Coupland †1791, a head carved in the tympanum of its curvy pediment. – To its S, an early C18 HEADSTONE decorated with a skull and crossbones, hourglass and angel's head (the soul) framed by lumpy vines. – S of the medieval chancel, GRAVESLAB of 1752 to Margaret Blackley, with a deeply cut coat of arms. – Between the old and new parish churches, MONUMENT to David Milligan †1798, a heavy pedestal carrying a very shallow pyramid roof instead of the expected obelisk; on its E face, relief of a ship.

MANSE (now KIRKSYDE) to the NW, built and perhaps designed by *John Nielson* in 1793–5. Two storeys, of white-painted rubble. Three-bay front, the r. window on the first floor a Venetian. The two-light l. window and gabled porch date from *James Barbour*'s alterations of 1894.

BUITTLE CASTLE AND OLD BUITTLE TOWER 8060
1.5km. W of Dalbeattie

An unpretentious tower house built on the S E corner of the bailey of a major medieval castle. Buittle, on the W bank of the River Urr, was the principal seat of the lords of Galloway at least from the C12, when a large motte-and-bailey castle (*c.* 2.2 hectares in area) was erected there, the river's natural defence supplemented by ditches and earthen ramparts. After the defeat of John Balliol, lord of Galloway and King of Scots, at the Battle of Dunbar in 1296, Edward I granted custody of the castle in quick succession to Henry de Percy, John de Hodelston and Sir John St John, the last gaining possession of the castle and lands in 1298. It was probably Sir John or his son who built a new stone-walled castle on the motte.

The castle seems to have been taken and partly dismantled by 'Patriot' forces *c.* 1310; fifteen years later, Robert I granted the lands of Buittle to his nephew, Sir James Douglas. However, the castle, presumably repaired, was back in Balliol hands by the mid-C14, Edward Balliol sealing two charters there in 1352. The next year David II granted the lands to Sir William Douglas (later first Earl of Douglas), in whose family they remained until the forfeiture of the Douglas earldom in 1455; by this time the castle may have been largely ruinous.

In the later C15 and C16 the feudal superiority of Buittle changed hands several times between the lords Maxwell and the Douglas earls of Morton, but the site of the castle itself seems to have been acquired before 1593 by the Gordons of Lochinvar. They were probably largely responsible for the construction of the present tower house.

BUITTLE CASTLE itself, built *c.* 1300 on the earlier motte, was roughly rectangular in shape (*c.* 45m. by 30m.), with round towers at the corners and, on the N W side, a gatehouse flanked by drum towers, each *c.* 8.2m. in diameter. There survive extensive but now overgrown and largely shapeless ruins of buildings which have been constructed of mortared rubble. The only architectural feature clearly visible is the precariously standing entrance arch of the gatehouse.

The tower house (OLD BUITTLE TOWER) on the edge of the bailey is L-plan, built of limewashed rubble, and clearly constructed in two stages. The first (perhaps of soon after 1535, when a charter to Robert, Lord Maxwell, included the condition that a mansion be built) seems to have comprised a rectangular two-storey block, the self-contained ground floor lit by slit windows in the N, E and S walls and perhaps entered by a door in the N wall's E end or possibly in the W gable, although the present door there is C18. The first-floor entrance (now blocked) was on the N side, originally reached by a ladder or forestair. This house was heightened to three storeys and an attic and given a rectangular NE jamb, probably in the 1590s, the work presumably carried out for Sir John Gordon of Loch-

invar's third son, John, who styled himself 'of Buittle'. At the
NW and SE corners were round turrets; only the lower courses
of their continuous corbelling now survive. In the inner angle
with the jamb, a bowed stair turret projected from the first
floor on continuous corbelling. Elliptical-arched entrance to
the jamb, perhaps C18 in its present form. Above the entrance,
a couple of windows (one decently sized, the other small),
both with roll-and-hollow mouldings. The other windows were
enlarged in the mid-C19, when the building, having stood
roofless since the later C18, was remodelled as a farmhouse,
losing its angle turrets but acquiring a new roof and new first-
floor S entrance approached by a stone forestair.

Inside, a rubble tunnel-vault over the main block's ground
floor; its door from the jamb looks late rather than early C16.
In the jamb was a stair to the first floor, removed probably in
the C19 but replaced with a wooden stair c.1990. At the first
floor, a W fireplace; the stone surround is of c.1990. To its N,
a small triangular-topped aumbry, its mouldings hacked off.
On the second floor, two rooms, each with a fireplace, the W
with a small aumbry. More living accommodation on the upper
floors of the jamb.

N of the tower house, three rubble-built single-storey ranges
forming a courtyard STEADING. They are probably early C19,
parts dating from work recorded here in 1819 and 1836. – N of
this court, an open-sided HAYSHED of c.1900, its corrugated-
iron roof carried on wooden posts. It is now a rare survival.

BURNFOOT HALL

2070

1.3km. E of Ecclefechan

Two-storey Tudor manor of c.1835, built of red sandstone ashlar.
Entrance (S) front of five bays, the two ends with broad spike-
finialled gables. Narrower gables at the intermediate bays flanking the centrepiece. This is castellated Gothic, apparently of
c.1820 and probably part of an earlier house on the site. Relaxed
W elevation with gables and gableted dormerheads, the broad
centre projecting and with a canted bay window. At the NW
corner, a square tower covered with a fishscale-slated pyramid
roof. Set-back and lower NE service wing.

BURNHEAD

8090

Tiny village.

PENPONT FREE CHURCH, Virginhall, 0.3km. E. Secularized.
Built in 1843–4 by *John Jardine*, *Messrs MacLauchlan*, masons,
and *Samuel Bell*, joiner. Tall box of painted coursed rubble, the
S wall's W end canted so as not to encroach on land belonging
to the Duke of Buccleuch, who had refused a site. Roundheaded
windows, the sill of the short window over the N porch inscribed
'For Christ's Crown'. On the W gable, a metal birdcage bellcote

with fluted columns and a steep ogee roof. w vestry and porch, probably additions dating from the remodelling of 1886.

MANSE on the other side of the road. Built in 1847, a Tudor L-plan with hoodmoulds and gablets.

RELIEF CHURCH. Disused. Painted rubble box of 1839, with big round-arched windows. The gables are missing their finials.

CROSS SHAFT, 0.7km. E. Standing in a field, the shaft (missing its arms and top) of a cross of generally Anglian type but also displaying apparent Celtic influence; it may be late C9. The surviving stubs of the arms have double concave curves, an Anglian detail, but at the centre of the head is a 'marigold' motif of Celtic type. On both fronts of the shafts, weathered carved decoration, mainly of affronted animals and interlaced work.

NITH BRIDGE, 0.9km. E. Built by *William Stewart*, 1777–8. Humpbacked ashlar bridge of two segmental arches, the pointed cutwaters forming pedestrian refuges at the parapet.

DESCRIPTION. The village is a mixture of white-painted rubble-built cottages, perhaps of the earlier C19, and politer and slightly later Tudor estate cottages with gabled porches and gableted dormerheads. The late Victorian HILLHEAD is bigger, with a canted bay window corbelled out to the square.

GROVEHILL HOUSE, 0.2km. S. Double-pile house of two periods and characters. The earlier part is the s block of *c*. 1800, originally a plain two-storey farmhouse, its canted bay windows added in the late C19. The piend-roofed N block of *c*. 1830 is a smart villa of three bays; the slightly advanced centre has a bullseye-windowed pediment carried on paired but widely spaced pilasters, the door now converted to a window. The outer bays have round-arched windows, their delicate decorative glazing intact. Another round-arched window in the bowed E end. – To the NW, an early C19 ashlar-fronted LODGE with hoodmoulded windows and diagonally set chimneys.

BURNSWARK HILL 1070

3km. N of Ecclefechan

Prominent hill with a complex history of occupation and fortification from the Bronze Age until its use as a trig point during the survey of southern Scotland in 1847.

HILLFORT AND ROMAN CAMPS. The earliest surviving monu- 4 ment is a Bronze Age round CAIRN of perhaps *c*. 1000 B.C. It stands within the now severely denuded ramparts of a HILLFORT constructed in the C6 or C5 B.C. *See* the Introduction, pp. 24–5. Also on top of the hill are the earthworks of a GUN EMPLACEMENT dating from the Civil War period of the mid-C17.

The hill is flanked by two ROMAN CAMPS. The N rampart of the N camp has been damaged but otherwise its defences survive, including two entrances in the s rampart. The s camp overlies a Roman fortlet of the mid-C2 and so probably dates from later in that century. Excavation in the S camp has produced evidence of semi-permanent occupation. In front of each of its three entrances are large mounds, probably the bases for stone-firing catapults aimed at the long-disused gates of the hillfort, where excavation has demonstrated that targets were laid. The distinctive type of lead sling shot discovered here has been found as far afield as Housesteads and Ambleside. Burnswark may have been one of the training grounds of the Roman army of North Britain.

To the E and W of the hill lie two Iron Age SETTLEMENTS. Earlier archaeologists suggested that these formed part of a circumvallation, but they are now seen as independent settlements.

0060

CAERLAVEROCK CASTLE
2.9km. S of Bankend

Powerful symbol of feudal strength enclosing some of the most ambitious early classical domestic architecture in Scotland. The position on the Solway plain and beside the mouth of the Nith is of clear strategic importance and the Romans constructed a camp beside an Iron Age fort on the hill of Ward Law behind the present castle (*see* the Introduction, p. 30). The first recorded mention of the lands of Caerlaverock was made *c.* 1160, when they were rented by the monks of Holme Cultram Abbey (Cumberland) from Ralph, son of Dunegal, lord of Nithsdale. Perhaps after being escheated to the Crown, they were acquired in the early C13 by John Maxwell (de Maccuswell), who was Chamberlain of Scotland *c.* 1231–3. It seems likely that Maxwell then built a stone-walled castle of enclosure ('Old Caerlaverock') 0.2km. SE of the present castle, its foundation resting on clay reinforced by wooden piles; the outline of this building is still marked by grassy mounds.

Perhaps because of this castle's relatively weak foundation John Maxwell's brother and heir, Aymer Maxwell, himself Chamberlain of Scotland *c.* 1258–60 and Justiciar of Galloway in 1264, abandoned it, perhaps still incomplete, and began the present castle, which is built on an outcrop of rock. Work seems to have been completed in the 1270s (a date provided by dendrochronological examination of wood used in the sole of the castle's first drawbridge) and certainly by 1299, when it was reported that the garrison of 'a castle called Caerlaverock' had done great damage to Lochmaben Castle, then held by the English. The next year Edward I himself commanded a successful siege of Caerlaverock, after which the castle was occupied by a pro-English force until 1312, when its constable, Sir Eustace Maxwell, Aymer Maxwell's great-grandson, changed sides and declared his support for Robert Bruce. In accordance with Bruce's usual policy of dismantling strongholds in case they should fall into the hands of his enemies and be garrisoned by them, the castle's defences were then slighted. Maxwell received in recompense '*pro fractione et pro prostratione castri de Carlaverok ad terram*' ('for the destruction and levelling to the ground of the castle of Caerlaverock') a remission of almost half the annual dues he owed to the Crown. Despite this slighting, the castle was again habitable by 1337, Sir Eustace Maxwell having in the meantime switched his allegiance from Bruce's son David II to Edward Balliol. However, in 1355 or 1356 Roger Kirkpatrick of Closeburn forced the whole of Nithsdale into submission to David II. Caerlaverock was again captured and again reportedly levelled to the ground.

With the virtual ending of the Wars of Independence in the late C14, the Maxwells regained both their allegiance to the descendants of Robert Bruce and possession of Caerlaverock. Between his succession in 1373 and his death in 1410, Sir Robert Maxwell is said to have built a new castle there, but it incorporated masonry of the mid- or late C13 castle on the site. Further work, almost certainly a remodelling and extension of the gatehouse, was carried out between 1454 and 1478 by Robert, second Lord Maxwell, who is said to have 'completed the bartizan of Carlaverock'. A new range was built along the courtyard's w side *c.*1500, and was joined to the gatehouse soon after by a stair constructed in the gap between the two blocks.

During the unrest which followed the Reformation and the forced abdication of Mary, Queen of Scots, the Maxwells were adherents of the Queen. In 1570 the Earl of Sussex, leading an English army into Scotland in support of the Protestant party, besieged and took Caerlaverock, which he was reported to have subsequently 'altogether overthrown' and 'demoleist and destroyit with gunpowder', probably blowing up the E tower of the gatehouse. Repair was under way by 1593, when John, eighth Lord Maxwell, was employing two hundred workmen on 'fortifyeinge at Carlaverock'; the work apparently included the reconstruction of the damaged gatehouse tower as an artillery fortification. This may have been intended as a defence against the Johnstones of Annandale, with whom the Maxwells were conducting a feud which led to the forfeiture and execution of John, ninth Lord Maxwell, in 1613 after his murder of the laird of Johnstone.

The Maxwells' fortunes revived after 1619, when Robert, tenth Lord Maxwell, married a first cousin of the King's favourite, the Duke of Buckingham. The next year Maxwell was created Earl of Nithsdale and in 1621 he received a new royal charter of the lands of Caerlaverock. Perhaps to celebrate his new position, and conceivably in the hope of entertaining Charles I on his intended progress to Scotland after his accession to the throne, the first Earl of Nithsdale built new ranges along the E and s sides of the courtyard, the work probably largely complete by 1634. Six years later the Maxwells' Catholicism turned to their disadvantage, Caerlaverock suffering a thirteen-week siege by the Covenanting army. After the castle's eventual surrender it was stripped of its furnishings and partly demolished. Never thereafter occupied, it was taken into government guardianship in 1948.

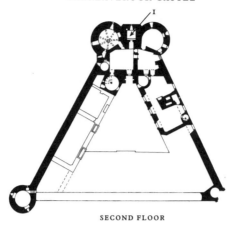

SECOND FLOOR

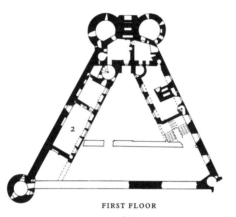

FIRST FLOOR

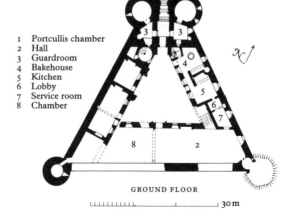

1 Portcullis chamber
2 Hall
3 Guardroom
4 Bakehouse
5 Kitchen
6 Lobby
7 Service room
8 Chamber

GROUND FLOOR

|⊔⊔⊔⊔⊔⊔⊔⊔⊔⊔⊔_____⌐ 30 m

Caerlaverock Castle. Plans

The SITE is a triangular outcrop of rock poking up through low-lying and boggy land, with Lochar Moss to the E, the Solway to the S and the Nith to the W precluding a landward approach from three quarters. The rock platform itself is defended by a moat and outer bank encircled by a second moat (now dry). N of these defences was the castle's outer ward, a rough rectangle enclosed by a low bank. At its NE corner, a rubble-built segmental-arched GATEWAY, perhaps of the late C16.

The castle's general appearance accords closely with its 61 description in a Norman-French poem (*La siege de Carlaverok*) by Walter of Exeter, who had been present at Edward I's siege in 1300:

> Its shape was like that of a shield, for it had only three sides all round, with a tower on each angle; but one of them was a double one, so high, so long, and so large, that under it was the gate with a drawbridge, well made and strong, and a sufficiency of other defences. It had good walls, and good ditches filled to the edge with water . . .

So it is a triangular castle of enclosure with round towers at the two S corners and a double-towered gatehouse at the N. The general concept, except for the triangular plan (probably dictated by the site), is similar to that of other late C13 Scottish castles such as Bothwell (Lanarkshire) or Kildrummy (Aberdeenshire), although at Caerlaverock the lord's living quarters were in the gatehouse, as at Tantallon (Lothian), and not in a donjon tower. *See* also the Introduction, p. 58.

The CURTAIN WALLS are evidence of the castle's long and complex history of construction, destruction and reconstruction. The lowest courses of the southern 29.16m. stretch of the 34.7m.-long W curtain are mid- or later C13, built of tight-jointed ashlar and having a plinth with a chamfered top and splayed base, all this usually below the water-level of the moat. Above this plinth is a second, its upper course steeply chamfered, which runs the full length of the curtain. Vertical walling below its N end suggests that this part of the wall had been demolished in one of the C14 dismantlings of the castle's defences. For a height of *c*. 1.2m. above this second plinth is ashlar masonry of rather coarser character than that of the mid-C13 work; this masonry and the plinth presumably date from Sir Robert Maxwell's reconstruction in the late C14. Probably contemporary are the similar masonry and widely splayed base at the bottom of the E curtain. The upper part of the W curtain wall and the very fragmentary S curtain (partly rebuilt in the C20) are of coursed rubble, the W curtain's coursing distinctly wavy. Clearly they belong to a third building phase, perhaps of *c*. 1400.* Near the W curtain's S end, a garderobe projected out on two heavy corbels. Slewed across the curtain's inner angle with the SW tower, a projection containing a passage. The upper part of the E curtain's northern two-thirds and the whole

---

* In this masonry, at the W curtain, is a blocked window which must pre-date the W courtyard range behind, to which it is quite unrelated.

of its southern third are early C17, rebuilt as the outer wall of the first Earl of Nithsdale's new E range. In this curtain wall, small horizontal ground-floor windows, the two at the N inserted in late C14 masonry and with a larger blocked window between them. Comfortably sized but plain windows at the two upper floors. Only the cornice, with its vertical bands of continuous corbelling, hints at the pretension of this range's courtyard front.

Of the castle's SOUTH-EAST TOWER only the lowest courses survive, probably work of the late C14. The ashlar-walled SOUTH-WEST TOWER is almost intact, the lowest masonry courses late C13, the less tightly jointed work above late C14. Small square windows at the three lower floors. Two of them, an (enlarged) SW-facing first-floor window and a S-facing second-floor window, have fishtail-ended arrowslits below them, both now built up and the upper one mutilated. Taller windows at the third floor. This may be an addition of the late C15, as must be its crowning machicolation.

63 The N GATEHOUSE is a formidable expression of baronial power but the building history is far from straightforward. The general concept of a U-plan building, with the projecting wings formed by round towers flanking the main block's central entrance, itself covered by the drawbridge when raised, corresponds to Walter of Exeter's description and must be mid-C13. Physical work of that date is most evident at the W tower whose battered base and lower two-thirds, perhaps the height of the original tower below its parapet, are built of tight-jointed ashlar like that of the lowest courses of most of the W curtain. The tower's top third, built of larger ashlar blocks, probably dates from the castle's late C14 reconstruction, as does the splayed side of the gatehouse's main block, which continues the line of the curtain but is higher. Late C15 machicolation on this wall and round the tower. At the first and second floors, comfortably sized W-facing windows, probably also late C15. Almost certainly of the late C15 is the N-facing horizontal gunloop with a broad chamfered margin; it has been inserted across the base of a mid-C13 slit window whose upper part has been utilized as an aiming sight. Cutting across the inner angle with the W side of the main block, a two-storey garderobe projection which serves the first and second floors; it looks late C14.

The gatehouse's balancing E tower is not an exact replica. The diameter is fractionally less (by about 0.35m.), its walling thinner by about the same amount, and its base has a more pronounced batter and rises a little higher. All this may be explained by the nature of the site but the masonry suggests that it is of three dates. A fragment of mid-C13 work on the tower's W side is visible inside the gatehouse, but much of its SW segment seems to date from the late C14. The ending of this work is marked externally by vertical joints near the N and S inner angles. Low down in the S inner angle, a slit window of the C14, or conceivably of the C13, with a gunloop (probably late C15*) inserted in its base. Higher up, quite large first- and second-floor windows adjoined by shotholes, all likely to be of 1593 or perhaps of the 1630s. The tower's NE semicircle between the vertical joints, its stone less red than the rest, seems to belong to a third building period. Was this the second phase of a two-stage reconstruction in the late C14, or a major repair of 1593 after the damage done by the Earl of Sussex twenty-three years before? There is no sign of arrowslits or slit windows, as might be expected if this were work of the late C14. Instead, facing N and W, are long horizontal gunloops, apparently contemporary with the walling and not insertions. They lack the chamfered margin of the W tower's gunloop and seem likely to be late C16. The chances must be that this part of the tower dates from a reconstruction (the 'fortifyeinge') of 1593. If so, the machicolation on top, which continues that of the front of the gatehouse's main block and E side, must either be re-used C15 work or a replica of it.

The gatehouse's front centrepiece is mostly of the late C15, covering the earlier work behind. Entrance set back between a pair of massive buttresses, their outer sides splayed, which project almost as far as the towers. Above the first floor the buttresses are linked by a narrow segmental arch supporting the front wall of a splay-sided portcullis chamber. Above that, the front wall is carried across from tower to tower and crowned by machicolation at the same height as that of the towers. Set back behind the parapet walk, remains of a two-storey caphouse with angle rounds; it is likely to be of the 1590s. The main entrance is through a pointed arch. In its soffit, a slot for a portcullis. Above the arch, a large weathered panel, its centre carved with a holly bush behind a stag couchant (the Maxwell crest), supporting a shield charged with the Maxwell saltire. Border of wreathed oak leaves. At each corner, an heraldic escutcheon charged with a coat of arms (the royal arms of Scotland, the double-headed eagle used by the Maxwells after 1581, the arms of Stewart of Garlies or of Dalswinton, and the arms of Maxwell impaling Mar). Above, the initials RM, presumably for Robert Maxwell, first Earl of Nithsdale, dating the panel to the early C17.‡ Over this panel, a smallish square hole, probably for a rope or chain to raise the drawbridge to cover the entrance.

Inside the entrance, a small lobby with a second and broader

---

* Its profile differs from that of other gunloops in this tower.

‡ The heraldry does not provide a conclusive date. The mother of Robert, fifth Lord Maxwell, who succeeded in 1513, was a daughter of Sir Alexander Stewart of Garlies, and his first wife, Janet † 1520 x 1525, was a daughter of Sir William Douglas of Drumlanrig, who bore the Mar arms in two quarters (a possible but not very convincing explanation for the Mar arms here). However, the Maxwells did not use the double-headed eagle in place of a saltire before 1581. Robert, tenth Lord Maxwell and first Earl of Nithsdale, was the only Robert Maxwell to have owned Caerlaverock between 1581 and the castle's destruction in 1640, but his connexion with the Stewarts of either Garlies or Dalswinton (the mother of the first Lord Maxwell was a daughter of Stewart of Dalswinton) was rather distant and he had no cause to impale the arms of Mar.

portcullis slot near its inner end. The s wall of this lobby was the front wall of the c13 gatehouse. Above its pointed doorway, a shovel-ended arrowslit under a second-floor window. Immediately behind the doorway, the slot of the c13 portcullis. Then the c13 tunnel-vaulted and ashlar-walled transe, its s end narrowed by late c15 masonry and covered with a semicircular vault, which ends with an obtusely arched doorway into the courtyard.

The courtyard front of the gatehouse is largely covered by the E and w ranges. At the exposed centre, late c15 buttresses project from the c13 wall. Above the second floor the buttresses' inner faces are corbelled inwards and rise into a moulded semicircular arch carrying a portcullis chamber, its floor pierced by a large slot. So, as remodelled by Robert, second Lord Maxwell, in the late c15, the gatehouse is massively strong, defended by its portcullises not only from frontal attack but also from the courtyard behind.

The courtyard's present two-storey WEST RANGE replaces an earlier range whose blocked windows have been seen in the curtain. It is of *c.* 1500, its surviving N two-thirds providing an organized procession of first-floor windows (originally mullioned and transomed) and hefty wallhead chimneys. Moulded surrounds to the openings. The ground floor's N and s windows have been crudely converted into doorways, the s presumably in the early c17, when the adjoining door was blocked by the building of the s range. This w range was integrated with the gatehouse in the early c16, when a stair tower was added, filling the width and most of the depth of the intervening space. Its front is a one-bay stack of windows above the door, all with simply moulded surrounds.

The early c17 s and E ranges were probably substantially complete by 1634, the date over one window. Of the SOUTH RANGE, the ground floor's front wall survives. It is of five bays. Fluted margins at the windows. The E window (a dummy) still has its entablature, the frieze decorated with a cherub's head. Central door set in a much altered classical frame. The pilasters are replacements, the r. without a capital, the l. with a weathered foliaged capital, probably not *in situ*. The cornice breaks forward at the centre, its projection supported originally by the door's now missing console keystone. The door itself is roundheaded, the arch springing from square capitals and carved with egg-and-dart ornament; roundels in the spandrels of the arch.

Much more survives of the EAST RANGE. It has been of three storeys and an attic and of six main bays; the two at the s are now very fragmentary. The N bay is a narrow stack of stair windows; so too was the southernmost bay. The four pedimented ground-floor windows of the centre bays, all with fluted surrounds, read as two pairs, divided by a central door and marked off from the end bays by two doors (the one at the s now distinguishable only by the bottom of one jamb). The doors are squeezed in between the main bays' windows to give a nervous rhythm of stair window/door/window/window/door/ window/window/door/stair window, the nervosity emphasized by the steepness of the pediments.

In the N door's pediment, two carved roses flank a weathered shield apparently bearing the Maxwells' double-headed eagle. In the pediment of the centre door, another worn shield in a strapwork cartouche and said to have been carved with the initials of Elizabeth, (Countess of) Nithsdale. In the pediment of the lowest stair window on the l., another strapwork cartouche containing a shield carved with the Maxwell saltire. In the broken pediments over the main windows, moulded triangles flank more strapwork cartouches bearing the double-headed eagle, roses and the date 1634, and the Maxwell crest of a stag couchant. The upper windows of the l. stair are framed by banded Ionic columns on conical bases. Their steep pediments are lavishly decorated. In the first, a pair of cherubs supports a coroneted shield bearing the double-headed eagle device; underneath, a human head, its mouth drawn into a grimace by an animal's paws. At the window above, dolphins support another coroneted shield, carved with the arms of Elizabeth Beaumont, wife of the first Earl of Nithsdale. At the top window, a shield with the Maxwell saltire. In the four centre bays, the rhythm of the taller first- and second-floor windows is uninterrupted by doors and so more relaxed than that of the ground floor. These windows have the same banded Ionic columns as at the stair, but here they are etiolated because of the greater height, and carry segmental pediments displaying heraldry, the initials of Robert, Earl of Nithsdale, and Elizabeth, Countess of Nithsdale, and scenes from Ovid's *Metamorphoses*. All this is very smart, described as a 'dainty fabrick' in 1640; but it is a façade disturbing to the functionalist: the vault behind it cuts across the top of the ground-floor windows, and the r. door must have been either a dummy or permanently locked, since it opens against the stair rising from the hall of the S range.

The castle's INTERIORS have been altered and rearranged in the course of its history. Their present unplastered masonry makes them hard to understand as the domestic accommodation of any particular period, although it provides clues as to how they have changed.

The ground floor of the gatehouse was probably always self-contained, with no direct connexion to the floors above. Each side of the transe, a guardroom, the one at the E entered through an obtusely arched door, probably of the mid-C13. The W guardroom's rectangular door with chamfered jambs looks C16. The stone under its lintel's N end has springings to both S and E which make no sense in its present position, so presumably it has been re-used. Both guardrooms are irregularly shaped, their vaulted ceilings insertions of the late C15 or C16. In the E guardroom's S wall, the stepped embrasure of a C13 slit window (now opening into the E range's stair). Quite large E window with a glazing groove, probably of 1593 or perhaps

of the 1630s. In the ground-floor room of the E tower, a SE
window of either the mid-C13 or the late C14 with a flattened
oval gunloop (probably late C15) pushed through its bottom.
This tower's other gunloops, both here and on the floors above,
are round holes internally and probably date from 1593. In the
W guardroom, a fireplace with a shouldered lintel. Small mid-
C13 window (now into the early C16 stair) with a stepped sill.
Another C13 window at the formerly vaulted ground floor of
the adjoining tower.

The construction of the early C16 stair at the gatehouse's
SW provided a grand approach to its upper floors, which had
probably been reached formerly by an external wooden stair to
the first floor, access to the floors above and the parapet walk
being by a tight turnpike in the wall thickness of the main
block's SW corner. The FIRST FLOOR of the gatehouse, as
constructed in the C13, was intended for the living quarters of
the lord. It contained a hall in the main block and a private
room in each tower, both now missing their wooden floors. In
the W tower's chamber, a garderobe at the SW. Plain C13
windows, the one at the E blocked by the forework built in the
late C15 when the W window was widened to the l. In the hall's
W wall, beside the door to the turnpike stair, an aumbry. In the
N wall, a broad segmental arch which gave access to the work-
ings of the original portcullis; the arch was presumably built up
when that portcullis became redundant with the construction
of the late C15 forework. Probably in the 1590s, the hall was
divided to form two rooms, perhaps an ante-chamber and
bedchamber.* The partition wall contains the W room's narrow
fireplace and a simply moulded doorpiece. The E room was
remodelled in the 1630s, when its present S chimneypiece with
consoled jambs was provided. At this room's SE corner, a recess
under a flattened segmental arch which springs from slender
attached columns to form a lobby at the entrance from the
adjoining stair in the E range. In the E tower's chamber, gunloops, but also the l. jamb of a C13 window blocked by the
forework. In the SE segment, an alcove equipped with a pistol-
hole; it is probably of 1593, or perhaps of the 1630s, and may
have been intended to house a close-stool screened by an arras.
There is an almost identical arrangement of rooms on the
SECOND FLOOR of the gatehouse, its hall having again been
divided into two rooms. In the N wall, doors to the W tower
and the forework's portcullis chamber, both with tall pointed
rear-arches. They are probably late C15. So too is the W chamber's domical ceiling with pointed ribs meeting at a shield
boss. Another domical vault in the E chamber, but cruder and
without ribs; it is likely to be of the 1590s. On the THIRD
FLOOR, probably a late C14 addition, another hall in the main
block, again subdivided. There is no access to the space above
the second-floor vaults of the towers, but a stepped wall passage

---

* One of these rooms, probably the one at the E, seems to have been the Earl of
Nithsdale's chamber in 1640.

climbs from the SW turnpike stair to a small room over the forework's portcullis chamber.

The 1630s EAST RANGE extended the accommodation on the first and second floors of the gatehouse. Each floor was provided with a further two rooms, perhaps a wardrobe and closet, producing two grand apartments or suites of rooms, one probably for the Earl and the other for the Countess of Nithsdale. In all these new rooms, stone chimneypieces with console-jambs. The jambs of the first-floor chimneypieces are fluted and, in the S room, decorated also with fleurs-de-lis, the armorial device of Elizabeth Beaumont, Countess of Nithsdale. Muscling into the NW corner of each N room is the curved wall of this range's NW stair which served the E room of each upper floor of the gatehouse. This stair, despite the grandeur of its façade and its comfortable size, must have been a secondary stair, since it is reached from the courtyard through a bakehouse at the N end of the E range's vaulted ground floor. Well in the floor of the bakehouse. In its S wall, a large elliptical-arched fireplace, an oven in its SE corner. S of the bakehouse, a short passage to the kitchen, whose fireplace has a pair of tall roundheaded arches. S of the kitchen, on the E side of this range, a lobby and service room opening into the hall of the S range. These were under a broad scale-and-platt stair which occupied the E range's S end and was entered from the S range's hall. This stair must been intended primarily as the principal approach to the first floor of the S range, but, at its first-floor landing, a door in the E window embrasure gave access to a short wall passage leading to the S room of the E range and also to a very tight turnpike stair to the floors above.

The early C17 SOUTH RANGE may have been designed in the hope that it would be the setting for a royal visitor. The ground floor has been divided into two rooms, a large E hall and a smaller W chamber which presumably connected with the S room of the W range. In the hall, one consoled jamb of a N chimneypiece. To its r., a large skewed segmental-arched door to the principal stair in the E range and a smaller door into the service room. A stone cornice and big elliptically arched window survive at the E wall. In the SE corner there has been a door to a now fragmentary turnpike stair, built (probably in the late C14) to serve the castle's SE tower.

The medieval SW tower has contained wooden floors, each supported on a scarcement in the wall and each entered from the W range or its predecessor, except for the top room, which was reached from the parapet walk. The present WEST RANGE is of c. 1500. Its S room, now almost entirely demolished, has contained a stair up to a NE door into this range's first-floor hall. Beside this door, the moulded jambs and capitals of a late medieval chimneypiece. The much better-preserved three ground-floor rooms to the N have each originally had a door and a window to the courtyard, but there is no communication between them. In the centre room, evidence of window seats. Each room has a smartly moulded chimneypiece, its jambs

decorated with rosettes and foliage. On the first floor, the large
s room has been a hall. Near the s end of its e wall, a well-
preserved stone chimneypiece, again with moulded jambs and
capitals but without rosettes. There may have been another
fireplace in the hall's n wall. Door into a n chamber, whose e
fireplace is centrally positioned. In this chamber's n wall, a
door to the early c16 stair linking this range to the guesthouse.
This door largely blocks an earlier basket-arched entrance, its
lintel's centre drawn up as a little concave-sided arch.

CAIRNRYAN

0060

Single-street village established along the shore of Loch Ryan by
the late c18.

HARBOUR. Begun in the mid-c19 but much expanded *c.*1939–
45. Long concrete pier at the n end, ferry terminal of 1973 at
the s.

LOCH RYAN LIGHTHOUSE. By *Alan Stevenson*, 1847. Painted
round tower with a domed cupola. Single-storey keepers'
houses.

PARISH CHURCH HALL. Disused. Humble Gothic, dated 1855.

DESCRIPTION. The village's n end begins with a GRAVEYARD,
the site where a chapel of ease stood from 1841 to 1990. Late
c19 headstones. Just to the s, on the edge of the harbour (*see*
above), a small early c19 battlemented TOWER. On the e
side of the road, the entrance to the drive of Lochryan House
(*see* p. 421). Further s, the white-painted early c19 OLD
MANSE, quite humble except for a ball-finialled gabled porch,
its scrolled skewputts decorated with rosettes. Then another
stretch of Lochryan House's garden wall before the village
houses really start. First a short terrace of very simple cottages,
probably of the early c19 and originally thatched, climbing up
the hillside to the e. The main street, open to the w, leads s,
following the line of the shore. On its e side, straightforward
housing of the early and mid-c19. In it, the old Parish Church
Hall (*see* above). After a gap, c20 houses. They and the village
end with THE HOMESTEAD, a neat late Georgian house, with
some cherry-cock pointing enlivening its whin rubble front,
overlooking the ferry terminal (*see* Harbour, above).

CRAIGCAFFIE CASTLE. *See* p. 195.
LOCHRYAN HOUSE. *See* p. 421.

CAIRNSMORE

4060

5.1km. N of Creetown

Small country house of *c.*1740, built of painted rubble. Piend-
roofed main block of two storeys over a high basement. Granite-
columned portico at the centre of the w front. Roundheaded
ground-floor windows with projecting keystones and imposts.

Slightly recessed flanking wings, each with a Victorian canted bay window.

CALLY PALACE

6050

1.3km. s of Gatehouse of Fleet

Georgian mansion built for the Murrays of Broughton and now 83 an hotel. It was clearly intended to stun the visitor with its importance but just fails to deliver a knock-out blow. The house was begun in 1763–5 by *Robert Mylne*.* This was a thriftily detailed Palladian composition. Piend-roofed main block of three storeys and a basement, built of grey granite ashlar with red sandstone dressings. Entrance (N) front of six bays, the centre four (the windows paired) slightly advanced under a pediment containing a large bullseye window. Small square second-floor windows. Parapet at the end bays and sides and along the back, which has a central bow, its ground-floor door approached by a concave-sided stair. Single-storey-and-basement links to boldly projecting single-storey pavilions. In 1794 *Thomas Boyd* heightened the links and pavilions by a half-storey and gave the E pavilion a rear bow.

A partial recasting of the house in a grandiose neo-classical manner was undertaken in 1833–8 by *J. B. Papworth*. To the centrepiece he added a flat-roofed block containing an entrance hall and stair up to the *piano nobile*, fronted by a porte cochère. Stark neo-Greek detail, with anta pilasters at the sides, unfluted Greek Doric columns at the front. The channelled masonry's ashlar blocks are much larger and more precisely cut than those of the C18 house; the porte cochère's columns are monoliths. At the same time Papworth recased the pavilions and the upper floors of the links in the same best-quality granite ashlar. Squat pilastrades along the upper floors, those of the links in not entirely happy contrast to the C18 walling below. At each pavilion the new ground-floor masonry is channelled. Boldly projecting anta pilasters; overall balustrades. Balustraded dwarf walls in front of the basement area tie the pavilions to the new centrepiece. At the back Papworth did much less, but he remodelled the central bow above the basement to form two unequal storeys in the height of the original three, with the *piano nobile*'s windows lowered to the floor and provided with balconies, and the upper windows' bottom parts being blind panels to conceal the height of the ground-floor room behind. In 1857 *Lanyon & Lynn* of Belfast added a chapel at the house's w end.

The mansion became an hotel in 1934 and the principal

* Alexander Murray of Broughton had built a pair of pavilions by 1742, when he received a design from *William Adam* for the centre block of a 'Great House'. This was not executed, and *c.*1755 *Isaac Ware* produced a grand Palladian design for James Murray of Broughton, who, however, in 1759 got the sketch design of another proposal from *Robert Mylne*, then in Rome. The construction of Mylne's executed design, quite different from this sketch, began in 1763.

external alterations for this use must be noted. Glazed dining room addition of 1955 at the back of the E link and pavilion. Lift tower on the W side of the main block, 1956. Large E addition of 1974. The chapel was demolished in 1990, leaving the W pavilion's gable looking sadly unfinished.

Papworth's entrance hall is a *nouveau riche* display of marble. This is the material used for the veined white floor slabs, their corners canted to allow the insertion of small grey squares. More marble covering the walls, with large pale panels above a reddish veined dado. Coffered plaster ceiling, with swags between the consoles of the frieze. The hall's S end opens onto the stair up to the *piano nobile* through a Roman Doric columned screen (marble again). The 1830s stair occupied the width of the screen's central opening and rose to a broad rectangular opening flanked by two huge unglazed windows. As part of the late C20 hotel alterations the stair was altered, with unfortunate effect, being broadened to the l. to fill this side of the stair hall, the l. window becoming a door opening, and, on the r., a flight made down to the basement.

The C18 entrance hall on the *piano nobile* was remodelled by Papworth and given a long and shallow central ceiling panel. To the l., the C18 stair hall, the stair balustrade now boxed in, but a high-relief plaster eagle surviving on the ceiling. The main block's principal rooms, all remodelled in the 1830s, are on the *piano nobile*'s S side. The E room (former dining room) has a compartmented ceiling enriched with lavish fruit decoration and an acanthus-leaf cornice. Bow-ended and high central room, its ceiling coffered, a deeply undercut rosette in each compartment. White marble chimneypiece with attached Ionic columns, an allegorical scene on the frieze. A less deeply coffered ceiling in the W room, again with rosettes in the compartments. Chimneypiece of buff and white marble, the jambs consoled, the frieze carved with a swagged urn. In the corridor link to the W pavilion the ceiling cornice is supported by plaster mermen and mermaids, probably modelled by either *Coffer* or *Wetherell*, who were paid for modelling ornaments in 1835. They supported transverse roundheaded arches between which were domes, all this now hidden by a suspended ceiling. In the W pavilion, a mid-C18 wooden stair, the steps with panelled sides and convex soffits.

The layout of the PARKLAND was begun by 1742, but the scheme was altered and extended *c.*1775 by *James Ramsay*. Since 1939 it has been almost swallowed up by commercial forestry, and it is now cut across to the S by an embankment carrying the new line of the A75. – For Cox's Lodge, at the park's NW, *see* Gatehouse of Fleet (Description). – At the main N entrance to the park, an asymmetrical pair of mid-Victorian crowstep-gabled LODGES, the E with a conical-roofed tower, the W with a triangular bay window. A little to the NE of the mansion house, the early C19 CROSS COTTAGE, with Gothick windows and a roll-moulded door; in the cross-finialled N gable, a Y-traceried two-light window. – SW of the mansion house, CALLY MAINS: the prosperous-looking piend-roofed farmhouse was built in 1838–9; the steading is mostly C20 but has one range of whitewashed rubble which looks early C19. – SE of the house, BELVEDERE LODGE, probably of 1832, with a broad-eaved and steep-pitched roof; Gothick glazing in the hoodmoulded windows. – To its E, the brick-walled GARDEN of *c.*1800, an early C19 cottage on its NE. – Further SE, THE TEMPLE of 1778, a battlemented two-storey Gothick folly (now roofless but formerly a gardener's house). Diagonal buttresses at the ground-floor corners; heavy stone spouts projecting below the parapet. Pointed door and windows. – To its S, another early C19 broad-eaved LODGE, now with a late C20 box-dormer. Latticed glazing in the hoodmoulded windows. Over the door, a panel carved with a coat of arms.

CANONBIE

3070

Curving village; much of the housing is C20, but there are some late C19 terraced cottages with bracketed eaves and a couple of late Georgian inns (the CROSS KEYS HOTEL and the RIVERSIDE INN), both with columned doorpieces.

PARISH CHURCH. By *William Atkinson*, 1821–2. Large buttressed and ashlar-walled box, with an uncrenellated parapet at the gables. Two tiers of windows, Tudor-arched below, four-centred above. N and S porches with low parapets. Projecting from the centre of the long W side, a tower with set-back buttresses and a battlement rising into square corner turrets. This is of three stages, the bottom and top with hoodmoulded four-centred openings, the second with a pointed light in each face. Inside, cast-iron columns supporting a GALLERY round the N, S and W sides, its front simply panelled. – Boxy PEWS. – Late C19 PULPIT in the centre of the E wall.

GRAVEYARD to the W. Across its centre, a long line of C18 HEADSTONES, some aedicular, decorated with heraldry, angels' heads (souls), and reminders of death, several with flowers spiralling up the sides, many given charm by the ineptness of execution. – E of this line, a large and square late Georgian battlemented MAUSOLEUM, with a hoodmoulded and pointed door in its N face. – E of this, the MONUMENT to the Rev. James Donaldson †1854. It is placed in a C13 round-arched recess, perhaps of a tomb, the only surviving fragment of Canonbie Priory, an Augustinian house founded in the C12 and abandoned in the C16. Dogtooth enrichment on the arch, its hoodmould's l. label stop with knotted zoomorphic carving, the r. floriated. – On the back of this monument, a small weathered WALL MONUMENT, probably of the C18. Aedicular, with a large coat of arms in the pediment.

BRIDGE. Built by *Gideon Boyd* and *Andrew Mein* in 1752–4. Three-span, with segmental arches and triangular cutwaters; steel footpaths of 1899 cantilevered out from the sides.

HALL. Dated 1912. Plain, with a hint of Scots Jacobean.

25

SCHOOL. Plain Tudor, by *James Burnet*, 1860. Addition of 1989, trying too hard to be in keeping. – To the NW, the piend-roofed OLD SCHOOLHOUSE, probably also of 1860. Two storeys and three bays with a projecting centre.

WAR MEMORIAL. Erected in 1921. Bronze statue of a mourning soldier, by *Thomas J. Clapperton*. Pink granite pedestal by *Beattie & Co.*

HOLLOWS MILL, 2km. N. Informal rubble-built STEADING, probably of the late C18 but extended in the earlier C19. – To the N, a CORN MILL of *c.* 1820, the main block heightened and given wings after a fire in 1867. The machinery survives inside.

PRIORSLYNN, 0.4km. SE. Rubble-built FARMHOUSE of the earlier C19, quite plain except for the pilastered and fanlit door. The rear block represents its late C18 predecessor linked to the STEADING behind, with courtyard ranges of several C18 and C19 dates; segmental-arched pend entrance in the W block. – To the S, a single-storey FARM BUILDING, probably of the later C18. Relatively long (17.3m.) and narrow (4.42m.), it is a framed structure, its wooden crucks resting on stone footings. The walls (now partly replaced in stone and corrugated iron) are of clay mixed with pebbles and straw. The roof, originally thatched, is now of corrugated iron. Interior divided by a clay partition into two compartments, each with a door from the outside. The W compartment's cobbled floor suggests it was a byre or stable; earth floor in the E apartment, perhaps a barn.

WOODSLEE, 1.9km. S. Straightforward early C19 piend-roofed mansion house built of coursed rubble. Main block of two storeys and a basement. Five-bay front, the windows grouped 1/3/1. Pilastered and fanlit doorpiece in a segmental overarch. Slightly advanced lower wings.

ROMAN MARCHING CAMP, Gilnockie, 2.7km. N. Only one rampart survives. It contains two gates, each protected by a traverse.

GILNOCKIE TOWER. *See* p. 319.

8090   CAPENOCH
                    0.9km. SW of Penpont

Mid-C19 red sandstone Manorial-Baronial country house designed in bits by *David Bryce* and incorporating a small Georgian mansion. The lands of Capenoch were acquired in 1727, through marriage, by the Kirkpatricks of Closeburn; they sold that estate in 1783 and retrenched to Capenoch, where they built a new house which was completed in 1795. In 1846 this was sold to James Grierson of Dalgonar, who in 1847–8 employed David Bryce to remodel and recase the C18 house and add a S extension. Two years later Grierson sold the house (at a loss) to Thomas Steuart Gladstone, a Liverpool broker, who brought back Bryce to enlarge the house to the N and add a W conservatory in 1854–7. Bryce was employed yet again in 1868 to extend the kitchen offices at the NW.

The main parts of the building form a U, the C18 house providing its shallowly recessed base between Bryce's additions. The starkly detailed N block of 1854–7, faced like the rest in red sandstone ashlar, is the first to greet the visitor. It is a three-storey-and-attic rectangle with fat conical-roofed turrets at the crowstepped E gable, but it contrives to suggest that it is an L-plan tower house with a crowstepped NW jamb. However, this 'jamb' is formed only by a gable jettied out twice from the main walling. The deception, if it is a deception, continues along the main block's N front and E gable, where the attic and angle turrets are brought forward on a continuation of the 'jamb's' upper tier of continuous corbelling to suggest a parapet. The martial impression is strengthened at the gable by moulded corbels under the continuous corbelling and by a stringcourse which drops under the gable and turret windows to form 'merlons'. Deeper 'merlons' under the rose-finialled dormers of the N front's attic. The lower floors are more reminiscent of a C16 Scottish palace. Stringcourse at the principal floor jumping up over the N front's mullioned and transomed three-light window and the armorial panel to its r., carried in a straight line across the E gable and under its large oriel window. At the E end of the N front, a plain corniced door; its design is apparently an afterthought, since Bryce's drawings show a porch, whose gable's E slope would have been directly aligned with the E slope of the 'jamb's' gable.

Externally, the C18 house forming the base of the U is now almost all by Bryce. Originally it was a double-pile of two storeys and an attic above a high basement, each of the long W and E sides of three bays. In 1847–8 Bryce recased its harled whin walling in red sandstone. To the W front he added angle turrets, the N square with a steep pyramid roof, the S conical-roofed and round. The attic windows were heightened with tall rose-finialled and steeply pedimented dormerheads rising above the eaves. At the E front, to which Bryce moved the entrance from the W, he was more thorough-going. Here he again added Jacobean dormerheads to the attic windows. The two l. ground- and first-floor windows were replaced by a tall three-light stair window. At the S corner, in the inner angle with his new S block, he placed a tower (intended for water closets), its lower part circular, the upper corbelled to a square under a steep pavilion roof whose bellcast eaves are broken by tall narrow dormers, their steep pediments again with rose finials. Projecting under the stair window, a single-storey battle-mented porch. Its entrance was made into a window in 1854–7, when a balustraded link between it and the new N block's entrance hall was built across the E front.

The S block of 1847–8 is low-key. Crowstepped gables again. On the S front, more rose-finialled dormerheads. Big off-centre bay window, its lower part canted, the upper corbelled to a square crowstepped gable. From this bay window, stone steps lead down from the drawing room to the garden. In the W gable, a three-light window.

The conservatory added to the C18 house's W side in 1855–6 is more aggressive. Stone-balustraded E end leading to four gabled bays, the detail punchy Jacobean. It gives access to a formal knot garden, laid out in 1856, with a balustrade at its W end overlooking the park.

The low NW service wing of 1854–7 has crowstepped gables and rose-finialled pedimented dormerheads. Its W end was heightened by Bryce in 1868.

The Victorian INTERIOR is remarkably complete. The front door opens into a large entrance hall-cum-billiard room. Plain chimneypiece of veined black marble, the opening round-headed. From this room's SE corner begins the toplit lower flight of the dogleg stair to the principal floor. At the landing in the 1840s porch, a panelled wooden ceiling. The upper flight rises under the main stair. Filling the E side of the centre block of the principal floor is a broad upper hall-cum-stair hall, its geometrically patterned wooden ceiling provided, like most of the woodwork, by the estate joiners, *Archie* and *John Grierson*, in 1857–8. Simple wooden chimneypiece at the W wall. The stair to the first (bedroom) floor is Jacobean, pendants dropping from the newel posts. Above it, a wooden ceiling boarded in decorative patterns.

The principal rooms form a U round the upper hall. At the SE corner is the morning room (the 1840s library, converted to its present use in the 1850s). Modillion cornice above an egg-and-dart frieze. Heavy white marble chimneypiece, big acanthus leaf capitals on the piers. To its W, the drawing room, well lit from the bay window in the S wall and the three-light window in the W. Cornice of the same type as the morning room's. Chimneypiece of white and brown marble in a late C18 manner, with upright acanthus leaf capitals on the piers topped by relief portraits of ladies; rosettes on the frieze. Occupying the two S bays of the centre block's W side is the 1850s library (the 1840s dining room). Dentil cornice above an egg-and-dart frieze. Chimneypiece of veined brown marble. Neo-Jacobean book-cases, grotesque human heads protruding from the cornice. The massive thickness of the C18 house's side walls (1.9m.) is clearly visible at the window. W door to the conservatory, its floor covered with tiles, brown-centred blue crosses enlivening the white ground. N of the library, but entered through a lobby off the upper hall and served also by a secondary stair from the floor below, the Bird Library (the 1850s business room), with a very broad pointed opening at its black marble chimneypiece. Occupying most of the N block is the dining room. It is higher than the other principal rooms and enjoys an E oriel window. Three-dimensional foliaged cornice. Chimneypiece of black marble veined with green.

The first-floor bedrooms are straightforward Victorian. In the attic can be seen the two parallel stone vaults which covered the C18 house (the E vault and outer wall cut into by the Victorian stair), each springing from the central spine wall and one of the long side walls. Were they a precaution against

Capenoch suffering the same fire damage as had affected the Kirkpatricks' previous mansion house at Closeburn Castle?

CARDONESS CASTLE   *5050*
1.3km. SW of Gatehouse of Fleet

Prominently sited on a hill, the tall oblong tower house built for 65 the McCullochs in the late C15. Unadorned rubble walling rising to a flush parapet behind which the attic's gables are set back to allow a wall-walk all round. In each face except the E there is an inverted keyhole gunloop at the ground floor; the N wall has a second gunloop at the first floor. The principal windows of the three main upper floors all have chamfered jambs, those of the first and second floors dignified with cornices. Small windows, mostly slits, light the stair and lesser rooms. Glazing grooves show that all have been fully glazed. In the S wall, a round-arched entrance, checked for an iron yett in front of a wooden door.

The doorway opens into a lobby. In its tunnel-vault, a hole through which an unwelcome visitor could be attacked from above. To the W, a guardroom with a gunloop to the S and an aumbry in the W wall. On the lobby's N side, a pair of doors sharing a chamfered jamb. They open into what is now a single tunnel-vaulted space, but the stub of a stone partition shows that it has been divided into two ground-floor store rooms with an entresol above; the rounded stone corbels which carried its floor joists survive. The W store has a slop drain under the gunloop in its N wall and round cupboards in the corners of its W gable. The entresol seems to have contained one undivided room. High-set W window flanked by cupboards.

Turnpike stair in the wall thickness of the house's SE corner. Off it, at the entresol level, a round-arched door into the main room. Beside this, a rectangular door to a prison in the wall thickness of the E gable. It is lit by a small window and provided with a seated garderobe. In the floor, a hatch to a pit prison below, much less comfortable, with only a ventilation slit for light and air. Just above the level of the entresol floor the stair gives access to a guardroom over the entrance lobby. S window overlooking the approach. *Meurtrière* hole in the floor. Crude aumbry in the W wall.

On the first floor, the hall, now with a concrete floor. In its N wall, a large fireplace with jambs of clustered shafts. Its straight lintel is now missing, but an engraving of 1760 shows its top decorated with carved foliage. Salt box on its E. W of the fireplace, an ogee-arched aumbry, probably a buffet for the display of plate. Rectangular aumbry at the W gable's N end, its walling grooved for a shelf. Another aumbry, its pointed arch now mutilated, at the S wall's E end. High up in the W gable and S wall, small horizontal windows, the one at the S with a stepped sill. They are set in deep segmental embrasures, as are the large windows to E and S, both with stone seats. In

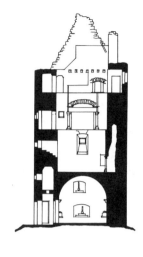

1 Hall
2 Stores
3 Pit prison
4 Guardroom
5 Prison

⊢⊣⊣⊣⊣⊣⊣⊣⊣⊣⊣⊣⊣⊣⊣⊣⊣⊣⊣⊣⊣⊣⊣⊣┤ 30 m

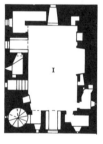

FIRST FLOOR

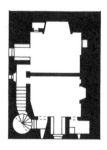

SECOND FLOOR

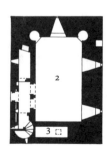

GROUND FLOOR

ENTRESOL

Cardoness Castle. Section and plans

the s window's E ingo, a door above the window seat into a small wall chamber whose floor steps up over the guardroom below. It is lighted by a narrow window and provided with a lamp stand. At the hall's sw corner, another wall chamber, dogleg in plan and with a recess at its N end. In the N wall's E end, a seated garderobe with a gunloop for light. At the E gable's N end, another wall chamber. Its N wall is grooved for a couple of shelves, so perhaps this was a steward's room. All the hall's doors have chamfered jambs and rectangular heads except for the round-arched entrance from the stair.

The now missing wooden floors above have been supported on scarcements in the walls. The second floor seems originally to have contained one main room entered from the stair by a roundheaded door. This door was built up, probably in the C16, when the room was divided in two by a stone partition carried on an arch, and an access to both the newly formed rooms made through a chamber in the s wall. In the w room, the C15 fireplace, its jambs again composed of clustered shafts. Above, two fragments of moulded cornice, the l. carved with stylized foliage and probably *in situ*, the r., with a rope moulding, re-used from elsewhere in the house. Salt box on the l. At the N wall's w end, an aumbry; it lacks the Gothic elegance of the similarly placed aumbry in the hall below. Big E and s windows in the same positions as those of the hall and also provided with seats. In the E gable, a garderobe. The E room's fireplace, presumably a C16 insertion, has splayed jambs. Fireplaces of the same type at the third floor and attic. At the third floor, big E and s windows, again with seats. Smaller window in the N wall's w end; in its w ingo, a door into a closet.

The house's hilltop site has been artificially extended to the s. Under this platform's s corners, heavily restored vaulted rooms, one with a stone bench along one wall.

CARDONESS HOUSE   *5050*
4.1km. sw of Gatehouse of Fleet

A Baronial mansion by *Kinnear & Peddie* was built here in 1889. In 1959–60 this was savagely reduced in size by *S. W. Burnage*, who retained a couple of bay windows and some neo-Jacobean dormerheads, now juxtaposed incongruously with a piended roof and bland neo-Georgian entrance front. – LODGE to the NE, smooth Baronial of *c.*1900, with a conical-roofed corner tower.

CARGENBRIDGE   *9070*

A handful of C19 houses along the main A711 road, the rest housing of the late C20. Large CHEMICAL WORKS to the NW, begun in 1941.

PRIMARY SCHOOL. Assemblage of flat-roofed boxes, by *Eric W. Hall*, 1959.

CARGEN, 2.4km. SE. The house is now a ruin. – U-plan STABLES (now CARGEN GROVE) by *Peddie & Kinnear*, *c*.1870. Across the open S side, screen walls running from between the crow-stepped S gables' angle towers. Each tower starts as a drum, with a dummy gunloop, and is then corbelled out to the square under a steep pavilion roof. – To the E, remains of a brick-walled GARDEN of *c*.1800. In its SE corner, an octagonal ashlar-fronted PAVILION topped by a square stair turret decorated with 'gunloops', its battlement mostly missing.

CARRUCHAN. *See* p. 163.
DALSKAIRTH. *See* p. 215.
GOLDIELEA. *See* p. 330.
MABIE HOUSE. *See* p. 430.
TERRAUGHTIE. *See* p. 538.

CARNSALLOCH HOUSE
9080

1.1km. S of Kirkton

84 Flashy but not very large Palladian mansion built for Alexander Johnston, a native of Galloway who had made money in London and bought the estate in 1750. The house was probably begun by June 1754, when there is mention of 'masons working at Carnsalloch', and completed in 1759 (the date displayed, together with the initials of Johnston's wife, Janet Gordon, on a plaque on the N wing's W gable). *Isaac Ware* may have produced or contributed to the design.*

Piend-roofed main block of three storeys, with a three-bay E front but only one bay deep. Stretched across its back and projecting for three bays each side, a single-storey corridor (its centre part now supporting two extra floors added in the later C20) which links to the low two-storey piend-roofed N and S wings which stretch back to form a U-shape. The 1750s masonry is all of red Locharbriggs ashlar, polished at the main block's upper floors but droved to a corduroy texture at its ground floor and on the links and the gables of the wings. At the main block, a first-floor belt course and stringcourse which continue as a polished ashlar parapet over the links; the belt course carries on across the wings, the strong horizontal effect weakened by the early C19 lowering of the sills of the first-floor windows. At the main block's ground floor, a pair of architraved and corniced windows flanking the heavy and boldly projecting pilastered and pedimented early C19 porch. The three first-floor windows are all large Ionic-columned Venetians set in overarches and with mutuled cornices above their side lights. Small square

---

* In *A Complete Body of Architecture* (1756) Ware illustrated a 'House built for Alexander Johnston, Esq., in Scotland', possibly a preliminary design for Carnsalloch.

second-floor windows under the heavy overall parapet. In the front of each link, a corniced door flanked by roundheaded niches. The wings' front gables are plain. The N wing incorporates an early C18 house,* a five-bay rendered block of two storeys and an attic, with a chimney-gabled centre projecting on the N and a less boldly advanced S centrepiece containing the entrance. The 1750s work added a piend-roofed ashlar bay at each end, making it the same length as the corresponding but wholly new S wing, whose W end's snecked rubble suggests that this part was rebuilt in the late C19. At the sides and back of the mansion, sizeable but insubstantial-looking single-storey additions built since the late 1960s, when Carnsalloch was acquired by the Leonard Cheshire Foundation.

Inside the main block, an entrance hall with a ceiling rose of acanthus leaves set in a surround of swagged husks. Behind is the main stair, its well now filled by a lift. Anthemion-patterned flat balusters. Over the first-floor landing, another ceiling rose of acanthus leaves set in husks; at the top, a coved ceiling. The main rooms have been much altered. In the ground-floor S room, a simple wooden chimneypiece, probably Edwardian, as is the swagged frieze. In the (subdivided) room above, a rinceau-decorated cornice of the 1750s. The long ground-floor corridor's tunnel-vault is now hidden by a suspended ceiling. Set into its E wall, a red sandstone slab carved with the date 1650 and the coats of arms and initials of Robert Maxwell and his wife, Agnes Irving, then the owners of Carnsalloch. The first-floor E room of each wing has been quite smart, with a coved ceiling. Both are now subdivided.

The early C18 house incorporated in the N wing is remarkably intact, three of the rooms still panelled, the W ground-floor room (probably the parlour) with a round-arched and console-keystoned china cupboard. The stair has turned balusters except for those at the top, which are of silhouette type.

To the SE, a large WALLED GARDEN, probably of the later C18, its walls of broached ashlar largely faced internally with brick. The E side is open, defended from animals by a ha-ha. At the NE corner, a square two-storey pavilion-roofed GARDENER'S HOUSE. – GLASSHOUSES mostly of the late C20, but one is Victorian, with a scrolly iron finial at one end.

E of the house, powerfully classical STABLES, presumably of the 1750s. The design may be derived from Chiswick House. Four rubble-built piend-roofed ranges forming a quadrangle, each of seven bays, with a tall advanced centrepiece containing a roundheaded archway under an open pediment. The centre of the quadrangle is not a court: it is filled by a square two-storey block with a Diocletian window in each face; the roof is a truncated pyramid. – Further E, at the start of the drive, an

---

* Probably this was a virtually self-contained wing added to an earlier house which was removed when the present mansion was built.

early C19 LODGE with pedimented gables and a stodgy Greek Doric portico.

55   CHAPEL in a wood, 0.5km. N of the lodge. Very sturdy Dec by *E. B. Lamb*, 1847. Two-bay nave and a low semi-octagonal apse, all with heavy stepped buttresses, their gablets now mostly fallen on the ground. Shields along the parapet. Stone slabbed and crested roof. Coat of arms of the Campbell-Johnstons of Carnsalloch near the top of the W gable, whose door is surrounded by high-relief foliage and topped by a pointed window filled with cusped loop tracery. (The interior is a tightly defined space bounded by a skeletal structure of piers and arches standing just clear of the walls.)

8090   CARRONBRIDGE

C19 estate village straggling along the A76.

DESCRIPTION. At the N end, a couple of mid-C19 broad-eaved *cottages ornés*, with mullioned windows and diagonally set chimneys. Behind them, a contemporary FARMHOUSE with gableted stone dormerheads and a porch. Then nothing much until just before the bridge, where, on the l., is a short row containing two cottages and a former smithy, probably of the earlier C19. On the r. and at right angles to the road, a mid-C19 terrace of five cottages (the two at the W now a single house) with depressed-arched doors in the gabled porches (one now removed) except at the lower and possibly earlier centre cottage. The BRIDGE itself, of one semicircular arch, was built in the mid-C18 but had its roadway widened with corbelled extensions (still surviving on the E) in the C19; both substructure and superstructure were again widened to the W in the C20. S of it, plain mid-C19 housing enlivened by a few bargeboards. Down a lane to the r., the former SCHOOL and SCHOOLHOUSE of 1844, the two-storey house enjoying gableted dormerheads and horizontal glazing. To the S, an informally grouped mid-C19 SAWMILL.

FARMS ETC.

ALTON, 4.1km. NW. Whitewashed farmhouse and steading built in 1829–31 to a design by *Walter Newall*, later published in Loudon's *Cottage and Village Architecture*. Single-storey farmhouse, its gabled porch and bargeboarded dormers added later in the C19. Courtyard of farm offices behind.

BURN, 3.4km. E. Prosperous crowstep-gabled and ashlar-walled Jacobean FARMHOUSE by *William Burn*, 1834, with a conical-roofed round turret corbelled out above a square projection. – Contemporary or near-contemporary STEADING, the ranges again crowstepped but built of whinstone rubble.

CARRONHILL, 0.4km. NE. House with two faces. The piend-roofed W part was built in 1827 by *William Dargavell*. Ashlar-

fronted, with a pilastered doorpiece. The asymmetrical Tudor
E block was added in the mid-C19.

SWEETBIT, 5km. NW. Farmhouse and steading built in 1829–31
and almost identical with Alton (*see* above), so presumably also
designed by *Walter Newall* and altered at the same time.

DABTON. *See* p. 208.

DRUMLANRIG CASTLE. *See* p. 222.

MORTON CASTLE. *See* p. 450.

CARRUCHAN

o.7km. S of Cargenbridge

9070

Mid-C19 H-plan house, probably incorporating some earlier work.
Crowstepped gables; mullions at some windows. Towers in the
N front's inner angles, one octagonal, the other round and
conical-roofed. – Contemporary L-plan STABLES, again crowstepped and with a conical-roofed round tower at one corner.

CARRUTHERSTOWN

1070

Architecturally undistinguished small village.

SCHOOL. By the Dumfries County Architect, *Alastair Macintyre*,
1974. Lightweight drydashed box, a touch of excitement given
by a taller bowed and monopitch-roofed projection, its artificial
stonework swept up to the front.

HETLAND HALL. *See* p. 339.

CARSCREUGH CASTLE

3.2km. NE of Glenluce

2050

Fragmentary remains of a mansion built by Sir James Dalrymple
of Stair (later the first Viscount Stair) *c.* 1670. It has been a tall
rubble-walled symmetrical U-plan, the main block lying on a
N–S axis, the short wings projecting W. Quite a lot of the S
wing still stands, containing large windows. In the SE inner
angle, a rounded stair tower. Part of the N wing is also extant.
For the rest, grassy mounds.

CARSETHORN

9050

Formerly the harbour for Dumfries, the present village was begun
in the early C19, when a wooden pier was erected and visited
regularly by a steam-packet from Liverpool. The one-sided
street following the line of the shore includes a two-storey
piend-roofed terrace of *c.* 1815, some of the houses enjoying
rustically smart fanlights, but several now with altered fenestration. The grandest is the HARBOUR MASTER'S HOUSE
near the N end, with rusticated quoins and a first-floor sill

course. At the village's s end, a late C19 COASTGUARD
STATION with a small look-out tower.

CARSLUITH CASTLE
4.8km. SE of Creetown

Roofless but substantial rubble-walled tower house, built for John
Brown of Carsluith in the 1560s and now forming the centre
range of a U-plan late Georgian steading. The tower house is
of three storeys and an attic, L-plan, with the stair jamb projecting at the NW and topped by a rudimentarily pedimented
caphouse. At the main block's NE, SE and SW corners, round
turrets, each projected on a course of continuous corbelling
surmounted by widely spaced rounded corbels. On the W, at
the join* of the main block and jamb, a shallow stair turret
corbelled out from the second floor. The main block's wallhead
survives at this end, its corbelling of the same type as that of
the turrets; one big stone spout remains of those which drained
the now missing parapet. Gables each set back to allow a wall-
walk, but these were only across the gable and not on the long
sides, whose wallheads are at a higher level; so presumably the
wall-walks were for show rather than defence. On the N front,
set at the level of the gables' and turrets' corbelling, are rounded
corbels to carry the ridge beam of a lean-to roof over a second-
floor wooden gallery; its joist holes are quite evident below. It
ran from a door in the jamb, where the access was eased by a
recess in the main wall, to a chamfered doorway in the main
block. The jamb door was later built up, probably in the C17,
and a window inserted, its sloping stepped sill carrying dirty
water from a slop hole clear of the house's entrance below. At
the main block's ground floor, small square windows and broad
utilitarian gunloops. First- and second-floor windows with roll-
and-hollow surrounds. In the s wall, a second-floor gunloop of
double-keyhole type; there was probably another gunloop to
its l, where the opening has been enlarged and robbed of
dressings. Small moulded windows to the jamb. Round gunholes under the caphouse and at the W stair turret.

In the inner angle, the moulded entrance opening into the
jamb. Placed above its cornice is the moulded frame of a badly
weathered panel on which are just discernible a coat of arms
(of Brown of Carsluith), the initial B and the date 156– (said in
the C19 to have been decipherable as 1564). Inside the jamb, a
comfortable turnpike stair. To its s, on the ground floor, a
small tunnel-vaulted lobby at the NW corner of the main block.
Off this lobby are two doors at right angles to each other. The
s door gives access to a tunnel-vaulted store lit by a small s
window and s and W gunloops. In the NW corner, a deep
cupboard. The lobby's E door opens into a short passage
leading to another store, again with a small s window and a
couple of gunloops.

* A notional rather than a physical join. The masonry is continuous.

The first floor is filled by the hall. Big but simply moulded N fireplace, a salt box in its l. side. Windows in segmental-arched embrasures. L. of the W window is a sink. To its r., a segmental-arched buffet recess; entered through its N side is a garderobe, lit by a small window. Aumbries in the S and E walls. The now missing floors of the two top storeys have been of wood, their joist holes clearly visible. At each gable of the second floor, a moulded stone fireplace with adjoining bed recess. Clearly this floor has contained two rooms, the W entered directly from the stair, the E originally via the wooden N gallery and then, after that was removed, presumably through the adjoining room. In the centre of the S wall, a pair of garderobes, one for each room, the E still lit and vented by a gunloop. In the E room's NE corner, two small aumbries, one above the other. Moulded fireplace in the attic's E gable. In the caphouse over the main stair, a room with a N fireplace and windows to the E and W.

Each of the two wings of farm offices added to the tower house c. 1800 is a piend-roofed two-storey block of whitewashed rubble, with a round-arched opening in the N bay of its inner face.

CARSPHAIRN 5090

Roadside village begun at the end of the C18, the buildings mostly C19.

PARISH CHURCH. Harled rectangle of c. 1815, with a birdcage bellcote on the E gable. The W end, originally semi-hexagonal, was made rectangular c. 1840 when a gallery was installed inside with a forestair for access. Both forestair and gallery were removed in 1931–2, when the low semi-hexagonal W porch (rebuilt in 1974–5) and E apse were added. Also of 1931–3, the neo-Romanesque lights in the round-arched windows.

Interior mostly of 1931–3, when the body of the church was divided into nave and aisles by thin iron columns. Stone chancel arch. – In the aisles, PEWS of 1931–3. – Occupying the nave, a long COMMUNION TABLE, probably of the mid-C18, with a pew on each side, all 'fenced' in a box enclosure. – The apse's COMMUNION TABLE and the PULPIT are of 1931–3. – CHAMBER ORGAN by the *Positive Organ Co. Ltd*, brought here in 1931. – In the N aisle, a BELL made in 1723 by *Robert Maxwell* of Edinburgh which hung in the bellcote until 1881. – STAINED GLASS. Three lights in the apse (St Paul, Our Lord as the Good Shepherd, and St Andrew), all by *R. Douglas McLundie*, the centre window of 1956, the other two of 1960.

GRAVEYARD. S of the church, plenty of C18 HEADSTONES carved with symbols of death and angels' heads (souls), one with a crowned hammer (the smiths' emblem), another with a coat of arms. – Near the SE corner, MONUMENT to Richard Yule † 1889, decorated with the relief of an old man (? Moses looking to the Promised Land). – At the NE corner, the BURIAL

ENCLOSURE, probably C18, of the Macadams of Waterhead. On its N wall, a weathered C17 TABLET carved with naked men flanking a coat of arms. – N of the church, beside the gate, the C18 HEADSTONE commemorating the Covenanting martyr Rodger Dunn †1689, but smarter and probably later than the standard early C18 Covenanter memorials. One side is carved with reminders of mortality, the other with an inscription including the verse:

> Pluck'd from Minerva's breast here am I laid
> Which debt to cruel Atropos I've paid
> Resting my clayey fabric in the dust
> Among the holy ashes of the Just
> My soul set sail for the celestial shore
> Till the last trump the same with joy restore.

SCHOOL. Georgian-survival of 1861.

CASSENCARIE
4050
1km. S of Creetown

Derelict and largely roofless mansion house. The earliest part, at the S, is a rectangular four-storey tower house of harled rubble built for the Muirs of Cassencarie, probably in the late C16 and almost certainly before 1593, when a tower is recorded here. Moulded window surrounds where not altered. This house was extended N, probably in the late C18, by the addition of a tall three-storey range of four bays, the piend-roofed N bay advanced to balance the tower. In this bay, a three-light ground-floor window. In *c.*1880 the house was bought by James Caird, who provided the C16 tower with a crowstepped gable and angle turrets (the l. square, the r. a pepperpot), added a granite portico in the inner angle of the Georgian wing and the tower, and built a gently Baronial back wing. To the N, crowstep-gabled low office houses of the earlier C19, one block with a ball-finialled gabled bellcote. They have recently been joined to the mansion house.

CASTLE DOUGLAS
7060

Planned gridiron village founded by Sir William Douglas of Gelston in the late C18 and made a burgh of barony in 1791, when the population was over six hundred. Cotton-spinning was at first the inhabitants' main occupation but the industry here was killed by the invention (*c.*1830) of the power loom, for whose operation Castle Douglas lacked a strong-flowing river or convenient source of coal. However, the burgh found prosperity as a market town and the site of the principal livestock auctions in Galloway; the C20 has added a role as a low-key tourist centre.

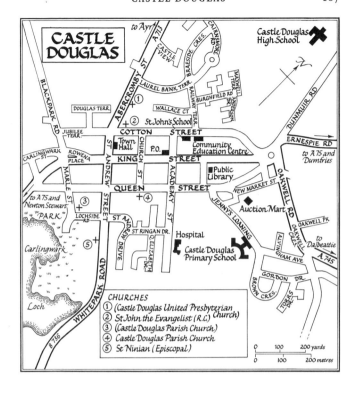

CHURCHES

Former CASTLE DOUGLAS PARISH CHURCH, Marle Street and Lochside Road. Converted to a theatre, 1992. Plain lancet Gothic by *James Barbour*, looking rather more unified than its building history warrants. It was begun in 1869 and much enlarged by *Barbour* in 1880–1. On each side of the nave a shallow projection whose window rises into a gablet. In the s gable, a stepped arrangement of three tall hoodmoulded lights; below them, panels carved with crosses and a trefoil. E and W transepts, their windows paired lights under a circular opening. In 1890 Barbour added a very tall tower to the end of the E transept. Big segmental-arched belfry openings set in thinly columned pointed overarches. Above, a crenellated parapet with a spired open-sided Gothic caphouse on its SE corner. Against the tower's S face, a semicircular conical-roofed stair tower serving the transept's gallery. Rectangular N chancel by *J. Jeffrey Waddell*, 1931.

Inside, an elaborate but curiously insubstantial nave roof with kingpost trusses, moulded hammerbeams and much bracing. The transepts' M-roofs are given central support by cast-iron columns. In the transepts, galleries of 1881, their front panels enclosing diagonal boarding decorated with simplified Gothic motifs. – STAINED GLASS. Chancel N window: three lights (the Ascension) by *Margaret Chilton* and *Marjorie Kemp*, 1948.

CASTLE DOUGLAS PARISH CHURCH, Queen Street. A building whose successive congregations have belonged to five denominations (Relief, Reformed Presbyterian, Free, United Free and Church of Scotland). Several of the denominational changes have been accompanied by changes to the fabric. The church was begun in 1801 as a Relief meeting house, and this origin is visible at the E front, which is built of brownish rubble, formerly harled, with simple pointed windows and a (blocked) pointed door. In 1870 the Reformed Presbyterians refronted the N gable and W front in red sandstone, hammerdressed at the front, and added hoodmoulds to their windows. At the same time they built the W tower, which rises sheer from a heavily battered base to corner machicolations from which gableted overarches break up to frame a round window on each face. Above this, a broached upper stage topped by a stringcourse and an octagonal stone spire rising between gablets. In 1923 the transepts (the W of stone, the E of brick) and shallow chancel were added. SW session house of 1929–30.

Inside, trussed roofs intersecting diagonally over the 1920s crossing. Deep N gallery. Stone chancel arch. – ORGAN by *Ingram & Co.* – STAINED GLASS. The chancel's three-light S window (Our Lord as the Good Shepherd, flanked by figures of *Unitas* and *Harmonia*) is of 1950. – In the session house, four lights (St Mary Magdalene, St Margaret of Scotland, the Presentation in the Temple, Our Lord among the Doctors in the Temple) by *Margaret Chilton* and *Marjorie Kemp*, *c.*1948–55, moved here in 1992 from the former Parish Church (q.v.).

CASTLE DOUGLAS UNITED PRESBYTERIAN CHURCH, Abercromby Road. Secularized. Big whin and sandstone Gothic box, by *James Barbour*, 1870. Broad gable front, its width disguised by the treatment of the centre, which is framed by buttresses joined by a pointed arch surmounted by the stub of the now missing bellcote. Inside this arched frame, an elaborate window, its dwarfish lights overpowered by a huge rose. Projecting from the centre, a wide porch, its parapet pierced by quatrefoils.

ST JOHN THE EVANGELIST (R.C.), Abercromby Road. Big and austere French Gothic, by *George Goldie*, 1867–8, all of local whin with red sandstone dressings. Nave ending in a semi-octagonal apse; SW steeple. Two-light side windows in hoodmoulded overarches, their tops decorated with blind quatrefoils. Large W window of two pairs of coupled lights, each under a circular opening, the whole surmounted by a rose. The tower is broached to an octagonal belfry topped by a stone spire. The interior's open roof was hidden by a wagon ceiling in 1992. Blind arcading along the windowless N wall and at the E apse, whose central bay is marble-clad. – STAINED GLASS in the windows of the S wall and apse

(Saints) by *William Wailes*, 1867–8. – Contemporary PRIEST'S
HOUSE at the E.

ST NINIAN (Episcopal), St Andrew Street. Craggy rogue Gothic,
by *E. B. Lamb*, 1856–61, built of aggressively hammerdressed
whinstone with granite dressings. Alternating bands of rounded
and rectangular slates covering the roof. Nave and a lower
chancel, with stone rhones carried on rounded corbels.
Windows with elongated trefoil heads. SW porch. At the join
of the nave and chancel, an organ chamber with a double-
pitched roof on the S. On the N, an immensely sturdy tower,
its E face buttressed by the lean-to vestry. The low top stage
projects on heavy rounded corbels and is decorated with roundels, the outer ones containing trefoils. Above, even heavier
chamfered corbels support the cornice topped by a set-back
battlement, with stepped merlons at its corners. There used to
be a spire. Inside, a braced kingpost-truss roof. Stone chancel
arch, its shafts carried on corbels. – Original FURNISHINGS. –
ORGAN by *Peter Wood & Son*, 1984. – STAINED GLASS. Four-
light E window (Our Lord blessing children; angels) by *James
Ballantine*, 1876. – In the nave S wall, three lights (Our Lord
blessing children; the Ascension; the Good Shepherd) of
c. 1880–1900. – In the N wall, a five-light window (the Parable
of the Sower) of *c.* 1885, stylistically mixed. – One late C19 light
(a very feminine angel) signed by *A. G. Taylor*.

PUBLIC BUILDINGS

AUCTION MART, New Market Street. Built *c.* 1900. Octagon of
buff brick with red sandstone dressings. Slated spire roof broken
by lucarne ventilators and large rooflights.

CASTLE DOUGLAS HIGH SCHOOL, Dunmuir Road. By *Stewartry County Council*, 1958. Three storeys of curtain walling.

CASTLE DOUGLAS PRIMARY SCHOOL, Jenny's Loaning. Built
in 1934.

COMMUNITY EDUCATION CENTRE, Cotton Street. Originally
Higher Grade School. By *J. A. Macgregor*, 1910. Tall two
storeys. Quite plain except for the porch's stylized urns.

HOSPITAL, Academy Street. By *Richard Park*, 1897. Single-
storey, built of glazed red brick with half-timbering in the
gables. E extension of 1934.

POST OFFICE, King Street. *See* Description below.

PUBLIC LIBRARY, King Street. Low-key Jacobean in hammerdressed red sandstone, by *George Washington Browne*, 1902–4.
L-plan, with a copper-clad and ogee-domed round tower in the
inner angle. At the E end, the ART GALLERY, added in 1938.

ST JOHN'S SCHOOL, Cotton Street. Opened in 1872 and now
rather altered. E-plan, with boys' and girls' porches in the outer
wings' inner angles. Round-arched windows in the projecting
gables.

TELEPHONE EXCHANGE, King Street. *See* Description, below.

TOWN HALL, St Andrew Street. Italianate in red sandstone,
by *James Barbour*, 1862–3. Broad recessed centrepiece with a

keyblocked window of three stilted round-arched lights. At the narrow pedimented ends, single-light stilted round-arched windows with consoled sills. On the l., a two-storey porch added in 1902, the anta-pilastered entrance surmounted by a high relief of the burgh arms. Set back to the l. of this, a contemporary extension with an open pediment and a window of three stepped and round-arched lights, extravagantly stilted.

DESCRIPTION

On the entry from the N and E the town's real beginning is marked by a tree-clad roundabout. On it, the WAR MEMORIAL of 1921, a granite mercat cross, its shaft topped by a shield displaying the burgh arms. From here three streets run S.

COTTON STREET on the W contains C19 workers' housing, two schools, St John the Evangelist (R.C.) Church (*see* Churches and Public Buildings, above) and the CO-OP SUPERSTORE by *Cameron Associates*, 1989–91, large and low with arbitrary post-Modern detail. In ABERCROMBY ROAD, the former United Presbyterian Church (*see* above). Some way further out, No. 39 (ROCKPARK) is a tall mid-Victorian Jacobean villa. The front has twin gables halted against corbelled chimneystacks which flank a small and steep centre gablet. From each front gable projects a bay window, the l. canted and parapeted, the r. rectangular with a sloping top. Tall spiral-decorated fireclay chimneypots at the back.

QUEEN STREET, the E of the three main streets, has a smarter mid-C19 beginning. Blocky classical doorpieces at Nos. 23 and 24. Nos. 25–28 form a short U-plan terrace of *c.*1850. Ball finials on the projecting gables, which have contained windows of three lights at the ground floor and two at the first. Then terraced cottages and houses, interrupted by the large forecourt of the Parish Church (*see* above) followed by the generous garden of ROSEBANK, a villa of *c.*1850, Georgian-survival but with canted bay windows flanking the porch. On the SW corner of St Andrew Street, the large but perfunctorily Art Deco PALACE CINEMA of *c.*1930. On the SE corner, the much prettier INVERGARRY LODGE, a mid-C19 *cottage orné* with broad eaves and horizontal glazing. To the E, ST ANDREW STREET's S side begins with a two-storey terrace (Nos. 52–60) of *c.*1840, with heavy anta-pilastered doorpieces. It is overlooked by a sloping field at whose top sits THE BRAE of 1803, with an anta-pilastered doorpiece at the advanced and battlemented centre of its main block. Straight links to lower piend-roofed pavilions, the l. with a big pedimented Victorian dormer, the r. overlaid by a conservatory. Across Lochside Street (for whose former Parish Church, *see* Churches, above), late Georgian detached houses. No. 66 St Andrew Street is quite grand. Panels on the frieze of its heavy pilastered doorpiece; ball finials on the ends of the overall cornice. No. 68 is a humbler version.

Rather smarter and with a front garden is the piend-roofed
BOTHWELL HOUSE, with rusticated quoins and a columned
doorpiece. Opposite St Ninian's Episcopal Church (*see*
above), THE GROVE, again with rusticated quoins, its Doric
doorpiece columned and pedimented.

KING STREET, the central street running s from the War Memorial, is the town's commercial thoroughfare. It begins with
buildings only on the w, a plain C19 terrace barely enlivened
by bracketed cornices over the doors of Nos. 15 and 16 and an
oriel window of *c.* 1900 on the late Georgian CROWN HOTEL.
Two more oriels, with bullseye windows between, at the late
C19 red sandstone Nos. 26–27. Also late C19 but friendlier,
with harling and broad-eaved gablets, are Nos. 28–30. Then the
IMPERIAL HOTEL of the earlier C19, with rusticated quoins,
Tudor hoodmoulds and a segmental pend arch. Opposite, the
Public Library (*see* Public Buildings, above), a large monkey-
puzzle in its garden. Now King Street becomes strongly commercial and predominantly Victorian and Edwardian. On the
w, a big asymmetrical Jacobean CLYDESDALE BANK, the
banking hall in its l. part marked by a balustraded balcony and
steep shaped gablets, the agent's office on the r. by a two-storey
rectangular bay window and a lion finial atop its semicircular
gablet. Opposite is No. 47 of *c.* 1900, its first floor with a
pair of rusticated bullseye windows under a pediment; steep
bargeboarded gablet above. At No. 48 on the w, a delicate
Victorian cast-iron shopfront. Then, on the e, No. 61, built as
the Union Bank in 1902, heavy Jacobean with red sandstone
dressings. No. 82 on the w is of *c.* 1930, tall two-storey Art
Deco-classical, with huge reliefs of thistles flanking the shields
over the doors. On the SE corner of Academy Street, a block
which looks late C18 but has a mid-C19 pilastered shopfront.
On the SW corner, the POST OFFICE of 1969–70, an undistinguished box, its cut-out corner sacrificing streetscape to
road safety. To its w, a blandly authoritarian TELEPHONE
EXCHANGE by *D. C. Ireland* of the *Ministry of Works*, 1956–7,
facing Nos. 7–11 ACADEMY STREET (STANLEY COTTAGES)
of *c.* 1900, built of red and white brick, with bargeboarded steep
gablets.

In King Street below the Post Office, another big red sandstone block of *c.* 1890, Jacobean again but with crowstepped
gables giving a strong Scottish accent; thistle and rose finials
on the steep triangular and semicircular dormerheads. Less
pompous the shopfront of No. 136, mixing cast-iron Gothic
columns with stone pilasters. On the e, the austere grey granite
crowstepped and gableted blockbuster of the ROYAL (former
NATIONAL) BANK OF SCOTLAND, dated 1864; high up in
one gable, a vesica containing a small relief of St Andrew. Vista
to the e along Church Street closed by the Parish Church (*see*
Churches, above). s of Church Street, nothing much until the
DOUGLAS ARMS HOTEL on the w, plain late Georgian. Set
into its front, a small stone in a moulded frame, inscribed
WC/MG/1779. A larger and plainer frame encloses a cast-

iron plaque, made by *J. Affleck* of Dumfries in 1827, which gives the distances from Castle Douglas to a selection of Scottish and English towns. On the NE corner with St Andrew Street, the MERRICK HOTEL of *c.* 1840, with corniced first-floor windows and an overall blocking course. On the SW corner, a small block of grey granite and red sandstone serving as the base for a very tall octagonal clock tower, its corbelled cornice surmounted by a cupola whose thin Roman Doric columns support a high ogee-roofed copper dome. It is by *W. F. Valentine*, 1934–5, a replacement for the late C18 Town House and steeple, which had been destroyed by fire.

In ST ANDREW STREET running W from King Street, the late Georgian DOUGLAS BAR with a Roman Doric columned doorpiece, followed by the Town Hall (*see* Public Buildings, above). Then two mid-C19 houses. One has a doorpiece whose modillion cornice breaks forward over end consoles, their sides carved with rosettes, the other a heavy anta-pilastered doorpiece.

VILLAS

CARLINGWARK HOUSE, 0.6km. S. Castellated villa of *c.* 1840, a round tower at the S corner. Gableted late C19 extension to the N; late C20 additions by *Dumfries and Galloway Regional Council* at the back.

ERNESPIE HOUSE (URR VALLEY COUNTRY HOUSE HOTEL), off Ernespie Road. Probably begun *c.* 1800 as an unpretentious harled house of two storeys and a basement. A little later in the C19 this was extended E in a castellated manner with hoodmoulded windows and, in plain fashion, to the N; this rear extension includes an unduly serious battlemented tower. The main block was dressed up in the mid-C19 with a Jacobean porch, overall balustrade and the addition of pedimented dormerheads to the first-floor windows. C20 single-storey SW addition, again battlemented.

HILLOWTON, off Dunmuir Road. The nucleus is a late Georgian house of two storeys and three bays. Mid-C19 remodelling provided a pedimented doorpiece, shallow rectangular windows at the ground floor, dormers on the roof, and a Georgian-survival addition at each end.

GREENLAW HOUSE. *See* p. 330.

THREAVE CASTLE. *See* p. 545.

1050   CASTLE KENNEDY

The older part of the village contains rubble-built terraced cottages of the 1860s; housing of the later C20 to the W. For the eponymous castle, *see* p. 409.

INCH PARISH CHURCH, 0.8km. NW. Austere lanceted Gothic by *J. Maitland Wardrop*, 1858–61. Big rubble-built nave, its W side buttressed; on the E, a broad transept. Lower short chancel; NE porch. Gableted bellcote at the N end, where a steeple was originally intended. The interior was completely recast by *Hamilton More-Nisbett* in 1895–6 after it had been gutted by a fire. Over the nave, a tunnel-vaulted wooden ceiling, its frieze studded with bosses carved with rosettes, fleurs-de-lis and other devices. Tall stone arch into the S chancel. This is rectangular but made to appear apsidal by a segment of minister's and elders' stalls backed by panelling, its canopied top surmounted by cresting. Above this rise the pipes of the ORGAN (by *Brindley & Foster*, 1897; rebuilt by *H. Hilsdon*, 1970). – Low metal CHANCEL RAIL with floral decoration. – Simple Gothic PULPIT on the chancel arch's W side. – The E transept, covered by an elliptical wooden vault, is filled by the STAIR PEW. Shouldered rectangular opening into the nave, its spandrels carved with coats of arms. – STAINED GLASS. Three-light E window (the Good Shepherd, with St John and St Peter) by *Heaton, Butler & Bayne*, *c.*1900, very competent but unexciting.

LOCHINCH CASTLE AND CASTLE KENNEDY. *See* p. 409.

CASTLEMILK
0.8km. NE of Kettleholm

1070

Scottish Baronial mansion designed in 1864 by *David Bryce* for Robert (later Sir Robert) Jardine, a partner in the opium-trading firm of Jardine, Matheson & Co. Work seems to have been completed in 1870, although the final bills were not settled for another three years.

Walls of coursed masonry, the buff-coloured stone brought from Cowdens quarry (Borders); slated roofs. The house is an asymmetrical composition of crowstep-gabled blocks, each of which housed, on the principal floor, rooms devoted to a specific aspect of the social and domestic life of a Victorian magnate. All the blocks (except the conservatory) are of at least two storeys above a fully exposed basement. The NE CORNER BLOCK, containing the principal entrance and the study and business room, is L-plan, the jamb provided by a huge round four-storey tower, its appearance derived from the early C17 Castle Fraser or Huntly Castle (Aberdeenshire). The windows are mullioned and transomed at the ground floor; at the first they enjoy aedicules with slender pinnacled columns and semi-circular pediments. The walling above is jettied out on heavy corbelling whose line drops below the second-floor windows. Overall, a corbelled-out balustrade. Ogee-roofed round turret rising above at the NW. Projecting E from the tower, a porte cochère with aggressively stepped buttresses at its corners, from which protrude carved dogs' heads (by *Thomas Borland*). Shouldered-arched openings; balustrade breaking into corbelled rounds. This part's main block is rectangular, with an attic projected on corbelling and pedimented stone dormers with scrolls on their sloping sides. Round corner turrets, their conical roofs topped by lead statuettes (by *Peter Drummond*) of

95

knights representing members of the Bruce family, the medieval
lords of the estate. At the E front's N end, a small gabled
projection containing an entrance for those visiting the owner
on business.

The PRINCIPAL BLOCK, intended for entertainment, abuts
the W side of the business block and projects far to its S. In
the inner angle with the round entrance tower, a conical-
roofed round turret whose tall mullioned and transomed
windows light the principal stair. On this E front, two-light
mullioned and transomed windows to the principal floor,
steeply pedimented dormerheads over the bedroom windows
above. At the basement, a luggage entrance opening onto a
stair which rises to the top of the house. At this block's N
end, a martially battlemented square tower and a parapeted
rectangular bay window. Symmetrical W front. Corbelled out
at each corner, a two-storey turret, its upper floor jettied;
lead statuettes of knights on the conical roofs. These sit next
to canted bay windows corbelled out to square gables at the
first floor. At the centre, a mullioned and transomed three-
light ground-floor window; steeply pedimented windows
above. Projecting from this block's S end, a single-storey
conservatory, the windows mullioned and transomed, urns
on the high parapet.

The third part of the house is the SE WING, which contained
the family's private rooms (bedroom, dressing rooms, boudoir
and bathroom). On the S front, at its join with the conservatory,
another canted bay window corbelled to the square, its E side
abutting another two-storey conical-roofed turret. Corbelled
out from the corners of the broad E end's top floor, a pair of
round turrets, their conical roofs once again surmounted by
statuettes of knights. In the centre of this end, another rounded
turret, its top squashed by a battlemented machicolation astride
the gable.

A low N service wing links to the STABLE COURTYARD to
the NE. This is of only one storey and an attic but the Baronial
dress is quite aggressive, the low height giving added pro-
minence to the tower and turrets.

The principal entrance opens into an ashlar-walled vestibule
in the round tower. Simple Jacobean ceiling and a short flight
of steps up to the bottom landing of the main stair. This is a
grand introduction to the PRINCIPAL FLOOR which it reaches
by a straight flight before doubling back on itself to continue
to the first floor. All of oak, except that between the main
balusters are slender ornamental railings of gilded wrought
iron. Scholarly Jacobean detail, the Ionic baluster design con-
flated from two examples published in C. J. Richardson's *Old
English Mansions* (1841).* Over the stair, a Jacobean compartmented plaster ceiling with large foliaged pendants (like
the rest of the plasterwork, the work of *James Annan*). At the

* The source noted, with much other information, in Alistair Rowan, 'Castlemilk,
Dumfriesshire', *Country Life*, 11 and 18 August 1977.

principal floor, two openings from the stair. One, straight ahead, is through a tripartite oak screen, its thin Corinthian piers with banded and faceted rustication copied from early C17 monuments in Greyfriars Churchyard, Edinburgh. On the frieze, carved human heads. The other opening is to the s through a semi-octagonal headed arch, its sides again with banded rustication, the keystones in the shape of human heads. Both these openings lead into the GALLERY which occupies 96 most of the E side of the house's principal block. It is T-plan, the broad tail (intended to house a billiard table) projecting E between the main stair and the service stair. Another Jacobean ceiling of the same type as over the stair. In the centre of the w wall, a very grand Jacobean Renaissance chimneypiece made by *William Patterson & Son* in 1869. Paired foliaged columns flank the opening. On its frieze, more foliage and *putti*. Overmantel containing a portrait of Robert W. B. Jardine painted *c.* 1877. On each side of the overmantel, a double tier of round-arched niches flanked by diagonally set terms; more foliage and *putti* on the overall frieze under a modillion cornice.

The PRINCIPAL ROOMS all open off the gallery. At its N end, the dining room, plain except for another Jacobean ceiling, which has strapwork enrichment in some of the compartments. At the main block's NW corner, the library. Another Jacobean ceiling, on which appear the monogrammed initials of Robert Jardine and his wife, Margaret Seton Buchanan Jardine. Oak bookcases with inlaid patterns of walnut veneer at the base, foliaged drops on the piers. Projecting from the cornice, carved heads by *William Patterson & Son*. Also by Patterson & Son is the Mannerist chimneypiece, with spirally fluted columns framing the opening. Barley-sugar columns at the overmantel. On top, a pediment broken by a strapworked cartouche. To the s, in the centre of the w front, an ante-room, completely refitted in 1928 to a design by *William Courtenay Le Maitre*, executed by *Vigor & Co.* of London. The character is late C17, with bleached panelling and fluted pilasters framing the N fireplace flanked by keyblocked roundheaded niches. Drawing room at the house's sw corner. The ceiling is again Jacobean but elaborately although delicately enriched. Plaster panelled walls, the effect late Georgian. Also Georgian of a sort is the white marble chimneypiece, with coupled Ionic columns and a deeply carved frieze. At the s corners, shell-headed round-arched niches made in 1928 from Bryce's bowed turret recesses. Opening off the gallery's s end and at a lower level is the conservatory, entered by a short flight of steps with neo-Jacobean strapwork balustrades. Along its w side, a row of sturdy marbled Doric columns introduced in 1928 when Le Maitre remodelled this as a billiard room.

In the garden, N of the house, a FOUNTAIN of *c.* 1870, again by *Bryce*. Bronze lions' heads on the basin. It is covered by a baldacchino, the Roman Doric columns at the corners re-used from the previous mansion house (of 1796) at Castlemilk. On each side, a roundheaded arch, the keystone carved as a human head. On the corners of the entablature, obelisk finials. Strap-worked dome top surmounted by a female figure. – At the beginning of the N drive, the NORTH LODGE of *c.* 1870, barge-boarded Tudor. Rusticated Jacobean GATEPIERS, the outer with ball finials, the inner with scrolled open spires. – Beside this approach, the WALLED GARDEN, probably also of *c.* 1870; the rubble masonry is swept up at the N. Spearhead cast-iron railings on the S side. – The S drive starts at Kettleholm with the SOUTH LODGE, again bargeboarded Tudor, and ball-finialled GATEPIERS of *c.* 1870. – Also of *c.* 1870, the S drive's BRIDGE, with pointed arches and bartizans serving as pedestrian refuges.

1050   CASTLE OF PARK
                          o.8km. W of Glenluce

73 Harled and crowstep-gabled tower house. The principal fact of its building history* is explained by a panel over the door, inscribed:

BLISSIT[.BE.]THE.NA[ME.]OF.[THE.]LORD.THIS
VERK.VAS.BEGUN.T[H]E.F[IR]ST.DAY.O[F].MARCH
1590.BE.THOMAS.HAY.OF.PARK.AND
JONET.MAK.DOVEL.HIS.SPOVS

The house was completed before the beginning of 1599, when it was described in a charter as newly built. It is of four storeys and an attic. L-plan, with a SE jamb; in the inner angle and projected on continuous corbelling, a shallowly bowed turret containing the stair from the third floor to the attic. A huge chimney rises from the wallhead of the main block's E side. Another massive chimney at the N gable, but the chimneys of the S gable and jamb are much more ordinary. The only signs of defence are two moulded round shotholes, one at the ground floor covering the entrance, the other at the top of the jamb's S face. Moulded windows, large at the first floor and comfortably sized at the upper storeys. Several of the attic windows break up through the eaves and perhaps were originally gabled or pedimented.

   Inside, the ground-floor rooms are all tunnel-vaulted. A passage runs along the main block's E side with moulded doors opening off it. The S room has a stair in the thickness of its SW corner leading to the first-floor hall, so presumably this was the wine cellar. At the passage's N end, a rather small kitchen with a serving hatch beside the door. In the kitchen's N gable, a huge segmental-arched fireplace. Off the fireplace's W side, a small room with a window to the W and its own tiny fireplace

---

* A couple of low E wings were added in the C18. These were removed as a preliminary to a programme of consolidation, reroofing and reharling undertaken *c.* 1965–8 by the *Ministry of Public Building and Works* (later transmogrified into the Ancient Monuments Branch of the *Department of the Environment* and then of the *Scottish Development Department*). Further work, mostly to the interior, was carried out for the Landmark Trust by *Stewart Tod & Partners* in 1992–3.

in the N wall. The principal stair is a broad turnpike in the jamb. The first floor of the main block is occupied by the hall, which has a huge moulded rectangular fireplace in its E wall; the stone floor slabs were introduced in the 1980s. In the NE corner, occupying the space between the kitchen flue and the side wall, a small closet, perhaps a close garderobe. In the corresponding NW corner, a tight turnpike stair (reinstated in wood in the 1992–3 alterations by *Stewart Tod & Partners*) to the floors above. In the E ingo of the S window's embrasure (segmental-arched like the others), a restored stone seat. Between this window and the door from the stair, an aumbry recess, apparently to hold trays or bowls of food before it was served, this end of the hall having presumably been cut off by a screen (now suggested by a line of kitchen units). The second floor originally contained two rooms, each with a moulded stone fireplace. The S room (subdivided in 1992–3 to provide a bathroom and passage to the N room) has a SW cupboard containing stone shelves and, in the NW corner, a garderobe complete with a lavatory drain. In the N room, one stone seat survives at the E window. Closets in the NE and SW corners. The ceiling boards were painted by *Jennifer Packer*, 1992–3, with stylized fruit, an evocation of what may have once existed but without danger of being mistaken for 1590s work. The third floor also originally contained two rooms (the S now subdivided), each with a moulded stone fireplace, both restored. Off the NE corner of the N room, a garderobe, still with a wooden seat over the drain. Tight turnpike in the house's inner angle to a small room over the main stair, with a fireplace in its E wall. Over the main block is an attic lit by a small S window.

CASTLE STEWART

3060

1.8km. N of Challoch

Ruined tower of *c.* 1500, the N and E walls mostly gone. It has been a four-storey rectangle, built of rubble, the corners thriftily rounded to economize on dressed masonry. Parapet on simply moulded corbels. Slit ground-floor windows in the S wall and what remains of the E; another at first-floor level, presumably to light a stair in the NE corner. Large S windows at the first and second floors; the second-floor windows still have chamfered jambs. In the W wall, a couple of small windows to the two top floors.

The interior was not vaulted. Stepped sills to the ground-floor windows. At the first floor, remains of a chamber inside the N wall. On the second floor, a W fireplace with moulded Gothic jambs. To its S, the entrance to another wall chamber. Segmental-arched embrasure at the S window. At the third floor, one Gothic capital survives of the S fireplace. W wall chamber.

CASTLEWIGG

3.3km. NW of Whithorn

Roofless ivy-clad ruin of a substantial mansion house of several dates. The earliest part, at the s, was built for Archibald Stewart of Barclye and Tonderghie, who had acquired the estate in 1584. It is L-plan, the jamb projecting at the NE corner. In the jamb's N face, a ground-floor gunhole and a large cornices first-floor window, its surround with a roll-and-hollow moulding. Another roll-and-hollow moulding at the entrance in the jamb's w face, its lintel bearing the date 1593, presumably the year of the house's completion. The main block's w gable is sufficiently free of ivy to show that its windows have been Georgianized. Inside the entrance, in the jamb, a tunnel-vaulted lobby with a vaulted store (converted to a wine cellar) to its E, its only external opening provided by the N wall's rectangular gunhole. S of the lobby, another tunnel-vaulted store at the main block's E end. The ground-floor rooms to the w are unvaulted. No evidence now of a stair. Probably it was attached to the jamb's NW corner, the position now occupied by a Georgian service stair. A small addition in the C16 house's inner angle is likely to be C18. N of this, a large extension of *c.* 1800: N front with full-height bows flanking the straight centrepiece, an anta-pilastered ashlar screen across its *piano nobile*.

CAULKERBUSH

No village. Only a church standing just outside the policies of Southwick House.

38 SOUTHWICK PARISH CHURCH. By *Kinnear & Peddie*, 1889–91, a sturdy mixture of Early Christian and Norman, built of local grey granite with dressings of red Gatelawbridge sandstone. Three-bay nave, transepts and a small apsidal chancel. Crossing tower derived from the C14 tower of St Monans Parish Church (Fife) but with two-light Norman belfry openings. Corbelled uncrenellated parapet with projecting cannon spouts; rising inside, a slated pyramid spire. Chaste Early Christian windows at the chancel and side walls of the nave. In the nave's N gable, a Norman window of three lights, the centre stilted. Two-light window, its tympanum carved with incised decoration, in the gable of the E transept. In this transept's s wall, a simple Norman door. More elaborate entrance, Norman again, at the NE porch.

Inside, a wagon roof over the nave; segmental rear-arches to the side windows. Roundheaded arches at the crossing, the w (liturgical s) blocked, the chancel arch enriched with chevron decoration. Over the crossing, a quadripartite vault. Panelled ceiling in the chancel. The arrangement is on best High Presbyterian lines, with the chancel raised two steps above the crossing and containing the communion table. On one side of the chancel arch, a neo-Norman FONT by *Cox & Buckley*, 1898, of white stone with marble shafts. – On the other, a neo-Jacobean PULPIT. – Wrought-iron Arts and Crafts LIGHT FITTINGS for oil lamps. – STAINED GLASS. Apse windows of c. 1891, filled with abstract patterns rising into Celtic crosses, except at the centre light, which contains a boy angel. In the nave's three-light N window, more 1890s glass, with patterns of the same sort forming a background for small panels containing angels and, in the centre, the boy Samuel. – The E transept's two-light window (the Baptism of Our Lord) looks a little later, its realism gently stylized. – In the chancel floor, an heraldic BRASS commemorating the contribution of Sir Mark Stewart of Southwick to the church's erection. – CHAMBER ORGAN of 1958 by *Solway Organs.*

SOUTHWICK CHURCHYARD, 2.2km. W. Enclosed by a rubble wall, its S end rounded, indicating that the graveyard may originally have been circular. It contains the ivy-clad ruins of a rectangular rubble-built CHURCH, perhaps of the C12 or C13 (*see* the Introduction, p. 35). There have been two round-arched windows in the E gable.

SCHOOL, Cushatgrove, 1.5km. NW. Now housing. Broad-eaved gently Gothic *cottage orné* of 1874, extended S in the same manner a little later. – Also of the 1870s, the detached two-storey gingerbread-style SCHOOLHOUSE.

CASTLE FARM, 1.9km. NW. In the steading, remains of AUCH-ENSKEOCH CASTLE, a house of c. 1600, presumably built by John Lindsay, whose charter of the lands in 1599 contained the condition that he build a mansion here. Part of the rubble E wall and round NE tower survive. In the main wall, a small square ground-floor window and rectangular windows, also quite small, at the floor above. Splayed rectangular gunloop at the ground floor of the tower; small square openings above. The house has been of at least three storeys.

GLENSONE, 3.4km. NW. Early C19 farmhouse, its main block of two storeys and three bays, built of white-painted rubble with rusticated quoins; end chimneys framing the piended roof. At each end, a single-storey pavilion.

SOUTHWICK HOUSE. *See* p. 522.

WREATHS TOWER. *See* p. 574.

CHALLOCH 3060

Just the church and rectory standing at a crossroads.

ALL SAINTS CHURCH (Episcopal). Geometric, by *W. G. Hab-* 33 *ershon & Pite* of London, 1871–2, built of whin with buff-coloured red sandstone dressings and red-tiled roofs, their eaves projected on wooden brackets. Nave and a slightly lower chancel from whose N side project the M-roofed transeptal organ chamber and vestry, all with stepped buttresses. Long SW porch, its wooden walls standing on a stone base. Tall spired metal bellcote over the nave. Plate-traceried windows at the gables, the others cusped single lights. The hoodmoulds of the

E window and vestry door have label stops carved with the heads of medieval men and women; foliaged stops at the w window.

35   Richly finished interior. Over the nave, an open queenpost-truss roof, its members moulded.* Coffered wooden roof at the chancel, its panels stencilled in gold with sacred monograms. Stone arches to the chancel and organ chamber. Nook-shafted rear-arches at the windows. The FURNISHINGS are almost all of 1872. – Wrought-iron CHANCEL SCREEN, the lower part a septum of 1872 by *Hart, Son, Peard & Co.*, the rood beam above added *c.* 1885. – Iron ALTAR RAILS decorated with painted and gilded roses. – Two-seat SEDILIA in the sanctuary. – REREDOS of three gableted arches, their backs painted with gold fleurs-de-lis on a blue ground. – ENCAUSTIC TILES by *Colla*, quite simple in the nave aisle, richer in the choir, and still richer in the sanctuary. – Each side of the altar, WALL TILES decorated with stylized foliage. – ORGAN, with stencilled pipes, by *Marston & Son.* – Stone PULPIT by *Cox & Son*, the faces of the bowl bearing blind arcading springing from marble columns, the base carved with angels. – FONT also by *Cox & Son*, an octagonal bowl on polished granite columns. – Brass LECTERN, the bookrest flanked by shamrock-decorated candlesticks. – On the w wall, a brass TABLET to the memory of Elizabeth Stopford Blair †1906, signed by *Jones & Willis Ltd.* and engraved with angels holding the inscription scroll.

STAINED GLASS. Three-light E window (Our Lord blessing children, David, and Our Lady) by *C. A. Gibbs*, 1872. – The chancel's s light (the *Agnus Dei* on a richly patterned ground) is also of 1872 by Gibbs. – So too are the E windows of the nave on each side (the Ascension on the N, Faith on the s). – Also by *Gibbs*, of *c.* 1875, is another N window (Samuel and Eli). – To its w, a late C19 light (the Good Shepherd). – Opposite, a richly coloured light of 1888 showing St Margaret of Antioch trampling on a snarling red dragon. It is probably by *C. E. Kempe*. – Certainly by Kempe are the w windows on each side of *c.* 1900, filled with heraldic emblems of apostles, virgins, martyrs and confessors. – Three-light w window (*Benedicite Omnia Opera*) of *c.* 1890.

Immediately outside the E end, an elegant white marble cross to the church's founder, Edward J. Stopford Blair, owner of the nearby Penninghame House, †1885. The slender octagonal shaft bears shields decorated with sacred emblems; the arms have foliaged ends, and the front of the head is adorned with an angel of the Resurrection.

ST NINIAN'S CHAPEL, 3.3km. N. Only the rubble-built ivy-covered E gable survives of a chapel built by John Kennedy of Blairquhan in 1508. In the gable's inner face, two roughly formed aumbries, the N placed higher than the s. The building has been *c.* 13m. by 7.2m.

CASTLE STEWART. *See* p. 177.

---

* The plaster between the rafters was intended to be painted sky blue and spangled with gold stars.

PENNINGHAME HOUSE. *See* p. 487.

CHAPELCROSS 2060

Just the nuclear power station, a powerful presence in the country-side.

POWER STATION. Built in 1955–60, with *Merz & McLellan* as 127 consultant engineers and *L. J. Couves & Partners* as associate architects. Four reactors, their squat round cooling towers rising in a tapering curve like huge concrete chimneys. Behind, four blocks of concrete and glass, the contrast of their crisp rectangular shapes emphasized by brightly painted metal work and slim black chimneys.

CHAPELKNOWE 3070

Hamlet containing the old United Presbyterian Church; Half Morton Parish Church stands by itself to the NE.

CHAPELKNOWE UNITED PRESBYTERIAN CHURCH. Disused. By *George Dale Oliver*, 1890. Minimal Gothic in red sandstone. Blocky bellcote with a pointed arch and crowstepped top.

HALF MORTON PARISH CHURCH, 1.3km. NE. T-plan kirk, its rubble walling mostly rendered and lined as ashlar. The body was built in 1744 and enlarged *c.*1795; the N 'aisle' was added in 1833. Big lancet windows of 1889; a blocked rectangular light in the W wall of the 'aisle' indicates what they replaced. Battlemented ashlar bellcote of 1839. Small vestry at the W added in 1848 by *R. Turner* of Hamilton. E porch of 1889.

CLACHANMORE 0040

Very short white-painted early C19 terrace, its centrepiece a two-storey three-bay house.

SCHOOL. School and schoolhouse of the later C19, with steep crowstepped gables and angular Gothic windows.

CLARENCEFIELD 0060

Small village along the road at the entrance to Comlongon Castle. Some C19 vernacular but largely C20 bungaloid.

McFARLAN MEMORIAL HALL. Plain with bracketed eaves, of *c.*1900.

POLICE STATION. Now housing. By *James Barbour & Bowie*, 1911. Small but heavily crowstepped; a sloping canopy over the paired doors.

SCHOOL. Now in other use. By *A. B. Crombie*, 1869. Battered chimney rising against the W front.

COMLONGON CASTLE. *See* p. 185.

CLATTERINGSHAWS

5070

8.3km. w of New Galloway

Humble farmhouse and steading of the later C19, built of painted rubble. The steading now houses the CLATTERINGSHAWS FOREST WILDLIFE CENTRE. In the entrance hall, a STAINED GLASS window ('The Galloway Window') by *Brian Thomas*, 1976, depicting wildlife of the area, a stag at the centre. Good strong colours and not kitsch. – To the NE, the reconstruction of a Romano-British HOMESTEAD discovered in 1974 when the level of the loch was lowered. The dwelling is circular, the low drystone rubble wall intended to support the timbers of the conical roof. In front of the entrance, a segmental forecourt, delineated by more rubble walling.

CLOSEBURN

9090

Village with a long line of terraced C19 cottages (No. 73 has a door lintel dated 1816) beside the A76. A second row to the w, the early C19 two-storey piend-roofed CORNER HOUSE filling the heel of the L-plan. Schools and Parish Church aloof to the E.

PARISH CHURCH. By *James Barbour*, 1878. Ambitious but not very inspired Gothic, in hammerdressed snecked rubble. It is cruciform, the E inner angles containing a vestry and organ chamber. Angle-buttressed NW tower of three tall stages, the lower two with narrow windows, the belfry with tall paired openings framed by overarches. Gablet over the door, one of its hoodmould's label stops carved with oak leaves, the other with thistles. Big dragon gargoyles at the open parapet, its corners topped by the buttresses' crocketed pinnacles.

The interior is spacious. The hammerbeam roof's braces spring from foliaged corbels; a display of intersecting carpentry over the crossing. – Pitch pine PEWS and PULPIT of 1878. – The COMMUNION TABLE of *c*. 1910 now has pride of place. – Elaborate little brass LECTERN of 1905. – ORGAN by *Henry Willis & Sons*, 1887. – STAINED GLASS. Abstract patterned designs of 1878 in most windows. – The two S windows contain narrative scenes (Our Lord and little children; the Good Shepherd; Our Lord and John the Baptist), also of 1878. – Window in the N transept (Our Lord blessing) by the *St Enoch Glass Studios*, 1948. – At the back, a medieval FONT brought here from Dalgarnock Churchyard. Large stone octagon containing a round basin with a central drain.

GRAVEYARD to the N. At its w entrance, mid-C18 rusticated and corniced GATEPIERS with ball finials. Inside them, a couple of small and crude shelters for elders receiving the collection. – In the middle of the graveyard, remains of the rubble-walled (formerly harled) OLD PARISH CHURCH, built in 1741 and heightened by *Archibald Cleland*, 1779. The E gable and the E bay of each side wall still stand. In the side walls, round-arched windows with moulded rectangular imposts and plain projecting keystones. E door of the same type, with a bullseye window above. On the gable, a ball-finialled birdcage bellcote with panelled piers. In it is hung a BELL bearing the initials G H (probably for *George Hog*, an Edinburgh founder) and the date 1606. The interior has contained an E gallery.

Immediately SE is the smart MAUSOLEUM built by Thomas Kirkpatrick of Closeburn in 1742. Ashlar walls pierced by large windows, the bays marked off by rusticated pilasters. The N entrance door has a basket-arched surround framed by thin panelled strips rising into tall flattened consoles which support the flat-topped pediment, its sides' bottom corners scrolled. Under the pediment, a frieze carved with a crude anthemion. Heraldic achievement in the tympanum. Round the walls inside, a frieze bearing the repeated warning '*Sic Transit Gloria Mundi*' and decorated with carved skulls and crossbones. – Leaning against the mausoleum's W wall, FRAGMENTS of C17 or early C18 memorials. Among them, part of a monument to Thomas Stoart †1673, carved with the relief of an angel's head (the soul) and a skull and crossbones. – A little to the S, an C18 TABLE STONE. Between its baluster legs, panels decorated with emblems of death and resurrection. The E panel is carved with a standing figure in C18 dress but he sprouts wings and a crown hovers over his head; on the W panel, a trumpeting angel's head, a corpse, skull and crossbones. – Beside this, the GRAVESLAB of Peter MacTurk †1670, with a crude skull and crossbones. – Propped against the retaining wall of the grave-yard's E extension, late C17 and early C18 SLABS, some prob-ably from table stones, a couple having foliaged borders and one (of *c.* 1700) carved with caryatids.

CLOSEBURN SCHOOL. By *James Barbour & Bowie*, 1909. Free-style. The main feature is the battered projecting centrepiece containing paired porches and crowned with a square pyramid-roofed open stone cupola.

Former WALLACE HALL ACADEMY. John Wallace †1723, a Glasgow merchant and native of Closeburn, left £1,400 for the building and endowment of a school here. By 1790 boarders were admitted, and the piend-roofed front block is the BOARD-ING HOUSE built for them in 1795. Three storeys and three bays, austere except for a corniced doorpiece. Behind, the SCHOOL itself; its present Scots Jacobean appearance, with crowstepped gables and hoodmoulded windows, dates from 1882, but it incorporates the school built by *William Lukup* in 1724–9 and remodelled in 1842 by *Walter Newall*.

CLOSEBURN CASTLE
1.1km. E

Rectangular rubble-built tower house of the Kirkpatricks, prob-ably dating from the earlier C15 but externally much altered *c.* 1800, when the irregularly positioned windows were enlarged with segmental heads and plain battlements (replacing battle-ments of 1689) were added to the tops of the tower and its NW caphouse. W door to the ground floor. At the W wall's N end, a roundheaded first-floor door, its jambs splayed, now approached by a stone forestair but originally by a ladder. Inside, a segmental tunnel-vault over the ground floor (divided into stores), formerly with a hatch for access to the floor above. Above, two round-arched tunnel-vaults, one over the first floor, the other (subdivided by entresols) over the three floors above. Tight turnpike stair in the wall thickness of the NW corner. Each of these floors has been subdivided into two rooms, perhaps in the C17 or C18, the partition wall containing the flues, which rise into a central stack.

To the N, a Victorian battlemented porch joining to a low piend-roofed block, probably of the later C18. – At the end of the S drive, an early C19 single-storey LODGE with a pedimented Roman Doric portico.

MOTTE, Dinning, 1.4km. SW. Motte and bailey, formed in the C12 or early C13 from a natural hillock close to the River Nith. The uphill approach from the SE is cut through by a ditch, 10m. wide and 3.6m. deep, with an earth rampart behind. The rampart returns on each side of the hillock to enclose an oblong bailey, c. 20m. by 17m. At the bailey's NW end rises the motte itself, a truncated cone, at least partly artificial, its circular summit c. 6m. in diameter.

COLLIN

Small village. The main street's cottages are mostly C19 (one dated 1827) but generally much altered; some C20 bungalows join in.

SCHOOL. Plain Tudor school and schoolhouse, dated 1876. Large pitch-roofed addition by *Dumfries and Galloway Regional Council*, 1993.

COLVEND

Hamlet with a school and hall, the Parish Church to the SW.

PARISH CHURCH, 0.5km. SW. Chaste Early Christian, by *P. MacGregor Chalmers*, 1910–11. The walls are of hammer-dressed granite with red sandstone dressings. Nave of five bays with a four-bay double-pitch-roofed N aisle and a S transept; very short rectangular chancel. W tower, sheer except for a sill course under the belfry openings, topped by a steep pyramid roof. Round-arched openings, all flush with the walling.

Inside, plastered walls make a foil for the red sandstone columns and window surrounds. Arcades into the aisle and transept, the roundheaded arches springing from cushion-capitalled columns. Braced collar roof over the nave, kingpost-truss roof in the aisle, a panelled wooden ceiling in the transept. The chancel is raised by three steps and entered through a roundheaded arch, the capitals of its responds carved with

dragons. Over the chancel, a wooden tunnel-vault. – FUR-
NISHINGS of 1911 in a High Presbyterian arrangement (the
communion table in the chancel, the font and pulpit flanking
the chancel arch). – Low boxy PEWS. – Stone FONT, the
round bowl carved with simplified foliage. – Plain neo-Jacobean
PULPIT. – STAINED GLASS. E window (the Ascension) by
Stephen Adam & Co., 1918, the colours quite deep. – In the S
transept, E and W windows (the Adoration of the Magi; the
Risen Lord on the road to Emmaus) of *c.* 1930 and apparently
by the same hand, the figures realistic but simplified. – Strongly
coloured W window in the N aisle by *Margaret Chilton* and
Marjorie Kemp, 1926, showing a fey-looking St John
accompanied by a determined eagle. – ORGAN of 1915.

In the GRAVEYARD S of the church, a large red sandstone
MONUMENT to the Rev. John Watson †1724, rather like a
wellhead. – Further S, a tall late C18 urn-finialled OBELISK to
members of the Cochran family. – To its W, the curly-topped
C18 HEADSTONE of the Donaldson family, carved with a lively
angel's head (the soul).

PUBLIC HALL. Dated 1933. Piend-roofed single-storey box with
a big gabled porch, the harled walls unenlivened by the cement
dressings.

SCHOOL. Of *c.* 1900, granite-walled with bracketed eaves.

KIPP HOUSE, 2.6km. NW. Villa of the earlier C19, built of
painted rubble with rusticated quoins. Verandah across the
two-storey main block. On each side, a single-storey link to a
pavilion-roofed single-storey wing.

COMLONGON CASTLE   0060
1.1km. W of Clarencefield

Tower house of the Murrays of Cockpool, with a Baronial mansion of *c.* 1890 tacked on to its E side. The tower itself certainly
existed by 1508, when the 'turris ac fortalicium de Cunlungane'
is recorded, and was probably built shortly before. Externally it
is severe, a five-storey rubble-walled rectangle rising from a
heavy base to a machicolation of heavily moulded corbels which
supports the battlement, the copes of its merlons simply
moulded. Chamfered window margins. Segmental-arched door
at the N wall's E end. At the base of the W wall, the opening of a
garderobe chute.

The top of the tower was remodelled, probably at the beginning of the C17,* with a crowstep-gabled gallery built on top of
the W parapet walk. At the same time a room was added over
the SE corner, its crowstepped gable matching that of the gallery
to produce a symmetrical S front. Behind this room was built
a battlemented look-out post, and the NE caphouse over the
stair acquired another battlement.

The entrance door at the NE corner opens into a short tunnel-

* And certainly before 1624, when the top-floor rooms are mentioned in an
inventory.

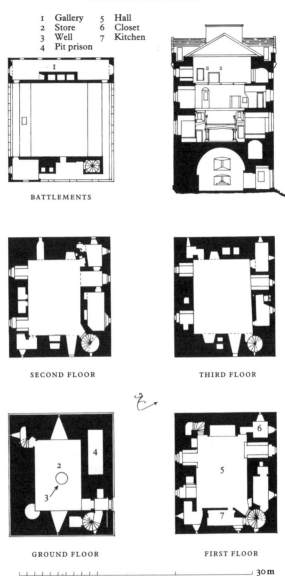

1 Gallery　5 Hall
2 Store　6 Closet
3 Well　7 Kitchen
4 Pit prison

BATTLEMENTS

SECOND FLOOR　　　　THIRD FLOOR

GROUND FLOOR　　　　FIRST FLOOR

30 m

Comlongon Castle. Section and plans

vaulted passage, its opening defended by an iron yett with
unusually strong bars. At the ends of one of the horizontal bars
are squarish brackets through which the bolt was pushed to
keep the yett closed. On the r. of the passage, a deep wall
recess; on the l., the entrance to the NE stair. Straight ahead is
the door to the GROUND-FLOOR room. This is now a single

space covered by a semicircular tunnel-vault, but scarcements in the side walls show that it has been divided by a wooden floor. In each gable below the level of this former entresol, a small window with widely splayed ingoes and a stepped sill. Rounded recess in the SE corner, apparently designed to contain a turnpike service stair. In the SW corner, the door to the stair serving the hall's dais end, again a turnpike but with a straight flight at the top. In the centre of the room's rough floor, a round ashlar-lined well, its top rebuilt in rubble. The entresol level also has a window with wide-splayed ingoes in each gable. This level was entered from a now blocked door off the main NE stair, which is also a turnpike but wider than the others and rises to the top of the tower.

At the FIRST FLOOR, two doors lead from the main stair: the SW opens into the hall; the S pierces one side of a huge segmental-arched kitchen fireplace. This fireplace was probably originally separated from the hall by a wooden screens passage, its position likely to be represented by the present stone wall, which may have been built as part of the early C17 alterations to the house. In this wall, a serving hatch from the narrow kitchen to the hall.

The hall itself is grand but not without comfort. Wooden ceiling, with beams carried on corbels, their heraldic carving largely obliterated and now suggested by recent paintwork. Stone window seats in the round-arched embrasures of the big side windows. The SW and NW window openings have contained fixed glazing above shutters; the smaller SE window has a glazing groove all round the opening. In the W wall, a big 69 fireplace, the capitals of its jambs decorated with foliated bands. On the l. side, a roll-moulded second jamb has been inserted, perhaps in the early C17, to help support the warped oak lintel. This lintel too may well be a replacement. Unusually, it is surmounted by rubble infill, presumably intended to be plastered, under the fireplace's ashlar cornice, whose C15 stones, carved with a vine scroll and flat-nosed human heads, seem to have been re-used. In the wall above each end of the fireplace, a corbel carved with an angel bearing a coat of arms. These corbels, although placed rather high, were probably designed as lamp sconces and look unhappy in their present job of supporting braces for the ceiling beams. Between them, an engagingly inept relief of the royal arms of Scotland, the unicorn supporters looking like toddlers who have sat down unexpectedly while learning to walk. Each side of the fireplace, a small window above a door, the l. to the service stair, the r. to a tunnel-vaulted wall closet, its small windows provided with stepped sills. At the W end of the hall's S wall, a large and elaborate aumbry, the late Gothic clustered shafts carrying a segmental-headed arch and an extrados carved with foliage. From the soffit hangs a foliated cinquefoil of wilfully irregular appearance, the foils of the r. side placed higher than those of the l. Above the SW and SE doors, small windows with exceptionally deep embrasures. The SE door opens into a doglegged wall closet covered with a segmental tunnel-vault and lit by narrow windows.

At the E end of the N wall, a door opens from the hall onto steps down to a vaulted room contained in the thickness of the wall. Stone seats at its small and narrow window. In the floor at the W end, the trap to a pit prison below. Beyond this room is another, also tunnel-vaulted and with a small window provided with seats. Off its SW corner, a garderobe. These two rooms were perhaps originally designed as a guardroom and prison; by 1624 they seem to have been used as charter rooms.

Off the main stair, just above the entrance to the hall, is a segmental-vaulted room in the thickness of the N wall. Small but quite comfortable, with a fair-sized window; in the NW corner, a garderobe, probably intended to be hidden behind a screen, with a lamp recess.

The SECOND FLOOR originally contained an upper hall or solar, off which were rooms in the thickness of the walls. Perhaps at the beginning of the C17, and certainly by 1624, this upper hall was divided in two. The partition wall (now missing) broke into the large C15 S fireplace, which was then converted into a pair of walk-in cupboards or perhaps close garderobes (one for each room), and new fireplaces were inserted in the gables, the W with a salt cellar in its r. jamb. Slit window in each gable. Large windows in the long walls. Both the S windows have seats. The N window lacks this luxury, not surprisingly since each of its ingoes is pierced by a door to a vaulted room in the wall thickness. The E of these rooms, possibly the chapel noted in an inventory of 1624, has two broad recesses in its S wall and a slit window in the N. Small windows again in the W room, which had had a second door directly into the upper hall; off its SW corner, a garderobe. At the upper hall's SE corner, the entrance to a third wall chamber, doglegged on plan and with a slit window in its E side.

The flooring of the original TOP STOREY is missing, but its oak beams were carried on scarcements in the long walls. A fireplace in each gable shows that it has contained two main rooms. Again, big windows to the N and S, all with seats, the SE with an aumbry in the l. ingo. Biggish closets in the N wall, both with slit windows, the E enjoying a garderobe. Small dog-legged closet, perhaps a garderobe, at the SW corner of this floor.

The NE stair rises into a CAPHOUSE. In its S wall, a door onto the E stretch of the parapet walk leading to the house's early C17 SE turret. From this turret a W door opens onto the S parapet walk, which gives access to the early C17 GALLERY, a long (12.17m.) and narrow (2.44m.) room created by roofing over the W parapet walk, whose stone gutters were left in place. A window in each gable, the S flanked by a lamp recess and a slop drain. In the W wall, five windows formed in the crenelles of the C15 battlement. Fireplace against the S side of the W chimneystack, which muscles into the gallery's centre. At the N end, a door onto the N parapet walk.

In the early C18 the fifth Viscount Stormont added an unpretentious laird's house on the E side of the tower. This was replaced *c.* 1890 by *James Barbour & Bowie* with the present mansion house, angled so that it just touches the tower. Unexciting plain Baronial. Entrance under a large coat of arms at the bowed NE corner, whose upper part is corbelled to the square and rises into machicolation carrying a crowstep-gabled caphouse, a deliberate reminiscence of the top of the tower. Stone verandah with block-rusticated columns across the S front. Inside, a panelled neo-Jacobean hall, with a coat of arms above its fireplace. Simpler panelling in the dining room. Adam-revival work in the drawing room.

CONHEATH   9060
1.1km. N of Glencaple

Small early C19 mansion house by *Walter Newall.* Two storeys over a basement, built of squared red sandstone rubble. Entrance (E) front of three bays. At the centre, a semicircular Roman Doric portico enclosing the tripartite fanlit doorway. Three-light window above, its centre sill lowered. At the W elevation, a bowed centrepiece, its French window an alteration of 1909. Balustraded single-storey and basement N addition by *James A. Morris*, 1909, with a multiplicity of leaded ground-floor windows at its bowed end.

Rubble-walled GARDEN to the W, with a roofless circular summerhouse in the centre of its W wall. This is probably contemporary with the house, but a blocked roll-moulded doorway may be re-used work of the C17, as perhaps are the bee-bolls.

To the N, a FARMHOUSE by *Robert S. Lorimer*, 1917. Symmetrical W front, with tile-hanging on its bay windows. – STEADING to its SE, the E entrance flanked by a pair of rubble-built blocks of the earlier C19. At the S block's NE corner, a broad-eaved octagonal DOOCOT.

In a spinney SW of the mansion house is the CHAPEL begun to a design of 1909 by *James A. Morris* but not completed until *c.* 1928, Morris's scheme having been amended and cut down by *Robert S. Lorimer*, *c.* 1914. Morris had intended an aisled nave and narrower chancel, with a jamb containing the organ and vestries on the chancel's N side and a porch on the nave's S. Lorimer omitted the nave and porch but provided a full-height 'vestibule' at the chancel's W end. Red sandstone masonry, of stugged and snecked squared rubble; slated roofs. The chancel is substantially to Morris's design. Two rectangular windows towards the W end of the S wall. Cross-finialled E gable. At its corners, clasping buttresses of channelled ashlar, their intended pinnacles omitted. Roundheaded E window with its projecting keystone and imposts left uncarved. The N jamb is a mixture of Morris and Lorimer. Prominent wallhead chimney on the E face as shown in Morris's design, but the roof's piend may be a Lorimer alteration.

The moulded W door with a depressed ogee-arched head is Lorimer's, moved to the N from Morris's chosen position at the S end of the wall. The 'vestibule', marked off from the chancel by a S buttress, is all by Lorimer and thrifty.* In its W front, another door with a depressed ogee-arched head. Scrolled skewputts.

The internal plan is mostly by Morris, the detail by Lorimer. Ashlar walls; boarded wagon roof. Segmental arch over the 'vestibule' (really a W recess). Another segmental arch at the opening into the choir area (the space originally intended for an organ) in the N jamb. In this arch, a neo-Jacobean wooden screen. To its E, a moulded rectangular door into the vestry, whose fireplace is also moulded. On the sanctuary's S side, a triple sedilia; the piers that carry the stone arches have Jacobean panelled decoration, their semicircular heads are Romanesque. A fourth but smaller arch encloses the piscina. – STAINED GLASS E window (the Madonna and Child) of *c.*1928, the figures in blue and gold on a background of mostly clear glass. It looks like the work of *Louis Davis*.

CORRIE

1080

Hillside graveyard marking the site of the church of a medieval parish which was joined to Hutton in 1609. Only a white-painted C19 farmhouse (CORRIEHILLS) for company.

CHURCHYARD. A good number of C18 HEADSTONES and a few TABLE STONES carved with heraldry and, rather sparingly, with emblems of death. The fullest panoply of motifs is shown on the headstone to Thomas Little †1761, its front decorated with inept Ionic pilasters framing a coat of arms above a skull and crossbones.

CORSEMALZIE HOUSE

3050

5.4km. NE of Elrig

Big and boring mid-C19 Tudor villa displaying a repertoire of hoodmoulds, bay windows and gables.

CORSEWALL CASTLE

9070

1.6km. SE of Corsewall Point

Badly ruined but still quite tall remains of the rubble-built, thick-walled rectangular tower of the Campbells, lords of Corsewall, probably erected in the C15. The ground-floor entrance has been at the E wall's N end, where there is now a large and crude opening, still with an original bar-hole on its S side. The ground-

---

* Morris's proposed nave would have had a W front of channelled ashlar topped by a steepled bellcote.

floor interior is largely intact. It contains a single high tunnel-vaulted room. Small rectangular windows with stepped sills in the S and W walls. At the W wall's S end, a recess containing a well; trapdoor in the vault above to allow water to be hoisted to the first-floor hall. There has been a turnpike stair in the wall thickness of the NE corner.

CORSEWALL HOUSE
0.3km. E of Kirkcolm

0060

Piend-roofed late Georgian country house which was thickened to double the size in the mid-C19. This Victorian addition has been partly removed, but what remains sticks out like a long nose ending in a Roman Doric portico. Angled rear wing by *C. S. S. Johnston*, 1905.

CORSEWALL POINT

9070

Just a lighthouse high above the Irish Sea.

LIGHTHOUSE. By *Robert Stevenson*, 1815–16. Tapering round tower of white-painted whinstone. A parapeted walkway is corbelled out above the bottom stage; at the top stage, blind quatrefoils. Cupola lantern. – Contemporary flat-roofed two-storey KEEPERS' HOUSES with prominent chimneys; single-storey lateral wings.

CORSEWALL CASTLE. *See* p. 190.

CORSOCK

7070

Small C19 village.

Former PARISH CHURCH (now KIRKLYNN), 1.2km. SE. Built as a chapel of ease in 1838–9, the design based on that of a chapel at Wharton (Cheshire). The architect may have been *Walter Newall*, who provided a design for the pulpit *gratis*. Buttressed box of white-painted rubble, the windows rectangular. At the N end, a gableted bellcote and porch.

PARISH CHURCH, 0.5km. SE. Built as Corsock Free Church in 1851–2 to a design by *William McCandlish* (*see* the Introduction, p. 43). Lancet-windowed buttressed box of whin rubble. SE porch; low semi-octagonal E apse. On the main E gable, a gabled bellcote-type finial. Tough NW tower with angle buttresses and a restless stringcourse under the triplet belfry openings.

Inside, a hammerbeam roof over the nave. The awkward Gothic stone chancel arch is an alteration of 1912 by *J. A. Macgregor*, adapting a design by *James Kennedy Hunter*. – Also of 1912 the PULPIT and COMMUNION TABLE. – In the SW corner, a plaster BUST of Alexander Murray Dunlop † 1870. – STAINED GLASS. Chancel E window (the Maries at the Tomb)

of 1923. – Nave N wall, memorial window of *c*.1950 to Briga-
dier-General Douglas McEwen, by *Brian D. L. Thomas* in
collaboration with the *Whitefriars Studios*, an arrangement of
rhododendron blooms and military decorations. – In the S wall,
a semi-abstract light ('The Spirit of the River') designed by
Alexander Hollweg and executed by *David Williams*, *c*.1985. –
To its W, an early C20 window (the Three Magi) signed by
Arthur J. Dix. – Three-light E window (the Good Shepherd)
by *Heaton, Butler & Bayne*, *c*.1905.
HALL. By *Grierson*, 1889–90, a ball finial on the front porch.
SCHOOL. Mid-C19 and harled. The school itself is plentifully
gabled. Georgian-survival schoolhouse at the E end.

CORSOCK HOUSE
0.9km. S

Early C19 house given a large Baronial addition by *David Bryce*
in 1853 and a second extension to the E in the same manner by
C. S. S. Johnston, 1910, all unified by harling. The early C19
building consisted of a broad-eaved two-storey main block.
Three-bay S front with open-pedimented ends. Lower two-
storey kitchen wing at right angles to the E and, beyond that, a
single-storey office court. Bryce provided a new neo-Jacobean
porch at the W bay in the inner angle with his addition. This
was pacific Baronial, with crowstepped gables, fat conical-
roofed turrets at the W corners, steep pedimented dormerheads,
and full-height bay windows, canted at the ground floor and
corbelled out to the square above. Johnston's E addition (replacing the E part of the original house) is again Baronial but
with an Arts and Crafts inflexion. Round tower on the S front;
gabled porch hiding what remains of the early C19 building.
    To the S, elaborate cast-iron Gothic GATES, their piers tra-
ceried open-sided octagons topped by crown spires.

9080   COWHILL TOWER
2.9km. N of Holywood

Conglomerate house of rather disjointed appearance. The
Cowhill estate was bought by George Johnston, a Liverpool
merchant, in 1783. In 1788–9 he demolished the existing house
and built a small mansion house some way to its N. This
comprised a plain two-storey main block with single-storey
wings, the ashlar-fronted gable of each containing a Venetian
window. The main block and E wing were recast in Baronial
dress by *W. F. Lyon c*.1867–71. Then in 1913–14 *Peddie &
Forbes Smith* added a crowstep-gabled imitation tower house at
the E end. This is of four storeys and an attic, built of crazy-
paved rubble. Across the E face, a parapet projected on continuous corbelling, with a NE angle round and a conical-roofed
SE turret. A flat-roofed drawing room protruded from the
tower's S front. Also of *c*.1914 is the crowstep-gabled upper

floor added to the Georgian w wing, its long side elevation displaying neo-Jacobean stone dormerheads. In 1942 a fire destroyed the centre of the house (i.e. the main block of 1788–9 as remodelled by Lyon), and six years later this was rebuilt to a design by *Antony Lloyd* but narrower than its predecessor, the line of whose front (s) wall is now marked by a terrace. A big bow projecting on the l. is the main feature of this work. In 1953 a small crowstepped extension (containing a stone turnpike stair) was added on the drawing room's e side. A second fire, in 1972, gutted the early c19 drawing room; it was remodelled the next year, acquiring a pitched roof and bowed end.

Unsurprisingly, the interior is eclectic. Entrance hall on the ground floor of the tower house, its walls covered with what looks like genuine early c18 panelling. Strapworked neo-Jacobean plaster ceiling, probably of 1914 but perhaps dating from alterations of 1923. On this hall's N side, a stair up to the principal floor, its ceiling again with strapwork decoration and a big pendant. In the drawing room, as remodelled in 1973, ceiling enrichment of mid-c19 Georgian-survival type. Big late Georgian marble chimneypiece with paired Corinthian columns, imported from Mabie House (q.v.). At the bottom of the centre block's stairwell, late Victorian or Edwardian panelling brought here from the demolished bank of Samuel Montagu & Co. in London. The main room in the late c18 w wing still has acanthus leaf capitals at the mullion piers of its Venetian window, but the simple panelling and strapworked and foliage-panelled plaster ceiling are of 1923. On the tower house's second floor, a bedroom (the White Room) with mahogany panelling of 1914, originally painted but now stripped.

SE of the house, STABLES AND COACHHOUSES (now housing), dated 1816 on an armorial stone in the centre of the w front. This front is of two storeys with rusticated quoins at the slightly advanced ends and taller centre. In each end, a segmental-arched coachhouse opening under a first-floor Venetian window which breaks up into the open pediment. The centre is pierced by a segmental pend arch. First-floor Venetian window, its side-lights blind. In the steep pediment, a semicircular recess containing round pigeon entries to the attic's doocot. Plain N and S ranges running back to a screen wall.

On the s axis of the house and on the site of its c16 or c17 predecessor, a FOLLY, perhaps of c. 1790; it was extended SE in the mid-c20. This is a picturesquely 'ruined' screen wall incorporating re-used fragments of the earlier house. At its w end, a roundheaded arch. Beside it, a rectangular unrebated doorway, its lintel a reset stone bearing the date 1579. Above the lintel, a stone whose weathered carving suggests a thistle growing from a saltire. On the s side of the screen wall above this door, two stones placed between the spiral-banded jambs of a panel frame. The upper stone is carved in high relief with a stag's head above a saltire (the crest and coat of arms of the Maxwells, who owned Cowhill from 1567 to 1783). The late

C16 lower stone displays a shield bearing a saltire and topped by a stag's head crest; flanking the shield are the initials RM and BM for Robert Maxwell of Cowhill and his wife, Barbara Maxwell. Set into the wall further E, a shallowly hogbacked late medieval gravestone incised with a sword; it came from the demolished Holywood Abbey. At the wall's E end, part of a turret carried on continuous corbelling.

At the end of the drive, a pair of piend-roofed early C19 LODGES, each with hoodmoulded windows and a lattice-sided Tudor-arched porch.

CRAICHLAW

2.2km. w of Kirkcowan

Disjointed L-plan country house developed by accretion and alteration from the C16 to the C20. In 1500 John Gordon of Lochinvar granted his recently acquired lands of Craichlaw to his second son, William, who built a tower here by 1506. The tower's accommodation was augmented or supplemented in the early C18 by the addition of a house on its E side. Then in 1864–6 *Brown & Wardrop* rebuilt the ruinous top floors of the tower, remodelled the C18 block, and added new E and N ranges enclosing a narrow back courtyard. Some remodelling was carried out by *Charles S. S. Johnston* in 1900. Finally, in 1954, *Ian G. Lindsay* demolished the 1860s N range and further altered Brown & Wardrop's work.

The crowstep-gabled tower dominates. It is a simple oblong with chamfered corners, built of whinstone rubble. The two bottom storeys are of *c.* 1500 but with round-arched S and W doors of 1864–6. The two floors above, also of whin with red sandstone dressings, were added by Brown & Wardrop. At the top floor, big pedimented dormerheads to the W and E. Fat conical-roofed round turrets at three corners. On the SE corner, a rectangular caphouse, its E side projected on continuous corbelling, its battlement rising flush with the walls.

The early C18 house E of the tower was of two storeys, with a shaped gablet at the centre of its five-bay front. Brown & Wardrop refaced this front's three E bays in stonework matching that of the tower, enlarged the ground-floor windows and carried the first-floor windows up through the eaves into stone dormerheads, the two outer roundheaded, the centre gableted and carved with the coat of arms of the Hamiltons, then the owners. Armorial panel over the ground-floor centre window. At the same time the two W bays were rebuilt as a projecting broad crowstepped gable, with a three-light window at its ground floor. The S gable of the 1860s two-storey E range, crowstepped again, is very slightly advanced. Projecting from it, a narrow rectangular bay window supporting a canted oriel. On this range's E front, a couple of crowstepped gablets. The one at the S is placed above a first-floor window which is framed by an Artisan Mannerist aedicule and fronted by a corbelled-out stone balcony, its parapet pierced by roundheaded arcading. Despite the Jacobean detail the effect is curiously Venetian. At this range's N end, a short stub of the 1860s N range.

Harled elevations to the courtyard. The back of Brown & Wardrop's work adjoining the tower was remodelled in 1954, when it was provided with a large round-arched entrance reminiscent of the garage door of a villa in some plush suburb. Attached to the back of the C18 house, a parallel but slightly shorter block, probably an early C19 addition. Granite margins to its windows, which are of three lights at the ground floor; those above have gabled dormerheads. Over the courtyard door into the E range, a re-used stone carved with the date 1644, two coats of arms, the initials 'WG.JC' (for William Gordon of Craichlaw and his wife, Jean Chalmers) and two hearts. N of the main courtyard, a service court formed by low crowstep-gabled ranges of the 1860s.

Inside the tower, the C16 ground floor and entresol were thrown together by Brown & Wardrop to form a tall Baronial vaulted entrance hall. Turnpike stair of the 1860s in the tower's SE corner, almost certainly in the position of the C16 stair. The entrance hall opens on the E into the 1860s stair hall, its ceiling of routine Jacobean character. The thinly detailed Jacobean stair itself was probably provided in 1900 as part of C. S. S. Johnston's alterations. On the W wall has been placed a large early C16 panel formerly on the outside of the tower, its centre carved with unicorn supporters flanking shields, one bearing the royal arms, another with those of Gordon of Craichlaw. In the top corners of the panel, two more shields which display the arms of William Gordon and his wife, Janet Baillie; human faces in the bottom corners. S of this hall, a double drawing room formed in the 1860s; big neo-Jacobean chimney-pieces.

CRAIGCAFFIE CASTLE
4.7km. SE of Cairnryan

0060

Thickly harled tower house built for John Neilson and his wife, Margaret Strang, in the 1570s; their initials and the date 157– are carved on the bottom skewputts of the N side. It is a crowstep-gabled rectangle of three storeys and an attic. On the unbattlemented long N and S sides, a moulded eaves course which becomes part of the continuous corbelling under the angle rounds, the bottom course broken by the tower's corners, and is carried across the gables to support their corbelled parapets. At the angle rounds, circular gunholes; on the NE round, a stone carved with hands holding a head. Large ornamental spouts (the best-preserved on the E gable) draining the end wall-walks. Big off-centre N chimney. The S front's swept dormers are late C20. At the ground floor, round gunholes to N and S. Inserted windows at this level. The upper windows' surrounds are moulded (some renewed). At the second-floor N window, dogtooth enrichment. Small roundheaded opening at the S front's second floor. Above the roll-moulded door in the N front's W end, the fragment of a panel frame. Another panel frame higher up. Directly over the door at eaves level, a machicolation projected on two moulded corbels.

(The entrance opens directly onto the foot of the turnpike stair at the NW corner. Tunnel-vaulted ground-floor kitchen, a fireplace in its E gable. In the SW corner, a chamber containing a well, a hatch in its domical vault. The first and second floors each contained one room.)

CRAIGCLEUCH
3080

1.3km. SW of Staplegordon

Small-scale mansion house of *c.* 1874–5 in the best Tudor manner of thirty or forty years before. Two-storey main block, its front of five bays. Shaped gables at the advanced ends from which project balustraded two-storey canted bay windows. Across the three inner bays, a round-arched loggia, its projecting centre an entrance porch which forms the lowest storey of a three-stage octagonal ogee-roofed tower. Single-storey-and-attic two-bay service wing to the W, its attic windows with semicircular dormerheads. Inside, a toplit central hall from which the principal rooms are entered.

CRAIGDARROCH HOUSE
7090

3.7km. W of Moniaive

Laird's house built in 1726–9 for Alexander Fergusson of Craigdarroch, the husband of Anna (Annie) Laurie. The architect was *William Adam* although the building, as executed, shows differences in detail from the elevation engraved for his projected *Vitruvius Scoticus,* and the intended flanking pavilions were omitted. It is a sturdy seven-by-four-bay piend-roofed rectangle, built of pink-washed rubble, the ashlar dressings and rusticated quoins picked out in white. Two storeys with an exposed basement and an attic; its pedimented wooden dormers are mid-C19 additions. The architectural display is concentrated at the centrepiece of the entrance (E) front, which is slightly advanced under a rather steep pediment* containing a blind bullseye and topped by urns on the centre and ends, the central urn's pedestal bearing the date 1729. In this centre-

---

* The *Vitruvius Scoticus* elevation showed a segmental pediment.

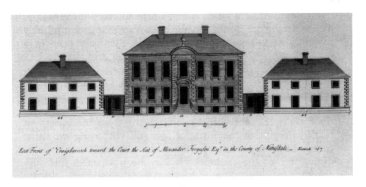

Craigdarroch House. East front.
Engraving of *c.* 1733

piece is the main door, approached by a broad and straight flight of steps, probably a C19 replacement for the narrower concave-sided forestair designed by Adam. The door itself is set in a rusticated ashlar surround, the consoled keystone carved as an acanthus leaf. It is framed by a pedimented aedicule, the Corinthian pilasters surprisingly inept, the tympanum carved with the arms of Fergusson and Laurie flanked by stylized flowers. Above, a segmental-arched window, again with an acanthus-leaf-consoled keystone.

The W (garden) front is plainer. Central door (now a window and missing its forestair) with a curvy-headed architrave topped by a consoled segmental pediment, in which is a panel bearing the entwined initials of Alexander Fergusson and Anna Laurie. The two S windows on each floor have been blocked. The three bays N of the centre were overlaid in 1854 by a W wing which tries hard to be tactful. At its W end's S side, a round-arched verandah with urns on the corners of its flat roof. Probably also of 1854 is the semicircular oriel window on the main block's S side. On the N side of the wing, a small apsidal-ended chapel added by *John Starforth* in 1889. Built into the main block's N gable, various stones, presumably from an earlier house on the site. One is early C17, inscribed with the injunction 'FEIR GOD', the initials WF and –G (for William Fergusson and his wife, Sarah Grierson) and a date, of which only the last numeral (7) survives. Another, also of the early C17, is carved with the arms of Fergusson and Maxwell (probably for Thomas Fergusson and his wife, Isabel Maxwell). A third is inscribed 'GOD SEND GRACE' above the arms of Fergusson and Grierson; at the bottom, the date 1631 flanked by the initials of William Fergusson and Sarah Grierson. To the W, on the C19 wing, two more heraldic stones; one has the date 1609, the Fergusson arms and the initials of Thomas Fergusson and Isabel Maxwell, the other has the Fergusson arms.

Inside, most of William Adam's plan survives but very little of his detail, the house having been Victorianized, probably in 1854, and then re-Georgianized in the early C20 in a manner of the later rather than the earlier C18. In the C18 the ground floor contained the family rooms (now reception rooms), the first floor a state apartment. On the r. side of the entrance hall, a C19 neo-Jacobean stair in the place of the C18 state stair to the first floor. Behind it, enclosed by thick walls, a stone turnpike stair rising from the basement to the attic. W of the entrance hall and occupying the three centre bays of the garden front was the early C18 private dining room (or parlour). It has been opened into the entrance hall with a broad but low rectangular arch, and the wall between it and a N bedroom has been removed. In the S wall, a very smart imported late C18 pine and gesso chimneypiece with fluted pilasters at the sides; on the frieze, Gothick arcading, the central arch filled with the relief of an allegorical scene. The private dining room originally had a door into the family bedroom (now a sitting room) at the SW corner. The early C18 stone chimneypiece (now marbled) survives, its basket arch tweaked up into a point at the centre. E of this were two dressing rooms (for the owner and his wife). They now form one room, again with an imported late C18 pine and gesso chimneypiece decorated with eagles and thistles. The state apartment was on the first floor, filling its S two-thirds. Its first and largest room, at the SE corner, was the dining room, now subdivided to form a bedroom and bathroom. It led into the drawing room (now a bedroom) at the SW, its stone chimneypiece apparently early C18 but quite plain. From this there was a door into the state bedroom in the centre of the W front, its appearance now Edwardian. A couple of closets to its N were converted to a passage giving access to the W wing in 1854. Across the house's N end in the early C18 was a suite of bedroom, dressing room and closet, an arrangement still intact but with the closet now a bathroom and the bedroom chimneypiece a replacement. In the W wing, a large drawing room (formerly a dining room), given its general late C18 character early in the C20.

The body of the chapel is entered from outside, its S gallery from the main floor of the W wing. Interior lined with wood from the estate; open wooden roof. – STAINED GLASS. Two windows in the N apse (Faith and Hope) by *Ward & Hughes*, 1890.

NW of the house, on a wooded hillside, an octagonal PRIVY, several of its mostly blind hoodmoulded openings decorated with crosslet arrowslits. It looks mid-C19. – To the W, a rubble-walled GARDEN, perhaps late C18. – Further W, a mid-Victorian cottagey STABLE block, now converted to housing.

CRAIGIEBURN

1000

3km. E of Moffat

Unpretentious rendered house standing on the edge of a ravine down to the eponymous burn, with an assortment of associated buildings in the well-wooded surroundings testifying to gentry status. The earliest part of the T-plan house seems to be the basement of the N jamb, its very thick walls built of rubble. This was probably the bottom storey of a C16 tower. The main block was put up *c.*1790. Two storeys and four bays, originally with a gablet over the S front's off-centre entrance bay. Additions were built in 1802, probably the raising or rebuilding of the jamb to the same height as the main block and the provision of a Gothick porch. In *c.*1865 the main block was extended E by one bay, the front gablet was removed and the Georgian porch was replaced by a two-storey projection. The overall low parapet is probably also of this date, as may be the two-light W window to the jamb's ground floor. The chimneys have been rebuilt in brick, probably in the C20.

The interior is largely of *c.*1865 and the C20, but early C19 plasterwork and marble chimneypieces survive in the ground-floor SW dining room and the jamb's first-floor drawing room. In the basement of the jamb, two parallel cellars (the E now subdivided), their rubble tunnel-vaults more likely to be late Georgian than C16.

SE of the house, built into a steep wooded bank overlooking the burn, a late Georgian ICE HOUSE, its front dressed up as a hermitage with a narrow and crudely pointed door. High in the gable, a small square opening, apparently designed as an outlet for water, which was carried by a partly surviving lead pipe through the ice house, to trickle down in romantic evocation of the melancholy of eremitical life. – Further SE, in the woodland garden, a small rubble-built BOTHY, perhaps early C19, extended in brick in the earlier C20. – STABLES SW of the house, the two-storey main block built of whitewashed rubble in 1794, with an elliptical pend arch under the central loft door. At the back the roof is carried down over a byre which forms part of the adjoining farm steading, its other buildings mainly C19. The stables were made L-plan in the early C19 by the addition of a piend-roofed wing. – At the end of the drive, a faintly Jacobean LODGE of *c.*1840 with a bay window as its main feature.

CRAIGIELANDS

0000

0.7km. SW of Beattock

Villa designed by *William Burn* for the brewer William Younger in 1817 (*see* the Introduction, p. 67). As first built it was well dressed in a stolid Greek-revival style, built of brick-shaped whin, the dressings of sandstone. Square tower rising in the centre of the piended roof. W front of one storey and a skylit attic, the basement appearing as a slightly projecting window-less plinth. At the centre, a pedimented portico, its four unfluted Doric columns just too slim to be powerful. Behind the portico, a door under a large semicircular fanlight and flanked by side lights. At the outer bays, tall corniced windows, a band course running under their sills. Boldly projecting mutuled eaves cornice. At each three-bay end elevation, a projecting gabled centrepiece helping to disguise the fact that the house's rear two-thirds contains two storeys in the height of the front's ground floor. At the garden (E) front the basement is exposed. This elevation was overlaid by painted brick outshots, including a central oriel window, in 1882. Also of 1882 the W front's attic, its small broadly pilastered windows sitting on top of the original cornice.

A vestibule, with a mosaic floor probably of 1882, opens into the central hall. This is a Greek cross on plan, the short limbs forming round-arched recesses. Over the centre, plaster-panelled pendentives supporting a circular lantern, its round-headed windows' soffits again plaster-panelled. More plaster panelling, in an austere wheel design, on the lantern's ceiling.

To the N, the former STABLES, probably of c.1820 but incorporating earlier work. Front elevation with a pend arch in the projecting broad-eaved centre gable. In the S gable, a pair of basket-arched coachhouse doorways. – S of the house, a rubble-walled GARDEN of c.1800, with walls extending like buttresses at the corners. – At each of the NE and (former) SE entrances to the drive, an identical piend-roofed single-storey LODGE of c.1820, with a projecting gable at the centre of each long side and a pedimented porch.

CRAWFORDTON HOUSE

1.5km. E of Moniaive

Baronial country house designed by *Peddie & Kinnear* for Colonel George Gustavus Walker and built in 1863–6 of hammerdressed red sandstone. It is now rather beleaguered by low additions put up for its late C20 use as a school. The major excitement is concentrated at the entrance (E) front. Boldly projecting off-centre T-plan porch, its W arms bowed, a leafy frieze carved under the parapet. In the porch's centre gablet, a pedimented panel bearing the date 1865. Behind the porch, a tall tower, its round-arched and rope-moulded first-floor oriel window flanked by foliage-capitalled attached columns and with stone cresting on its slabbed roof; under the window, a semicircular stone parapet with dumpy Gothic balusters. At the tower's second floor, a rope-moulded stringcourse projected on con-tinuous corbelling which jumps up over a blind central 'machicolation' and rises above a plain panel on the l. Overall, a machicolated parapet; on the SW corner, a conical-roofed caphouse topped by a weathervane. To the r. of the tower, a pair of steeply gabled dormerheads. At each end of this front, a crowstepped gable. The r. is cut into by a round NE tower, the cone of its fishscale-slated roof truncated by a wooden cupola, pointed arches springing from its wooden columns, its witch's hat of a roof also truncated and topped by a stalk-like finial. Across this tower and the end gables runs a moulded stringcourse, dropping below the window sills. Conical-roofed SE turret.

The other elevations are a little more relaxed. At each end of the S front, a crowstepped gable, square at the bottom, broached to a semi-octagon at the principal floor, and then corbelled out to become square again under the eaves. As if fearful that their general resemblance might bore a spectator, each is detailed differently, the SW gable rising higher than the SE, its corbelling to the square placed higher up, and a stringcourse carried over the second-floor window. In this gable's E inner angle with the main block, a fat round tower, its second floor jettied out on simply moulded stone corbels, the conical roof covered with fishscale slating. Between the two gables, a balcony projected on bold machicolation, its parapet pierced by roundheaded arches springing from squat Gothic columns. At this centre section, a stringcourse jumping up between the gableted second-floor windows. The round turrets on the outer corners have trefoil 'gunloops'.

The W front is almost symmetrical, but the Jacobean dormerheads and wallhead chimneys are all placed a little to the r. of where they should be were the centre line respected. Off-centre to the l., a rectangular two-storey bay window. The SW angle turret is more than balanced by that at the NW, which is corbelled out to a circular shape at the principal floor and, above that, to a diagonally set and gabled rectangle at the second floor. Utilitarian N elevation with a low service wing.

Inside, the main rooms have deep cornices decorated with three-dimensional plaster flowers. Thin barley-sugar balusters at the neo-Jacobean stair.

CREETOWN   4050

Small burgh at the mouth of the Cree. A planned village, on the site of an earlier settlement, was laid out in 1785 and made a burgh of barony seven years later; but attempts to establish industry here had little success, and by the mid-C19 it was famed chiefly for its gardens. Formerly a harbour, it is now cut off from the river by land reclamation which enabled construction of a by-pass to the W.

CHURCHES AND PUBLIC BUILDINGS

KIRKMABRECK PARISH CHURCH, Kirk Brae. Simple Perp, by *John Henderson*, 1831–4. Large and tall four-bay box of whin rubble with red sandstone dressings. The tower projects from the advanced and pedimented centre of the front (W) gable. It is of three stages, with a heavy Tudorish door at the first, a very tall pointed window at the second, and paired belfry openings at the third. The battlement's corners rise as gableted square piers topped by foliaged finials. Inside, a Tudor-arched plaster ceiling. On three sides, deep galleries supported by marbled cast-iron columns. – PEWS and PULPIT of 1893. – Behind the pulpit, an ORGAN by *Ingram & Co.*, 1912.

ST JOSEPH'S R.C. CHURCH, Hill Street. Designed by *Peter McKie*, it was built as Creetown Free Church in 1858–9 and converted to a Roman Catholic church in 1876. Plain whinstone rectangle with diagonally set pinnacled buttresses at the corners and pointed windows. Low E addition of 1876.

GEM ROCK MUSEUM, Chain Road. Built as the Parish School by *Peter McKie*, 1857. Tall single-storey and T-plan in a simple *cottage orné* manner, with broad eaves and horizontal glazing.

SCHOOL, Chain Road. By *Stewartry County Council*, 1965. Brick-built, in the Festival of Britain manner.

DESCRIPTION

Entry from the N is across a rubble-built early C19 viaduct with segmental arches and curving parapets. Then JOHN STREET'S C19 vernacular houses of one or two storeys establish the architectural norm, the material mostly rubble, often harled. The roadway widens on the W to form ADAMSON SQUARE. In its centre, a battlemented granite CLOCK TOWER erected to commemorate Queen Victoria's Diamond Jubilee of 1897. In BARHOLM STREET to the W, BAYVIEW of *c.*1840, with rusticated quoins and a pilastered doorpiece. At the end of Barholm Street and closing the vista, an early C19 LODGE to the demolished Barholm House. In its advanced and gabled centre, a pointed door under a bullseye window. HIGH STREET climbs uphill from Adamson Square's SE corner. On its corner with Chain Road, St Joseph's R.C. Church (*see* above). At the top, the plain early C19 KILBUCHO HOUSE.

After Adamson Square, John Street has buildings on both sides, the W starting with the ELLANGOWAN HOTEL by *George W. Webb* of Reading, 1898. Three broad gables crossed by a balconied verandah supported by bay windows. Up CHURCH STREET on the E, a glimpse of the bowed end of Hill of Burns (*see* below). Opposite, HARBOUR STREET'S late C18 and C19 vernacular housing. Off it, in MILL STREET, the ivy-clad ruin of a two-storey-and-attic MILL, built of thinly harled rubble, the date 1819 elegantly incised on one lintel. Near John Street's S end, CRISPIN STREET opens to the l. In it ST CRISPINS, a two-storey house with heavy chimneys and smallish windows grouped 2/1/1. The date of 1736 over the door looks plausible. In KIRK BRAE behind, Kirkmabreck Parish Church (*see* above). It faces a small mid-C19 granite-built HALL (former Female School); broad eaves and lattice glazing in the two-light windows.

HILL OF BURNS
off High Street

Smart late Georgian villa with an earlier back wing, the interior mostly Edwardian. The two-storey front (N) block is of 1811. Three bays of granite ashlar with a Doric portico and bowed ends. Balcony under the W end's deep first-floor windows, which light the former drawing room. The SW wing behind is a rubble-built early C18 house, also of two storeys and three bays but quite humble. The SE inner angle is filled by a harled two-storey block, probably of 1811 but heightened and given an E bow in 1911 by *Dunn & Findlay*.

Inside, the dining room on the W of the entrance hall retains its black marble chimneypiece and cornice of 1811, but the Tynecastle Tapestry frieze is of 1901. On the other side of the hall, a billiard room made by Dunn & Findlay, a neo-Jacobean chimneypiece its principal feature. Also by Dunn & Findlay is the present drawing room at the house's SE corner. Best-quality Early Georgian-revival wooden chimneypiece, its lugged architrave carved with egg-and-dart ornament; heavy consoles under the mantel shelf, a leafily carved panel at the centre of the frieze. Stair also of 1901, but the first-floor landing's delicate plasterwork is probably of 1811.

STONE CIRCLE, Glenquicken, 3.4km. E. Probably formed in the second millennium B.C., a circle of twenty-four (perhaps originally twenty-five) boulders. A larger boulder in the centre.

CARSLUITH CASTLE. *See* p. 164.
CASSENCARIE. *See* p. 166.

CROSSMICHAEL   7060

Roadside village, mostly of C19 single-storey terraced cottages built of harled or painted rubble.

PARISH CHURCH. Painted rubble kirk, the piend-roofed body built in 1749–51. The slim round tower projecting from its S side is almost certainly earlier, perhaps of 1611, the date of the bell (by *John Burgerhuys*) which it contains. In 1822–3 the mason-architect *David McLellan* designed and built the N 'aisle', piend-roofed again, with a chimney on its gable. He may also have given the body its narrow pointed windows. Then, in 1824–5, *John Graham* and *William Laurie* heightened the tower by *c*.0.7m. and added a conical spire whose present fishscale slating must be late C19, probably part of the alterations made by *John Starforth* in 1880–1. E vestry of 1965; W porch of 1971.

Remarkably complete and well-finished Georgian INTERIOR. Coomb plaster ceilings, galleries on Tuscan columns at the E and W ends and in the N 'aisle', their fronts and those of the box pews panelled; all this work is probably of 1822–3. In the S corners, the mid-C18 LAIRDS' PEWS of the Gordons of Kenmure and the Copelands of Danevale, each with a basket arch towards the pulpit, the SE pew's arch flanked by fluted pilasters without capitals, the SW'S pilasters Ionic. – C20 PULPIT and COMMUNION TABLE. – STAINED GLASS in the S wall flanking the pulpit. W window (the Risen Lord) by *Heaton, Butler & Bayne*, 1898. – E window (Our Lord stilling the Storm) of *c*. 1920.

Immediately W of the church, the mid-C18 BURIAL ENCLOSURE of the Gordons of Culvennan. Rusticated quoins and acorn finials at the corners. In the E wall, a basket-arched door under a panel carved with a skull and crossbones in an egg-and-dart border. On the enclosure's S wall, huge MONU-MENT to William Gordon of Greenlaw †1757. Urn-finialled Corinthian aedicule, the tympanum carved with a deeply undercut coat of arms. Inscription tablet in a lugged architrave topped by an angel's head (the soul) and flanked by pendant flowers dropping from shells. The inscription itself records that the monument was 'erected By his disconsolate Widow' and recites Gordon's virtues as a husband, father and master. – S of the E end, a HEADSTONE erected in the early C18 but restored in 1917; it commemorates the Covenanting martyr William Graham, a skull and bones above the inscription. – To its E, the HEADSTONE of Robert Rivan †1781, its front carved with a hand-held hammer under a crown (the smiths' emblem).

DANEVALE PARK, 1.4km. S. The Victorian mansion house has been replaced in unexciting fashion. – Mid-C19 STABLES court-yard, the front, its battlement partly removed, mixing basket-arched cart openings and blind Gothic windows. Small doocot tower over the basket-arched pend.

CULGRUFF HOUSE. *See* p. 205.

See p. 205.

4040   CRUGGLETON

Church hidden in a copse.

CHURCH. Small but relatively tall church, probably built in the earlier C12; restored from a ruin *c*. 1890 by *William Galloway* acting for the third Marquess of Bute. The extent of the rebuild-ing is indicated by a tiled line, but much of the work consisted of taking down and re-erecting what still stood.

Nave (*c*. 10.4m. by 6m.) and a lower chancel (*c*. 6m. by 4.95m.), the rubble walls rising above a chamfered plinth, the roof slated. The plinth and quoins are missing from the W corners of the nave and the chancel's E corners, so these may originally have been covered with dressed stone pilasters. Flori-ated cross of *c*. 1890 on the W gable. The openings are a mixture of C12 and 1890s work. Tiny round-arched E window, the monolith head C12, the dressed jambs a conjectural restoration. In the chancel's S wall, two more tiny windows and a narrow round-arched door, its surround chamfered; all these are con-jectural both as to their appearance and their previous existence here. Similarly conjectural slit-like windows, round-arched again, in the S wall of the nave. This wall's W door, round-arched and with cushion-capitalled nook-shafts, is a restoration but based on evidence. Another tiny round-arched window in the w gable, its monolith head original, the jambs of the 1890s. At the w end of the N wall, a plain round-arched door with a chamfered surround; it was restored from evidence of an existing door in this position.

Inside, the roundheaded chancel arch is partly made up of 8 medieval work. Towards the nave, two orders of shafts with bulbous bases; the inner order's cushion capitals are reeded, the outer ones are cubical. The arch's inner side to the chancel is quite plain.

CULGRUFF HOUSE 7060
0.6km. E of Crossmichael

Hugely overgrown multi-gabled red sandstone villa with a tall martial tower. It is dated 1889.

CUMLODEN 4060
2.2km. NW of Newton Stewart

Very large and rambling rendered *cottage orné* built *c.* 1825 for Sir William Stewart, the second son of the seventh Earl of Galloway. Carved bargeboards and exceptionally broad eaves; latticed glazing. Verandah along the entrance (s) front. In this front's centre gable, a stone decorated with an ogee arch under the inscription 'ALNS STEVARD MILES FEC.', brought here *c.* 1890 from Garlies Castle (q.v.). At the house's NW section, hoodmoulds over the ground-floor windows, oriel windows above.

CUMMERTREES 1060

Small village near the Solway, its two personalities split by a railway bridge.

PARISH CHURCH. T-plan church of 1777, now covered with render lined out as ashlar. Plain roundheaded windows; in the w gable, a bullseye above the moulded doorpiece. On the gable of the N aisle, a birdcage bellcote, its stepped top now surmounted by a fleur-de-lis finial, probably a Victorian alteration. Also probably Victorian are the 'aisle's' angle buttresses carrying stone drums topped by truncated spires. At the 'aisle', a semi-octagonal apse, perhaps of *c.* 1930. Low E vestry of 1924. (Interior recast and refurnished by *John Starforth*, 1875–6; the furnishings were altered again in 1924.)

Immediately E of the church, the large and battlemented early C19 BURIAL ENCLOSURE of the Douglases of Kelhead (later Marquesses of Queensberry); Tudorish detail at the mostly blind openings. – To its E, a HEADSTONE to William

Riddle †1739, a curvy-topped Ionic aedicule; in the tympanum, an angel's head (the soul) above reminders of death. War Memorial LYCHGATE of c. 1920.

SCHOOL. Plain, by *James Tweedie*, 1905; extended by *Dumfries and Galloway Regional Council*, 1992.

DESCRIPTION. The village's W part beside the Parish Church (*see* above) is mostly composed of single-storey C19 cottages, generally rather altered. The road under the RAILWAY BRIDGE of 1848 leads to the fifteen-house QUEENSBERRY TERRACE, built *c.* 1900, by General Brook of Kinmount as the first phase of a projected holiday village; *F. J. C. Carruthers* was the architect. The terrace, despite the alterations marring its symmetry, is a piece of seaside fun. Brick-built, the top floors harled and half-timbered, with red-tiled roofs. Variegated display of balconies, jettying, bay and bow windows, bracketed canopies and ogee lead domes. The architecture deserved to bring success but the presence of the railway immediately across the road must always have deterred holiday-makers.

KINMOUNT HOUSE. *See* p. 357.

CUMSTOUN
6050

2km. SE of Twynholm

Mansion house by *Thomas Hamilton*, 1828, extended and remodelled by *Kinnear & Peddie* in 1891.

Hamilton's house, built for Adam Maitland, who had acquired the estate *c.* 1819, was a large Tudor-Gothic villa, the dourness of its whin rubble walling and red sandstone dressings saving it, perhaps unfortunately, from frivolity. The main block was a shallow U-shape, symmetrical on plan but with the E range a storey higher than the W, the balance restored by a low SW service range.

At the entrance (N) front's recessed centrepiece was a large flat-roofed Tudor porch with battlemented octagonal corner buttresses. It projected from a two-storey block, the first-floor windows' hoodmoulds rising from Gothic corbels. Set back behind this block's parapet, the second floor was treated as a tower: semi-octagonal front with battlemented octagonal buttresses at the corners and pointed windows. The advanced ends of the E and W ranges were given determinedly different treatments. At the end of the three-storey E range, battlemented clasping buttresses, a canted and battlemented bay window at the ground floor and three-light windows above, the first floor's hoodmoulded. Aggressive stepping at the centre of the parapet. At the two-storey W range, octagonal corner buttresses, again battlemented. A pair of Gothic windows to each floor, the upper floor's hoodmoulded. Empty image niche above. Crenellated parapet following the lines of the gable. The E and W elevations seem both to have been plain. The low service wing (altered in the C20) extends W from the SW corner.

The garden (s) front repeated the tripartite arrangement but with a basement exposed by the falling site. Slightly advanced three-bay centrepiece, again with battlemented octagonal corner buttresses. At its centre, a canted and battlemented two-storey bay window. Pointed windows at the ground and second floors, hoodmoulded rectangular openings to the first floor. The ends of the E and W ranges were undemonstrative, clasping buttresses their principal feature.

The 1890s remodelling was most severe at the entrance front, where *Kinnear & Peddie* shifted Hamilton's porch from the centrepiece to the end of the W range and, in its original position, added a plain single-storey block. In front of the E range they provided a boldly projecting two-storey block; its battlemented clasping buttresses and hoodmoulded windows (the three-light ground-floor window since converted to a garage door) are half-hearted attempts to make it other than utilitarian. On this addition's E side, a canted bay window. At the same time Kinnear & Peddie broadened the E range's s half to the E, providing a new three-light ground-floor s window, badly aligned with the openings above, and a two-storey canted bay window to the E.

Inside, the principal rooms are on the ground floor. In the centre of the N side, a large Jacobean hall of the 1890s, the main stair opening off its E end. Behind the hall is the s-facing drawing room (probably its original function, but it was used as a billiard room for a time after 1891). Here Hamilton's work survives. Ribbed plaster vaulting at the canted bay window. Gothic panelling on the arched soffits of the other windows, the shutters, and the door. Cornice with delicate Tudor-Gothic traceried panels on the flat. Plain white marble chimneypiece. The unsatisfactorily L-shaped dining room (the 1890s drawing room) at the SE corner is by Kinnear & Peddie. Baroque chimneypiece, doorcase, china cabinet and pelmets. The 1890s dining room at the NE corner is now a garage.

In front of the house, the crude bowl of a medieval FONT, said to have come from Dundrennan Abbey. It sits on a fluted pedestal, probably also medieval, but the two pieces do not belong together.

On a mound, perhaps partly artificial, the ruin of CUMS-TOUN CASTLE, a tower house probably built in the C15. It has been a simple four-storey rectangle, *c.* 9.8m. by 6.4m. The W gable and stubs of the N and s walls survive, constructed of rubble with in-and-out quoins. Big slit windows on the s side at ground floor level. Large N and s windows to the first and second floors, smaller W windows at the first and third (now blocked), all with chamfered jambs. The interior seems to have been unvaulted. At the second floor, segmental-arched window embrasures.

NW of the house, a narrow single-storey rubble-built BYRE range of the earlier C19, with latticed glazing. At the centre of the broad-eaved piended roof, a square pavilion-roofed cupola containing a doocot. – NE of the house and again early C19, the rubble-walled GARDEN. On its S side, a contemporary *cottage orné*, the ground-floor windows hoodmoulded, the gableted first-floor N windows pointed. – Early C19 NORTH LODGE at the end of the drive, with broad eaves, hoodmoulded windows and a piend-roofed Tuscan-columned portico.

8090   DABTON
                         0.6km. SE of Carronbridge

Small-scale but quite smart group formed by a villa-classical country house and its appendages, designed by *William Atkinson* in 1820 to accommodate the Chamberlain of the Drumlanrig estate. The house itself, built of stugged pink sandstone ashlar, is an interlocking jigsaw. At the W end, an L-plan main block. Filling the SE inner angle but with its S front slightly recessed, a rectangular block. Attached to the E end, a third block, its N and S fronts both recessed. A fourth block, again with set-back fronts, was added at the E *c.* 1840. The arrangement of the different parts forms a hierarchy descending from W to E: the main block contains the principal rooms, the second block the estate office, the third block a tenants' waiting room and the kitchen, the fourth block (of *c.* 1840) the servants' hall, scullery, larder and knife room. The hierarchy is emphasized by the detailing. At the two-storey main and second blocks, piended roofs, tall ground-floor windows, a first-floor sill course and a moulded cornice. The third block is lower, its ground-floor windows smaller, the sill course is omitted, the cornice reduced to a plain band, and the roof straight-gabled. The fourth block is lower again, with small windows but a piended roof.

The main block's S (entrance) front is of three broad bays, the centre recessed but the eaves carried across in an unbroken line on the plane of the ends. Unmoulded round-arched entrance, now containing a fanlit double door but originally opening into a porch. Atkinson's N front was a restrained classical elevation of five bays. The advanced and pedimented centre has a three-light ground-floor window under a blind semicircular fanlight. *c.* 1860 canted bay windows lighting the drawing room were added to this front's W end and the W side's N; the stone mullions of their central lights were removed in the late C20 at the same time as a couple of originally dummy windows to the W were opened up. Irritating intrusions are the two small windows (one to the W perhaps of *c.* 1900, the other of 1944 to the N) made to light a bathroom and lavatory.

The second (estate-office) block appears from the S like a respectful senior civil servant standing at his minister's shoulder but half a step behind. The third block has a round-arched S door, but as this was for tenants it is much narrower than the principal entrance.

In the main block, an entrance hall with small panels and rosettes on the cove of its ceiling. Plain stone chimneypiece at the W wall. In the house's SW corner, the dining room (now sitting room), its Adam-revival chimneypiece an import of *c.*1900. This is off-centre in the E wall, perhaps to compensate for the projection of a sideboard from the N end, where Atkinson provided a recess (now filled in). At the NW corner, the drawing room, its egg-and-dart cornice probably a replacement of *c.*1900. Very smart imported late C18 pine and gesso chimneypiece, with swagged foliage on the frieze; at the ends, ladies holding lyres. Next door, in the centre of the N front, the library, whose pine and gesso chimneypiece may well be of the 1820s. Thistles at the centre of the frieze; at the ends, paterae, their bosses modelled as lions' heads. At the NE corner of the entrance hall, a roundheaded arch filled with a fanlit door. This opens into a corridor off whose S side opens the plain business room (now dining room) in the main block's SE corner. On the N side of the passage, a pair of roundheaded arches; the W arch is a recess, the taller E arch opens onto the stair, at whose top a segmental arch gives access to the corridor serving the first-floor bedrooms.

Projecting E from the house's NE corner, a single-storey DAIRY block, an early addition if it is not of the 1820s. This forms one side of an informal early C19 service court. – E of this, a more formal court of STABLES AND KENNELS, presumably contemporary with the house. Plain low ranges on its N, E and W sides. On the S, a pair of two-storey piend-roofed blocks, the E with round-arched openings (some now built up) to the court. At the main entry between these blocks, a sturdy pair of corniced gatepiers. – E of the stables, an extensive GARDEN, the irregular ground rising sharply to the N, bounded on three sides by high walls constructed of rough ashlar, probably in the 1820s. In the E wall, a round-arched recess or summerhouse. – Piend-roofed single-storey LODGE of *c.*1820 at the entrance to the drive from the W, a blocking course over the centre bay, which contains the pilastered door.

DALAWOODIE
0.5km. E of Newbridge

Villa of polished red sandstone ashlar, by *Walter Newall, c.*1830. Italianate, the windows each of two round-arched lights; bracketed broad eaves. Flattish pyramid roof over the central tower. Plain late C20 E addition.

DALBEATTIE

A planned village was laid out on both sides of the Dalbeattie Burn in 1781 by two local landowners, and employment was

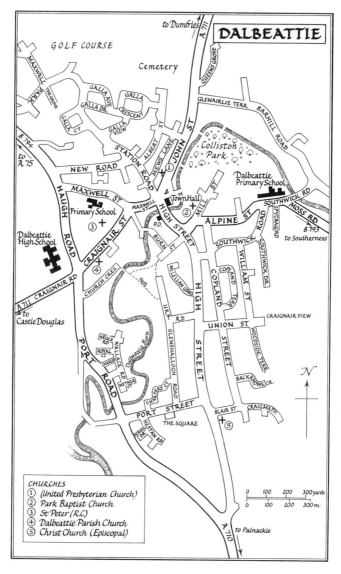

DALBEATTIE

GOLF COURSE

Cemetery

to Dumfries

CHURCHES
① (United Presbyterian Church)
② Park Baptist Church
③ St Peter (R.C.)
④ Dalbeattie Parish Church
⑤ Christ Church (Episcopal)

provided from *c.* 1790 by a paper mill, followed in the early C19 by other mills of various types and a forge. The Craignair granite quarries to the w were worked on a large scale between 1826 and 1832 to supply stone for the construction of Liverpool Docks. A granite-polishing industry was begun in 1841, and something of a boom period ensued; Dalbeattie became a police burgh in 1858, when its population was almost 1,700. The C20 has seen industrial decline, although granite continues to be quarried, and the population is now almost 4,000.

CHURCHES

CHRIST CHURCH (Episcopal), Blair Street. First Pointed, in grey granite, by *Francis Armstrong*, 1875. Shallowly buttressed nave; small semi-octagonal apse and NE vestry added in 1955. Squat angle-buttressed tower of 1875. It is of two stages (the lower a porch, the upper a belfry) finished with a heavy corbelled parapet but intended to have a spire. Narrow lancet windows with elongated trefoil heads. W window of four lights under a cusped rose. Inside, a collar-braced roof. – STAINED GLASS. In the nave, one light (St Michael) signed by *I. McQueen*, *c.*1950, colourful but bitty. – In the apse, two lights (Our Lady; St John) by *Margaret Chilton* and *Marjorie Kemp*, 1954–5, more powerful than usual for those artists.

DALBEATTIE PARISH CHURCH, Craignair Street. Big but plain Gothic cruciform of granite rubble, by *Kinnear & Peddie*, 1878–80. SW steeple, its tower's angle buttresses sloping in under the belfry, whose faces are filled with chunkily detailed paired openings; broached stone spire. Spacious unaisled interior with a gallery at the W end over the narthex. – In the E apse, five STAINED GLASS lights (the Ascension) of 1882. – In the N transept, an ORGAN, its pipes stencilled, by *Forster & Andrews*, 1887.

PARK BAPTIST CHURCH, Mill Street. Originally Dalbeattie Free Church. By *Francis Armstrong*, 1880–1. Broad grey granite box, the slight central projection of the front gable suggesting a nave and aisles. On the r., a four-stage tower under a tall broached slate spire enlivened with small lucarnes. Round-arched windows, but not weighty enough to be Romanesque.

ST PETER (R.C.), Craignair Street. Built in 1814 as a plain hall church, of pinky granite with red sandstone dressings; large rectangular windows. At the end, a slightly recessed and crow-step-gabled one-bay link, with a pointed attic window above its pointed and hoodmoulded door, to the tall, single-storey piend-roofed priest's house. The grey granite ashlar tower on the church's E side was added *c.*1850. Three intaken stages under a gabled and pinnacled parapet.

UNITED PRESBYTERIAN CHURCH, John Street. Now Colliston Boys Club. By *James Barbour*, 1860–1. Bullnosed granite box, its breadth disguised because the centre of the front gable is slightly advanced under a gableted bellcote. At the front corners, angle buttresses with steeply sloping tops. Angular pointed windows.

PUBLIC BUILDINGS

COLLISTON PARK. The land was given to the town in 1900. – Cast-iron Edwardian octagonal BANDSTAND. – WAR MEMORIAL of *c.*1920 in local grey granite, a very simplified version of the Edinburgh Mercat Cross, the octagonal drum base supporting a column topped by the lion rampant of Galloway. – BRIDGE of *c.*1900 over the Dalbeattie Burn, a single elliptical

span. The parapet's latticed sides are held by curvaceous
U-frames passing under the roadway and rising to each top
rail.

DALBEATTIE HIGH SCHOOL, off Haugh Road. Low and archi-
tecturally lightweight in buff brick, by the County Architect,
Archibald T. Caldwell, 1958. – SPORTS HALL by *Dumfries and
Galloway Regional Council*, 1984.

DALBEATTIE PRIMARY SCHOOL, Southwick Road. Three tall
single-storey grey granite broad-eaved blocks joined by flat-
roofed links of 1965. The H-plan centre block was built in 1876.
In the centre of its W front, a square tower broached to an
octagonal belfry covered by a slated spire. E block, its roof with
a ridge of red tiles, of 1900. The W block was added by *James
Barbour & Bowie* in 1912.

POST OFFICE. *See* Description, below.

TOWN HALL, High Street. Built in 1861–2. Two storeys and
quite plain except for a small Italianate clock tower on the NW
corner.

DESCRIPTION

JOHN STREET is the entry from the N. Only a plain Victorian
villa (the BURNSIDE HOTEL) on its E side. On the W, six
blocks of granite-built council houses (PARK TERRACE) by
W. F. Crombie, 1920, their steep piended roofs cutting down
across the gables; bracketed cornices over the doors. Then
two long late C19 terraces of granite-walled cottages, many
with their dormers replaced by boxes. After them, detached
and set back, the former United Presbyterian Manse (No. 5)
by *Robert Baldie*, 1872, Georgian-survival but with bracketed
eaves and a bay window. Beside it, the old United Presbyterian
Church (*see* Churches, above). At John Street's S end, the
villa-like BANK OF SCOTLAND of *c.*1890, with an outsize
basket-arched door. It faces a small bow-ended and battlemented Victorian block (THE ROUND HOUSE) on the
corner of Water Street.

MAXWELL STREET carries on to the W. On its N, a two-
storey terrace (Nos. 10–22) of *c.*1900, with bargeboarded dormerheads at the first-floor windows. Then a late C19 terrace of
cottages; anta-pilastered doorpiece on No. 26. CRAIGNAIR
STREET goes S. On its r. side and set well back is St Peter's
(R.C.) Church (*see* Churches, above). Further down on the
l. and facing another late C19 cottage-terrace is a mid-C19
Georgian-survival house, followed by the Parish Church (*see*
above). In BURN STREET, running E from Craignair Street's
N end, rubble-built C19 former mills. Just across the burn, the
mid-C19 WOODBURN, single-storey, with an anta-pilastered
doorpiece. Beside it, HALLBURN, built as a working men's
club in 1877 and now much altered, but still with pointed doors
in the gables and diagonally set corner buttresses topped by
chimneys.

HIGH STREET makes an alternative route from the corner

of John Street and Maxwell Street. At its top, on the l., is the
Town Hall (*see* Public Buildings, above). On the r., across the
BURGH BRIDGE, whose granite balustrades were acquired
when it was widened in 1930, is a gingerbread POST OFFICE
by *J. A. Macgregor*, 1902–3. Then High Street settles down into
late C18 and C19 vernacular. On the NW corner with Mill
Street, a block of 1883 with iron cresting on its small Frenchy
tower. In front, a triangular space, its centre filled by a columnar
FOUNTAIN of grey and pink granite erected by *D. H.
& J. Newall* in 1887 to celebrate Queen Victoria's Golden
Jubilee.

On MILL STREET's l. side, the mid-C19 piend-roofed ALMA
HOUSE, its projecting r. bay topped by an Italianate tower.
This looks like an addition of *c.*1860, as may be the consoled
pediment over its door and the consoled cornices over the
ground-floor windows. On the corner with Alpine Street, a
faintly Art Deco former CINEMA of *c.*1930, followed by a
late C19 cottage-terrace (Nos. 14–30) facing the Park Baptist
Church (*see* Churches, above). Further on, a semi-detached
pair (Nos. 40–42), also late C19 but in red and white brick.
Alpine Street leads E from Mill Street to SOUTHWICK ROAD.
On its N side, the Primary School (*see* Public Buildings, above).
Further E, the piend-roofed BARRBRIDGE MILL of 1837, two
storeys of whitewashed rubble; behind, a detached kiln which
has been heightened in brick and given a ship's ventilator.
Near Southwick Road's W end, the ROYAL BRITISH LEGION
(former Conservative Club) by *J. A. Macgregor*, 1896–7. Tall
two storeys, with bargeboards at the front gables. Facing down
Southwick Road from High Street is the plain ROYAL BANK
OF SCOTLAND of 1858, its ground floor clad in polished granite
*c.*1930. The S stretch of High Street is more domestic, a
rather ragged version of much of the rest of the town. Near
the end, Christ Church (Episcopal), for which *see* Churches,
above.

BUITTLE CASTLE AND OLD BUITTLE TOWER. *See* p. 137.
EDINGHAM CASTLE. *See* p. 303.

DALGARNOCK   8090

Isolated graveyard of a medieval parish which was united with
Closeburn (q.v.) in 1697.

GRAVEYARD. The rubble-built enclosing WALL is probably
C19. Set into one gatepier of the E entrance is a stone,
probably C18, one of whose faces is carved with a skull and
crossbones, another with a flaming urn. – Straight ahead,
MONUMENT to the Nithsdale Martyrs (i.e. Covenanters) by
D. J. Beattie & Son, 1925, a cross carved with a thistle,
crown, book, sword, and scroll of the Covenant. – Beside
the wall, N of the entrance, the well-preserved GRAVESLAB
of Andrew Houetson †1675, with a marginal inscription. At
the top, an angel's head (the soul) in very shallow relief; a

skull and crossbones at the bottom. – Just s of the entrance, nestled in the roots of a tree, a crude stone FONT, presumably medieval. – To its s, a better-dressed rectangular FONT, now standing on a pedestal made up of fragments from C18 monuments, some upside-down, decorated with emblems of mortality. – To the w, a group of C18 and C19 TABLE STONES. Among them, the GRAVESLAB of the Covenanter James Harknes †1723, with the inscription:

> Belo this stone this dust doth ly
> who indured 28 years porsecution by tirrany
> Did him persue with eko & cry
> through many a lonsome place
> at last by Clavers he was tane
> Sentenced for to dy
> But God who for his soul took car
> Did him from prison bring
> Because no other Cause they had
> but that he ould [*sic*] not give up
> with Christ his Glorious king
> and Swear alligence to that beast
> the duke of York I mean.
> In spite of all there hellish rage
> a natural death he died
> in full asurance of his rest
> with Christ eternaly

– A little to the w, HEADSTONE to Robert Miller †1732, its front with a wavy top and panelled pilasters framing a grinning angel's head above emblems of death, including a pair of scissors, a corpse, and bones flanking a hand which holds a book inscribed 'I SHAL BE SATISFID [*sic*] WITH THY LIKNESS WHEN I AWAKE'. – Just to the NW, a SLAB, perhaps the top of a table stone, commemorating John Hoatson †1717, its border carved with angels' heads and rosettes; at the bottom, a skull, crossbones and hourglass. – To the w, an innocently baroque SLAB to Mungo Gilein †1715, with caryatids at the sides, an angel's head and emblems of death at the top. – Beside it, a similar slab to John Gilein †1684, but with scrolled foliage instead of caryatids. – Immediately to the w, HEADSTONE of James Gilchrist †1758, the figure of a standing man on the front. – Behind, an C18 TABLE STONE, the uprights decorated with panelled pilasters; between them, panels carved with grisly reminders. – To its s, the HEADSTONE of John Addison †1732, with a caryatid and human figure flanking an angel's head above a book and flaming urn. – Near the graveyard's sw corner, a GRAVESLAB inscribed 'IOHN MVLIGAN 1640', its stark simplicity a contrast to the elaborate carving of the late C17 and C18. – A different contrast is provided by a fair number of late C18 and early C19 HEADSTONES of a standard type found in nearby parishes, their fronts carved with polite reliefs of classical urns.

KIRKBOG, 0.4km. NW. Farmhouse and steading built and perhaps designed by *James Thomson*, 1827, the house a piend-roofed ashlar box, the steading buildings less formal and painted white.

DALSKAIRTH

2.2km. SW of Cargenbridge

Early Georgian laird's house extended into a lopsided small mansion. It began in the earlier C18 as a piend-roofed rectangle of two storeys and a basement. Five-bay front, with rusticated painted quoins, architraves and a stringcourse under the ground floor all in contrast to the white harling. Perhaps a little later the house was extended by one bay at each end, the full-height wings set slightly back from the main block. Some remodelling was carried out *c.* 1830, when a new fanlit door was provided at the E front, the windows were enlarged and a bow was built on the N wing's W side. In 1897 *John A. Campbell* produced designs for a Baronial replacement to be built on a more elevated site, but what was executed in 1899 was a remodelling and extension of the N wing, giving the front its unbalanced appearance, the addition of flat-roofed dormer windows and the provision of a baroque portico. The interior was gone over at the same time.

In front of the house, an octagonal baluster SUNDIAL, the bronze dial dated 1734 and signed by *Edward Narriel* (?) of London. – Also in front, a stone WELLHEAD of 1900 in an Arts and Crafts manner. – On the wooded Dalskairth Hill behind, LENNOX'S TOWER, a rubble-built round folly of *c.* 1800. Pointed door under a weathered crest; slit windows. – What was probably a second WELLHEAD now stands beside the drive; it is a corniced and domed ashlar cylinder, dated 1824. Above its hoodmoulded door, a re-used panel bearing the initials I G and MM and the date 1572 (?). – Near the entrance to the drive, plain U-plan STABLES of *c.* 1800. – At the entrance itself, an early C19 T-plan LODGE, its N gable's blind window dignified with a consoled pediment. – Contemporary tall rusticated and ball-finialled GATEPIERS.

DALSWINTON

Unpretentious but remarkably well-kept hamlet of two terraces of rubble-built and painted housing of *c.* 1790, the row on the S of the road single-storey, that on the N heightened to two storeys, probably in the C19.

CHURCH, 0.6km. SE. Mission church of 1881, constructed of red-painted corrugated iron. Gothic windows; a steeply spired E bellcote. Timber-lined interior with an open roof; chancel formed between a vestry and laird's pew at the W end. – STAINED GLASS. Semi-abstract W window (scenes in the life of King David) by *Cyril Wilson*, 1975. – In the N wall, one light (David), much more realistic, of *c.* 1950.

TOWER, Clonfeckle, 1.8km. E. Round rubble-built tower (now roofless) erected in 1810 by Patrick Miller of Dalswinton as a monument to the Rev. Dr William Richardson, of Clonfeacle in Ireland, who had discovered the use in agriculture of fiorin grass, which Miller introduced to Scotland.

DALSWINTON HOUSE
1.4km. SE

Late C18 mansion house on the site of a C13 castle, the remains of a C16 or C17 laird's house standing as a garden folly on lower ground to the SE. The site, close to a ford across the River Nith, one of the principal routes N from the Solway Firth, was of obvious strategic importance in the medieval period, and a castle belonging to the Comyns stood here, almost certainly on the mound occupied by the present mansion, until 1355, when it was taken by Roger Kirkpatrick of Closeburn and dismantled. The lands then passed to the Stewarts of Garlies (later Earls of Galloway), who seem to have built a tower house, probably SE of the old castle's site, by 1542, when a fortalice is recorded here. In 1624 the estate was bought by John Rome, a Dumfries merchant, whose son sold it (rechristened Dalswinton-Rome) eighteen years later to James Douglas of Mouswald; from him it passed to a branch of the Maxwells. In 1785 Dalswinton was bought by Patrick Miller, a director and later Deputy Governor of the Bank of Scotland. He built the present house, created the loch, which he used for the maiden voyage of a cumbersome multi-hulled and paddle-wheeled boat (the design left unpatented), and introduced fiorin grass to the estate farms. His son sold the estate, *c.* 1830, to James Macalpine-Leny, from whose grandson it was acquired in 1919 by David Landale, a director of the Shanghai and Hong Kong firm of Jardine Matheson.

DALSWINTON HOUSE itself was built by Patrick Miller soon after he acquired the estate in 1785. It is an austere rectangle of three storeys and a basement, all faced with polished Locharbriggs ashlar, the basement's masonry channelled. Overall mutuled cornice carrying a balustraded parapet. At the principal (E) front, architraves with block-consoled sills to the first- and (square) second-floor windows. The windows of the ground floor are taller and corniced to denote the *piano nobile*. In the centre was a portico, replaced by *James Barbour & Bowie* in 1919–20 with a single-storey-and-basement bow, its pilasters supporting a boldly projecting cornice. At the centre of the rear (W) elevation, a full-height bow. The architectural severity has been accentuated by the replacement of the windows' C18 small panes by plate glass, perhaps in 1919–20, when James Barbour & Bowie provided a new entrance at the N gable. This N extension is set back from the house's E front but not, unfortunately, from the W. In its N side, a broken-pedimented doorpiece, the capitals of the columns of a simplified Art Deco-like order. Above, and lighting the new stair behind, a tripartite opening under a Diocletian window, a reworking of the C18 stair window at this end.

The late C18 interior contained a large entrance hall with a room (the parlour and business room) each side. Behind the hall, a small inner hall with the principal stair to its r. On the hall's l., and occupying the SW two-thirds of the house, the drawing room. Bow-ended dining room in the centre of the W front. The main rooms still contain white marble chimney-pieces, probably of *c*.1790. The C18 entrance hall was converted to a sitting room in 1919–20, when it was given plain wooden panelling. The drawing room's plaster-panelled walls and enriched ceiling are in a late Georgian manner but more likely to be of *c*.1890 than *c*.1790. The C18 stair was removed in 1919–20 to form a passage to the new N entrance and stair hall, where James Barbour & Bowie's stair is routine neo-Jacobean.

On lower ground to the E, the remains of DALSWINTON OLD HOUSE. Rectangular main block; only its ground floor, now turfed over, still stands. Inside, a room (originally two) covered with an ashlar tunnel-vault. Large segmental-arched kitchen fireplace in the W gable. This may be C16. At the NW corner, a round stair tower, entered at the present ground level through a moulded and corniced door. Flanking the door but at different levels, a pair of recumbent double-keyhole gun-loops. The stair inside goes both up, with a moulded door into the missing hall, and down to the basement. This very unusual arrangement and the awkward join to the main block suggest that the tower has been an addition, perhaps built for John Rome *c*.1624, and that its construction may have been accompanied (unless there was a forestair to the tower) by the raising of the ground level to cover the main block's lowest floor. N of this house, foundations of a rectangular building, perhaps the mansion house or offices said to have been built here *c*.1760.

To the N, DALSWINTON LOCH, formed by Patrick Miller *c*.1785. On its E shore, a GARDEN of *c*.1790, its rubble walls faced internally with brick. – At the N end of the loch, a round DOOCOT of *c*.1790, its ashlar walling relieved by a band course. – W of the loch, DALSWINTON MAINS, a stable and coachhouse courtyard of *c*.1790. Low two-storey ranges of polished ashlar. Over the S range's pedimented centrepiece, a tower, its bottom stage a square pedestal. Above, a taller octag-onal clock stage. This is now topped by a truncated pyramid roof finished with iron cresting, clearly Victorian, perhaps replacing a dome.

Two entrances to the parkland from the NE. The W is the BACK LODGE, built in the earlier C19, with a battlemented bow at the centre of its front. – To the E, EAST GATE, a pair of late C18 lodges. At each front gable, a pedimented centrepiece containing an overarched window. Cylindrical gatepiers with rosettes on their fluted friezes. They carry big stone urns.

DALTON

Small L-plan village. Its painted or harled rubble cottages are mostly Edwardian, but one is dated 1760 on its door lintel.

FREE CHURCH. Disused. Tall lanceted box of 1866. In the w gable front, a triangular build-up from the quatrefoil lights flanking the door to a stepped three-light window and a vesica under the gableted bellcote.

LITTLE DALTON CHURCH, Kirkhill, 2.5km. W. Roofless remains in an unwalled graveyard overgrown with trees. The rubble-built church is perhaps of the early C16. T-plan with an off-centre N 'aisle'. Near the w end of the main block's N wall, a plain round-arched doorway. Three windows, all with rectangular rear-arches, survive intact. One, at the s wall's w end, is a small lancet. To its E, a round-arched light. At the E end of the N wall, a rectangular window. Roundheaded arch with projecting imposts from the body into the 'aisle'.

PARISH CHURCH. Simple Early Christian, by *J. M. Dick Peddie*, 1894–5. Sturdy nave with a narrower and lower short chancel, all built of snecked red sandstone rubble. At the nave's NE corner, a squat square tower, its two-light belfry openings with cushion-capitalled columns.

Inside, a kingpost-truss roof over the nave, scissors roof in the chancel. Segmental-headed rear-arches to the windows. Plainly moulded semicircular chancel arch. – STAINED GLASS three-light E window (the Ascension, with St Peter and St John) by *A. Ballantine & Gardiner*, 1896.

To the SE, the roofless shell of the OLD PARISH CHURCH built in 1704, its N, E and W walls incorporating the bottom courses of the stonework of its medieval predecessor. Rubble-built rectangle with surprisingly smart detail. Square-headed windows and doors, their surrounds embellished with V-jointed rustication. In the long N wall, two tall windows flanked by doors which have been converted to windows. At each gable, a forestair to a gallery door; over the E door, a bullseye window. The gables' ground-floor doors are insertions, perhaps of the early C19. On the w gable, a birdcage bellcote topped by a weathercock; chimney on the E gable. The interior has had a gallery round three sides.

Just NW of the Old Parish Church, a late Georgian BURIAL ENCLOSURE. Round-arched entrance and rusticated angle quoins. – s of the Parish Church, C18 HEADSTONES, two carved with pilasters and reminders of death, a third omitting the pilasters but multiplying the grisly emblems in compensation. – To their W, the suave classical MONUMENT to the Carruthers of Whitecroft, probably of the late C18. Tall plinth carrying an urn-finialled obelisk.

HALL. Dated 1898. Glazed red-brick walls and bargeboards.

SCHOOL. Now a house. Built in 1854–5; *James Richardson* was the mason. Single-storey T-plan, of whin with red sandstone dressings.

STANDING STONE. Narrow block, *c.*1.95m. high, probably
erected in the second millennium B.C. and now painted
white.
BENGALL HILL, 3.8km. N. White-painted farmhouse of *c.*1860
with bargeboarded gables. The steading complex behind looks
a little earlier.
DENBIE. *See below.*
KIRKWOOD. *See* p. 395.
MURRAYTHWAITE. *See* p. 455.

DAVINGTON 2000

Observatory, church, temple, and a few houses scattered in moorland.

ESKDALEMUIR AND ETTRICK REFORMED PRESBYTERIAN
CHURCH. Disused. Probably designed by *Walter Riddell*, who
made out the specification; built in 1835–7. Humble rubble
box, its lancet windows perhaps dating from alterations of
1882.
KAGYU SAMYE LING TIBETAN CENTRE, Garwaldwaterfoot,
1.6km. S. Simple FARMHOUSE of *c.*1860, with bracketed
eaves. – Brightly coloured TEMPLE of traditional type, by
Sherab Palden Beru, 1979–88, in pink 'Fyfestone'. Three
receding storeys, the ground floor verandahed, balconies in
front of the upper floors. Pagoda roof, the swept-up eaves
ending in carved wooden beasts. It looks kitsch to Western
eyes.
ESKDALEMUIR OBSERVATORY. By *W. T. Oldrieve*, 1904–7, in
dark whinstone rubble. Austere neo-Jacobean main block with
a low tower. Small two-storey buildings on the approach, in a
blocky Arts and Crafts manner.

DENBIE 1070
1.2km. SW of Dalton

Laird's house of modest but marked pretension. The front (S)
block was built in 1706 for John Carruthers, an Edinburgh
lawyer whose father had acquired the estate. Two-storey piend-
roofed rectangle of five bays by two, the front windows grouped
1/3/1. Red sandstone dressings, now painted but intended to
contrast with the rendered walling, probably originally harled.
Rusticated quoins at the corners and, less usually, the front
windows, looking very like those of the nearby Dalton Old
Parish Church of 1704. The entrance is in the centre, its door's
lugged architrave framed by a Roman Doric aedicule, with
attached columns supporting a frieze whose metopes are carved
with fleurs-de-lis, a quatrefoil and a rosette. In the steep open
pediment, a panel carved with a coat of arms, the initials of
John Carruthers and his wife, Margaret, and the date '6th APRIL
1706', probably that of the house's completion. Rising from the

centre of the roof, a pair of corniced chimneystacks. Chamfered
surrounds to the side windows.

All this seems straightforward enough, but was the house
originally a simple rectangle, or was it, perhaps, U-plan with
N wings? And was the main entrance at the S, as now, or at
the N and the doorpiece moved here *c.* 1800 when the house
was almost doubled in size? This piend-roofed late Georgian
rear block is plain, the N elevation an asymmetrical arrangement of two- and three-light windows.* Late C19 extension
built against the W side and protruding to the N. It is set
well back from the early C18 front, with which its W gable
windows try to be in keeping; two-storey canted bay window
on the W side.

Inside, the entrance hall in the 1706 block and the stair
hall of *c.* 1800 now form a long passage in which the stair
rises. Simple decoration with mutuled and rosetted cornices;
the stair hall's ceiling is enriched with an acanthus-leaf rose
set in a husked quatrefoil. The entrance hall may originally
have been divided, one corner of it perhaps filled with a fairly
tight circular or oval stair as at Newhailes House (Lothian)
of 1686. E of the entrance hall, the drawing room (originally
family parlour or low dining room), its walls covered with
early C18 panelling, possibly altered at the N end, where
there may have been presses. Around the simply moulded
stone chimneypiece, a lugged architrave; overmantel with
stumpy pilasters. S of the fireplace, a china cupboard with a
lugged architrave; it seems to have been formed in the original
entrance to the room; the present NW door was probably
made *c.* 1800. Another door in the N wall. It is in the position
of an early C18 window or door, perhaps into a NE wing. In
the dining room W of the entrance hall, another early
C18 stone chimneypiece. Ceiling enriched with a big circle
decorated with fruit, its character late C17, its date probably
late C19 or early C20.

An elliptical arch of *c.* 1800 opens from the stair landing into
the first floor of the early C18 house. Here the rooms are higher
than those below and seem to have formed a state apartment.
The E (now a bedroom), presumably the state dining room,
has been Victorianized. It would have had a door into the room
across the centre of the S front, which is now a bathroom but
was originally a small drawing room or ante-room. From this
was entered the state bedchamber. Panelling on the walls: that
of the N wall is on two planes and perhaps altered; the E has a
door cut through at the N end. At the original SE entrance, a
lugged and corniced architrave; the panel above, its frame
enriched with beading, seems designed to contain a painting.
Full-height panelled pilasters flanking the E fireplace, its stone
surround like those of the ground-floor rooms, the overmantel
with a long mirror framed by stumpy panelled pilasters and

---

* The r. ground-floor window widened to three lights in the 1980s.

topped by another panel intended for a painting and with a beaded frame.

Immediately E of the house, a rubble-walled GARDEN, its date given by the inscription over the W entrance: 'JOHN CARRUTHERS [fifth of Denbie]/1814'. – SE of the house, the U-plan STABLES, probably C18 in origin if the stop-chamfered doors at the E range's S end are *in situ*; but remodelled and probably enlarged in 1817–18. Straightforward ranges of whitewashed rubble, rather altered in the C20; ball finials on the N and S blocks. – To the S, an octagonal DOOCOT, again built of whitewashed rubble, its slated roof topped by a lantern. Over the N door, a transomed roundheaded opening, the keystone inscribed 'J.C. [for John Carruthers, fourth of Denbie]/1775'. This opening contains two tiers of roundheaded flight holes, of stone below the transom, of wood above; fanlight at the top. Circular interior, the nesting boxes formed by brick piers supporting stone slabs. – Piend-roofed LODGE of *c.* 1840 at the entrance to the drive. Gabled porch at the side; on the front, a battlemented bay window.

DORNOCK   *2060*

Little more than a hamlet but containing the two farm steadings of Dornock House and Dornocktown. The church and manse stand aloof at the W end.

PARISH CHURCH. T-plan church, built of sneck-harled rubble in 1793. Round-arched windows with projecting imposts and keystones; a bullseye in the gable of the N 'aisle'. On top of this gable, a birdcage bellcote, rebuilt by *Hugh Ker*, 1855, with a ball finial on its stepped roof. More ball finials, probably of 1793, on the other gables. Tall N porch added in 1884–5 by *James Barbour*. The small W porch and E vestry are later additions. Inside, the shallow-relief but quite elaborate ceiling rose is presumably of 1793. – FURNISHINGS by *Barbour*, 1884–5, the front of the N gallery and the pulpit both neo-Jacobean. – STAINED GLASS. Two lushly coloured lights (Our Lord as the Good Shepherd; the Agony in the Garden) flanking the pulpit. They are by *A. Ballantine & Gardiner*, 1893–4. SE of the church, three hogbacked GRAVESTONES, possibly C16, carved with panels containing fleurs-de-lis.

Former MANSE to the W, Tudorish of 1844–5.

DORNOCK HOUSE. Incorporated in the early C19 farm steading is the small early C18 mansion house. The two-storey four-bay front has been quite smart. Moulded surrounds and projecting sills at the windows. Round-arched doorpiece with projecting imposts; carved tendrils each side. The moulded cornice is continued across the adjoining building but a joint in the stonework suggests that this is an addition, perhaps late Georgian, despite apparently re-using window surrounds from the earlier house.

STAPLETON TOWER. *See* p. 527.

DRUMCOLTRAN TOWER

8060

1.6km. NE of Kirkgunzeon

Sturdy C16 tower house of the Maxwells of Drumcoltran, sitting on the edge of a farm steading. It is L-plan, built of local whin rubble, with the main corners rounded to avoid the need for dressed stone, which is used only at the door and window openings. High parapet, its uncrenellated coping renewed, carried on individual crudely moulded corbels round the three-storey-and-attic main block. The NW jamb rises into a gabled third floor projected across the inner angle. At the main block's upper floor and the top room of the jamb, domestic windows. The two doors (one now a window) and one window at the main block's ground floor are insertions, perhaps of the C18, probably replacing small openings. C16 gunloop in the S wall and another in the N wall, covering the entrance. This door is in the jamb's E face. Above it, the empty moulded frame for an armorial panel. Over this, and perhaps not *in situ*, a stone inscribed with platitudinous Latin injunctions ('Keep secrets. Speak little. Be truthful. Avoid wine. Remember you must die. Be merciful'). Slit windows light the stair in the jamb.

The tunnel-vaulted ground floor contains two rooms, the E presumably the kitchen though its simply moulded large stone chimneypiece is an insertion blocking a gunloop. Smaller store room to the W, the partition wall perhaps an insertion. Broad turnpike stair in the jamb. Just before it reaches the first floor there is a large recess in the E wall, perhaps for a tray from which a meal was served. The first floor seems originally to have been one room, subdivided (the partition walls since removed) in the early or mid-C18 when the E fireplace was contracted and given a plain rectangular chimneypiece and a second fireplace with a basket-arched chimneypiece was made in the SW corner. The second floor, now a single space and lacking its wooden floor, has contained two bedchambers, each with an off-centre fireplace and with a garderobe in the S wall. In the thickness of the N wall, a passage from the stair to the W room; it may have been a closet. At the attic, a fireplace in the W gable. The room over the stair in the jamb, perhaps a study, has a fireplace in the N gable.

DRUMLANRIG CASTLE

8090

Fantastic pink sandstone edifice built for the first Duke of Queensberry *c.* 1675–97. The contrast between its Baroque opulence and the bareness of the surrounding hills shocked early visitors ('like a fine Picture in a dirty Grotto, or like an Equestrian Statue set up in a Barn', wrote Defoe), and, though the hills are now softened by massive plantations, theatrical excitement is still abundantly present.

The lands of Drumlanrig, commanding the passes from the N into the Nith valley, and the site of a Roman fort in the C1 and

C2, were granted by James, second Earl of Douglas, to his natural son, William Douglas, c. 1383. A castle had been built here by 1429, its site of such great natural strength, with almost sheer drops on three sides, that major defences were needed only on the N. In the mid-C16 James Douglas of Drumlanrig rebuilt 'the haill house and pallice of Drumlanrig', which by 1618 made an irregular quadrangle with a projecting NW tower. In that year Sir William Douglas of Drumlanrig (later the first Earl of Queensberry) obtained plans for remodelling the S range, containing the principal rooms, and adding towers at the SW and SE.

There is no evidence that any part of the 1618 scheme was executed, though estimates of materials were obtained, and in 1673 the third Earl of Queensberry (later the first Marquess and first Duke) noted on those plans that they were 'to be looked over and advised be Sir Wm Bruise'; the note continues, in a different hand: 'As also Mr. Mills draughts both for the house and bridge'. It seems clear that *Sir William Bruce*'s opinion was being sought on a new design by *Robert Mylne*,* and that the plans of 1618 were regarded either as still providing a possible alternative or as supplying Bruce with a survey of the existing house. No further documentation directly links either Bruce or Mylne (both then engaged in the reconstruction of the Palace of Holyroodhouse in Edinburgh) with the rebuilding of Drumlanrig begun two years later. But in 1686 the Dutch carvers *Peter Paul Boyse* and *Cornelius van Nerven* moved to work there after being employed on Bruce's own Kinross House, and work at Drumlanrig was directed in 1686–90 by Mylne's son-in-law and successor as the government's principal architect and building contractor in Scotland, *James Smith*. *William Lukup* was master of work and presumably in day-to-day charge.

The old house was demolished, except for the E range, which was to be remodelled, in 1675. In August 1684 no fewer than thirty-one masons and eight wrights were recorded as working 'at the Castell of Drumlangrige', and by 1690 the interior was being finished, although work on the principal stair continued until 1697. With such a protracted building period it is not surprising that the design seems to have been modified in the course of construction.

The general model for the house is George Heriot's Hospital (now School) in Edinburgh, begun in 1628 and mostly completed by 1659, the largest building put up in early C17 Scotland. Like Heriot's, Drumlanrig is quadrangular, with an ogee-roofed round stair tower in each corner of the courtyard and a rectangular tower at each outer corner. But the emphasis here is more vertical; the outer towers are unrelieved by stringcourses and their pepperpot bartizans squat on the corners, not projected on corbelling. Rubble-built E and W ELEVATIONS, plain except for rope-moulded eaves courses studded with cannon spouts under the overall balustrades and Y-shaped lead down-

---

* That 'Mr. Mill' was Robert Mylne is clear from his surviving design and estimate for Drumlanrig Bridge.

pipes on the towers. The basement windows were deepened
c. 1815. The E front's C16 origin is betrayed by blocked windows
and gunloops. The severe S FRONT is relieved only by the
segmental-pedimented Doric doorpiece at the head of a double
stair, its wrought-iron balustrade decorated with roses, thistles
and tulips and, in the centre, the Douglas emblem of a winged
heart and the coronetted monogram of the first Duke of
Queensberry. This ironwork is probably by *William Baine* or
William Gairdner, the smiths employed here in 1684. The
landing is supported by Tuscan columns identical with those
at the entrance (originally garden) stair of James Smith's own
Newhailes (Lothian) of 1686 and those at the entrance (again
originally garden) portico of Caroline Park House (Edinburgh)
of 1696. The stair was extended E and W in the mid-C19.

It is the N FRONT which gives Drumlanrig its theatrical
glamour. The approach, at the end of a great avenue, is through
a long forecourt, its S end marked by a low balustrade, probably
provided by *William Elliot* in 1813. Screen walls on the E and
W sides; at their S ends, heavy early C18 rusticated gatepiers
with huge ball finials. Outside the gatepiers, on each side, a
square early C18 pavilion which lost its ogee roof and acquired
a parapet in 1813. Groin-vaulted ground-floor room inside the
E pavilion. From the pavilions, discreet office ranges (probably
by *William Burn*, c. 1830–4, with some late C19 additions),
replacing screen walls, run back to swallow up a second pair of
early C18 pavilions, also deprived of their original ogee roofs.

All this is a gentle introduction to the Baroque bravura of
the main house, skied above a terrace which is loggia-fronted
before the main block; at the corner towers the terrace breaks
forward with flat-roofed pavilions demarcating an inner court,
its centre filled by the horseshoe-shaped perron sweeping down
from the terrace. The effect must have been still tauter before
the removal of the balustrade which tied the perron to the
pavilions. Above the terrace rises the castle. Between the corner
towers, one-bay three-storey links which provide a step down
on each side to the two-storey pilastered centrepiece, its
entrance bay projecting boldly and carried up into a ducally
coronetted clock tower. It works through sheer swagger; but
closer inspection, richly rewarded by the quality of carved
detail, reveals astonishing inconsistency of design.

Under their diagonally set balusters, the terrace's loggia front
and end pavilions sit awkwardly together. The pavilions are
treated very simply, their inner faces decorated with carved
animal heads (one apparently a hippopotamus), their N fronts
with the heads of hounds and relieved by niches.* The loggia's
round-arched and key-blocked openings are framed by fluted
Doric pilasters of the same type (derived from Vignola) as used
by Bruce and Mylne at the Palace of Holyroodhouse. As at
Holyroodhouse, the pilasters carry a frieze carved with heraldry

---

* Formerly filled by lead statues of the Four Seasons; figures of gladiators stood
on the terrace above.

Drumlanrig Castle. North front (*Vitruvius Britannicus*, i, 1715)

(here of the Douglases); above each pilaster sticks out the head of a hound. This is very smart, but the frieze collides ineptly with the pavilions. More surprising is to find the loggia covered inside by groin vaults whose heavy ribs spring from corbels in the manner of *c.* 1500; the rosetted bosses are slightly more up-to-date. Far from archaic is the perron (rebuilt to the original design in 1860 by *Charles Howitt*), copied from a plate in Pierre Le Muet's *Manière de bien bastir*; but, though wonderfully effective in itself, it makes the porch under the clock tower pass for almost nothing as the visitor ascends.

The clock tower itself, magnificent in composition and adorned with superb carving, is distinctly odd in detail. The two lower storeys form an immensely tall but narrow aedicule, the fluted Corinthian columns stretched to ridiculously skinny proportions; on top, a segmental pediment filled with a huge coat of arms pushing up from the frieze. Inside this aedicular frame, a giant overarch, its base lost in the carved swags and bunches of fruit surrounding the entrance, whose pediment is carved with ladies reclining against shields, a ducal coronet above, a grotesque head below. On the E and W sides of the clock tower, pedimented doorways from the terrace are framed 79 by crisply carved swagged curtains: the one at the W bears a marquess's coronet, so is datable to 1682–4; the one at the E has a duke's coronet, giving a date after 1684.* The coronetted cupola, clearly cribbed from the crowned cupola over the entrance to Holyroodhouse, is an effective expression of ducal power but sits oddly on the segmental pediment of the aedicule below. Surely it must be an afterthought.

The possibility of afterthoughts cannot be confined to the central bay. The giant order applied to the two bays each

---

* The third Earl of Queensberry was created Marquess of Queensberry in 1682 and Duke of Queensberry in 1684.

side does not look at ease; its skinny pilasters are squeezed
uncomfortably between the windows, and the upper floor's
surprisingly steep window pediments break into the entablature
which stretches across the three-storey end bays. May not the
whole front between the corner towers have originally been
designed to be without pilasters and of three storeys, and
the five centre bays later reduced to two storeys to allow the
application of the classical order? If so, the original design
would have been very close to that of the N front of George
Heriot's School, and the old-fashioned steepness of the window
pediments (filled with excellent heraldic carving) would look
less out of place.

INTERIOR. In the basement of the E RANGE, tunnel-vaults,
probably C16. Perhaps of the same date, but more likely to be
late C17, are the iron yetts at the N ends of the corridors along
the E and W ranges.

The door of the main entrance from the porch is guarded by
another yett. It opens into a hall made in 1875 from what had
been a loggia. Wooden chimneypiece painted to imitate stone.
C17 gilded leather wall hangings stamped with the Douglas
winged heart, perhaps moved here from the former ground-
floor drawing room in the S range. The C17 progression from
the loggia was into the COURTYARD whose five-storey corner
towers (bearing dates from 1679 to 1687) hint that Drumlanrig
is still a real castle. The steep-pedimented windows of the main
ranges give a politer message. All is tied together by moulded
stringcourses above the two lower floors and a mutuled eaves
cornice over the second floor, slightly incongruous decoration
on the towers. Architectural inconsistencies appear. The tower
doors are provincial Doric with excessively deep friezes. A more
correctly Doric door to the S range but with a huge armorial
panel crudely breaking the segmental pediment. At the N
ground-floor arcade (its arches now windows), the same polite
Doric order* as on the N terrace, but with steep pediments
over the end arches; above the centre arch, the Douglas emblem
of a winged heart.

The interior of the S RANGE was originally occupied by two
identically planned apartments or suites of rooms, the lower
intended for the Duke's occupation, the upper a state apartment. The courtyard's S door opens into the dining room,
which was formed c. 1840 by throwing together the W end of
the C17 stair hall and Low Dining Room. Thinly modelled
Jacobean ceiling of c. 1840, a type that reappears in the other
principal rooms remodelled at the same time. The panelling
too is C19, but on the overmantels and overdoors are late C17
carvings of dead birds and fruit, probably re-used from the
gallery. To the W, a service room (originally drawing room),
still with its C17 shutters and wooden cornice. Panelled nursery
(originally bedchamber) in the SW tower. Instructive late C17
overmantel painting, perhaps by *Jacob de Witt*, of Lot fleeing

---

* The pilasters were renewed in the C19.

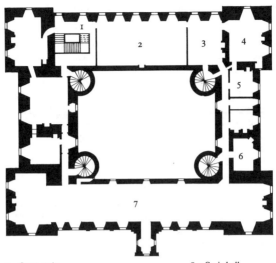

I	State stair	8	Stair hall
2	State dining room	9	Low Dining Room
3	State drawing room	10	Drawing room
4	State bedchamber	11	Bedchamber
5	Dressing room	12	Duke's closet
6	Charter room	13	Loggia
7	Gallery		

FIRST FLOOR

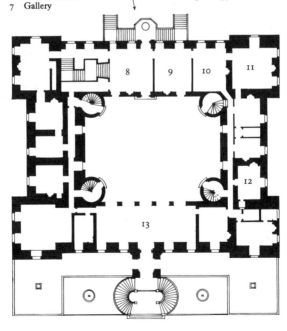

GROUND FLOOR

|—————————————————| 30 m

Drumlanrig Castle.
Reconstruction of early eighteenth-century plans

the Cities of the Plain. More carved birds on an overdoor. At the N of the W range, a groin-vaulted bedroom (originally the Duke's closet), its central boss carved with the monogram and coronet of William, Marquess of Queensberry, and so datable to 1682–4. The morning room in the SE tower was given a Corinthian pilastered sideboard recess in 1813 when it was fitted up as a dining room for the Duke's agent. Its Jacobean ceiling, with the Douglas heart prominently displayed, is of *c.*1840. In the parlour to the N, an early C19 Frenchy marble chimneypiece.

80   The state stair to the first floor looks a bit cramped since the C19 curtailment of the stair hall. Simple twisted wooden balusters and a heavy twisted newel post. The first floor was the C17 *piano nobile*. In the centre of the S range is the drawing room (the C17 state dining room), the first room of the C17 state apartment. C19 Jacobean ceiling but the rest looks original. Panelling with Corinthian pilasters frames the veined marble chimneypiece carved with the Queensberry coat of arms in deep-cut relief. On the overmantel, superbly executed deeply undercut foliage and birds looked down upon by cherubs. More carving of the same type and quality in the doors' segmental pediments and the panels above. Ante-room (originally state drawing room) to the W. In two panels over the console-pedimented doors, carved limewood foliage with monograms of the first Duke of Queensberry, so executed between 1684 and his death in 1695; originally they were in the state bedchamber. Lugged overmantel (designed for a painting) at the chimneypiece which is off-centre to allow for the *enfilade* into the state bedchamber in the SW tower. Here, tapestries framed by panelling. Corinthian pilasters at the chimneypiece, whose overmantel is filled with a scene of Hercules killing the dragon (again perhaps by de Witt). Narrow vaulted passage along the W range. Off it, above the vaulted bedroom (former Duke's closet), the charter room, also vaulted and with a foliaged boss. Iron inner door, a precaution against fire spreading from outside to destroy the charters recording the Duke's legal right to his huge estate. Oak-lined walls; above the plain stone chimneypiece, an overmantel designed for a painting.

When Drumlanrig was first completed, the whole of the N RANGE's first floor was filled by a gallery such as John and Robert Mylne (with advice from Sir William Bruce) had provided at Leslie House (Fife) in 1667–72 (*see* the Introduction, p. 65). At both Leslie and Drumlanrig the gallery was the setting for a magnificent display of portraits; at Leslie it opened off the state stair, but at Drumlanrig it was isolated on the other side of the house. Is this because it was an afterthought, decided upon when the other ranges had been nearly or completely finished internally? The gallery was divided up to form bedrooms in 1813. In the central bedroom, a huge chimneypiece brought *c.*1930 from Dalkeith House (Lothian). It is of *c.*1710, perhaps the work of *Richard Neale*, marble-cutter, and *Isaac Silverstyn* and *William Morgan*, carvers. Grey and pink veined

Drumlanrig Castle. Elevations and plan of gardens and plantations.
Engraving by J. Roque, mid-eighteenth century

marble under a mirror whose white marble frame is carved in
high relief with fruit, birds and cherubs. Wooden overmantel
frame (for a painting) carved with birds and fruit and
surmounted by two cherubs' heads leaning against a ducal
coronet.

The Castle has FORMAL GARDENS on its E, W and S sides.
To the E and W are formal parterres, as there have been certainly
since 1738 and probably since the C17. At the centre of the W
parterre and the outer corners of the one at the E stand bulbous
red sandstone pedestals, their panelled fronts carved in high
relief with fruit-filled vases. These may be late C17. So too may
be their crowning white marble vases; those on the E are each
carved with cartouches, foliage and grotesque human heads,
that on the W with a low-relief classical scene. These parterres
are linked by a broad terrace S of the castle, its balustrade
probably late C17, the balusters diagonally set. S of this terrace
was a steeply sloping bank down to the Marr Burn. In the late
C17 the bank was terraced but *c.* 1750 the two lower terraces
were converted to a slope. Terraces were reinstated *c.* 1840. On
the upper of these two terraces, another parterre, again with an
urn in the centre. The lower terrace is now grassed over. – On
the N side of the Marr Burn, a couple of SUMMERHOUSES of
1844, both octagonal and with tree-trunks supporting their
roofs (now slated but probably thatched originally). The sides
of the one at the W are faced with heather and pierced by
pointed openings; the one at the E has sides with geometrical
patterns of split logs and with cusped openings. Inside, the E

summerhouse is lined with moss in patterns including the Queensberry coat of arms, the w with split branches. – s of the mid-C19 ST GEOFFREY'S BRIDGE over the burn, a third mid-C19 SUMMERHOUSE, again octagonal and constructed of tree-trunks, the roof now slated. Three sides are open, the others faced with geometrically patterned split branches.

The surrounding PARKLAND rises steeply to the w. The heavily wooded hillsides' plantations were begun in the early C18 and recreated after the profligate fourth Duke of Queensberry had felled most of the mature trees in 1810. The main approach from the NE is across DRUMLANRIG BRIDGE over the Nith, built in the late C17 but repaired in 1710 (by *William Lukup*) and again in 1747. Two roundheaded arches, of pinky ashlar, the central pier ending in triangular cutwaters, their tops sloped. Parapets by *Charles Howitt*, 1860, projected on continuous corbelling. On the E side of the abutment, two cast-iron lions' heads, probably of 1860. – On the N side of the river, BRIDGE COTTAGE of 1841, a gently picturesque single-storey lodge, is almost certainly by *William Burn*. – Upstream to the NW, CREEL BRIDGE of c.1840, a narrow lenticular footbridge carried on pairs of slender cast-iron columns. – Overlooking the main drive is DRUMLANRIG MAINS, with a Tudor house of the earlier C19 standing at the SE corner of an extensive sawmill and workshop complex. – To the s, LAUNDRY COTTAGES, built as the Castle's laundry, again in the earlier C19, but remodelled by *Charles Howitt* c.1871. L-plan; at the corner, a buttressed and gabled tower originally of three storeys but later cut down to two, probably by *J. Laird*, c.1924.

c.1.1km. s of the Castle is the KITCHEN GARDEN, its ashlar-coped brick wall built c.1825. In the centre of the w side, a small triumphal-arched gateway; pedimented N entrance with coupled pilasters. – Outside, to the w, LOW GARDENS HOUSE, a bargeboarded *cottage orné* by *William Burn*, 1831, with mullioned and transomed windows and an E-facing verandah. – To its N, the mid-C19 HEATHER HOUSE, a summerhouse whose conical roof (now slated) is carried on tree-trunks, the walls between made of split logs. Inside, walls faced with split twigs in geometrical patterns. – SW of this, a tall and square battered stone CHIMNEY which served the kitchen garden.

DRUMMORE

Village beside Luce Bay, mostly C19 but with C20 local authority housing to the NW.

ST MEDAN'S CHURCH, Stair Street. Built as Kirkmaiden United Free Church in 1903. Plain Gothic buttressed rectangle of whin with red sandstone dressings, a red tiled ridge on the roof. Square NE tower of three stages, the lower two battered, the pyramid-roofed top a belfry with two-light rectangular openings, stumpy columns attached to their mullions. Inside, a gallery over the E vestibule; pulpit at the W end. – STAINED GLASS. In the S wall, one light (King David), by *Douglas Hamilton*, 1953.

HARBOUR. Rubble-built N pier of *c.* 1845, extended from *c.* 106m. to 134m., probably in 1889; breakwater on the W.

PRIMARY SCHOOL, Shaw Lane. Neat flat-roofed package, by the Wigtown County Architect, *John G. Sowerby*, 1974–5.

DESCRIPTION. LOW DRUMMORE on the village's SE edge is an informal white-painted grouping of farmhouse and steading, the buildings mostly C19. MILL STREET is the main street, generally C19 vernacular of one or two storeys, with a good supply of bargeboarded dormerheads. Rather grander than the norm is the mid-C19 QUEEN'S HOTEL, with consoled cornices over the windows and a large recumbent stone lion on top of the Roman Doric columned doorpiece. In STAIR STREET to the NW, St Medan's Church (*see* above). Opposite, the former KIRKMAIDEN FREE CHURCH by *William Todd*, 1843, now a hall and featureless. In front, an OBELISK commemorating the Rev. John Lamb † 1855, signed by *Mossman* of Glasgow. At the foot of Mill Street, on the r., the eponymous MILL, mostly of *c.* 1865 and built of painted brick, though the rubble base may be early C19; wheel on the side. Opposite, a mid-C19 rubble-built WAREHOUSE with brick surrounds to the doors and windows. In SHORE STREET, painted and rendered C19 vernacular. Quite elaborate window architraves on the SHIP INN of *c.* 1860; over its door, the carved and painted relief of a ship. At the beginning of HARBOUR ROAD to the E, a big early C20 WORKSHOP of corrugated asbestos sheeting.

DUMCRIEFF

1000

2.5km. SE of Moffat

Restrained piend-roofed mansion house built *c.* 1820–8, the work begun by Dr John Rogerson † 1823, the former physician to the Russian imperial court. Rubble-built two-storey U, the S range incorporating some mid-C18 fabric from the building's predecessor. W-facing entrance front. At the deeply recessed three-bay centre, a door with sidelights and an overall elliptical fanlight, framed by broadly spaced Doric columns *in antis*; three-light window above. S elevation of seven bays, the centre three closely spaced under a pediment, a Diocletian window in its tympanum. Across this centrepiece's ground floor, a balustraded Doric columned loggia.

DUMFRIES

By far the largest town of the region (with a population of over
31,000), and its undoubted metropolis, strategically sited astride
the main E–W route between the English border and the Irish Sea,
and also on the route N up the valley of the Nith. Dumfries is first
mentioned in 1160, when Radulf, son of Dunegal, granted land
there to the Hospice of St Peter at York. Probably it was a royal
burgh by 1174–5, when William I signed a charter there. By this
time there seems also to have been a royal castle, apparently sited
at the present Castledykes Park. That the town was a centre of
some local standing in the C13 can be inferred from the foundation
there in 1265 of the Convent of the Greyfriars by Devorgilla, Lady
of Galloway, who is also reputed to have erected a bridge across
the Nith. In the unrest of the early C14 the Church of the Greyfriars was the scene for the murder in 1306 of John Comyn of
Dalswinton (the 'Red Comyn') by Robert Bruce (later King
Robert I). Soon after 1313 the castle of Dumfries was destroyed;
no new royal castle took its place.

In the C15 and C16 the town was burnt several times by the
English and once by accident but was already notable as a centre
of textile industry. Reasonable prosperity in the C17 and the
beginning of the C18 is attested by the erection of a new town
house (the Midsteeple) in the centre of the broad High Street in
1705–7. The town's commercial importance was at its height
between *c.* 1720 and the 1750s, when it became the most important
port for the tobacco trade (the harbour itself was at Carsethorn),
so that in 1752 it could be described as the 'Scottish Liverpool'.
However, that trade had ended by 1760, when Bishop Pococke
noted that the inhabitants had lately invested their profits from it
in the erection of 'beautiful buildings of the red hewn sandstone'.
More long-lasting was the trade in livestock, Dumfries being a
major C18 and C19 centre for the sale of cattle, horses and pigs.
The wealth of what in the mid-C19 was the commercial and
administrative centre of the region was accompanied for the more
prosperous by a social life of which an observer in the 1860s wrote
that 'Dumfries has altogether an intellectual and polished tone,
which invests it with an importance far paramount to the bulkiness
of its population [*c.* 14,000]. It has also, in a considerable degree,
a character . . . for gaiety and fashionable dissipation.'

Woollen manufacture developed considerably in the later C19
but declined soon after. The C20 has seen varied attempts to
promote new industries, including the manufacture of cars and
rubber goods. At the same time the prosperous Victorian suburbs
of both Dumfries itself and Maxwelltown on the W side of the

Nith (created a burgh of barony in 1810 but amalgamated with Dumfries in 1928) have been hugely supplemented by housing estates, one almost engulfing the medieval Lincluden Collegiate Church; and the commercial centre of the town has undergone extensive redevelopment, perhaps necessitated by the competition from the now easily accessible city of Carlisle, just across the English border.

LINCLUDEN COLLEGIATE CHURCH
Abbey Lane

Set in a bend of the Cluden Water near its junction with the River Nith, the substantial remains of a flashy French-influenced late medieval church and the domestic buildings which housed its college of canons. A priory of Benedictine nuns was founded at Lincluden *c.*1160, reputedly by Uchtred, son of Fergus, lord of Galloway. In 1389, on the petition of Archibald ('the Grim'), third Earl of Douglas and lord of Galloway, Annandale and Bothwell, the Pope commissioned the Bishop of Glasgow to suppress the priory and replace it with a college of secular canons. The establishment consisted originally of a provost, eight prebendaries and twenty-four bedesmen, who presumably took over the existing church and conventual buildings.

In 1429 the Princess Margaret, widow of the fourth Earl of Douglas (and Duke of Touraine) and daughter of King Robert III, endowed an additional prebend, and four more were erected later in the C15, one endowed by William, eighth Earl of Douglas, *c.*1445, and at least one other by the Maxwell family about the same time.* The enlargement of the establishment seems to have been followed by a rebuilding of the choir, probably on a larger scale, to house both the canons' altars and the show-off tomb of the Princess Margaret †1450. This work was accompanied by a rebuilding of the s nave aisle with a transeptal chapel projecting from its E bay and the construction of a new range on the N side of the cloister garth. Stylistically the new work is so close in spirit, and in some of its detail, to the French-influenced early C15 work at Melrose Abbey (Borders) and Paisley Abbey (Renfrewshire) that a common author must be presumed; the Paris-born *John Morow* is the most likely candidate.‡ Given the similarities of the remodelling at Lincluden to what was done at Melrose and Paisley, it is hard to argue for a date after the mid-C15 for its completion. However, the evidence of its abundant heraldry suggests that work continued until the end of the century, or was resumed then, perhaps after a substantial interval which had seen the forfeiture of the Douglas earldom and the growing local importance of the Maxwell, Herries and Douglas families, all

* One of these, the prebend of Kirkandrews, was annexed to the Chapel Royal at Stirling in 1501.

‡ An inscription at Melrose Abbey records the work of John Morow both there and elsewhere: 'IOHN MOROW SVM TYM CALLIT WAS I AND BORN IN PARYSSE CERTANLY AND HAD IN KEPYNG AL MASON WERK OF SANTANDROYS YE HYE KIRK OF GLASGW [*sic*] MELROS AND PASLAY OF NYDDYSDAYL AND OF GALWAY'.

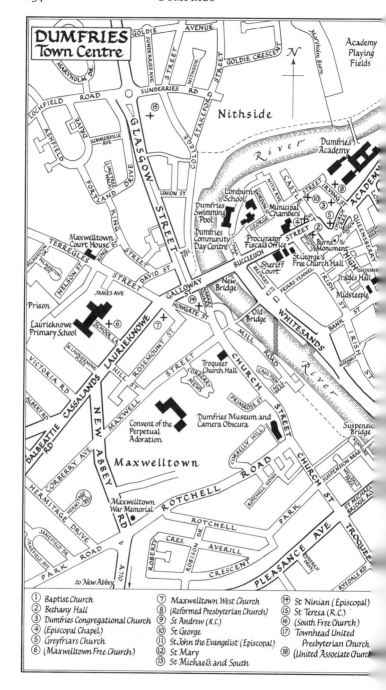

DUMFRIES Town Centre

① Baptist Church
② Bethany Hall
③ Dumfries Congregational Church
④ (Episcopal Chapel)
⑤ Greyfriars Church
⑥ (Maxwelltown Free Church)
⑦ Maxwelltown West Church
⑧ (Reformed Presbyterian Church)
⑨ St Andrew (R.C.)
⑩ St George
⑪ St John the Evangelist (Episcopal)
⑫ St Mary
⑬ St Michael's and South
⑭ St Ninian (Episcopal)
⑮ St Teresa (R.C.)
⑯ (South Free Church)
⑰ Townhead United Presbyterian Church
⑱ (United Associate Church)

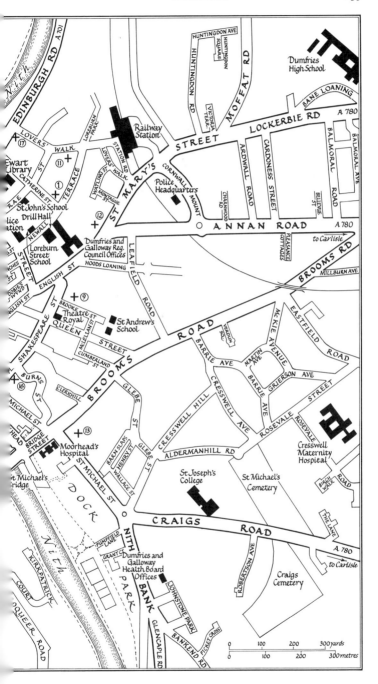

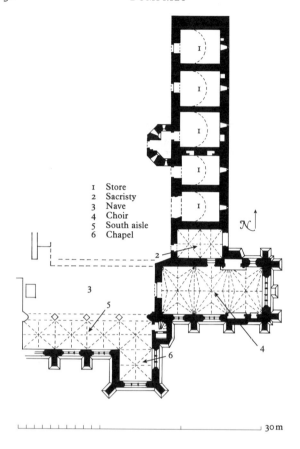

1 Store
2 Sacristy
3 Nave
4 Choir
5 South aisle
6 Chapel

Lincluden Collegiate Church. Plan

expecting to be honoured in the fabric of this church. Unspecified
work was still in progress in 1505–6, when payments of drinksilver
were made to the masons.

The church was apparently attacked by Protestant reformers
c. 1560, when it was saved from destruction and subsequently
repaired at a cost of £3,000 by William Douglas, younger of
Drumlanrig. In 1564 he recouped his expenditure by obtaining
from his half-brother, the last Provost of the college, a grant of
the Mains of Lincluden together with the principal 'mansion' of
the college extending N from the choir. Soon after, the 'mansion'
and church were in the possession of John, eighth Lord Maxwell
and Earl of Morton, whose grandson Robert Maxwell, first Earl
of Nithsdale, carried out a partial reroofing of the church in 1629.
However, the buildings were abandoned by 1700 and thereafter
were used as a quarry until 1882, when the proprietor, Captain

Alfred Constable Maxwell of Terregles, had the ruins tidied up. They are now in the care of the Secretary of State for Scotland.

The late C12 NAVE and N aisle have gone, except for foundations marked out in the grass; but enough remains were discovered in the 1880s to establish that they were of four bays, like the S aisle, and that the W door was roundheaded and enriched with chevron ornament. More is visible of the C15 SOUTH AISLE and its transeptal SOUTH-EAST CHAPEL, built, like the choir, of best-quality red sandstone ashlar with a splayed plinth. The outer wall of the two central aisle bays still stands in ragged fashion. In it, hoodmoulded three-light windows whose heads have contained elaborate tracery. Sill course carried across the walling and the unstepped buttresses. It is continued round the three outer walls (the W windowless) of the much better-preserved chapel, where it steps up at the E of its two diagonally set corner buttresses to continue under the E window, which was placed at a higher level than the others to allow for an altar below. On each corner buttress, a splayed stringcourse. In both the main three-light E and S windows, remains of tracery with fat quatrefoils in the heads (the tracery of the S window having apparently been very similar to that of a window in the early C15 N aisle at Paisley Abbey); hoodmoulds with carved label stops, now badly eroded. High in the S gable, a small window of two pointed lights. In the inner angle with the choir, a stair tower, its corner canted and crossed by the chapel's sill course, which steps up to the height of the sills of the choir windows.

The CHOIR is roofless, but the walls are intact and have a

Lincluden Collegiate Church. South side
(from R. W. Billings, *The Baronial and Ecclesiastical
Antiquities of Scotland*, Vol. iv, 1852)

cornice decorated with carved foliage. It is a three-bay rectangle. The buttresses are again unstepped and crossed by the
sill course; each has a splayed stringcourse at the height of the
label stops of the hoodmoulds over the windows. The s side's
two-light w window is squeezed uncomfortably against a stair
tower in the inner angle with the nave's SE chapel, and the
window's hoodmould and concave splay are halted abruptly
against the tower. In the window, two lights under a circlet.
The other s windows are each of three lights, with elaborate
curvilinear traceried heads; the tracery in the l. of these two
windows is almost identical with that found in early C15
windows in the s chapels added to the nave of Melrose Abbey
and the N nave aisle of Paisley Abbey. The label stops of the
two w windows' hoodmoulds are carved with shields bearing
the arms of Stewart of Garlies, Herries and Maxwell; the first
perhaps refers to Agnes Stewart, who married John, fourth
Lord Maxwell, c. 1491, and the second to the daughter of Sir
Herbert Herries of Terregles, who married Herbert, first Lord
Maxwell, c. 1450.* On the label stops of the E window on this
side, badly weathered angels. Back-set buttresses at the E gable.
It contains a five-light window with the same concave-splayed
surround as at the s windows but here with slender nook-shafts
with stiffleaf capitals at the outer ends of the splay. On the
hoodmoulds' label stops, the arms of Maxwell and Stewart of
Garlies, perhaps for John, fourth Lord Maxwell, and Agnes
Stewart, his wife. Rising under the window, a central buttress.
Above this main window, a rectangular opening which lit a
room in the space between the choir's vault and the roof.
On the choir's N side, only the E bay projects clear of the
sacristy and the N range of domestic buildings, which housed
the College's canons. In it, an off-centre two-light splay-sided
and hoodmoulded window, its label stops carved as shields.
The bases of the E nook-shaft and central mullion survive. The
w light's lower part is blocked by the cavetto-splayed back of
the E corner of the monument inside the church to Margaret,
Countess of Douglas, †1450. Beside the window, filling this
bay's w half, a huge buttress-like projection, with the top of its E
face sloping inwards, which houses the recess of the monument.
The position of the window in this bay and its relation to the
projection suggest that a recessed monument was intended here
when this bay was built but that it was decided to make its
surround more magnificently large after construction of the
window. In the two w bays of this side, only pointed window
heads above the flat roof of the sacristy.

14   INTERIOR. NAVE. The late C12 N arcade is no more, but
investigation in the 1880s discovered that it had had cylindrical
piers carrying pointed arches. Of the s arcade there survives
the E respond, its moulded capital suggesting a late C12 date.

---

* But the Stewart arms could be those of William Stewart, Provost of Lincluden
from 1529 to 1535, and the Herries arms those of George Herries, who was Curator
of Lincluden in 1494. However, the conjunction of the Herries and Maxwell arms
at the same window suggests some link between them.

The piers, as rebuilt in the late C15, were square-plan and diagonally set. Both the s aisle and its chapel have been covered with sexpartite stone vaults. The surviving wallshafts are chunky and have prominent foliaged carving at the capitals. At the aisle's E end, a turnpike stair to a room over the chapel. There have been stone seats at the ingoes of its s window.

The stone PULPITUM dividing the nave from the choir has survived. Above its basket-arched moulded doorway, a broad arch with foliaged capitals topping its shafts. The w face of the sill of this arch is carved with two rows of figures. The upper contains alternating cherubs and angels, their hands folded. In the badly worn lower row, scenes from the life of Our Lord (the Annunciation, Nativity, Adoration of the Magi, and possibly the Adoration of the Shepherds, the Purification of Our Lady, and Our Lord in the Temple). On the E face of the sill, a single deep line of foliage.

The CHOIR has been covered with elaborate late Gothic vaulting. The wallshafts rise from deeply carved corbels, the E corbel on the N side set higher than the others to allow room for the monument below. This corbel bears the royal arms of Scotland. On the opposite corbel, the arms of the duchy of Touraine, which had been held by the fourth Earl of Douglas, husband of the Princess Margaret, and was claimed by his descendants. All the windows have cavetto-splayed ingoes. Their hoodmoulds' shield labels are carved with heraldry. Most of the coats of arms are associated with the Earls of Douglas, two of them (one with the impaled arms of Douglas and Galloway, the other with those arms quartered) probably for the eighth or ninth Earls of Douglas, successive husbands of Margaret, daughter of the sixth Earl of Douglas and heiress of Galloway ('the Fair Maid of Galloway'), providing a date of c.1450 for their erection. Two shields are exceptions. One, at the s side's w window, bears the arms of Haliburton, probably for John Haliburton, Provost of Lincluden c.1430. The other, at the E window on the N side, displays the arms of Herries, perhaps for George Herries, Curator of Lincluden in 1494. In the N wall, w of the tomb, the door into the sacristy. Pointed surround, nook-shafted and elaborately carved; the foliage carving ends at the bases with grotesque apes. The door itself is rectangular. In the trefoiled tympanum above, deeply cut but badly weathered heraldry, the coats of arms those of the Earls of Douglas. There has been a room above the vault; the stone corbels which supported the floor joists are still in place. It was covered with a pointed tunnel-vault (whose lower part survives), strengthened by splayed ribs. Under the choir's E bay was a vaulted crypt reached by a stair entered outside the s wall. – At the E gable, three corbels which supported the slab of the HIGH ALTAR.

In the s wall's E end, a PISCINA, its surround an elongated and simplified version of the Countess of Douglas' monument (*see* below). On the back, two tiny cusped niches. – Immediately to its w, a triple SEDILIA, its outer frame again like that of the

monument but with pointed arches. – The N wall's E end is
15 filled by the grandiose MONUMENT to the Princess Margaret,
Countess of Douglas and Lady of Galloway and Annandale,
†1450. It is formed by a sarcophagus set in a recess. The
sarcophagus projects, and is topped by a rectangular superstructure or outer framework whose slender pinnacled piers
support a foliaged cornice above a deep band carved with blind
cusped arches. On the front of the sarcophagus, more blind
cusped arcading, here filled with shields, their weathered heraldry including the coats of arms of Douglas, Galloway, Annandale, Bothwell and Drummond (for the Countess's mother)
but also of Stewart of Atholl, suggesting that the tomb was not
completed until after 1460 when Margaret Douglas ('the Fair
Maid of Galloway') married, as her third husband, Sir John
Stewart, first Earl of Atholl. On the sarcophagus, a weathered
female effigy.* The recess itself is covered by a depressed arch,
with an ogee-profiled and crocketed outer order rising into a
finial at the centre of the arcaded upper band of the framework.
Nook-shafts with elaborate but worn carved decoration. The
inner order has been cusped. At the back of the recess, an
incised Latin inscription recording this as the tomb of the Lady
Margaret, daughter of the King of Scotland and sometime
Countess of Douglas and Lady of Galloway and Annandale.‡

N of the choir is the SACRISTY. It has been of two sexpartite-
vaulted bays with a room above. At its W end, a door into a
lobby at the E end of the N nave aisle. N of the sacristy, the
remains of the canons' DOMESTIC RANGE. On the ground
floor, five stores. All have been tunnel-vaulted and entered by
outside doors from the W, but the external masonry of the S
two is of the same high quality as that of the sacristy and
probably is contemporary with it; that of the N three is rougher,
and they are likely to be part of a later addition. Above the
stores, two upper floors reached by a stair on the W side. Only
the base of its octagonal tower now survives, but it was recorded
in 1789 as bearing the royal arms and those of William Stewart,
Provost of Lincluden between 1529 and 1535, who is likely to
have been responsible for the N extension of this range. Above
the N end, a third floor making a plain rectangular rubble-
walled tower, its gables formerly crowstepped. Excavation in
1882 discovered evidence of a second range extending N from
the W end of the church, possibly part of the convent buildings
and perhaps later adapted for the college. None of this is now
visible, nor is there any evidence of the range which could be
expected to have closed the cloister garth's N side.

To the E and overlooked by the N range, a sunken GARDEN
enclosed by grassy banks. It was probably made in the C16 or
early C17, and its general appearance was restored in 1938. –

---

* It probably belongs here but was discovered, not *in situ*, during the tidying up of
the ruins in the 1880s.
‡ 'hic:iacet:d[omi]na:margareta:regis:scocie:filia:quo[n]da[m]
   comitissa:de:douglas:do[mi]na:galwidie:et:vallis
   ana[n]di[e]'.

Adjoining the garden's SE corner, a now wooded MOTTE, formed (perhaps in the C12) by severing the W end of a ridge by a broad externally ramparted ditch, which curved between the River Nith on the S and the River Cluden on the N. Some of the ditch's N stretch is now covered by the garden. The motte's oval summit is exceptionally small (c. 7.6m. by 4.6m.); perhaps it was reduced in size in the C16 or early C17, the likely date for the terracing of its sides and its conversion into a garden feature.

CHURCHES

BAPTIST CHURCH, Newall Terrace and Catherine Street. By *Francis Armstrong*, 1880–1. Two-storey front of polished ashlar, with a pedimented centre.

BETHANY HALL, Buccleuch Street. Originally Buccleuch Street United Presbyterian Church. Simple Dec, by *Alexander Crombie*, 1861–3.

CHURCH OF JESUS CHRIST OF LATTER DAY SAINTS, Edinburgh Road. By *Paul Oliver*, 1963–6. Big shed with brick and panel walls and a roof of asbestos tiles. Modernistic thin steeple.

CRICHTON MEMORIAL CHURCH. *See* p. 256.

DUMFRIES CONGREGATIONAL CHURCH, Irving Street. Flat-fronted Italianate of 1835. Façade of red sandstone ashlar. In each end bay, a round-arched door, the l. under a window of two roundheaded lights, the window over the r. a large rectangle with a moulded architrave. Inside these bookends, a centrepiece of three bays, each marked off by piers and containing a window placed in a rectangular overarch. The outer windows are single lights, and the window at the broad centre is of three lights; all are roundheaded. Overall parapet, projected at the centre bays on arcaded corbelling.

EPISCOPAL CHAPEL, Buccleuch Street and Castle Street. Disused and roofless. By *T. F. Hunt*, 1817 (*see* the Introduction, p. 42). Looking very like a prosperous two-storey villa, built of ashlar (now painted), the ground-floor masonry rusticated. Overall cornice and balustrade. In the centre of the S front, a giant Ionic columned and pedimented portico. On the E front, consoled cornices over the first-floor windows. This front's semi-octagonal apse, with anta pilasters wrapped round its corners, is an addition of 1848.

GREYFRIARS, High Street. A replacement for the 1720s New 32 Church, it is by *John Starforth*, 1865–8. Large-scale and inventively detailed Dec with plenty of crisply carved detail, all in red sandstone snecked rubble. Aisled nave and broad transepts at the N end. At the S end, and dominating both the building and the townscape, is the steeple. Tall tower with stepped angle buttresses, their three lower intakes gableted, their tops sloping into the tower. In the centre, a broad bipartite door of two pointed arches under an ogee hoodmould, its label stops carved with crowned male and female heads, the inner spandrels decorated with high-relief foliage. The door's central pillar is topped by a tabernacle niche containing the figure of a female saint bearing a cross. Blind arcading above the hoodmould. At the belfry stage, overarched three-light openings, with gableted clockfaces at their base. Squat pinnacles on the tower's corners. From inside these and from the main faces of the tower there rises an octagonal stone spire studded with lucarnes. Each side of the steeple, a round stair tower circled by crowstepped and pinnacled buttresses. A diagonal line of narrow pointed lights marks the ascent of the stair inside. Beyond these stair towers are the aisle ends, each canted, with a big octagonal pinnacle at the join with the nave. Cusped loop tracery in their lower windows.

The interior is a huge, almost square space. Collar-braced and kingpost-truss roofs over the nave and transepts, the S corbels at the crossing carved with angels' heads, the boarded ceiling decorated with faded abstract stencilling. Flat ceilings over the short aisles, which are separated from the nave by cast-iron columns. The lower stages of the columns have clustered shafts under the gallery topped by bell capitals; extravagantly foliaged capitals at the upper stage, except in the transepts, where this stage is omitted. The fronts of the S, E and W galleries are rich, with inlaid decoration, a blind quatrefoil in each panel. At each supporting column the fronts break forward and have attached paired columns. In the S gallery, a row of MAGISTRATES' SEATS with inlaid roses on their backs. The focus is on the PULPIT, again decorated with blind quatrefoils and coloured inlay. – Behind the pulpit, the ORGAN by *Ingram*, 1921,* its case again with blind quatrefoils and inlay. – STAINED GLASS. In the N window above the organ, brightly coloured scenes from the life of Our Lord, by *James Ballantine & Son*, 1868. – Under the W transept gallery, two three-light windows (the Ascension; the Good Samaritan) of 1884 by *Powell Bros.*, again brightly coloured and rather crowded. – In the W aisle, the S window under the gallery is by *L. C. Evetts*, 1970. Semi-abstract coloured symbols of Baptism, the Burning Bush, and Holy Communion on a background of textured clear glass. – Gallery window of the E transept (Old Testament scenes) by *Camm Bros.*, *c*.1880. – Gallery window of the W transept (Our Lord teaching) by *James Ballantine & Son*, 1873.

LINCLUDEN PARISH CHURCH, Margaret Walk. By *M. Purdon Smith*, 1953. Rendered walls above a red sandstone base; shallow-pitched copper roof. Unassertive belfry tower.

LOCHSIDE PARISH CHURCH, Lochside Road. Begun by *J. C. Miller* in 1961–2 as a plain hall church dignified by a small and blocky red sandstone belfry. In 1964–5 *Miller* added a new and taller cruciform church at the E. Rendered walls with rubbly red sandstone trim; open pedimented gables. Over the crossing, an open metalwork *flèche*.

---

* It incorporates pipes from the previous organ, built by *Robson* in 1873 (*see* the Introduction, p. 48). That organ stood at the back of the S gallery.

MAXWELLTOWN FREE CHURCH, School Lane. Now a hall. By *John Thomson*, 1843. Rectangle, with fat pointed windows and foliage-finialled shallow buttresses. Just projecting from the centre of the s gable, a three-stage battlemented tower gripped by clasping buttresses, now missing their finials. Ogee hood-mould over the door; two-light belfry openings.

MAXWELLTOWN WEST CHURCH, Laurieknowe. Built as Maxwelltown Free Church in 1865–6, it is by *James Barbour*. Big box of stugged red sandstone ashlar, with barely projecting s transepts and semi-octagonal N stair towers. The main (N) front is a firescreen, still Georgian in feeling despite its correct Dec detail. Gableted corner buttresses topped by gableted and crocket-finialled pinnacles. Parapet pierced by cusped vesicas. At its apex, an octagonal stone-spired bellcote with gabled openings. In the centre, a gabled door, the tympanum carved with a rose containing cusped vesica tracery; more tracery of the same sort in the flanking round windows. Above the level of the door, a pair of hoodmoulded three-light windows separated by a thin diagonally set buttress topped by a foliaged finial.

The interior continues the Gothic detail and Georgian feel. Gallery round three sides, its pot-bellied fronts decorated with a frieze of cusped vesicas and stencilled foliage. The supporting slender cast-iron columns rise through the gallery to carry broad pointed arches marking off very narrow N and s aisles, and also to provide the springing for the ribs of the ceiling. The ceiling ribs from the s transept bays intersect at a pendant ventilator. The s focus is on the early C20 PULPIT, backed by the ORGAN (rebuilt in 1948). Behind the organ, an apsed recess, its windows containing coloured patterned glass. More patterned glass in the other windows.

REFORMED PRESBYTERIAN CHURCH, Irving Street. Now an auction room. Built in 1831–2 but remodelled in 1866. Cheap Gothic.

ST ANDREW (R.C.), Shakespeare Street. By *Sutherland & Dickie*, 1963–4. Concrete-framed square with cut-out corners, the exposed uprights crossed by bands of square-jointed red sandstone ashlar. The roof provides excitement, sweeping down from the clearstoreyed E corner, the position of the altar. – Behind, an unexciting late C19 Gothic HALL.

To the w, two towers survive from the former ST ANDREW'S PRO-CATHEDRAL, destroyed by fire in 1961. This had been designed and built by *John McCracken* in 1811–13; it was given a w tower and NW school extension in 1842–3, and was enlarged by *George Goldie* in 1871–2. The southern tower is the w steeple of the Pro-Cathedral. Its lower part, the tower proper, is by *John H. Bell*, 1843. Three stages, each face panelled; the lowest contains the entrance, the two above each have an overarched window of two lights under a circlet top. The broached octagonal stone spire was added in 1858 by *Alexander Fraser*. The lower N tower, more Italianate in appearance, belonged to the school addition of 1842 and is said to have been designed by *Marmaduke Constable-Maxwell*, not otherwise known as an architect.

St George, George Street. Built as St George's Free Church in 1843–4 but almost completely remodelled by *James Halliday*, 1892–3. Its piend-roofed box shape survives from the 1840s, but the ambitious Italianate front of red sandstone ashlar is all of the 1890s. Five bays, each marked off by boldly projecting piers, their lower ends fluted. They are topped by individual entablatures projecting from the main cornice. Panelled parapet topped by huge square urns above the piers. Tall windows, each of two stilted round-arched lights under a circular light, set in a stilted roundheaded arch with a console keystone. Small curly-topped w porch to the vestry; the main door is at the e end.

Inside, the church is almost square but with n and s aisles marked off by superimposed Corinthian columns, the lower supporting the panelled gallery fronts, the upper topped by foliaged consoles from which spring the ribs of the compartmented and coved main ceiling. Under the raked floors of the side galleries, sloping beams which spring from pilasters along the walls. An e gallery shoots back over the vestibule. In the centre of the w wall, a recess, its roundheaded arch carried on stumpy Corinthianish columns framed by piers, their lower ends fluted. The lavish painted decoration of the 1890s has not survived. – pews of 1892–3. – pulpit and communion table of 1966.

St John the Evangelist (Episcopal), Newall Terrace and Lovers Walk. By *Slater & Carpenter*, 1867–8. Austere First Pointed, built of aggressively hammerdressed Locharbriggs ashlar. Nave and buttressed narrow aisles. Rectangular chancel, lower than the nave, with stepped buttresses and simple rounded corbels under the eaves. Lean-to w narthex, its long wall pierced by squat lancets, added in 1888 by *Alexander Ross*. Lancet windows, those of the chancel and w gable dignified by hoodmoulds. nw steeple, the walling of its tower broken only by a sill course under the tall belfry openings; two rows of rounded corbels under the eaves. Semi-octagonal stair turret projecting from the e face. Broached octagonal stone spire, the starkness relieved by lucarnes. To the s, and at an angle to the church, a low lancet-windowed hall, by *W. F. Crombie*, 1923. Against its w gable, a flat-roofed and parapeted porch, a figure of St John standing above the door.

Solidly expensive Tractarian interior, the walls of diagonally tooled pinkish local stone. Five-bay nave covered by a braced kingpost-truss roof. Pointed arcades, their pillars' stiffleaf caps of pink stone, their shafts and bases and the arches' inner order of buff-coloured Prudham stone. One-light windows in the aisles, triple lancets in the clearstorey. In the nave's w gable, three lancets under a rose window. A single light at the w end of each aisle, and another at the n aisle's e end. The s aisle opens into the organ chamber. Pointed chancel arch, its attached columns' shafts of Prudham stone. The chancel is of two bays, its roof a collar-brace pierced by a cusped opening. In the S side's W bay, an arch filled by organ pipes. In the other side bays, paired lancets. The E wall has a roundheaded recess containing three lancets, the centre taller than the others, under a quatrefoil light. In the sanctuary N wall, a stone CREDENCE provided by *Alexander Ross*, *c.* 1885, its pointed arch's hoodmould carved with foliage; deeply undercut foliage on the corbel supporting the slab. – In the sanctuary S wall, a double SEDILIA, probably also of *c.* 1885. Polished granite shafts and foliaged capitals at the columns; more foliage on the front of the pointed arches.

FURNISHINGS. At the W end, an alabaster FONT of *c.* 1905, a version of Thorwaldsen's Kneeling Angel font in Copenhagen. – Wooden eagle LECTERN, perhaps of 1868. – Stone PULPIT of 1868, very simple Gothic. – CHANCEL SCREEN, again probably of 1868 and Gothic, the central gablet topped by a cross and flanked by figures of Our Lady and St John. – Gothic CHOIR STALLS by *Alexander Ross*, 1884. They are of oak, carved with subjects including fruit, angels and saints. On the back of the N stalls (the S stalls are backed by the organ), blind arcading with angels' heads in the spandrels. – ORGAN by *Hill & Son*, 1872–3; rebuilt by *Forster & Andrews*, 1889, when a third manual was added, and again in 1903 by *Wadsworth*. Major rebuild of 1938 by *Harrison & Harrison*, who also extended the pedal organ and added the positive organ in the S aisle in 1969.* – ORGAN CASE. Restrained late Gothic, designed by *H. O. Tarbolton* and executed by *Scott Morton & Co.*, 1938. – Oak ALTAR RAILS, probably of 1868. Gothic, carved with foliage including wheat and vines, the *Agnus Dei* and a Dove. – In the sanctuary, ENCAUSTIC TILES designed by *Slater & Carpenter*, 1872; in front of the altar they are decorated with elaborate abstract patterns. – Oak ALTAR of 1905, with carved angels at the ends. It has been pulled forward but was intended to stand against the wall, flanked by red marble pillars and surmounted by an alabaster RETABLE, also of 1905, its front covered with gold mosaic. – Above the retable is a REREDOS of 1868, filling the width of the chancel. Five arched compartments. The mosaic work is an embellishment by the *Venice and Murano Glass & Mosaic Co. Ltd*, 1881. In the spandrels, angels' heads on a blue ground. In the arches, a gold ground setting off naturalistically coloured figures of Our Lord and the four Evangelists.

STAINED GLASS. Extensive scheme of strongly coloured glass complementing the architecture, installed in 1868–1912. It seems all to be by *Clayton & Bell*. In the W and main E window, scenes from the life of Our Lord; the *Agnus Dei* surrounded by angels in the W gable's rose. – In the chancel side windows, saints. In the S aisle, Old Testament figures, except for the W window (the Good Samaritan) of 1872. – In the N aisle, New Testament scenes, with St John in the E gable.

In the S aisle, a WAR MEMORIAL by *Robert S. Lorimer*, 1922.

* Information about the organ was given me by Colin Menzies.

Green marble inscription tablet set in a Hoptonwood stone frame carved with routine Lorimerian flowers and foliage. – On the W wall, three mosaic MEMORIAL PANELS of *c.* 1905.

28 ST MARY, St Mary's Street. Built in 1837–9 as a chapel for members of a Relief congregation who had joined the established Church of Scotland in 1835; *John Henderson* was the architect. It is a prominently sited tall Perp rectangle of polished ashlar. Firescreen E front; at its outer corners, octagonal buttresses topped by gabled and foliage-finialled pinnacles. The centre is advanced between buttresses, their octagonal pinnacles again gabled and foliage-finialled. Over the Tudorish door, three tall lights, the centre one framed by slender buttresses which rise above to grip the corners of a tall spired and foliage-finialled bellcote. Each side of this bellcote, a concave-sided open parapet. Lower W chancel added in 1896; stodgy late Gothic.

The interior is divided into a nave and aisles by segmental-headed arches springing from cast-iron columns. In the aisles and across the E end are galleries, their elaborately panelled fronts provided as part of *A. B. & J. Crombie*'s alterations of 1878. Probably also of 1878, the boarded and panelled ceilings. Big stone chancel arch of 1896, springing from heavily foliaged corbels. The encaustic-tiled chancel is raised by four steps. At its W end, a stone dais intended for the communion table, the wall behind with recesses containing three pointed wooden arches. – On the chancel arch's S side, a big but plain Gothic wooden PULPIT of 1896, skied on an octagonal pedestal of polished pink and grey granite. – On the chancel's N side, the ORGAN by *James J. Binns*, 1896. – STAINED GLASS. Five-light W window (the Ascension) of 1896, signed by *J. T. Stewart & J. E. C. Carr*, strongly coloured, the drawing now rather eroded. – In the three E lights, early C20 depictions of singing angels.

22 ST MICHAEL'S AND SOUTH CHURCH, St Michael Street. Built as a replacement for the medieval St Michael's Parish Church in 1742–9 by the masons *Alexander Affleck* and *Thomas Twaddell* and the wright *James Harley*, the body of the church being to their own design,* the steeple to a design by *William Hanna*, mason, and *Henry Wilkinson*, wright. The church itself is a big piend-roofed box of orangey rubble, with rusticated quoins. At the N and S sides, a two-tier arrangement of rusticated windows, roundheaded above, rectangular below; at the end bays, doors in Gibbs surrounds; the S front's E door is now a window and its W is covered by a pedimented early C19 porch. Another porch of the same type at the W door of the N front; its E door is hidden inside a late C19 vestry. At the E gable, tall round-arched centre windows with plain surrounds; the outer windows are again arranged in two tiers and rusticated. Tall round-arched windows, their surrounds rusticated, flank the W tower. This is of four stages, each marked off by a stringcourse; rusticated quoins. At the bottom stage, a Gibbsian round-

---

* A design produced by *William Adam* was rejected as too expensive.

arched door (converted from a window in 1827). Then two stages of rectangular windows, their surrounds again rusticated. At the top stage, roundheaded belfry openings, partly covered by clockfaces of 1887. Overall cornice and parapet. On the parapet's corners, stumpy pinnacles; the centre of each face supports one side of the octagonal stone spire. On the spire, three tiers of roundheaded lucarnes, diminishing in size towards the top. The effect is almost Gothic.

The INTERIOR is divided into a nave and aisles by stone arcades, the roundheaded arches carried on Tuscan columns. Over the nave, a shallowly coved ceiling with a modillion cornice. The focus is on the PULPIT; its body is a replacement of 1869, but the Corinthian-pilastered back and urn-finialled heavy sounding board are of 1746. – GALLERIES in the N and S aisles and the W end, their fronts and the PEWS all of 1869. – In the W gallery, an ORGAN by *Henry Willis & Sons*, 1890 (rebuilt by *Henry Willis III*, 1933) in a simple Baroque case. – It replaced a large CLOCK, now resited on the back wall of the N gallery. This is dated 1758; the octagonal face is bordered by egg-and-dart enrichment and supported by a small pedestal with angle columns.

STAINED GLASS. In the two tall windows flanking the pulpit, pictorial glass of 1878 (Moses in the bulrushes; Our Lord in the manger). – The E gable's outer windows above and below the galleries (the Transfiguration, Crucifixion, Raising of Lazarus, and Ascension) are all of 1891. – Under the N gallery, two windows ('Blessed are the Pure in Heart'; Our Lord and the Centurion) by *A. Ballantine & Gardiner*, 1901 and 1903. – Under the S gallery, late Victorian outer windows (Our Lord walking on the Water; the Maries at the Tomb); centre window (Our Lord blessing children) of *c.* 1880. – In the N wall's upper tier, one richly coloured early C20 window (Melchizedek and Aaron) and one modern-traditional window (Our Lord) of *c.* 1935. – Above the S gallery, a dark window (Abraham) designed by *Alfred A. Webster* and executed by the *Stephen Adam Studio*, 1910, and a characteristically colourful work of *William Wilson* (the Good Shepherd), 1958.

MONUMENTS. In the S gallery, a mid-C19 marble TABLET to John Cunningham †1800, with a relief bust. – Beside it, a MEMORIAL to Burns' biographer, Allan Cunningham, by *M. L. Watson*, 1843, carved in relief with a mourning figure of Literature; it is a replica of the monument erected to Cunningham in Kensal Green Cemetery (London). – On the S wall of the vestibule under the W tower, a forbidding BUST of the Rev. Alexander Scott †1830, by *David Dunbar, elder.* – Also by Dunbar, the marble STATUE of *c.* 1830 depicting a sleeping girl. It commemorates Edith Dunbar, who died in infancy. Inscription:

> Like a dew-drop kiss'd off by the sun's morning beam,
> A brief but a beauteous existence was given:
> Her soul seem'd to come down to earth in a dream,
> And only to wake when ascended to heaven!

GRAVEYARD. At the NW corner, tall painted ashlar mid-C18 hollow GATEPIERS, designed also to shelter elders receiving the collection for the poor. Panelled pilasters on their fronts and doors in their long inner faces. The urn finials look rather too small.

The graveyard is crammed with MONUMENTS: the earliest, of the C17, are placed along the walls, many of the table stones of the earlier C18 have piecrust borders, and there is a good number of early C19 memorials designed in Commissioners' Gothic. At the w wall, near the entrance, a badly worn long monument to John Corsane †1629, with fluted end pilasters supporting the cornice. – To the s, a monument to Francis Irving †1633, heavily restored in 1838 but probably reproducing the design of the original. Advanced ends with leafy Composite capitals (the column shafts now missing) which support pediments. In the centre, a segmental top panel carved with angels' heads (souls) flanking a skull and crossbones. Recut inscription including:

ANE EPITAPHE
KING IAMES AT FIRST ME BALIVE NAMED
DRVMFREIS OFT SINCE ME PROVEST CLAMED
GOD HAST FOR ME ANE CROVNE RESERVED
FOR KING AND COVNTRIE HAVE I SERVED

On the back of the monument, another inscription (probably recut) under a skull and flanked by panels decorated with crossed bones and an hourglass. – Next to this, the monument to the Gilchrists, its back carved with the relief of an obelisk; it looks to be of c. 1800. From it projects a heavy Baroque sarcophagus commemorating Marion Ewart †1849. – A little further s, the monument to John Crosbie of Holm †1720; the centre panel bears a high relief of tasselled curtains suspended from an angel's head. – Big but boring pedimented and urn-finialled memorial to William Thomson †1847. – Then an Ionic aedicule to George Lowthian †1735, an angel's head in the tympanum; it was restored in 1845. – At the w wall's s end, a frivolous Composite aedicule commemorating Susanna Muir †1710, the inscription tablet crowned by a flurry of angels' heads. On top of the open segmental pediment, a flowery-bordered cartouche flanked by urns. Mourning cherubs on the sides; drapery and a skull at the base. The back is staider, carved with a winged hourglass and a skull and crossbones. – In front, a headstone of c. 1700 to William Murhead, gunsmith, the sides carved with high-relief human figures; on top, an angel's head above a winged hourglass, wreath, bones and skull. It is signed by *William Lookup (Lukup)*. – To the E, a big Roman Doric aedicule to John Gibson †1856. – To its N, the monument to Robert Johnston of Kelton †1715, the combined sarcophagus and headstone, looking remarkably like a bed. On the headstone, a coat of arms. The top of the sarcophagus has a carved piecrust border, the sides heraldic shields, the end a crossbones. – Behind it, two early C18 table stones with piecrust borders.

On the church's s wall, a weathered scroll-sided aedicule of 1733 to the Rev. Patrick Linn, with emblems of death at the base; on top of the cornice, an angel's head above an open Bible. – Leaning against this wall, a stone commemorating Marion Archibald †1735, an angel's head at the top. – Beside it, a stone to Elizabeth Key †1709, with inept Ionic columns. – Attached to the s wall, a scrolly pedimented aedicule to Margaret Walls †1739, the pilasters decorated with skulls, drapery and angels' heads. More angels' heads over the inscription panel; a coat of arms breaks through the pediment. – Near this wall's e end, James Ewart †1799, with an urn-finialled flattish obelisk above the inscription panel. – In front, the graveslab of John Mitchell †1708, with a cartouche containing crossbones and an hourglass. – On the church's e wall, a Tudor Gothic monument to Alexander Herries Maxwell of Munches †1815, with a large heraldic achievement.

se of the church, a slab to Andrew Hunddle (?) †1677, an inscription round the margin; in the centre, a shield bearing a mason's mark. – To its s, on the edge of the churchyard's oldest section, the monument to Hugh Lawson of Girthead †1781. In the rusticated ashlar base, a niche containing an urn. Above, an obelisk bearing weathered marble panels carved with a relief bust and a crest; the urn finial is now missing. The design may be by *Robert Adam*, to whom it was attributed by the early C19 architect Walter Newall. – Some way to its e, an C18 table stone to five children, the slab carved with five heads above the text: SUFFER LITTLE CHILDREN TO COM UMTO ME. – Further N, the headstone of Robert Hunter †1735, the front carved with reminders of death under an angel's head. On top, two reclining figures form a pediment. – A little to the se, behind a pair of yew trees, THE MARTYR'S MONUMENT erected in 1834 to commemorate C17 Covenanters. Sturdy grey granite obelisk on a battered base. – Beside it, two stones to Covenanters, both replacements of 1873, probably for early C18 stones. One is to William Welsh †1675, the inscription commanding:

STAY PASSENGER. READ
HERE INTERR'D DOTH LY
A WITNESS 'GAINST POOR
SCOTLAND'S PERJURY.
WHOSE HEAD ONCE FIX'D UP
ON THE BRIDGE-PORT STOOD.
PROCLAIMING VENGEANCE
FOR HIS GUILTLESS BLOOD.

The other is to William Grierson †1667, the inscription confident of his salvation and the equally important damnation of his enemies:

UNDER THIS STONE LO
HERE DOTH LY DUST
SACRIFICED TO TYRANNY:
YETT PRECIOUS

IN IMMENULL'S SIGHT
SINCE MARTYR'D FOR
HIS KINGLY RIGHT:
WHEN HE CONDEMNS
THESE HELLISH DRUGES,
BY SUFFRAGE SAINTS
SHALL JUDGE THE JUDGES.

– To the SE, against the graveyard's old E wall, an elegant late C18 obelisk, its inscription now illegible and its finial missing. – Near the old N wall's E end, a larger and heavier urn-finialled obelisk to John Bushby †1781. – To its W, a monument to Sarah Cutlar †1759, the scroll-sided and open-pedimented base supporting an obelisk dressed up with consoles on the sides, a cartouche on the front, and a swagged urn at the top. – Beside it, two chaste neo-classical monuments, James Hill †1776 with Ionic pilasters and a ball finial, and Mary Heron †1772 with Roman Doric columns and a pediment. – In front, two table stones: one is to Edward Maxwell †1740, an angel's head and hourglass at one end, and a skull and bone at the other; the other commemorates Grissal Maxwell †1733, its foliaged border having skulls and bones at the top corners and angels' heads at the bottom.

On the S wall of the graveyard's S extension, a neo-Greek monument to James Crichton †1823, with Empire garlands on the frieze; eagles' heads decorating the urn finial. – To its E, identical Commissioners' Gothic monuments to Watson Stott †1822 and Ebenezer Stott †1828.

In the graveyard's Roman Catholic section at the NE, opened in 1852, a buttressed and crowstepped MORTUARY CHAPEL by *William McGowan*, 1855. Acutely pointed door and windows except at the N (liturgical E) gable which contains a round window.

At the graveyard's old SE corner, the BURNS MAUSOLEUM, by *T. F. Hunt*, 1815–16, is a white-painted octagon, the general concept borrowed from James Wyatt's mausoleum for the fourth Earl of Darnley, erected *c.*1783–4 at Cobham Hall (Kent). At each of the four short sides, a projection of coupled Ionic columns (Wyatt's were Doric), originally intended to be surmounted by sarcophagi as at Cobham. In each of the three longer sides (the fourth is solid), a big rectangular opening (now glazed) containing heavy iron gates. Above the boldly projecting cornice, the domed attic (in place of Wyatt's pyramid), with a blind lunette in each long side. Inside, on the floor, the red sandstone slab of the table stone which was erected over the poet's original grave *c.*1805. Behind it, a marble high relief by *Hermon Cawthra*, 1936, replacing a relief of 1817–19 by *Peter Turnerelli*. Turnerelli's relief, inspired by Burns' dedication to the Caledonian Hunt ('The poetic genius of my country found me, as the bard Elijah did Elisha – at the plough, and threw her inspiring mantle over me'), showed the poet summoned from the plough by the poetic genius of Scotland. Cawthra's relief is very similar, but he shows Burns dressed in ploughman's garb instead of Turnerelli's tailcoat and buckled shoes; a little mouse looks on.

ST NINIAN (Episcopal), Howgate Street. Secularized. Mission church of 1891. Simple rectangle with an apsed E end and round-arched windows, built of hammerdressed red sandstone.

ST TERESA (R.C.), Glasgow Street. By *John Sutherland* of *M. Purdon Smith & Partners*, 1956–8. Broad rendered box under a slated double-pitch roof, gablets projecting at the sides; a low flat-roofed porch across the full width of the W front. SW steeple, its tower little more than a red sandstone base for the extravagantly tall broached spire. Inside, the N aisle is divided from the nave by thin piers. – Stretched across them are semi-abstract STATIONS OF THE CROSS by *Norman J. Forrest*, 1958. – STAINED GLASS. Two windows by *William Wilson*, 1958: one (St Joseph) in the porch, the other (the Baptism of Our Lord) in the former baptistery (now a meeting room).

SOUTH FREE CHURCH, Nith Place. Now a church hall. By *James Barbour*, 1863–5. Earthbound Dec in red sandstone. The front is dressed up with a pair of gables, the l. pierced by a big five-light window, its tracery formed of large flattened quatrefoils, the r. containing a low entrance squashed beneath a huge rose window. On the r. gable, a tall steeple Gothic birdcage bellcote.

TOWNHEAD UNITED PRESBYTERIAN CHURCH, Lovers Walk and Academy Street. Now a hall. Energetic but dumpy Gothic, by *James Barbour*, 1867–9; of hammerdressed red sandstone ashlar. Interior with an elaborately braced roof and boarded ceiling. – STAINED GLASS E window of two lights (Enoch and Simeon) by *Stephen Adam & Son*, 1899–1900.

TROQUEER PARISH CHURCH, Troqueer Road. Plain preaching box by *Andrew Crosbie*, 1770–1, but entirely recast in 1886–8 by *James Barbour*, who heightened the walls, added a shallow S transept or chancel and provided porches at the SE and SW. At the same time the windows were given transoms with arched lights above and below, and the main corners acquired heavy pinnacles. At the E gable Barbour produced a heavy buttress, partly supporting his absurdly heavy oversailing Gothic birdcage bellcote. S of the SW porch, a vestry of 1954.

The interior is mostly of the 1880s, with an open wooden roof. D-plan gallery on slim classical columns round three sides of the body. The focus is on the S 'chancel', entered through a pair of four-centred arches springing from a central column. – In front of the 'chancel', a COMMUNION TABLE by *Scott Morton & Co.*, 1949. – At the back of the 'chancel', the ORGAN by *Norman & Beard*, 1903, brought here from the former Buccleuch Street United Presbyterian Church in 1948 and rebuilt by *Hill, Norman & Beard*, 1954. – STAINED GLASS. In each of the E and W walls, two Second World War Memorial windows, with Christian symbols and figures of St Andrew and the Good Shepherd, all by *Douglas Hamilton*, 1950. They came from the now demolished Maxwelltown Laurieknowe Church.

GRAVEYARD. SE of the church, some slab tops from C18 TABLE STONES; badly weathered but high-relief reminders of death are still visible on two of them. – Against the w wall, MONUMENT commemorating William McDowall †1881, a battered red sandstone pedestal topped by a draped urn. On the face of the pedestal, a white marble high-relief portrait bust by *Dods & Sons*. – Near the churchyard's N entrance, the late C19 Gothic MAUSOLEUM of the Kirkpatricks. It is sturdy, with walls of hammerdressed red sandstone ashlar, a roof of stone slabs and buttressed corners. Blind quatrefoil in the E gable; in the w, the hoodmoulded pointed entrance containing an elaborate iron door.

UNITED ASSOCIATE CHURCH, Loreburn Street. Disused. Built in 1829 and extended to the rear by *A. B. & J. Crombie*, 1879. Firescreen front of polished red sandstone ashlar, divided by pinnacled buttresses into a gabled nave and aisles, their parapets panelled with blind arcading. Hoodmoulds over the large pointed windows; small Tudor Gothic porches of 1879 at the ends. It is a little too serious-minded to be enjoyable.

CEMETERIES, MONUMENTS AND PARKS

BURNS MONUMENT, Church Place. By *Mrs D. O. Hill* (*Amelia Robertson Paton*), 1882. Carrara marble statue of Robert Burns sitting on a tree stump. A recumbent collie rests its head on the poet's right foot. On the pedestal, carved quotations from Burns' works.

CRAIGS CEMETERY, Craigs Road. Laid out in 1874, the date of the Gothic GATEPIERS and the stolid LODGE. – MONUMENTS. Just inside the entrance, Ellen Cameron †1915, who is depicted by a life-size white marble statue, a dove perched on her wrist; it is signed by *W. Birnie Rhind*. – Rather coyer, Mary McLaren †1919: a polished granite pedestal topped by a girl dressed in a nightgown and dowsing a torch. – At the E corner, John Hutton Balfour Browne, surmounted by the bronze of a kneeling angel, by *G. H. Paulin*, 1923. – A little to its SW, a painted bronze to William Alexander Francis Browne †1885, with a boldly sweeping relief of an angel.

DOCK PARK. Green space beside the Nith. Formality is provided by a lime AVENUE first planted in 1748. – MONUMENT to John Law Hume and Thomas Mullin, a musician and steward on the *Titanic*, by *Kirkpatrick Bros.* of Manchester, 1912–13. Grey granite obelisk; on the pedestal, a bronze relief of the *Titanic* and a bronze scroll bearing the words and music of 'Nearer my God to Thee'. – Octagonal BANDSTAND erected in 1906, of cast iron with a wooden roof; harps are depicted in the spandrels.

DUMFRIES WAR MEMORIAL, Lovers Walk and Newall Terrace. Designed by *J. S. Stewart* and executed by *Stewart & Co. Ltd* of the *Bon Accord Granite Works*, Aberdeen, 1921–2. Granite statue of a King's Own Scottish Borderer, his rifle reversed.

FOUNTAIN, High Street. By *George Smith & Co.*, of the *Sun Foundry*, Glasgow, 1882. The lowest basin is of stone, all the rest of cast iron. The bottom basin is filled with water coming from the mouths of crocodiles held by little boys. Basin above in the form of a lotus leaf and filled with water from dolphins' mouths. In the centre of the top basin (another lotus leaf), a stalk surrounded by birds.

McGOWAN FOUNTAIN, Castle Douglas Road and Dalbeattie Road. Erected in 1913 as a memorial to Jean McGowan †1864. French Renaissance, clad with pale green tiles. Central round stem decorated with foliage and joined by four roundheaded arches to panelled piers, again with foliage decoration and topped by leafy consoles. Above, a circular fluted bowl from whose centre rises a bulbous stem carrying a second bowl decorated with naturalistic flowers and foliage.

MAXWELLTOWN WAR MEMORIAL, New Abbey Road and Rotchell Road. By *Henry Price*, 1920. Gigantic bronze of a King's Own Scottish Borderer, his arms outstretched as in crucifixion.

QUEENSBERRY MONUMENT, Queensberry Square. Tall and 56 elegant memorial erected in 1780 by the Commissioners of Supply of the County of Dumfries to commemorate Charles, third Duke of Queensberry. The designer was *Robert Adam*, the contractor *Thomas Boyd*. Red sandstone ashlar column, 6.4m. high, with Prince of Wales feathers at the necking and a flaming urn on the top. Carved rams' heads at the corners of the pedestal. On its w face, a high relief of a lady (Scotland) mourning over an urn. This is of the Adam Brothers' 'patent stucco' and, unsurprisingly, is badly weathered. The monument was removed from Queensberry Square in 1934 and re-erected there in 1990.

ST MICHAEL'S CEMETERY, Aldermanhill Road and Craigs Road. Laid out *c.*1890. At the N end, GATEPIERS topped by outsize blocky urns. – On the E side of the central walk, a MONUMENT to William Ord Pinder, 'equestrian and circus proprietor', †1941, topped by the statue of a grieving horse. – Nearby, the HEADSTONE of Robert Stevenson †1967, carved with the relief of an armchair and the inscription: 'WE NEVER KNEW HIS VALUE TILL WE SEE [*sic*] HIS VACANT CHAIR'. It is signed by *Gibson* of Glasgow.

CRICHTON ROYAL HOSPITAL
Bankend Road and Glencaple Road

Large complex, looking at first glance like a village of country houses set in immaculately maintained gardens, with a church at the centre. Under the will of Dr James Crichton †1823, who had made a fortune in the service of the East India Company, a sum of about £100,000 was left to his wife and trustees to be spent on charitable purposes. Mrs Crichton's first idea was to found a university at Dumfries, but the money was insufficient and the government refused to contribute the required balance. Then in

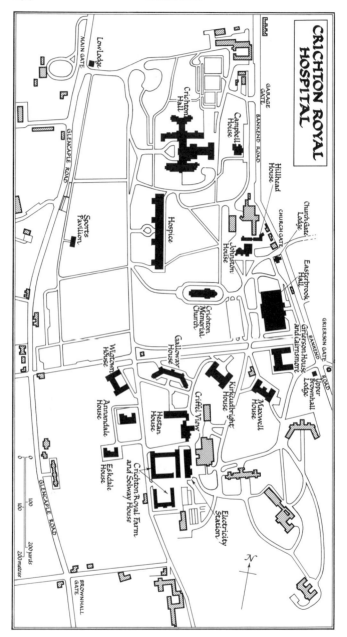

CRICHTON ROYAL HOSPITAL

Low Lodge

MAIN GATE

GARAGE GATE

BANKEND ROAD

Crichton Hall

Campbell House

Hillhead House

Church Gate Lodge

CHURCH GATE

Sports Pavilion

GLENCAPLE ROAD

Hospice

Johnston House

Easterbrook Hall

Grierson House and Cairnsmore

GRIERSON GATE

Crichton Memorial Church

BANKEND ROAD

Upper Brownhall Lodge

Wigtown House

Galloway House

Kirkcudbright House

Maxwell House

Annandale House

Hestan House

Criffel View

0

0

100

100

200 yards

200 metres

GLENCAPLE ROAD

Eskdale House

Crichton Royal Farm and Solway House

Electricity Station

N

BROWNHALL GATE

1833 she and the trustees decided to spend the bulk of the sum available on the erection and endowment of a lunatic asylum near Dumfries, 'upon the most approved plan and capable of accommodating 100 patients'.

In February 1834, forty acres of land were bought and plans commissioned from *William Burn*, who had designed Murray's Royal Asylum at Perth and additions to the Dundee Lunatic Asylum. Burn produced a design for the new Crichton Institution which proved to be beyond the resources of the trustees, and they decided to build only a little more than half of it (*see* Crichton Hall, below). The foundation stone was laid on 27 June 1835, the first patient was admitted in June 1839, and the Institution obtained a Crown charter (naming it the Crichton Royal Institution*) the next year.

The Institution which opened in 1839 was charitable but did not confine its ministrations to the poor. An advertisement of June 1839 announcing its opening proclaimed that:

. . . every facility will be given for the admission of individuals whose condition requires confinement, whatever their rank or means may be; and it has been determined that the maintenance, classification, and general treatment, shall be regulated more by what the Patients have been accustomed to, and what their present happiness and ultimate recovery may demand, than by the sum of money that is paid. At the same time, the building is so constructed, and such arrangements have been made, as to admit of individuals of the most elevated rank in society enjoying all the comforts, luxuries, and privacy, which their tastes, habits, or station, may render agreeable or necessary.

The patients were divided into five main classes;‡ the annual charge per head for treatment and accommodation varied from £10 to £350. Every patient had a private bedroom, but one in the lowest class made do with an 'iron bed; no curtains, no carpets, &c.', was fed on 'Animal soup every day; animal food thrice a week', and might be granted the 'luxuries' of tea if female or tobacco and beer if an 'industrious' male. A patient paying £100 was given a 'Parlour and Bed-room . . . furnished in American birch', ate at a 'separate table, with wine, desert [*sic*], &c., three times a week', and had the 'Use of a carriage as an indulgence, a piano, &c. as a right.' Those in the top class received for their £350 a 'Parlour and Bed-room, Bath-room, &c., elegantly furnished', ate at a separate table with 'wine, desert every day; game in season', and had 'Use of a carriage or horse every day'. In the lower classes, one keeper ('enjoined to soothe, encourage, amuse, or employ') cared for ten patients; a patient in the top class had a personal keeper.

In 1848–9 the Institution was enlarged by the erection of a second building (the Southern Counties' Asylum), designed (by *William McGowan*) principally to house pauper patients from

* The name was changed to Crichton Royal Hospital *c.* 1943.
‡ There were seven classes in total, but three of these consisted of paupers, differentiated by whether or not they had been nominated by Mrs Crichton or whether or not they were natives of Dumfriesshire or Galloway.

Dumfriesshire and Galloway. Extension and remodelling of the original building, by *W. L. Moffat*, followed in 1867–71.

The 1890s saw major expansion. Among the more important new buildings was the Crichton Royal Farm, a big steading which included accommodation for 80 male patients, the Institution's Secretary declaring that 'Insanity is a disease which demands a stimulus, and there is no stimulant equal to fresh air and exercise . . .' At the same time the Institution ensured its own supplies of good-quality water by making an artesian well and of power by the construction of an electricity station.

Architecturally the most impressive contribution of the 1890s was the construction of the Crichton Memorial Church, in slightly belated celebration of the Institution's fiftieth anniversary. Equally significant for the development of the complex was a change in the way of treating patients. The Physician Superintendent, Dr James Rutherford, who had been impressed by reports of a continental system which grouped different categories of patient in different buildings, was accompanied by the church's architect, *Sydney Mitchell*, on a study tour of Germany in 1897. After their return the continental system was adopted at the Crichton Royal, and new detached blocks, each designed for a specific category of pauper patients but looking far from cheap, were built up to 1914.

The present gardens were laid out in 1923–6 by *Sir George Watt*, donations of cuttings and seed being received from local landowners as well as from the Royal Botanic Gardens in Edinburgh and from Darjeeling. In 1925–7, after demolition of the Southern Counties' Asylum, a large new ward block (The Hospice), with accommodation for 100 patients, was put up. Further broadening of the hospital's facilities was marked by the opening in 1938 of Easterbrook Hall, containing a large hall, canteen, library, gymnasium, swimming pool and squash courts. The late C20 move towards provision of psychiatric care in the community has brought a lessening of the hospital's residential function and the closure of some buildings.

The entries for individual buildings below describe the church first, followed by the other buildings in alphabetical order.

36 CRICHTON MEMORIAL CHURCH. By *Sydney Mitchell*, 1890–7. Stylish Dec mini-cathedral, built of red sandstone snecked rubble. Seven-bay nave with low aisles and a five-bay w porch. Transepts and crossing tower. Two-bay choir, its aisles covered by double-pitch roofs, with a semi-octagonal sanctuary. The site slopes steeply from E to W, so the nave is raised above a crypt (intended as a mortuary chapel) and the porch contains a great flight of steps up to the level of the church. Entrance to the porch is through a rather narrow pointed arch in a broadly splayed surround with foliaged capitals on the attached columns which support alternately plain and foliaged orders; the carving was all executed by *William Vickers*. Flanking the door are pointed blind windows, each of two lights under a quatrefoil. Over the door, an ogee-headed hoodmould, its finial

rising into corbelling carved with foliage and flanked by angels holding shields. This corbelling supports the base of a narrow tabernacled and crocket-finialled niche (originally containing a statue of Charity) placed in the centre of a row of narrow windows covered by continuous hoodmoulding. Gableted angle buttresses. Heavy gableted octagonal pinnacles on the w corners of the low battlement.

Under the nave is the crypt. Its three w bays have broad pointed three-light windows, their detail angular. Each bay of the aisles above is marked off by a sturdy stepped and gableted buttress rising clear of the uncrenellated parapet; octagonal pinnacles on the w corners. Tiny rectangular side windows, each containing a cusped light; hoodmoulded rose windows in the gables. The aisles counterpoint the height of the nave, whose tall clearstorey soars above, its walling gently relieved by shallow buttresses, their gableted tops kept below those of the tall three-light traceried windows. Five-light w window, its tracery elaborate late Gothic. On the sides of the nave, a low battlement with exceptionally long merlons. At the w corners, gableted angle buttresses topped by crocketed octagonal pinnacles; a cross on the gable's apex.

In the gable of each transept, a tall four-light traceried window. Narrow pointed windows in the two-bay sides. Battlements and pinnacled angle buttresses like those of the nave.

At three corners of the crossing tower, angle buttresses topped by slender octagonal pinnacles. The sw corner has an octagonal stair turret, again slender but rising higher, gargoyles projecting from the eaves of its bellcast spired roof. In each face of the tower, a pair of tall two-light belfry openings is flanked by Gothic image niches and separated by a slim buttress which rises across the face of the parapet to a pinnacle; projecting from each buttress at the point where it interrupts the continuous carving-studded corbelling of the parapet is a dragon gargoyle.

The choir aisles are sturdy and plain, their buttresses gableted. The choir itself has stepped buttresses with slender pinnacles, an uncrenellated parapet and tall two-light clearstorey windows. Even taller windows, also of two lights, at the apsed sanctuary.

The INTERIOR is easily the most accomplished work of late 37 Victorian ecclesiastical architecture in Dumfries and Galloway. The walling is all of pink Gatelawbridge sandstone ashlar. The PORCH is aisled. Tall and and slender quatrefoil columns with foliaged capitals carry the sexpartite vaulting's ribs, which meet at foliaged bosses. Door into the church in a broad pointed arch of four orders enriched with foliage. Each side, a tabernacle niche.

The pointed NAVE arcades have columns with foliaged capitals attached to the piers. Wallshafts rise up the piers and through shaft rings projecting from the stringcourse under the clearstorey windows, to end with simply moulded capitals. These carry wooden ribs crossing the panelled coomb ceiling, its bosses and friezes carved with stylized foliage. Segmental rear-arches containing the windows of the aisles, each of whose bays is marked off by a stone half-arch. Marble floor (by *Allen & Young*), with a rectangular pattern in the aisles, a diagonal design in the nave.

At the CROSSING, an immensely tall arch into each limb springs from piers of clustered shafts with foliaged capitals. In each of the corners, a single attached column from which sprout branches forming the outer order of the arches; the column continues up to a simple moulded capital bearing a beam which runs diagonally across the flat Perp panelled oak ceiling to one corner of its centre panel, carved with the hospital's coat of arms. Under the crossing, a geometric-patterned marble floor; triangular patterns on the transept floors.

Two black marble steps up to the CHOIR. Its floor is also laid with triangular patterning, but here purple and black marbles are dominant rather than the white prevailing to the w. Arches opening either side into vestries and an organ chamber. Hoodmoulds above the windows. Two more black marble steps up to the SANCTUARY. Over both choir and sanctuary, oak boarded sexpartite vaults give a forward thrust to the E, a contrast to the static quality of the nave.

FURNISHINGS mostly of 1897 in a High Presbyterian arrangement.* N of the chancel arch, an octagonal oak PULPIT, with carved cherubs' heads projecting at the corners of the foliaged frieze. – LECTERN with a large brass angel supporter; it was supplied by the *Army and Navy Auxiliary Supply*, c. 1910. – In the sanctuary, an oak COMMUNION TABLE, good-quality but routine Perp. – The canopied STALLS behind take the place of a reredos. – ORGAN by *Lewis & Co. Ltd*, 1902, the Perp case designed by *Sydney Mitchell*. – Hanging from the centre of the crossing, an Art Nouveauish wrought-iron LAMP with fleur-de-lis decoration. – STAINED GLASS by the *Glass Stainers Co.* (probably the work of *Oscar Paterson*). Black patterns relieved by a few touches of pale colour and stylized figures, all on a clear background which allows views of the trees outside.

In the CRYPT under the church, quadripartite vaults springing from piers with attached shafts.

ANNANDALE HOUSE. Originally a closed ward. By *Sydney Mitchell*, 1906–9. Scots Jacobean, with heavy crowsteps and curly pedimented dormers.

ARTESIAN WELL, 0.9km. SW. By *John Davidson*, 1890–1. Plain single storey of red sandstone, the E front a parade of piended roofs; the tall chimney was demolished in 1948. Inside, the main water storage tank is covered by a boarded roof braced with metal tie-rods. Terrazzo walkway round the tiled pool. Stained glass in the door.

CAMPBELL HOUSE. Originally Crichton House, the residence of the Medical Superintendent of the Institution. It is by *William McGowan*, 1841–2, but was enlarged by *W. Moir* in

* The church is undenominational.

1888–9. Asymmetrical villa, its architecture an unassertive mixture of Georgian-survival and Jacobean. Eclectic, largely neo-Jacobean interior of 1889. Bay-windowed drawing room with flowery motifs on the compartmented plaster ceiling. C18-revival chimneypiece. In the library, a heavier chimneypiece, its mantelshelf supported on corbels carved as male and female terms.

CHURCH GATE LODGE. 1896. Would-be picturesque, with a projecting pediment-gable centrepiece on the N and the roof swept over a wooden porch.

CRICHTON HALL. Of the buildings in the complex, this is the earliest and by far the largest, and was originally intended to stand alone. *William Burn*, who was appointed architect of the new asylum in 1834, produced a design for a three-storey palace, its general appearance Elizabethan, most of the detail Georgian-survival. The plan, almost identical to that of Watson & Pritchett's West Riding Lunatic Asylum at Wakefield (Yorkshire) of 1816–18, was formed by two crosses joined at their heads, each cross with an octagon at its hub. The trustees found the scheme too expensive and decided to build only one of the crosses (the N) and what should have been the centrepiece at the join of the two. Work was begun in 1835 and completed four years later. In 1867–71 *W. L. Moffat* extended Burn's building s with a T-plan addition, its tail completing Burn's centre range, but its cross-bar shorter than Burn's intended cross arms; Burn's cross shaft was omitted.

The walling is all of stugged red sandstone ashlar. The principal entrance is in the w front of Burn's intended central range. At this range, a three-bay centrepiece (the s end of the work executed by Burn), the windows all with lugged architraves cut across by keystones, those at the first floor aproned and corniced; the centre window has a scrolly broken pediment. Parapet pierced by intersecting circles. Burn's entrance was replaced in 1910 by a big Jacobean Renaissance door under an open segmental pediment. His intended large stone cupola was never executed, depriving the building of a much-needed touch of excitement.

Each side of this centrepiece, a slightly recessed three-bay unparapeted link (the N by Burn, the s by Moffat) to the projecting cross arms. In each link, the central first-floor window is tripartite, with a scrolly broken pediment over the centre light. At the hub of the N cross, an octagon with a circular parapet, within which rises a second and taller octagon, again with a parapet and with a three-light window on each face lighting the former stair hall inside. Moffat produced only a semi-octagon for the s link and omitted the inner octagon.

The s front of Burn's w arm is of eleven bays, the centre seven recessed and without a parapet, the w two boldly advanced. Broken pediments over the two first-floor windows at each end and over alternate windows of the centrepiece, the central pediment scroll-sided; cornices and aprons at all these windows. The N front of Moffat's W wing repeats most of Burn's detail, but it is of only six bays and the two W are only slightly advanced. The main fronts of Burn's straight E wing and T-plan N wing have long, slightly recessed centrepieces and parapeted ends. At the N fronts, broad and prominently keystoned segmental arches (now glazed and partly built up), originally onto open galleries.

Moffat's S front (the entrance front from 1870 until 1896, when the main entrance reverted to its original W position) largely ignores Burn. The general impression is of a pompous palazzo. Seventeen bays, the ends and centrepiece boldly projecting and parapeted. At the ends, tripartite windows, those of the first floor with scrolled pediments over their centre lights. At the seven-bay centrepiece, the two bays at each end are slightly advanced, with scrolled pediments over the first-floor windows. In the middle three bays, Mannerist first-floor windows with consoled open pediments; heavy Jacobean porch. Baroque overall parapet, scrolls flanking the urn-finialled centre.

At the back of Burn's S range, a plain E wing, begun in 1852 by *William McGowan*, enlarged in 1857 and 1868–9, and again in 1901–4 by *Sydney Mitchell*, who heightened it and added a circular stair tower. It ends with a T-plan NURSES' HOME by *James Flett*, 1923–6, quoting Burn's detail in simplified form.

The INTERIOR is predominantly a mixture of Burn, Moffat and Sydney Mitchell. The W front's main door opens into an entrance hall remodelled by *Mitchell* in 1896. Terrazzo floor with an abstract-patterned border. Elliptical neo-Jacobean ceiling with enrichment and a frieze of the type produced by *Scott Morton & Co*. Stair hall behind, again of 1896, grand but small-scale Jacobean; woodwork by the *Albert Works Co*. Off the stair, on the first floor of the E wing, is the baroque Dining Hall made by Mitchell in 1902–4. Round the walls, Ionic pilasters with swagged volutes; swags and cartouches on the deep frieze. Compartmented ceiling supported on heavy foliaged brackets. At the centre of the W front, the Board Room. Its position is that of Burn's Board Room, but its Jacobean decoration was provided by Mitchell in 1895, when it was the *table d'hôte* dining room. Shallow-compartmented Jacobean ceiling enriched with foliage and cherubs' heads. Oak chimneypieces with mirrored overmantels, the N framed by coupled baluster pilasters, the S canopied.

Burn's central octagon contained a stair hall composed of three concentric rings, the outer a circular passage at each floor, the second the circular stair, and the inner a round core of storage space. The arrangement survives (together with 1830s stone wine racks) only in the cellar. At the floors above it was all removed in 1870–1 by *Moffat*, who created a single space ringed by tiers of octagonal galleries carried on elaborate Corinthian columns, the balusters surmounted by decorative latticed grilles with fleur-de-lis finials. The shallow glass dome above was provided in 1861. Off this hall run broad corridors, each serving a ward ('Gallery') which begins with large communal rooms followed by smaller bedrooms.

The corresponding hall of Moffat's S extension of 1867–71 is again toplit, with tiers of galleries and the same decorative grilles, but it is square and much smaller. In the centre of the S range's first floor is Moffat's Recreation Hall, two storeys high, with a heavy rose-ventilator on the compartmented ceiling. There used to be galleries on three sides, but the E and W were partitioned off and (together with the spaces below) converted to sitting rooms in 1908. The N gallery survives, supported on a basket arch flanked by figures of 'Comedy' and 'Tragedy'. High on the S wall, a MONUMENT of 1834 commemorating the foundation of the Crichton Institution. Stumpy balusters under a segmental pediment broken by the coat of arms of Dr James Crichton. It used to be over the W entrance but was moved here in 1870.

BOWLING GREEN to the N, overlooked by an octagonal Gothic PAVILION of 1884.

CRICHTON HOUSE. *See* Campbell House, above.

CRICHTON ROYAL FARM AND SOLWAY HOUSE. Big and powerful farm steading and patients' accommodation (now workshops) designed by *John Davidson* with advice from *Colonel R. F. Dudgeon* and built in 1890–2. The N range originally contained dormitories for 80 patients, with housing for the farm manager and keepers in the end blocks. It is of fifteen bays, the centrepiece a crowstep-gabled four-storey tower whose three lower stages contain hoodmoulded windows, all set in a giant overarch and with each floor slightly projected on corbels; at the top stage, a clock. Two-storey-and-attic links, again with giant overarches; semicircular-headed dormers. Crowstep-gabled two-bay ends, the windows in their three lower floors also overarched. The E and W ranges are each of a tall single storey; the N range is quite plain except for a cupola and weathervane; the S has overarches containing small segmental-headed windows under bullseyes. At the S corners, tall crow-step-gabled blocks like those at the N. S of the courtyard, powerful crowstep-gabled ranges, the W with overarches, the centre with huge crosslet arrowslits.

CRIFFEL VIEW. Originally day accommodation for male patients sleeping at Crichton Royal Farm. Cottagey, by *Sydney Mitchell*, 1898–9. It was enlarged in 1908–9, when the verandah was added to the S front.

EASTERBROOK HALL. Built as the central therapeutical and recreational building (containing a canteen, library, hall, gymnasium, swimming pool and squash courts); by *James Flett*, 1934–8. Long and blocky, the detail unexciting Art Deco. Two-storey centrepiece topped by a small cupola; single-storey lateral wings. Dry Art Deco interior; coffered ceiling over the main hall.

ELECTRICITY STATION. 1894–5. Large and muscular, with crowstepped gables. At the W end, a huge chimney, its polished ashlar an effective contrast to the hammerdressed masonry of the rest.

ESKDALE HOUSE. Originally a closed ward. By *Sydney Mitchell*, 1906–9, a repeat of his contemporary Annandale House (*see* above).

GALLOWAY HOUSE. Originally a hospital for men. By *Sydney Mitchell*, 1910–12. Red-sandstone-walled and piend-roofed on a butterfly plan; semi-octagonal ends to the wings. Plain and single-storey, except at the centrepiece which is of two storeys with a cupola-ventilator. Across the centre, a sun lounge replacement for a verandah.

GRIERSON HOUSE AND CAIRNSMORE. Designed as an observation villa for male patients. By *James Flett*, 1932–4. Neo-Georgian with Art Deco touches.

HESTAN HOUSE. Nurses' home, by *James Flett*, 1922–3. Heavy-handed neo-Georgian, with corniced windows and oversized balustrades on the centre and ends.

HILLHEAD HOUSE. Built as staff accommodation in 1862, it is probably by *Alexander Crombie*. Small suburban villa, its heavy hammerdressed rusticated quoins contrasting with the rough ashlar walling. Vestigial pediment on the porch.

HOSPICE. Long ward block for 100 patients, by *James Flett*, 1925–7. Neo-Georgian contemplating Art Deco.

JOHNSTON HOUSE. By *Sydney Mitchell*, 1897–1901, designed as a laundry block to be staffed by female pauper patients. In 1909–11 it was converted to house the hospital's administrative centre, stores and post-mortem department. Relaxed free Scots Jacobean in red sandstone. Shaped gables and bay windows with angular strapwork parapets. On the W front, a round tower crossed by stringcourses. About halfway up the tower, a band of panels carved with cartouches. At the top, corbels carrying attached Roman Doric columns under the eaves cornice; between the columns, alternating strapwork cartouches and heavily keystoned round-arched openings. Low ogee lead dome with an Art Nouveauish finial. The tower's projecting porch and the NE wing were added in 1909–11. Inside, a stair hall with brown flower-decorated tiles and a thin neo-Jacobean ceiling. The first-floor laboratory still has its furnishings of 1911.

KIRKCUDBRIGHT HOUSE (KINDAR, FLEET AND MERRICK). Originally an observation villa for male patients. By *Sydney Mitchell*, 1911–12. Red sandstone H-plan, with shaped gables on the SE front, its verandah replaced by a sun lounge. Prominent ventilators on the bellcast roof.

LOW LODGE, Main Gate. By *James Barbour*, 1906–7. Blocky Tudorish; battered tops to the large chimneys.

MAXWELL HOUSE. Originally a convalescent men's ward. By *Sydney Mitchell*, 1910–12. H-plan, the centre of the S front filled with a glass-roofed verandah. Neo-Georgian but with Jacobean shaped gables at the centre of the E and W sides; small octagonal cupola on the roof.

SOLWAY HOUSE. *See* Crichton Royal Farm, above.

SPORTS PAVILION. Lightweight picturesque of *c.* 1923.

UPPER BROWNHALL LODGE, Grierson Gate. By *James Barbour*, 1904–5. On the N front, a shaped gable rising to an absurdly narrow and steep top; gingerbread porch to its W.

WIGTOWN HOUSE (MONREITH AND MOCHRUM). Originally a women's observation villa. By *Sydney Mitchell*, 1911–12, and just like his contemporary Kirkcudbright House (*see* above).

PUBLIC BUILDINGS

BUS SHELTER, Glasgow Road. Ordinary enough were it not topped by the fibreglass statue of a rhinoceros by *Robbie Coleman*, 1992. This marks the beginning of a bicycle trail.

BY-PASS. Constructed in 1988–90. *Hugh Murray* of *Dumfries and Galloway Regional Council* was the engineer. *Babtie, Shaw & Morton* were the consultant engineers, responsible for the design of the major structures. Their bridges are of concrete, with thin slab-like piers. More dramatic are two metal-decked pedestrian bridges by *Murray*. One, off Criffel Road, is a single-mast cable-stayed suspension bridge. The other, off College Road, supported on concrete piers, is curved and approached by a spiralling ramp.

CALSIDE SCHOOL, Calside Road. By *Dumfries and Galloway Regional Council*, 1979. Inventive display of tiled roofs above the brick walls.

CONVENT OF THE PERPETUAL ADORATION, off Maxwell Street. Now in other use. The convent was founded by Marcia, Lady Herries; the first nuns were brought from Arras. Chapel and main buildings by *Pugin & Pugin*, 1880–4, all built of bullnosed and coursed red sandstone rubble. Tall plain Dec chapel at the NW, a statue of Our Lady in the NW (liturgical W) gable, a tall gableted bellcote at the SE end. L-plan conventual building, its NW wing incorporating a cloister passage. Mullioned and transomed windows, some with steeply pointed cusped lights; rose windows in the gables. SW wing (a girls' boarding house) added in the same manner by *James Barbour*, c. 1890. At one corner, an undemonstrative tower, with a small slated spire rising within its pierced parapet.

The CHAPEL INTERIOR is austere. Chancel marked off from the nave by a tall arch. – Large and heavy oak REREDOS by *Pugin & Pugin*, 1884, with tabernacle niches and carved angels. – Small SW (liturgical SE) Lady Chapel, its stone ALTAR probably of 1884, the front carved with the Immaculate Conception. – STAINED GLASS. Colourful NW (liturgical W) window (the Immaculate Conception and saints) by *H. S. Meteyard*, 1934. – In the (liturgical) W window of the N aisle, a window (the Nativity) of 1945. In the corresponding window of the S aisle, biblical scenes, after 1971.

CRESSWELL MATERNITY HOSPITAL, Rosevale Street. Lightweight architecture, by *Sutherland, Dickie & Partners*, 1962–8.

CRICHTON ROYAL HOSPITAL. *See* p. 253.

DOCK PARK. *See* Cemeteries, Monuments and Parks, above.

DRILL HALL, Newall Terrace. By *Alan B. Crombie*, 1890. Small-

scale but quite aggressively Scottish front block, built of hammerdressed red sandstone. Over the entrance, an oriel window
topped by a truncated octagonal spire finished with an open
iron crown. Flanking this centrepiece, a pair of crowstepped
gables with pyramid-roofed square bartizans at the outer
corners. Long and low drydashed hall behind.

DUMFRIES ACADEMY, Academy Street. Sprawling conglomeration, developed from the 1890s. The earliest block, at
the SW, is by *F. J. C. Carruthers*, 1895–7. Two storeys of
exuberant English Baroque, built in red sandstone ashlar.
Square-jointed rustication at the ground floor, some of the
stones incised with a Greek key pattern. Grandiose centrepiece
with a portico of giant Ionic columns, the frieze partly pulvinated; the pediment's tympanum was intended to be filled
with high-relief figures of local celebrities. Flaming urns on the
ends of the attic behind. Over its centre, a cupola, whose
diagonal corner buttresses rise from winged lions. In each face,
a roundheaded arch with Corinthian pilasters and a consoled
keystone. On top of the cupola, an ogee dome covered with
fishscale-patterned stone slabs and topped by a gilded teak
figure of 'Learning', carved by *James H. Douglas*. Behind the
portico, the main door, framed by attached Greek Doric
columns supporting an entablature, its frieze carved with Greek
key; winged lions sitting on the ends. Above, two tiers of
carved panels in place of a centre window. Under the flanking
windows, carved lyres. Each side of this centrepiece, a broad
one-bay link to a slightly advanced end. All the windows are of
three lights. At the ground-floor windows, plain circles decorate
the capitals of the classical mullions. In the links, the first-floor
windows have mullions in the form of tall pedestals carrying
stubby fluted piers. The ends' upper windows have Corinthian
columns *in antis*. Under all these first-floor windows, panels
carved (by *Douglas*) alternately with lyres containing anthemion
and with emblems of learning, the arts, science and commerce.
Further emblematic panels in the blind centre lights of each of
the links' windows. Over each end, a small circular louvre-
sided and lead-domed ventilator-cupola. Much simpler detail
at the side elevations and even simpler at the back.

Big two-storey NE ADDITION by the Dumfries County
Architect, *John R. Hill*, 1936. Art Deco in polished red sand-
stone ashlar, but not much fun. – To its NE, a red-brick GAMES
HALL, by *Dumfries and Galloway Regional Council*, 1983. –
Behind the original block, a curtain-walled office-like EXTEN-
SION by *Dumfries and Galloway Regional Council*, 1982.

DUMFRIES AND GALLOWAY COLLEGE OF TECHNOLOGY,
Herries Avenue. By the *Dumfriesshire County Architect's Department* (County Architect: *Alastair D. Macintyre*), 1971–5. Large
group of neatly wrapped parcels in brown brick and dark
glass.

Former DUMFRIES AND GALLOWAY COUNTY POLICE BAR-
RACKS. *See* Dumfries and Galloway Regional Council Offices,
below.

DUMFRIES AND GALLOWAY HEALTH BOARD OFFICES, Nith 110
Bank. Built as the Dumfries and Galloway Royal Infirmary in
1869–73; designed in a North Italian medieval manner by *John
Starforth*. Fifteen-bay W front, the end bays advanced and
pyramid-roofed. This is of two storeys, except at the boldly
projecting three-bay centrepiece, which has an extra floor, a
pierced parapet and a steep central gablet carved with foliage.
Over the principal entrance, a mullioned and transomed
window of four roundheaded lights with circular tracery; it is
flanked by statues of St Luke and Hygeia carved by *John Currie*.
In each of the bays immediately flanking the centrepiece there
has been a round-arched door (one for access to the accident
ward, the other to the dispensary), flanked by narrow windows
with extravagantly stilted heads, all the openings now drastically
reduced in size. Above these are balconies pierced by roundheaded arcading. The rest is mostly simple, with round-arched
windows, those of the first floor of two lights under a circled
head. The ends return E for five bays, each with an advanced
centre. Long and plain back wing. Plain interior with long
corridors. The centre W room above the entrance hall was the
Infirmary's Board Room. It has had a floor inserted but originally rose through two storeys to a coved ceiling. Stained glass
borders survive in the top of its window.

To the NE, a plain two-storey block (now TREASURER'S
DEPARTMENT) by *G. Ramsay Thomson*, 1911–12. A few details
culled from the main building, but the general idiom is Scots
Renaissance. W of this, a block of 1897, Scots Renaissance
again, with segmental and triangular pediments, finialled
respectively with stars and roses. Immediately E of the main
infirmary, a piend-roofed two-storey building designed by
James Barbour and built in 1894–7 as an infectious diseases
hospital; it was converted to a nurses' home in 1912. – A brick
bridge links the main building to NITHBANK HOSPITAL, an
extensive assemblage of prefabricated huts erected in 1947–8.
DUMFRIES AND GALLOWAY REGIONAL COUNCIL OFFICES,*
English Street. Authoritarian neo-Georgian, by *J. M. Dick
Peddie*, 1912. U-plan of polished Locharbriggs ashlar. The
ground floor's channelled masonry is carried up at the one-bay
gables and centrepiece to form broad pilasters framing three-
light first-floor windows; they have mullions shaped as thin
Roman Doric columns *in antis*. At each of these bays, a concave-
sided attic containing a Diocletian window. The rest is balustraded.

To the S, the former COUNTY POLICE BARRACKS by
James Barbour, 1876, aggressive Baronial in red hammerdressed
sandstone. – W of the main block, an assertive but mannered
low extension in red brick with black trim, by *Dumfries and
Galloway Regional Council*, 1980.
DUMFRIES AND GALLOWAY ROYAL INFIRMARY, Bankend

---

* The building was transferred to the ownership of the new Dumfries and Galloway
Council in 1996.

Road. By *Boswell, Mitchell & Johnston*, 1970–4. Large, sensible
and unexciting, of brown brick with shuttered concrete con-
trasts at the fascias and stair towers. – By the main entrance,
two red sandstone female TERMS, perhaps of the later C17.
They originally flanked the entrance to Christy's Well, were
built into an icehouse at the old Infirmary in 1873–4, and moved
here in 1974.

For the old Infirmary, *see* Dumfries and Galloway Health
Board Offices, above.

DUMFRIES COMMUNITY DAY CENTRE, George Street. Originally a masonic hall, the basement intended to be let as a
school; by *Alan B. Crombie*, 1889. Single storey over a deep
basement, built of red sandstone ashlar. Three-bay front, the
outer windows each of two round-arched lights with upturned
volutes at their Corinthian columned mullions. In the centre,
an Ionic portico, its entablature topped by a scroll-sided pedimented panel carved with masonic symbols supported by
mermen. Over the outer bays, a swagged frieze and balustrade.

DUMFRIES HIGH SCHOOL, Bane Loaning. Built in stages: the
first (classrooms and other accommodation) is of 1948–51; a
second (technical and science and art blocks, assembly hall
and two gymnasia) followed in 1957–61. – DAVID KESWICK
CENTRE (stadium, two gymnasia and a sports hall) by *Dumfries
and Galloway Regional Council*, 1989.

DUMFRIES MUSEUM AND CAMERA OBSCURA, Church Street.
The dominant feature is the strongly battered tower of whitewashed ashlar, built as a windmill in 1798. In 1835 this was
acquired by the Dumfries and Maxwelltown Astronomical
Society and converted by *Walter Newall* to an observatory and
camera obscura, opened in 1836. Newall provided a pedimented door and windows, their architraves displaying exaggerated but enjoyable entasis. Extravagantly corbelled sill at
the window over the door. Also by Newall is the tower's top,
projected on simplified corbels and crowned with a lantern
cupola. At the back, a utilitarian brick museum added in 1862
and extended E in 1981 with drydashed walls and a big 'mansard' roof.

N of the tower, a cast-iron Victorian FOUNTAIN in the shape
of a lotus. – W of this, a Roman Doric columned octagonal
'rotunda', by *John Gregan*, 1841. Inside it, sandstone figures
of 'Old Mortality' and his pony carved by *John Currie*. The
inscription on the rotunda's back wall relates that:

The Sculptures here deposited were conceived and executed by our
Native artist, MR JOHN CURRIE, disposed of by Lottery, 25th
October, 1840, and the prize drawn in name of DR JOHN SIN-
CLAIR, a youth beloved by all, of high promise and superior talents.

By a mournful accident. he died the following day; and the Figures
of OLD MORTALITY AND HIS PONY were presented to the
Dumfries and Maxwelltown Observatory, in fulfilment of his intentions.

They are here finally placed, a memorial to departed worth, a present
to the public, and a token of attachment to the place of his birth.

DUMFRIES SWIMMING POOL, off Nith Avenue and Park Lane.

By *Gordon J. Kinghorn*, 1960–3, the front a faint echo of the 1951 Royal Festival Hall in London.

DUMFRIES WORKSHOP, George Street. Originally a school. By *Alan B. Crombie*, 1897–9. Free Jacobean in hammerdressed red sandstone.

DUMFRIES YOUNG OFFENDERS INSTITUTION. *See* Prison, below.

EWART LIBRARY, Catherine Street. Unexciting free Renaissance by *Alan B. Crombie*, 1900–4. Two storeys and seven bays of polished ashlar, the ground-floor masonry channelled. At each of the broad and slightly projecting ends, a mullioned and transomed three-light ground-floor window. On the floor above, a pedimented Ionic aedicule with pilaster shafts of polished pink granite; it frames a Venetian window, the centre light's spandrels topped by seated emblematic ladies (Knowledge, Music, Art and Truth) carved in high relief. At the five central bays, plain transomed ground-floor windows. Door framed by heavy banded piers on which sits another pair of emblematic ladies flanking a pedimented aedicule. Between the round-arched first-floor windows, granite-shafted Ionic columns rising to the urn-topped neo-Jacobean parapet. Cheap-looking rear extension by *R. S. Osbourne*, 1936.

The internal character is North European Renaissance. Elaborate green tiles on the vestibule walls. Behind, an imperial stair with, at the landing, a STAINED GLASS window of 1903, its central figure a bishop. More stained glass in the cupola of the ornate plaster ceiling above. Ionic columned screens in the stair hall and principal rooms.

GEORGETOWN LIBRARY, Gillbrae Road. Cottagey post-Modern with brick walls and big tiled roofs. By *Dumfries and Galloway Regional Council*, 1991.

GEORGETOWN SCHOOL, Gillbrae Road. By *Dumfriesshire County Council*, 1974.

LAURIEKNOWE PRIMARY SCHOOL, James Avenue and School Lane. Plain red sandstone Jacobean of *c.*1900. Flat-roofed additions by *Dumfriesshire County Council*, 1963.

LINCLUDEN SCHOOL, Priory Road. By the Dumfries County Architect, *George Bartholomew*, 1951–5.

LOCHARBRIGGS SCHOOL, Wallacehill Road. By *George Bartholomew*, 1954.

LOCHARBRIGGS VILLAGE HALL, Main Road. By *Alan B. Crombie*, 1891–2. Built of hammerdressed red Locharbriggs stone. Jacobean gablet topping the front gable; in it, a rose window.

LOCHSIDE SCHOOL, Lochside Road. Three-storey curtain-walled main block by the *Dumfriesshire County Architect's Department*, 1960–2; the baby-blue panels fail to be cheerful. Later single-storey brick extension.

LOREBURN SCHOOL, George Street. Plain ashlar block of *c.*1930.

LOREBURN STREET SCHOOL, Newall Terrace. Now in other use. By *R. K. Kinnear*, 1876. Thrifty, with a hint of Tudor.

MASONIC CLUB, George Street. Built as the Dumfries Assembly

Rooms in 1825. Dignified plain classical in polished red sandstone ashlar. Two storeys and a basement, five bays, the ends
slightly advanced and with aprons to their first-floor windows
and cornices to those of the ground floor. In the inner bays,
console-corniced ground-floor windows flanking the heavy
Doric portico surmounted by a balustrade.

MAXWELLTOWN COURT HOUSE, Terregles Street. Disused.
By *Alan B. Crombie*, 1892–3. Small-scale Jacobean in hammerdressed red sandstone. Three projecting shaped gables, the
outer two with broken segmental pediments over the first-floor
windows; in the centre, a large window of three round-arched
transomed lights under a semicircular pediment. Cupola-
topped tower in the w inner angle.

MAXWELLTOWN HIGH SCHOOL, Lochside Road. By *Dumfriesshire County Council*, 1971, with later extensions, patterned
brick and render the main materials.

105 MIDSTEEPLE, High Street. The burgh's town house, built in
1705–7; its position in the middle of the street, the modernity
of its architecture and its tall steeple all proclaim its civic
importance.

In 1703 the Burgh Council decided:

> that whereas the toun is not at present provided with sufficient prisones,
> whereby several malefactors guilty of great crimes, and others for debt,
> have made their escape, to the dishonour and imminent perill of the
> Burgh; as also that there is not ane steeple in the whole toun, nor ane
> suitable council-house and clerk's chamber for keeping the charter
> chist and records of the Burgh, nor ane magazine house, nor room for
> the sure keeping of the toun's arms and ammunition thereto belonging;
> therefore it is our opinion and unanimous advice . . . that the said sum
> of twenty thousand merks* be disposed of and employed for the uses
> foresaid . . . and that the same be built on the waist ground at the
> back of the Cross, being in the middle of the toun and highest place
> thereof.

A committee set up to put this scheme into execution commissioned a Liverpool architect, *John Moffat*, to come to Dumfries and 'furnish a modall' for the building and also 'to visit
Glasgow steeple', presumably the mid-C17 steeple of the Old
College. In April 1704, Moffat was paid £104 Scots 'for drawing
the steeple scheme, and in name of gratification for his coming
to Dumfries'. However, he refused to act as contractor for the
building and nothing further was done until the beginning of
the next year, when the committee, 'considering how long the
designed building is retarded for want of an architect . . .
resolved to send for one Tobias Bachup, a master builder now
at Abercorn, who is said to be ye good skill'. In February
1705, the committee signed a contract with *Tobias Bachop*,
who undertook to complete the work ('conform to the scheme
drawn, and the alterations of the dimensions which the Committee had made') within two years for a price of 19,000 merks
Scots (£1,041 13s. 4d. sterling). Bachop was subsequently

* By the C18, £1 Scots was worth one-twelfth of £1 sterling, and 1 merk Scots
(two-thirds of £1 Scots or 13s. 4d. Scots) was consequently 13⅓d. sterling.

referred to in the committee minutes as 'architect and builder of the steeple and Council-house'. How far the design should be credited to Moffat and how far to Bachop is unclear. Certainly the steeple, as executed, bears a strong general resemblance to that of the Old College in Glasgow, but the resemblance is closer still to the steeple of the Town House in Stirling, built in 1702-3 to the design of Sir William Bruce, who had regularly employed Bachop as a master mason since 1686. The position of the steeple at one corner of the town house is a further parallel with the Stirling Town House, which Bachop, who was based at Alloa, must almost certainly have known. Bachop should probably be regarded as partly, if not wholly, responsible for the design.

Three-storey ashlar-faced main block, the ground-floor masonry channelled.* Rusticated quoins at the corners of the two upper floors, moulded stringcourses under their windows' projecting aprons. At the first-floor windows, lugged architraves and cornices (the cornice now missing from the E front's S window). In the l. bay of the S end, a segmental-pedimented and Ionic pilastered doorpiece of c. 1880. The stone forestair to it was restored in the early C20, but its wrought-iron balustrade decorated with flowers is early C18 and by *Sibbald*. In the S gable's centre bay, instead of windows, a couple of moulded frames containing panels, that at the first floor carved with a depiction of St Michael trampling a dragon, the panel above bearing the royal arms of Scotland. Two more panels were placed in the W wall in the early C20, both originally from the burgh's prison of 1579. One bears the coat of arms of the Browns of Carsluith and the burgh motto 'A LORBVRNE'. On the second, the initials of Herbert Raining and Robert McKinnell, one set flanking a pair of shackles, the other a bow and arrow, their status made clear by the word 'BAIllies' (*sic*).

The steeple projects from the NE corner. Tower built of polished ashlar with rusticated quoins. Six stages marked off by stringcourses, the course under the fourth stage being a decorative band carrying on the main block's parapet detail. Pierced parapet of the same design at the top. Within this, a louvre-sided belfry-cupola, its lead roof rising as a steep convex-sided square spire under an ogee-profiled cap surmounted by a weathervane. In the tower's W face, an unobtrusive basket-arched door reached by a narrow forestair.

MOORHEAD'S HOSPITAL, St Michael Street and Bridge Street. Endowed as an almshouse by James and William Moorhead, merchants in Dumfries and Carlisle, and built in 1751-3 by *Alexander Crombie*, mason, and *James Harley*, wright. Rendered two-storey H-plan. At the three-bay centre block, a rusticated doorpiece under a curvy-sided panel recording the hospital's endowment and erection. Above, a three-light window con-

---

* Most of the stonework was replaced in a restoration by *James Barbour*, completed in 1910.

verted to a single large opening. Small rectangular cupola on
the roof. Rear extension of 1963.

MUNICIPAL CHAMBERS, Buccleuch Street. By *James Carruthers*, 1931–2. Wrenaissance going Art Deco, the front faced
with red sandstone ashlar.

NEW BRIDGE, from Buccleuch Street to Galloway Street. Originally by *Thomas Boyd*, 1791–4. Five segmental arches with
rounded cutwaters. In 1892–3 *James Barbour* and *Sir William
Arrol* widened the carriageway, laying a new deck cantilevered
out beyond the face of the arches; they also added piers to the
cutwaters, their tops corbelled out to form individual stone
parapets, each decorated with an oval panel and topped by a
shell-headed niche which forms the pedestal for an ornamental
lamp standing on eagles' legs; main parapets of ironwork
studded with rosettes. The parapet and deck were renewed and
the E arch broadened to the S (in concrete faced with ashlar)
by *Babtie, Shaw & Morton*, 1985.

NITHSDALE DISTRICT COUNCIL HOUSING SERVICES
DEPARTMENT. *See* Perambulation 1, below.

NOBLEHILL SCHOOL, Annan Road. Blocky Jacobean H-plan,
by *Edward J. W. Dakers*, 1904, set back from the road. C20
drydashed extension at the rear. Fronting the road is a school
by *A. Crombie & Son*, 1874, with an adjoining detached schoolhouse (No. 245 Annan Road) in the same punchy Gothic
manner.

101 OLD BRIDGE, from Whitesands to Mill Road. Built *c.* 1430–2,*
reconstructed in 1620 after being wrecked by a flood, and
shortened from nine arches to six in the early C19 following
reclamation of land on the east bank of the Nith. Slightly
humpbacked, built of rough ashlar with rubble parapets pierced
by weepholes draining water from the walkway. The W arch is
obtusely pointed, the others almost roundheaded but irregular.
Triangular cutwaters with sloping tops; the central cutwater on
each side is carried up as a pedestrian refuge, to whose W the
parapet rises to the same height.

POLICE HEADQUARTERS, Cornwall Mount. By *Dick Campbell*
of *Dumfries and Galloway Regional Council*, 1992–3. Cheerful
but restrained post-Modern in red brick and blue glass with
red sandstone trimmings. This is the friendly public face of
policing.

POLICE STATION, Loreburn Street. By *Dumfriesshire County
Council*, 1938.

POST OFFICE, Buccleuch Street. *See* Procurator Fiscal's Office,
below.

POST OFFICE, Galloway Street. *See* Perambulation 2, below.

PRISON, off Terregles Street. Castellated but utilitarian, by
Major-General *T. B. Collinson*, architect and engineer to the
Scottish Prison Department, 1883. Additions of 1988 in a more
domestic but no less thrifty manner.

---

* A papal grant of indulgences was given in 1432 to subscribers for the completion
of the bridge, said to have been recently begun.

PROCURATOR FISCAL'S OFFICE, Buccleuch Street. Built as the Post Office in 1887–9; the architect was *W. W. Robertson*. Large-scale but quiet Scots Renaissance, of red sandstone ashlar. Fleur-de-lis, rose and thistle finials on the steeply pedimented dormerheads over the second-floor windows. Advanced off-centre gable, the royal arms carved over the centre light of its tripartite first-floor window.

RAILWAY STATION, Station Road. Plain buildings of red sandstone; decorative cast-iron columns supporting the platforms' glazed canopies. The W range is of 1858–9, the E of 1885.

ST ANDREW'S SCHOOL, Brooke Street. Two red sandstone blocks. One is of two storeys, by *James Barbour & Son*, 1895–6; unexciting Wrenaissance. The other is of 1908, single-storey with faintly Art Nouveau touches.

ST GEORGE'S FREE CHURCH HALL, Buccleuch Street. Now in other use. By *James Halliday*, 1883. Scots Jacobean, the gables and centre gablet crowstepped. Star and crescent finials on the steeply pedimented attic dormers.

ST JOHN'S SCHOOL, Rae Street. Now Careers Office. Built in 1884–5 and originally single-storey, the three-bay front elaborately detailed Tudor Gothic, the centre marked off by battlemented octagonal buttresses. The much plainer upper floor was added in 1908–9 by *James Barbour*.

ST JOSEPH'S COLLEGE, Craigs Road. By *Charles Hay*, 1907. Large and plain, three storeys and an attic, built of hammerdressed and snecked red Locharbriggs rubble. Thirteen-bay fronts to N and S, each with an advanced centrepiece. The S centrepiece containing the main entrance is carried up as a tower, topped by a consoled parapet of stone latticework. Inside the parapet, a short but steep slated pyramid roof with a steeply pedimented neo-Jacobean window projecting from each face. On the long ranges to each side, tall dormers with bellcast roofs and wrought-iron finials. At the E end, a three-storey brick extension of 1984, incorporating an addition by *John Sutherland*, 1957–60. Shorter and taller pitched-roofed W extension by *Dumfries and Galloway Regional Council*, 1981, clad in dark glass. – SW of the main block, THE BRO. JOHN JOSEPH HALL, dated 1934, built of snecked rubble. Low and broadeaved, a verandah across the front. – NE of the main block, the former BOARDING HOUSE (now HOLYWOOD TRUST), also of 1907 and by *Hay*. Four storeys and nine bays, with a gabled bellcote on the advanced centre. Segmental-arched windows to the first and second floors, except at the centre, which has paired roundheaded lights and a top-floor Venetian window.

CHAPEL, NW of the main block, by *Charles J. Menart*, 1923, built of hammerdressed red sandstone. Nave with low aisles, transepts (lower than the nave) and a chancel. SE vestry; W tower. The chapel is in a simplified Romanesque manner, the rounded corners corbelled to the square under the eaves of the nave, transepts and chancel. The tower contains the main entrance, its cushion capitals carved with neo-Celtic motifs, the semicircular arch decorated with foliage. Above the door, a tall but austerely detailed window. Corbelled stringcourse under the belfry, which is pierced by paired roundheaded arches. Angle rounds at the uncrenellated parapet, within which rises a slated phallic dome. In the transepts' gables, tall windows like that of the tower. Small windows at the aisles and in the nave clearstorey; tall clearstorey windows at the chancel. Inside, open wooden roofs over the nave and transepts; a coved ceiling in the chancel. Roundheaded nave arcades, simplified Romanesque capitals on the piers. Capitals of the same type at the tall arches into the transepts and chancel. In the chancel's apsed E recess, a pastrycook Gothic ALTAR and REREDOS of 1903, white-painted with marbled columns. The altar front is carved with a high relief of the Last Supper flanked by Old Testament types of the Eucharist. On the reredos, high reliefs of Abraham about to sacrifice Isaac and a woman receiving the Holy Communion, together with sculptured angels. – STAINED GLASS of c. 1923. In the bigger windows, figures of saints; heraldic glass in the nave clearstorey.

ST MICHAEL'S BRIDGE, St Michael's Bridge Road. By *J. Boyd Brodie*, 1925. Sloping bridge, of concrete faced with red sandstone. Three segmental arches and a smaller roundheaded arch at the S end; sturdy triangular cutwaters. On the sides, large grey stone plaques bearing the arms of Dumfries and Maxwelltown.

ST MICHAEL'S SCHOOL, Glebe Street. School Board Gothic by *A. Crombie & Son*, 1876, in hammerdressed red sandstone. Gablets and a spire-topped octagonal turret provide vertical emphasis. Flat-roofed C20 additions.

ST NINIAN'S SCHOOL, Lochside Road. Two storeys of curtain walling, by the Dumfries County Architect, *George Bartholomew*, 1964–6. Single-storey extension by *Dumfriesshire County Council*, 1972, of reddish brick with a wooden fascia.

ST TERESA'S SCHOOL, off Osborne Drive. Three-storey curtain-walled main block by the County Architect, *George Bartholomew*, 1962–4. Single-storey brick extension of the 1970s.

SHERIFF COURT, Buccleuch Street. By *David Rhind*, 1863–6. Tall and starkly purposeful Baronial, built of hammerdressed red sandstone. Roundheaded entrance under an outsize rope moulding; above, a huge pepperpot turret with giant cannon spouts. The two bays l. of this centrepiece are large-scale but almost domestic, the second-floor windows rising into steeply pedimented dormerheads; pepperpot angle turret. To the r. of the entrance the building is taller and more austere, with a high corbelled-out and pierced parapet and another pepperpot turret on the W corner. The effect is rather weakened by the gentility of the plain late C20 E extension.

SOCIAL SECURITY OFFICE. *See* Perambulation 1, below.

SUSPENSION BRIDGE, from Dockhead to Suspension Brae. By *John Willet*, 1874–5; reconstructed to the original design but using modern methods by *W. A. Fairhurst & Partners*, 1985. The cables are suspended from very tall pairs of Doric columns,

each pair crowned with an entablature; latticed sides to the
walkway.

TELEPHONE EXCHANGE, Loreburn Street. By *H.M. Office of
Works*, 1958–63. Stone-clad bureaucratic architecture at its
most boring. Rear extensions of 1970.

THEATRE ROYAL, Shakespeare Street. By *C. J. Phipps*, 1876,
incorporating and remodelling the body of a theatre designed
by *Thomas Boyd* and built in 1790–2. The rendered front is
entirely by Phipps, who added a narrow block in place of Boyd's
portico. Giant angle pilasters. Three roundheaded ground-
floor arches; a row of simplified pilasters at the attic. Interior
by *Colin Morton*, 1959–60, but retaining Phipps' gallery front
of cast-iron acanthus leaves.

TRADES HALL, Queensberry Square. By *Thomas Boyd*, 1804–6.
Polite three-storey ashlar-faced block. N front of five bays, the
centre three slightly advanced under a pediment. Corniced
first-floor windows, a consoled pediment over the central one.
At the three-bay W side, three-light centre windows in the
upper storeys, the first-floor windows with Doric columns *in
antis* and a cornice.

TROQUEER CHURCH HALL, Church Street. By *Sutherland &
Dickie*, 1963, remodelled in 1993 by *Sutherland, Dickie &
Copland*, with a big pitched roof and new frontage.

PERAMBULATIONS

1. Central Dumfries

BRIDGE STREET runs E from St Michael's Bridge, the S crossing
of the Nith into the old burgh. Parallel to St Michael's Bridge,
the Suspension Bridge (for both, *see* Public Buildings, above).
On Bridge Street's S side, Dock Park (*see* Cemeteries, Monuments and Parks, above) and, at the corner with St Michael
Street, Moorhead's Hospital (*see* Public Buildings, above),
looking across to St Michael's and South Church (*see* Churches,
above), its steeple and gatepiers very prominent. To the S, St
Michael Street leads out to the Dumfries and Galloway Health
Board Offices in Nith Bank and St Joseph's College in Craigs
Road (for these, again *see* Public Buildings, above).

In BURNS STREET off the N section of St Michael Street, BURNS
HOUSE, a quite unassuming mid-C18 house occupied by the
poet for the last three years of his life. Its rubble walls (stripped
of render in *M. Purdon Smith*'s restoration of 1934–5) conspire
with the roadway's cobbles to give an Olde Worlde look. In
ST MICHAEL STREET, Nos. 129A–153B, a long four-storey
flatted block by *Dumfries Town Council Architect's Department*,
1963–4, has continuous balconies giving a strong horizontal
emphasis at both front and back; vertical punctuation is provided towards the street by heavy stone-fronted stair towers.
Muscling into the N vista, an outsize corner pavilion of the
LOREBURNE CENTRE, a very large shopping development by
Scott, Brownrigg & Turner, 1988–91. It seems sadly conscious

that it is too bulky for the site but tries many tricks to disguise
both its corpulence and its late C20 date. This end is post-
Modern, containing the entrance to a mall which stretches
through the centre of the building. The W side to Irish Street
begins by stepping forward with a boldly cantilevered floor in
parodic reminiscence of C16 Scots architecture.

IRISH STREET's W side starts off happy enough to be Georgian.
No. 9 looks late C18. Key-blocked round-arched entrance,
intersecting tracery in the fanlight. A couple of heavy pilastered
and corniced doorpieces at Nos. 15–19 of *c.*1840. To their N,
a high stone wall, behind which lies No. 29, a large two-storey
town house of the earlier C18. Brick-built above a sandstone
basement exposed in the fall of the ground at the back. Front
divided by rusticated stone quoins into a five-bay centre and
one-bay piend-roofed ends. Lugged and key-blocked margins
to all the ground-floor windows. Margins of the same sort and
with consoled sills to the upper windows of the centrepiece,
but at the ends the first-floor openings are plain. After a short
gap provided by a garage, the piend-roofed ALBERT CLUB
(No. 61) of 1828, built of red sandstone ashlar. To the street it
presents a Doric portico and corniced ground-floor windows.
At the back, facing the river, a second Doric portico; the
cornices of the ground-floor windows are supported on consoles. The Loreburne Centre opposite now incorporates the
mid-C19 façade of the former DUMFRIES AND GALLOWAY
CLUB, by *John Starforth*, 1874. Tall three-storey five-bay red
sandstone N front, with consoled sills under the weakly lugged
window architraves and a tall Roman Doric portico. To its N,
the breeze-block backside of MARKS AND SPENCER, 1982–3.
At Nos. 63–65 of *c.*1830 on the W side, delicate fanlights. A
mid-C19 Roman Doric aediculed porch is all that survives of
the C18 town house which stood at Nos. 73–75. NITHSDALE
DISTRICT COUNCIL HOUSING SERVICES DEPARTMENT*
is by *Nithsdale District Council*, 1992.

On the E side of Irish Street, after the Loreburne Centre's
breeze-block end, the three-storey mid-C19 former BRITISH
LINEN BANK, its front remodelled in 1872 by *John Starforth*.
Projecting from the advanced two-bay centre, a heavy piered
portico, pairs of urns on the ends of its balustrade. The centrepiece has first-floor windows with pulvinated bayleaf friezes
under consoled open segmental pediments, their tympana filled
with small-scale carving. Shouldered architraves, again with
carved enrichment, at the windows above. In the outer bays,
segmental-arched ground-floor windows; consoled pediments,
alternately segmental and triangular, at the first floor. On the
SE corner with Bank Street, the OLD BANK, built as the
Commercial Bank *c.*1830. Three storeys of painted ashlar, the
end bays slightly advanced and with pedimented windows.
Across the ground floor of the two-bay centrepiece, an attached

* The building was transferred to the ownership of the new Dumfries and Galloway
Council in 1996.

screen of fluted Doric columns. On the SW corner, No. 93 Irish Street of the later C18. Three storeys again, with a Roman Doric aediculed doorpiece. In each gable, a pair of bullseye windows lighting the attic.

BANK STREET's W stretch down to the river starts on the S with No. 16 of c. 1840, which has an anta-pilastered doorpiece for emphasis. Then the former NATIONAL BANK OF SCOTLAND's tall red sandstone palazzo, by *Alexander Fraser*, 1862. Vermiculation at the ground-floor window surrounds and angle quoins. Decorative cornices over the first-floor windows surmounted by segmental panels carved by *William Flint* with figures of SS Michael and Andrew (patron saints of Dumfries and Scotland) and two coats of arms. Overall entablature, its frieze studded with a variety of rosettes, under a balustrade. On the S corner with Whitesands, ROYAL BANK OF SCOTLAND by the *Rowand Anderson Partnership*, 1982. Low and horizontal; dark glass sandwiched between a battered sandstone ashlar base and a boldly oversailing slated roof. On the N corner, the broad gable of the late C18 vernacular COACH AND HORSES INN. Going back up Bank Street, on the N Nos. 5–11, a harled C18 tenement to which Robert Burns moved in 1791 when he left Ellisland. No. 17, built as the Royal Bank of Scotland in 1856, is by *Peddie & Kinnear*. Politely detailed red sandstone palazzo, its ground floor given a thinly Art Deco granite facing in 1939–40. On the corner with Irish Street, the single-storey Burnetian Baroque CLYDESDALE BANK of c. 1914.

On the E side of Irish Street, N of Bank Street, No. 98, late Georgian with widely spaced Roman doric columns at the door. On the W, Nos. 105–107 (BANK OF SCOTLAND CHAMBERS) by the *Bank of Scotland Architects' Department*, 1966, trying to be polite but uncomfortably large. Beyond it, the former GREYFRIARS HALL of c. 1860, small-scale Tudor Gothic in red sandstone ashlar. Then the mid-C19 SKYLINE HOTEL, the consoles of its segmental-pedimented doorpiece carved with fruit. The two-storey vernacular No. 135 is probably early C18. Single-storey Georgian-survival outshots towards the street were added in the mid-C19. It is overlooked by the grimly utilitarian late C20 SOCIAL SECURITY OFFICE (No. 124). No. 139 is a tall town house of c. 1800, built of broached ashlar with rusticated quoins. Three storeys and a basement. Slightly advanced centre under a pediment, its tympanum decorated with a blind oval oculus. Crushingly heavy and austere portico, a mid-C19 addition. In the W stretch of FRIARS VENNEL, exiting at right angles towards the river, an agreeably unpretentious medley of C18 and C19 vernacular. More of the same at the N end of WHITESANDS overlooking the Nith. For the Old Bridge and the New Bridge, *see* Public Buildings, above.

BUCCLEUCH STREET's W end begins with unassuming and rather altered late Georgian buildings. Then, on the S, Nos. 24–36 by *James Barbour*, 1878–9, a long gently French Renaissance department store. Thinnish detail but enlivened by carved

swags, cornucopia and fleurs-de-lis. It looks down George
Street to the Dumfries Workshop and Dumfries Community
Day Centre (*see* Public Buildings, above). On the E corner with
Charlotte Street, a punchier but small French Renaissance
block of *c.*1870. Small carved heads over the ground-floor
windows. Part is topped by a French pavilion roof, its tall iron
cresting still in place. Then more late Georgian, again altered.
On the S side, the Sheriff Court, Procurator Fiscal's Office and
St George's Free Church Hall (*see* Public Buildings, above).
There follows the CLYDESDALE BANK of 1892 by *James
Thomson* of Glasgow. This palazzo has swallowed the bottle
labelled 'Grow'; its centre soars up from a tall balustraded
portico (the capitals of its pink granite columns carved with
tight foliage but suggestive of a Doric order) by way of a first-
floor oriel window framed by Ionic columns to a recessed
second-floor window, its framing columns Composite, all
topped by a heavy Baroque panel breaking into the overall
balustrade. This panel is carved with a half-shell framed by
consoled pilasters which carry a cornice surmounted by scrolls
and a central acroterion; foliage-decorated corner pinnacles.
Opposite, a rebuke to such exuberance, the Municipal Chambers (*see* Public Buildings, above), followed by three late Georgian houses, Nos. 75 and 79 faced with broached ashlar (now
painted), No. 77 with a ground floor of polished ashlar. Each
is two-bay, of two storeys and a basement, with a fanlit door
and overarched window (No. 79's altered to a Venetian) at the
ground floor. On Buccleuch Street's S side, the Bethany Hall;
on the N, at the Castle Street corner, the former Episcopal
Chapel (for these, *see* Churches, above).

CASTLE STREET, running N from Buccleuch Street, was laid
out in 1806 by *Robert Burn*; he probably provided elevations,
although they were not necessarily strictly adhered to in the
execution. On the E, a two-storey-and-basement terrace of
houses (Nos. 14–22), built *c.*1810, each of three bays, faced
with broached ashlar (now painted). Sill course at the ground
floor, a band course at the first; pilastered doorpieces, their
friezes decorated with roundels. The terrace ends with the
slightly later five-bay No. 24; it is generally similar to the others
but its first-floor windows are less deep and provided with
aprons. Opposite, another terrace (Nos. 25–37), again of *c.*1810
and similar to Nos. 14–22; but each house is of only two bays,
with panelling on its band course and its doorpiece decorated
with egg-and-dart enrichment at the necks of the pilasters but
a plain frieze. No. 39 at the end is mid-C19 and a floor higher,
with heavily consoled cornices over some windows. N of George
Street, another terrace on the E (Nos. 26–30), the first two
houses like those of the terrace to their S but perhaps a little
later, the door friezes plain and the first-floor windows deeper
and balconied. No. 30 is another five-bay house, very like No.
24 but with a plain frieze at the door and a pedimented N gable.
The W terrace (Nos. 41–47) of *c.*1820 is almost identical to the
E terrace in the S stretch but without roundels on the doorcases.

The five-bay end house (No. 47) has first-floor windows of the same size as the others and without aprons; on its N gable, again pedimented, a procession of diagonally set chimneystacks. The street's N end is filled by a building of 1993–4; the design by *A. C. Wolffe & Partners* was altered by the developer in execution. Bullseye-windowed large gable, suggestive of a pediment, on the axis of the street but, rather disconcertingly, off-centre on the building.

GEORGE STREET is more mixed. On the S side of its W stretch, a late Georgian terrace (Nos. 34–40) with a rusticated terrace and basket-arched pend; an over-heavy Victorian portico has been added to No. 34. At the early C19 Nos. 35–37 opposite, again a rusticated ground floor but also pilastered doorpieces. E of Castle Street, on the S side, St George's Church and the Masonic Club (*see* Churches and Public Buildings, above). On the N, a very lightweight CHURCH HALL built by *Robison & Davidson Ltd*, 1961. Then J. M. BARRIE HOUSE (Nos. 39–99), by *Robert Potter & Partners*, 1984–6, post-Modern but without either wit or conviction. At this side's E end, No. 101 (MOAT BRAE) by *Walter Newall*, c. 1832, is a two-storey-and-basement villa faced with polished ashlar. Pedimented Greek Doric portico. Consoled cornices and aprons to the ground-floor windows, aprons at the first floor. Heavy cornice and parapet.

IRVING STREET leads S. On the E side, Nos. 9–15, a late Georgian terrace built of broached ashlar (some fronts now painted). Ground-floor band course; sill courses at the ground and first floors. Some variations of detail. Pilastered doorpieces at Nos. 9, 11 and 15, but the door of No. 15A has a consoled cornice. Another consoled cornice over No. 9's ground-floor window, its bottom roll extravagantly large. Then the Dumfries Congregational Church, keeping the flat-fronted Georgian character, unlike its Reformed Presbyterian rival opposite; for these, *see* Churches, above.

ACADEMY STREET's beginning is dominated by the bulk of Dumfries Academy (*see* Public Buildings, above) on the W. Opposite, the early C19 Nos. 26–30 enlivened by an elegant late C19 Jacobean shopfront with broad pilasters and slender fluted columns. For the former United Associate Church in Loreburn Street and the Ewart Library and Baptist Church in Catherine Street, *see* Churches and Public Buildings, above.

On Academy Street's S corner with LOVERS WALK, the old Townhead United Presbyterian Church (*see* Churches, above). On the N corner, the garden wall and lodge of ELMBANK, a villa of c. 1860, its bargeboards enjoyably carved. Lovers Walk continues to the E with prosperous villas of the later C19 along its N side. Pedimented centres at the Georgian-survival Nos. 15–17, 27–29 and 31–33. Nos. 19–21 have two-storey bay windows, their parapets topped by curly pediments broken by strapwork-bordered shields. On the corner of Newall Terrace, St John the Evangelist Episcopal Church (*see* Churches, above). In front, the Dumfries War Memorial (*see* Cemeteries, Monu-

ments and Parks, above). Then the railway station (*see* Public
Buildings, above), which is eclipsed from view and in scale by
the STATION HOTEL, by *Milwain*, 1896–7, villa-like despite
its size, with bracketed eaves, half-timbered dormers, a broad
bargeboarded porch facing the station, and an octagonal
pagoda-like cupola on the roof.

Turning s into ST MARY'S STREET the character becomes more
urbane. On the r., No. 9 (NITHSDALE HOUSE) of *c*.1860
has Jacobean detail. Sparing Gothic touches at the roughly
contemporary Nos. 3–7. Then St Mary's Church (*see* Churches,
above) looking down on its HALL of 1888 on the corner of
Annan Road. After the hall, big but barely detailed rubbly late
Victorian Scots manorial villas, now making up the CAIRN-
DALE HOTEL. In English Street to the s, the Dumfries and
Galloway Regional Council Offices (*see* Public Buildings,
above). For Shakespeare Street's St Andrew's (R.C.) Church
and the Theatre Royal, *see* Churches and Public Buildings,
above. In QUEEN STREET to the e, the mid-C19 No. 60 has
carved foliage at the corners of its first-floor windows. Round-
arched door decorated with rosettes, the keystone carved as a
female head. To the w, past the plain late Georgian Nos.
24–34, a return to ENGLISH STREET. On its s side, the
QUEENSBERRY HOTEL by *James Barbour*, 1869, the pilasters
on its elaborate frontage carved with trophies and foliage in
high relief. Over the first-floor windows, roundheaded panels
bearing high-relief *putti* and a satyr; keystones carved as human
heads. A shaped Victorian gable separates it from the less
outgoing former UNION BANK (No. 8), a dignified palazzo of
1875–7 by *William Railton*. Over the round-arched ground-floor
windows, the heads of three bearded ancients (two awake and
one asleep); bayleaf friezes above the portico and first-floor
windows. To the w, informal variety. At No. 19 of *c*.1800, a
console-pedimented doorpiece; small-scale Victorian columned pub front adjoining. The low two-storey Nos. 29–31
may be early C18. Cast-iron-columned late C19 shopfront on
No. 36. At No. 41 one bulbous column of another Victorian
shopfront has avoided being boxed in. A small chimneyed
pediment on the late C18 No. 49. Nos. 48–50 opposite, also
late C18 but with a Victorian pub front, its Composite columns
improbably slender. w of Loreburn Street, JUBILEE BUILD-
INGS of 1887 on the N, with a bust of Queen Victoria displayed
in a niche. Beyond, more late Georgian development, No. 75
with a pediment.

LOREBURN STREET, dominated by the boredom of the Telephone Exchange and Police Station (*see* Public Buildings,
above), leads back to Academy Street. At Academy Street's sw
end, a glance down QUEENSBERRY STREET to the jolly free
Flemish upper storeys of No. 120 of *c*.1900. On CHURCH
CRESCENT's w side, the TRUSTEE SAVINGS BANK by *John
Gregan*, 1847. Two storeys but large, the rusticated ground
floor a plinth for the Ionic columns which frame the first floors'
end bays. At the recessed centre, a first-floor Venetian window

whose blind centre light is a niche containing a statue by *John Currie* of Dr Henry Duncan, the founder of the savings bank movement. Overall mutuled cornice and parapet. At the end of Church Crescent, on the axis of High Street, the commanding presence of Greyfriars Church with the Burns Monument in front (*see* Churches and Cemeteries, Monuments and Parks, above). To the E, No. 7 CHURCH PLACE is free Flemish of 1895, with an oriel window rising into a cupola-topped octagonal turret flanked by shaped gablets.

HIGH STREET was pedestrianized in 1989, with the usual concomitants of small-scale concrete paving and 'Quality Street' signposts, litter bins and benches. The N end is low-key and plain Georgian, Victorian and C20. Interest begins where the street broadens to the E to form QUEENSBERRY SQUARE, the setting for the Queensberry Monument (*see* Cemeteries, Monuments and Parks, above) first erected here in 1780. At the NE corner, the TRUSTEE SAVINGS BANK, busy post-Modern by *Sutherland, Dickie & Copland*, 1993. On the E side, the BANK OF SCOTLAND (former BRITISH LINEN BANK) by *H. O. Tarbolton*, 1933–4 and very old-fashioned. Polite English Baroque, a domed cupola on the corner. On the square's S side, the Trades Hall (*see* Public Buildings, above), a gentle assertion of civic dignity.

Immediately S of Queensberry Square, High Street's middle is largely filled by the more assertive Midsteeple (*see* Public Buildings, above). Just S of it, on the E, the three-storey Nos. 120–124 High Street, dated 1809, with a balustrade broken by a central pedimented attic. Then the uninspired Art Deco BURTON of 1934. Opposite, a small mid-Victorian ashlar-fronted block, the panels in the heads of its round-arched first-floor windows carved with human heads. Beyond it, Nos. 107–109 by *Walter Newall*, 1827. Tall but gentle Jacobean with hoodmoulded windows and octagonal chimneys; a bowed corner to Bank Street. Then High Street broadens again to form a square, its centre occupied by the brightly painted Fountain (*see* Cemeteries, Monuments and Parks, above). To its E, plain late Georgian buildings, one with a pedimented attic breaking the balustrade just as at Nos. 120–124. On the W side, the five-bay No. 79, its lower two floors built in the early C18 as the town house of Richard Lowthian of Staffold; the upper two storeys, with larger windows and a cast-iron second-floor balcony, were added *c.*1860, when this became the County Hotel. It was redeveloped behind the façade by *Baxter, Clark & Paul* in 1984–5. Inside, re-used early C18 panelling, Corinthian pilasters framing the fireplace and round-headed and keyblocked door.

High Street's S end was redeveloped in the 1970s and 1980s. On the E side, 'infill' architecture which would be respectful of its elders had any survived. On the W, the Loreburne Centre of 1988–91 (*see* also St Michael's Street, above); this side begins with a couple of replicated late Georgian frontages, followed by fidgety neo-vernacular and ending with tithe barn commercial.

115   The vista is closed by No. 24 NITH PLACE, built in 1753 for
       Archibald Maxwell, the Town Clerk, and ponderously smart,
       the walling set off by rusticated quoins. Two storeys and five
       bays, the centre three advanced under a pediment pierced by a
       bullseye window. Urns on the ends of the parapet. Lugged
       window architraves with projecting keystones and consoled
       sills. Corinthian aedicule at the door, its lintel carved with a
       lady's head flanked by swags. Just as ponderous but much less
       smart, the adjoining former South Free Church (*see* Churches,
       above).

2. Maxwelltown

On the W side of the Nith, Maxwelltown was a separate burgh of
barony from its creation in 1810 until its absorption by Dumfries
in 1928.

MILL ROAD at the W end of the Old Bridge (*see* Public Buildings,
   above) is the starting point. Hard beside the bridge, OLD
   BRIDGE HOUSE, built for James Birkmyre, a cooper, *c*.1660.
   Single-storey over a basement, rubble-walled, with a picturesquely irregular E gable. The windows and doors are now
   mostly C19, the older openings built up. Propped against the
   gable, a large fragment of a steeply pedimented C17 dormerhead
   carved with the relief of a stylized tree and the initials II. Mill
   Road leads N and W up to Maxwelltown's HIGH STREET,
   now a garden overlooked by the former St Ninian's (Episcopal)
   Church (*see* Churches, above) on the corner of Howgate Street.
   MARKET SQUARE, an undistinguished mixture of the C19 and
   later C20, leads to Galloway Street.
GLASGOW STREET, beginning on the N side of Galloway Street,
   starts with simple early and mid-C19 buildings on the W but
   collapses architecturally almost at once into late C20 shanty-
   town. A little further N, partial redemption is provided by Nos.
   81–83 (ST ANDREW'S COURT), by *Crallan & Winstanley*,
   1988–90, a four-storey piend-roofed block of flats, the three
   lower floors of bright red brick, the top floor's brown brick
   marking it off as an attic. The general impression is of a late
   C20 reworking of the Georgian manner, but the recessed two-
   storey glazed entrances, their astragals painted bright blue, are
   a joyful escape from neo-Georgian politeness. A little further,
   on the r., St Teresa's (R.C.) Church (*see* Churches, above), its
   spire hitherto a half-noticed landmark.
In GALLOWAY STREET itself, simple two-storey buildings of the
   earlier C19. Pilastraded ground floor at Nos. 29–30 on the r.
   On the l., the POST OFFICE of *c*.1900, wedge-shaped, with
   an ogee-domed oriel on the corner to Howgate Street. On the
   corner with Terregles Street, HOPE PLACE, an L-plan terrace
   of three mid-C19 houses, Georgian-survival but going Italianate.
TERREGLES STREET's r. side is a procession of garages. On the
   l., an austere early C19 terrace (Nos. 1–13) followed by a
   comfortably set-back double house (Nos. 15–17) of the earlier

C19 but now drydashed; No. 15 has an anta-pilastered door-piece. Further out, the former Maxwelltown Court House (*see* Public Buildings, above).

LAURIEKNOWE continues the line of Galloway Street to the SW. On its l. side, Maxwelltown West Church (*see* Churches, above). On the r., an austere early C19 two-storey terrace (Nos. 2–12), the doors of Nos. 4 and 6 paired within a basket-arched recess. Then No. 14, Georgian-survival, its windows of two lights and heavily architraved; a segmental pediment on consoles over the door. There follow villas on both sides. They begin on the r. with the prominently sited and large CHAPEL-MOUNT HOUSE (No. 16) of 1834, built of cream-painted ashlar. Elaborately carved bargeboards. Gently Gothic tower, its pyramid roof with bracketed eaves and some fishscale slating. Set back in School Lane, the former Maxwelltown Free Church and Laurieknowe Primary School (*see* Churches and Public Buildings, above). After Nos. 24–28 Laurieknowe, which are plain mid-C19 Georgian-survival, the much more stylish No. 30 of *c.*1840. Single-storey-and-attic, in a sort of Jacobean manner, with a small lion standing on the anta-piered portico. Across the front gable and round the side, a verandah with elaborate but delicate ironwork. On the corner opposite, No. 1 HILL STREET, by *John A. Copland* of *Sutherland, Dickie & Partners*, 1966. Flat-roofed and blocky, with dark brick dressings at the drydashed walls; a rounded stair tower counterpoints the angular geometry. Further up Hill Street, a pair of prosperous late C19 red sandstone villas, the Italianate No. 3 with a small tower, RUBISLAW with a Gothic porch. In MAXWELL STREET, just off the axis of Hill Street, No. 29, a late Victorian Gothic villa, formerly part of the Convent of the Perpetual Adoration (*see* Public Buildings, above). Maxwell Street leads downhill through late C20 speculative housing to Church Street.

CHURCH STREET'S N end begins with humane but boring four-storey flat-roofed blocks of flats on the E. They are by the *Dumfries Town Council Architect's Department*, 1961–6. For Troqueer Church Hall on the W, *see* Public Buildings, above. Then flatted terrace blocks of *c.*1900, DEVORGILLA TERRACE on the W and Nos. 139–207 Church Street on the E, their stugged red sandstone masonry not especially cheerful. Much jollier is MILLBANK, a low late Victorian bargeboarded villa. It is followed by Nos. 1–5 CORBERRY TERRACE of *c.*1840, with very broad anta-pilastered doorpieces, overlooked by the Dumfries Museum and Camera Obscura (*see* Public Buildings, above). In the otherwise unexciting ROTCHELL ROAD, the early C19 ROTCHELL HOUSE, with a fluted Doric-columned and pedimented portico. A bay window has been added to the l. At the far end of the road, the Maxwelltown War Memorial (*see* Cemeteries, Monuments and Parks, above).

INDUSTRIAL BUILDINGS

GATES FACTORY, Main Road, Heathhall. Built in 1913 for the
Arrol Johnston Motor Company on the model of designs by
Albert Kahn. Reinforced concrete frame filled with brick and
glass; flat roof. Additions in the same manner by *Kerr & Watson*,
1924.

ROSEFIELD MILLS, Troqueer Road. Massive woollen mill by
Alan B. Crombie, 1885–9, all of red brick with sandstone dressings. The main block overlooking the Nith is a huge Venetian
palazzo. Gothic overarching at the centrepiece, its parapet's
central merlon rising into a small obelisk-finialled pediment.
End towers with machicolated parapets. At the links, pairs of
two-light windows set back from the main walling; wallhead
projected on arcaded corbelling. Office block with a central
pyramid-roofed tower, and another mill range fronting
Troqueer Road in the same style.

TOWN MILLS, Mill Road. Originally a grain mill. Rubble-built
main block, by *Andrew Meikle*, *c.*1781, and quite straightforward. Higher transverse addition of *c.*1840 at the S end.
Crowsteps were added to the gables *c.*1900. Now the Robert
Burns Centre.

WINDMILL, Church Street. *See* Public Buildings, above: Dumfries Museum and Camera Obscura.

VILLAS ETC.

ALBANY LANE. No. 1 (ROSEVALE) is mid-C19 piend-roofed
Georgian-survival, with a Tuscan-columned portico.

ALDERMANHILL ROAD. ALDERMANHILL HOUSE is neo-
classical of the earlier C19. Two storeys and three bays of
painted ashlar. Pediment topped by stone tureens at the slightly
advanced centre, from which projects a heavy Greek Doric
portico, its columns unfluted. Doric mullions to the ground
floor's three-light outer windows.

BANKEND ROAD. ELLANGOWAN, an asymmetrical cottagey
Gothic villa, was built in 1869 for James MacGowan, the
Burgh Chamberlain of Dumfries. In the inner angle of the
main block and S wing, a tower of four stages, the lowest
square, the others octagonal; corbelled bowed balconies at the
first-floor corners, spired roof with lucarnes and topped by a
weathervane.

COLLEGE ROAD. Lincluden House of 1824 has been demolished, but its STABLES survive. They are by *Walter Newall*, 1821.
Two-storey U-plan of red sandstone ashlar. At the principal (S)
front, the hoodmoulded and Tudor-arched pend is placed in a
broad battlemented tower flanked by smaller towers at the ends
of the other ranges. In the central tower's rear elevation, the
flight holes of a doocot.

COLLEGE STREET. Marooned in C20 housing is OLD STAKE-
FORD of *c.*1830. Pink-painted ashlar; one storey and an attic
over a high basement. Asymmetrical Tudor, the end bays

gabled, the windows hoodmoulded; tall slit window to the r. of
the arched door.

CRAIGS ROAD. In the grounds of St Joseph's College, the single-
storey MOUNT ST MICHAEL'S by *Walter Newall*, c.1820.
Lighthearted Jacobean. Tall flat-topped buttresses at the
gables, the S with a bay window. – Much further out, and set
well back on the S, MAIDENBOWER, a two-storey three-bay
villa of the earlier C19, built of squared red sandstone rubble.
Pilaster strips at the corners. Fanlit door under a corniced
window at the barely advanced centre. Bracketed antefixae-
finialled pediments over the windows. Late C19 rear addition. –
A little further, on the E, is CRAIGS HOUSE, again of the
earlier C19. Single storey, basement and attic, built of painted
ashlar. Five-bay W front. Pedimented Roman Doric portico at
the broad centre. Aproned windows. Pedimented gables over
the outer bays. The attic windows are additions, perhaps of
1896 when the interior was altered.

EDINBURGH ROAD. On the E, No. 28 (GRACEFIELD ARTS
CENTRE) is a mid-Victorian red sandstone villa, with elaborately carved bargeboards and broad eaves. Three-bay front,
the l. windows (the first-floor one blind) with cornices, a bay
window on the r. In the centre, a recessed entrance under
an extravagantly corbelled glass-fronted projection. Corniced
windows at the sides. – No. 30 of c.1860 is a long asymmetrical
red sandstone spread. Unimaginative Baronial with crowstepped gables and a conical-roofed round tower at one
corner. – No. 32 (IVY LODGE) is dated 1841. Small-scale
Elizabethan, the broad r. bay advanced and gabled. Over
the two l. bays, pedimented gablets, each stepped and having
scrolls at the base and a spiky finial on top. Another gablet of
the same sort at the floor over the S porch. – Further out,
and set well back on the W, NUNFIELD HOUSE, a large red
sandstone villa of the later C19. Pompous Renaissance, the
pavilion-roofed centre speaking with a pronounced French
accent.

GEORGETOWN ROAD. The GEORGETOWN COMMUNITY
CENTRE near the N end occupies a rendered early C19 house.
Piend-roofed main block of two storeys and three bays, with
rusticated quoins and a Roman Doric portico; its crude battlement is a later addition. Recessed links to tall pedimented
wings, perhaps slightly later additions; blind bullseyes in their
tympana.

GLENCAPLE ROAD. The rendered LADYFIELD WEST
(originally HANNAYFIELD) by *Walter Newall*, 1812, is showy.
Single storey over a basement which is fully exposed by the fall
of the ground at the back. Piend-roofed block of three bays by
three, panelled piers at the corners. Pedimented Ionic portico
at the front's advanced centre. Also advanced is the centre bay
of each side, with a window in a roundheaded overarch. –
LADYFIELD EAST is another smart early C19 villa. Two storeys
and a basement. Three-bay front of painted broached ashlar.
Recessed and segmental-pedimented centrepiece, a Venetian

window at its first floor; at the ground floor, a heavy porch with pilastered canted corners.

NETHERWOOD, 3.6km. SE. Early C19 two-storey villa by *Walter Newall*. Painted ashlar with rusticated quoins. Shallow bows projecting each side of the entrance, whose fanlit door and sidelights are framed by a screen of attached Roman Doric columns *in antis*. Narrow links, their roundheaded windows with intersecting tracery, to single-storey wings, each with a window in a segmental-headed overarch.

NETHERWOOD BANK, 3.9km. SE. Rendered villa of two storeys and a basement, begun *c*. 1820. W front originally of three bays, the centre door set behind a screen of Roman Doric columns *in antis*. Three-light windows in the outer bays of the ground floor and the first floor's centre. In the late C19 a parapet was added, the house was extended at each end with a full-height balustraded bay window, and a conservatory was built at the S.

NUNHOLM ROAD. Early–mid-C19 Georgian and Georgian-survival terrace (Nos. 2–22) comprising ALBANY PLACE. Bay-windowed Nos. 2–6 of *c*. 1860. The rest is plain, the broached ashlar fronts mostly painted. Heavy anta-pilastered doorpieces are the norm. No. 22 is more ambitious, with a three-light ground-floor window; door and sidelights under a big segmental fanlight, all contained in the broad doorpiece's relatively light frame. – Then Nos. 26–28 (ALBANY HOUSE) of *c*. 1840, with canted bay windows flanking the pilastered doorpiece. Slightly later E addition with a pedimented centrepiece on the side. – Set back on the other side of the road, Nos. 37–39, an early C19 piend-roofed double house. No. 37 has hoodmoulded windows and a pilastered porch, No. 39 a shallow rectangular bay window; both share a boldly projecting eaves cornice.

9080   DUNCOW

Now little more than the school on the edge of the policies of Duncow House, but there was a village here in the C18 and C19.

SCHOOL. Broad-eaved, with a few thrifty Gothic touches; built *c*. 1875 and extended N at the end of the C19. – Adjoining two-storey SCHOOLHOUSE, also of *c*. 1875, its masonry hammer-dressed. Projecting from the front, a canted bay window scooped up to the square at the upper floor.

DUNCOW HOUSE. The mansion house has been demolished; it was by *Alexander Crombie*, 1860. The contemporary STABLES survive. Italian Gothic, built of aggressively hammerdressed stone, with a tower over the courtyard's entrance.

CASTLEHILL, 1km. NE. In a field, the big tapering rubble-built circular tower which formed the base of a WINDMILL of *c*. 1700.

QUARRELWOOD, 1km. NW. House of two storeys and three bays, built of painted rubble and with Venetian windows flanking the round-arched door. It was built *c*. 1798 as the manse for the adjoining CAMERONIAN CHAPEL of 1798. This is a large octagonal pavilion; it was reconstructed as a library for the house by *A. C. Wolffe* in 1969, when it had been reduced to a fragment. In the s front, tall roundheaded windows (the centre light formerly a door).

RIDDINGWOOD HOUSE, 1.2km. NE. Decidedly prosperous piend-roofed villa of *c*.1830, by *Walter Newall*. Painted ashlar w front of two storeys and three bays. Heavy pedimented doorpiece. Aprons under the console-corniced ground-floor windows; moulded architraves to the windows above. Five-bay elevation to the s, a canted bay window at the slightly advanced centre; the other ground-floor windows are still corniced, but the aprons were lost when their sills were lowered. – Contemporary or near-contemporary GARDEN HOUSE to the s, battlemented and with bartizans at the corners.

NEWLANDS. *See* p. 469.

DUNDRENNAN 7040

Pleasant village whose architectural distinction would be small were it not for the presence of the Abbey.

DUNDRENNAN ABBEY

Carefully tended ruin of an important C12 Cistercian monastery. According to a C13 interpolation in the *Melrose Chronicle*, it was founded in 1142. The majority of writers and lists state that it was endowed by David I (reigned 1124–53), although some ascribe the endowment to Fergus, lord of Galloway (†1161). However, the Cistercian family tree places the foundation of Dundrennan after that of Revesby Abbey, which was founded in 1143, and in his mid-C12 *Vita Sancti Malachiae* Bernard of Clairvaux states that Malachy, Bishop of Armagh, founded a Cistercian house at '*Viride Stagnum*' in Galloway in 1148. '*Viride Stagnum*' has been generally identified as Soulseat, but Soulseat Abbey was a Premonstratensian house and Bernard is unlikely to have confused such an establishment with one of his own order. It must be at least possible that Dundrennan was the abbey founded in 1148 by St Malachy (with an endowment from the King or the lord of Galloway), the monks being brought from Rievaulx, of which this was a daughter house.*

The first phase of building work, comprising the presbytery and transepts, was probably completed shortly before 1165, when construction of the cloister's permanent buildings had been recently begun. The whole church was probably completed by *c*.1200, by which date the transepts had been remodelled and

* An alternative explanation of the documentary evidence has been suggested by J. G. Scott ('The Origins of Dundrennan and Soulseat Abbeys', *Transactions of the Dumfriesshire and Galloway Natural History and Antiquarian Society*, 3rd ser., lxiii (1988), 35–44), who argues that Malachy may have founded a Cistercian house at Soulseat in 1148, its monks being moved to Dundrennan in or soon after 1156, Soulseat then being taken over by the Premonstratensians.

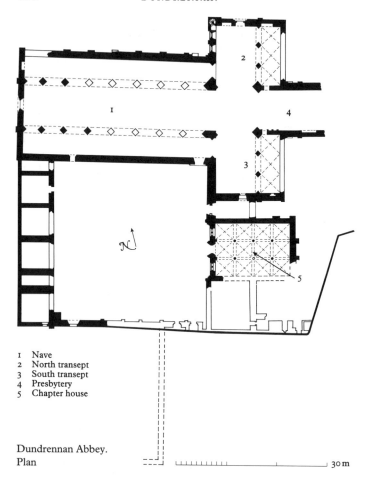

1   Nave
2   North transept
3   South transept
4   Presbytery
5   Chapter house

Dundrennan Abbey.
Plan

30 m

provided with E chapels. Alan, lord of Galloway, was buried at
Dundrennan in 1234, probably in the N transept's NE chapel; but
subsequent medieval references to the abbey are few. In 1529 the
buildings were reported, perhaps with some exaggeration, to have
suffered from neglect and English attacks, and in 1543 the W end
of the abbey church was said to be ruinous. After the Reformation
most of the buildings seem to have been abandoned and used as
a quarry, although the abbey church's E end was used as a parish
church until 1742. Some repairs were made in 1838 by the sixth
Earl of Selkirk, and three years later the ruins were taken into the
care of the government, whose architect *William Nixon* began a
more extensive programme of repair.

The abbey buildings, presumably all laid out at the time of
the foundation, conformed to the standard C12 Cistercian plan,
having a square cloister garth with accommodation for the choir
monks on its E and S sides, the lay brothers' quarters on the W,

and the abbey church on the N, its S transept filling the cloister's
NE corner and its presbytery projecting E of the cloister. There
survive most of the presbytery and transepts, very little of the
nave, and fragments of the cloister buildings.

The church

The unaisled rectangular PRESBYTERY was of four bays. The
three W bays still stand to the wallhead; they are built, like
the rest of the church, of good-quality grey sandstone ashlar.
Admirably simple and solid, they have large round-arched
clearstorey windows; their sill course is carried across the
straight buttresses, and a stringcourse has returned across the
transepts' chapels.

Of the TRANSEPTS, the S is fragmentary, the N much more
complete. At the corners, straight clasping buttresses, the NW
containing a stair. In the N transept's W wall, two disconcertingly unaligned tiers of tall round-arched windows. The
lower pair, divided by a buttress, are centred in the walling
between the nave and the N end of the transept, the upper pair
in the walling between the N corner and the line of the nave
roof, logical enough perhaps but visually unsatisfactory. Over
the lower windows, hoodmoulds carried on nook-shafts, their
bell capitals still in place. The upper windows are plain. Under
the windows, sill courses which return across the N gable. So
too does the splayed base. It is topped by a stringcourse which
jumps up at the gable to form a hoodmould over the central
door. This door is round-arched, of two moulded orders; the
foliaged capitals of the nook-shafts survive. Above the door,
another pair of tall round-arched windows at the same level as
the upper pair on the W wall. Higher up, a pair of nook-shafted
pointed windows (the W fragmentary). C18 engravings show
the gable's apex complete and having a small rectangular
opening. At the top of the N transept's E wall above the transept
chapels, round-arched windows of the same type as in the N
and W walls but shorter, probably curtailed when the chapels
were added.

The walls of the TRANSEPT CHAPELS, added shortly before
1200, have been largely removed but each trio formed a rectangular aisle the full length of the transept, covered by a
monopitch roof sloping up to the W. The roofs obscured the
already existing clearstorey windows of the presbytery's W bay,
which were partly built up when these chapels were added.
Enough survives of the N chapels' N and E walls to show
that they had hoodmoulded round-arched windows with nook-
shafts and bell capitals, conservative for their likely date of
c. 1180. A sill course round the N transept chapels links the
presbytery's stringcourse to the lower stringcourse of the transept.

The NAVE'S side walls are represented only by their lower
courses, almost wholly C19 restoration. Built into the S wall, a
few foliaged and moulded capitals, apparently of the late C12

and probably from the cloister walk. The extant lower part of
the W gable was largely rebuilt in 1841–3. It seems originally to
have had a door to each aisle; the one on the N is now blocked
externally, but its nook-shafts are still in place. The S door is
no longer visible. The central great W door was unblocked and
restored in the 1840s. It looks late C12. Pointed arch, the
abaci of the detached nook-shafts decorated with lots of small
nailhead ornament; the rounded S abaci are medieval, the
square abaci on the N replacements of the 1840s.

The INTERIOR of the presbytery and transepts, still relatively
complete, is austere but not mean. Pointed arch from the N
transept into the nave aisle. A wall passage runs from the NW
stair across the windows. Sill courses under the N transept's
W windows are carried round the N wall, the lower as a
stringcourse rising into a hoodmould over the door. They may
originally have returned across the E wall and joined the sill
course and stringcourse in the presbytery. The same detail was
presumably repeated in the S transept. In the presbytery, triple
vaulting-shafts rise from plain corbels; it was probably vaulted
or intended to be vaulted from the start. In the W bay of the
presbytery's S wall, the three arches and one capital of a blind
arcade which backed the SEDILIA. Unusually, its seats must
have projected from the wall. In the bay to its E, a badly
mutilated double PISCINA. The W bay's N and S doors are
insertions of 1838, the S door's much-restored trefoil head
enriched with nailhead ornament re-used from the cloister
buildings.

The late C12 remodelling of the crossing and transepts gave
the presbytery's W corners elegant responds of clustered shafts
with simple bell capitals. In each transept's E wall were inserted
three tall pointed arches into the new chapels. Again they have
clustered shafts and bell capitals but they look uncomfortably
squashed, apparently because of a decision to make them the
same height as the slightly broader arches from the transepts
into the nave aisles. Above each arcade, and tightly contained
by stringcourses, a low triforium, its presence a departure from
earlier Cistercian practice, which had deemed such a feature
an unnecessary luxury. The S transept triforium is unexciting,
three pairs of pointed openings to light a passage in the roofspace above the chapel vaults. The triforium of the N transept
is more ambitious, with four pointed blind arches over each
arch of the arcade below. Between each quartet of arches, the
sill course breaks forward in a ring-like projection, presumably
intended to contain a vaulting-shaft rising from a foliaged corbel
below. More evidence of intended vaulting at the N gable, which
has vaulting-shafts in the corners and centre and a vaulting
line clearly evident above the clearstorey windows. Between
the W wall's clearstorey windows, a foliaged corbel carrying
a clustered vaulting-shaft. But the idea of vaulting this transept must have been given up before construction of the
apex or this gable, since its two pointed windows would have
been above the originally intended vault and they are too

large to have been designed to light only a roofspace. The transept chapels have been covered with quadripartite vaults, the shafts and some of the vaulting surviving in the N chapels. In the N wall of this N group of chapels, a round-arched window. In both groups of chapels, the lower stringcourse of the transept is carried round the walls. Grooves in the piers of the arcades show that there have been wooden screens both between one chapel and another and between each chapel and the transept.

The lower parts of the W crossing piers survive, restored in the C19. Both have flat inner faces against which were placed the stalls of the choir monks. Only the bases of some piers of the seven-bay nave remain. All have pointed angle shafts and intermediate semicircular attached shafts. SW respond of similar plan. The NW respond is quite different. Is it a C19 restoration?

The monastic buildings

The nave and cloister buildings enclosed a 31m.-square court. On its E side, the CHAPTER HOUSE W wall still stands to the height of one storey. It is of three bays, panelled with pointed and moulded overarches springing from attached shafts, their caps and bases moulded; on the arches, very small and close-set nailhead enrichment. In the centre, an elaborate cinquefoil-headed door, its spandrels carved with badly weathered foliaged scrollwork. In each outer bay, a two-light window, the central shaft now missing, the attached side shafts again with moulded caps and bases. Over each pair of lights, a panel carved with a foliaged star to the exterior, a fleur-de-lis to the inside. Above, a few surviving corbels of the cloister walk's roof, over which is part of one jamb of a window* which lit the monks' dormitory on the first floor of this range. Inside the chapter house, the surviving parts of the columns and wallshafts show that it contained three vaulted four-bay aisles of equal width. All this looks mid-C13, and probably indicates a reconstruction or rebuilding of this part of the cloister. Not much more than foundations remain of the rest of the E range.

The S range is just as ruined, but at its W end is a pointed door with moulded capitals, probably the entrance to the kitchen. The W range originally housed lay brothers, but presumably they were dispensed with by the late C15 (as at other Cistercian houses) and the range was then rebuilt; it was much repaired in 1840–3. On the ground floor, tunnel-vaulted stores, now housing cusped arch heads from the arcades of the cloister walk.

---

* Shown as pointed in Adam de Cardonnel's *Picturesque Antiquities of Scotland* (1788).

Monuments

In the N transept gable, the pointed and moulded broad arch of
a TOMB RECESS. It looks late medieval. – In the N wall of
the N transept chapels, a moulded semicircular arched recess
containing the now limbless figure of a knight, likely to be the
EFFIGY of Alan, lord of Galloway, †1234. – Placed against the
nave's W wall, a GRAVESLAB commemorating the lady of Orch–
(? Orchardton) †1440, incised with the figure of a woman,
her feet resting on a small dog. – In the recess of the blocked W
door to the N nave aisle, two GRAVESLABS, one to Sir William
Livingstone of Culter †1607, decorated with his initials and
16   coat of arms. The other, probably C13, is carved with the
recumbent figure of an abbot, depicted as having been stabbed
in the chest. His feet rest on the small figure of a man dressed
only in a kilt and shoes, whose intestines spill out of a large
wound in his side. Does this recall the murder of an early abbot
of Dundrennan and the subsequent retribution meted out to
his assassin? – In the chapter house floor have been set stone
COFFIN LIDS. One, probably C14, commemorating an Abbot
Giles, is carved with a central cross, its head enclosed in a ring
within which the arms are decorated with traceried panels; in
the spaces between the arms, flowers sprout from the cross's
corners. More traceried panels on the stepped Calvary below.
To the l. of the cross, a crozier, again sprouting flowers; to the
r., rosettes alternating with fleurs-de-lis. – N of this, the C13
coffin lid of another Abbot Giles, with an incised Gothic-
lettered inscription. – On the coffin lid of Abbot William,
probably late C12, a cross and crude crozier. – Deeply cut
Lombardic inscription on the late C14 coffin lid of Abbot Brian.

CHURCH, GRAVEYARD, PUBLIC BUILDINGS

RERRICK PARISH CHURCH. Germanic Gothic, by *W. R.
Corson*, 1864–6. Broad buttressed whinstone box, the front (E)
gable bisected by a buttress halted under a huge plate-traceried
rose window. Saddleback-roofed and crowstep-gabled NE
tower.

GRAVEYARD, 1.5km. SE. The site of Rerrick Parish Church until
1865, when it was moved to Dundrennan village. There still
stands part of the W gable of the CHURCH, which was built or
enlarged by *John Mack* and *Thomas Kerr*, masons, in 1743 and
given an 'aisle' by *John Graham* in 1827–8 (*see* the Introduction,
p. 38). It is built of rough ashlar. In it, a round-arched window,
probably of the 1740s although its internal splay might suggest
an earlier date. – Several C18 TABLE STONES and HEAD-
STONES, a couple decorated with angels' heads (souls).

OLD SCHOOL. Built of whitewashed rubble by *John McClure*
and *Gilbert Liviston*, 1783, 'upon the same plan of the Schoolhouse at the Ronehouse of Kelton'. Tall single-storey schoolroom, with a blind bullseye window in the gable from which
projects a parapeted porch, probably an addition. Attached at

the s and forming an L-plan is the gableted schoolhouse, a consoled cornice over its door.

SCHOOL. N block by *Bennet*, 1851–2, with a chimney gablet at the front and a ball finial on the E gable. SW wing added by *Robert Wallace*, 1911.

FARMS ETC.

HAZLEFIELD HOUSE, 3km. NE. Early C19 main block of two storeys and three bays, built of painted rubble. The entrance pediment is of 1994. At each gable, a set-back wing, the r. single storey. The l. wing has been heightened to two storeys and given a piend roof, perhaps in 1870 when William Graham did work here.

PORT MARY HOUSE, 2.3km. S. Late C18 rendered laird's house. Main block of two storeys, a basement and attic, with a full-height gabled central projection of hammerdressed ashlar added to the front in the late C19. Screen walls (the N now masking a corridor) join this block to single-storey-and-attic piend-roofed and Venetian-windowed pavilions, the s marred by C20 dormer windows.

ORROLAND. *See* p. 485.

DUNRAGIT HOUSE

1050

5km. W of Glenluce

Ragbag of a house. The tall three-storey rendered main block is substantially late C18. Front of four bays, the centre two advanced under a chimney-topped pediment, a bullseye window in the tympanum. Moulded architraves to the first-floor windows. Victorian porch. In the S gable, a couple of windows whose moulded surrounds look C17, so presumably earlier work is incorporated. Long rear extensions, mostly C19.

DUNROD

6040

Small rubble-walled graveyard in a field.

PARISH CHURCH. Now reduced to an outline marked out by low heaps of rubble; it has comprised a nave and chancel, perhaps built in the C12. – Just outside the graveyard entrance, a crude FONT bowl formed from a hollowed lump of granite.

KING'S BARRACKS, 0.6km. NW. Flat-roofed and unexciting, by *A. C. Shallis* of the *Ministry of Works*, 1958.

DUNSCORE

8080

Small triangular-plan village, the houses mostly C19 and unpretentious, the Parish Church occupying the highest point. For the demolished Parish Church of 1649, *see* the Introduction, p. 37.

PARISH CHURCH. Innocent Gothic, by *James Thomson*, 1823–
4. Whinstone box, the red sandstone dressings now painted
white. Tall spiky pinnacles on the buttresses and E gable. Y-
traceried and transomed two-light windows, their hoodmoulds
linked by stringcourses. The main cornice is carried around the
buttresses and across the gables, where it forms the base of
their pediments. The W gable's pediment is broken by the
three-stage tower, across which the church's main cornice is
carried as a sill course. Gableted pinnacles on the corners of
the tower's uncrenellated parapet.

Inside, a coved ceiling with Gothic ventilator roses. – U-
plan GALLERY on cast-iron columns. – W PULPIT, its heavy
sounding board topped by a crown. – A few BOX PEWS in the
NW corner.

GRAVEYARD. Just W of the church, a curly-topped HEAD-
STONE to John Paton † 1750, its panelled pilasters framing the
figure of a man who holds a skull and a bone. – Small BURIAL
ENCLOSURE of the Griersons of Dalgonar, probably early C18.
Low walls topped by oblong blocks instead of balusters. Ball
finials at the corners and on top of the scroll-flanked inscription
panel over the entrance.

BOGRIE, 5.5km. W. Quite unpretentious two-storey farmhouse
built of painted rubble, its present form probably dating from
1860, when the tower of Bogrie was demolished and its stone
was used to repair the farm steading, but incorporating earlier
work. Off-centre round-arched broad doors to E and W (the W
now glazed) which could be C17 work. So too could be the
windows' roll-moulded margins. Over the E door, two stones,
one carved with a coat of arms, the other with the date 1770.
Also in the E wall, a steep pediment decorated with a thistle; it
looks C17. Over the W door, another stone bearing the date
1660 and the initials IK and IM (probably for John Kirko of
Bogrie and his wife, Jean Maxwell). S sun lounge of 1974.
Single-storey office wing, probably of 1860, at the NW.

SPEDDOCH, 2.4km. SW. Overgrown and not very gainly rendered villa, by *John Lessels*, *c.*1860. Heavy pilastered porch
flanked by a pair of bay windows which become semi-octagonal
at the upper floor but are scooped back to the square under the
eaves. Some early C20 alterations.

SUNDAYWELL, 5.6km. W. Harled farmhouse, its three-storey N
two bays converted from a square tower house, probably in the
late C18. Late C19 porch, its gable containing a reset heraldic
stone, probably from the tower, bearing the initials of James
Kirko of Sundaywell and his wife, S– Welsh, and the date 1651.
Mid-C19 two-storey S addition with gabled dormerheads over
the first-floor windows. Behind, a whitewashed U of FARM
OFFICES, probably of the earlier C19.

LAG TOWER. *See* p. 399.
STROQUHAN. *See* p. 538.

DUNSKEY CASTLE

0050

0.8km. SE of Portpatrick

Substantial ruin of a house which belonged to the Adairs of
Kinhilt. It was probably built in the mid-C16 but incorporates
some earlier walling. The site is a cliff-edged promontory jutting
into the Irish Sea, its landward (NE) side cut off by a ditch. A
causeway gives access across the ditch to the house, which
stretches across this side of the promontory. The early C16
building seems to have been a tower house at the SE corner of
the site, with a wall continuing the line of its E front to the NE
corner, all built of whinstone rubble with lots of pinnings. The
tower house is L-plan, the SW jamb higher than the main block;
rectangular projection in the inner angle. Turrets at the main
block's E corners, a chimney breast protruding from its W wall.
Over the door in the inner angle's projection, three empty
frames for armorial panels. Inside the door, a short tunnel-
vaulted passage. Off its E side, another vaulted passage along
the W side of the main block, giving access to two very narrow
vaulted cellars under the jamb's stair and to two larger stores
(again vaulted) in the main block. The N store is windowless;
the S, which has a turnpike stair in the wall thickness of the
house's SE corner, was presumably the wine cellar. In the SW

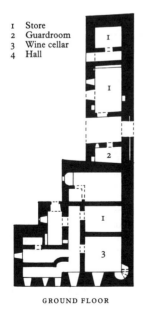
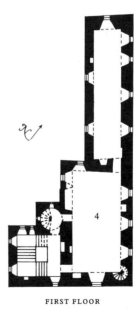

1 Store
2 Guardroom
3 Wine cellar
4 Hall

GROUND FLOOR   FIRST FLOOR

⌐————————————————————————————————————⌐ 30 m

Dunskey Castle. Plans

jamb, a broad scale-and-platt stair to the first floor, where the
main block is filled by the hall. Fireplace near the N end of the
W wall. Immediately S of the fireplace, a door to the remains of
a turnpike stair in the inner angle's projection, which originally
served the floors above. The second floor of the main block
contained two rooms, each with an off-centre fireplace in the
gable; one of the moulded jambs of the S fireplace survives. In
the SW jamb, one room on each of the upper floors, each with
an off-centre fireplace in the W gable.

It was probably as part of the additions traditionally said to
have been made to the castle by Hugh, first Viscount Montgomery of the Great Ardes (who had acquired Dunskey in 1620),
that the narrow three-storey wing was built N of the tower
house, its E wall formed by the earlier defensive wall of the
castle. Large first-floor windows to the E, N and W. On the E
side's ground floor the only opening is the entrance (now
robbed of dressings) from the causeway. On the S side of the
vaulted entrance passage, a windowless vaulted guardroom,
with an aumbry in its W wall. N of the entrance passage are two
windowless vaulted stores, both entered from the courtyard,
the N store via a passage. On the first floor there has been one
long room entered through the hall of the tower house; fireplace
at the S end.

DUNSKEY HOUSE
1.8km. N of Portpatrick

Large but gaunt mansion house by *James Kennedy Hunter*, 1901–
4, in a stripped Scottish manorial style, crowstepped gables and
the jettying of the top floor the principal embellishments. Paired
straight gables over the S entrance, a cannon spout projecting
between them. The interior is lavishly appointed. In the
entrance hall, a plain stone chimneypiece; its lintel bears the
date 1903 and the initials of Charles Lindsay Orr Ewing and
his wife, Lady Augusta Helen Elizabeth Boyle, for whom the
house was built. In the overmantel, a stone from the building's
predecessor, recording that it had been 'PERFECTED 1706'
by IB and IAG (John Blair of Dunskey and Jean Agnew, his
wife) and also with the initials IB and IH, perhaps for the late
C18 owners, Jean Blair and her husband John Hunter. Ahead
is the stair hall; stair balusters of C17 silhouette type. To the W
of the stair hall, the main hall (now dining room) with a beamed
ceiling. Depressed-arched niche over the basket-arched stone
chimneypiece. N of the main hall, the bay-windowed billiard
room, with another beamed ceiling. Large inglenook recess on
the W. In the house's SW corner, the drawing room. L-plan,
the jamb marked off by a screen of heavy Ionic columns.
Opulent plasterwork in a free French-accented late C18
manner. Cherubs' heads on the main part's swagged frieze.
Boudoir to the N, the plasterwork of its coved ceiling and
fireplace overmantel of rather earlier C18 and more Scottish

inspiration; musical instruments in the ceiling corners. Severe segmental-vaulted study to the N, its fireplace plain Gothic. E of the stair hall is the former dining room, the ceiling decorated with swagged husks of late C18 type. In the library at the SE corner, shallow ceiling enrichment of very best late C18 type.

DURISDEER

8000

Hamlet beside the unexpectedly smart church, the cottages predominantly mid-C19. A little apart is the plain MANSE, built in 1763 but extended and altered in the C19.

PARISH CHURCH. Cruciform church with, at its W end, a two-storey block of session house and retiring rooms intended for the use of the Duke of Queensberry, the owner of Drumlanrig Castle and patron of the parish. The church's N jamb (the Queensberry Aisle) is the earliest part, built for the first Duke of Queensberry between 1695 and 1708 as a mausoleum attached to the medieval parish church; the architect was *James Smith*. It is a tall square pavilion, the walls of pinky ashlar with rusticated quoins, a moulded base and boldly projecting cornice. Ogee-domed lead roof,* its dumpy profile and spiked-ball finial dating from 1883, when the roof's height was lowered.‡ Originally, the jamb had a large Gothic N window, but this was replaced *c*.1711 by a shallow N projection to accommodate the monument inside; at the same time rectangular windows with splayed jambs were inserted in the E and W walls.

In 1716 the medieval church was demolished and construction of the present church and the W cross-bar began. *John Farr*, mason, was master of work, *James Anderson* the foreman, and *Robert Heslop* and *John Hills* the wrights. It seems likely that *James Smith* was again the architect. Work was mostly finished in 1720 but the tower was not completed until nine years later. The church itself is T-plan and built of harled rubble. The rusticated quoins, base and cornice all quote the detail of the Queensberry Aisle, but the line of the top quoin is continued across each face as an ashlar band course under the cornice. Big and chunkily moulded round-arched windows in the N and S walls of the body, their leaded lights replaced by wooden sashes in 1784. In the S and E gables, windows of the same type but truncated to allow for the rusticated doorpieces below. In the side walls of the S 'aisle', tall rectangular windows like those inserted in the Queensberry Aisle a few years before. A utilitarian door (now blocked) has been inserted just E of the Queensberry Aisle, perhaps *c*.1870, when the pulpit was moved to this side of the church. Originally, the body was roofed with a piended platform, and the S 'aisle' had an ogee lead dome balancing that of the Queensberry Aisle; but both the body and

---

* This is a deviation from the contract of 1695, which specified a roof 'theaked with thackstone' and with a 'flameing urn' finial.

‡ The roof was releaded in 1983 but the 1883 profile was retained.

Queensberry Aisle. Drawing of 1695

the s 'aisle' were given simple piended roofs in the alterations
made in 1784 by *Andrew Watson*, joiner in Dumfries.* Set into
the gable of the s 'aisle', a small stone sundial in an egg-and-
dart border, dated 1699.

The w cross-bar has the appearance of the town house of
some small burgh. Moulded base, cornice and rusticated
quoins, all like those of the church, but it is of two storeys in
the height of the church's one. Front elevation of three widely
spaced bays, the gables each of four narrow bays. All the
windows are linked vertically by ashlar panels making a gentle
contrast to the main walling's harled rubble. In the centre of
the w front, a door with a lugged architrave and mutuled
cornice. Above it, a short round-arched window which has
moulding of the same profile as at the windows of the church
but cut across by a keystone and imposts. Rising from the
centre of the piended platform roof, a coursed rubble tower of
two stages, the lower with a blind bullseye window in each face;
in each face of the upper stage, a round-arched belfry opening
containing a pair of pointed lights. Channelled strip quoins,
cornice and a parapet within which once rose a lead-covered
spire, removed in 1825.

Inside the church, the s, e and w arms have galleries on thin
cast-iron Roman Doric columns, the w a replacement of 1784
with a dentil cornice, the s and e perhaps early C19. – Bow-
fronted PULPIT of the earlier C19, its pedimented back a 1950s
alteration. Attached to the pulpit are C18 wrought-iron brackets, one carrying a baptismal basin, the other an hourglass. The

---

* The church was re-roofed to the 1784 design in 1957.

pulpit's present position in front of the arch to the Queensberry Aisle dates from *c.* 1870; previously it had stood at the E corner of the body of the church and the S 'aisle'. – Mid-C19 pine PEWS. The two rows of table seats in front of the pulpit convert into communion pews.

The interior of the QUEENSBERRY AISLE, entered by an E door, is sumptuous Baroque. In its S wall, a broad segmental arch into the church; its jambs are chamfered and moulded, the apex of the hoodmould broken by a coroneted strapwork cartouche. All this looks old-fashioned for the 1690s and by comparison with the rest of the aisle; so was there an earlier 'aisle' or chapel here? In the arch, a foliaged wrought-iron screen of *c.* 1700. Floor of black and cream marble. Ashlar walls rising to a bold cornice. In the attic above the cornice, large carved stone panels on the S, E and W walls. The E and W panels bear reliefs of winged skulls from which hang swags decorated with emblems of death. On the S wall, a trumpeting angel holds a big medallion bearing a portrait of the second Duke of Queensberry. On the l. of the angel, a pyramid-topped tomb, its finial the winged-heart emblem of the Douglas family; on the front of the tomb chest, the Queensberry coat of arms. On the r. of the angel, a globe. Coved plaster ceiling with an octagonal hatchment hanging from the centre.

In the middle of the Aisle, a black marble slab covers the entrance to the burial vault below. Over this stands a tall BALDACCHINO. Smith's design of 1695 clearly derives from that of Bernini's baldacchino over the high altar in St Peter's, Rome. At the four corners, tall fluted and acanthus-topped bases carry the barley-sugar columns ornamented with spiralling bands of laurel leaves, all executed in grey-veined white marble. Deeply undercut Corinthian capitals of white statuary marble, formerly gilded. On each face of the deep entablature, a central panel, the E and W panels each carved with a skull and crossbones, the N and S with the winged-heart Douglas emblem. Foliaged brackets under the cornice; the intervening soffit panels are decorated with motifs from the Queensberry coat of arms. On each face above, a forward-leaning pediment, its base prolonged in James Smith's characteristic manner, the tympanum carved with a cartouche. The underside of the canopy is decorated with a sunburst surrounded by cherubs' heads peeping through clouds.

In the N wall of the Queensberry Aisle, a big segmental-arched recess of *c.* 1711 breaks through the cornice. In the recess, the huge MONUMENT to James, second Duke of 48 Queensberry, †1711 and his wife Mary †1709, for which *John van Nost* was paid £400 in 1713. It is lavish Baroque, executed in variegated marbles. At the top, a ball-finialled semicircular marble canopy, from which hang white marble curtains pulled open to drape the monument's sides. At each side of the bottom, a weeping cherub, the l. resting one foot on a horribly realistic skull and both with teardrops glistening on their cheeks. Below and between the curtains is an aedicule; its projecting

Corinthian columns have fluted grey marble shafts standing on bases of a paler grey marble and surmounted by white marble capitals. Below the columns, tall panelled pedestals, each with a carved pendant of foliage and crossbones. Behind, attached piers with simply fluted capitals. Entablature of pale grey marble, crowned by vases on the advanced ends. Above the entablature, an heraldic achievement, the shield left blank. At the back of the aedicule, high-relief pendants of flowers and leaves flank a pilastered and roundheaded Roman Doric arch which frames three cherubs holding the inscribed scroll commemorating the Duke. Projecting from the aedicule is a double sarcophagus, its taller back part topped by a figure of the reclining Duke dressed in Garter robes, his legs crossed, his chin resting on his right hand. He looks down bemusedly on the effigy of his dead Duchess lying flat on her back, wearing a jewelled dress, coronation robes and a tiara.

CHURCHYARD. Built into the s wall's E end, FRAGMENTS of C17 or C18 monuments, several carved with angels' heads (souls) and one with an hourglass, crossbones and a skull. – E of the church, the HEADSTONE of Marren Poirglas †1739, its fluted pilasters topped by a skull and hourglass; in this frame, the high relief of a woman, her hands demurely clasped, standing on crossed bones. It may be the work of her husband, the mason *Robert Kerr*. – Beside this, the HEADSTONE of David Scott †1747, aedicular with fluted pilasters and a ball-finialled steep pediment, skulls on its sides, a coat of arms in the tympanum, an angel's head on the entablature. – Immediately to the N, another C18 HEADSTONE, to James Sands, again with panelled pilasters and decorated with an angel's head. – To the NW, the HEADSTONE of William Ire †1756, the front carved with a crowned last (the emblem of the shoemakers) above an hourglass, skull and crossbones. – To its N, the HEADSTONE to John Patterson †1826, the best of several similar early C19 monuments, with acanthus-capitalled pilasters and a scrolled pediment framing the relief of a suave urn under a swag. – Propped against the NE corner of the church, three C18 HEADSTONES. One has a stack of reminders of death between panelled pilasters, another (to Robert Palley †1702) the relief of a boy standing under an angel's head. – A little SE of the church, the MONUMENT to William Corsan †1802, a tall pedestal with swags on the frieze and a dainty urn finial.

At the E end of the church's s wall, a railed enclosure. Inside it, now attached to the church wall, the GRAVESLAB of James Lorimer †1683, decorated with an hourglass lying on top of gravedigger's tools. – Also the GRAVESLAB of James Lorimer †1729, with a piecrust border and coat of arms. – Beside the s gable of the church's w cross-bar, an early C18 TABLE STONE commemorating the Covenanter, Daniel McMichael, inscribed:

AS DANIEL CAST WAS IN LYONS DEN FOR PRAYING UNTO GOD
AND NOT TO MEN SO LYONS THUS CRUELY DEVOURED ME FOR

BEAIRING [*sic*] WITNES TO TRUTHS TESTIMONY I REST IN PEACE
TILL JESUS REND THE CLOUD AND JUDGE TWIXT ME AND THOSE
WHO SHED MY BLOOD

– To its W, an C18 TABLE STONE. Between the baluster legs,
panels carved with symbols of death and an angel's head. –
Beside it, a tall aedicular HEADSTONE dated 1778, commemorating Isobel Lorimer. Fluted pilasters flanking an angel's
head; concave-sided pediment. – W of the church, the HEAD-
STONE of 1685 to the children of *William Lukup*, master of
work at Drumlanrig, who probably carved it. Scroll border
round a pilastered aedicule containing a niche in which stands
the figure of a mason, presumably Lukup himself, holding a
skull; in the segmental pediment, an angel's head. On the back,
the incised relief of a winged hourglass and crossbones. – Near
the churchyard entrance, the HEADSTONE of Robert Lorimer
†1756, carved with an untidy array of grisly emblems under an
angel's head.

DALVEEN, 3.4km. N. Farmhouse and steading of 1836, probably
to a design provided by *William Burn*. Substantial but unexciting crowstep-gabled house, some of the windows enlarged
to two lights. In the low W wing's gable, a reset panel bearing
the arms of the Douglases of Dalveen; it is probably C16 or
C17. U-plan steading behind and a detached barn to the N. – On
the hillside to the N, an urn-finialled pedimented MONUMENT
erected in 1836 to commemorate two Covenanters killed here
in 1685.

ROMAN FORTLET, 1.4km. NE. The site is a hog-backed ridge at
the S entrance to the Dalveen Pass which carried the Roman
road from Nithsdale to Clydesdale. In the mid-C2 the ridge
was levelled and a fortlet erected, its turf rampart protecting
timber buildings which perhaps accommodated a century of
eighty men. The survival of the ramparts, single ditch and
protective traverse in front of the entrance render this one of
the best-preserved Roman fortlets in Britain.

EAGLESFIELD   *2070*

Long roadside village, begun early in the C19 but the houses now
predominantly C20.

CHURCH. Very simple harled hall church opened in 1953; sloping
buttresses along the side walls. – LYCHGATE at the entrance,
a picturesque touch.

PUBLIC HALL. By *Peter Chapman*, 1892–3. Plain except for a
pedimented doorpiece.

SCHOOL. By *F. J. C. Carruthers*, 1907. Long, with shaped gables.

BLACKET HOUSE. *See* p. 129.

SPRINGKELL. *See* p. 525.

EARLSTOUN CASTLE
2.9km. N of St John's Town of Dalry

Unmartial tower house now attached to the N end of a C19 steading range. It was probably built in the late C16, almost certainly before 1601, when John Gordon of Earlstoun was granted a charter of the lands together with the 'fortalice'. Rubble-walled L of three storeys and an attic. Unusually for a house of this type and date, the gables are not crowstepped and there is no gunloop. At the main block's ground floor, small windows. Good-sized openings to the floors above, those of the first floor with roll-moulded surrounds, perhaps to designate that floor's primacy, those of the second chamfered. In the main block's S wall, a re-used wedge-shaped stone pierced by a round hole and bearing the date 1655 together with the initials W G and M H (for William Gordon of Earlstoun and his wife, Mary Hope). It came from a mid-C17 two-storey E extension; its roof raggle is visible on the tower's gable. In the inner angle, a stair turret corbelled out at the first floor and corbelled out further at the second.

The entrance in the jamb's E face opens onto a lobby at the foot of the turnpike stair to the first floor. On the main block's ground floor, two vaulted stores. The first-floor hall (now in poor condition) has contained quite grand panelling, perhaps of the late C17, with Ionic pilasters flanking the E fireplace. N of the fireplace, a blocked door which opened into the now missing mid-C17 E addition.

EASTRIGGS

121Township built in 1916–18 to house munitions workers, the layout plan by *Raymond Unwin*. Brick-built piend-roofed housing, now badly altered and the uniformity lost; a row of shops at the W end.

39 CHURCH OF ST JOHN THE EVANGELIST (Episcopal), Lady-smith Road. 1917, by *C. M. Crickmer*, who had been associated with Unwin at Hampstead Garden Suburb in London and was resident architect for the townships of Gretna and Eastriggs. Sturdy Early Christian cruciform with a few late Gothic touches, built of snecked squared rubble. Aisled nave and chancel, N transept. Over the strong S tower a slated bellcast pyramid roof with cat-slide-roofed lucarnes.

BAXTER MEMORIAL HALL, Annan Road. Mission hall of 1930, with slim buttresses and bracketed eaves.

EASTRIGGS COMMUNITY SCHOOL, Hobart Terrace. By *Dumfries and Galloway Regional Council*, 1987. A restless jumble. Dark brick base and a ribbed metal roof; much use of clearstorey lighting.

ECCLEFECHAN 1070

Sizeable village, famous as the birthplace of Thomas Carlyle, at the centre of a medieval parish whose church (on the site of Hoddom Church, *see* below) was abandoned in 1609. It enjoyed a weekly market in the C18, when weaving was the inhabitants' principal activity, but declined as a market centre after 1815 in the face of competition from Annan; weaving was abandoned in the 1870s. The A74 runs noisily close to the N.

ECCLEFECHAN FREE CHURCH. Now a hall. Big and broad Gothic box by *George Laidlaw*, 1877–8, with a rose window and gableted bellcote at the front gable.

HODDOM CHURCH, Hoddom Road. Built as Johnstone United Presbyterian Church in 1864–6; the architect was *James Barbour*. Big, plain Gothic in red sandstone. Nave, transepts and a saddleback-roofed NW tower. Very broad single-span interior, a gallery round three sides. At the E end, a pointed arch to the apse from which projects an exceptionally roomy PULPIT, its wooden front decorated with delicate Gothic blind arcading; it was probably made by *William Gillies*, who was contractor for the church's joinery. – In the windows, STAINED GLASS patterns of fleurs-de-lis.

ECCLEFECHAN COMMUNITY EDUCATION CENTRE, Hall Road. Built as a Good Templars Hall in 1906. Single-storey, with thistle finials.

HODDOM SCHOOL, Langlands Road. By *Dumfries and Galloway Regional Council*, 1975–7. Single-storey, built of synthetic stone bricks, with a 'belfry' feature and clearstorey.

DESCRIPTION. BURNBANK STREET, entering from the W, begins with a bronze STATUE of Thomas Carlyle, cast by *McDonald & Creswick Ltd* in 1929; it is a replica of *J. Edgar Boehm*'s statue of 1882 in Chelsea (London). It looks down the hill towards Carlyle's birthplace. Burnbank Street is mostly C19 vernacular. On the corner of Hall Road and High Street, the Ecclefechan Community Education Centre (*see* above). Further along HALL ROAD and set well back, THE FIRS, a mid-C19 two-storey and three-bay house of painted rubble. HIGH STREET is mostly simple C18 and C19 housing. Among it, the white-painted ECCLEFECHAN HOTEL, which has taken over several buildings, one early C19 with three-light windows and a first-floor lintel course. Its late C19 E block has an ogee-domed rounded corner to Langlands Road. In HODDOM ROAD to the S, HODDOM COURT on the r., by *Russell & Bryce*, 1988–9; gentle post-Modern housing on the site of the Victorian Hoddom School whose awkward Gothic campanile of 1875 has been retained; it is a skinny tower broached to an angle-buttressed belfry, with a weathercock on the pyramid roof. On the l., Hoddom Church (*see* above). Immediately S of the church, one wall of the single-storey OLD SCHOOLHOUSE of 1731; it now forms part of the graveyard's boundary wall rebuilt in 1881–2.

On the N side of High Street, a block on the E corner of Langlands Road, perhaps of *c.* 1800, with rusticated quoins and big scrolled skewputts; the corniced shopfront (now fronting a house) looks like a mid-C19 addition. A little further down, CARLYLE HOUSE, again of *c.* 1800, with rusticated quoins; its pedimented Roman Doric portico and two-light ground-floor windows are mid-C19 embellishments. The street is now divided by an open culvert containing the Ecclefechan Burn. On its S side, No. 1 CARLYLE PLACE, a cottage, probably of the mid-C19; set into the front wall a re-used lintel carved with a scrolly cartouche bearing a crown and last, flanked by the initials Wp MC and the date 1749. Beside it, the two-storey CARLYLE'S BIRTHPLACE, built by Thomas Carlyle's father and uncle, both masons, in 1791. It is a double house with a broad, almost depressed-arched central pend under a Venetian window (the centre light blind). Over the l. house's door, a re-used stone carved with impaled coats of arms, the initials II and the date 1673.

SHORTRIGG, 3.1km. W. Asymmetrical but unexciting late C19 FARMHOUSE. – Adjoining the informal and rather altered rubble-built C18 STEADING is an C18 WINDMILL. Tall strongly battered round tower, its conical slated roof probably a late C19 replacement. Beside it, a conical-roofed early C19 circular HORSEMILL, the two mills exemplifying changes in technological fashion.

BURNFOOT HALL. *See* p. 138.
KIRKCONNEL HALL. *See* p. 364.
KNOCKHILL. *See* p. 398.

ECCLES
1.4km. N of Penpont

8090

Georgian country house complex which has developed around the barmkin of a tower house. The tower house, which was in existence by 1605 and ruinous by 1776, stood at the SW corner of a courtyard. Probably in the earlier C18, single-storey ranges of whitewashed rubble were built along the courtyard's S, E and N sides, with two-storey pyramid-roofed pavilions at its SE and NE corners. In *c.* 1830 the tower house itself was replaced by a new block, probably incorporating some of the earlier fabric. This is L-plan, of two storeys and piend-roofed. Main S front of two bays, the r. containing the entrance, the l. a shallow bow with a Venetian window at each floor. The buildings were repaired and partly remodelled by *Gordon J. Kinghorn*, 1965, when the N stable range was demolished and the NE pavilion was made into a garage.

GARDEN to the SE, a rubble-walled irregular hexagon, probably of the early C19. – Also early C19 is the LODGE to its E, single-storey, with a pointed door and windows.

EDINGHAM CASTLE

1.4km. NE of Dalbeattie

Ruined tower house built for the Livingstones of Little Airds, probably in the earlier C16. Most of the W gable and substantial parts of the other walls still stand. It is a rubble-built three-storey rectangle. Slit windows at the ground floor. In the gable, a comfortably sized first-floor window and a square window above. One first-floor window, robbed of its dressings, survives in the S wall. Near the N wall's E end, a door with chamfered jambs. It opens into a lobby off which the turnpike stair rises in the wall thickness of the house's NE corner. On the lobby's S side, two doors, sharing a central jamb, give access to what is now a single tunnel-vaulted room but may originally have been divided by a wooden partition. No fireplace, so presumably the ground floor was used for storage.

ELIOCK HOUSE

1.2km. SW of Mennock

A big three-storey H-plan house, standing on a natural platform overlooking the Nith, much more complicated than it looks. The earliest part, at the N end, is a massive tower, probably of the later C16, with shotholes to N and S. Probably also C16 was its W extension by two bays, originally of two storeys. This N range was badly damaged by fire *c.* 1940 and its E end partly demolished. In 1658 the house was made T-plan by the building of a S wing, its S end marked by a large wallhead chimney on the harled E side and a projecting conical-roofed round stair tower, its top stage a doocot, on the W. On the lintel of the tower's moulded door, the date, probably recut, 'MDCLVIII'. In *c.* 1770, James Veitch, Lord Eliock, extended the T to an H, lengthening the tail and adding a new wing across its S end. The E face of his extension of the cross-bar is harled; the rest is of ashlar, droved on the S range's piended E gable and six-bay S front but polished on the N elevation of that range and the W front of the cross-bar extension. Polished ashlar also on the C17 stair tower's S half, so presumably this was refaced at the same time. However, the N half of the tower and the walling to its N are of broached ashlar; this is also apparently a late C18 refacing, but the difference in treatment is hard to understand. In *c.* 1910 the house was further altered: a red sandstone single-storey porch filling the E side's open centre (its Renaissance door juxtaposed with a crenellated parapet) was added, the N range's W end was raised in pinkish sandstone to the same height as the rest, and an orange sandstone bullseye window was inserted in the centre of the S range's top floor.

ELRIG

Small village. The C18 and C19 houses (some originally weavers' cottages) are mostly single-storey, built of white-painted rubble; several were formerly thatched.

CHAPEL FINIAN, 4.4km. W. Low remains of a small rectangular rubble-built chapel, probably of the C10 or C11. The long N and S walls have been buttressed. Door in the S wall's W end. The chapel has stood in a walled enclosure, with a well on the W side.

HIGH MILTON, 0.3km. W. Early C19 farmhouse of two storeys and three bays; low courtyard steading on the S.

HOUSE OF ELRIG, 2.1km. NW. Low-key but accomplished Arts and Crafts Scots manorial by *Stewart & Paterson*, 1912, with crowstepped gables and gableted dormerheads.

CORSEMALZIE HOUSE. *See* p. 190.

ELSHIESHIELDS TOWER
2.8km. NW of Lochmaben

72 C16 tower house of the Johnstones of Elshieshields, extended in the C18 and C19 to make a modest country house. The tower house itself is plausibly said to have been built in 1567, probably incorporating a C15 two-storey rectangular house. Harled crow-step-gabled L-plan of three storeys and an attic, the main block's walling unbroken by stringcourses. At its SE, SW and NW corners, fat conical-roofed round turrets projected on continuous corbelling. In the centre of the S front, a steep gablet containing the attic window. Higher NE stair jamb, its roof ridge running N–S in contrast to the main block's E–W roofline, giving a disjointed look to the whole. At the top of the jamb, a turret corbelled out in the inner angle. This contains a second stair to the jamb's two floors above the main stair. Each floor is marked off by a rope-moulded stringcourse, the upper serving as an eaves course to the turret and a sill course to the jamb's top windows. At the two top floors of the jamb and the SE and NW turrets of the main block, windows with rounded jambs. Rounded jambs again at the door in the jamb's inner face; it is guarded by a gunhole in the main block. Over this door, a sill-like projection, presumably part of the frame for a panel. Higher up, an empty panel frame decorated with nailhead enrichment. Another moulded panel frame on the main E gable. Projecting from the jamb's E side just below second-floor level, a moulded slop drain. Corbelled out at the jamb's S gable, a stone look-out post, a shothole in each side; its flat-roof may have been intended for a beacon.

Inside the tower, an unvaulted ground-floor store. Turnpike stair to the floors above. The first floor is occupied by the hall (now study). In its W wall, a simply moulded stone chimneypiece, probably of the later C17. Moulded rectangular aumbry in the E wall. In the N wall, another rectangular aumbry but its surround's soffit forms a pair of roundheaded arches with a central pendant (broken off) in place of a mullion (cf. the aumbry at Fairgirth House). The second floor again contains one room, presumably the principal bedchamber (now lower library). Quite large C16 moulded stone chimneypiece in the E wall. Contained in the thickness of the S wall, a pair of garderobes, each with a scat over the chute, the W garderobe also enjoying a window. On the main block's attic floor, again one room (now upper library), its boarded segmental vault introduced by *W. Schomberg Scott* in 1967. The jambs of the moulded C16 E fireplace bulge out at the top to form crude corbels. In each of the three turrets off this room, a round closet. In the jamb's small room directly over the main stair, a N fireplace. Attic room without a fireplace above.

A sizeable extension, effectively a second house, was added to the tower's W gable in the mid-C18 and enlarged and altered in the early and mid-C19. It is now smooth-rendered in contrast to the harling of the tower. Originally of two storeys and five bays, it was given an extra floor with steeply gableted windows in the 1830s. Probably at the same time, a flat-roofed and ball-finialled porch was added to the S front, and, either then or a little later, each pair of ground-floor windows on that front was converted to a broad canted bay window. Also in the 1830s, the rectangular C18 stair jamb at the back of this block was heightened and its gable was provided with crowsteps. The large Tudor porch on the E of this jamb may be slightly later. Single-storey W wing at right angles to the house built in 1848. Inside the main addition, simple mid-C18 panelling in the drawing room and first-floor bedrooms. Basket-arched bedroom chimneypieces. The drawing-room chimneypiece is late C18 (brought here in the mid-C20), of pine and gesso, its fluted pilasters with acanthus leaf capitals; shells, thistles and eagles on the frieze.

ESKDALEMUIR

Upland hamlet of C19 and C20 cottages.

PARISH CHURCH. Built in 1826, probably to a design by *John* 26 *Smallwood*, who had prepared plans the year before (*see* the Introduction, p. 40). Tall box, now drydashed, of three bays with mullioned and transomed Y-traceried pointed windows. At the S gable, an ashlar tower of four diminishing stages, the first with a pointed door, the second with a Gothick window matching the others; at the third a blind quatrefoil; hood-moulded belfry openings at the top. Octagonal stone spire by *Walter Miller*, 1853, replacing the original, which had been struck by lightning. Inside, round three sides, a semi-octagonal GALLERY on very thin cast-iron columns. – In the centre of the W wall, a high PULPIT with a sounding board. – CHAMBER ORGAN by *The Positive Organ Co. Ltd*, 1907. – Drily expression-

ist STAINED GLASS window (Our Lord and St Francis of
Assisi), signed by *W. J. R. Cook*, after 1938.

Small GRAVEYARD across the road to the E. Its centrepiece
is a large red sandstone MONUMENT to the Rev. William Brown
†1835. Cruciform pedestal carrying swagged urns flanking an
obelisk, its W face and urn finial carved with more swags. The
pedestal's inscription panel is framed by dowsed torches. –
Near the SW corner, HEADSTONE to John Elliot †1820, a
pedlar murdered by his travelling companion. The inscription
records the murder, the criminal's apprehension, trial and
execution and that the stone was erected in 1821 by the inhabitants of Eskdalemuir: 'in order to convey to future ages, their
abhorrance [*sic*] of a crime, which was attended with peculiar
aggravations; and their veneration for those laws, which pursue
with equal solicitude, the murderer of a poor friendless stranger,
as of a Peer of the realm . . .'

GRAVEYARD, 1.3km. S. Several C18 HEADSTONES, some aedicular, enthusiastically decorated with emblems of death,
several with angels' heads (souls) at the top or with lumpy
vines.

BRIDGE. Rebuilt in 1878. Of rubble, with two segmental arches.

SCHOOL. By *James Burnet*, 1872. Small, with bracketed eaves.

FORT, Castle O'er, 4.9km. S. Iron Age hillfort of the first millennium B.C., now surrounded by a forestry plantation. The
site is a steep rocky hill around whose roughly oblong summit
(*c.*120m. by 60m.) have been constructed a pair of ramparts
with a ditch between; entrances through the ramparts at the E
and SW. Rather later, a smaller inner enclosure (95m. by 35m.)
was formed on the NW area of the summit by the erection of a
drystone wall. Inside this second enclosure, traces of the stances
of nine round houses. More banks and ditches to the S and W
of the summit, not all necessarily defensive.

ROMAN FORT, Raeburnfoot, 1.2km. N. Fort of the mid-C2. The
earthworks of two enclosures, one inside the other, make this
unusual. The inner enclosure, surrounded by two ditches, contained timber buildings. The outer enclosure, with a single
ditch, may have been an annexe or a temporary camp.

ESKDALEMUIR AND ETTRICK REFORMED PRESBYTERIAN
CHURCH. *See* Davington.

ESKDALEMUIR OBSERVATORY. *See* Davington.

3090   EWES

Little more than the church and old manse standing beside the
A7.

PARISH CHURCH. By *James Burnet*, 1866–7. Grey rubble box with
hoodmoulded lancet windows, the S gable window of three lights
with attached shafts. Tall gableted bellcote. NE porch.

   In the graveyard to the SW, C18 HEADSTONES carved with
emblems of death. – MONUMENT to George Malcolm †1805.
Pedimented sarcophagus with free-standing Doric columns at

the corners, like the model of a Greek temple. MANSE to the S; mid-C19 with a corniced doorpiece.

BRIERYSHAW, 0.3km. E. Single-storey and attic *cottage orné* farmhouse of the earlier C19. Bargeboards and bracketed eaves; horizontal glazing. – Piend-roofed late Georgian STEADING to the N.

FORT, Brieryshaw Hill, 0.9km. N. Hillfort of the first millennium B.C. On the E side of the hill's flat summit, two broad ramparts of earth and stone, with a ditch, *c.* 9m. wide, between. The entrance has been on the E, where the ditch and outer rampart are discontinued. Outer ditch to the W.

ARKLETON. *See* p. 110.

FAIRGIRTH HOUSE

8050

1.2km. NW of Barend

Small limewashed laird's house. Its general appearance is late Georgian, but it has developed from a monastic grange traditionally said to have been associated with a chapel dedicated to St Laurence. The earliest part is the W end, perhaps built in the early C16. This seems to have been a freestanding rectangular block of two storeys and an attic, with a turnpike stair in the NE corner. In the S wall, the top of a door, its margin rounded. Small ground-floor window with a similar margin to the l. Good-sized first-floor window, the margin again rounded. In the W gable, a small first-floor window and a tiny light to the attic, both probably late Georgian insertions or replacements. Inside, an unvaulted ground-floor room. No fireplace, so probably this was a store. Moulded E fireplace in the room above. Probably in the later C16, the house was extended E by the addition of a hall. In the centre of the hall's S wall, a door with a roll-and-hollow moulding. The flanking windows and those of the first floor are all late Georgian, perhaps dating from the addition of the upper floor if it is not contemporary with the hall. Inside the hall (now sitting room), a very broad W fireplace with moulded stone jambs and a wooden lintel. In the N wall, an aumbry much like one at Elshieshields Tower (q.v.); its head is formed by a pair of round arches sharing a central pendant (now broken off). It is painted with stylized floral designs. The house's E end was added in the C19. Broad canted bay window of the 1920s at the W gable's ground floor. C20 brick additions at the back.

FOURMERKLAND TOWER

9080

1km. NW of Newbridge

Small (only *c.* 7.2m. by 5.8m.) and unpretentious rectangular, rubble-walled and crowstep-gabled four-storey tower house, built probably in 1590 for Robert Maxwell. Corbelled out at the NW and SE corners are round turrets, their upper masonry and conical roofs late C19 restorations. These turrets and the shothole-like gable openings lighting the roofspace are the only martial hints. Slit windows to the ground floor. Quite comfortably sized openings above, one at the first floor enlarged in the C19 when the top-floor dormers were provided. Simply moulded door at the s wall's w end. Above it, a panel bearing the Maxwell arms, the initials of Robert Maxwell and his wife, and the date 1590. Above the panel, a slop drain from the stair inside. The entrance opens onto the foot of the turnpike stair in the house's sw corner. Tunnel-vaulted store occupying the ground floor. At each of the upper floors, a single room equipped with a fireplace and one or more aumbries. The top floor is also provided with closets in the turrets.

FRENCHLAND TOWER
1.6km. E of Moffat

Ruin of a rubble-built three-storey-and-attic L-plan laird's house, the main block likely to have been constructed in the mid-C16 by the Frenches of Frenchland, its upper part remodelled and the sw jamb added probably early in the C17. Most of the main block's w wall and a large part of the E have fallen. At the N gable, four rounded corbels showing that, before the remodelling, there was a parapet here, the building's only sign of martial purpose. In this main block, rectangular windows with rounded margins. Chamfered margins at the windows of the later jamb. Inside, the C16 stair was a turnpike contained in the wall thickness of the sw corner; it was partly superseded in the C17 by a scale-and-platt stair (since removed) in the jamb which gave access to the first floor. The whole of the main block's first floor has been occupied by the hall. Part of its s fireplace's relieving arch survives; in the N gable, an off-centre segmental-arched recess. Rectangular aumbry, checked for a door, near the E wall's N end. In the jamb, there was a room on each of the two upper floors above the stair.

FRIARS CARSE
1.9km. SE of Auldgirth

The neat little piend-roofed laird's house, with a pediment over its front door, which was built in 1771–3 for Robert Burns' friend, Robert Riddell, has been submerged in a substantial but unimaginative castellated Baronial sprawl of 1873 by *James Barbour*. This was further extended by *James Barbour & Bowie* in 1909. – STABLE COURTYARD to the sw. Three of its ranges are rubble-built and early C19; the roof of the N range is straddled by a slated doocot. The front (E) range is of 1905, its masonry hammerdressed. Jerkin-headed gables projecting at the ends. In the centre, a piend-roofed tower over the segmental-arched pend. On the front, a reset armorial panel of

1598. – s of the mansion house, THE HERMITAGE, built
c.1785 but remodelled and refaced in 1874. Small rectangular
building, the gables crowstepped, shouldered arches to the
windows.

GALDENOCH CASTLE
4.3km. W of Leswalt

9060

Roofless rubble-built tower house, probably built in the mid-C16.
L-plan, the NE wing containing the principal stair. The gables'
crowsteps are built up with small stones covered with slates. A
SW turret projects on continuous corbelling but the corner of
the main block pokes through the arc. Dressings have mostly
been removed, but enough remain to show that the first-floor
windows have had simply moulded margins, those of the second
floor plain sandstone surrounds. Entrance in the N face of the
wing, with part of the moulded l. door jamb surviving.

Inside, on the ground floor of the main block, a tunnel-
vaulted room with a small window in each gable and indications
of a fireplace in the E wall. Aumbries at the NW and SE corners.
The turnpike stair rises in the wing to the second floor; another
stair off it serves the attic of the main block and a room at the
top of the wing. First-floor hall, only the r. jamb of the fireplace
in its E wall surviving. Aumbries in the other walls. In one ingo
of the E wall's S window, a door opening onto a very tight
turnpike, which is partly contained in the wall thickness of the
SE corner but also, as it rises, nudges into the hall and the
floorspace above. On the second floor have been two rooms,
the one at the S reached by this tight turnpike from the hall,
the one at the N from the main stair. Each has a gable fireplace
and an aumbry. Door above a high sill from the S room into
the SW turret.

GALLOWAY HOUSE
1km. S of Garlieston

4040

Set in a park, a huge barrack-like spread, all built of rubble
with rusticated quoins and dressings of polished red sandstone
ashlar, begun in 1740–2 by Alexander, Lord Garlies (later sixth
Earl of Galloway), but since altered and enlarged at least five
times. *John Baxter* was both contractor and architect for the
1740s house, adapting a design by *John Douglas*. This consisted
of a main block of three storeys over a basement, linked by
curved quadrants to two-storey-and-basement pavilions. The
W front of the piend-roofed main block was of five bays, the
centre three slightly advanced, with coupled giant Corinthian
pilasters at the corners carrying a modillion cornice. Above
the cornice, panelled pilasters supporting a pediment. Gibbs
surrounds to the ground-floor windows. Over the door, a consoled broken pediment, its tympanum carved with a coat of

arms by *Samuel Hyslop*, 1846, perhaps replacing an earlier
heraldic device. Above this, a first-floor window set in an egg-
and-dart surround flanked by large scrolls. The window each
side has a bracketed sill. Bracketed sills also under the windows
of the outer bays. The attic windows were originally of the same
size as those below: those of the centrepiece have bracketed
sills. The 1740s E elevation to the garden may originally have
been a simpler version of the front. Curved quadrants, each of
two storeys over a basement, with round-arched and key-
blocked ground-floor windows and square windows to the first
floor. The end pavilions were of three bays by two and plain.

Some alterations were made in 1764 for John, Lord Garlies
(later seventh Earl of Galloway) by *Robert Mylne*, but more
important seems to have been work carried out in 1808 and
costing over £2,000. This may have included the addition to
the centre of the E side of a large full-height bow with a ground-
floor stone balcony supported on Doric columns.

In 1842–9 a major enlargement of the house was undertaken
for Randolph, ninth Earl of Galloway, by *Burn & Bryce*. They
added an additional storey to each pavilion, the new second-
floor windows topped by pediments pushing up into the overall
balustrades. The main block was extended at each end by one
bay, continuing the C18 building line of the garden elevation
but set back behind the C18 quadrants on the W side. Across
each end of this extended main block was placed a two-storey-
and-basement wing, projecting in front of the main block to
the E. At the same time the first-floor windows in the outer
bays of the C18 W front were raised to correspond with a new
floor level behind; aprons were provided between the openings
and the original sills. The attic windows on this front were
shortened. On the garden front, the C18 outer bays' ground-
floor windows were enlarged to three lights to correspond with
those of the additions, and the upper-floor windows were also
altered.

Further work was carried out in 1870, perhaps the reconstruction or rebuilding of a low service wing to the N. Finally
in 1909 *Robert S. Lorimer* infilled the gap between the 1840s SE
wing and the SW pavilion with a single-storey bow-fronted and
balustraded extension.

98   Inside, the grandest room is Lorimer's entrance hall, created
in 1909 by throwing together the space behind the main block's
centrepiece formerly occupied by the C18 entrance-cum-stair
hall and a secondary stair. This new hall rises through two
storeys, with a first-floor wooden-balustraded balcony cantilevered out the length of its E side, and two tiers of window
on the W. Panelled walls and ceiling form a display of fibrous
plasterwork by *Thomas Beattie*, an opulent mixture of late C17
and early Georgian motifs. At the S end, two roundheaded
arches sharing an Ionic pier open into Lorimer's stairwell; its
plasterwork continues that of the hall, but the C17 influence is
stronger at the ceiling. Behind the hall, the bow-ended ground-
floor drawing room, with cornice and doorcases of the 1840s.

Inlaid marble chimneypiece, probably of 1909; the central panel of the frieze is carved with a bird and a fox. N of the drawing room is the suite of principal rooms (billiard room, library and dining room) provided by *Burn & Bryce* along the garden front; the first two survive substantially intact. To the S of the drawing room were the 1840s family rooms (study, bedroom, boudoir and, to the W, dressing room).

S of the house, a pilastered ARCHWAY flanked by giant scrolls; probably mid-C18. – Polygonal GARDEN to the SW, its walls built in 1809, the main wall of rubble, the internal division walls of brick. – Bow-ended WHITHORN LODGE at the main SW entrance to the policies. Mid-C19 picturesque, the overhanging eaves supported by wooden posts to form a verandah.

GARLIES CASTLE
3.7km. NE of Newton Stewart

4060

Low remains of a tower house built *c.*1500 for the Stewarts of Garlies (later Earls of Galloway). It has been a rubble-walled rectangle, *c.*9.1m. by 12.2m. The long S wall's W half and the NW corner are still quite high; of the rest, only the ground floor remains. In the N wall's E end, an inverted keyhole gunloop. Entrance in the centre of the N wall, opening into a wall passage which has been slab-lintelled. At the passage's W end, a small windowless guardroom, its side walls coved to carry lintel slabs over the top; aumbry in the W end. At the passage's E end, remains of a turnpike stair in the wall thickness of the house's NE corner. On the passage's S side, a pair of doors with chamfered surrounds and sharing a central jamb. They open into the main space of the ground floor, which has been divided into two rooms by a stone partition; the stubs of its ends are still in place. Both rooms have been vaulted. The one at the W has been a store lighted by slit windows in the S and W walls. Recess in the SW corner. The E room is much smaller, with only a S slit window. At its E wall, but not *in situ*, a large and smart fireplace of *c.*1500. Moulded Gothic jambs. Deep lintel under the frieze and cornice, the frieze carved with a relief of foliage coming out of the mouths of human heads. N of the fireplace, an aumbry. In the walling of the house's SE corner, a prison entered from above. The house formerly stood on the S side of a courtyard; its other ranges are now represented by heaps of stones.

GARLIESTON

4040

Substantial village on the shore of a bay, founded *c.*1760 and named after John, Lord Garlies (later seventh Earl of Galloway).

INDEPENDENT CHAPEL, Cowgate. Now a house (THE OLD CHURCH) and rather altered. Rendered piend-roofed box of 1804, the windows rectangular.

SORBIE PARISH CHURCH, o.8km. W. By *David Thomson* of
Glasgow, 1873–6. Big and bare Gothic, built of whin with red
sandstone dressings. Nave and E transepts; SW steeple with tall
and narrow belfry openings and a pyramidal slated spire. –
STAINED GLASS. E window (the Ascension) of *c.* 1876. – In
the S transept, a window (St Paul) by *Morris & Co.*, 1927, the
figures taken from a design by *Edward Burne-Jones.*

HARBOUR. Big rubble pier built in 1838 and extended in 1855.
On it, rubble-walled mid-C19 granaries and a big brick C20
grain mill. Stone breakwater to the S, constructed in 1843.

SCHOOL, off North Crescent. Late C19 Board school. Sparing
Tudor detail, with a few hoodmoulds; ball finials on the gables
and gablets.

DESCRIPTION. Along the shore, NORTH CRESCENT and
SOUTH CRESCENT form a shallow U-plan of terraced houses,
its long bottom a straight line, its ends bowed. Generally
straightforward C19 vernacular buildings, with a few of the
C20, mostly harled or rendered or of painted rubble. On the N
corner of MILL ROAD, which divides the two crescents, a late
C19 MILL WHEEL by *J. & F. Wallace* of Castle Douglas; it is
still in working order but to no purpose, since the mill itself has
gone. At Nos. 4–6 South Crescent, three early C19 two-storey
houses with club skewputts. The late Georgian No. 17 is modestly ambitious, the painted rubble walling framed by an ashlar
basecourse, strip quoins and an eaves band; Roman Doric
columns at the door. In CULDERRY ROW, behind North
Crescent, Victorian villas on the W side. The E side is mostly
single-storey early C19 vernacular, in whose company No. 15
(LINCOLN COTTAGE) of *c.* 1840 appears shockingly sophisticated. Neo-Jacobean, with intricate glazing in the hoodmoulded windows. Tudor-arched and hoodmoulded door at
the centre, with a finialled gablet flanked by corbelled-out
octagonal buttresses; in the gablet, an attic window, its sill
supported on semi-octagonal corbels, the hoodmould's label
stops carved with human heads. Behind South Crescent is
COWGATE, the architecture fragmentary but including the
former Independent Chapel (*see* above). HIGH STREET behind
has a better-preserved row of C19 vernacular houses on the E
side. At the corner with Mill Road, the early C19 QUEENS
ARMS HOTEL, with rusticated quoins and a cornice under the
eaves. Housing of the later C20 to the W.

GALLOWAY HOUSE. *See* p. 309.

GALLOWAY HOUSE. *See* p. 309.

0090   GARVALD

Isolated ruin of the church of a parish which was united with
Kirkmichael in 1674.

PARISH CHURCH. Remains of a rubble-built oblong, *c.* 18.4m.

by 6.8m. Rectangular door in the s wall's w end; its lintel is said*
to have been carved with the date 1617, presumably the year of
the church's erection or reconstruction. One moulded jamb
survives of the E window, which was two-light, of late Gothic
character.

BURRANCE OF COURANCE, 0.3km. E. Prosperous-looking
farmhouse. Front block of 1823 built of pinky-coloured rubble.
Two storeys and three bays, with a pilastered doorpiece. Big
early C20 rear extension with gableted stone dormerheads.

COURANCE HOUSE, 1.2km. E. Laird's house of *c.* 1840. Ashlar-
walled main block of two storeys over a basement, its piended
platform roof now with concrete tiles. Entrance front of three
bays, the slightly advanced and parapeted centre with a porch,
its frieze decorated with arcading. Two-light windows, those
of the ground floor corniced and set in minimally projecting
rectangular bays. Lower back wing, its basement and principal
floor C18, the first floor probably a mid-C19 addition.

ROSS MAINS. *See* p. 502.

GATEHOUSE OF FLEET   6050

Small burgh begun in the 1760s as a planned village on the estate
of James Murray of Broughton. A tannery was established here
in 1768 and breweries followed in the 1770s and 1780s; but rapid
growth began with the establishment of a cotton mill in 1785, the
year the village was made a burgh of barony. Seven years later the
population had reached 1,150, with four cotton mills providing
the principal employment. Industrial prosperity was short-lived:
two of the cotton mills closed in 1810 and the other two soon
after. Although cotton manufacture was begun again in 1832,
it was abandoned eighteen years later, and the town's population declined steadily during the second half of the C19, from
1,750 to a little over 1,000. The burgh now appears pleasantly
sleepy, the early industrial promise discernible only at second
glance.

CHURCHES

CHURCH OF THE RESURRECTION (R.C.), Riverbank. By *Sutherland, Dickie & Copland*, 1971. Church and hall contained in
a tall single-storey drydashed box with a deep wooden fascia;
the church's windows are vertical, the hall's horizontal. On the
E side of the church's N end, a monopitch-roofed clearstorey,
intended to light the altar; but this has been moved out from
the wall, on which still hangs a CRUCIFIX of 1971 by *Arthur
Dooley*.

* By the RCAHMS, whose Investigators visited the site in 1912.

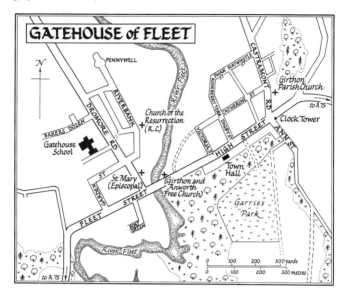

Former GIRTHON AND ANWOTH FREE CHURCH, High Street.
Secularized and the interior much altered. Built in 1844; an
M-roofed rectangle with pointed Gothic windows. At the E
gable, a confident four-stage square tower with three-light
belfry openings and sharp pinnacles on the parapet.

GIRTHON PARISH CHURCH, Castramont Road. As built in
1817–18, this was a harled box, plain except for the rectangular
windows' rusticated quoins. A reconstruction by *Thomson &
Menzies*, 1895–6, provided the windows with transomed round-
arched lights. At the S end it added a red sandstone ashlar
tower of three unadorned stages under a battlement with angle
rounds; inside the battlement, a low slated spire. Apse-ended
vestry projecting S from the tower; battlemented porch in the
inner angle. Inside, a plaster ceiling, presumably of 1818, with
a couple of swagged roundels enclosing large pendants. – FUR-
NISHINGS of 1896. – ORGAN by *Henry Finch*. – STAINED
GLASS. Three-light N window (the Nativity, Crucifixion and
Ascension), probably of 1896.

ST MARY (Episcopal), Dromore Road. Broad Gothic box, built
in 1840 as a United Associate chapel and acquired by the
Episcopalians early in the C20. – Mid-C19 STAINED GLASS,
the windows containing roundels framing portraits of heroes of
the Old Testament (Daniel and Isaiah), the New Testament
(SS. Peter, Paul, John the Baptist and Stephen) and the Reformation (Martin Luther and John Knox).

PUBLIC BUILDINGS

BRIDGE. Two segmental rubble arches built by *John Frew*,
1729–30. The bridge was widened in 1779 and again in 1811,
presumably the date of the present sturdy triangular cutwaters.
The roadway was further widened by the *Stewartry County
Council*, 1964–5, with a concrete deck of slab and cantilever construction, and the parapets replaced by utilitarian metal railings.

CLOCK TOWER, High Street. 1871, by *F. T. Pilkington* and 57
predictably wild. Above a tall battered base of schist and granite
the tower rises, broken only by a tall round-arched slit window
on each face, to a granite ashlar clock stage. Its corners are
corbelled out, in an inversion of the lower stage's batter, to
carry the springing of a segmental arch over the clockface of
each front. Above, an open belfry with heavy granite piers
supporting machicolation; parapet formed by stylized antefixae.

GATEHOUSE SCHOOL, Dromore Road. By *Stewartry County
Council*, 1964.

TOWN HALL, High Street. By *J. Robart Pearson*, 1884–5, of red
sandstone with a broad crowstepped centre gable. The hall was
reconstructed by *Stewartry District Council*, 1993–4, a pend
being punched through its centre, the Victorian roundheaded
entrance and sidelights converted into an arch flanked by rectangular openings containing Tuscan columns. The contrast of
late C20 classicism with C19 Scots is disconcerting.

DESCRIPTION

HIGH STREET begins at the WAR MEMORIAL by *Scott & Rae*,
1921, a granite Celtic cross, the faces carved with Pictish motifs.
On the r., the single-storey TOLL HOUSE of *c.*1823, L-plan
with bowed ends, bracketed broad eaves and diagonally set
chimneys. Then WOODSIDE TERRACE establishes a norm of
harled or rendered houses of one or two storeys. Opposite, a
garage followed by the long rear wing, set obliquely to the
street, of the Murray Arms Hotel (*see* below) and the Clock
Tower (*see* Public Buildings, above) where the street forms a
little square. In CASTRAMONT ROAD to the N, Girthon Parish
Church (*see* Churches, above).

ANN STREET to the SE is smarter. On its NE side, the MURRAY
ARMS HOTEL, its main block probably built in 1766 by *David
Skimming*, with rusticated quoins and a pilastered doorpiece.
The interior retains a large C18 kitchen fireplace with a pro-
jecting keystone and a broad pointed oven opening in each
ingo. The recessed SE wing combines with the humble mid-
C18 THE GATEHOUSE, to form a three-sided court. Then the
late Georgian MASONIC ARMS, smart with rusticated quoins. 117
Tripartite door under a three-light window, the centre openings
linked by a carved and painted heraldic achievement signed
'HYSLOP SCULP.' and dated 1812. Opposite, the CALLY
ESTATE OFFICE, harled late Georgian with additional

windows now inserted in the front. ROSEVILLE, of cherry-cock-pointed rubble, on the NE is early C19; inverted loop tracery in the fanlight. To its SE, NELSON SQUARE, a short and simple terrace dated 1812, with extra windows made in 1953. At Ann Street's SE end, ball-finialled early C19 GATE-PIERS to the park of Cally Palace (*see* p. 151) and the two-storey COX'S LODGE, built in 1824–5, with bracketed broad eaves and lattice glazing, the brick porch an addition of 1858–9. Beside it and set back, a tall mid-C19 house. To the NE, SCOTT'S MILL, built as a cotton mill, *c.*1790, three storeys of pa ited rubble. It was converted to three flats by *A. C. Wolffe & Partners* in 1994.

High Street SW of Ann Street is mostly early or mid-C19, the two-storey buildings generally painted or rendered. At Nos. 18–22, exposed granite ashlar masonry with cherry-cock pointing. No. 21 opposite is also of granite, but the ashlar is very rough and galleted with slivers of stone and brick. Simple pilastered doorpieces on Nos. 28 and 29. The late Georgian Nos. 34–40 comprise a provincially smart block with a basket-arched central pend and every other first-floor window a Venetian. It faces down DIGBY STREET, whose very simple early C19 houses and workshops are of rubble and brick. Passing under the street is the town's mill lade. At the N end, ROSE-BERRY TERRACE and SWAN STREET, an angled terrace of early C19 two-storey brick-built housing leading to the contemporary and quite utilitarian brick millworkers' houses of BIRTWHISTLE STREET.

In High Street SW of Digby Street, the BANK OF FLEET HOTEL with an aedicular doorpiece under a three-light first-floor window. On the l., immediately below the Town Hall (*see* Public Buildings, above), the mid-C19 No. 56, with hood-moulds over the ground-floor door and windows. In VICTORIA STREET, sitting beside the mill lade from the Water of Fleet, is a former BRASS FOUNDRY (now BURNSIDE) of the earlier C19, a two-storey U-plan of brick, with granite gables fronting the street. No. 65 High Street is Edwardian in its present form, a narrow front with a pedimented door; at the wallhead, a semicircular Jacobean pediment flanked by pinnacled dormer-heads. Just to its SW, BRUACHMORE, a piend-roofed harled house fronting an L-plan brick-built brewery of 1784. At the early C19 BRAE COTTAGE, round chimneys grouped on the centre of the roof. On High Street's l. side, the piend-roofed three-storey ANGEL HOTEL of *c.*1800, the outer windows of its three-bay SW front all of three lights; Venetian windows at the first floor. At the bottom of High Street, the former Girthon and Anwoth Free Church (*see* Churches, above), its tower a solid vertical accent. A path beside it leads NE to the rubble-built three-storey BOBBIN MILL, built as a cotton mill *c.*1790 and reconstructed in 1841 after a fire; at the S gable, a wheel signed by *W. Hay*, millwright, and *J. Affleck*, founder, 1824. To its SE, the ruin of another late C18 mill, to which a large wheel has been attached.

On the s side of the Fleet (for the bridge, *see* Public Buildings, above), DROMORE ROAD off to the r. leads past St Mary's Episcopal Church (*see* Churches, above). The main road is FLEET STREET. At its beginning, the ANWOTH HOTEL, mid-C19 with a pilastered doorpiece. Then plain terraced housing of the earlier C19, mostly rendered or harled, though the exposed masonry of Nos. 14–18 shows the independence of individual feuars; each of the three houses is built of stone from a different quarry and the rubble masonry is butt-jointed. On No. 29, an early C19 doorpiece with heavy columns and a small pediment.

FARMS

BARLAY MILL, 0.8km. N. Informal row of chunky painted rubble buildings, stepping up from a cottage at the s end to the mill itself at the N. Some of this may be C18, but a barn was built here in 1815 and further work was carried out in 1839 and 1854–5.

LOW BARLAY, 1.6km. N. Cottagey farmhouse built in 1850. Hoodmoulded windows and broad eaves.

VIADUCT

BIG WATER OF FLEET VIADUCT, 8.9km. NW. By *B. & E. Blyth*, 1861. The longest viaduct (*c.* 275m.) on the Portpatrick Railway's line from Castle Douglas to Stranraer and Portpatrick. Twenty spans, the seven at the E end built on a curve. Granite piers (now encased in brick), the segmental arches of brick, now braced with old rails.

CALLY PALACE. *See* p. 151.
CARDONESS CASTLE. *See* p. 157.
CARDONESS HOUSE. *See* p. 159.
RUSCO TOWER. *See* p. 502.
RUSKO. *See* p. 504.

GELSTON CASTLE
2.6km. SE of Kelton

7050

Galloway's most ambitious essay in the late Georgian castle style, now a roofless tree-surrounded shell. It was built *c.* 1805 for Sir William Douglas of Castle Douglas and Gelston; the architect was probably *Richard Crichton*. The general shape is that of a toy fort, with a round tower at each corner and, in the centre of each side, a tower feature rising above the standard height of two storeys over a high basement. The masonry is all of droved red sandstone ashlar, immaculately dressed. The corner towers are identical, each of four stages, marked off by band and string courses, under a corbelled battlement. Inside the battlement, a narrower short round turret, also battlemented. Each tower has tall slit windows, plain rectangles at the battered basement, rectangular but overarched at the second stage,

roundheaded and overarched at the third stage; at the top stage
and the turret, decorative circular panels. The band and string
courses of the towers stretch across the walling of the house's
four sides, tying up a tidy package.

At the outer bays of the entrance (s) front, a corbelled
battlement; round-arched windows to the *piano nobile*.
Forward-thrusting tripartite centrepiece of three storeys above
the basement. Its narrow ends are advanced as battlemented
square towers; their ground- and second-floor slit windows are
roundheaded and overarched, the first-floor lights hoodmoulded rectangles. These towers clasp the broad centre, its
piano-nobile door and flanking sidelights all roundheaded; the
perron is now missing. Above, a giant roundheaded overarch
enclosing the three close-set and aproned roundheaded first-
floor lights and elliptical-arched second-floor window. Uncrenellated corbelled parapet. Plain side elevations but with a hefty
battlemented chimneystack rising from the centre of each. At
the garden (N) front, the outer bays form two broad bows, their
battlements the only martial hint. Projecting between them, a
taller semi-octagon, its *piano-nobile* door and windows roundheaded and overarched. Hoodmoulded rectangular windows
to the first floor, roundheaded windows to the second. Corbelled but uncrenellated parapet, a tiny round turret at each
corner.

99			STABLES (now housing) to the SW, also of *c.* 1805, in the
same manner and clearly by the same architect as the house.
The courtyard is on the same alignment as the mansion but
slipped to one side, the effect of this asymmetrical relationship
now lost as a result of later planting. Front range again of
broached ashlar. Two-storey advanced ends, each with a broad
segmental-arched coach entrance under a trio of roundheaded
windows. Corbelled parapet, its front pierced by small crosslet
'arrowslits', the sides by circles; round turrets at the corners.
Tall single-storey battlemented links to the centrepiece. This is
an extravagant display. Octagonal tower of three tall stages, the
upper two inset. At the lowest stage, pierced by a segmental
pend arch, a corbelled battlement, its corner turrets taller versions of those at the ends. Second stage with a two-light hoodmoulded window in each face; solid stone cannon 'spouts' at
the parapet. At the top stage, each face is pierced by a window
crossed by a stringcourse, below which the window's bottom
part forms a blind panel decorated with blind double keyhole
'gunloops'. More 'gunloops' at the parapet; round turrets at its
corners. Battlemented rubble screen wall to the r., dressed up
with huge double keyhole 'gunloops' and a low battlemented
tower. – W of the stables, the early C19 Gothick COACH HOUSE,
extended from three to five bays in the later C20. – Behind the
stables, a rubble-walled GARDEN, probably of *c.* 1805. – On the
drive from the NE, a small BRIDGE, perhaps mid-C19, its
battlement formed by merlons stuck on top of the parapet. –
At the end of this drive and of the W drive, mid-C19 LODGES
of painted rubble, consoled cornices over the windows.

GILNOCKIE TOWER
3070
2.3km. N of Canonbie

Sometimes called Hollows Tower; a tower house beside the Esk, built for the Armstrongs probably in the mid-C16. After many years of dereliction it was reroofed in 1979–80 by *W. G. Dawson* and the interior was subsequently made habitable. It is a rubble-built rectangle, *c.* 10m. by 7.6m., with four storeys and an attic. Immediately above the projecting base, in each of the W and S walls, a rectangular gunloop; two gunloops, one above the other, in the N wall. Roll-and-hollow moulded door at the W wall's S end. Roll-moulded windows to the upper floors. Slit stair windows at the S wall's W end. The parapet (now missing, its place taken by a rail) was originally projected on rows of corbelling, the lower ones continuous, the two upper with alternately recessed and projecting moulded corbels. Immediately under the parapet, a rope-moulded stringcourse which has jumped up at the centre of each of the four round angle turrets. Rising within the parapet is the crowstep-gabled attic. Chimney at its N gable. Corbelled out from the S gable is a stone stand on which a warning beacon could be lit in the event of an English invasion.

Inside, each floor was originally filled by a single room, the turnpike stair nudging into its SW corner. Ground-floor store covered by an ashlar tunnel-vault and lighted by a high-set window in the N gable. The sill of the door into this room is a re-used sandstone slab, incised, probably in the second millennium B.C., with carving (now worn) of spirals and a key-like symbol. The first-floor hall has windows to E and W in round-arched embrasures; their stone seats have been restored. A third much smaller window high in the S gable. In the N gable, a fireplace with moulded jambs (the lintel missing) flanked by aumbries. The second floor probably contained the principal bedchamber. Windows like those of the floor below in the side walls, their stone seats original. At the N gable's E end, a plain fireplace. In the E wall, a garderobe, with the stone seating in place. The room's S end has been partitioned off as a bathroom. On the third floor, rectangular E and W window embrasures, their slabbed tops sloped towards the exterior. Window seats again. No visible evidence of a fireplace. The S end was again partitioned off in the 1980s. Featureless attic; its floor was raised in the 1980s when the door lintel was removed.

GIRTHON
6050

Little more than the old Parish Church and its manse (now Girthon Kirk).

Former PARISH CHURCH. Roofless since 1818, but the rubble-built walls, formerly harled, are largely intact. Much of the E gable and the immediately adjoining stretch of the S wall is late medieval; the rest is probably early C17 (*see* the Introduction,

p. 37). In the E gable, a stepped arrangement of three medieval round-arched windows. The gable's roundheaded door with a chamfered surround looks early C17. Door of the same type under a contemporary roundheaded window in the W gable, which is now missing its bellcote. Also apparently early C17 are the chamfered-margined and roundheaded windows in the long S wall which flank the central (minister's) door; over this door, a large rectangular fanlight. In the N wall, a door to a deep E gallery. Inside, at the S wall's E end, a weathered late medieval ogee-arched piscina.

Near the church's SW corner, a HEADSTONE to Richard Moray †1759, decorated with a pair of angels' heads (souls) above skulls and crossbones. – On the outside of the church's S wall, near its E end, an early C18 MONUMENT, the keystone of its lugged architrave carved with a cherub's head, the base with skulls and crossbones; on top, a broken pediment and urn finial. – Nearby, the HEADSTONE of Alexander Gordon †1760, the top carved with an angel's head above emblems of death. – Against the E gable, a worn STONE, perhaps C17, carved with the Maxwell coat of arms. – Next to it, a HEADSTONE, probably early C18, commemorating the Covenanting martyr Robert Lennox †1685. – A little to the E, the HEADSTONE of Robert Glover, late gardener at Cally, †1776, with a panel carved with reliefs of a rake, hoe and spade. – Near the graveyard's S wall, the HEADSTONE of David McTaggart †1773, aedicular with panelled pilasters and a curly pediment, the top carved with roses, an angel's head and foliage.

The harled GIRTHON KIRK to the N was built as the manse by *Patrick Blain* and *Samuel Kennan* in 1738–9 but has been enlarged and altered since. To its E, a single-storey range of FARM OFFICES, probably of 1812–14.

GIRTHON AND ANWOTH FREE CHURCH. *See* Gatehouse of Fleet.

GIRTHON PARISH CHURCH. *See* Gatehouse of Fleet.

4030   GLASSERTON

Church sitting by itself in the parkland of the demolished Glasserton House (*see* the Introduction, p. 67).

PARISH CHURCH. The body of the church was built by *William Lahwoor*, mason, and *Patrick Dunlop*, wright, in 1732. Simple rubble rectangle with round-arched windows, a forestair at the N wall's E end, and a ball finial on the E gable. On the W gable, a birdcage bellcote, probably C16 and traditionally said to have been re-used from the church of the suppressed parish of Kirkmaiden (*see* Monreith). Stumpy columns; ball finial on top of the ogee roof. The N 'aisle' and tower were added by *J. B. Papworth* in 1836–7. The 'aisle' itself is courteously similar to the 1730s church but has much taller windows. The three-stage tower, again of rubble, introduces unfussy late Georgian Gothic. Angle buttresses with massive copes over their intakes

1. New Abbey

2. Isle of Whithorn

3. Kirkdale, cairn (Cairnholy I), third and second millennia B.C.

4. Burnswark Hill, hillfort, sixth or fifth century B.C., and Roman camp, second century A.D.

5. Ruthwell, Ruthwell and Mount Kedar Church, Ruthwell Cross, probably early eighth century

6. Isle of Whithorn, St Ninian's Chapel, *c.* 1300, restored by P. MacGregor Chalmers, 1898

7. Buittle, Old Parish Church, probably twelfth and thirteenth centuries, altered probably in sixteenth and seventeenth centuries and in 1743–5

8. Cruggleton, Church, chancel arch, probably early twelfth century, restored by William Galloway, *c.* 1890

9. Whithorn, Whithorn Priory, south door of nave, made up in early seventeenth century from twelfth-century carved masonry

10. Dundrennan, Dundrennan Abbey, late twelfth century

11. New Abbey, Sweetheart Abbey, thirteenth and fourteenth centuries

12. New Abbey, Sweetheart Abbey, thirteenth and
fourteenth centuries

13. Glenluce, Glenluce Abbey, chapter house,
later fifteenth century

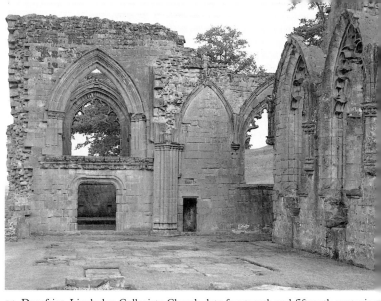

14. Dumfries, Lincluden Collegiate Church, late fourteenth and fifteenth centuries

15. Dumfries, Lincluden Collegiate Church, monument to Princess Margaret, Countess of Douglas, mid-fifteenth century

16. Dundrennan, Dundrennan Abbey, graveslab, probably thirteenth century

17. Sanquhar, St Bride's Parish Church, statue, probably early fifteenth century

18. Kirkcudbright, High Street, Selkirk Arms Hotel, font bowl, 1481 or 1482

19. Portpatrick, Old Parish Church (St Andrew's Kirk), tower, probably sixteenth century, with cupola of 1791

20. Anwoth, Old Parish Church, 1627, probably altered 1710

21. Annan, Old Parish Church, 1789–90

22. Dumfries, St Michael's and South Church, 1742–9

23. New Galloway, Kells Parish Church, by William McCandlish, 1822

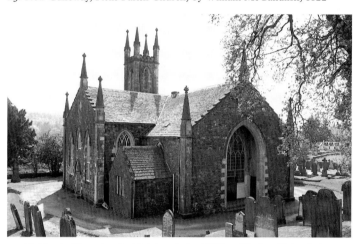

24. Kirkland, Glencairn Parish Church, by William McCandlish, 1836–7

25. Canonbie, Parish Church, by William Atkinson, 1821–2

26. Eskdalemuir, Parish Church, probably by John Smallwood, 1826

27. Lochmaben, Parish Church, by James Thomson, 1818–20

28. Dumfries, St Mary's Church, by John Henderson, 1837–9

29. Langholm, Langholm Parish Church, by Burn & Bryce, 1842–6

30. Annan, Old Parish Church, magistrates' pew, 1789

31. Kirkcudbright, Kirkcudbright Parish Church, pulpit,
by William Burn, 1838

32. Dumfries, Greyfriars Church, by John Starforth, 1865–8

33. Challoch, All Saints Episcopal Church, by W.G. Habershon & Pite, 1871–2

34. Moffat, St Andrew's Parish Church,
by John Starforth, 1884–7

35. Challoch, All Saints Episcopal Church,
by W.G. Habershon & Pite, 1871–2

36. Dumfries, Crichton Royal Hospital, Crichton Memorial Church,
by Sydney Mitchell, 1890–7

37. Dumfries, Crichton Royal Hospital, Crichton
Memorial Church, by Sydney Mitchell, 1890–7

38. Caulkerbush, Southwick Parish Church, by Kinnear & Peddie, 1889–91

39. Eastriggs, Church of St John the Evangelist (Episcopal),
by C.M. Crickmer, 1917

40. Gretna, St Ninian's (R.C.) Church, by C. Evelyn Simmons, 1918

41. Gretna, St Ninian's (R.C.) Church, by C. Evelyn Simmons, 1918

42. Dumfries, Crichton Royal Hospital, Crichton Memorial Church,
stained glass, by Glass Stainers Co., 1897

3. Lockerbie, All Saints Episcopal Church, altarpiece, by J. Ninian Comper, *c.* 1920

44. Anwoth, Old Parish Church, monument to the Gordons of Cullindoch, *c.* 1635

45. Kirkcudbright, Greyfriars Episcopal Church,
monument to the MacLellans of Bombie, *c.* 1635

46. Tundergarth, Parish Church, headstone of George McLean †1760

47. New Galloway, Kells Parish Church,
headstone of John Murray †1777

48. Durisdeer, Parish Church, monument to second Duke of Queensberry and his wife, by John van Nost, 1713

49. Newton Stewart, Monigaff Parish Church, monument to
Patrick Heron †1761 and Patrick Heron jun. †1761

50. Terregles, Parish Church, chancel, 1588

51. Bentpath, Westerkirk Parish Church, Johnstone Mausoleum, by Robert Adam, 1790

52. Kelton, Parish Church, Douglas Mausoleum, probably by William Douglas, 1821

53. Kirkland, Glencairn Parish Church, Gillespie Mausoleum, early nineteenth century

54. Dumfries, St Michael's and South Church, Burns Mausoleum, by T.F. Hunt, 1815–16

55. Carnsalloch House, chapel, by E.B. Lamb, 1847

56. Dumfries, Queensberry Monument,
by Robert Adam, 1780

57. Gatehouse of Fleet, clock tower, by F.T. Pilkington, 1871

58. Moffat, High Street, Colvin Fountain,
by William Brodie, 1875

59. Glenkiln, 'Glenkiln Cross',
by Henry Moore, 1955–6

60. Haugh of Urr, motte, Mote of Urr, probably mid-twelfth century

61. Caerlaverock Castle, thirteenth century to seventeenth century

62. Morton Castle, probably early fourteenth century

63. Caerlaverock Castle, gatehouse, mid-thirteenth century, reconstructed in later fourteenth century, fifteenth century and 1593

64. Threave Castle, late fourteenth century

65. Cardoness Castle, late fifteenth century

66. Orchardton Tower, late fifteenth century

67. Rusco Tower, c. 1500

68. Comlongon Castle, probably *c.* 1450, the top remodelled
in the early seventeenth century

69. Comlongon Castle, hall, probably *c.* 1450

70. Repentance Tower, 1565

71. Hills Tower, early sixteenth century, with addition of 1721,
and gatehouse of 1598

72. Elshieshields Tower, probably of 1567, incorporating fifteenth-century work

73. Castle of Park, 1590

74. Amisfield Tower, 1600

75. Stranraer, Castle of St John, *c.* 1510, remodelled *c.* 1600 and 1821–2

76. Kirkcudbright, MacLellan's Castle, begun 1581

77. Caerlaverock Castle, east range, early seventeenth century

78. Drumlanrig Castle, north front, 1675–90

79. Drumlanrig Castle, carving on north range, by Peter Paul Boyse
or Cornelius van Nerven, *c.* 1686

80. Drumlanrig Castle,
state stair, 1697

81. Tinwald, Tinwald House, by William Adam, 1738–40

82. Moffat, Moffat House, by John Adam, 1762–7

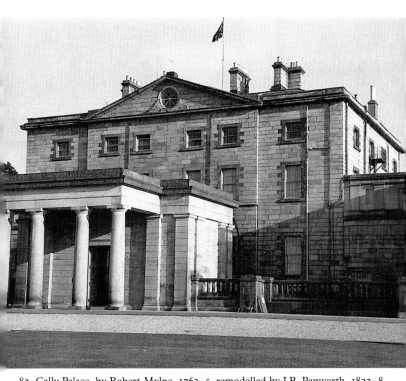

83. Cally Palace, by Robert Mylne, 1763–5, remodelled by J.B. Papworth, 1833–8

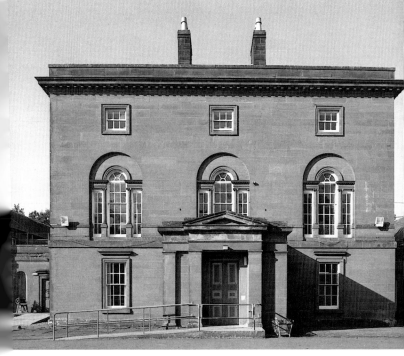

84. Carnsalloch House, 1754–9

85. Knockhill, 1777

86. Rammerscales, 1768

87. Raehills House, by Alexander Stevens jun., 1782

88. Kirkdale, Kirkdale House, by R. & J. Adam, 1787–8

89. Kinmount House, by Robert Smirke, 1812–18, with balustrades added by James Barbour & Bowie, 1899

90. The Grove, by Thomas Rickman, 1825, enlarged by Peddie & Kinnear, 1869

91. Barwhinnock, *c.* 1830

92. Barwhinnock, entrance hall, *c.* 1830

93. Lochinch Castle, by Brown & Wardrop, 1864 8

94. Threave House, by C.G.H. Kinnear, 1871–3

95. Castlemilk, by David Bryce, 1864–70

96. Castlemilk, gallery, by David Bryce, 1864–70

97. Old Place of Mochrum, by Richard Park, 1873–c. 1880, incorporating remains of fifteenth and early seventeenth-century work

98. Galloway House, entrance hall, by Robert S. Lorimer, 1909

99. Gelston Castle, stables, probably by Richard Crichton, *c.* 1805

100. Barjarg Tower, lodge and gatehouse, early nineteenth century

101. Dumfries, Old Bridge, *c.* 1430–2, reconstructed 1620, and shortened early nineteenth century

102. Auldgirth, Old Bridge, by David Henderson, 1781–2

103. Southerness, lighthouse, 1748–9, heightened *c.* 1785
and by Walter Newall, 1842–3

104. Port Logan, harbour, 1818–22

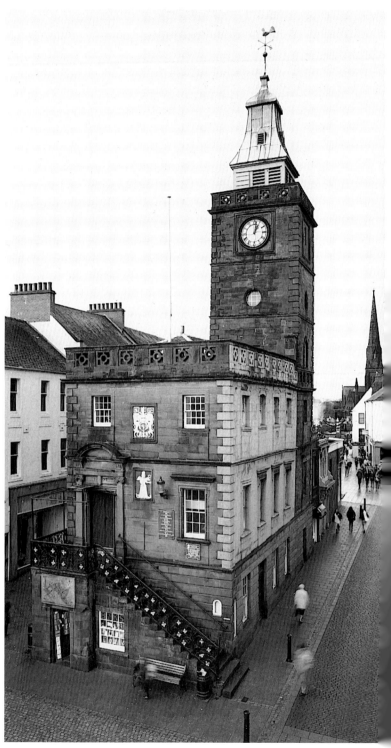

105. Dumfries, Midsteeple, by Tobias Bachop, 1705–7

106. Kirkcudbright, Tolbooth, 1625–7, with east tower of 1642 and mid-eighteenth-century west extension

107. Whithorn, Town House, steeple, probably of 1708

108. Sanquhar, Tolbooth, by William Adam, 1735–7

109. Lochmaben, Town Hall, by D. & J. Bryce, 1876–7, with tower of 1722–3, its spire of 1743–5

110. Dumfries, Dumfries and Galloway Health Board Offices (former Dumfries and Galloway Royal Infirmary), by John Starforth, 1869–73

111. Wigtown, County Buildings and Town Hall, by Brown & Wardrop, 1862–3

112. Dumfries, Crichton Royal Hospital, Crichton Hall, central octagon, by William Burn, 1835–9, remodelled by W.L. Moffat, 1870–1

113. Newton Stewart, Samuel Douglas' Free School, by John Henderson, 1834

114. Whithorn, George Street, Pend Arch, probably late fifteenth century

115. Dumfries, No. 24 Nith Place, 1753

116. Ecclefechan, Carlyle's Birthplace, Carlyle Place, 1791

117. Gatehouse of Fleet, Ann Street, Masonic Arms, 1812

118. Kirkcudbright, High Street, No. 117, *c.* 1790, and No. 119, early nineteenth century

119. Dumfries, Castle Street, probably by Robert Burn, *c.* 1810

120. Annan, former Southern Bank of Scotland, No. 73 High Street, *c.* 1845

121. Beattock, Old Brig Rest Home, probably by Thomas Telford, 1822

122. Moffat, Sidmount Avenue, Sidmount Cottage, by Walter Newall, 1832

123. Parton, cottages, 1901

124. Ecclefechan, Shortrigg, windmill, eighteenth century, and horsemill, early nineteenth century

125. Kirkandrews, Corseyard, steading, 1911–14

126. Tongland, Tongland Power Station, by Sir Alexander Gibb & Partners, 1934

127. Chapelcross, Power Station, by Merz & McLellan and L.J. Couves & Partners, 1955–60

and surmounted by big crocketed pinnacles. A gableted bellcote in the centre of each face of the battlement. In the E face, an off-centre pointed door inserted in 1891 by *David Henry* of St Andrews. The interior was remodelled in 1891, when Henry reduced the size of the E and W galleries and introduced the N gallery, pews and pulpit.

Attached to the church's SE corner is a roofless MAUSOLEUM dated 1834. Set into the blocking of its entrance are two stones carved with a coat of arms and the inscription 'HEIR LYIS D.G.G. [Dame Grizel Gordon] LADY GARLEIS.QVHA. DECEISSIT. THE. XII. DAY. AVGVST. YE. ZEIR. OF. GOD 159–.' – Immediately to its E, an C18 HEADSTONE, the front carved with a leafy border framing the depiction of an angel's head (the soul) above an hourglass flanked by skulls; crossbones at the bottom. – S of the mausoleum, the HEAD-STONE of William Hannay, tenant in Upper Ersock, †1773, with the verse inscription:

> Stop Passenger the humbler virtues know
> Of one in life, that never made a foe.
> Honest and plain, and still as light was giv'n
> He trod with willing steps the path to heav'n.
> What tho' the Rich dispise the lowly kind,
> They not in God a partial Judge shall find.
> Beyond the grave all vain distinctions cease
> And only Saints are crown'd with endless peace.

– Just S of the church, another C18 HEADSTONE carved with an angel's head above an hourglass-flanked skull. – At the graveyard's NE corner, the early C18 MAUSOLEUM of the John-ston Stewarts of Physgill and Glasserton. Rubble-built with rusticated quoins. Ball finials on the corners of the cornice. Empty panel-frame over the off-centre N door. – At the church-yard's entrance, a picturesque SESSION HOUSE AND STABLE of *c*.1830.

PHYSGILL HOUSE. *See* p. 489.
ST NINIAN'S CAVE. *See* p. 510.

GLENAE

9080

2.1km. NW of Amisfield Town

Creeper-clad small mansion house built in 1789–90 for the laird and advocate John Dalzell of Glenae. *Thomas Boyd* was the architect, *William Hyslop* the mason. It is all of broached red sandstone ashlar. Main block of two storeys over a high base-ment marked off by a band course. Five bays. The ground- and first-floor windows' architraves are delicately moulded; those of the ground-floor *piano nobile* have cornices and dentil friezes. Concave-sided stair to the entrance, its segmental-fanlit opening framed by an Ionic-columned aedicule. Recessed single-storey-and-basement links to piend-roofed pavilions. Each pavilion is again of one storey and a basement, but they are treated differently. In the E pavilion's front, a three-light window to the basement. The window above is of three lights, the outer blind, and would be a Venetian were the central opening arched. Big and blind three-light window in the w pavilion.

The principal rooms on the ground floor have high-quality carved pine chimneypieces, the one in the dining room decorated with foliaged drapes and urns. In this room, a round-arched and keyblocked sideboard recess, rosettes on the soffit, acanthus leaf capitals at the piers, their panelled fronts adorned with carved grapes. Large but shallow ceiling rose set in husked swags over the semicircular stair.

On the lawn in front, four weathered mid-C19 STATUES of gryphons, removed from the Palace of Westminster in the 1950s.

9060   GLENCAPLE

Village near the mouth of the Nith. In the C18 and C19, ships too large to sail higher up the river loaded and unloaded here, and there was a small boat-building industry. Glencaple was also a destination for Victorian strollers from Dumfries. It consists largely of C19 terraced cottages, many now with box dormers.

CHURCH, off Church Street. Built as a Free church in 1856; designed by *William McGowan*. Red sandstone box, the windows rectangular. At the front gable, a slightly advanced buttress-like centre containing a round-arched door and supporting a gableted bellcote with roundheaded openings.

BARBOUR MEMORIAL HALL, Church Street. Dated 1938. Unexciting, the front rendered with brick dressings.

CAERLAVEROCK SCHOOL, Church Street. By *Dumfries and Galloway Regional Council*, 1978–9. Brown brick walls, the huge pitched roof sweeping down to brick flying buttresses.

PIER, Shore Road. Large rubble-built pier of 1836–40.

Former SCHOOL, Church Street. Late C19, with broad eaves.

KIRKCONNEL LEA, 1.9km. S. Large and determinedly asymmetrical villa of *c.* 1870, built of bullnosed red sandstone. Broad eaves and carved bargeboards. Octagonal towers and turrets at the corners, now without their cresting. Also missing is the verandah which used to stretch along two sides. – In the garden, a battlemented and machicolated late C19 semicircular TOWER. – Also late C19 is the GARDEN SHED N of the house, built of brick with red sandstone dressings, a partly 'ruined' tower at its centre.

CONHEATH. *See* p. 189.

GLENKILN

2.9km. NW of Shawhead

Hill-farming estate. The HOUSE at the E end of Glenkiln Reservoir is a quite unpretentious cottage farmhouse, probably of the mid-C19. To it were added in the later C20 a couple of octagonal pavilions, one a rebuilt lodge of *c.*1770 from the demolished mansion house of Mollance, near Castle Douglas, the other a copy. – On the surrounding moorland, and seeming almost a natural part of it, is a collection of SCULPTURE, all bought by the estate's owner, Sir William Keswick, between 1951 and 1976. Beside the road running SE towards Kirkpatrick Durham from just E of the house, the 1.93m.-long 'Two Piece Reclining Figure No. 1' by *Henry Moore*, 1959 (the fibreglass cast erected here in 1976), the human figure suggested by two sculpted masses, the space between asserting a presence of its own. It is, according to the artist, 'a mixture of the human figure and landscape, a metaphor of the relationship of humanity with the earth, just as a poem can be.' – Beside a second road which runs NE past the house and reservoir, another work by Moore, the 'King and Queen' of 1952–3, a pair of seated hieratic figures, stylized except for naturalistic hands and feet.* – A track (the 'Covenanters' Road') goes over the hill to the S. In a clump of pines below it, the 'Visitation' by *Jacob Epstein*, 1926, the 1.65m.-high bronze figure of Our Lady an expression of humility, with bowed head and folded hands. – *c.*0.9m. W of the 'King and Queen', set on the top of a hill, the 'Glenkiln Cross', a 3.35m.-high bronze of 1955–6, again by *Moore*. Emblems of the Crucifixion on the tapering rectangular pedestal, which carries a craggily rounded conflation of the cross and the human form. – At the reservoir's W end, the tall bronze statue of an urgently striding 'John the Baptist' by *Auguste Rodin*, 1878–80. – A little further on, another bronze by *Henry Moore*, his 'Standing Figure' of 1950, a surprisingly sensuous composition of voids and curving pin-headed solids.

GLENLEE PARK

1.4km. SW of St John's Town of Dalry

Country house-villa of 1823, incorporating and remodelling a small C18 house. A picturesque design provided by *Robert Lugar* and illustrated in his *Villa Architecture* was modified in execution (not to its benefit), and alterations have been made since, including the rendering of the main walling and painting of the dressings and rusticated quoins. The roofs were deprived of their broad eaves and the heavy corniced chimneystacks were replaced with rows of octagonal chimneys *c.*1860.

The house is made up of an assemblage of two-storey blocks,

---

* At the beginning of 1995 vandals decapitated the figures, and the heads have not been found. The Henry Moore Foundation is to mould and cast replica heads in late 1995 but will only attach them to the figures if fully satisfied with the result.

almost all piend-roofed, of different sizes and heights. On the
W, three unequal-sized blocks. At the taller and advanced centre
of these, a porch, its pediment unexecuted or later removed,
with a hoodmoulded round-arched door to the front and roundheaded windows in the sides. The N block is of one bay by
three, presenting to the front its short side with a three-light
ground-floor window, which is console-corniced like most
other windows of this storey. The S block is square, again with
a three-light front window. E of this, what remains of the C18
house, which was gripped at each end by a higher and advanced
block of 1823. The W block was intended by Lugar to be fronted
by a bold bow rising as a round tower above the eaves of the
blocks each side. In execution the bow was omitted, so this
block appears as a tall but staid pavilion. The second tall
rectangular pavilion at the other end is broader than originally
intended. The front half of the C18 house between these pavilions was removed in the 1950s, producing a deep U-plan. The
house's N and E sides are informal: parts of the E side were
demolished in the 1950s; at the N side, a corbelled first-floor
oriel window, probably of *c*.1860.

GLENLUCE

Large village, its appearance almost that of a small burgh. It
developed in the early C19, principally as a local centre, and now
makes an agreeable base for visitors to western Galloway.

GLENLUCE ABBEY
1.8km. NW

Fairly fragmentary ruin of a Cistercian abbey founded by Roland,
lord of Galloway, in 1190 or 1192; the first monks were brought
from Dundrennan. After 1544, when the Earl of Cassilis expelled
the abbot from the monastery, possession of the buildings was
disputed between the Earls of Cassilis and the Gordons of Lochinvar; the monks may have been deprived of their residence even
before the Reformation of 1560. By 1602, when Laurence Gordon
obtained a charter, the buildings were named the 'manor or place
of Glenluce called of old the monastery of Glenluce', their use
apparently wholly secular.

Little remains of the ABBEY CHURCH of *c*.1200 other than the
bottom courses of rubble-built walls. It has been cruciform on
the standard Cistercian pattern, with a six-bay aisled nave, two-
bay transepts, each with a pair of E chapels, and an unaisled
rectangular presbytery of two bays. The W front has had clasping buttresses at the corners and buttresses marking off the
nave from the aisles; three W doors. The NAVE's four W bays
have been partitioned off, the central vessel and N aisle forming
one space, the S aisle another, the dividing walls perhaps put
up in the C16, when this part of the nave was no longer required

1 Nave
2 North transept
3 South transept
4 Presbytery
5 Sacristy
6 Slype
7 Chapter house

30 m

Glenluce Abbey. Plan

for lay brothers, but it is more likely to be of the later C16. The
bottom of the N nave arcade's E pier survives; it is a plain
octagon. To its E, the base of the NW CROSSING pier, rectangular, with a rounded attached column on the W face, shafts
on the E. Attached columns at the surviving bottom of the
crossing's NE respond. Much of the PRESBYTERY's S wall still
stands. At its W end, the upper part of a respond. Clustered
shafts with elided caps on the W face; on its N face, a slender
shaft with a weathered foliaged capital from which rises a
vaulting-shaft, again with an elided cap. In this S wall, the W

jamb of the E window with its internal hoodmould springing from a carved corbel; the window used to be round-arched.

Very little remains of the N transept. The SOUTH TRANSEPT and its chapels are much more complete. The chapels were each covered with a quadripartite vault, its ribs springing at the E wall from conical shafts with elided caps supported by corbels, at the W from corner responds, and a central pier between the chapel entrances. In the C15 or C16 this pier was swallowed up in a partition wall. Perhaps at the same time the lean-to roof over the chapels was heightened to give a gallery above the vaults, blocking the transept's clearstorey, a jamb of whose N window is still visible. Lighting the gallery, a small pointed window in the S wall. In the E wall of each of the chapels, just S of where the altar stood, evidence of an aumbry. The S wall of each has contained a trefoil-headed piscina: the S is *in situ*; fragments of the N were re-erected *c.* 1910 on top of the remains of the partition wall. In the N chapel's N wall, an aumbry checked for a door; it may be a C16 insertion.

In the S transept itself, at the E end of the gable, a simply moulded door to the adjoining sacristy. Beside this door, a large recess, possibly for a tomb but now robbed of dressings. In the SW corner, the base of the night stair from the monks' dormitory, the W jamb of its moulded door, *c.* 2.1m. above the ground, still *in situ*. Higher up, in the centre of the gable, the projection of a turnpike stair entered from the dormitory to the S. This turnpike, together with the upper part of the gable, dates from a C15 or C16 remodelling which provided three floors above the transept, their joists supported on wall scarcements. The first floor was at the same level as the gallery over the chapels. The second floor has been well lit from two pointed windows which flank the door from an attic above the dormitory. At the top floor, a rectangular window almost at the apex of the gable.

At the N end of the cloister's E range has been the SACRISTY. Small aumbry in its N wall; evidence of a built-up pointed door in the S. To its S, the tunnel-vaulted slype, a C20 rebuild. At the E end of this passage, some medieval red floor tiles.

S of the slype is the CHAPTER HOUSE, by far the best-preserved of the abbey buildings (it was repaired in 1910–11 by *P. MacGregor Chalmers*). It almost certainly dates from the later C15, when the whole E range may have been rebuilt. Entrance through a semicircular arch springing from nook-shafted piers; the capitals are carved with rather blocky stylized foliage. Inside, more stylized foliage on the capitals of the central pier's clustered shafts, from which spring the sturdy ribs of the sexpartite vault. At their other end, the ribs rose from corbels; most are decorated with bands of horizontal moulding, but two are carved with the heads and trunks of human figures, one holding a scroll inscribed 'REQUIESCAT IN PACE'. The ceiling bosses are carved with foliage, rosettes surrounded by faces, and two have coats of arms (the royal arms of Scotland with angel supporters, and the arms of Galloway flanked by grotesque heads). The door's hoodmould springs from corbels carved with human heads. On the central stone of its arch's soffit, a line of five rosettes. At the E wall of the chapter house, the back of the abbot's stall, its trefoil head surmounted by a mitre flanked by rosettes. The stall is placed between two rather short windows, their mullions renewed, each of three trefoil-headed lights under a quatrefoil, very like the E windows in the chapter house of Crossraguel Abbey (Ayrshire), suggesting that the same masons may have worked at both buildings. In the centre of the floor, medieval tiles, not very happily surrounded by quarry tiles.

s of the chapter house are a pair of tall tunnel-vaulted rooms, the s entered from outside the cloister. Each has contained a wooden entresol floor, the joists of the N held by wall sockets. The s room's joists have been supported on crude corbels and this floor seems to have been an insertion, cutting across the splayed embrasure of the narrow s window and leaving insufficient headroom for an adult to stand upright below.

The cloister's s (refectory) range was subdivided in the C16 and is now fairly fragmentary. At the w end, a kitchen fireplace. The w range, also fragmentary, is probably largely C16. In it, a couple of tunnel-vaulted stores. On this range's w side, a rectangular tower, perhaps late C16, of three storeys under a double-pitch roof. Ground-floor doors to E and W, the w blocked. At the first floor, an E door (blocked) and a w window. The top has been a doocot.

The arcading of the CLOISTER WALK has been reconstructed on the E side of the garth, with a dwarf wall carrying plain pointed arches. At the E walk's N end, a book press. On the s side of the garth, the bottoms of round piers on tapering octagonal bases.

A little s of the cloister, the bottom courses of the rubble walls of OUTBUILDINGS; their date and function are uncertain.

MONUMENTS. Inside the choir, on the s wall, an heraldic stone commemorating Thomas Hay of Park and his wife, Jane Hamilton; it is dated 1663 or 1683. – In the N transept, the GRAVESLAB of Robert Gordon of Lochinvar †1548.

CHURCHES AND PUBLIC BUILDINGS

GLENLUCE FREE CHURCH, North Street. Secularized and altered. Built in 1846 by *Alexander McLelland*, mason, and *Edward Sproat*, wright. A harled box with roundheaded windows, the w bellcote now missing.

OLD LUCE PARISH CHURCH, Church Street. T-plan kirk of 1814, the walls now drydashed and the roof slates replaced by tiles. Birdcage bellcote on the w end; a large round window in the E gable, perhaps an insertion. In the s wall and the w and N gables, roundheaded windows with projecting keystones and imposts, the s windows surmounted by an upper tier of horizontally proportioned rectangular lights. The windows in the other walls are simple rectangles. Forestair against the N aisle's

E side. Two other forestairs (at the E and W gables) were
removed in 1967–8.

(Interior much altered in 1967–8 by *Hill, Macdonald & Potter*,
who removed the E gallery to form a 'chancel', extended the W
gallery and partitioned off the back of the N gallery for a session
house above a vestry. – STAINED GLASS. In the porch, two
lights (the Light of the World, the Good Shepherd) by *William
Meikle & Sons*, 1905, imported from the demolished Glenluce
United Presbyterian Church. – ORGAN by *Casey & Cairney*,
1968.)

E of the church, an ivy-covered BURIAL ENCLOSURE,
perhaps early C19, with a coat of arms over the entrance. – S of
the church, a weathered GRAVESLAB incised with a skull and
the date 1677. – To its W, the HEADSTONE of William Tem-
pleton †1724, the front decorated with an angel's head (the
soul) above reminders of death framed by climbing roses.

PUBLIC HALL, Main Street. By *Richard Park*, 1878. Broad gable
front, with a stumpy spired clock turret corbelled out at the
apex.

RAILWAY VIADUCT, 0.4km. W. By *B. & E. Blyth*, 1858–61.
Built of whinstone and much repaired in dark red brick. Eight
segmental arches carried on trapezoid piers.

DESCRIPTION

MILLBANK at the E end of the village is a mid-C19 *cottage orné*.
Hoodmoulds over the windows, those of the upper floor with
rosette labels. Carved wooden trefoil pendants hanging from
the broad eaves; lacily fretted bargeboards. Then not much
until the junction with North Street (for the former Glenluce
Free Church there, *see* above), which marks the start of tight-
knit terraced development in MAIN STREET, a mostly two-
storey mix of commerce and housing. On the r., KELVIN
HOUSE HOTEL, mid-C19 Georgian-survival, has a pilastered
doorpiece and three-light windows at the ground floor, but the
outer windows above are of two lights. The ROWAN TREE
GUEST HOUSE opposite is a little earlier; it has a heavy flattened urn finial on its advanced and pedimented centre. Also
early C19 and with a pilastered doorpiece is No. 30, jutting
forward as the street bends. *See* above for the Public Hall and
for Old Luce Parish Church, which stands aloof in Church
Street. On the corner of Church Street, the ROYAL (former
NATIONAL) BANK OF SCOTLAND by *T. P. Marwick*, 1899–
1900, with mullioned and transomed windows, big and round-
arched at the ground floor. Then the scale drops and the village
peters out.

CAIRNS, Mid Gleniron, 3.2km. N. Two long cairns; their
development in the fourth or third millennia B.C. was established by excavation in 1963–6. The N (MID GLENIRON I)
began as a small roughly square cairn, *c.*6m. by 5.8m., built
of small stones and containing an orthostat-sided rectangular
chamber, *c.*2.9m. by 0.62m., entered from the N. There was

then built, *c*. 4.3m. to the N, a second oval-shaped cairn, *c*. 7m. by 4.6m. It contained a chamber *c*. 2.3m. by 1m. and 1.4m. high; each of its side walls were built of a single slab, the S end stone placed askew between them. The chamber was later extended N to a length of 3.2m.; the extension's walls were of drystone construction and carried out to the portal stones of the cairn front. The next development was the erection of a third trapezoidal-shaped cairn sited between the two earlier ones. Its chamber was again rectangular, *c*. 2.2m. by 0.76m., and built of orthostats, but it is at right angles to the earlier chambers. Probably contemporary with this chamber's construction was the unification of all three in a single cairn, its crescent-shaped N front faced with orthostats linked by drystone masonry. Nine Bronze Age cremations in urns were later inserted into the E flank. The ruin of an almost square CAIRN, *c*. 10m. by 9.1m., lies *c*. 4m. S.

120m. S of Mid Gleniron I is the much more ruined MID GLENIRON II, again a long cairn, trapezoidal in shape, *c*. 12.8m. long, 11.3m. broad at the N end and 7.3m. at the S. It began as a small E-facing oval-chambered cairn at the S end. There was later added, just to its N, a larger S-facing rectangular chambered cairn, the two then being united as a long cairn. To the S, a round BURIAL CAIRN, *c*. 17m. in diameter and 2.75m. high.

CARSCREUGH CASTLE. *See* p. 163.
CASTLE OF PARK. *See* p. 176.
DUNRAGIT HOUSE. *See* p. 291.
SINNINESS CASTLE. *See* p. 520.

GLENTROOL

Village for Forestry Commission workers. It is laid out round a green on which squats the school. Single-storey-and-attic harled houses with steep-pitched tiled roofs. They are of 1952–4.

SCHOOL. By the Stewartry County Architect, *Archibald T. Caldwell*, 1954–6.

CAIRN (KING'S CAIRN), Kirriemore, 7.3km. NE. Much robbed but still impressive cairn of the third millennium B.C., now surrounded by trees. It is roughly oval, *c*. 30m. by 35m. In the centre, a slab-walled chamber approached from the SE by a lower passage of the same breadth.

CAIRN (SHEUCHAN'S CAIRN), 5.8km. NW. Round cairn of *c*. 16.5m. diameter, constructed of small stones in the third millennium B.C. It contains a slab-walled trapezoidal chamber; the entry passage from the SW is of the same breadth as that end of the chamber.

CAIRN (THE WHITE CAIRN), 0.5km. W. In the middle of a forestry plantation, a round boulder-built cairn of the third millennium B.C. The diameter is 13.7m., the height now reduced to a maximum of 1.4m. Now exposed are its rectangular central chamber, reached by a passage from the S

which broadens along its approach to the full width of the
chamber. The walls of both are constructed of large split boulders, their flat faces fronting the interior, which support drystone walling which carried the massive roof slabs. Two
capstones are *in situ* over the chamber.

GOLDIELEA
2.3km. SW of Cargenbridge

Small rendered mansion house (formerly Woodley Park)
described in 1794 as 'lately built'. Main block of three storeys
and five bays, with sill courses across the upper floors. Single-
storey links to low two-storey piend-roofed pavilions. The
house was altered in pompous fashion *c*.1857, when a Roman
Doric portico was erected and the second-floor windows were
given alternately segmental and triangular pedimented dormerheads breaking through the eaves cornice. Of the same date are
the links' three-light windows, balustrades and pedimented
dormerheads. Brick billiard room and a glasshouse range added
at the back in 1895.

Behind the house, a disused VIADUCT by *John Miller Jun.*,
built for the Castle Douglas and Dumfries Railway in 1859.
Eighteen roundheaded arches springing from battered piers.
Pilaster strips rising across the channelled and bullnosed red
ashlar masonry to form pedestrian refuges at the parapet.

GREENLAW HOUSE
2.2km. NW of Castle Douglas

Roofless shell of the rustically smart mansion house built for
the Gordons of Greenlaw in 1741. Walling of rubble, the red
sandstone rusticated quoins and dressings a contrast to the
rendered finish. Two storeys over a fully exposed basement
which projects as a plinth. S front of seven bays, the centre five
advanced, their tall ground-floor windows and those of the first
floor with block-brackets under the sills. Broad concave-sided
flight of steps to the entrance, a tripartite arrangement of a
door flanked by sidelights in a frame of fluted Ionic pilasters
supporting a segmental pediment. The fanlight is contained in
a key-blocked roundheaded arch; over each sidelight, a circular
niche. Projecting from the gables are full-height bows, the one
at the W containing the stair. On the *piano nobile* of each bow,
a round-arched opening linked by a lintel course to rectangular
lights forms a broadly spaced version of a Venetian window.
Plain rear elevation, the centre five bays again advanced; an
early C19 pilastered doorpiece at the basement.

GRETNA   *3060*

Substantial township built during the First World War to house munitions workers at the large cordite factory (since demolished) which had been erected between Gretna and Eastriggs to the W. The chief architect, responsible for the layout and general direction, was *Raymond Unwin*, with *C. M. Crickmer* acting as resident architect. After the First World War the township lost its factory and purpose. It now forms a dormitory of Carlisle, the Registration Office the main attraction for visitors.

CHURCHES

ALL SAINTS (Episcopal), Annan Road and Central Avenue. Powerfully austere and small-windowed Early Christian in snecked rubble, by *Geoffrey Lucas*, 1917. Five-bay nave, its roof swept down with an extravagant bellcast over the aisles, its buttressed W end projecting clear; SW porch. Narrower and slightly taller chancel, a small gableted bellcote at its W end. High in the buttressed E gable, a round window. Projecting from the chancel's W end are a N transept and the lower part of an intended square S tower. E of these, a double-pitch-roofed Lady Chapel (N) and organ chamber (S). Inside, the octagonal piers of the nave arcades are corbelled to the square to carry the pointed arches. The N aisle's two W bays were partitioned off in 1992. Over the nave, a pointed tunnel plaster vault crossed by rosetted transverse ribs. Over the aisles, braced roofs with kingpost trusses set at an angle to support 'ridge pieces' placed two-thirds of the way down the slope. Big pointed arch into the choir. Smaller arches from the choir and the aisles into the Lady Chapel and organ chamber. Simple oak PANELLING in the sanctuary. In its S wall, a segmental-arched SEDILIA and round-arched PISCINA. – FURNISHINGS designed by *Lucas*, the wood carving executed by *Lawrence Turner*. – Stone ALTAR, its wooden riddel posts topped by gilded angels. – Blocky Arts and Crafts CHOIR STALLS, COMMUNION RAIL, LECTERN and PULPIT. – Big and simple octagonal stone FONT, the sides of its steepled oak cover decorated with stiffleaf crockets, its top surmounted by a pelican in piety. – Late Victorian CHAMBER ORGAN with stencilled pipes.

GRETNA PARISH CHURCH. *See* Gretna Green and Springfield.

ST ANDREW, Central Avenue. By *C. M. Crickmer*, 1917. Studiedly simple cruciform, the harled walls enlivened by brick dressings and red-tiled roofs. Nave and narrow aisles under a single large roof; slightly lower transepts and an apsidal-ended chancel. In the S transept's E inner angle, a tower covered with a broad-eaved flattish pyramid roof topped by a big weathervane. Round-arched openings at the tower. Rectangular nave windows with sloping tiled sills. The nave's W gable extends clear of the aisles; pushing out from its centre, a semi-octagonal projection flanked by roundheaded arches, each of which contains an entrance surmounted by a brick tympanum. Inside, roundheaded nave arcades, the piers without capitals. More roundheaded arches into the choir and apse. Over the nave, a panelled elliptical tunnel-vault, its stiles decorated with vine reliefs. – Imported ORGAN of 1890, by *Forster & Andrews*.

40 ST NINIAN (R.C.), Victory Avenue. By *C. Evelyn Simmons*, 1918. Byzantine, built of brown pressed brick with red-tiled roofs. Nave flanked by low windowless aisles which stop short of the W end. Short full-height transepts, each ending in a lower projection (chapel on the S, sacristy on the N). Over the crossing, a low tower which begins square and is then broached by four small piended roofs to a pavilion-roofed octagon. Tall choir ending in a lower semi-octagonal apse, with a large roundheaded blind arch on each face. The detail is all of the simplest. Small roundheaded lights with steeply sloping sills in the nave clearstorey, the choir and the transepts' projections. Round windows high up in the gables of the nave and transepts.

41   The interior was acclaimed by Sir Robert Lorimer in 1918* as showing 'how if a man has a feeling for rhythm and proportion and fitness, and is able to handle his materials, quite excellent results can be obtained by the knowing use of ordinary brick and plain white plaster.' The materials are indeed without ostentation – limestone flags on the floor, brick for walling, plaster for ceilings. Gently Baroque gallery over the entrance vestibule at the nave's W end. Low groin-vaulted passage-aisles divided from the nave by paired roundheaded arches under paired clearstorey windows. These double bays are divided from each other by attached piers from which spring the groin vaults of the nave ceiling. Along the nave's N and S walls, and reappearing in the transepts and chancel, brick stringcourses projected on square brick ends serving as primitive corbels. Square saucer-domed crossing, higher than the nave. It opens into each limb through a tall roundheaded arch. Short tunnel-vaulted transepts. On the S transept's S side, a pair of arches, roundheaded again, into a two-bay groin-vaulted chapel. In the E wall of each transept, a blind oculus over a low roundheaded arch which opens into a domed square chapel, one containing a statue, the other now a baptistery, each with blind arches on the outer walls and an open arch to the chancel, on whose inner face each of these is paired with a blind arch under a pair of clearstorey lights. Groin-vaulted chancel ceiling. At the E end, a half-domed apse framed by another roundheaded arch.

PUBLIC BUILDINGS

GRETNA COMMUNITY EDUCATION CENTRE, Central Avenue. Originally The Institute, built *c.*1916. Two-storey brick-built U-plan, now partly drydashed. At the parapeted main block, a slightly advanced centre with giant anta pilasters carrying an open pediment.

GRETNA PRIMARY SCHOOL, Victory Avenue. By *Dumfries and*

* In *Country Life*, 17 August 1918.

Galloway Regional Council, 1981. Horseshoe of single-storey classrooms around a taller octagonal hall. Brick walls and dominant tiled roofs.

REGISTRATION OFFICE, Central Avenue. By *Peter Nelson* of *Dumfries and Galloway Regional Council*, 1989–91. Post-Modern, with brick walls and pitched roofs. Over the entrance, a gable suggestive of a pediment; big round windows in the end gables.

DESCRIPTION

ANNAN ROAD enters from the W past the GABLES HOTEL, originally the township doctor's house, accomplished neo-Georgian by *C. M. Crickmer, c.* 1916, with tall segmental-arched ground-floor windows and a canopied door at the piend-roofed main block; single-storey piend-roofed wings. The gentility is rather marred by the recently introduced solar panels and a large rear addition. Housing built for First World War munitions workers follows along the road and up Central Avenue to the N. The general pattern is two-storey, with brick walls and piended slate roofs, in a neo-Georgian manner. Some touches of decoration are provided by door canopies, a little decorative patterning in the brickwork, the occasional porthole window or segmental fanlight, but Sir Robert Lorimer's comment in 1918 that 'all is plain, practical, straightforward, of pleasant and reasonable proportion and mercifully devoid of ornament and prettiness' is accurate enough – or, rather, was, before home ownership brought do-it-yourself ornamentation and prettification.

On Annan Road's NW corner with Central Avenue, All Saints' Episcopal Church (*see* Churches, above) and its contemporary brick-built neo-Georgian former RECTORY (also by *Geoffrey Lucas*). E of Central Avenue, on Annan Road's S side, a long two-storey block (originally the Police Station) by *Henry A. Saul, c.* 1916, with a segmental-pedimented door in its main range's advanced and pedimented centre. In the ends, also advanced and pedimented, Venetian windows on the ground floor. A subtle rhythm is established by the windows being set in slightly recessed vertical strips of walling. Further out, on the N side, SURRONE HOUSE, a two-storey piend-roofed late Georgian dwelling extended E by one bay.

CENTRAL AVENUE S of Annan Road is the township's commercial and public centre, but the Community Education Centre and Registration Office (*see* Public Buildings, above) fail to provide the necessary touch of pomp and circumstance. On the W, opposite them, a block of First World War shops under flats. They flank the slightly set-back CINEMA (now BINGO HALL) of 1916, by *C. M. Crickmer.*

STANDING STONE (LOCHMABEN STANE or CLOCH-MABENSTANE), 1.2km. SW. Huge rounded granite boulder, *c.* 5.5m. in circumference and 2.3m. high. It was erected in the third or second millennium B.C., possibly as part of a stone circle but perhaps as a solitary marker of the N end of a ford across the River Esk.

3060   GRETNA GREEN AND SPRINGFIELD

Two small settlements, almost touching each other but kept apart by the A74. The village of Gretna Green was rebuilt 'after a new modell' *c.* 1720; but, despite its being described in 1723 as 'pleasant and fine', Sir William Burrell, visiting thirty-five years later, found it 'produced a strong mark of the Poverty of its Inhabitants', whose clay-built houses he dismissed as 'miserable Cots'. Perhaps unsurprisingly these were cleared or rebuilt in the C19. The adjoining Springfield was founded in 1791 by Sir William Maxwell as a formally planned village, soon to be principally occupied by cotton weavers; it has been almost all rebuilt in the C20. Both were, for a time, famous for their trade in enabling eloping English lovers to take advantage of the relatively lax Scottish marriage law.

GRETNA FREE CHURCH, Springfield. Now a hall. Plain Gothic, by *T. Taylor Scott*, 1894–5, the E gable now bereft of its bellcote.

GRETNA PARISH CHURCH, Gretna Green. T-plan kirk of sneck-harled red sandstone rubble, built in 1789–90 but transformed into a lumpy Gothic edifice in 1909–10 by *James Barbour*. He thickened the main block with the addition of a S aisle, almost swallowing up the C18 jamb, blocked the gable doors and provided new windows throughout. Also Barbour's is the E side's slim bell tower, a red-tiled spire rising within the battlement, a spired caphouse, again red-tiled, at its NW corner.
    NW of the church, a large MONUMENT of *c.* 1840 to members of the Weild family, topped by four blunt obelisks, two carved with coats of arms.

STORMONT HALL, Springfield. By *John T. Laidlaw*, 1906. Of hammerdressed rubble, its plainness just relieved by barge-boards and a Venetian window.

DESCRIPTION. GRETNA GREEN itself is a tiny settlement, with some small late Victorian villas E of Gretna Parish Church (*see* above) and its very plain MANSE (by *A. B. & J. Crombie*, 1880–1). To the N, set well back in a park-like garden, is GRETNA HALL. Its five-bay main block, two storeys and an exposed basement of white painted rubble, was built for Colonel James Johnstone in 1710 (the date on the door lintel). Moulded surrounds to the ground-floor windows and again at the low horizontal windows above. In the centre of the first floor, a large panel carved with the Johnstone arms and said to have been brought from Old Graitney, the family's previous residence. The central porch is probably an early C19 addition but its basket-arched doorpiece looks early C18, perhaps re-used. At each end of this block, a one-bay piend-roofed addition of *c.* 1792, when the house was fitted up as an inn. In the front of each, a Venetian window, the r. deeper than the l. Large drydashed hotel extension of 1967 on the E. To the W, a basket-arched entrance into the stable courtyard of *c.* 1765.

SPRINGFIELD to the W is virtually cut off by the bridge carrying the A74. It is mostly C20, but at its E end there is a short rubble-built single-storey early C19 terrace including THE OLD BLACKSMITH'S SHOP (with a re-used datestone of 1713). Brick-built and bargeboarded front addition, perhaps mid-C19, with a Gothick window. Behind, a bronze SCULPTURE ('Smith-God') by *R. & L. Lauren*, 1989, the spikily expressionist depiction of a smith beating out weapons.

GRIBTON   *9080*

2.9km. NW of Newbridge

Big and rambling villa (now subdivided) by *Walter Newall, c.* 1830. Generally Tudor in style but with a prominent pair of Dutch gables. Are they intended to suggest an English manor house which has grown by accretion? – At the beginning of the drive, contemporary urn-finialled GATEPIERS and a Tudor LODGE.

THE GROVE   *9070*

1.5km. NW of Terregles

Two-storey Tudor mansion, designed in 1825 by *Thomas Rickman* 90 for the Liverpool merchant Wellwood Maxwell, and enlarged by *Peddie & Kinnear* in 1869. Used as a hospital for much of the C20. Rickman's house was U-plan, the NW wing provided by a small C18 house which already stood here. The 1830s work is all of red sandstone broached ashlar. Symmetrical S (entrance) front of seven bays, with a tall three-bay centrepiece containing a pointed door. Over the door, a rectangular hoodmould, which has contained an heraldic panel, flanked by quatrefoils. Each side of the door, an ogee-arched cusped window. At the centrepiece's upper floor, three tall round-arched and cusped windows. Architraved rectangular windows in the outer bays, those of the ground floor two-light with stone mullions and transoms.

Rickman's E façade, enjoying the view over the Nith valley, is much less formal. Three sections. The S section is the gable end of the main S front, from which projects a two-storey canted bay window rising in three slightly diminishing stages, the second stage formed of blind panels. The middle section is slightly recessed. At its ground floor, a very shallow rectangular bay window with cusping in its four tall ogee-arched lights. Plain architraved first-floor windows. Overall parapet, its central panel decorated with a blind quatrefoil. The third section, slightly set back again, is of three bays; cusped heads to the narrow ground-floor windows, the upper windows again architraved. On top, a cornice rises at the centre into a gablet containing a lozenge panel. On this section's N end, another rectangular bay window, again with cusping in the round-arched lights.

In 1869 *Peddie & Kinnear* filled in the open court of Rickman's U and covered the C18 house's N gable with the E end of a new service range. At the same time they provided an L-shaped SW block. Its S gable projects S of Rickman's entrance front but continues its broached ashlar and Tudor manner, in rather simpler form, with mullioned and transomed three-light windows. In this block's inner SW angle they placed a conservatory, its polished ashlar framing big mullioned and transomed windows; ball-finialled parapet pierced by quatre-foils. Its two-tier double-pitched and glazed covering was replaced by a flat roof in the C20.

In the E and W sides of Rickman's entrance hall, large pointed recesses forming overarches into the rooms each side. Behind, a large toplit stair hall; the stair balustrades are now represented by C20 plywood. Rickman's principal rooms, ranged along the E wing, probably consisted of a drawing room, library and dining room. The drawing room at the S contains plain fin-ishings of 1869. The others, like the rest of the interior, were altered in the C20.

<!-- marginal: 0080 -->

HALLEATHS
1.4km. E of Lochmaben

The mansion house by *David Bryce*, 1866, incorporating a house of *c*.1773 (*see* the Introduction, p. 68), has been demolished. The rubble-walled STABLES of 1843 survive, the front block converted to housing, the rest to stores and workshops. The altered main block in the S range is of two storeys. Three-bay front, the outer bays containing paired roundheaded windows at each floor (those of the upper floor blind). Shallowly pro-jecting centrepiece, with wide pilasters of polished ashlar flan-king the (blocked) pend arch. Recessed low wing at each end. The other three ranges form a single-storey U. Parapeted S ends, each with an advanced gabled centre containing a blind round-arched window. The courtyard has rounded corners, where Doric columns, their masonry tooled to suggest fluting, support the overhang of the broad-eaved roof. – To the S, a picturesque bargeboarded LODGE, dated 1868 and presumably by *Bryce*.

HARDGATE *see* HAUGH OF URR

<!-- marginal: 0010 -->

HARTFELL SPA
6.3km. N of Moffat

The chalybeate spring was discoved in 1748 by John Williamson, a copper prospector. The spa building itself, now heavily restored, was put up by the third Duke of Queensberry in 1754. Externally it is covered with turf. Inside, a small and irregular tunnel-vaulted room. The central boss is carved with the human heart crest of the Douglases, their motto 'Forward', the initials CDQ (for Charles, Duke of Queensberry), and the date 1754. The lettering and date are in mirror-writing, designed to be reflected in the water welling up below.

HAUGH OF URR   8060

Begun in the late C18 as two villages, Haugh of Urr on the B794 and Hardgate to the NE, which now almost touch each other. Mixture of C19 vernacular with some C20 local authority housing, the earliest of 1921 by *W. F. Crombie*. For the medieval burgh of Urr, *see* the Introduction, p. 74.

ANTIBURGHER CHAPEL, Hardgate. Now a house. Built in 1798, remodelled in 1860, when it was widened and heightened, and reroofed in 1910 after being gutted by fire. It is a humble whitewashed rectangle with pointed windows; stump of a bellcote on the W gable.

URR PARISH CHURCH, 0.6km. SE. By *P. MacGregor Chalmers*, 1914–15, and studiedly simple in hammerdressed red sandstone. Nave with a short and low chancel. N aisle shorter than the nave, the NW inner angle filled by a tower. At the tower, a stringcourse under the belfry; spouts projecting from the parapet, with martial effect. Pointed door in the tower's base, its hoodmould's labels carved with tiny cherubs' heads. Paired pointed windows to the aisle. The nave's side windows are alternately of roundheaded and pointed lights. Gothic three-light windows in the gables.

Ashlar-walled interior. Nave arcade of segmental arches springing from columns of clustered shafts. Kingpost-truss roofs, the nave's braced. – FURNISHINGS all of 1914–15, in a High Presbyterian arrangement with the communion table in the chancel, whose entrance is flanked by the pulpit and font. – Behind the pulpit, a dove FINIAL from the pulpit of the previous church (built in 1814–15). – ORGAN at the aisle's E end and with an arched opening into the chancel. – Round stone FONT with Iona marble columns.

STAINED GLASS. In the tower porch, one light (David) in rich blue and mauve, after 1924. – The nave's W window (scenes from the life of Abraham) is of 1917, brightly coloured with small-scale drawing. – In the S wall, two lights (the Agony in the Garden; Our Lord washing St Peter's feet) signed by *Alexander Strachan*, after 1937. – To their E, engraved glass (the Resurrection) by *David Gulland*, *c.* 1978. – E window (the Crucifixion) by *Douglas Strachan*, 1921. – In the N aisle's side wall, one light (Our Lady) of *c.* 1917. – The aisle's W window (Our Lord and Apostles) is of 1901, re-used from the previous church. – In the vestry, a wooden PANEL from a pulpit carved with the date 1606 and the initials I^M T for Master John Thomson, then the minister of Urr.

GRAVEYARD. S of the church, a worn SLAB to Robert Herries

†169[5?], its border carved with reminders of death. – N of the church, a MONUMENT to the Rev. James Muirhead †1808. Pedestal with a fluted frieze. It supports an urn-finialled obelisk, one face decorated with a crest framed by a swag. – To its E, the Herries of Spottes BURIAL ENCLOSURE of 1793, its front pierced by a round-arched and key-blocked door flanked by similarly detailed blind windows framing inscription panels.

HALL AND LIBRARY, Haugh of Urr. Dated 1908. Harled, with bracketed eaves and bargeboards.

HARDGATE SCHOOL. By *Alexander Crombie*, 1866. Plain except for a flaming urn finial on one gable. Late C20 addition.

60 MOTTE, Mote of Urr, 1.8km. S. Well-preserved remains of a grandiose motte-and-bailey castle, probably constructed in the mid-C12 for Walter de Berkeley, the King's chamberlain. Bailey of 152m. by 66m., surrounded by a 15m.-wide ditch. Near its E end, a 7m.-wide ditch around the motte. This is a truncated cone, originally 8.17m. high but raised to 10m. following a fire in the C12 which destroyed the surmounting wooden buildings. Roughly circular summit of 27m. by 23m. Pottery finds suggest it continued to be occupied until the C14.

FARMS

CHAPELTON, 1km. W. Large but plain Georgian-survival farmhouse of *c.*1865. – Across the road, FARM STEADING dated 1866. On the W, a single-storey rubble-built byre range, with an attic gable over the centre pend. On the E, a tall U-plan piend-roofed complex built as a grain storage depot.

WEST GLENARM, 2.9km. NE. Harled farmhouse of two storeys and three bays, the windows altered. It looks early C19, but over the door is a mid-C18 consoled pediment, its fluted frieze decorated with rosettes, the cornice carved with egg-and-dart ornament; in the tympanum, the stag couchant crest of the Maxwells.

SPOTTES HALL. *See* p. 523.

6060   HENSOL
             4.9km. N of Laurieston

Large Tudor villa designed by *Robert Lugar* and built in 1822–4 for John Cunninghame of Lainshaw. All of rock-faced local granite. Main block of two tall storeys at the S, a lower long T-plan service wing stretching back to the N. The main block is almost square, with a slim ogee-roofed square tower at each outer corner. Hoodmoulded mullioned and transomed windows. The 1820s main entrance was on the W side through a porch projecting from a boldly advanced gabled centrepiece, with an oriel window above. The porch was moved from here and a conservatory erected *c.*1960. S front of two parts, each gabled, the r. slightly recessed and with another first-floor oriel. Three-bay E front, the outer bays gabled, the centre recessed.

Three-light ground-floor window on the r. which Lugar had intended to be balanced by one on the l. The tail made by the service wing is low, with stone gablets over the upper windows. Single-storey flat-roofed extension of *c*. 1920 in front of the W side. On the E side at the S end, the original entrance porch, re-erected here *c*. 1960. Taller plain cross-bar at the house's N end.

Inside, the original entrance hall on the W opens into an inner hall, its ceiling ribbed. Tudor-arched recess to the E. On the N side, an open Tudor arch into the stair hall. Cast-iron fleur-de-lis finials on the stair balusters.

In the garden, S of the house, a SUNDIAL of *c*. 1675, formerly at Lainshaw (Ayrshire) and very similar to one of 1674 at Ladyland (also Ayrshire). Badly damaged shaft, now appearing as a truncated obelisk rising from a bulbous base. On the shaft, the arms and initials of Sir Alexander Cunninghame of Lainshaw and his wife, Dame Margaret Stewart. Faceted double head, the dials hollowed or heart-shaped, their lead gnomons 1980s replacements.

LODGE at the W end of the drive. Again Tudor, probably of *c*. 1825.

HETLAND HALL

1.1km. W of Carrutherstown

0070

Main block said to have been built in 1868 but looking forty years earlier. Harled, with buff-painted dressings. The S front had a central door flanked by full-height bows. In 1925–7 this was extended by one bay at each end and a T-plan wing was added at the NE, all in a neo-Georgian manner, with rusticated quoins and flat-roofed dormers; red sandstone doorpiece on the E, with Doric columns and a steep open pediment. Blocky brick extension added at the W by *Sutherland, Dickie & Copland* in 1965, when the house was used as a seminary. It is now an hotel. Expensive but eclectic interior of the 1920s.

HIGHTAE

0070

Tight-knit village including a couple of mid-C19 farmhouses and steadings standing beside the curving street. The earlier cottages are mostly C19, of painted or harled rubble. Several C20 intruders and many window alterations.

CHURCH. Built as a Relief chapel in 1796 and remodelled for the Reformed Presbyterians in 1865, when the windows were enlarged and the gableted W bellcote and small porch were added. – MANSE of 1865–6 adjoining.

THE ROYAL FOUR TOWNS HALL. By *John T. Laidlaw*, 1910. Harled piend-roofed rectangle, with architectural display concentrated at the front gable. Here, corniced windows flank a doorpiece dignified by panelled pilasters and a semicircular pediment. Its keystone provides the base for an engagingly inept statue of King Robert the Bruce framed by a gablet.

WAR MEMORIAL. Of *c.* 1920. Battered pillar of rusticated ashlar topped by a crown.

RAMMERSCALES. *See* p. 496.

HILLS TOWER
9070
1.6km. SE of Lochfoot

71 Satisfying combination of a C16 tower house adjoined by an early Georgian wing, these forming the S range of a courtyard which is entered through a gatehouse of 1598 (the date was visible until the earlier C19).

In 1527 Edward Maxwell, then the tenant of Breconside (*c.* 3km. to the SW), bought the lands and mill of Hills from James Douglas of Drumlanrig. Probably soon after, Maxwell built the tower at the courtyard's SW corner, adorning it with a panel showing the arms and initials of himself and his wife, Janet Carson. The W entrance to the courtyard (probably formed at the same time as the erection of the tower) was dignified by his grandson and namesake, who constructed its gatehouse in 1598. The last major stage in the group's development was the addition in 1721, by yet another Edward Maxwell, of a low wing on the tower house's E side; the mason *John Selkrig* was the contractor and possibly the designer.

The rubble-built GATEHOUSE is small but smart. Two

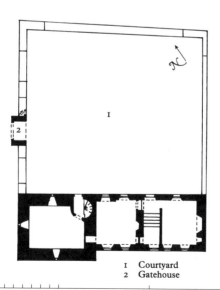

1 Courtyard
2 Gatehouse

30 m

Hills Tower. Plan

storeys, the upper floor jettied out on continuous corbelling. In the W face, a roundheaded arch, its hoodmould continued as a horizontal stringcourse across the front and sides. At the first floor, two pear-shaped gunholes flanking a panel carved with the royal arms of Scotland. The ashlar band course under the eaves is carved as chequer-set corbelling. Segmental-vaulted pend. At the back, an inserted first-floor crosslet 'arrowslit', probably an early C19 embellishment; forestair to the upper floor.

The TOWER HOUSE itself is a plain rubble-built rectangle, its sturdy W buttress clearly an addition. At its N front's E end, a moulded door. Quite high above it, and not directly aligned, a stone carved with the Maxwell crest above two shields separated by a thistle and surmounting the initials EM and IC (for Edward Maxwell and Janet Carson). Comfortably sized windows (two of them blocked) with chamfered margins lighting the first and second floors; at the second floor's SE corner, a dumbbell-shaped slit to a garderobe. Moulded corbelling, alternately recessed and projecting, under the crenellated parapet and its barely emphasized angle rounds; the stone-flagged vault behind is drained by cannon spouts. Inside the parapet, a crowstepped attic, with a large chimney at its W gable and a bowed caphouse over the stair at the NE corner.

Inside the tower, one room on each floor, with the turnpike stair nudging into the NE corner. The ground-floor room, covered with a segmental-arched rubble vault, has been a store; small W fireplace inserted in the C20. At each of the first and second floors, a simply moulded stone fireplace in the W gable, that on the second floor smaller and off-centre; garderobe in the SE corner. The first floor's fireplace is flanked by low and narrow rectangular aumbries. In the second floor's N and S window embrasures, stone seats. On the third floor (the floor itself now missing), another W fireplace with moulded jambs. Stone seat at the small S window. The attic floor was originally supported on stone corbels but has been replaced at a higher level.

The EAST WING, added by *John Selkrig* in 1721 (the date carved on the surround of the window over the door), is built of whitewashed rubble. Two-storey four-bay front (the first floor's r. window now blocked). Above the door, an empty panel frame. Between the first-floor windows, a row of four armorial panels. One, containing the arms of Sir John Maxwell, Lord Herries, and his wife, Agnes, Lady Herries, must be of the later C16. Another, carved with the initials and impaled arms of Edward Maxwell of Hills and his wife, Agnes Maxwell, is of the late C16 or early C17. The interior of the wing has been much altered in the C20, but the ground-floor's E room, with a large fireplace in the gable, was the C18 kitchen. In the first-floor W room, a fireplace incorporating a re-used moulded lintel of the C16 or early C17.

At MAINS OF HILLS to the W, a plain gableted FARM-HOUSE of 1860, probably by *Alexander Fraser*. – Whin-walled STEADING built in 1809–12 by *Robert Brown*, mason, and

William Wilson, joiner, the piend-roofed main block solidly elegant.

HODDOM

Former PARISH CHURCH. *See* Hoddomcross.
HODDOM CHURCH. *See* Ecclefechan.

1070   HODDOM CASTLE
                       3.7km. NW of Brydekirk

Large but stark C16 tower house, scarred by the removal of additions but still joined to a rambling late Victorian wing. In 1547 Sir John Maxwell married Agnes, Lady Herries, the eldest daughter and co-heir of William, third Lord Herries of Terregles. Fourteen years later he bought the two-thirds of the Herries lands, including Hoddom, which had not been inherited by his wife, and in 1562 he took his seat in Parliament as Lord Maxwell of Herries. Three years later he was reported to be building two forts within two miles of Annan, 'the one great – the other a watchtower of great height'; the first is almost certainly identifiable as Hoddom Castle, the second as the nearby Repentance Tower (q.v.). Hoddom must have been completed by 1568, when, following the Battle of Langside, it was besieged by the Regent Moray and quickly surrendered, although it was 'a strong fort' whose defenders 'mycht haif holdin long enewcht, yf thai had bene gud fellows within it'. Two years later it was reported that the Earl of Sussex, during a week's incursion into southern Scotland, had thrown down ten of the principal castles, including 'two of which are most strong – Annand and Hodoun'; this is more probably a reference to a slighting of the outer defences than to major destruction.

In 1627 John Maxwell, sixth Lord Herries, sold Hoddom to Sir Richard Murray of Cockpool; on his death in 1636 the lands and tower passed to his younger brother, Sir John Murray, first Earl of Annandale, who before his own death four years later was said to have 'greatly increased' the Castle 'with additional buildings', almost certainly including the heightening of the tower house's jamb by an extra floor. After passing into the ownership of the Earl of Southesk in 1653, Hoddom was sold in 1690 to a Dumfries burgess, John Sharpe. It may have been soon after this that a two-storey W wing was added. Charles Kirkpatrick Sharpe inherited in 1769, and in 1793 it was reported that he had repaired the tower, possibly building a central wall rising through the main block, and added several rooms, perhaps the N wing. Probably *c.* 1810 he extended the existing W wing and added a S wing. In 1826 his son, Lieutenant-General Matthew Sharpe, commissioned designs from *William Burn* for a big castellated new S addition and a remodelling and heightening of the W wing. Work was completed in 1832, the N wing having apparently been demol-

ished as part of the scheme. In 1877 Hoddom was bought by a
Huddersfield millowner, Edward Brook, who in 1878–91 added
large extensions tenuously linked to the N side of the tower. The
s and w wings were demolished c. 1953–75, leaving the tower and
the latest extensions forming a rather incoherent group.

The site, in a bend of the River Annan, is defensive; the ground
falls steeply on the E and there is a gully, probably artificial, on
the s. These defences were almost certainly supplemented from
the C16 by a wall. The best approach is along an avenue from
the w. At its end, a segment of large and smartly detailed neo-
Jacobean piers, probably dating from Burn's work of 1826–32,
which have enclosed a FORECOURT. On this forecourt's E side,
a screen wall with a battlemented round tower at each end.
The s tower is wholly of c. 1830. So too are the N tower's
battlement and flat roof, but the rubble walling below contains
two blocked gunloops (facing NW and sw) and must be of the
late C16 or early C17, as is the vault over the ground-floor room.
The E segment of the tower was refaced in the 1970s after
demolition of the abutting w wing of the house.* The screen
wall between these towers is again largely late C16 or early C17,
but its battlement looks to be of c. 1830. In the centre of the
wall, a GATEWAY, perhaps of c. 1636–40, with a broad elliptical
arch and topped by a small round-arched bellcote flanked by
ball finials. This gateway opens into the courtyard surrounding
the tower house, its s and E walls rebuilt in the C19, its N side
now largely bounded by additions of the 1880s.

The TOWER HOUSE itself is a large L-plan. Main block of
four storeys, the rough ashlar walling rising, unbroken by stringcourses, to a course of continuous corbelling surmounted by
alternately recessed and projecting corbels carrying the
sparsely crenellated parapet, which is drained by boldly projecting stone spouts. Machicolations in the centre of the E face
and at the N face's join with the NW jamb. SW, SE and NE
angle rounds, projected on corbelling of the same type as
under the main parapet but with two additional lower rows of
continuous corbelling broken by the house's corners. At the
ground and third floors, purposefully utilitarian horizontal
gunloops (mostly blocked). Tall moulded windows, enlarged
to their present size in the C17, at the first and second floors.
At the N end of the attic's w wall, a buttress-like chimney,
heightened in the C17 and topped by an angle round in the
late C19, when it was closed off. The s gable's chimney was
broadened outwards in 1826–30 to accommodate extra flues.
On top of the N gable, a beacon stack, the 0.72m.-wide crowsteps providing easy access.

The NW JAMB was originally of four storeys, the top floor
projected on corbelling like that carrying the parapet of the
main block and with turrets at the w corners but all set at a
slightly higher level. A parapet machicolation over the door in

---

* C18 views show round towers with octagonal pavilion roofs at the NW, SW and
SE corners of a barmkin.

the inner angle. Almost certainly as part of the work carried out *c.* 1636–40, the jamb was heightened by one floor, and the corner turrets were finished with conical roofs (since replaced, probably in 1889) rising within the parapet. The parapet itself, jettied out on a cornice and meanly crenellated, is a replacement of the late C19, when the E angle rounds were added, both projected on continuous corbelling, only the top course of the one at the NE circling the corners, the corbelling of the one at the SE much bolder. Stone spouts drain the flat roof. At the jamb's SE corner, but inside the parapet, a round C19 battlemented caphouse, probably of *c.* 1830, above the secondary stair. In each of the jamb's W and S faces, a gunloop of the same utilitarian type as at the main block. Door in the inner angle, its segmental-arched and rope-carved hoodmould clearly not original and probably of the late C19. Above the door, a boldly rounded surround designed to contain a huge armorial panel but now filled with a dummy window, perhaps of *c.* 1830. It is jostled by the inner angle's first-floor window which was enlarged from a slit *c.* 1830.

(INTERIOR. From the entrance to the jamb, a passage covered by a segmental tunnel-vault leads to the foot of the main stair. From here a second segmental-vaulted passage goes E with, at its end, four steps down into the main block. Off the S side of this second passage, a small guardroom in the thickness of the wall. Off the passage's N side, a low and narrow door to a prison under the stair. There has been a ventilation shaft rising through the segmental vault near the SE corner. Lamp recess in the NW corner. The main block's ground floor originally contained one large tunnel-vaulted store (subdivided, perhaps in the later C18) with gunloops in all four walls. Small windows, both now blocked, in the gables; under the N window, a built-up cupboard.

The broad turnpike stair in the jamb rises to the second floor, where it is covered by a very shallow vault. S of the FIRST-FLOOR landing in the jamb, a small irregularly shaped room (perhaps a guardroom), the S side of its tunnel-vault cantilevered out from the wall on a continuous course of masonry. In the main block, the unvaulted hall, again now subdivided. In its W wall, a broad C16 fireplace with moulded jambs but a plain lintel; its N side was altered in the C18, when the fireplace was blocked and the SE corner of the room in the jamb squared up. Off the NW corner, a garderobe lit by a slit window. The E and W windows, originally high-set and small, have been deeepened. The N window's E ingo was removed *c.* 1830 to form a recess. On its l., an C18 door (now a window) into the demolished N wing. The S window was converted to a door into the S wing of *c.* 1810 and then blocked *c.* 1830 when Burn's new S wing was built; a new door approached by a flight of steps was made to its W.

The SECOND FLOOR of the main block again originally contained one large room or upper hall, lit by small high-set windows. In the S gable, a moulded fireplace, its opening reduced in size when the room was divided into two. s of the fireplace, an aumbry, its wooden surround and boarded door probably c16. Smaller aumbry or lamp recess at the e wall's s end. At the w wall's n end, a large aumbry checked for a door. In the wall thickness of the ne corner, a garderobe lit by a very narrow slit window (now blocked) and entered originally from the w through a moulded door but now from a s door inserted in the ingo of the adjoining window. Another garderobe in the centre of the e wall, again with a moulded c16 door and a second door, probably c18, to its s.

Access to the floors above and the roof of the jamb is by a second turnpike stair in the jamb's se corner. On the jamb's THIRD FLOOR, a tunnel-vaulted room, its nw fireplace an insertion of c.1830. Off the room's e side, a narrow wall chamber, possibly a garderobe, lit by a slit window. The main block's third floor, now two rooms with fireplaces in the partition wall, was originally a single space and without a fireplace, perhaps intended as a barrack room for use if attack threatened. Gunloops, now blocked except for one converted to a window, in all the walls. The windows, except for one in the s wall, were enlarged or inserted c.1830. In the ne corner's wall thickness, an irregularly shaped garderobe with a drain and slit window.

The main block's ATTIC FLOOR seems again originally to have contained one large room, later subdivided and with a fireplace and comfortably sized window inserted in the s gable c.1830. In the n gable, a c16 slit window. To its w, at floor level, a low door into a wall safe. The jamb at this level originally contained one room (later subdivided), with closets in the w corner turrets. In the centre of the w wall, a distinctly smart mid-c16 moulded fireplace with two semicircular arches joined at a central pendant, the opening partly infilled c.1830. At the room's se corner is the entrance to the machicolation over the door to the house. In this room, windows with segmental-headed embrasures, except for the e wall's n window, whose embrasure is round-arched. Similar room on the floor above; its turrets' central windows are c17, but their other openings were probably inserted c.1830. e fireplace, its stone surround incorporating an inverted fillet between edge-roll and cavetto mouldings, confirming a likely date of c.1636–40 for this floor.)

N of the tower house, a COURTYARD closed by a battlemented screen wall on the w. On its e side, a substantial collegiate Tudor range, with its main elevation facing e, by *Wardrop & Anderson*, 1886–8. Lower ranges, the n of 1878, the s of 1886, on the other two sides. N of this, small-scale but quite aggressively Baronial service buildings of 1891. At their ne corner, a conical-roofed round tower, one of its stringcourses decorated with foliage, human heads and a cock, the other rope-moulded. Above the archway of a screen wall which has extended n from this tower, a re-used stone incised with the motto, date and initials '16 GOD BE M^M R MC HERE 77'. The initials are almost certainly those of Mr Matthew Reid, then minister of Hoddom, and his wife, Margaret Crichton; perhaps the stone came from the former Hoddom Manse (demolished in the early C18).

HODDOMCROSS

Place-name marking the site of an Anglian monastery (of which nothing is now visible above ground), the former Hoddom Parish Church and its graveyard.

Former HODDOM PARISH CHURCH. Roofless since a fire in 1975. T-plan kirk of sneck-harled rubble, designed by the mason-architect *John Park* in 1816 and built the next year. Hoodmoulded and Y-traceried two-light windows. Pinnacles on the corners of the E and W gables. Another pinnacle on the W gable's apex, but the E gable is topped by a battlemented finial. The gable of the N 'aisle' is crowstepped and carries a tall birdcage bellcote with shallow crenellations. Another shallow battlement on the W side of this 'aisle'. The chunkily crow-stepped porches either end of the S wall look like later additions, perhaps dating from alterations made by *Robert Douglas* in 1913–14. The interior contained galleries and, in the 'aisle', a retiring room for the Sharpes of Hoddom.

In the graveyard, three BURIAL ENCLOSURES, probably all Georgian, but the one immediately SW of the church (containing a memorial tablet to the Rev. Alexander Orr † 1767) has stumpy attached columns corbelled out along the W and S sides. Also built into the W side, a purposeless console. – On the outer face of this enclosure's W wall, a large urn-finialled Roman Doric aedicular MONUMENT with foliaged scrolls at the sides. It was erected in 1779 by James Clow to commemorate his wife, Mary Hunter, of whom the inscription relates: 'And to be short to her Praise she was the wife that Solomon speaks of in the XXXI Chap of the book of Prov. from the 10th verse to the End'. – SE of the church, an urn-finialled OBELISK on a big pedestal; it is a monument to John Jeffrey † 1799. – Good number of C18 HEADSTONES, carved with coats of arms and emblems of death.

HODDOM BRIDGE, 1.7km. W. Humpbacked ashlar bridge built by *Andrew Laurie* in 1763–5. Three segmental arches with large triangular cutwaters.

HOLLOWS TOWER *see* GILNOCKIE TOWER

THE HOLM
0.8km. NW of Balmaclellan

The main block of the mansion house, which was Tudor of *c.* 1840, was demolished *c.* 1970 when *A. C. Wolffe* converted the service wings into a new house. They form a single-storey-and-attic parapeted U, built of cherry-cock-pointed whin with red sandstone dressings. Hoodmoulded windows and spiral-carved chimneys. At the open W side (formerly closed by the mansion), straightforward rendered walling, the gables topped by urns from the mansion's parapet. Five-bay N and S ranges, rather bare since Wolffe removed their bargeboarded gabled dormers. The E front is enjoyable. Panelled parapet carved with stylized reliefs. At each end, an advanced gable, shaped by scrolls and flanked and topped by urns. In the centre, a canted bay window; above, an urn-finialled steep pediment decorated with strapwork. Set into the gable of the l. end, a stone carved with the coat of arms of the Gordons, the initials RG and EG, and the date 1525.

Early C19 GATEPIERS close to the house with stylized scrolls at the sides and recumbent but watchful lions on top. – At the entrance to the drive, a LODGE of c. 1840 with the same-shaped gables as the house. Hoodmoulded door and windows placed in rusticated surrounds. – Contemporary octagonal GATEPIERS, again topped by recumbent lions, one awake, the other fast asleep. – In a copse S of the house, STATUES of 'Old Mortality' and his pony, versions of the group of 1840 by *John Currie* at Dumfries Museum.

HOLYWOOD

Small village of late C20 local authority housing, the Parish Church and its bow-fronted former MANSE (now KIRKLAND) of 1773 standing to the E, roughly on the site of the now vanished C12 or C13 Holywood Abbey.

PARISH CHURCH. Built in 1779 of rough ashlar. Piend-roofed T-plan, made cruciform by a tower projecting from the S side. At the body, tall round-arched windows with projecting keystones. Round-arched windows light the jamb's gallery, rectangular lights the area below. E and W porches added by *Alexander Fraser*, 1864. Also of 1864 the tall plain sneckedrubble addition to the end of the jamb. The tower is of three stages. The two lower, built of the same rough ashlar as the church and containing small rectangular openings, are of 1779; band course between these stages, a cornice above the second. The top stage is an addition, probably dating from repairs of 1821. Ashlar corner piers and a parapet pierced by roundheaded arcading make a framework at each face containing a pair of rectangular belfry openings separated by a slim Roman Doric column.

The interior was remodelled in 1864 by *Alexander Fraser*, who strengthened the ceiling with wooden beams and provided new pews. The gallery is now partitioned off as a meeting room. – C20 COMMUNION TABLE, LECTERN and FONT. – Over the communion table, a stainless steel LAMP crowned with thorns, designed by *John Young* and executed by *Henshaw*, 1969. – CHAMBER ORGAN of 1896 by *Wilkinson & Sons*, placed here in 1920. – STAINED GLASS. The four S windows, with

diaper patterns containing sacred and floral motifs, are of 1864–
c. 1880. – NW window (coloured crests and drawings of flowers
and foliage) of *c.* 1980.

GRAVEYARD. At the W entrance, C18 rusticated and ball-
finialled GATEPIERS, with a rubble-built HEARSE HOUSE,
probably C19, to the S. – Near the E wall, MONUMENT to
the Johnstons of Cowhill. The centrepiece is a Roman Doric
columned aedicule, with a coat of arms rising into the open
pediment. Its earliest inscription, to George Milligen Johnston
†1801, provides a likely date. Side wings with strapwork finials
on the consoled cornices; they look mid-C19. – Beside this, a tall
and elegant urn-finialled OBELISK to the Rev. Bryce Johnston
†1805. – At the graveyard's NW corner, the earlier C19 MAUSO-
LEUM of the Youngs of Lincluden. Pediment to the front, its
frieze supported by boldly projecting angle pilasters; in the
tympanum, a coat of arms. Exaggerated entasis to the lugged
architrave round the doorway. More boldly projecting pilasters
along the sides; roof of huge sandstone slabs.

SCHOOL. By *Dumfriesshire County Council*, 1967.

STONE CIRCLE (TWELVE APOSTLES), 0.4km. SW. The largest
stone circle in Scotland, formed in the third or second millennium B.C. It is *c.* 88m. in diameter, composed of eleven
(probably twelve originally) standing stones, of which five are
still upright. The tallest, 3.2m. long, lies on the ground. It has
diametrically faced the tallest (*c.* 1.9m. high) of the upright
stones. *See* the Introduction, p. 23.

COWHILL TOWER. *See* p. 192.
ISLE TOWER. *See* p. 350.
PORTRACK HOUSE. *See* p. 493.

INCH

OLD PARISH CHURCH. *See* Lochinch Castle and Castle
Kennedy.
PARISH CHURCH. *See* Castle Kennedy.

4030   ISLE OF WHITHORN

Picturesque large village with a deep and sheltered harbour used
from the C16 to the late C18 as the principal port of eastern
Wigtownshire, exporting barley and importing Swedish wood
and iron.

CHURCHES AND PUBLIC BUILDINGS

ISLE OF WHITHORN CHURCH, Main Street. Built as a Free
church in 1843–4. Rectangle of white-painted rubble, with
intersecting glazing-bars in the pointed windows. Birdcage
bellcote and club skewputts. The E porch and W vestry look
like early additions.

St Ninian's Chapel. Roofless but largely intact small rec- 6
tangular rubble-built church of *c.*1300, heavily restored by
P. MacGregor Chalmers in 1898. The entrance, robbed of dressings, is near the S wall's W end. In the W gable and N and S
walls, narrow windows, their sides splayed to the inside; they
are now rectangles but may originally have been lancets. The
E window, originally of two lights, has lost all external dressings;
pointed rear-arch internally. Inside the church, a small square
aumbry near the N wall's E end. Opposite, in the S wall,
two irregular recesses, conceivably vestiges of a piscina and
credence. On the r. of the E window, a projecting stone, its
purpose unclear. There seems to have been a bench along the
W end. The surrounding churchyard has had a stone wall.

HARBOUR. Formed in the C16, but the present rubble quay is of
1790. At its W end, a late C19 or early C20 concrete pier with
wooden rubbing posts.

SCHOOL, off Main Street. Now in other use. Tudor of 1872, with
hoodmoulds over the windows and a diagonally set chimney.

ISLE OF WHITHORN CASTLE
off Main Street

Harled three-storey tower house, perhaps built in 1674 for Patrick
Houston of Drummaston.* It is L-plan, with the inner angle of
the main block and the crowstep-gabled NE jamb almost filled
by a broad stair tower. On the main block's S corners, rounded
turrets projected on individual moulded corbels; their roofs
slope into the gables and under the main eaves. Large windows
at the first and second floors; the r. first-floor window in the S
front has a moulded surround. Plain single-storey N wing added
in the C19.

DESCRIPTION

MAIN STREET'S entry from the N sets the tone, with brightly
painted and often rendered C18 and C19 vernacular terraced
houses of one or two storeys. More of the same in TON-
DERGHIE ROW to the W, but here the norm is broken by
the taller mid-C19 DUNBAR HOUSE, its bipartite windows
containing round-arched lights. S of this, MAIN STREET
becomes bitty, with just a few buildings on its E side watched
over by Isle of Whithorn Castle (*see* above). LOW ISLE HOUSE,
which has a rusticated blind bullseye in the advanced and
chimney-gabled centre, may be late C18. Then a gap (the
causeway to the isle proper) before the street starts again with 2
terraced cottages on both sides, much as at its beginning. A
lane between Nos. 58 and 60 on the E leads to the former
school (*see* above). Then, round the corner to the r., C19
warehouses overlooking the harbour (*see* above).

---

* A stone, not *in situ*, carved with that date and the initials of Patrick Houston and
his wife, Margaret Gordon, has been re-used in the C19 wing.

FARM

ISLE FARM, 1km. N. Broad-eaved Tudor *cottage orné* of *c.* 1840,
with sloping stone canopies over the mullioned and transomed
windows. – Simple whitewashed STEADING, probably early
C19, on the other side of the road.

TONDERGHIE. *See* p. 553.

0060

ISLE TOWER
0.4km. N of Bankend

Ruined tower house, probably of *c.* 1565 and reconstructed by
Edward Maxwell in 1622.* It has been a three-storey-and-attic T-
plan, with the stair jamb projecting from the centre of the N wall.
The E gable, the S wall's E end and a fair amount of the N wall
(its W end reinforced by later buttresses) still stand; they are
pierced at all levels by a splendidly purposeful array of wide-
mouthed oval gunloops and circular shotholes. In the gable, a
quite comfortably sized ground-floor window. At the first floor,
a large window with a roll-and-hollow moulding; beside it, a
blocked horizontally proportioned opening. Small second-floor
window, the surround again moulded. Rising through the eaves
cornice, one jamb, also moulded, of an attic window. The
arrangement of these openings appears quite random.
    Inside there survive the moulded jambs of a door from the
stair jamb into the main block, whose ground floor may have
been vaulted. Segmental-arched embrasures to the first- and
second-floor windows of the E gable. Small second-floor E
fireplace.

9080

ISLE TOWER
2.6km. NW of Holywood

Diminutive C16 tower house, now attached to an unpretentious
laird's house of the C18 and C19. The tower itself, built for
John Ferguson of Isle in 1587 (the date over the entrance),
is a simple three-storey-and-attic crowstep-gabled rectangle,
c. 5.86m. by 6.78m., its rubble walls built of a mixture of whin
and red sandstone. No parapet, but fat round turrets at the NE
and SW, each carried on continuous corbelling whose top
course alone projects clear of the corner; the adjacent skews of
the gables are cut back to allow room for the turrets. In the SW
turret, a round gunhole. Chimney on top of the W gable; at the
apex of the E gable, a small arched doocot opening, with a
flight ledge below. Gableted dormerhead on the S front. Roll-
moulded surrounds to the upper floors' N and S windows. At
the SE corner, small slit windows lighting the stair. Over its

* That date, together with the arms and initials of Edward Maxwell and his wife,
Helen Douglas, used to be displayed on a panel on the stair jamb; but there was a
fortalice here by 1614.

roll-moulded entrance (now inside the later house to the s), a stone carved with the date 1587, the arms of Ferguson of Isle, and the initials of John Ferguson and his wife. The entrance itself is unusually defensive, perhaps to compensate for the tower's shortage of gunloops and lack of a parapet. It has contained an external wooden door with an iron bar across its inner face. Behind the door, an iron yett, still *in situ*, behind which were two more bars. On the tower's ground floor, a store (subdivided) its vault removed. Quite smart first-floor hall, its E window provided with stone seats. High-set rectangular opening in the N wall. In the E wall, an aumbry, its soffit pierced by a hole giving access to a safe above. Two more aumbries in the N and W walls. In the NE corner, a close garderobe lit by a small window. The neo-Jacobean woodwork was provided by *Kinnear & Peddie* in 1891. Probably also of 1891 is the wooden corbel carved as a grotesque head under one end of a ceiling joist. The second floor has again contained a single room. Its w aumbry is probably c16, the N (contained in boarding rather than stonework) probably late c19. More woodwork of 1891. No fireplace at the attic floor, but it enjoys access to the turrets, the NE with a small window, the SW having a larger window as well as a gunhole. Loft above.

Attached to the S side is a mid-c18 two-storey house built of whitewashed rubble. The corniced doorpiece looks Georgian, except for its chamfered surround, perhaps altered in 1882, when *Kinnear & Peddie* added neo-Jacobean dormerheads and crowsteps. Perhaps at the same time or a little later, the r. ground-floor window was enlarged to two lights, and the c18 house was extended at the back and given a single-storey S addition and SW wing. Inside, the drawing room contains a late c19 dado, its panels carved with c16 motifs, and a neo-Jacobean wooden chimneypiece.

Extending from the w gable of the tower house, a two-storey office wing by *John Milligan*, 1806. Set into its masonry are two earlier moulded panels; both are now illegible but the S is said to have borne the initials MAA and the date 1700.

JARDINE HALL   *1080*
3.6km. N of Applegarth

The mansion house (built in 1814 but much altered and enlarged by *E. J. May* in 1892–7) was demolished in 1964. The large quadrangular STABLE COURT of 1825 survives. Ashlar-faced showfront to the W. Rusticated base below the ground-floor sill course. At each end, a pedimented two-storey tripartite-windowed pavilion. Single-storey links, their round-arched windows blind, join the pavilions to the centrepiece, a square tower whose bottom stage is pierced by a tall roundheaded and pilastered pend arch. Above, a clock-stage with Roman Doric columns in its cut-out corners. On top, a circular domed lantern, its walling pierced by round openings. The other elevations are plainer. The N and S ranges have pedimented centrepieces. – To the NW, a WALLED GARDEN of c.1820, divided into two compartments by a central wall. The inward-curving S wall of the E part has a pair of Roman Doric columned and pedimented aedicules flanking the gateway (the wrought-iron gates themselves are of 1927); more aedicules in this part of the wall but they are pilastered and mostly blind. In the centre of the W part's S wall, a pedimented and urn-finialled gateway, the tympanum carved with a swag.

1090   JOHNSTONEBRIDGE

Tiny village, mostly of the C20.

JOHNSTONE PARISH CHURCH, 0.8km. S. Piend-roofed L-plan kirk of 1818–19, by the mason-architect *John MacDonald*, incor-porating the S wall and gables of the church built here in 1743–5 and one wall of the earlier Annandale Aisle. All of red sandstone rubble with rusticated quoins. Big round-arched windows with projecting imposts and keystones. At the main block's NE corner, a square two-storey tower, its first-floor window again round-arched. On the church's E gable, a ball-finialled birdcage bellcote with panelled piers. In the inner angle of the tower and church, a flat-roofed and parapeted session house and porch, its present appearance dating from an alteration of 1907 by *F. J. C. Carruthers*. Very simple interior, the FURNISHINGS introduced in 1881–2 by *James Barbour*, but his pine pulpit is now altered and the E gallery partitioned off. – In the porch, a BELL, perhaps C17, said to have come from Lochwood Tower.

To the SW, piend-roofed MANSE of c.1795, made L-plan by the addition of a wing in 1809.

SCHOOL. By the architect-builder *Alexander Morison*, 1862–3. Single-storey school, a consoled cornice over its door. Two-storey Georgian-survival schoolhouse at the W end.

TOLLHOUSE, Dinwoodie, 1.8km. SE. Single-storey tollhouse designed by *Thomas Telford* and built by *John MacDonald*, 1822–3. Projecting bow at the E front; in the W, pointed windows, the centre one of three lights. Broad-eaved piended roof.

RAEHILLS HOUSE. *See* p. 495.

8090   KEIR MILL

Tiny village founded in the late C18, though most of the houses are now C19. The eponymous MILL of 1771 was much altered on its conversion to a house, but it retains its scrolled skewputts.

KEIR PARISH CHURCH. Stolid Gothic, by *William Burn*, 1813–15 (*see* the Introduction, p. 40). Broad three-bay box built of pinkish Capenoch ashlar. Gableted buttresses; three-light Tudorish windows, their tracery renewed in *James Barbour*'s alterations of 1880. Battlemented but dumpy W tower, the

belfry corners chamfered. Barbour added a slim stair turret
with an octagonal stone-roofed top at its SW corner. Also of
1880 is the stugged-ashlar E chancel and the adjoining lean-to
vestry.

SCHOOL. Now in other use. Built in the later C19. Prominent
front gables, mullioned windows and a Gothic door.

FARMS ETC.

MORTON HOLM, 1km. NE. Prosperous mid-C19 ashlar-fronted
farmhouse. Pilastered and corniced doorpiece; stone gablets
over the first-floor windows. Whitewashed farm buildings
behind.

NETHER KEIR, 3.1km. SE. White-painted farmhouse of two
storeys and three bays, the windows grouped 1/2/1/1; gabled
porch. It was probably built as part of *William McCaig*'s work
here in 1841.

OLD MANSE. Built in 1777–8 by *Archibald Cleland* but enlarged
and recast in 1828. Piend-roofed main block of white-painted
rubble, a band course dividing the ground and first floors. Plain
corniced doorpiece.

PENFILLAN, 0.5km. W. Two-storey three-bay piend-roofed
farmhouse of *c.* 1830. The gabled porch may be an addition.

CAIRN, Capenoch Moor, 2.1km. W. Rising from moorland, a
long cairn of the third or second millennium B.C., the mound
formed of angular stones. It is *c.* 34m. long, the width tapering
from *c.* 17m. at the higher SW end to *c.* 11.6m. at the NE, which
has been badly robbed. Parts of the internal construction are
exposed, showing walls of flat slabs, some founded on rubble.
The present cairn is almost certainly a unification of several
originally separate chambered cairns.

BARJARG TOWER. *See* p. 120.

KELLOHOLM *see* KIRKCONNEL

KELTON   7060

Handful of houses near the church.

PARISH CHURCH. Built in 1805–6; a big box of harled rubble
with rusticated quoins. Round-arched windows, bullseyes in
the gables. Gabled bellcote added by *R. Rowand Anderson*,
1879. Short jamb of 1895. N porch of *c.* 1930. The interior was
remodelled in 1879 by Anderson, who faced the walls with red
tiles and provided an open kingpost-truss roof. – ORGAN by
Forster & Andrews, 1895, the pipes stencilled. – On the wall to
the r. of the organ, a MONUMENT to the Rev. Samuel Cowan,
with a high-relief portrait bust by *T. Stuart Burnett*, 1887.

   A little to the N, the MAUSOLEUM of Sir William Douglas, 52
said to have been designed by his nephew, *William Douglas*, the
friend of H. W. ('Grecian') Williams, and built in 1821. Very

best Ægypto-Greek in white ashlar. Boldly battered sides and a Doric entablature; entrance with Greek Doric columns recessed between the inclined jambs. On top, a panelled attic under a boldly projecting roof.

CHURCHYARD, to the SE. The site of the OLD PARISH CHURCH, which was rebuilt in 1743 and given an 'aisle' forty years later. Only a tiny fragment survives, kept as the backing for a pilastered MONUMENT to the Rev. William Falconer †1727. – A couple of late Georgian BURIAL ENCLOSURES.

INGLESTON, 2.7km. SE. Two-storey painted rubble late C18 farmhouse, originally L-plan with a SW jamb. The pedimented Roman Doric N portico is probably an addition of the early C19, when the flanking ground-floor windows may have been enlarged to three-light. Also early C19 is the addition filling the SE inner angle, a full-height bow window on its E face.

GELSTON CASTLE. *See* p. 317.

KENMURE CASTLE
                    1.4km. S of New Galloway

Derelict harled remains of the C16 and C17 courtyard house of the Gordons of Lochinvar (Viscounts of Kenmure after 1633), much altered in the C19 and abandoned in the C20. The site, a conical knoll near the head of Loch Ken, was probably artificially strengthened in the early medieval period. The house now occupying its summit seems to have developed from the late C16. Two drawings by Francis Grose show its appearance in 1790, when it consisted of a courtyard with its N (entrance) and E sides bounded by high walls, the W side filled by a tall range and the S by a lower block. Projecting at each of the S corners was a rectangular tower with angle rounds, probably of the later C16. These two towers, depicted by Grose as roofless and described by him as ruinous, may have been demolished in 1817, when a new approach was made and the courtyard's N and E walls were pulled down.

Rather later in the C19 (probably in the 1840s, when *William McCandlish* worked here), the S range (formerly stables) was remodelled and heightened as domestic accommodation and the W range was extended to the S. This range was remodelled by *M. E. Hadfield & Son* in 1879, when the S range was thickened to the S. In 1908 *Christian Eliot* extended the W range to the N.

The oldest and by far the most interesting part of the house is now the main portion of the three-storey W range, almost certainly built *c.* 1630 for Sir John Gordon of Lochinvar, first Viscount of Kenmure, who is said to have 'brought Kenmure to the perfection of a complete fabric as it was never before'. Plain outer (W) front, with simply moulded window surrounds and gunloops which are now rectangular but may originally have been circular or oval.

The E front to the courtyard is the showpiece. Projecting NE stair tower, its S face canted. C18 and C19 views show tusking on the tower's N front (now hidden by the early C20 addition), suggesting that it may have been intended to sit in the inner angle formed by a range across the courtyard's N side which was never built. Rope-moulded stringcourses, their decorative gymnastics displaying the inventiveness of a master mason, run across the upper floors of both the tower and the main block, jumping up as a hood over each window. The baseline of the lower stringcourse is placed at first-floor sill level; that of the upper stringcourse runs just above the sills of most of the second-floor windows, but at the stair tower it is brought down to the window sill and held in place there by a couple of high-relief terms. At one of the main block's windows, the stringcourse is not content to join a procession of hoods but also drops down between a pair of carved human heads to form an inverted ogee arch under the opening. The importance of the door in the S face of the stair tower is emphasized by the lower stringcourse being broken by two superimposed rope-moulded ogee arches; the lower arch frames the door itself, the inverted upper arch surrounds an empty panel frame. At the main block, an eaves cornice of small moulded corbels, alternately advanced and recessed. This cornice is carried across the stair tower as a stringcourse supporting a shallowly projected caphouse and jumping up over its E window. The sturdy stepped buttresses against the main block's ground floor were added in 1865 by *Hugh H. Maclure*; the walling between them is of 1879.

Projecting from the end of the E front in the inner angle with the S range is a sizeable octagonal stair tower, possibly also of *c.* 1630 but more likely to be an addition of the later C17. The lines of the main block's stringcourse and cornice are continued across it as sill courses, but, instead of being rope-moulded, they are plain projections above a ball moulding. Over the door, a large panel carved with an heraldic achievement.

The S range is probably largely of the 1840s in its present form, but the two lower floors may have been built or remodelled in the C18 (perhaps *c.* 1743, when repairs were made), and the range was lengthened 3m. to the E in 1879. It is now plain except for gableted dormerheads (one surviving on the N front) and for its entrance (now a window). This looks like re-used work of *c.* 1630, possibly taken from one of the demolished S towers. Moulded stone door surround. This is framed by an arched rope moulding. Inside the top of the arch has been placed a stone carved with the Gordon coat of arms flanked by a pair of cusped blind arches, each containing the relief of a human figure; this may be the stone which Grose showed over the N entrance to the courtyard.

The W range's S end as remodelled in 1879 attempts to suggest the tower shown here by Grose, an angle turret giving Baronial emphasis. The addition of 1908 at the N end of the W range tries hard to fit in by quoting the C17 detail, without much conviction; a large chimney corbelled out at the W gable is its most memorable feature.

The interiors were mostly destroyed by fire *c.* 1950. On the ground floor of the C17 W range there is an E passage off which open tunnel-vaulted stores with round shotholes in their W wall. Another shothole, blocked by the early C20 addition, in the W side of the stair tower.

KETTLEHOLM

Hamlet, its trim late Georgian housing built for workers on the Castlemilk estate.

ST MUNGO PARISH CHURCH. Muscular late Scots Gothic, by *David Bryce*, 1875–7. Broad buttressed box with a NE tower, all built of bullnosed grey Brookholm ashlar. At the corners, diagonally set buttresses with crocketed pinnacles; shallowly crenellated battlement. Plain lancet windows in the long sides. At the W gable, a pinnacled-buttressed porch decorated with grotesque carved heads. Above it, two-light Dec windows under a big wheel window. In the E gable, two fat lancets under a large rose window. Simple S porch. The tower is also diagonally buttressed and battlemented. At its SW corner, an octagonal caphouse with a crocketed stone spire; octagonal stair turret clasping the SW corner.

The interior is a single broad space under a magnificently elaborate open roof. – PEWS of 1876. – The small PULPIT, decorated with linenfold panelling, looks like a replacement of 1905, when the ORGAN (by *Abbot & Smith*) was introduced behind it. – Windows all with STAINED GLASS by *James Ballantine & Son*, 1876. In the side walls the glass is obscured and plain except for red foliage-patterned borders. Abstract patterns in the end windows, the central roundel in the W wheel window displaying a Star of David, the E a dove. – WAR MEMORIAL in the porch, a bronze tablet with a relief of two angels holding a scroll. It is by *F. M. Taubman*, 1922.

HALL. By *D. W. Campbell*, 1907–8. Smartly white-harled, with red sandstone dressings. Steep shaped gablet in the centre of the front. Octagonal cupola, bellcast eaves at its spire.

ST MUNGO SCHOOL, 0.2km. N. Built as St Mungo Parish Church in 1841–2; *William McGowan* was the architect. Harled T-plan, with round-arched windows and a birdcage bellcote on the E jamb. It was converted to a school in 1876–7 by *James Barbour*, who added a W classroom in the same manner as the church. Later lean-to additions against the jamb.

CASTLEMILK. *See* p. 173.

KILLUMPHA
1.5km. E of Port Logan

Plain harled tower, perhaps of *c.* 1600, with Georgian windows and dummy bartizans probably provided in 1823, when *John McConnel*, mason, and *James McTaldroch*, joiner, built the low farmhouse which almost engulfs it. That house has itself been dressed up in the C20 with bay windows and crudely battle-mented porches.

KINMOUNT HOUSE

1060

2.2km. N of Cummertrees

Severely rational mansion house of 1812–18, the first to be 89 designed by *Robert Smirke** in what Pugin described as 'New Square' style (Greek-revival stripped of ornament). It was built for the fifth Marquess of Queensberry, who had inherited the title but very little else from a distant cousin in 1810. It is made up of a three-storey cross with arms of varying breadths at whose intersection there rises a four-storey square tower. In the inner angles, two-storey blocks. Single-storey service wing to the W. All this is built of honey-coloured polished ashlar from Cove quarry, the precisely dressed masonry reinforcing the austerity, although this is now belied by Baroque urn-topped balustrades added by *James Barbour & Bowie* in 1899. At the tower's exposed top stage, round-arched windows.

The entrance front faces N. Here the cross's arm is three bays wide, the centre slightly advanced. Projecting from this, a porte cochère with coupled pilasters at the corners; round-arched entrance behind. At the E side the barely projecting arm is only one bay broad; segmental-headed overarch to its ground-floor window. To the S, a broader arm, its five-bay front slightly recessed behind the corner blocks, each with a three-light window in a segmental-headed overarch. The slightly projecting W arm of the cross is three bays wide. In its S bay, an overarched three-light window. The other two bays are overlaid by the service wing, along whose S front *Barbour & Bowie* added a conservatory in 1899. This is single-storey, with tall pilastered and pedimented end pavilions. Between them, five mullioned and transomed three-light windows with pilasters between. Behind, the join of Smirke's service wing to the main block is marked on the N side by a slightly advanced one-bay section, its window overarched, its piend roof just softening the austerity of the rest. Projecting from the house's E corners, pilastered and pedimented gates to the garden, probably by *J. M. Bowie*, *c.*1922.

The interior, like the exterior, is grouped round the central tower, which contains a three-storey hall. On its E and W sides, first-floor galleries carried on rather tall Greek Doric columns. Over each gallery is a semicircular coffered arch recess, at the hall's N and S sides blind semicircular arches, all these walls containing roundheaded subsidiary openings. Above, pendentives forming a dome topped by a lantern from whose roundheaded windows and cupola the light floods down. Cantilevered stair to the W. The original severity of the principal rooms was softened a little in 1899 by the introduction of some

* *William Burn* was the job architect.

oak woodwork. In the s-facing dining room, simple plaster panels on the walls. Austerely compartmented ceiling with rosettes on the beams and a central rose. Black marble chimneypiece with Empire-style garlands on the jambs. Drawing room at the SE corner, its ceiling a panelled elliptical vault.

w of the house are the STABLES of 1820, also by *Smirke*. Two-storey N range (converted to a house by *Wheeler & Sproson, c.*1981), with the outer bays shallowly advanced and pedimented. Single-storey E and W ranges, each with a pedimented door and gable. – Beside the stables, the MOTOR HOUSE of 1907, its E front with a pair of pedimented gables flanking a canopied shelter in front of the garage doors. – To the SW, QUEENSBERRY HOUSE, a very simple single-storey cottage built *c.*1815, extended from three bays to four later in the C19. Its original door and window openings have moulded surrounds of *c.*1700, apparently re-used from the previous mansion house here (known as Kelhead). Of the same date and from the same source is the large Douglas family crest set in the wall beside the door. – SW of Kinmount House, a late C19 brick-built AVIARY composed of five gabled shelters opening into wrought-iron cages, the outer two forming large octagonal pavilions. – To the SE, across an ornamental lake, a free Jacobean Renaissance BATHING HOUSE of *c.*1900. Shaped gables to E and W, balustraded bows to N and s. – At the s entrances to the parkland, HANNAH LODGE and HITCHILL LODGE, both of *c.*1900, with wooden verandahs. They stand beside elaborate wrought-iron gates. – At the NW entrance, the Edwardian WEST LODGE. Two storeys with a Tudor-arched pend over the drive. Half-timbering and an octagonal turret in the inner angle of the L-shape. – A little E of the main drive's start from the NE, the EAST LODGE, early C19 with horizontal glazing. In the N gable, a round-arched panel carved with the heraldic achievement of the Marquesses of Queensberry. – To its W, quadrants linking square GATEPIERS of *c.*1815, all topped by flattened pyramids; the massive inner two piers are a powerful foretaste of the mansion house.

KIRKANDREWS

6040

Hamlet begun in the late C18 beside the site of a medieval church.

CHAPEL. Built in 1906 by a Manchester businessman, James Brown, who had bought the nearby estate of Knockbrex. On the approach, a lychgate of stone and wood with a red tile roof. The chapel itself is a small rectangle crushed by a corbelled parapet, with a round tower projecting at the NE corner. Round-arched windows. Buttressed and battlemented W porch. Inside, walls of ribbon-pointed rubble partly masked by a high panelled dado, the windows and door framed by attached columns, their capitals enriched with neo-Celtic decoration. The focus is on the N end's rubbly fireplace, a weathered heraldic panel in its overmantel.

CHURCHYARD. The medieval parish church has been demolished, but two rubble-built BURIAL ENCLOSURES mark its
position and may incorporate fragments of its walling. – To
their s, a curly-topped late C18 heraldic HEADSTONE erected
by John Campbell of Croyeard to the memory of members of
his family.

FARMS ETC.

BARMAGACHAN, 1.7km. NE. Unpretentious early C18 harled
two-storey laird's house with vestigially stepped gables to the
steep roof. At the back, irregularly placed windows, most
reduced to their putative original size in 1972. The front faces
N into a courtyard. Three-bay centrepiece, with roll-moulded
surrounds to the openings. Recess above the door, presumably
for an heraldic panel. Lower wings (the w one heightened in
1972), perhaps of the later C18, project s and are joined by a
flat-roofed N range of 1972.

  W of the house, a small 6m.-high MOTTE, of truncated cone
shape, the summit enclosed by a bank. Some remains of a ditch
and counterscarp round the base.

CORSEYARD, 1km. W. Prominently sited courtyard steading built 125
for James Brown of Knockbrex in 1911–14, the heavy detailing
imparting a nightmare quality. The main (s) block is the
milking parlour, with lean-to buttresses and roundheaded
entrances and overarches; the E door has a heavy hood. Nave
and aisles treatment, the gables of the segmental-arched 'nave'
pierced by big crosslet 'arrowslits'. On the N side, a tall water-
tower, with a rounded merlon in the centre of each face, little
battlemented turrets on the corners and a battlemented circular
caphouse. E range (stables) with a small but very martial tower.
Less aggressive low ranges on the N (barn) and w (cartshed)
sides. Inside the dairy, the walls are patterned with glazed
faience bricks; glazed terracotta tiles on the floor. To the s, a
boundary wall. Ball-finialled gabled gateway, the horseshoe-
shaped arch under a crosslet 'arrowslit'. At the W corner, a
small battlemented turret (tool shed).

DUN, Castle Haven, 0.7km. W. On a rocky sea-girt promontory,
naturally defensible on the W and s. The w end is enclosed by
a D-plan wall from which is carried out a second wall of the
same shape, providing an inner and outer enclosure. The inner
is perhaps of the first century B.C., the outer perhaps a little
later; both walls were 'restored' and heightened in 1905. The
outer enclosure, c.39m. by 20m., was surrounded by a solid
wall, c.2.7m. thick, pierced by entrances at the NE and SE. On
the inner face, three sets of slab steps which gave access to the
wallhead. The inner enclosure's area is c.18.3m. by 10.7m.
maximum. Surrounding wall mostly composed of two skins of
masonry enclosing narrow galleries or passages. Main entrance
to the enclosure at the NE, aligned with the outer enclosure's
entrance. At its outer end's E side, an upright stone, probably
a doorcheck. Halfway through this entrance passage, a pair of

upright stones which clearly are doorchecks. Inside the enclosure, doorways into the galleries and, at the NE, slab steps to
the wallhead. At the enclosure's SW corner, a narrow stepped
passage through the wall giving access to more steps on a path
down to the shore.

MOTTE, Roberton, 0.3km. NE. Formed, probably in the late C12,
by cutting a ditch through a bank overlooking the Pulwhirrin
Burn to isolate a roughly oblong area of *c.*27m. by 14m.

KNOCKBREX. *See* p. 397.

PLUNTON CASTLE. *See* p. 489.

KIRKBEAN

Hamlet of picturesque but simple early C19 cottages.

PARISH CHURCH. Harled T-plan kirk of 1776, said* to have
been designed by *William Craik* of Arbigland. Tall round-
arched windows in the S wall of the tail, which has a Venetian
window in its E gable; in the gables of the cross-bar, rectangular
windows over the doors. N porch added by *Samuel Hunter* in
1881–3, perhaps the date of the boiler house at the E end. In
the W wall, tall round-arched windows flank the tower. Its two
lower stages are of 1776; the second has a Diocletian window.
The two upper stages were added in 1835–6 by *Walter Newall*,
the first with a clock in its front, the top a big octagonal belfry
cupola of polished ashlar under a lantern, now missing its finial.
Inside, plain FURNISHINGS of 1881–3.

At the entrance to the CHURCHYARD, GATEPIERS, dated
1835, with stepped ashlar tops and ball finials. – Immediately
SW of the church, a HEADSTONE to Marian Costine †1756, its
front topped by an angel's head (the soul). On the back, the
high-relief figure of a woman under the inscription: 'All you
young women as you pass by As you are now so once was I
Remember tho that you must die'. – To its S, bits of a TABLE
STONE, probably C18, the ends carved with baluster columns
framing high reliefs of ladies. – At the churchyard's E end, an
aedicular red sandstone MONUMENT to William Maxwell of
Preston †1741; the orderless fluted pilasters carry a scrolled
broken pediment carved with a small coat of arms; inscription
tablet of white marble.

MANSE (now WOODSIDE HOUSE) to the SW, built in 1798;
low piend-roofed offices (converted to a dwelling) on its W.

SCHOOL. Dated 1885. L-plan, of squared granite rubble with red
sandstone dressings. Curvaceous neo-Jacobean hoodmoulds
over the S gable's two-light window.

TORRORIE, 2.8km. SW. Prosperous farmhouse of *c.*1770, built
of white-painted rubble. Main block of three storeys and three
bays, the parapeted porch added in 1808. Two-storey lateral
wings, each with a one-bay front.

ARBIGLAND. *See* p. 104.

* By *The New Statistical Account of Scotland* (1845).

KIRKCOLM   0060

A burgh of barony (Stewarton) was founded here in 1623 but had disappeared by the 1780s, when the present village was begun. MAIN STREET's houses are mostly C19 vernacular; in and off CHURCH STREET to the W, the Parish Church and C20 housing.

PARISH CHURCH, Church Street. Harled T-plan kirk of 1824, wooden Y-tracery in the big pointed windows. Diagonal-set buttresses at the corners. More buttresses (two now removed) against the long E wall. On the gable of the W 'aisle', a birdcage bellcote, a C20 concrete replacement for the Georgian original. Plain and altered interior, the 'aisle' partitioned off.

Immediately E of the church, the KILMORE STONE CROSS, said to have come from a graveyard around the former St Mary's Chapel at Kilmorie (2.9km. S). In the C18 it was built into the former parish church as a door lintel; after that church was demolished, it was erected in the grounds of Corsewall House before being moved to its present site in 1988. Each face is carved but the reliefs are so different in style that they must be assumed to be by different hands and of different dates, probably in the C9 or C10. On the S face, the relief of a cross, with a chalice and host at the intersection of the arms; below the cross, two snakes. Interlaced decoration on the cross and under the snakes. All this shows Celtic influence. The other face is cruder and the stylistic influence Norse. Incised depiction of the Crucifixion above the figure of a man or god accompanied by two birds, the symbolism probably intended to display the triumph of Christianity over a heathen god, either Odin or Sigurd. – W of the church, a tall red sandstone STATUE of c.1920, the stylized representation of a woman with a child clasping her skirt.

MARIAN TOWER, 3.3km. W. Small but prominently sited phallic stone tower erected in 1802 by Sir John Ross, the Arctic explorer, in memory of his wife.

PUBLIC HALL, Church Street. Built in 1928. Harled, with sparing Jacobean detail.

CORSEWALL HOUSE. See p. 191.

KIRKCONNEL   7010

Large village begun in the later C18 but with few buildings earlier than the late C19, when coal mining (now abandoned) began in earnest. Kelloholm to the SE, a development begun in 1921, is a suburb which has now outgrown its parent in size if not interest.

CHURCHES

PARISH CHURCH, Main Street. The body was built in 1728–30 by *John Weir*, mason in Carcoside, following instructions from the first *Earl of Glasgow*; N jamb added by *Adam Laidlaw*, 1805–

6. It forms a rubble-built and sneck-harled T, with rectangular side windows and bullseyes (now blocked) in the E and W gables. At the corners, strip quoins surmounted by urns. More urns on the apex of the W gable and the corners of the E gable's birdcage bellcote. At the centre of each face of the bellcote, a broad ogee-topped panel carved with a winged heart, the armorial bearing of the Duke of Queensberry, the parish's principal C18 landowner; stone ogee roof. In 1896 the church was recast by *MacGibbon & Ross,* who gave the roof a red tile cresting, lengthened the N jamb, placing a Venetian window in its new gable, and added a vestry at the E end and an apse with round-arched windows in the centre of the long S wall. Built into the apse are four carved stones from the graveyard of St Connel's Church (*see* below). Two are Corinthian capitals, a third is carved with an angel's head (the soul), the fourth shows a book. They probably belonged to C18 monuments. W porch of 1923; in its ball-finialled but simplified pediment, a stone bearing the date 1729.

The interior is largely by MacGibbon & Ross. Kingpost-truss roof; broad low arch into the apse. – FURNISHINGS of the 1890s. – The font is an C11 rectangular CROSS BASE found near St Connel's Church (*see* below) and placed here in 1896. In the top, a socket hole. On two sides, weathered carving of interlaced work. – STAINED GLASS. In the apse, the centre light (the Crucifixion) is by *Stephen Adam,* 1901, the two flanking lights (the Risen Lord, the Nativity of Christ) of 1914 by *Alfred A. Webster,* all in strong dark colours. – The main S wall's W window ('The Harvesters') is by *James McPhie,* 1967; stylized realism. – Similar and contemporary window (Christ the King) E of the apse. – In the main block's N wall, one window ('Go ye therefore and teach all nations'), more expressionist, by *Crerar,* 1969. – The jamb's N window (St Conal) is by *R. Douglas McLundie* of the *Abbey Studio,* 1964. – MONUMENTS on the S wall. W of the apse, a grey marble tablet by *George Webster,* 1894, carved with a relief portrait and commemorating the Rev. John Donaldson. – E of the apse, a bronze relief portrait to the Rev. Charles Forbes Charleson, by *C. d'O. Pilkington Jackson,* 1955.

Just outside the churchyard, a tall MONUMENT of 1912 to Alexander Anderson, 'surfaceman' and poet. Two craggy blocks of red sandstone, the upper bearing a bronze plaque with a relief portrait by *H. S. Gamley.*

On Main Street's S side, the very plain CHURCH HALL of *c.* 1900.

ST CONAL (R.C.). Dated 1921. Gentle Gothic, in white harl with brick dressings.

ST CONNEL, 1.6km. N. The outline of the medieval parish church of Kirkconnel, perhaps dating from *c.* 1300, was revealed by excavation in 1926. It has been a simple rectangle, *c.* 22.5m. by 8.2m., containing a nave and a chancel raised by two steps. The present low rubble walls are mostly of 1926 but incorporate stones carved with emblems of death (skulls, crossbones and an hourglass), presumably from C18 monuments. – In the graveyard wall, FRAGMENTS of dressed stonework, including bits of cross shafts.

SALVATION ARMY HALL, Main Street. Built as Kirkconnel United Free Church in 1911. Humble except for a fleur-de-lis finial on the front gable.

PUBLIC BUILDINGS

KELLOHOLM SCHOOL. By the Dumfries County Architect, *George Bartholomew*, 1954–6, incorporating a building of 1925 which was enlarged in 1952.

KIRKCONNEL ACTIVITY AND RESOURCE CENTRE, Main Street. Built as a school in the later C19. Single-storey and U-plan with mullioned and transomed windows in the front gables. In 1910 *W. F. Crombie* filled the hollow centre with a twin-gabled addition.

KIRKCONNEL COMMUNITY EDUCATION CENTRE, Main Street. Small Tudor school of 1907, by *David Stitt*. Behind, a blocky detached extension by *James Crombie*, 1912–14.

POLICE STATION, Main Street. By *James Barbour*, 1897. Picturesque, with bracketed broad eaves.

RAILWAY STATION, off Main Street. *Cottage orné* of 1850. – Lattice-sided FOOTBRIDGE over the track.

DESCRIPTION

The village consists of little more than the long MAIN STREET running from the Parish Church at the W end to St Conal's (R.C.) Church at the E (for these, *see* Churches, above). Just before the Parish Church, THE SCHOOL HOUSE by *Charles Howitt*, 1856, Georgian-survival with overlapping skews. Immediately after the church, the Kirkconnel Activity and Resource Centre facing the Kirkconnel Community Education Centre (*see* Public Buildings, above). Beside the latter, the WAR MEMORIAL of *c.*1920, a granite statue of a youthful soldier. Then, one- and two-storey housing of the C19 and early C20. In it, a few incidents. The QUEENSBERRY ARMS HOTEL of the earlier C19 boasts a corniced doorpiece. Red sandstone BANK OF SCOTLAND (former BRITISH LINEN BANK) of 1925, its doorpiece pilastered. MAC'S BAR, built as a hall in 1922, has vaguely Jacobean detail and a broad front gablet. On the S side of the street, the MINERS' MEMORIAL of 1983–4, designed by *Tom Sandilands*, its principal feature the bronze bust of a miner by *Michael Williams*. After the Police Station and Salvation Army Hall (*see* Public Buildings and Churches, above), a late C19 terrace, quite picturesque with bargeboarded dormers.

FARMS

BUTTKNOWE, off the W end of Main Street. Piend-roofed ashlar-walled farmhouse of the earlier C19. Hoodmoulded windows. The Douglas coat of arms is carved on a stone in the front wall. – Contemporary STEADING behind.

KELLOSIDE, 0.4km. S. Gableted Tudor farmhouse of the 1870s; horizontal glazing in the windows. – Contemporary STEADING behind.

KIRKCONNEL CHURCHYARD
see SPRINGKELL

1070   ## KIRKCONNEL HALL
0.4km. N of Ecclefechan

Ungainly country house of two periods, now an hotel. The earlier part, at the E, was built in 1838. Two storeys, with an anta-piered and pedimented portico (partly bricked up) at its three-bay E front. This part was demoted to the status of a wing in 1870, when the tall three-storey main block of three bays by three was added. It is built of stugged red sandstone ashlar. Corniced windows to the ground floor, those of the S front of two lights. This front's r. bay is slightly advanced, with a plain pilastered porch; above this the windows are set in a shallow projection topped by a diminutive pediment. Late C20 brick additions at the back. Eclectic but charmless interior of 1870 in the main block.

Behind the house's NW corner, remains of the NW corner of a TOWER HOUSE, probably of the mid-C16, its walling constructed of large boulders. The springing of a ground-floor vault survives.

9060   ## KIRKCONNELL HOUSE
2.4km. NE of New Abbey

Laird's house of considerable complexity, the product of hap-hazard growth and change from the C15 to the C19. Documentation is sparse, and any account of the history must be partly conjectural; but the main stages of the building sequence seem fairly clear. Aymer de Maxwell, brother of the first Lord Maxwell, married Janet de Kirkconnell, the heiress of this estate, *c.* 1430, and in a charter of 1448 he was styled lord of Kirkconnell. It may have been about this date that the earliest part of the present house was built. This seems to have been a plain rectangular tower, perhaps of only two storeys, probably standing at the SW corner of a courtyard.

In the early or mid-C16 the tower acquired substantially its present form, being heightened to three storeys and an attic and made L-plan by the addition of a stair tower, with a door in its E face, at the NW corner. The next stage was the erection, probably in the mid-C17, of a detached block, perhaps a jointure house, N of the tower. This C17 block was given a NE wing c.1700. Then in 1755–60 a substantial brick addition was built to fill the SE inner angle of the C17 house and join it to the tower. Probably at the same time, the courtyard on the E was removed and a new brick-walled court formed on the W side of the house. The last major extension was the building in 1815 of a long chapel wing filling the N side of the new courtyard.

The TOWER HOUSE at the courtyard's SE corner is built of rubble masonry to which patches of thin harling still adhere. Main block of three storeys and an attic. In the E gable, a blocked ground-floor door with no dressings to suggest a date, but this may have been the C15 entrance. Above it, a blind rectangular moulded opening, probably C16, which makes no sense in relation to the room behind (if an opening, it would be from the fireplace's hearth), so probably it was always decorative. A similar blind opening, again with little obvious purpose, in the S front, where moulded C16 windows, now blocked, used to light the first and second floors; they were superseded c.1760 by two-light windows, the first floor's tall and with a fluted central column, the second floor's low. In each of the S, W and N walls, a ground-floor opening (the W and N hidden externally by later additions), perhaps originally a gunloop, now filled with a crosslet 'arrowslit' (probably an early C19 insertion). In the main block's W gable, another blocked C16 window at the first floor and one which is still open at the second. Round the main block, a parapet projects on a continuous course of corbelling surmounted by individual moulded corbels; big stone spouts for drainage. The stonework above, with one immensely broad crenelle on each face, may be a late C18 replacement. Inside the parapet rises the crowstep-gabled attic lit by small end windows. The NW stair tower is quite plain except that, at the top, the S end of its W wall is slightly jettied out on a continuation of the main parapet's continuous corbelling; the extra thickness allows space for a secondary stair rising from the top of the main stair up to the crowstep-gabled caphouse. In the stair tower, small C16 windows and some larger ones inserted in the C18.

The originally detached MID-C17 HOUSE, just to the N, is a harled two-storey block. The l. and r. of its first-floor W windows are moulded; the l. has a steeply pedimented dormerhead, as the r. one probably did before it was given the present swept top. Between these windows, a third, which is off-centre and again has a swept top, but it is unmoulded and looks like a C19 insertion. The broad NE wing added c.1700 is also harled and quite plain. In its N wall, what look like very early sixteen-paned sash windows with thick astragals. The wing's wallhead has been raised, probably in the late C18, when projecting bricks were inserted under the eaves and the gable windows enlarged and given brick margins.

The ADDITION OF 1755–60 which fills the gap between the NE wing and the tower house is a polite but plain symmetrical block of three storeys with a five-bay E front. Unusually for its date in Scotland it is built of brick, although the rusticated quoins and lintels are of stone. Overall cornice bracketed out on a course of diagonally set bricks between the second-floor windows. At the S gable's exposed E end, a brick-lintelled dummy door. It is not in a position where a door was ever likely to be required; so was it formed as an experiment in brick construction? The back (W) wall of this block's stair jamb, which is aligned with the W wall of the mid-C17 block, must, at least in its lower part, pre-date the rest of the block, since it contains a blocked arch that was made useless as an entrance by the C18 stair inside. Perhaps this and the short stretch of wall to its S are remnants of a C16 barmkin wall.

On the courtyard's N side, the long CHAPEL BLOCK of 1815. Brick-walled again but without stone dressings. Two storeys and six bays, the ground-floor windows segmental-headed, those of the first floor round-arched. Projecting brick mutule-blocks under the eaves. This range is joined to the main house and partly obscured by a lean-to corridor, probably a C19 addition.

INTERIOR. In the tower, a tunnel-vaulted ground-floor store room. Comfortable turnpike stair in the jamb. The first-floor hall became a dining room c. 1760, when the ceiling was raised. In the E wall, a big white marble chimneypiece of late Adam type, probably of 1788; it came from the demolished Terregles House. The second floor, now one room, was originally divided into two, the S reached from the stair by a passage in the N wall. The W fireplace looks mid-C17. In the E gable, a moulded C16 fireplace with, to its S, a segmental-arched recess, perhaps for a bed. In the N wall, another segmental-arched recess, but this is the embrasure of a blocked window. On the attic floor, a single room with a plain W fireplace. In the caphouse over the main stair, reached by the secondary stair in the thickness of the W wall, a room, again with a fireplace.

In the S ground-floor room (now a kitchen) of the mid-C17 house, a simple moulded stone chimneypiece, much like that in the tower's second-floor room. In the NE wing, the two first-floor rooms both contain two-panelled doors of c. 1700.

The addition of 1755–60 forms a virtually self-contained house. On the r. of its entrance hall, the library, its walls covered with mid-C18 panelling. To the l. of the hall, the morning room, now plain Victorian. A three-bay drawing room occupies the S end and centre of the first floor; it has a cornice of upright leaves. Behind, a corridor with a plaster tunnel-vault and a door at its S end opening into the first-floor hall/dining room of the tower. On the second floor, bedrooms with coved ceilings.

The courtyard's N range of 1815 contained a kitchen and other offices on the ground floor. On the upper floor's E end, two rooms intended as accommodation for a priest. The rest is filled by a long rectangular Roman Catholic chapel (now secularized). Coved ceiling. At the E end, a D-plan apse framed by marbled and fluted pilasters with acanthus leaves at their necks; marbled acanthus leaf cornice. At the chapel's W end was the family pew, again framed by pilasters.

W of the house, two rubble-built and whitewashed OFFICE RANGES, one topped by a cupola-like doocot. They may be early C19. – SW of the house, a large brick-walled GARDEN, perhaps late C18, with cottages at its corners.

KIRKCOWAN 3060

Sizeable village on flattish land N of the River Bladnoch.

Former PARISH CHURCH, Main Street. Only the ivy-clad rubble E gable survives of the church built in 1732. In it, a rectangular door and window above.

Enjoyable collection of C18 HEADSTONES in the surrounding graveyard. Just SE of the church, a mid-C18 stone to John Douglas, with rosetted individual friezes over its pilasters. More rosettes and an angel's head (the soul) above. – To its S, another headstone commemorating members of the Douglas family, with panelled and foliaged pilasters failing to support the shaped top. Within this frame, a full panoply of emblems, including a corpse, a winged hourglass, and a skull and crossbones. – Immediately W of the church, William Dalrymple †1757, carved with another lavish display of grisly emblems; at the top, an angel's head, the wings rising as an oval frame to the face. – Further W, Ellizabeth [sic] McCormick †1726. Foliaged sides; front framed by panelled pilasters. In the curly top an angel's head with outstretched wings. Main panel carved with reminders of mortality in an egg-and-dart border. – To the S, Thomas McIlnay †1737, again with an angel's head and egg-and-dart bordered panel. – S of this, James McWilliam †1789. Rosetted friezes above the panelled pilasters; front carved with an angel's head and incised foliage. – To the SW, John McTaggart, dated 1743, the scrolly broken pediment flanked by grotesque heads. On one face the tympanum is decorated with a skull and hourglass, on the other with an angel's head. At the base, on one side an angel's head, on the other a coffined corpse and the inscription 'MEMENTO MORI'. Carved bones on the sides. – Further SW, two mid-C18 stones very like that to Ellizabeth McCormick, one commemorating members of the Douglas family, the other Daniel McClure †1737.

PARISH CHURCH, Main Street. Simple Perp in harled rubble but not without pretension; it was built in 1834. T-plan, with forestairs at the E and W gables, the N jamb ending in a tower. Tall diagonally set buttresses at all the corners, those of the body jostling the tower. Big floriated crosses on the gables. Cornices on the side walls where parapets might have been expected. In the centre of the S wall, a pair of buttresses;

squeezed between them, a shallow outshot, its pedimented top squashed by another floriated cross. The tower is of two stages, the lower very tall, the upper intaken. On top, a battlement with corner pinnacles. – Simple hall addition on the w.

Inside, N, E and W galleries on marbled cast-iron columns. – Plaster ceiling rose with spiralling acanthus leaves in a swagged husk circle. – Tall PULPIT of 1834, the alcove behind opened into the church by *J. Sandford Kay*, 1910. – Late C19 CHAMBER ORGAN by *J. & A. Mirrlees*, brought here in 1966.

SCHOOL, Station Road. Broad-eaved school and picturesquely gableted schoolhouse of *c.* 1900.

DESCRIPTION. At the village's s end and set well back, KIRKLAND HOUSE, built as the Parish Manse in 1741 and now with Victorian dormers and a lean-to porch. Then the graveyard, over which towers the gable of the former Parish Church (*see* above). On the other side of Main Street, a pair of late Georgian gables belonging to the harled TARFF HOTEL. MAIN STREET is mostly C19, quite picturesque in whinstone and render, with some C20 infill. A few houses are a little grander. On the r., the two-storey No. 37 of *c.* 1840, with rusticated quoins, a first-floor band course and a pilastered doorpiece. No. 33, perhaps a little earlier, is of only one storey but has rusticated quoins and big club skewputts. A mid-C19 pilastered granite doorpiece on No. 13. At the street's N end, the Parish Church, with the school behind (*see* above).

CRAICHLAW. *See* p. 194.
OLD PLACE OF MOCHRUM. *See* p. 478.
SHENNANTON HOUSE. *See* p. 519.

KIRKCUDBRIGHT

Small burgh, its population less than 3,500, at the mouth of the Dee; the county town of the old Kirkcudbrightshire and the administrative centre of the former Stewartry District. There was a royal castle here by 1288, when it was under the guardianship of John Comyn; the royal burgh had been founded by 1330. Kirkcudbright was probably relatively sizeable and affluent when a Franciscan convent was founded within its walls *c.* 1455, but it may have been in decline by the later C16, when Thomas MacLellan of Bombie took over the convent garden as the site of his intimidating tower house–mansion and gave the convent church to the town as a replacement for the former parish church *c.* 1km. away.

The town had clearly fallen into decay by 1692, when its council

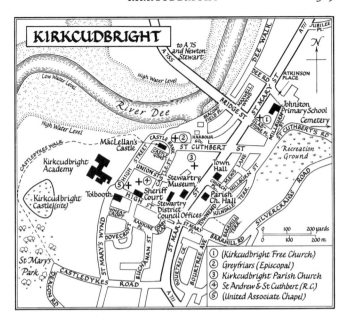

reported that the inhabitants 'have no forraigne trade, and that ther inland trade is verie inconsiderable; all they have they bring from Leith, Dumfreise, and other free burghs on horseback', and asserted that more than half of the houses were 'aither waste or ruinous'. Nor had matters improved in 1724, when Daniel Defoe found 'a Harbour without Ships, a Port without Trade, a Fishery without Nets, a People without Business'. Attempts to introduce industry were at last begun in the 1790s but never met much success. The town's C19 prosperity came largely from its popularity as a residence for people enjoying private incomes, who were joined in the early C20 by a group of artists, notably E. A. Hornel, Sir James Guthrie, W. Y. McGregor, S. J. Peploe, E. A. Taylor and Jessie King, attracted by the picturesque quality of the burgh's closes, the variety of housing available and the surrounding scenery. An artistic reputation still lingers but there is little sign of bohemianism.

CHURCHES

GREYFRIARS (Episcopal), St Cuthbert Street. Humble rubble-built irregular cruciform, with simple Gothic windows and stylized flaming urn finials on the gables. In its present form it is by *P. MacGregor Chalmers*, 1919, but the component parts are earlier. The chancel is a late C16 laird's 'aisle', added by the MacLellans of Bombie on the S side of the late C15 Franciscan convent church which had been taken over as the parish church in 1571. That church was rebuilt except for the 'aisle' in 1730,

and the C18 successor was in turn demolished *c.*1838 to be
replaced by a school, converted by Chalmers into the present
church's transepts and nave. In the screen wall to the E, a
round-arched GATEWAY, probably late C16, its keystone
carved with the relief of a head.

Inside, the nave walls are plastered, but those of the transepts
and chancel are of exposed rubble. Roundheaded late C16
chancel arch with imposts on the piers. In the tunnel-vaulted
chancel's S gable, a trefoil-headed PISCINA, found nearby and
almost certainly from the late C15 convent church. – STAINED
GLASS. In the chancel, a three-light S window (the Adoration
of the Magi) of 1921. – In the E transept, two brightly coloured
and decorative lights (St Francis and St Cuthbert) by *Gordon
Webster*, 1961. – At the nave's N end, a stylized window (St
Michael), signed by *Isabella Douglas*, 1951. – ALTAR CROSS and
candlesticks of beaten brass set with semi-precious stones, by
*Mabel Braunton, c.*1925.

45   The E side of the chancel is filled by the MONUMENT erected
*c.*1635* to Thomas MacLellan of Bombie and his wife, Grissel
Maxwell, by their son. It is a mixture of Gothic and classical;
the general form is still medieval, with the effigy of a knight
placed in a recess, its segmental arch carved with dogtooth
ornament. Only the rose on top hints that this is not C15 work.
On the back of the recess, three panels carved with popular
post-Reformation reminders of death. On the centre panel,
a skull, hourglass, crossbones, and the motto 'MEMENTO
MORI'. On each outer panel, a hand pointing to an inscription,
the l. reading 'RESPICE FINEM' (Look to your end), the r.
'MORS MIHI VITA EST' (Death is life to me). This recess is
contained within a rectangular classical frame although the
leafy capitals of the paired columns observe no accepted order.
In the spandrels, carved foliage and the portraits of a man and
woman in C16 dress, each placed above a flower. On the ends
of the cornice, triangular ball-finialled panelled pinnacles, their
fronts carved with half-wheels, perhaps intended as stylized
shells. Scrolls join the pinnacles' inner sides to the rectangular
inscription tablet at the centre. On the tablet's ends, more ball-
topped pinnacles, carved with chevron decoration. They flank
an aedicule (its columns' capitals now missing) which frames
an heraldic achievement. Above, a scroll-topped semicircular
pediment carved with a bird and an angel's head (the soul). On
top, a pudgy cherub leaning forward under the chancel vault.

KIRKCUDBRIGHT FREE CHURCH, St Mary Street. Now
housing. Geometric Gothic, by *John Honeyman*, 1872–4. Gable
front flanked by a SE steeple and NE stair tower.

KIRKCUDBRIGHT PARISH CHURCH, St Mary Street. Big and
bare angle-buttressed cruciform; by *William Burn*, 1835–8. The
W end, which originally only just projected beyond the transepts, was given an apsidal-ended vestry in 1886. The general

* The inscription records that it was put up by Robert MacLellan, Lord Kirkcudbright, so it must date from between 1633, when he was granted the peerage,
and his death in January 1639.

impression is Tudor, although the hoodmoulded windows are lancets. Large gargoyles at the corners. Shallow porches at the transepts. E tower, its buttresses topped by conical pinnacles. Y-traceried two-light window in each face of the second stage, three-light belfry openings at the third. Octagonal stone spire with big gablets on four faces of its broaching; smaller lucarnes higher up. In the inner angles of the tower and nave, low rounded projections containing the gallery stairs.

Inside, a Tudor-fronted gallery on cast-iron columns in each of the three main limbs. Tudor-arched ribbed plaster ceilings with foliaged bosses. – Boxy PEWS. – Canopied PULPIT AND 31 READING DESK, again Tudor, at the E end. – This is now flanked by the pipes of an ORGAN by *Wilkinson & Sons*. – STAINED GLASS. In the S transept, one light (the Good Shepherd) by *William Meikle & Sons*, 1920. – MONUMENTS. High up on the E wall, a tablet to the Rev. John Underwood, with a high-relief bust by *T. Stuart Burnett*, 1886. – In the porch, a draped urn (now painted) commemorating the Rev. Dr Robert Muter, dated 1846 and signed by *Nelson* (i.e. *Thomas & James Nelson*) of Carlisle.

ST ANDREW AND ST CUTHBERT (R.C.), off High Street. Plain Gothic of 1886. – STAINED GLASS. Three-light early C20 W (liturgical E) window (the Annunciation and Nativity of Our Lord), bright but bad. – In the baptistery and Lady Chapel, two windows (the descent of the Holy Spirit, and an abstract), both designed by *J. Faczynski* and executed by *J. O'Neill & Son*, 1967.

UNITED ASSOCIATE CHAPEL, High Street. Secularized. Gothick of 1822 with hoodmoulded windows, the porch a later addition.

CEMETERY
St Cuthbert's Road

This was the site of the medieval Parish Church, of which no trace now remains.* – The principal ENTRANCE is early C17, a segmental arch topped and flanked by ball finials. – Beside it, and at right angles, a pair of corniced and ball-finialled GATEPIERS, probably dating from the graveyard's early C19 enlargement. – Immediately W of the C17 entrance, the large wall MONUMENT erected in 1644 by John Ewart to commemorate his sons, John and Andrew. It is a medieval-classical mixture. The lower part consists of a tomb chest surmounted by a broad and shallow pointed-arched recess, its back carved with an inscription and reminders of death. All this is Gothic-survival, but it is placed in a would-be classical frame of leafily capitalled columns carrying a cornice. On the cornice's ends, segmental-arched stones. Over its centre, a stone of the same pointed shape as the recess below and bearing an inscription which begins:

---

* It is said (by *The New Statistical Account of Scotland*, iv (1845), 21) to have been c.18.3m. by 9.2m.

WELCOM.SOFT.BED.MY.SWEIT.REPOS
AND.SO.FOR.CHRIST.FROM.HENCE.AROSE
WELCOM.SWEIT.SLEIP.FROM.ꟻHE.I.WAKE
FOR.ENDLES.IOYES.FOR.TO.PARTAKE

On the back of the monument, reliefs of an hourglass, cross-bones and a skull, and the inscription:

OUR.TYME.RVNNES.FAST.AS WE MAY.SIE
WHICH.BEING.SPENꟻ ꟻHEN MVST.WE DIE

– Immediately in front, a worn GRAVESLAB, perhaps early C18, its top decorated with a coat of arms, the bottom with a skull and crossbones. – A little to the NE, the mid-C18 HEADSTONE to David Thomson and members of his family, with an angel's head (the soul) carved at the top. – E of this, a TABLE STONE to Samuel Herries †1793, with a piecrust border round the slab. It is supported on six legs carved with high-relief emblems of life (trees, clothed figures, and angels' heads) and death (a corpse, a skeleton, the reaper, skulls, an hourglass, and crossbones). – To the NW, the C18 HEADSTONE of John Gordon, adorned with reminders of mortality and a hand holding a crowned last (the emblem of the shoemakers). – NE of this, a couple more HEADSTONES bearing angels' heads, one late C18, the other to Robert — †1808. – To the SE, a broken GRAVESLAB commemorating Andrew Carsane, dated 1626, with two coats of arms and a worn inscription. – Beside it, the weathered GRAVESLAB of Isobel Maxwell †1627, an heraldic achievement at the top, crossbones at the bottom. – Immediately to the N, a TABLE STONE, perhaps early C18, but the inscription probably recut in the early C19. It commemorates two Covenanters, William Hounture and Robert Smith, †1684, and proclaims:

ꟻHIS MONUMENT SHALL SHEW POSTERITY
TWO HEADLES MARTYRES UNDER IT DOꟻHE LY
BY BLOODY GRHAME WERE TAKEN AND SURPRISED
BROUGHꟻ TO ꟻHIS TOUNE AND AFTERWARD WERE SAIZ'D
BY UNJUST LAW WERE SENꟻENCED TO DIE
ꟻHEM FIRST ꟻHEY HANG'D ꟻHEN HEADED CRUDLY
CAPTANS DOUGLAS BRUCE GRHAME OF CLEVERHOUS
WERE ꟻHESE ꟻHAT CAUSED ꟻHEM BE HANDLED ꟻHUS
AND WHEN ꟻHEY WERE UNꟻO ꟻHE GIBBET COM
TO STOPE ꟻHEIR SPEECH ꟻHEY DID BEAT UP ꟻHE DRUM
AND ALL BECAUS ꟻHAT ꟻHEY WOULD NOT COMPLY
WIꟻH INDULGENCE AND BLOODY PRELACIE
IN FACE OF CRUEL BRUCE DOUGLAS AND GRHAME
ꟻHEY DID MANꟻAINE ꟻHAT CHRIST WAS LORD SUPREAM
AND BOLDLY OUNED BOꟻH ꟻHE COVENANꟻS
AT KIRKCUDBRIGHꟻ ꟻHUS ENDED THESE TWO SANꟻS

– To the S, the HEADSTONE of Margaret McGown †1755, decorated with an angel's head and grisly emblems. – Further S, the TABLE STONE of John Halliday of Castle Mains †1756, with a well-preserved piecrust border and coat of arms on the slab. – To its SE, the HEADSTONE of a smith †1749, the front framed by panelled pilasters and a curvy top and carved with reminders of death and a hand-held crowned hammer. – Beside the cemetery's N wall, a large pale sandstone HEADSTONE to William H. Clarke †1924, carved in relief with an Isadora Duncanish lady and a stylized tree, very much in the manner of Eric Gill.

PUBLIC BUILDINGS

BRIDGE, Bridge Street. By *Blyth & Blyth* and *L. G. Mouchel & Partners*, 1924–6. Five-span bow-truss concrete bridge with no pretension to prettiness.

JAIL. *See* Sherriff Court, below.

JOHNSTON PRIMARY SCHOOL, St Mary Street. Small-scale Italianate of 1847–8. Single-storey, of five bays with three-light windows in the slightly advanced ends. Over the centre, a tower with a low pyramid roof. The school was enlarged in 1933 by *W. A. MacKinnell*: the fronts of the additions try to fit in; their sides and backs make no such effort.

KIRKCUDBRIGHT ACADEMY, St Mary's Wynd. By *Alan B. Crombie*, 1901, incorporating the school built in 1815–18. Plain, with sparing classical detail and a cupolaed clock tower. Large additions by the *School Building Development Team* of the *Scottish Education Department*, 1958. – To the NW, the red sandstone COCHRAN MEMORIAL GYMNASIUM by *W. A. MacKinnell*, 1930–1, with a pedimented Corinthian centrepiece.

PARISH CHURCH HALL, St Mary Street. By *Alan B. Crombie*, 1892. Blocky late Gothic with rather small-scale detail, in red sandstone. Octagonal cupola.

POLICE STATION, High Street. *See* Description, below.

SHERIFF COURT, High Street. By *David Rhind*, 1866–8. Asymmetrical toy fort but not at all frivolous. Over the entrance, a tower with a big battlemented oriel window. At the back, the castellated OLD JAIL of 1815, its tall tower and octagonal caphouse more important in distant views than close up.

STEWARTRY DISTRICT COUNCIL OFFICES,★ off St Mary Street. By the *Stewartry County Council*, 1949–52. Lightweight, with a few *moderne* touches.

STEWARTRY MUSEUM, St Mary Street. By *Robert Wallace*, 1892. Baronial in whin and red sandstone; a squat battlemented tower over the entrance. – Attached to the front railings, cast-iron plaques bearing the burgh arms. They come from the former bridge over the Dee, designed by *H. J. Wylie* in 1868.

TOLBOOTH, High Street. Long three-storey rubble block built 106 in 1625–7, with an E tower added in 1642, and a mid-C18 one-bay W extension. The tower of 1642 is of rubble up to the eaves level of the main block. Then two stages of ashlar, the first containing a rectangular window, the second with a pointed belfry opening now partly covered by the clock made by *J. McSkimming* in 1897. Above a stringcourse, round-arched corbelling carrying a tall parapet drained by stone spouts;

★ The building was transferred to the ownership of the new Dumfries and Galloway Council in 1996.

obelisks on the parapet's corners. Inside it, a conical stone spire
with a boat weathervane. The forestair is an addition of 1742
and blocks a door into the prison at the tower's base. The 1620s
main block's first-floor windows have moulded jambs (the one
without them looks like an insertion); narrow windows and
two gunholes at the second floor. Small and crudely formed
windows in the w extension; the lower part of its corner to St
Mary's Wynd is chamfered to ease the passage of carts. The
interior is mostly by *Stewartry District Council*, 1992–3, with a
metal spiral stair in the tower. In the c18 w extension, rubble
tunnel-vaults over the two lower floors.

On top of the forestair, the MERCAT CROSS. Crude base
supporting a 1.95m.-high shaft from whose top protrude curved
projections, possibly intended as volutes. Triangular finial, its
N face carved with the date 1610 and the initials EME.

TOWN HALL, St Mary Street. Renaissance in red sandstone
ashlar, by *Peddie & Kinnear*, 1878–9. Two tall storeys. Consoled
balcony over the door. Coupled pilasters at the first floor, whose
outer windows are round-arched and key-blocked; Venetian
window at the centre.

KIRKCUDBRIGHT CASTLE
off Castledykes Road

Only substantial grassy mounds now disclose the presence of the
royal castle first mentioned in 1288, when John Comyn of
Buchan was appointed its Keeper. The site is a roughly oblong
mound surrounded by a ditch. Excavation in 1911–13 showed
that the castle itself had been a rubble-built rectangular enclosure with a round tower at each corner. On the N front a fifth
tower combined with the NE tower to form a gatehouse of
considerable strength. The big sw tower was presumably a
keep. Pottery found here suggests that the castle was built in
the late c13 and abandoned early in the c14.

MACLELLAN'S CASTLE
St Cuthbert Street

76 Roofless but substantial remains of the large and gaunt late c16
mansion, a tower house come to town, built by Thomas MacLellan of Bombie, who had been granted the site of the abandoned
Greyfriars Convent in 1569. The house, its rubble masonry wholly
or partly taken from the conventual buildings, was begun in 1581;
the masons were *Robert* and *Alexander Couper*.

The main building is L-plan, of three storeys and an attic. Cradled
in its NW inner angle, a small three-storey L-plan projection
which ends at the w with a taller crowstep-gabled stair tower.
Attached to the main building's SE corner is a square four-
storey-and-attic tower on whose w abuts another stair tower,
whose monopitch roof is at right angles to that of the principal
tower. Corbelled out from the main building's E front, a
rounded stair turret topped by boldly projecting corbels which
probably carried a rectangular caphouse. Another stair turret

on continuous corbelling, but more shallowly bowed, projects from the SE tower's third floor. At the main W and N gables, round angle turrets carried on vertical corbel bands placed above continuous horizontal corbelling. In these turrets, narrow vertical slits and, at the W gable's N turret, a cross-shaped gunloop. Round shotholes in the half-gable above the SE stair. Purposeful wide-splayed gunloops all round the ground floor, as if ready to deal with any disturbance in the town. The surviving cornice on the main S and E sides is of cavetto profile. On the L-shaped NW angle projection, chequer-set corbels carrying a parapet whose walk has been drained by stone cannon spouts. Comfortable-sized windows even at the ground floor; the first floor's are larger to emphasize its importance.

Expensive detail is reserved for the NW inner angle. Here the surrounds of the door and principal windows are moulded. First-floor W window with dogtooth enrichment on its inner face; above, a finialled would-be pediment without a base. Over the door a blind first-floor window, the base of its pediment provided by a transom. On this pediment's apex and ends, weathered finials, the top one carved as a thistle. The bottom half of the window is divided by a mullion into two panels, each bearing an heraldic achievement, the l. badly worn, the r. carrying the quartered arms of Maxwell and Herries sur-mounted by the initials G M (for Grissel Maxwell, Thomas MacLellan's second wife) and the date 1582,* with the motto 'DO[MI]N[U]S DEDIT' below. The attic windows' frag-mentary moulded surrounds rise from conical pendants.

The main entrance in the NW inner angle opens onto the foot of the straight principal stair. Gunloop on the l. To the r., a door into a tunnel-vaulted passage along the S range's N side. Off this passage, two tunnel-vaulted stores, both with S windows; the E store has an aumbry in its W wall, the W a gunloop under the window. At the passage's W end, a lobby at the foot of a now missing turnpike service stair. S of this lobby is another store; its proximity to the service stair, which gave access to the dais end of the hall above, suggests that it was the wine cellar. Entrance cutting awkwardly into its vault. S window again. Gunloops in the N and W walls, an aumbry in the N. The other end of this passage meets a second which runs along the house's E side, lit by a couple of windows and a gunloop in its outer wall. At this second passage's N end is the kitchen, its entrance again badly related to the vault. Beside the door, a service hatch. In the kitchen's S wall, an aumbry; in the E a slop hole. Large elliptically arched N fireplace, a small high-set window in its E side; in its W side, an oven. At the S end of the E passage, a small lobby at the foot of a rebuilt turnpike stair, a gunloop on its S. On the lobby's W side, a door from outside. On its E side, a tunnel-vaulted store on the ground floor of the SE tower, with a window and gunloop in its E wall.

* The arms and initials seem certainly to be those of Grissel Maxwell, but she did not marry Thomas MacLellan until 1584, so it seems likely that the date, improbably early if it marks the completion of the house, has been recut and altered.

The straight stair from the main entrance is the formal approach to the first floor. From its landing a gallery runs back w to a small wall-chamber whose s wall contains an opening (a 'laird's lug') into a corner of the hall fireplace, allowing an occupant of this room to overhear conversation in the hall. N of the landing, a comfortable room, probably a guest chamber, with a fireplace in its w wall, a close garderobe in the NE corner, a closet in the NW.

The hall itself has a broad simply moulded N fireplace and large windows set in segmental-arched embrasures. On the w side of the N window's very deep embrasure, a door to the service stair. A second door from this stair and a door directly from the hall open into the bedchamber at the house's w end. w fireplace, a salt box on its r. side. Large windows again; the s window's E embrasure contains the door to a garderobe. In the SE tower, entered from the adjacent turnpike, is another bedchamber. Large window beside its E fireplace; a horizontal window high in the s wall. Garderobe at the NW corner.

The floors above were once reached by the NW and SE turnpike stairs and by an E turnpike (its bottom treads surviving) which begins at the first floor. On the second floor, above the main stair hall, a room with a s fireplace. Over this room's w end, a semicircular arch like a sideboard recess. Small closet on the w. The other rooms on the upper floors have been very like those below but more simply detailed.

DESCRIPTION

ST MARY STREET is the entry from the s. On the l., the piend-roofed OAKLEY HOUSE of c. 1805. Its s front was originally of two bays, the l. bowed and containing a ground-floor Venetian window and a three-light window above. This bow became the centrepiece when the house was extended w in the later C19. After the junction with High Street, the Stewartry Museum on the l. and the Parish Church Hall (*see* Public Buildings, above) are followed by the large open green around Kirkcudbright Parish Church (*see* Churches, above). The church looks over to the Town Hall (*see* Public Buildings, above), which abuts a prosperous mid-Victorian terrace (Nos. 9–13) of hammer-dressed grey granite with broad-eaved front gables, columned flat-roofed canopies over the doors, and heavy sloping stone canopies at the windows. Then the yellow sandstone BANK OF SCOTLAND, unexciting Ruskinian Gothic by *William McEwen*, 1895, and a low late C19 block, whose pilastered doorpieces are Georgian-survival although the ashlar masonry is hammerdressed and many of the windows bipartite. On the corner with St Cuthbert Street, the rubble-built three-storey ROYAL BANK OF SCOTLAND and ROYAL HOTEL, late C19 again, with two-light windows.

N of St Cuthbert Street, St Mary Street becomes commercial. On both sides, unassuming mid-C19 two-storey terraces, mostly painted or rendered, the w beginning with a 'tower' formed by the slightly later addition of a battlemented top floor. Corinthian columned shopfront at Nos. 28–30; at Nos. 34–40, shopfronts whose fluted pilasters carry consoles carved with acanthus leaves. On the NW corner of Bridge Street, THE INGLE RESTAURANT, the cottagey main block surviving from the former RAILWAY STATION designed by *Peddie & Kinnear* in 1864. Bracketed eaves and bargeboards at the gables and dormerheads; over the central ground-floor window, a sloping stone canopy on moulded brackets. Beside and behind, sturdy housing of 1972 by the *University of Edinburgh Architectural Research Unit*. After the steepled former Kirkcudbright Free Church (*see* Churches, above), on the NE corner of Gladstone Place, and Johnston Primary School (*see* Public Buildings, above), a lane leads E to MILLBURN STREET, at whose E end is the MILL POTTERY, an L-plan former corn mill of *c.* 1800, built of whitewashed rubble, nudging into the hillside; cowled round ventilator on the back jamb.

In St Mary Street's final stretch, ATKINSON PLACE, a three-sided courtyard of almshouses built *c.* 1870 of whin with red sandstone dressings. Gabled and gableted, with bracketed broad eaves and bargeboards. On the gates at the courtyard's NW entrance, the motto 'AS FOR ME AND MY HOUSE WE WILL SERVE THE LORD'. Immediately N is the OLD MANSE of 1900, a sizeable asymmetrical bay-windowed villa. Console-pedimented doorpiece; a shell-tympanum in the l. attic window's pediment.

ST CUTHBERT STREET is the town's broad central space. On its S corner, at the edge of the Parish Church's garden, a granite Celtic CROSS commemorating Dunbar James, Earl of Selkirk. It was designed by *J. Aldam Heaton* and carved by *Farmer & Brindley* in 1885. To its W, a squat battlemented Tudor WELL of 1854, the water issuing from a cast-iron lion's mask signed by *T. Leadbetter*. Simple C19 two-storey range opposite. Then the street's balance is redressed: the N side is open to Harbour Square and the river, the S built up with a terrace of C18 and C19 houses, straightforward vernacular except for the red ashlar No. 4 of *c.* 1900, two tall storeys of shopkeeper's Renaissance. For Greyfriars Episcopal Church opposite, *see* Churches, above. The street's W end is filled by the dour rubble mass of MacLellan's Castle (*see* above). In front, the WAR MEMORIAL by *G. H. Paulin*, 1921. Bronze of a scantily draped swordsman defending a crouching boy; tall plinth of craggy granite. In CASTLE GARDENS to the SW, an early C19 rubble-built terrace with rusticated corner quoins. At its W end, the conical roof of a late Georgian GARDEN HOUSE poking over the back wall of No. 3 High Street.

CASTLE STREET is a diversion. Generally simple late Georgian houses, their rubble walls often painted or rendered. Some are grander. On the E, the early C19 No. 7 is ashlar-fronted with a rusticated ground floor and skinny columns at the door. Tudor hoodmoulds over the ground-floor windows, a moulded architrave at the centre window of the first floor. To its S, the

MASONIC ARMS bears an egg-and-dart bordered panel carved
with the arms of St Cuthbert's Lodge of Kirkcudbright and the
date 1790. No. 16 opposite was built *c.*1860 as the National
Bank of Scotland. Two tall storeys of red ashlar; elaborate
and heavy consoles supporting the cornices over the door and
windows. The piend-roofed early C19 No. 22, on the Union
Street corner, has a delicate cast-iron fanlight above the door and
moulded architraves to the first-floor windows. Late Georgian
tall corniced doorpieces at Nos. 35 and 37; No. 35's frieze is pulvinated, No. 37's fluted and rosetted. No. 39 is dated 1806.

In CASTLE BANK to the N of MacLellan's Castle, under the
eaves of the the harled Nos. 1–3, a couple of carved grotesque
heads, perhaps C17. To the W, the broad rubble gable of an
M-roofed warehouse of 1880 with its own quay to the river;
converted to tidy housing (RIVERSIDE COURT) by *Bryce &
Hastings*, 1983.

HIGH STREET's W side kicks off with the early C19 piend-roofed
No. 2, which has an oval panel on the horizontally fluted frieze
of its doorpiece. The air of late Georgian gentility is reinforced
by Nos. 3–5 opposite. Pedimented double door with tall acanthus leaves at the necks of the columns. No. 8 of 1817, set back
behind arrowhead railings, is decidedly prosperous, its fanlit
tripartite door framed by Ionic columns supporting a rather
mean entablature. At the back, a battlemented semi-octagonal
projection.

   Also recessed from the street, behind spearheaded railings
and late C18 cast-iron gateposts decorated with rosetted panels,
is BROUGHTON HOUSE (No. 10 High Street), the C18 town
house of the Murrays of Broughton and later the home of the
painter E. A. Hornel. It was built by *Thomas Mirrie*, mason,
c. 1735. Rubble-walled, of two storeys and five bays, the centre
rising into a gablet containing a blind bullseye window. Scrolled
skewputts on the gables and gablet. Keyblocked corniced door
with a lugged architrave. On it, an elaborate brass name-plate of
*c.*1910. Projecting early C19 wing on the r. Behind it, fronting
a lane to the river, a broad-eaved and bargeboarded extension
of 1910 by *John Keppie*. On the main house's rear elevation, a
full-height bow at the S bay, an addition of the early C19. Inside
the house, the wall between the entrance hall and the r. room
was replaced by a Jacobean screen in Keppie's 1910 alterations.
In both the r. and l. ground-floor rooms, good quality but plain
marble chimneypieces of *c.*1820. The l. (dining) room's simple
panelling looks mid-C18. In Keppie's NE extension, a gallery
(restored in 1992 after a fire). The walls are panelled below
a plaster copy of the Parthenon frieze. Big stone Jacobean
Renaissance chimneypiece. Toplighting through panels of
engraved glass. At the NE corner, an Artisan Mannerist screen
into a recess provided with window seats. The room opens at
the N into a studio. Open wooden roof. Gothic door and
window to the garden. The garden itself is largely *Hornel*'s
creation, but the acorn-finialled gatepiers at its entry from the
house look C18. In the garden, huge flower-crammed borders

divided by narrow paths. One part is Japanese, with a small bridge.

In GORDON PLACE on High Street's E side, a small block of c.1840 with rusticated quoins and Tudor hoodmoulds. Immediately S of Broughton House, the mid-C18 rubble-built No. 14 High Street. Its doorpiece has rusticated and corniced pilasters carrying balusters which support a pediment. On the l., an early C19 extension with a basket-arched pend. Nos. 21–25 may be late C18, but the anta-pilastered and pedimented double door of Nos. 23–25 looks an early C19 embellishment. Another pilastered and pedimented door on the early C19 No. 16. No. 18 looks late C18, with Greek key decoration on the console-corniced doorpiece. Then the houses become more humdrum. No. 42 is unequivocally Victorian, of whin with red sandstone dressings and a conical-roofed slim turret. No. 48 is late Georgian but has a late C19 granite doorpiece with tiny Gothic columns squeezed into the classical architrave. Opposite, the old United Associate Chapel (*see* Churches, above). At the W side's S end, the red ashlar No. 54 of c.1840, with a pilastered doorpiece and aprons under the windows.

High Street now turns E. On its S, the Tolbooth (*see* Public Buildings, above). Squashed between its tower and Steeple Close, the C18 gable of No. 58. Then two C17 rubble-built blocks (Nos. 66–72), both with round-arched pends to closes behind; on No. 72, the moulded frame for a now missing armorial panel. There follow plain early C19 houses fronting the street and the long POLICE CLOSE running back to the S. On High Street's N side, the Sheriff Court (*see* Public Buildings, above) accompanied by the primly suburban 1950s POLICE STATION and police houses; on the houses, a weathered armorial panel, perhaps C17. They do nothing for the corner with Castle Street. Much more effective for that street is the late Georgian No. 110 High Street, whose open-pedimented doorpiece provides a formal axial feature. Next to it, the GORDON HOUSE HOTEL of the earlier C19, with an anta-pilastered shopfront of four bays, the cornice bowed over two of them.

E of Castle Street, High Street begins again, with simple two-storey vernacular houses. They continue to the end on the S. On the N, genteel pretension resumes with No. 115, a house of c.1830 set back behind railings. Heavy block-pedimented doorpiece and rusticated quoins. Much suaver is No. 117 of c.1790, with a pair of shallow segmental bows flanking the centre whose tall columned and pedimented doorpiece is sur-mounted by a lugged architraved first-floor window. The battle-mented early C19 No. 119 is of only two bays; over the door, a cornice skied above a pulvinated frieze. Mid-C19 anta-pil-astered doorpiece on the SELKIRK ARMS HOTEL near the street's E end. In its garden, an octagonal FONT BOWL, dated 1481 or 1482; its carvings include the depiction of a bird holding the leash of a fox; on a shield, the MacLellan coat of arms. It used to be at St Mary's Isle, 2.4km. SW.

INDUSTRIAL BUILDING

CREAMERY, Bridge Street. By *Alexander Mair*, 1934–5. The main
block is a tall rendered box with vertical windows and narrow
buttresses.

FARM ETC.

CANNEE, 1km. S. Informally grouped mid-C19 steading with
crowstep-gabled ranges (some converted to housing). In this,
a round WINDMILL TOWER, perhaps of the late C18. Four
stages, each marked off by a ratcourse and with a brickwork
band below the top. The upper part was a doocot.

CUP-AND-RING MARKS, High Banks, 3.2km. SE. Low rock
outcrop, *c.*30m. long, carved in the second millennium B.C.
with groups of cups and cups circled by rings. Several of the
ringed cups are surrounded by clusters of plain cups. *See* the
Introduction, p. 24.

5050   KIRKDALE

The name of a medieval parish which now marks a hillside with
a mansion house at its bottom, a steading (Kirkdale Mains) above,
and a churchyard higher up still.

CHURCHYARD. Small and overgrown. In it the remains of a small
rubble-built medieval CHURCH abandoned after the union of
Kirkdale parish with Kirkmabreck in 1618. Featureless except
for a rectangular door, perhaps a late C16 insertion, near the S
wall's E end. – To the W, a MAUSOLEUM erected by Sir Samuel
Hannay of Mochrum in 1787. Square pavilion. The entrance
front is of granite ashlar with an open pediment and a segmental-arched inscription panel in its tympanum. Consoled
cornice over the door. A pointed window in each side wall. The
date of the mausoleum raises the possibility that it was designed
by *R. & J. Adam*, the architects for the contemporary Kirkdale
House (*see* below).

KIRKDALE BRIDGE. Built *c.*1788, its design a drastically simplified version of one by *R. & J. Adam*. Rubble-built with a
granite ashlar band course and a high parapet. Three semicircular arches, the centre spanning the Kirkdale Burn, the
outer two over footpaths. Cone-topped cutwaters. Bullseye
panels in all the spandrels except the E on the N side. The
bridge was widened to the S in 1857 by *William McGowan*, who
repeated the C18 elevational design.

KIRKCLAUGH, 2.4km. SE. Asymmetrical Baronial manor of
*c.*1860 incorporating a late Georgian house. Crowstepped
gables, stone-finialled dormerheads, and a corner turret. On
the S front, a canted bay window corbelled out to a gabled
square upper floor.

KIRKDALE HOUSE

On a wooded hillside overlooking Wigtown Bay, the austerely accomplished mansion house built in 1787–8 by Sir Samuel 88 Hannay of Mochrum, a Galloway laird who had acquired an additional fortune as a London merchant. *R. & J. Adam* were the architects. *Corps de logis* with lateral links to pavilions. The masonry is all of grey granite ashlar, hammerdressed at the basement, polished at the floors above. Piend-roofed main block of two and a half storeys over a sunk basement. Five bays by five, but the N and S fronts are longer than the side elevations. Mutuled cornice and first- and second-floor sill courses all round; ground-floor sill course at the sides and garden front.

At the entrance (N) front, band courses over the basement and ground floor. Broad ends, with tall ground-floor windows set in roundheaded overarches. Projecting from the slightly recessed centre, a balustraded portico, its Roman Doric columns paired. At the back of the portico, attached columns framing the door and sidelights; the width of their openings is repeated at the windows above. The side elevations are plain (one first-floor window enlarged), except that each has a rather awkward Venetian window, the top of its centre light blind, at the ground-floor *piano nobile*. The garden (S) front's centrepiece is a canted bay. In the end bays of the *piano nobile*, overarched and console-pedimented ground-floor windows fronted by stone balconies whose balustrades (now missing) hid the windows' breaking of the sill course. At the centrepiece, a console-pedimented door flanked by corniced windows, their sills lowered, probably in the early C19. Cornices over the first floor's centre and end windows.

Extending each side of the main block, a narrow three-bay balustraded link of one storey over a basement, slightly recessed from the N front and set well back from the S. They join to square pyramid-roofed pavilions, each of two low storeys and a basement, their small scale emphasizing their subordinate status. Three closely set windows (some blind) at each floor of their outer elevations. At the pavilions, the eaves cornices are simply moulded, a further mark of deference to the main block.

The interior was gutted by fire in 1893 and then reconstructed by *Kinnear & Peddie*, their neo-Jacobean manner not an entirely happy counterpoint to the Adams' exterior.

KIRKDALE MAINS to the NW. Smart harled steading of *c.* 1790 and perhaps again by *R. & J. Adam*. It is octagonal. The N, S, E and W sides each have a two-storey piend-roofed block with a central roundheaded arch or overarch. The other four sides have, or had, single-storey blocks, two still with segmental-arched cart-shed openings; the NE block has been rebuilt, the SE demolished. To the N, a small detached gazebo-like tower, now in ruins.

CAIRNS, Cairnholy, 0.5km. NE. Two long cairns, both badly robbed of their overlying covering of stones and earth but the main slabs still standing. Each seems to have begun in the third millennium B.C. as a single chamber covered by a mound and been extended in the next millennium by an ante-chamber, forecourt and a long mound of stones behind. The s cairn (CAIRNHOLY I) has been *c.* 43m. by 10m.; its w end is now cut off by a track and appears only as a low rise in the grass. Its N and s sides have been revetted with upright slabs, displaced from the vertical by a southwards slippage of the cairn material. At the E end, a shallow concave forecourt delineated by eight tall orthostats; those of the s half are graded in height towards the centre. Here a pair of stones forms the 0.46m.-wide portal to the slab-walled ante-chamber, *c.* 1.8m. by 0.76m. A large slab lying on the N side may have been part of the roof and is decorated with a weathered cup-and-ring mark. Immediately behind, but divided off by the ante-chamber's end-stone, is the original rectangular chamber, *c.* 1.9m. by 0.76m., its slabs lower but more massive than those of the ante-chamber. – CAIRNHOLY II, 0.15km. uphill to the N, almost entirely robbed of its covering material, has been *c.* 21m. by 12m. Because of the slope of the ground there was little room for a SE ceremonial forecourt, which seems here to have been a V-shape, only 0.9m. deep at the centre. Entrance, *c.* 0.38m. broad, flanked by stones; the r. is *c.* 2.9m. high, the l. (perhaps broken) 1.5m. Lying on the ground in front, the large stone which closed the entrance. The portal stones project back to form a short passage into the ante-chamber behind. This is *c.* 1.5m. square, the NW wall formed of one long slab, the SE of a shorter slab supplemented by a pillar-like stone whose height of 1.7m. must presumably have been the minimum for the roof. The inner chamber is *c.* 1.3m. by 0.7m., its sides and end each formed by a single massive slab. Remains of the heavy corbelling which carried the roof, its capstone still in place.

BARHOLM CASTLE. *See* p. 118.

8060   KIRKGUNZEON

Small village bisected by a burn (the Kirkgunzeon Lane).

PARISH CHURCH. White-painted rectangle of 1790 with tallish roundheaded windows in the s wall; the N window is perhaps an insertion. Birdcage bellcote on the w gable, a ball finial on the E. Originally there was a door in the centre of each gable, but in 1869 *Alexander Fraser* added a porch at the E door, built up the existing w door and made a new door and porch to its r. Lean-to vestry converted from a hearse house in 1959.

In the graveyard, s of the church, an OBELISK (now missing its finial) which commemorates John Wightman †1812. – To its E, the much larger early C19 MONUMENT to members of the McWhire family, probably erected for Robert McWhire, late merchant in Halifax, †1831. Obelisk with a flaming urn finial. In the rusticated pedestal's w face, a niche containing an urn.

s of the church, the former MANSE (now MANSEPARK) of 1804, quite plain in white-painted rubble.

MAXWELL MEMORIAL HALL, 0.4km. E. Dated 1906. Of grey granite with red sandstone dressings. Broad eaves; a bowed E porch.

SCHOOL. By *Stewartry County Council*, 1964.

DESCRIPTION. The village's older houses and cottages, mostly C19 and rather altered, lie across the burn from the church and manse, reached by a humpbacked early C19 BRIDGE. At their E end, LANESIDE, the much altered granite-built and broad-eaved mid-Victorian school. Housing of the later C20 E of the church.

CORRA CASTLE, 0.5km. S. In the badly altered C19 steading, remains of each end of a rubble-built house, probably of the early C17. It has been a straightforward rectangle, *c*. 15.5m. by 6.7m., of two storeys and an attic.

DRUMCOLTRAN TOWER. *See* p. 222.

KIRKINNER

4050

One-street village, its terraced cottages mostly C19, a few perhaps a little earlier; several now have box dormers. The church stands aloof to the E.

PARISH CHURCH. Tall rubble-built and crowstep-gabled box of 1828. Stepped buttresses along the sides and placed diagonally at the corners. Pointed two-light windows with angular tracery in their heads. Above the E gable window (partly blocked *c*. 1900), the cusped heads of two (blind) lights under a trefoil. Is this a re-used medieval fragment? Battlemented W tower of two stages, the lower buttressed and with a tall pointed Y-traceried W window; pointed belfry openings above.

Inside, a quite elaborate but delicate plaster ceiling rose. – Slim cast-iron columns carrying a gallery round three sides, its fronts panelled. – PULPIT at the W end, its octagonal body supported on an octagonal stem. It is reached by steps behind it which rise from the N side to a curved landing on the E and S. Attached to the pulpit, two pierced metal bowls, each decorated with foliage and a cherub. They presumably held a baptismal basin and hourglass. – Plain late C19 PEWS. – The other furnishings (FONT of 1948, COMMUNION TABLE of *c*. 1950, and LECTERN of 1967) are C20. – STAINED GLASS. Two lights (the Sower; an Angelic Reaper) of *c*. 1900 behind the pulpit.

In the NE corner of the church, a C10 stone CROSS SLAB, brought inside from the churchyard in 1967. Gently curved slightly tapering shaft, its principal faces carved with interlaced reliefs. Circular head of typical Whithorn-school type; each front is incised with a cross, the spaces between its curved arms are pierced with holes, and its centre is marked by a boss, the W boss incised with a cross. (*See* the Introduction, p. 32.)

In the SE corner of the graveyard, the late C18 MAUSOLEUM

of the Vans Agnews of Barnbarroch. It is now damaged but has been very smart. Tall N and W fronts, each of three bays, the outer containing roundheaded niches. Higher centrepieces, each with paired Ionic pilasters carrying an entablature and pediment; the N's tympanum is carved with a saltire of up-ended torches. Parapets over the end bays. The swagged urns which stood on top are now on the ground.

SCHOOL. Single-storey cruciform of *c*. 1860. Large hoodmoulded two-light windows; ball finials on two gables. Behind, a plain detached block by *Andrew Thomson*, 1924, now linked by a late C20 extension. The playground boasts a monkey-puzzle tree.

BARNBARROCH. *See* p. 122.

8090   KIRKLAND

Small village, with Glencairn Parish Church at the W end.

24 GLENCAIRN PARISH CHURCH. Innocent Gothic of 1836–7 by *William McCandlish* and very similar to his slightly earlier church at St John's Town of Dalry. Tall T-plan, built of whin with red sandstone dressings. On top of the clasping buttresses, gableted pinnacles with leafy ball finials. Hoodmoulded windows; blind quatrefoils high up in the gables. The gable of the N 'aisle' is treated like the N gable at St John's Town of Dalry, being given a huge arched recess, its back almost filled by a six-light window. Projecting from the centre of the long S wall, a tower, each of its four stages marked by a bold stringcourse which is carried across the clasping buttresses. Tall openings in the two lower and top stages; the short third stage is relieved by a blind quatrefoil. At the belfry the buttresses become octagons topped by pinnacles above the battlement. Vestry addition against the E wall of the 'aisle'.

Inside, each arm is marked off by a basket arch and contains a gallery supported by wooden columns. – In the galleries, BOX PEWS of the 1830s. – PEWS of 1902 in the area. – The COMMUNION TABLE is now the focus. Both it and the PULPIT are early C20, of oak with Lorimerian decoration. – ORGAN (now without a console) of 1902 in the W arm. – STAINED GLASS. One window (the Good Shepherd) by the *Abbey Studio*, 1948, colourful modern-traditional. – MONUMENTS. In the centre of the E wall, a white marble tablet to Dr Walter Ross Munro †1816, signed by *Henry Rouw* of London, bearing the relief of a lady mourning over a sarcophagus; Dr Munro appears in a cloud above. – On the E gable, a bronze relief bust of the Rev. Patrick Borrowman by *James Paterson*, 1900. – On the W wall, a neo-classical bronze tablet of 1928 to Captain Robert Cutlar Fergusson of Craigdarroch and his daughter Ella. Aedicular frame with fluted pilasters and a coat of arms in the segmental pediment. A mourning angel each side of the inscription tablet and an angel's head (the soul) below.

CHURCHYARD. In the SE corner, the rubble-built gables of

the medieval OLD GLENCAIRN PARISH CHURCH. It has
been a large rectangle (*c.* 27.2m. by 8.2m.). The W gable has a
splayed base; its N corner's buttress is probably an addition. In
this gable, two blocked narrow lancets, perhaps C13. Above
them, a broad lancet with a segmental-headed rear-arch which
looks much later, possibly a post-Reformation insertion. Off-
centre C17 roundheaded door (later converted to a window),
its roll-and-hollow moulding crossed by chamfered imposts. In
the E gable, a pair of very narrow round-arched windows (the
N blocked) with wide internal splays. – Inside the church area,
three GRAVESTONES, probably C19 replacements of early C18
originals, which commemorate Covenanting martyrs. One, to
John Gibson, proclaims:

> MY SOUL'S IN HEAVEN
> HERE'S MY DUST
> BY WICKED SENTANCE
> AND UNJUST
> SHOT DEAD CONVICTED
> OF NO CRIME
> BUT NON-COMPLYANCE
> WITH THE TIME
> WHEN BABELS BASTARD
> HAD COMMAND
> AND MONSTEROUS TYRRA
> NTS HAD THE LAND

– A second, to Robert Edger and Robert Mitchell, enjoins:

> HALT PASSENGER TELL IF
> THOU EVER SAW
> MEN SHOT TO DEATH
> WITHOUT PROCESS OF LAW
> WE TWO OF FOUR WHO IN
> THIS CHURCHYARD LY
> THUS FELT THE RAGE OF
> POPISH TYRANY

– The third, to James Bennoch, announces:

> HERE LYES A MONUMENT
> OF POPISH WRATH
> BECAUSE I'M NOT PERJUR'D
> I'M SHOT TO DEATH
> BY CRUEL HANDS MEN
> GODLES AND UNJUST
> DID SACRIFICE MY BLOOD
> TO BABELSS [*sic*] LUST

– Just to the E, the broken original of Bennoch's stone.
   Against the W gable of the old church, the BURIAL ENCLOS-
URE of the Fergussons of Craigdarroch, dated 1675. Low ashlar
walling surmounted by a balustrade of diagonally set plain
rectangular blocks supporting a moulded cornice. There have
been ball finials on the corners; they are still in place over the
inscription panel. – Built against the E gable of the old church,
a large aedicular MONUMENT to Stephen Lawrie of Maxwelton
† 1637. On the projecting ends of the base, panels carved with
geometrical designs. The main frame has fluted pilasters; fluted

frieze at the entablature. Ball-footed dumpy pinnacles on the ends of the cornice; over the centre, a panel carved with reminders of death, its pediment displaying a chalice flanked by the initials of Stephen Lawrie and his wife.

53   N of the present Parish Church, the tall early C19 MAUSO-LEUM of the Gillespies of Peelton. Adamish neo-classical, beautifully executed in very finely jointed red sandstone ashlar, with fluted acanthus-capitalled pilasters at the canted urn-topped corners. On each main face, a round-arched recess (the S containing the entrance) under a swag. Domed stone roof with a smart urn finial. – SE of the church, the HEADSTONE to the centenarian John Mcubin †1663, the front carved with a very crude relief of an angel's head above emblems of death. – In the graveyard's SE corner, a few C18 HEADSTONES decorated with reminders of death. – In its NE corner, the MONU-MENT to Walter Ross Munro †1816, a big pedestal-tomb of red sandstone with marble inscription panels in the two long faces; on the ends, a bronze bust of Munro and a coat of arms. Swagged urn on top.

DESCRIPTION. At the village's E end, hidden in a well-treed garden, is the former MANSE, by *Walter Newall*, 1840–1, a white-painted *cottage orné* with bay windows, a bracketed door pediment, horizontal glazing and Tudor chimneys. On the S side of the main road stands its straightforward harled pre-decessor (now CAIRNSIDE), built in 1776–7 and extended S in 1802–3. Just E of Glencairn Parish Church (for which, *see* above), a mid-C19 terrace of cottages with hoodmoulds over the doors and windows. At their E end, a Victorian cast-iron PUMP, the water flowing from a lion's mouth.

OLD CRAWFORDTON, 1.7km. SE. L-plan farmhouse of white-washed rubble. At first glance it seems of no especial interest, but it is largely late C17, and the original door and window openings (several now blocked) have roll mouldings. The S range's W end has clearly been reduced in height in an C18 or C19 remodelling. Piend-roofed brick addition, probably of the C20, on the NW block's W side. Projecting W from the house's SW corner, the roofless ground floor of a tower house, probably of the C16 or early C17. It has been a straightforward rubble-walled rectangle, *c.* 10.4m. by 5.9m. Small windows; two doors in the N wall. Inside, two tunnel-vaulted stores. There has been a turnpike stair in the NW corner.

E of the house, a plain detached range of FARM OFFICES, again of whitewashed rubble, probably built in the C19.

MOTTE, Lower Ingleston, 1.1km. SW. Motte and bailey con-structed in the C12 or early C13 on low-lying land beside the Cairn Water, from which rises a long triangular-shaped and steep-sided ridge. The approach is from the triangle's E angle, which is cut across by a V-shaped ditch, *c.* 11m. wide and over 3m. deep, and a counterscarp. Beyond these, the bailey, *c.* 65m. long. At its W end, another ditch, *c.* 7.6m. wide and 3.7m. deep, in front of the motte, whose truncated cone shape has been formed by scarping the sides of the ridge's highest point.

MAXWELTON HOUSE. *See* p. 431.

KIRKMABRECK   *4050*

Just the ruin of a church in a wooded hillside graveyard overlooked by a large granite quarry.

Former PARISH CHURCH. Only the E gable and the lower parts of the walls survive of the rubble-built medieval church which was abandoned in 1637. In the gable, a sizeable rectangular window, robbed of its dressings. The church's interior has been divided to form burial enclosures. – To the S, a large and simple neo-classical MONUMENT to Professor Thomas Brown † 1820. Tall pedestal carrying a stone shaft, the lid-like cornice surmounted by an urn.

PARISH CHURCH. *See* Creetown.

KIRKMADRINE   *0040*

Just the church in a small graveyard, probably the site of a monastery in the early Christian period and later of a medieval parish church.

CHURCH. Built as a mausoleum-chapel by Lady McTaggart Stewart of Ardwell in the late C19, it is a determined evocation of the C12; Cruggleton Church is the obvious inspiration. Rubble-built nave and lower chancel; simple round-arched windows and doors. Inside, a semicircular chancel arch springing from clustered shafts, their capitals incised with decoration.

In the W porch, a collection of STONES, some fragmentary, from the graveyard. Among them are three PILLAR STONES. One, of the C5, commemorates the bishops or abbots ('chief priests') Viventius and Mavorius, the top of its front carved with a circle enclosing a cross whose r. arm loops to form the Chi-rho monogram. Above the circle, the inscription 'A et [O]'. – Similar C5 stone to –s and Florentius, again with a circled cross forming the Chi-rho but without the Alpha and Omega inscription. – The third pillar stone, probably of *c.* 600, has a heavier cross above the Latin inscription:

INITIUM
ET FINIS

– HEADSTONE, probably of the C8 or C9 and of Anglian design. At the top, a cross whose short shaft rises from a large base divided by diagonal lines into four panels, each containing a small incised cross. – Another HEADSTONE, perhaps of the C9 or early C10 and Northumbrian-influenced, is carved with three crosses, the top one Maltese and with horns (?) under the arms. – A third HEADSTONE, wedge-shaped and possibly C11, bears an ornamented cross with circles separating the arms; below, a plain cross above a lozenge. – Small PILLAR decorated with a cross; springing from the base are curved lines which join to the shaft. It may be C12. – SLAB of the C12 or C13. Top panel carved with irregular interlace; in a panel below, a cross with T-shaped ends to the head and arms and a leafy foot to the shaft.

KIRKMAHOE see KIRKTON

KIRKMAIDEN

Hamlet beside the Parish Church.

Former FREE CHURCH. *See* Drummore.

PARISH CHURCH. Begun in 1638 but not completed until some years later. Rubble-built T-plan with a N 'aisle'. On the E and N gables, ball-and-spike finials. Gableted W bellcote of 1885. The low W vestry was added in 1921. The windows are plain rectangles, the one in the N wall a late C19 insertion. Off-centre round-arched S door, now blocked. This looks C17; so are the doors in the E and W gables C18 or C19 insertions? Very simple interior, the coomb ceiling probably of 1885, the date of the PULPIT and its brass oil lamps. The N 'aisle' contains the burial vault of the McDoualls of Logan, which forms a dais for the gallery made here in 1885. – BELL, its inscription relating that it was made for Nicholas Ramsay, lord of Dalhousie, by *John Morison*, 1534. – On the N wall, a wooden PANEL carved with the coat of arms and initials of Patrick Adair of Alton and his wife, together with the inscription: O GOD MAK ME TO HEIR IN FAITH AND PRACKTEIS IN LOVE THY HOLY WIRD AND COMA[N]DEME[N]TIS THOU ONLY ART MY SUPOIRT GOD MAK ME THANKFUL 1618.

GRAVEYARD. SW of the church, the MONUMENT to James Scott †1852, son of the keeper of the Mull of Galloway lighthouse. It is a miniature replica of a lighthouse. – Very near it, the HEADSTONE to Patrick McGoffog †1768, with an angel's head (the soul) at the top. – To its S, the HEADSTONE of Samuel Paterson †1731 but looking late C18. It is an accomplished pilastered aedicule, the shaped pediment broken by an urn, the metopes of the Doric frieze carved with rosettes and rams' skulls. Swagged drapery at the top of the inscription tablet. – Behind it, the HEADSTONE of Jenn [*sic*] Corkran †1733 (?), crudely lettered and with a face incised on the front.

UNITED FREE CHURCH. *See* Drummore: St Medan's Church.

SCHOOL, 0.4km. E. Now in other use. H-plan school and schoolhouse of 1877, with a big double-keyhole gunloop in one front gable.

FORT, Crammag Head, 4.5km. SW. Sea-girt promontory site, fortified probably in the late first millennium B.C. or early in the first millennium A.D. Outer defence provided by a low curving stony bank, a gap between its S end and the cliff edge providing a passage. *c.*21m. to the W the promontory's N and S sides have been cut away to leave a path *c.*3.35m. wide. W of this artificial pinchpoint, the ruin of a round enclosure, probably a broch, of *c*.18.3m. diameter, the base of its wall formed of massive stone blocks. Before this sector was removed the wall thickened towards the E, making the interior roughly oval.

KIRKMICHAEL   0080

Just the church and churchyard beside the mid-C19 farmhouse and steading of TOWNHEAD.

PARISH CHURCH. T-plan kirk of sneck-harled rubble, by *John McCracken*, 1813–15. Piend-roofed body; birdcage bellcote on the N jamb's straight gable. Big round-arched windows. N vestry added in 1871. Inside, the N gallery, with a deep panelled front, is carried on cast-iron columns. – Late C19 PEWS and PULPIT, perhaps dating from 1880s alterations. – STAINED GLASS. The two S windows flanking the pulpit (Our Lord stilling the storm; Our Lord as the Good Shepherd) are probably of 1882; they look like scenes from a children's Bible. – NE window (Our Lady flanked by Faith and Hope) of *c*.1935, brightly coloured and crowded but not without discipline.

E of the church, an C18 TABLE STONE, one of its supporting slabs carved with an angel's head (the soul), the other with a skull and crossbones. – To its S, the HEADSTONE of William Johnston † 1741, aged 1 year and 8 months, the front displaying the figure of a woman flanked by emblems of death; above, an angel's head. – To the SE, a HEADSTONE to Mary Barton † 1760, its front with an angel's head and winged hourglass placed between panelled pilasters. – S of the church, the half-buried GRAVESLAB of John –head † 1512 or 1513, carved with a skull and bones. – To its W, a late C18 urn-finialled OBELISK commemorating Dr John Burgess.

THE BARONY. *See* p. 123.

KIRKPATRICK DURHAM   7070

Sizeable village founded *c*.1785. It was intended to attract a cotton or woollen industry which failed to arrive.

FREE CHURCH, Victoria Street. Now Village Hall. Built in 1843 but completely remodelled by *Alexander Crombie* in 1870. Awkward Gothic rectangle, of whin with red sandstone dressings. S gable front, its centre very slightly advanced and topped by a gableted bellcote. Heavy pinnacles on the stepped angle buttresses. Mutule blocks under the eaves.

PARISH CHURCH, 0.3km. S. Late Georgian Gothic despite its Victorian date, by *Walter Newall*, 1849–50. Tall and T-plan, a tower at the end of the W jamb. Mostly harled with red sandstone dressings. At the sides, big pointed windows containing Y-traceried wooden mullions. The main block has a window of three pointed lights in each gable. The centre light in each is larger than the others and Y-traceried, with a circular stone

panel above. High in the N gable, an heraldic panel, the coat
of arms perhaps that of William Kennedy, who was Abbot of
Crossraguel between 1520 and 1547. Also carved on the panel
is the date 1748, that of the previous church on the site. The
jamb's gable, angle-buttressed and parapeted, is built of
coursed whin with red sandstone dressings. Minimally
advanced from it is the front of the tower, again angle-buttressed. At its lowest stage, a Tudor door. Big rectangular
window above. Circular panel at the third stage. Jumping
stringcourse which forms hoodmoulds over the rectangular
openings of the belfry which rises clear of the church. Spike-
topped gableted finials on the battlement.

The interior was refurnished in 1949, when the jamb was
partitioned off to form a hall. Huge plaster ceiling rose, presumably of 1810. – STAINED GLASS. High up in the centre of
the E wall, a two-light window (St Luke and St Patrick) of
1896, clearly drawn and coloured. – Much darker and messier
window (the Sower and the Reaper) at this wall's E end, by *The
Glass Stainers Co.*, 1888.

GRAVEYARD. SE of the church, a few C18 HEADSTONES.
The front of one is a pilastered aedicule framing a coat of arms,
with a skull at the base; in the open pediment, an angel's
head (the soul). It commemorates Margaret Heron †1749, the
inscription recalling that

> ... she delivered the poor that cried
> The fatherless & him that had none to help
> She looked well to the ways of her household
> And did not eat the bred [*sic*] of idleness ...

– To its S, a stone to Andrew Johnston †1775, with a curly-headed
front whose panelled pilasters frame an angel's head above a
piecrust-bordered panel. – E of the church, a TABLE STONE to
Mary McLellan †1697, a Covenanting heroine. The slab's
fluted sides are carved with skulls, reminders of death and an
angel's head; on top, a coat of arms and the inscription.
SCHOOL, St David Street. Disused. Dated 1885. Aggressive whin
and granite asymmetrical T-plan, the tail flanked by gabled
porches. Gabled and round-arched bellcote feature where the
tail joins the cross-bar.
DESCRIPTION. On the S approach, after the Parish Church (*see*
above), which faces the unpretentious C19 farm steading of
KIRKSTYLE, the village is heralded on the W side of the road
by DURHAM HOUSE, built as the Parish Manse in 1837–
8. Two storeys and three bays, the anta-pilastered doorpiece
flanked by minimally projecting and corniced rectangular bay
windows; the horizontal glazing pattern survives. The village
proper is L-shaped, its houses and cottages mostly vernacular
of the late C18 or C19. At the beginning of the W side of ST
DAVID STREET, running to the N, the two-storey ST DAVID'S
LODGE, piend-roofed and rubble-walled. At its upper floor, a
round panel displaying a coat of arms and the date 1813. Also
on the W, the early C19 No. 7, with a moulded eaves cornice,

and the taller No. 9, with big first-floor windows and a mutuled cornice. A little further on the same side, standing well back, is the school (*see* above). Near the N end of the E side, the mid-C19 No. 10, built of painted rubble with rusticated quoins. Spike-finialled gableted dormerheads over the first-floor windows. Shallowly bowed porch, its walling swept up to a central spike finial.

VICTORIA STREET runs E from St David Street's S end. The early C19 No. 1 on the S side has a console-corniced door and mutuled eaves cornice. Carved bargeboards on Nos. 6–8, probably mid-C19, though the chimneys are of C20 brick. Near the street's bottom end, the former Free Church (*see* above).

DURHAMHILL, 0.4km. NE. Three-storey three-bay laird's house of *c.* 1820. Rusticated quoins, the main walling now pebbledashed. Aedicular Roman Doric doorpiece. All the front windows are of three lights. Each side of the house, a detached single-storey-and-attic piend-roofed steading building with a central round-arched cart entrance under a bullseye window.

KILQUHANITY, 2.2km. W. Piend-roofed villa of *c.* 1820 by *Walter Newall*. Two storeys and a basement, three bays. Broad doorpiece with engaged Roman Doric columns. Lower L-plan SE wing added *c.* 1840.

WALTON PARK, 2.6km. NW. Villa of two storeys and a basement built in 1816 for Major James A. Campbell. Entrance (S) front with broad bows flanking the centre, which is surmounted by a flat-topped 'pediment'. Attached Roman Doric columns at the door. Late C19 E addition in hammerdressed masonry, with a battlemented tower and another full-height bow. – STABLES dated 1817. Four rubble ranges around a courtyard. Unpretentious showfront to the S; its ends are formed by the gables of the E and W ranges, each with a round light at the top. Tall gabled centrepiece containing the pend arch. Above, a pointed doocot opening.

BROOKLANDS. *See* p. 134.

KIRKPATRICK-FLEMING

Straggling roadside village of the C19 and C20.

PARISH CHURCH. T-plan kirk built of snecked rubble. The body may well incorporate medieval walling, but the church was enlarged, probably including the addition of the N jamb, in 1726, when the roof's heather thatch was replaced by slates; partial rebuilding took place *c.* 1775. Round-arched windows, those in the S front with projecting imposts and keystones. They all look to be of *c.* 1775, as do the ball finials on the E and W gables. On the gable of the jamb, a tall birdcage bellcote of 1733. In the inner angles, gallery forestairs and porches, perhaps added in *John B. Leslie*'s alterations of 1892–3. Certainly of 1892–3 are the E vestry, the bargeboards and red-tiled roof ridge. W porch added in 1911.

Built against the N jamb is the Irvings' BURIAL ENCLOSURE, probably of the earlier C18. V-jointed ashlar base; panelled superstructure with pilasters supporting the cornice. Moulded door surround, its lintel carved with a skull and crossbones. – Against the W gable, the BURIAL ENCLOSURE of the Grahams of Mossknowe, dated 1678 (?). Rusticated quoins; on top, a balustrade with ball finials on the corners. Inscription panel over the moulded entrance. – Fair number of C18 HEADSTONES decorated with heraldry and reminders of death. Among them, S of the church, the stone commemorating John Armstrong †1701, the pedimented front carved with a pair of hands. – HEADSTONE to John and James Lam †1748 and 1752, both in infancy, embellished with the relief of two children standing above a pair of coffins.

MANSE to the W, by *A. Crombie & Son*, 1878–9. Georgian-survival, but some of the windows are rectangular bays and others are of two lights.

PRIMARY SCHOOL. Dated 1881. Plain except for a sort of Gothic Venetian window.

VICTORIA HALL. By *George Dale Oliver*, 1898–9. English Baroque in bullnosed ashlar; Venetian window in the pedimented gable.

BROATS, 2.7km. SW. Smart piend-roofed early C19 farmhouse, skinny columns at its portico.

MOSSKNOWE. *See* p. 453.

KIRKPATRICK-IRONGRAY

Rural parish, with the church sitting by itself.

PARISH CHURCH. Built in 1803, a whitewashed rubble box with red sandstone dressings. In 1872–3 *James Barbour* provided mechanically detailed Romanesque trimmings with the insertion of new windows and the erection of a squat SW tower; of the same date, the flèche ventilator. The interior is mostly Barbour's. Open wooden roof, the collar-braces springing from carved stone corbels. Romanesque recess at the W end. In front of it, a mid-C20 COMMUNION TABLE. – Simple PEWS of 1872–3. – STAINED GLASS. High in the W gable, a two-light window (the Good Shepherd and (?) St John), after 1904. – In the N wall, a strongly coloured window (Faith and Hope), after 1880. – S wall: W window, 1873, with bright patterns enclosing medallions of Our Lord and little children; E window (the Maries at the Tomb; the Ascension), c.1890 and realistic. – Realistic again but crude the E gable's S light (Our Lord as the Light of the World), c.1925.

The CHURCHYARD WALL was built in 1838. – Just SE of the church, a TABLE STONE to Katrin Mill or Browne †1633, the slab carved with a marginal inscription, the initials KB and a coat of arms. Between the uprights, later panels bearing C19 inscriptions, armorial motifs and fleurs-de-lis. – Beside it, the TOMB-CHEST of Helen Walker, the original of Jeanie Deans in Sir Walter Scott's *The Heart of Midlothian* (1818), who refused to lie to save her sister from a charge of infanticide but then walked to London to petition the Duke of Argyll for a reprieve from the death sentence. The monument was designed in 1831 by *William Burn*; the inscription is written by Scott. – To the E, the TABLE STONE of Bessie Edgar †1707, its bottom end carved with the high relief of a woman holding a book. – To its S, an elegant urn-finialled OBELISK commemorating Captain James Finan †1796, aged seventy-two, the inscription on the tall pedestal relating that:

CAP.T FINNAN *maintained unsullied the character of a* British Officer. *on the late War of* Great Britain *with revolutionary* France. *the hoary Veteran hastened, among the earliest of his Countrymen to* Arms: *and headed a Compn. of the Royal Dumfries Volunteers, during the awful* struggle of Treason & Anarchy ag.st Loyalty & Order.

MANSE, 0.2km. S. Built in 1801, of white-painted rubble with three-light ground-floor window. The flat-topped dormers are C20 additions. Extensive outbuildings behind.

BRIDGE, 0.2km E. By *William McGowan*, 1855. Two segmental arches of hammerdressed rough ashlar; bulbous-topped rounded cutwaters.

MARTYRS' MONUMENT, Hallhill, 0.3km. W. Erected in 1851. Small railed enclosure. At its back, a pedimented monument with a flaming urn finial; a pair of hands is carved on the frieze. In front of this, the contemporary GRAVESLAB commemorating the Covenanters Edward Gordon and Alexander McCubine, inscribed:

AS LAGG AND BLOOD[Y] BRUCE COMMAN'D
WE WERE HUNG UP BY
HELLISH HAND
AND THUS THER FURIO
US RAGE TO STAY
WE DY'D NEAR KIRK
OF IRON GRAY:
HERE NOW IN PEACE
SWEET REST WE TAKE
ONCE MURDER'D FOR
RELIGEON'S SAKE

DRUMPARK, 3.7km. W. The mansion house designed by *John Cunningham* of Liverpool in 1859 has been rebuilt. The STABLES survive, heavily detailed, with crowstepped gables and cupolas. Also of *c.* 1860 the gingerbread LODGE.

HALLHILL, 0.8km. W. White-painted farmhouse and steading built by *Thomas Edgar* and *James Herries*, masons, and *Frederick Maxwell*, joiner, in 1803–6. Unusually, the gables are topped not by chimneys but by little ball finials. The porch is an addition.

KIRKTON

Small village, its unpretentious houses of the later C19 surrounding a triangular green on which stands a pump. Kirkmahoe Parish Church is just to the w, late C20 housing to the e.

KIRKMAHOE PARISH CHURCH. By *Walter Newall*, 1822–3. Big box with a w tower, all built of red sandstone stugged ashlar. Gableted sharp pinnacles on top of the diagonal buttresses. Three-light side windows with Perp tracery and hoodmoulds. In the e gable, a four-light window, a pair of blind crosslet arrowslits and a quatrefoil in the apex. Projecting from this gable, a pair of Tudor porches. The w tower is of three stages, its diagonal buttresses again with pinnacles which rise well clear of the battlement. Low s vestry, probably an addition, enlarged to the w in the 1960s.

The interior is a single space, the ceiling's huge span crossed by ribs springing from corbelled wallshafts. – PEWS provided in *James Barbour*'s reseating of 1889. – Neo-Jacobean PULPIT of 1823, with a small canopy now bereft of its spired finials. It was moved from the s wall to the NE corner as part of the alterations made in 1966–7, when the FONT, LECTERN (by *Ian Douglas*) and COMMUNION TABLE (by *William Russell*, with carved work by *Norman J. Forrest*) were introduced and a plain w gallery was erected with a glazed screen below. – STAINED GLASS. At the s wall's e end, Our Lord and saints, by *H. W. Lonsdale*, 1895. – E window (the Revelation of God to Man, from the Fall of Adam to Pentecost) by *William Wilson*, 1967, with typically strong but unusually dark colours. – MONUMENTS. On the s wall, a white marble tablet of 1838 commemorating Peter Johnston of Carnsalloch, with a draped urn at the top, a coat of arms at the bottom. – Black and white marble monument of *c.*1825 to the Maxwells of Dalswinton, with a flaming urn. – Over the door from the vestry, a wooden PANEL bearing the date 1614.

GRAVEYARD. In the w inner angle of the church and vestry, a MONUMENT to the Rev. John Wightman †1817, a fat fluted column, its acanthus leaf capital carrying a swagged urn. – SE of the church, the large urn-finialled HEADSTONE to Mary Lindsay †1832, inscribed:

> Stranger! one fleeting moment save,
> For this is MARY LINDSAY'S GRAVE,
> Who practised, in her low estate,
> Virtues that well become the great:
> Who, self-denying, chaste, and kind,
> An honour was to womankind,
> Near yon rude cot she first drew breath,
> And there she closed her eyes in death
> – Pattern to all who wish to thrive –
> At the ripe age of eighty-five.
>
> No husband Mary ever had,
> Nor offspring age's ills to glad;
> Yet all the children round and round

In her a foster-parent found.
Their eggs she boiled, their Josephs dried
And soothed and coaxed them when they cried
And when the burn was wide and wild,
She ferried over every child.
Proficient in each nurturing art,
The *fremit* had a mother's heart;
A Janitress from love not hire -
How blest was Mary's winter fire!

Disturb not but respect this stone,
Raised to her memory by one
Who even in death would Mary shield
– *Hannah of Bayhall Huddersfield*

– Behind it, a curly-headed C18 HEADSTONE to James Thomson, the front carved with a crowned hammer (the emblem of the smiths). – Near the churchyard's SE corner, the GRAVESLAB of Archibald Wright †1700, with emblems of mortality at the bottom. Inscription:

WEEP.NOT.FOR.ME.WHO.HERE.DO.LY
WEEP.FOR.YOUR.SINS.BEFORE.YOU.DY
FOR.DEATH.IS.NOT.TO.BE.LAMENTED
BUT.SIN.IS.STILL.TO.BE.REPENTED

– Some way SW of the church, a TABLE STONE, one end of its slab bearing a panel carved with an angel's head (the soul) and a counter display of reminders of death; below this, the initials CW and the date 1713. The inscription is to Joseph Robson †177– and Christiana Wallace †1769; a late C18 date would fit the style of the slabs, decorated with rosetted oval panels, which have been added between the legs. – At the graveyard's E entrance, late Georgian corniced GATEPIERS with half-globe finials.

HALL. Dated 1902. Built of red sandstone, with a Venetian window above the gabled porch.

ROMAN FORT, Carzield, 0.7km. NW. The base of a cavalry regiment in the mid-C2. The SE corner of the fort, which covered 2.56ha., is clearly visible in the field beside the entrance to Carzield House.

CARNSALLOCH HOUSE. *See* p. 160.

MILNHEAD. *See* p. 435.

KIRKWOOD   *1070*
1.3km. NE of Dalton

Sprawling red sandstone mansion house, by *Walter F. Lyon*, 1880. Baronial, with a strongly detailed display of crowstepped gables, Jacobean pedimented dormerheads, and mullioned and transomed windows. Tower projecting at the SW, a bartizan on one corner, a conical-roofed round turret in the inner angle.

KIRROUGHTREE HOUSE

4060

1.2km. E of Newton Stewart

Mansion house (now an hotel), begun in the early C18, but much extended at the end of the C19 and the beginning of the C20. At the S end is the Georgian house, built in 1719 for Patrick Heron of Kirroughtree with the 'advice and contrivance' of his uncle, *Andrew Heron* of Bargaly, and remodelled *c.*1775. Harled, like the rest, with painted ashlar dressings. Three storeys and a basement. Full-height canted bay at the centre of the S front; a full-height bow, probably of *c.*1775, at each gable. The lugged window architraves and broken segmental pediments are either of *c.*1890, when the house is said to have been 'rebuilt', or of 1907 when *Peddie & Washington Browne* did work here. Big N additions of the late C19 or early C20. Boldly projecting E portico with stumpy Ionic columns. Octagonal tower at the NE corner. Quite lavish but not especially exciting late Victorian or Edwardian interior.

KIRTLEBRIDGE

2070

Small C19 village.

KIRTLE CHURCH. By *James Gillison*, 1840–1, but completely remodelled in 1896–8 by *Hardy & Wight*. Tall box of sneck-harled rubble with round-arched windows of the 1890s. Also of the 1890s are the S apse and the square four-stage tower. This is of snecked squared rubble with lancet openings. Uncrenellated parapet; at its NE corner, a pyramid-roofed finial looking like a miniature caphouse and carrying a weathervane. Inside, Hardy & Wight replaced Gillison's flat plaster ceiling with an open queenpost-truss roof. Ribbed and panelled wooden ceiling over the apse, entered through a pointed stone arch. – FURNISHINGS of 1896–8. – STAINED GLASS. In the W wall, one light (the Risen Lord) by *Clayton & Bell*, 1898; disappointing. – S window (Our Lord stilling the Tempest) by *Douglas Strachan*, *c.*1920; characteristically expressionist and strongly coloured. – CHAMBER ORGAN by *The Positive Organ Co. Ltd*, 1890.

RAILWAY VIADUCT. Of nine segmental arches; built in 1847. The masonry is aggressively bullnosed.

SCHOOL. Dated 1906 and humble.

THE BRAES, 0.4km. N. Laird's house of whitewashed rubble, built in 1737 (the date over the door). Two-storey main block, a lintel course under the eaves. Chamfered windows. Lugged and moulded doorpiece under a steep pediment, the tympanum carved with a monogram. The house was extended to an L by the addition of a W wing, probably early in the C19. More additions of the C20. – To the SE, a BYRE and BARN of the earlier C18 forming an L. In the byre's N gable, flight holes for a doocot. – To the s, a WALLED GARDEN; the lintel of its blocked E door is dated 1731. Ball-finialled gatepiers, probably of the late C18.

LANGSHAW HOUSE, 0.4km. E. Unassuming laird's house, the product of accretion. The earliest part, at the back, is an E-facing mid-C18 rendered two-storey range, with early C20 pediments over the upper windows of the outer bays. In 1787 the house was made T-plan by the addition of an informal block to the s end. Pedimented portico near the centre of its front. In the E gable's pediment, an elliptical-arched panel. Plain addition of 1901 on the w side of the original house. Billiard room extension of 1907 at the w end of the 1787 block.

WYSEBY, 0.4km. SE. Unpretentious rendered laird's house, said in 1797 to have been 'built within these few years', although it looks rather earlier. Three storeys and originally of three bays. Corniced doorpiece with a pulvinated frieze; same cornice and frieze at the window above. The door was given a pedimented Roman Doric portico in the early C19. Perhaps at the same time the house was extended E by one piend-roofed bay. Probably later is the addition's canted bay window, its centre light now a door. – To the w, whitewashed STABLES, probably of the later C18. Adjoining on the N, an octagonal early C19 DOOCOT, the ground floor occupied by a pigsty, the first by a henhouse; the pigeons' stone nesting boxes survive at the top.

CROSS, Merkland, 1.2km. SE. C15 stone cross 3m. high, with its base renewed. The arms and head each end in a carved fleur-de-lis.

BONSHAW TOWER. *See* p. 131.
ROBGILL TOWER. *See* p. 500.
WOODHOUSE TOWER. *See* p. 573.

KNOCKBREX

2.2km. NW of Kirkandrews

Plain neo-Georgian rubble-walled manor house built in 1900 for the Manchester businessman James Brown, and incorporating at the E end a refaced and remodelled early C19 house. (Neo-Georgian and Arts and Crafts interiors, the main rooms panelled.)

STABLES to the E, also of 1900. Four ranges round a courtyard, with broad eaves to the gabled dormers. Cupola over the round-arched pend entrance. Pavilion-roofed tower at the back. – Contemporary WALLED GARDEN behind. – Further E, the granite-built 'TOY FORT', again of *c.* 1900. Battlemented square folly of a house. Corner towers, two of them octagonal, one square with a conical-roofed round turret, the fourth circular with a candlesnuffer roof.

1070   KNOCKHILL
                      2.6km. w of Ecclefechan

85 Laird's house built in 1777 for Andrew Johnstone of Knockhill
   after his return from the West Indies, where he had been
   transported for his part in the 1745 Jacobite rising. It is distinctly
   old-fashioned for the date: a piend-roofed, white-painted,
   rubble-walled box of two storeys over a basement, with rusticated quoins at the corners. Five-bay s front; the ground-
   floor windows were always larger than the others to denote the
   piano nobile, but they were deepened, probably in the early C19.
   At the centre, a recessed Venetian door framed by a doorcase of
   engaged Roman Doric columns *in antis*, with a small pediment
   above the cornice. On the frieze, the date 1777, together with
   the initials of Johnstone and his wife and the inscription: 'Too
   Small for Envy/for Contempt to [*sic*] Great.' Additions (two
   rear and two lateral wings), all probably of the earlier C19.
   The single-storey-and-basement w wing is bow-ended. Semi-
   octagonal end to the almost full-height E wing; its very shallow
   rectangular oriel window is perhaps a mid-C19 alteration. Low
   NE wing, with a Venetian window in the centre of its E side.
      To the N, U-plan STABLES of *c.*1780. Each of the two s
   gables has a segmental-arched cart entrance under a small
   bullseye window.

5080   KNOCKNALLING
                   4.3km. NW of St John's Town of Dalry

Tudor-style house of *c.*1840. Five-bay s front with advanced
   and ball-finialled gabled ends. Hoodmoulds over the two-light
   ground-floor windows (one now a door); first-floor windows
   rising into ball-finialled gablets. Boldly projecting gabled E
   porch. – STABLES to the N. Two ranges forming the N and s
   sides of a courtyard. The s range, probably of the earlier C19
   but much altered, is single-storey and humble. Two-storey late
   C19 N range, with pedimented dormerheads over the first-floor
   windows. Stodgy Gothic tower at the E end. Screen wall with
   ball-finialled gatepiers on the E side of the court. – Rubble-
   walled BARN, probably of the mid-C19. In each wall, regularly
   spaced triangular vents. Depressed-arched doors in the E and w
   sides (the w blocked). In the gables, pointed doocot openings.

9080   LAG'S TOMB

Small graveyard, the site of Dunscore Parish Church until 1649.
   The present name is taken from the monument erected here in
   1897.

GRAVEYARD. In the centre, the ashlar-walled C18 BURIAL
   ENCLOSURE of the Fergusons of Isle, with rusticated quoins
   and a cornice. – To its w, a broken GRAVESLAB to someone

†1671, carved with a crude skull and crossbones. – Just w of this, the SLAB of a table stone (now stuck upright in the ground) to someone else †1719, also with emblems of death. – A little further w, the pilastered and open-pedimented HEADSTONE of William and Isobel Thomson †1772 and 1773, aged 4 months and 12 days, and 4 days, inscribed:

> The Tender Babe that Sleepeth here
> Was much belov'd of parents dear.
> Few were there Days Short was there race,
> But heaven we hopes there dwelling place.

– Against the E wall of the burial enclosure, a MONUMENT erected in 1897 to commemorate Sir Robert Grierson of Lag, the scourge of the Covenanters. It incorporates a worn heraldic stone inscribed with the initials I G (perhaps for John Grierson), which came from Lag Tower. – N of this, the crude but well-preserved TABLE STONE of James Grierson †1676, incised with a skull and crossbones. – Near the graveyard's E wall, a HEADSTONE to John Grierson, smith, †1732, its front carved with an angel's head (the soul) above a hand holding a crowned hammer (the emblem of the smiths).

LAG TOWER   *8080*
2.2km. NE of Dunscore

Sizeable fragment of a rectangular tower house built for the Griersons of Lag, perhaps shortly before 1526, when a tower here is first recorded. Most of the N and E walls still stand but only stubs of the S and W. Rubble-built with dressed quoins. Windows now robbed of dressings. The house has been of four unvaulted storeys served by a SE turnpike stair. Each of the first and second floors has contained a N fireplace and a garderobe.

LANGHOLM   *3080*

Small town beside the Esk, founded as a burgh of barony in 1621; its first substantial stone houses were erected a few years later. In 1778 the burgh's superior, the Duke of Buccleuch, laid out a gridiron 'New Town' extension (New Langholm) on the w side of the Esk, and a cotton mill (since demolished) was established there at the same time. Woollen mills on both sides of the river, a brewery and small distillery followed. The population was about 1,400 by 1850 and over 4,000 by 1880. Since then industry and population have declined.

CHURCHES

ALL SAINTS (Episcopal), 0.4km. N, in the grounds of Langholm Lodge. By *James Burnet*, 1887. Of corrugated wood with a slate roof. Rectangular side windows containing Gothic lights; a quatrefoil window in the W gable.

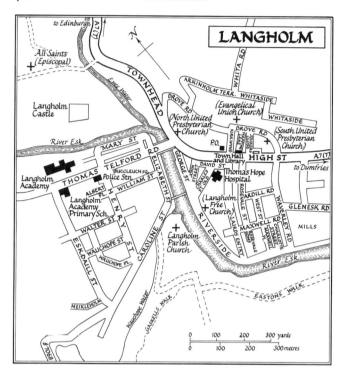

Evangelical Union Church, Drove Road and Kirk Wynd.
Disused. Lanceted box by *James Burnet*, 1870. In the broad
gable front, a hoodmoulded window of three lights; trefoil
opening at the top.

Free Mission Hall, Riverside. Now Community Centre. By
James Burnet, 1881. Buttressed rectangle with hood-moulded
lancet windows. In the front gable, a window of three stepped
lights with slender attached shafts. On top of the gable, a Gothic
bellcote. 1990s addition on the N.

29 Langholm Parish Church, off Caroline Street. Big
Georgian-survival ashlar-clad and parapeted Gothic kirk, by
Burn & Bryce, 1842–6. Nave and aisles of seven bays, with fat
hoodmoulded lancets and sturdy gableted buttresses along the
sides. Angle buttresses topped by octagonal pinnacles. Large
Gothic birdcage bellcote on the E gable. At both E and W
gables, the nave and aisles are marked off by pinnacled buttresses. Three-light window at each end of the nave, the centre
light stilted. The W (liturgical E) window is very tall. E entrance
of three orders with bell-capitalled nook-shafts, flanked by blind
quatrefoils. SW porch; NW session house enlarged by *R. B.
Burnet*, 1913.

The interior is a huge barn. Neo-Jacobean wooden-faced
piers divide off the aisles, which, together with the E end, are
filled with galleries. Hammerbeam roof, its braces springing

from the wallhead. – The w focus is *Burn & Bryce*'s PULPIT,
big and Jacobean, with strapwork cresting on the sounding
board. – Simple boxy PEWS of 1915 by *P. MacGregor Chalmers*. – ORGAN in the E gallery, by *Henry Willis & Sons*, 1893. –
Strongly coloured STAINED GLASS w window of three lights
(Scenes from the life of Our Lord) by *Morris & Co.*, 1925.* – s
of the pulpit, the BELL from this church's predecessor, cast in
1795 by *Armstrong & Co.* of Edinburgh.

NORTH UNITED PRESBYTERIAN CHURCH, High Street.
Disused. Ungainly E.E. of 1867, by *Robert Baldie*. Broad box,
its bulk disguised at the front (w) gable by a slight recession on
the r. to suggest an aisle and, on the l., by a steeple, also set
back. In each face of the tower, a window of two very tall lancet
lights under a rose. Stone spire, with an octagonal upper part
plonked down on the square lower stage without broaching;
only lucarnes to mitigate the awkwardness.

SOUTH UNITED PRESBYTERIAN CHURCH, Drove Road.
Secularized. By *Michael Brodie*, 1883–4. A plain buttressed
rectangle with lancets and a slender octagonal flèche with a
lead spire. sw porch with foliaged capitals on the columns of
the double door; above the door, a roundel containing a portrait
bust in high relief.

PUBLIC BUILDINGS

BRIDGES. *See* Langholm Lodge and Description, below.

LANGHOLM ACADEMY, Thomas Telford Road. Three storeys
of pale curtain walling, by *Dumfriesshire County Council*, 1962.

LANGHOLM ACADEMY PRIMARY SCHOOL, Thomas Telford
Road and Eskdaill Street. Begun in 1854–6, gently Tudorish
and U-plan, with a bell hanging at the sw gable. *George Scott*
was the contractor. The centre was rebuilt in 1894 as a tall
two-storey block in plain School Board Tudor. – Detached
GYMNASIUM of 1911, by *J. P. Alison*.

LIBRARY, High Street, back-to-back with the Town Hall. By
James Burnet, 1875–8. Smart Jacobean with slim ogee-roofed
corner towers, mullioned and transomed windows, and simplified buckle quoins. s front with a stepped gable flanked by
pinnacled ball finials and with a rectangular oriel window.
Shaped gables on the w side to High Street.

In the small garden on the s, the old MERCAT CROSS,
perhaps early C17. Round shaft carrying a red granite boulder,
its top incised with a rough cross. – STATUE of Admiral Sir
Pulteney Malcolm, originally erected in Market Place in 1842
and moved here in 1878. Tall granite pedestal; Italian granite
statue (now whitewashed) by *David Dunbar yr.* – Attached
to the garden's E wall, a DOORPIECE with Roman Doric
columns and a segmental pediment, probably from the old
King's Arms Hotel in Market Place, traditionally said to
have been worked on by the engineer *Thomas Telford* during

---

* The subjects were drawn by *J. Henry Dearle*, adapting earlier designs by *Edward
Burne-Jones* for some of the scenes.

his apprenticeship as a mason at Langholm in the 1770s. MISSION HALL, Charles Street Old. Now a house. Minimal Gothic, by *James Burnet*, 1881.

POLICE STATION, Buccleuch Square. By *Alexander Fraser*, 1865. Scots Jacobean of a sort, in red sandstone. Energetically crow-stepped gables, one with a coat of arms surrounded by thistles.

POST OFFICE. *See* Description, below.

THOMAS HOPE HOSPITAL, David Street. By *Woodd & Ainslie* of London, 1894–6. Plain low Jacobean for the most part but with a squat square tower. This has a large rope-course under its high and martial battlement from which protrude big stone spouts. On each of its E and W faces, a battered chimney is corbelled out from the wall and rises above the parapet like an additional defence. At its SW corner, a round turret corbelled out to a battlemented octagonal caphouse. – Contemporary two-storey LODGE to the street, in the same Jacobean manner. On its rounded front, a cartouche in an Artisan Mannerist aedicule.

TOWN HALL, High Street. Built on the site of the Tolbooth in 1811–12. Two-storey ashlar-fronted piend-roofed block with a band course and rusticated quoins. Centre advanced as a tower with an anta-pilastered and corniced second stage, its window round-arched with a projecting keystone and imposts. Above this, an intake to the third stage, again with a round-arched window. Then another intake to the panelled clock-stage and yet another intake to the belfry, its openings again round-arched. On top, a concave-sided spire and weathercock.

LANGHOLM CASTLE
0.5km. N

Badly ruined remains of a tower house built for the Armstrongs at the beginning of the C16 and largely demolished in 1725. It has been a rubble-walled rectangle. A fair amount of the S gable survives; in it, a rectangular first-floor window. Stubs of the E and W walls. No evidence of vaulting inside.

LANGHOLM LODGE
1km. NW

The main block of the mansion house designed by *James Playfair* for the third Duke of Buccleuch in 1786–7, and rebuilt *c.*1790 after a fire, was demolished in 1953. Playfair's lateral wings survive, each like a small country house in its own right. The front of the N wing is relatively unaltered: it has a piend-roofed centre of two storeys and three bays with a single-storey two-bay wing at each end. The wings of the S block were raised to two storeys in the late C19. – To the S, the DUCHESS BRIDGE, a cast-iron footbridge over the Esk, designed by *William Keir Jun.* and erected in 1813. Elegant lattice-girdered segmental span, the railings of the balustrades tied down by iron scrolls to the projecting deck. – LODGE at the entrance to the drive from the E, a broad-eaved *cottage orné* of the later C19.

DESCRIPTION

Langholm

On the entry of the A7 from the N, the first incident is the EWES BRIDGE, carrying a minor road W to the parkland of Langholm Castle and Langholm Lodge (*see* above). It is probably of 1763, humpbacked with two segmental arches and triangular cutwaters. Then an early C19 TOLLHOUSE, with the centre of its front projecting as a battlemented semi-octagon; broad-eaved piend roof with a central chimney.

HIGH STREET begins with CLINTHEAD, a smart villa of *c.* 1800. One storey above a tall basement (which becomes a ground floor at the back); the basement is dressed up at the front with pebble rustication. At the main floor, moulded architraves and rusticated angle quoins. Less smart the rubble-built early C19 No. 8, but it has panelled pilasters at the door and a D-plan S gable. To its W, the sloping TOWNHEAD BRIDGE over the Esk, built by *Robin Hotson* in 1775. Three segmental arches and triangular cutwaters. Its stone parapets were removed in 1880, when *John Hyslop* added cantilevered steel footpaths with lattice-girder parapets. On High Street's E side and looking down to the bridge, the old North United Presbyterian Church (*see* Churches, above). Beside it, No. 9, of 1816, has a classy doorpiece with concave ingoes, a fluted frieze decorated with two panels carved with urns, and a mutuled cornice. High Street then jinks l. to focus on the Town Hall further down; the buildings are largely plain two-storey Victorian but some are rather grander. On the W, at the corner with John Street, the BANK OF SCOTLAND (former BRITISH LINEN BANK), a three-storey palazzo by *Wardrop & Reid*, 1876. Rusticated ground floor with a tall pedimented Ionic doorpiece; over the door, a window with an open segmental pediment. Almost opposite on the E, the ROYAL (former NATIONAL) BANK OF SCOTLAND by *Alexander Fraser*, 1863–4, in a sort of austere Scots Jacobean, the l. corner canted at the bottom and ending in a tall conical-roofed turret at the top. Ruskinian Gothic doorpiece with leafy capitals. Paired segmental-arched first-floor windows under a Tudor hoodmould; above, a restless stringcourse studded with little carved human heads. Next door, the CROWN HOTEL is also of three storeys but much lower, rendered and crisply painted in black and white. It looks late C18 but the wackily classical doorpiece is early C19. Exaggerated entasis to the fluted pilasters, their individual friezes carved with urns; concave-sided pediment with mutules. Opposite, a two-storey Jacobean block of *c.* 1840, with its parapet scooped up into shaped gablets, one taller than the others and carrying a chimney. On the E side again, the POST OFFICE by *H.M. Office of Works*, 1935, with a rubbly crow-stepped gable.

MARKET PLACE is formed by High Street's broadening to the W in front of the Town Hall (*see* Public Buildings, above). View down David Street to the Thomas Hope Hospital (*see* above) and up Kirk Wynd to the old Evangelical Union Church (*see* Churches, above). Just before the Town Hall, on the r., the three-storey ESKDALE HOTEL of 1865–7 by *Habershon, Spalding & Brock* of London, with Gothic windows and carved bargeboards (*see* the Introduction, p. 81). Beyond the Town Hall and Library (*see* above), the entry to DROVE ROAD on the l. At its foot, some humble C18 houses, No. 30 with a forestair. Further up, the former South United Presbyterian Church (*see* Churches, above). Back on High Street, further along and set well back in a steeply rising wooded garden, ASHLEY BANK HOUSE is in a smooth mid-C19 Elizabethan style, with strapworked parapets over its bay windows and clustered octagonal chimneys; it has been rather altered. Beside the road, its LODGE, dated 1886, aggressive with a crowstepped gable and battlemented round tower. At the s end of the town, a TOLLHOUSE just like the one at the N end.

GLENESK ROAD leads NW towards the River Esk. On its l., the WAVERLEY MILLS. The eight w bays of the double-pile four-storey main block and the s stair tower are of 1865–7, designed by *Thomas Aimers*. He was also responsible for extending it to seventeen bays and heightening the tower (since cut down again) in 1871. On the corner of Waverley Road to the N, the late C19 BELL'S MILLS; the surviving buildings are mostly single-storey and plain, but there is a fat chimney behind the engine house, whose roof supports a cast-iron tank. On the N side of WAVERLEY ROAD, late C19 two-storey red sandstone terraces of workers' housing, with bracketed eaves. From here a path beside the Esk leads to another late C19 WOOLLEN MILL, its low buildings a mixture of brick and red sandstone. Slim round chimney beside another engine house with a roof-tank. In RIVERSIDE, near the corner with Charles Street Old, the former Langholm Free Church (*see* Churches, above).

New Langholm

BOATFORD BRIDGE, which crosses the Esk to New Langholm, is a suspension bridge by *E. Hernulewicz & Co.* of London, *c.*1871,* the cast- and wrought-iron pylons standing on masonry piers. From the foot of Elizabeth Street, at the bridge's w end, another BRIDGE, presumably of the 1840s, to Langholm Parish Church (*see* Churches, above); it is slightly hump-backed, of two broad segmental arches with low triangular cutwaters and a stringcourse under the parapet. At Elizabeth Street's N end, THOMAS TELFORD ROAD leads w with plain houses of the mid- and late C19. The road broadens at BUCCLEUCH SQUARE, whose sw corner is filled by the Police Station (*see* Public Buildings, above). On the N side, a PUMP, probably early C19, an octagonal stone shaft with spouts

---

* It replaced another suspension bridge which had both opened and collapsed in 1871.

protruding from the mouths of cast-iron lions' heads; on top, a weathered stone vase. At the NW corner, THE SCHOOL HOUSE, ashlar-fronted Georgian-survival by *James Burnet*, 1862–3, with chamfered window margins and a very heavy pilastered doorpiece. Further W, Langholm Academy and its Primary School (*see* Public Buildings, above).

AUCHENRIVOCK, 3km. S. Fragment of a rubble-built tower house, probably of the late C16 or early C17. The W wall still stands almost to the height of one storey. In it, a round shothole. Another shothole in the surviving W stub of the N wall.

MONUMENTS, Whita Hill, 1.5km. E. On the summit of the hill, a tall granite OBELISK on a square pedestal, erected in 1835 to commemorate General Sir John Malcolm. It was designed by *Robert Howe,* with *Thomas Slacks* as engineer and contractor. – To its N, the bronze and cor-ten steel MONUMENT TO HUGH MACDIARMID by *Jake Harvey*, 1982–4. A giant open book with stylized reliefs and cut-outs, their subjects evoking the poet's life (a thistle, pipe, whisky glass with the image of a female form, eagle, eclipse, flock of birds, hand guddling trout, the warp and weft of Langholm weavers, the Border hills).

SKIPPER'S BRIDGE, 1km. S. Rubble-built bridge over the Esk, built *c.*1700 but widened to the N by *John Hotson* in 1808–9. Three unequal-sized segmental arches, the outer two small and designed to cope with flood water. Pointed ashlar cutwaters. On the S side, corbelling which steps up over the arches. Pilaster strips above the N cutwaters. Both parapets are of 1808–9.

LANN HALL   8090
0.4km. S of Tynron

Laird's house of the later C18. Harled with rusticated quoins. Three-bay main block of two storeys over a high basement. Piended platform roof with bellcast eaves. At the centre, a Roman Doric columned doorpiece approached by a perron. The gableted dormer windows were added by *James Barbour & Bowie, c.*1900. Set well back at each side, a lower piend-roofed wing. In the inner angles, flat-roofed square projections. – Behind, a rubble-walled GARDEN of 1807.

LAURIESCLOSE   2070

Just the church standing beside the road.

CHURCH. Now a house. Sturdy and picturesque, built in 1905. Nave with low aisles under a single swept roof; battered buttresses. Tower over the entrance, the broad eaves of its slate spire broken by a gablet.

LAURIESTON
6060

L-plan village of white painted or harled vernacular houses, mostly C19. The novelist S. R. Crockett (1860–1914), author of *The Raiders*, was educated at the village school.

FREE CHURCH. Now a house (BEECHMOUNT) and much altered. Painted rubble rectangle, dated 1845 on the ball-finialled s porch. Another ball finial on the E gable. The W gable's bellcote was replaced by a chimney in 1966, when the windows were enlarged.

MEMORIAL TO SAMUEL RUTHERFORD CROCKETT. By *J. Jeffrey Waddell*, 1932. Square whinstone tower, its sides battered, the top domed.

SCHOOL. Built in 1879 and enlarged in 1965.

AIRDS OF KELLS, 5.4km. N. Two-storey farmhouse (now with a brick porch) linked by curved screen walls, each with a door flanked by blind windows, to two-storey pavilions, their piend roofs halted against chimneystacks. All of painted rubble. The pavilions were described in 1743 as 'lately built'. The farmhouse is probably a little earlier.

LAURIESTON HALL
1.1km. NW

Large house which has grown from the C17 to the C20. The earliest part, at the N, is a harled square tower, probably of the early C17. The walling of its lower three storeys is probably original, although the windows are all C19. The top two floors were added in 1893 by *Sydney Mitchell & Wilson*, with restless sill courses and conical-roofed angle turrets. Square ogee-roofed caphouse at the SE corner. Balustrade around the wall-walk; wallhead chimney on the W side. A sizeable extension was built in 1777 but has not survived. The next development seems to have been the low SW wing, probably part of additions made in 1825–9. Central crowstepped gable containing a large pointed entrance, flanked by battlemented bows, with hood-moulded windows. The rest is neo-Georgian of 1906, harled with sandstone dressings. Giant Ionic pilasters at the corners of the main block. At its E (entrance) front the two r. bays are advanced. Of these, the taller s bay is covered by a semicircular pediment flanked by ball finials; projecting from it, a porte cochère.

Mid-C19 STABLES to the E, with a squat clock tower over the pend in the centre of the s range.

HENSOL. *See* p. 338.

LESWALT
0060

Village of C20 local authority housing, with the former Parish Church at the W end and the present Parish Church at the E.

Former PARISH CHURCH. Ivy-clad ruin of a rubble-built nave,

probably medieval in origin but much altered in the C18.*
Rectangular windows, one with a round-arched embrasure.
There has been a chimney on the E gable, dating from the
church's use as a school after 1827. The NE 'aisle', now walled
off from the rest, was built to contain the burial vault and
laird's loft of the Agnews of Lochnaw in 1644, according to the
inscription on the armorial panel over the N door.‡ Higher up,
a mullioned and transomed window.

S of the church, a few C18 HEADSTONES decorated with
emblems of death and angels' heads (souls). – Against the
graveyard's N wall, the late C18 BURIAL ENCLOSURE of the
Agnews of Lochnaw. Pedimented front, with an oval panel in
the tympanum. There have been ball finials on the pediment's
apex and ends; one survives.

PARISH CHURCH. Harled T-plan kirk of 1827–8, with a forestair
at the gable of the N 'aisle'. Buttresses at the corners and along
the S wall. Big roundheaded S windows, the others smaller and
segmental-arched. Birdcage bellcote on the W end. Inside, the
N gallery seems to be of 1828; the rest is of 1953.

MEMORIAL HALL. Dated 1927. Harled, with sparing Jacobean
detail.

MONUMENT, Tor of Craigoch, 1.1km. NW. Built in 1850–1 to
commemorate Sir Andrew Agnew of Lochnaw † 1849, a former
Member of Parliament for Wigtownshire. Battlemented square
tower of three battered stages, the upper two intaken.

PRIMARY SCHOOL. Minimal Tudor school and schoolhouse,
by *S. H. Taylor*, 1875.

CHALLOCH, 0.6km. E. Harled early C19 farmhouse of two
storeys and three bays. The flat-roofed porch probably dates
from the alterations made in 1868. In the E gable, a MARRIAGE
STONE bearing the date 1573 flanked by coats of arms.

FORT (KEMP'S WALK), Larbrax, 5.8km. SW. Large promontory
fort of the late first millennium B.C. The only landward
approach is from the N. The W half of this approach is defended
by three earth and gravel ramparts with ditches between; at the
E half, only two ramparts and one ditch. The enclosure behind
is 83m. by 44.5m. On a W spur, remains of a round hut.

GALDENOCH CASTLE. *See* p. 309.
LOCHNAW CASTLE. *See* p. 419.

LINCLUDEN *see* DUMFRIES

LOCHANS

Village with some C19 vernacular houses (mostly rather altered);
the rest is of the later C20.

---

* Some of the alterations may date from 1776, when a scheme prepared by *Thomas Hall*, wright, and *Archibald Paterson*, mason, was agreed by the heritors; but, if executed, it was in modified form.

‡ As reported by the RCAHMS. It is now covered in ivy.

Former SCHOOL. White-painted school and schoolhouse of
*c.*1900.

GARTHLAND MAINS, 1.6km. SE. Early C19 piend-roofed farmhouse of two storeys and three bays, rusticated quoins the main
decoration.

KILDROCHET HOUSE, 1.4km. SE. White harled piend-roofed
two-storey laird's house of *c.*1800. The W front was originally
symmetrical, with a pair of shallow bows flanking the corniced
door. It has been extended S by one bay, the addition displaying
a Diocletian window at the ground floor.

8070   LOCHFOOT

Undistinguished small village.

LOCHRUTTON PARISH CHURCH, 1.3km. E. Whitewashed
rubble rectangle of 1819, with intersecting wooden tracery in
the pointed windows. The red-tile cresting of the roof, the W
bellcote and the W vestry are all Victorian, perhaps dating from
the alterations made in 1889.

On the E gable, two identical Ionic pilastered and pedimented
MONUMENTS, commemorating the Rev. George Duncan
†1765 and his son and namesake †1807. – Propped against a
table stone to the S, the upper half of a GRAVESLAB carved
with two weathered figures; it may be C17. – HEADSTONE to
William Carson †1772, decorated with high-relief reminders of
death under an angel's head (the soul). – HEADSTONE of Hellin
Anderson †1755, also carved in high relief, with a column
surmounted by a flaming urn; flowery border, an angel's head
at the top.

HILLS TOWER. *See* p. 340.

0000   LOCHHOUSE TOWER
                            1km. NE of Beattock

Tower house built for the Johnstones of that Ilk, probably in the
early C16 and certainly by 1562. It is a rubble-built oblong, with
the corners rounded to economize on dressed stonework. Three
storeys and an attic. Projecting plinth under the ground floor's
wide-splayed gunloops. Good-sized windows at the upper
floors; the second-floor walling is set back on an intake.
Moulded corbels at the wallhead, though the parapet they
supported is missing. The house was reroofed *c.*1973, when a
C19 entrance in the S gable was built up. At the E wall's N end
is the moulded C16 door. It opens into a small lobby in the
thickness of the wall. Off this lobby's S side, a guardroom.
Tunnel-vaulted ground-floor store. Turnpike stair in the wall
thickness of the NE corner of the house.

LOCHINCH CASTLE AND   *1060*
CASTLE KENNEDY

Magnificent parkland and two large houses, the ruined Castle Kennedy of *c.*1600 and the Victorian Lochinch Castle, standing at either end of an isthmus between two lochs (the White Loch on the W and the Black Loch on the E).

There was a house on the site by 1426, when a charter was signed there. It was replaced *c.*1600 with the present Castle Kennedy, built for John Kennedy, fifth Earl of Cassilis. In 1674 the house and estate were sold to Sir John Dalrymple, later the first Viscount of Stair, whose eldest son was created Earl of Stair in 1704. The second Earl, a soldier and politician, inherited in 1707, but in 1716 the mansion house of Castle Kennedy was gutted by fire, and it was never subsequently inhabited.

In 1722, perhaps as the prelude to an intended repair or rebuilding of the house, Lord Stair commissioned plans for a garden layout from *William Boutcher*. Work, possibly to Boutcher's design or perhaps to one by *William Adam*, who laid out the park at Stair's estate of Newliston (Lothian) in 1725 and designed a temple for Castle Kennedy, was begun in 1730 under the supervision of the head gardener, *Thomas McAlla*, and continued until shortly before the Earl's death in 1747. The gardens covered the isthmus with a formal pattern of radiating and criss-crossing rides of trees; the Round Pond (formed by cutting off a bay of the White Loch) made a hinge at which the design's axis skewed round from the N to the NW following the shape of the land. Along the E shore were constructed large terraces and banks with regularly spaced mounds serving as look-out points over the Black Loch to the hills beyond. The SE end of the isthmus was cut through by a straight canal joining the two lochs. SE of this, a belt of trees was planted along the shores of both lochs, making a boundary between the gardens and the farmland beyond; more planting, set back from the lochs' other sides, was added in the mid-C19.

The gardens fell into dereliction in the early C19, but restoration began after the accession in 1840 of the eighth Earl of Stair. In 1841 he commissioned *J. C. Loudon* to restore the gardens according to the C18 plan but using different species of trees, largely imported from North America (including the monkey-puzzles which line the main avenue running NW from the Round Pond).

In 1864 the tenth Earl of Stair began the erection of a new mansion house, Lochinch Castle, sited on the axis of the Monkey Puzzle Avenue but with its drive passing along the west side of the White Loch, from which at the same time were cleared the houses of estate workers, who were moved to the new village of Castle Kennedy (q.v.) S of the enlarged park. Under the tenth Earl and his successors, the Castle Kennedy gardens have been developed as an outstanding plant collection contained within the framework of the C18 layout.

LOCHINCH CASTLE, designed by *Brown & Wardrop*, was built 93 in 1864–8 in a relaxed Baronial manner with a few French touches, the mingling of styles perhaps an allusion to the Franco-Scottish alliance of the clients, the tenth Earl of Stair and his wife, Louisa, daughter of the Duc de Coigny. It is of two storeys with a basement (exposed on the garden fronts) and attic, built of cream-coloured Lancashire stone. Long asymmetrical entrance (N) front, stepping forward and back. An off-centre tower covered with a tall French pavilion roof is its main accent; the others are crowstepped gables, with rounded corners corbelled to the square under the eaves. Some windows are emphasized by aedicules with banded attached columns or pilasters, their segmental pediments topped by finials, and the tympana carved with foliage motifs in high relief. Steep Jacobean triangular pediments, again finialled, rise above the eaves over the first-floor windows. Small attic windows with cottagey wooden bargeboards carved by *James Annandale*. The boldly projecting entrance gable has fat conical-roofed and fishscale-slated angle turrets. The entrance itself is a rope-moulded segmental arch crowned with the heraldic achievement of the tenth Earl of Stair and his wife, carved by *John Rhind* from a drawing by *Henry Laing*. Also by Rhind are the baroque lions flanking the door, each rearing up on top of a rock (the Stair crest).

Irregular U-plan w front, the N gable projecting much more boldly than the s. Each gable has conical-roofed angle turrets decorated with quatrefoils. Projecting from the gables are bay windows, the N canted and with a plain parapet, the s with shallow crenellations and ball-finials. Stretched between the gables, a balustrade over the ground-floor window; a Jacobean pediment above the attic window.

The s front continues the diversity. At its w end, a pair of crowstepped gables from which projects the drawing room's canted and balustraded bay window. Then a three-bay section fronted by a Jacobean imperial stair. The central ground-floor window is framed by attached banded columns; on the frieze, coroneted Ss and Cs (for Stair and de Coigny) and the date 1867. Over the first-floor windows, Jacobean pedimented dormerheads, the outer two steep triangles, the central one shaped and topped by the small statue of a C17 soldier. To the r. of this section, a large tower, its plain walling broken by a canted oriel window at the principal floor, a sloping stone-flagged roof over its banded cornice. On top of the tower, a machicolated battlement with cannon spouts, and at its s and NE corners, conical-roofed turrets, the SE beginning much lower down than the others; at the NW corner, a big flat-roofed round turret. Inside the battlement rises the attic storey, with a crowstepped gable on each face. Quiet stretch E of the tower.

Attached to the E end of the house, a service range, now roofless and gutted. It is part of Brown & Wardrop's design but its character is late Georgian castellated. Angle rounds and cannon spouts project from the battlement, whose crenelles are exceptionally long. Big slit windows pierce the walls. Near the

E end of the S front is a small tower, its square base broached
to an octagonal stone-roofed top; carved gryphons protrude
from the eaves.

At the NE corner of this range, the stable court, also completed in 1867. Elliptical-arched entrance in a crowstepped
gable flanked by drum towers; their bases are decorated with
large gunloops, and their upper storeys project on simply
moulded corbels, with fishscale-slating on the bellcast conical
roofs. Inside the court, straightforward Jacobean ranges.

INTERIOR. The entrance hall of the mansion house is plain
Jacobean, with pendants on its grained ceiling. This plasterwork, like the rest in the house, is by *James Anderson*. Floor
covered with encaustic tiles by *William Hawley*. Each side of
the front door, a niche containing a slab of veined purplish
marble supplied by *Andrew Wallace & Co*. Stair up to the
principal floor, where a hall/corridor runs along the N side.
Rectangular bay-window projection to the N containing a billiard table. Plain Jacobean plaster ceiling. Big oak chimneypiece, again Jacobean, with Artisan Mannerist pilasters
flanking the fireplace. On the overmantel, the coats of arms
of Stair and de Coigny (carved by *Davidson & Reid* from a
drawing by *Henry Laing*); female heads at the top corners.
Above, cherubs holding garlands and, in the centre, a central
cartouche containing entwined Ss. At the hall/corridor's NE
corner, an organ. At the E end, the principal stair. The panels
of the heavy Jacobean balustrade, with rosettes, lions' masks
and other devices, were also carved by *Davidson & Reid*. On
the bottom baluster, a gryphon holding a shield; this was
executed by *Alexander Hill*.

S of the hall/corridor are the principal rooms. The W is the
drawing room, its ceiling again Jacobean but quite light, with
coronets on its elaborate frieze. Overdoors decorated with
reliefs of a nymph and cherub. Coroneted Ss on the white
marble Frenchy chimneypiece by *Andrew Wallace & Co*. In the
E wall, double doors into the library, where the ceiling and
frieze are repeated. Very similar white marble chimneypiece
(again by Wallace & Co.), a coroneted rock (the Stair crest) at
its centre. Built-in bookcases, the doors of walnut, the friezes
decorated with female heads. E of the library is the dining room,
its height greater than that of the other rooms. Coved plaster
ceiling, again Jacobean, its pendants rather small. Huge wooden
chimneypiece dated 1864, the fireplace framed by Artisan Mannerist pilasters. In the overmantel, a portrait of the second Earl
of Stair (by *Allan Ramsay, c. 1740*), topped and tailed to fit and
flanked by shell-headed niches. On top, a pediment broken by
a coroneted circle carved with Ss. At the ends of the overmantel,
lions holding plain shields.

In the garden W of the house, a SUNDIAL, its squat Ionic-
capitalled column carved with spiralling vines. It was brought
here from Castle Kennedy and looks late C17. The faceted top
is a replacement of 1889.

S of the house, beside the White Loch, a BOATHOUSE of

1869, built of whin rubble with granite dressings. Broad-eaved jerkin-head roofs with fleur-de-lis cresting.

The now roofless CASTLE KENNEDY at the S end of the isthmus, described as the 'novum castrum de Inche' (the new castle of Inch) in a charter of 1605, is a remarkable fusion of the tower-house tradition and classicism. From the tower house it takes its compact form and verticality, from classicism its ruthless symmetry. It is rubble-built and Y-plan, with an oblong four-storey-and-attic main block from whose E gable full-height square wings project to the front and sides. In the W inner angles, taller square towers, the S containing the stair. The principal (E) front is of three bays, the main block providing a deeply recessed gabled centrepiece. The top windows of the wings were almost certainly all surmounted by pedimented dormerheads. One of these survives on the N wing's outer side, its pediment broken by a finialled pedestal. In the S face of this wing, a ground-floor gunhole covering the door which is squeezed into the SE inner angle. To the r. of the door, a water inlet beside a large blocked window, perhaps an insertion of c. 1700. In the W face of each tower, a ground-floor gunhole. The ground floor has been vaulted. The main block had a passage along its S side, and the rest was occupied by a large store room. W and N additions, both of two storeys and perhaps of c. 1700.

Immediately S of Castle Kennedy, a rubble-walled GARDEN, probably of the C17. Entrances in the centre of the N and S walls: the N entrance has ball finials, the one at the S has obelisks standing on balls. – E of the house, the KITCHEN GARDEN, its brick walls built in 1733, those on the E and W scooped up to the N. A range of glasshouses (mostly demolished) was built against the N wall in the 1860s. – At the SE entrance to the landscape gardens of Castle Kennedy, a pair of early C18 cornised GATEPIERS carrying balls topped by obelisks. – The road is carried across the canal by a BRIDGE of 1739, built of brick with stone dressings and rusticated quoins. Single segmental arch. Humpbacked roadway but straight parapets, each surmounted by three ball-finialled stone stalks. At the ends of the parapets, scroll-sided stones, the front of each carved with a coat of arms, monogram or floral motif, the back with a thistle.

On the W side of the White Loch, a graveyard containing the roofless INCH OLD PARISH CHURCH designed and built by *Thomas Hall* in 1770. Rubble-walled T-plan. The W 'aisle' (now bricked off from the rest) has rectangular windows and a chimney. On the S gable of the body, a birdcage bellcote. In the E wall, roundheaded windows with projecting keystones and imposts. Round-arched door in each gable, the N with chamfered jambs, suggesting that this wall may survive from the church's C17 predecessor.

LODGES. Both by *Brown & Wardrop*, 1867–9, the N broad-eaved and with 'half-timbering' hung in front of its stone walls, the S with carved bargeboards and latticed glazing.

LOCHMABEN   *0080*

Small town squeezed between lochs (Castle Loch, Kirk Loch and
Mill Loch) to the S, W and N. It was founded before 1296 as a
burgh of barony under the feudal superiority of the Bruces, lords
of Annandale, whose principal castle stood here. After the
accession of Robert Bruce to the throne in 1306, the lordship
of Annandale, including the superiority over Lochmaben, was
granted to his nephew, Thomas Randolph, Earl of Moray, from
whose descendants it passed to the Earl of Douglas in 1409.
Following the forfeiture of the earldom of Douglas in 1440,
Lochmaben came to be accepted as a royal burgh, and was
formally enrolled as one in 1605. Despite this, it never became
more than a local trading centre with a small woollen industry.
Even by the mid-C19 the town consisted of little more than one
long and broad street and a second shorter street leading off to
the W. In 1851 *The Parliamentary Gazetteer of Scotland* found it
'dingy, desolate and leaden-eyed'. During the C20 Lochmaben
has expanded to the N, and its appearance now is clean, neat and
respectable, if a little lacking in excitement.

CHURCHES

OLD CHURCHYARD, off High Street. The site of the demolished
medieval parish church; well stocked with large headstones (the
earliest of *c.*1750, but mostly C19) and a few Georgian table
stones. – At the NW corner, a big urn-topped red sandstone
OBELISK commemorating Dr James Mounsey of Rammerscales †1773.

PARISH CHURCH, High Street. Large but simple Gothick 27
preaching box, by *James Thomson*, 1818–20. Hoodmoulded and
Y-traceried mullioned and transomed windows. Crowstepped
S gable, its lean-to extension added by *Colin Morton* in 1958–9.
At the ashlar-fronted N gable, a parapet with cusped blind
arcading and sharp corner pinnacles. In the centre of the
gable, a tower, its parapet pierced by roundheaded arches, the
corners again pinnacled. It is of three stages; the window
and doors (one blocked) of the lowest stage have quatrefoil
heads; at the upper stages, hoodmoulded and Y-traceried
openings.
  Inside, a U-plan gallery on straight Tuscan columns. Plaster-
panelled neo-Georgian ceiling by *Peter Chapman*, 1896. – The
focus is the Perp PULPIT made in 1903, when the ORGAN by
E. F. Walcker & Co. was installed behind it. – PEWS of 1843,
brought here from the demolished Free Church in 1959. – Over
the S door, a gilded wooden DOVE, probably of 1814, from the
demolished Burgher Chapel. – In the NE corner, part of a
GRAVESLAB, perhaps of *c.*1300. It is carved with a floriated
Celtic cross; under the l. arm, a pair of shears.

PUBLIC BUILDINGS

FREEMASONS' HALL. *See* Description, below.

HOSPITAL, 0.7km. W. Begun as a fever hospital by *F. J. C. Carruthers*, 1908, and extended in 1922 (by *Evan Tweedie*) and 1936 (by *John R. Hill*); later alterations. Low harled blocks, several with verandahs.

PARISH CHURCH HALL, Princes Street. Dated 1926 and quite plain.

POLICE STATION. *See* Description, below.

SCHOOL, Annandale Crescent. By *Dumfries and Galloway Regional Council*, 1980–2, and extended in 1991. Interlocking pavilions with brick walls and shallow pitched roofs.

109 TOWN HALL, High Street. By *D. & J. Bryce*, 1876–7, incorporating the steeple and other parts of its early C18 predecessor. The Georgian town hall, built in 1722–3, was a piend-roofed two-storey main block from whose centre projected an ashlar-faced tower flanked by single-storey porches whose roofs and a band course formed a pediment, broken at the base by the roundheaded and keyblocked arches of the porch and tower entrances. Rusticated masonry below the band course. At the tower's second stage, a Venetian window with panelled pilasters and large fluted consoles under the sill. Above the corniced clock-stage was an octagonal belfry, its domed roof topped by a cupola, replaced in 1743–5 by a dumpy stone spire.

Bryce's work in the 1870s converted the porch entrances to windows and heightened the porches themselves to form a narrow flat-roofed two-storey front block, with recumbent lions on the corners of its crowning balustrade. Probably at the same time the central light of the tower's Venetian window was made into a niche. This was filled in 1887 with a statue by *John W. Dods* of the Rev. William Graham, the historian of the burgh. Bryce replaced the 1720s main block with a taller and larger Georgian-survival block, its straight gables containing Venetian windows and topped by a chimney and stone eagle. Interior of the 1870s. In the end windows of the first-floor hall, STAINED GLASS portraits of Robert the Bruce and Sir William Wallace, by *James Ballantine & Son*, 1879.

CASTLES

There have been two castles at Lochmaben, one a motte on the neck of land between the Kirk Loch and the Castle Loch (now a golf course), the other standing on the promontory which juts into the S end of the Castle Loch. The first is now only a site; the second is badly ruined.

The motte, of characteristic C12 Anglo-Norman type, was constructed by the Bruces, lords of Annandale, probably by *c.* 1172, when William I signed a charter at Lochmaben. It is likely that the motte continued in use for some years after its capture by Edward I in 1298; its keep, probably originally of wood, was later replaced in stone.

However, in 1298 Edward began the construction of a palisaded enclosure, known as the 'pele' or the 'palisade of the close', said to have been located 'outside the castle of Lochmaben'. This 'pele' must have been substantially complete by August 1299, when it successfully withstood an attack by Robert Bruce. The erection of such a palisade, which could provide protection for men and materials, was the usual preliminary to the building of Edward I's castles in Wales, and the presumption must be that the 'pele' constructed in 1298–9 adjoined the site of the second castle of Lochmaben, 1.2km. SE of the original motte, and was intended to house its builders.

An indenture of 1346, when William de Bohun, Earl of Northampton,* appointed Richard de Thirllewalle keeper of Lochmaben Castle, provides some evidence that the second castle was habitable by then; it distinguishes between the 'cloisture' of the 'piel', in which camp followers were allowed to live and work, and the 'piel' itself, which was to be entered only by members of the garrison. The implication is that the new castle was then known as the 'piel', perhaps to distinguish it from the motte castle, and that the palisade had become its 'cloisture' or outer ward.

On the death of Humphrey de Bohun, Earl of Hereford, without a male heir in 1373, the lordship of Annandale reverted to the English Crown, and in 1374–6 Edward III carried out repairs and alterations to Lochmaben Castle, including the strengthening of the 'new front called la Pele', repair of the bretasche, reroofing of two towers and the construction of a new bridge.

The English occupation of Annandale in 1384 was ended with the capture of Lochmaben Castle by a Scottish force under Archibald ('the Grim'), lord of Galloway, and George Dunbar, Earl of March. Both the *Scotichronicon* and John of Fordun state that the castle was then rased to the ground; but this is apparently a much exaggerated description of the slighting of its defences. Whatever damage was done in 1384, the castle must have been habitable again by 1414, when Archibald, Earl of Douglas and lord of Annandale, signed a charter 'apud castrum de Lochmabane'.

In 1440, after the execution of William, Earl of Douglas, Annandale and Lochmaben Castle passed again into the hands of the Crown. Repairs to the castle were made in 1491, and more extensive building work, including the erection of a hall, was carried out in 1504–6. During the Earl of Hertford's invasion of Scotland (the 'Rough Wooing') in 1544–5, Lochmaben Castle was besieged and taken, but there is little indication that it was much damaged. However, in 1579, when John, Lord Herries, Warden of the West Marches, recommended to the Privy Council that the castle should be the Warden's usual residence, he also requested money for repair of 'the Kingis Majesteis rewynous hous of Lochmaben ... for na honest man can have being thair now.'

---

* Whose father had been granted the lordship of Annandale forty years before.

Whatever its failings as a comfortable residence, the castle remained a formidable defensive structure, described in 1585 as 'of the greatest strength of any in this west border of Scotland', and continued to be garrisoned until the union of the crowns in 1603. Seven years later, defence against English invasion now unnecessary, the lands of Lochmaben were made a barony, granted, together with the hereditary office of keeper of Lochmaben Castle, to George Home, Earl of Dunbar. He sold the barony and office in 1612 to the King's favourite John Murray, later Viscount Annan and Earl of Annandale. Twelve years later, James VI ordered payment to Lord Annan of the large sum of £1,600 sterling 'for reedifieing and reparation of our castle of Lochmaben', but only £700 of the sum had been paid by 1628, and it is not clear how much work was carried out. Later in the C17 the castle seems to have been abandoned and by 1793 it was in ruins: 'nothing now standing but a small part of the heart of the wall. The fine ashlar work is all stripped off, and there are few houses in the neighbourhood, in which some of the stones are not to be seen . . . '

LOCHMABEN OLD CASTLE, off Kirk Loch Brae. Motte site of the castle built by the Bruces in the mid-C12 and abandoned in the C14. It occupies the high S end of a natural ridge between the Kirk Loch and the Castle Loch. Approaches from all directions have been cut off by a ditch (now partly destroyed by the road on the S and E), probably originally filled with water. Its counterscarp is still clearly evident to the SW and N. A pathway leads across the ditch at the SE end and winds up to the summit, which is now used as one green of a golf course. Among trees on the N side of the summit, remains of a mound said to have been partly composed of mortared rubble.

LOCHMABEN CASTLE, 1.2km. SE. The site is a wooded promontory jutting into the Castle Loch. Its middle forms a roughly oblong plateau, c.167m. by 90m., artificially heightened (at least in part) to stand c.3m. above the rest of the promontory, whose edges may have been covered by the loch in medieval times. The landward (S) approach to the promontory has been defended by a doglegged ditch running from the promontory's SW corner to the Valison Burn on the E. About 100m. N of this are two more ditches, presumably filled with water from the loch when they were first dug, probably in 1298–9. The N of these ditches bounds the plateau's S end, and from this ditch two narrower ditches run N beside the plateau's steeply scarped E and W sides for a distance of c.70m. They end at another ditch which cuts across the promontory, bisecting the plateau. The two parts of the plateau formed the outer and inner wards of the castle. The outer ward, at the S, was probably the site of the palisaded enclosure formed in 1298–9. There are traces of stone building, perhaps late medieval, round its edge.

The inner ward, at the plateau's N end, has been a rectangular castle of enclosure, c.45m. by 36.5m. Excavation has suggested

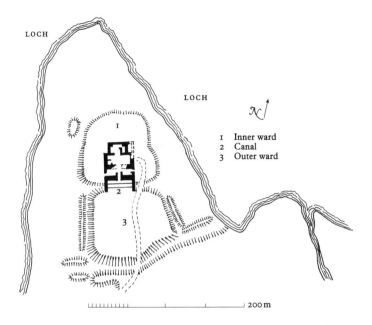

LOCH

LOCH

1 Inner ward
2 Canal
3 Outer ward

200 m

Lochmaben, Castle. Plan

that its main (s) front is probably the product of three changes of mind during the c14. In the first phase the castle's s wall was built *c.* 13.7m. behind the present front; it was probably intended to have square towers at its outer corners as well as a pair of towers flanking the central entrance. This scheme may not have been completed because the design was changed to replace the intended flanking towers* by a boldly projecting rectangular barbican containing the entrance passage. This work might well have been finished by 1346, when Richard de Thirllewalle was appointed keeper of the castle.

The final phase of construction of the s front, perhaps in the 1370s, when the 'new front called la Pele' was strengthened, entailed the building of a new s wall on the line of the barbican's s end and rising from the ditch between the two wards. At the same time the inner ward's e and w walls were extended s, not just to meet this new wall but stretching beyond it and carried over the ditch on arches large enough to allow boats to pass through. This U-plan forework,‡ unparalleled in Britain, was presumably designed as a safe haven for boats patrolling the loch and servicing the castle, whilst the forward projection of the e and w walls also provided narrow 'towers' (2.7m. broad)

* Their bases were discovered by excavation.
‡ An etching of 1780 by John Clerk of Eldin and copies of it apparently show a wall on the ditch's s side with two towers flanking the entrance; but these seem to be artistic fantasies rather than topographical records.

commanding the area of the outer ward, which seems to have
been abandoned as living accommodation by c. 1400. The forework's walls still stand to a height of 12m. Their diagonally
tooled ashlar facing survives only at the double-splayed plinth,
the rest now consisting only of the exposed core of mortared
rubble. The entrance has been in the centre, approached by a
drawbridge, the pit of its counterpoise constructed of ashlar.
Of the building behind the front, only fragments remain. The
entrance has opened into the stone-walled central passage of the
early or mid-C14 barbican; it originally had a narrow guardroom
each side, and was flanked by small courtyards between the
barbican and the late C14 extensions of the castle's E and W
walls. N of the W guardroom and courtyard, i.e. behind the
original S front, there are two tunnel-vaulted rooms side by
side, both ashlar-faced internally and probably entered from a
central court. On this court's E side, another room. On the N
of the court, remains of four more rooms; the largest has a
drain in its N wall.

DESCRIPTION

ANNAN ROAD and LOCKERBIE ROAD lead in from the S and
SE. At their junction, the WAR MEMORIAL by *Beattie &
Co.*, 1921, a marble statue of a youthful King's Own Scottish
Borderer standing at 'Arms Reversed'. To its W, the Parish
Church (*see* Churches, above), closing the end of HIGH
STREET, which starts off with detached Victorian and C20
villas on the E. On its W side, CHURCH PLACE, an early C19
terrace of three white-painted or harled houses, each with a
chunky pilastered and corniced doorpiece. Then the old FREE
CHURCH MANSE, plain late Georgian, with an austere Elizabethan block of 1867 added by *James Barbour* to its S end.
Across the road and a little to the N, the mid-C19 BIRCHLEA
with a heavily consoled cornice over the door. Set behind a
front garden, ANNANDALE HOUSE of c. 1840 is a large villa
with two- and three-light windows overlooking the street;
gabled canopy on big brackets above the N door. Then the
development becomes tighter-knit, with terraced single-storey-
and-attic or two-storey buildings of the C19 and C20. At the end
on the E side, the mid-C19 Georgian-survival FREEMASONS'
HALL with a Roman Doric columned doorpiece. Beside it, a
late C18 pair sharing a moulded cornice: the harled S house
(DALVEEN) has an Ionic doorpiece and a ground-floor window
enlarged to two lights; the door of the N house has a lugged
architrave and moulded cornice. High Street's N end is filled
by the Town Hall (*see* Public Buildings, above). In front, a
large sandstone STATUE of Robert the Bruce in armour, by
John Hutchison, 1876–9, on a pedestal of polished Dalbeattie
granite.
BRUCE STREET eases out to the W. On its corner with Castle
Street, a heavily crowstepped but small late Victorian POLICE
STATION. On the S, the smooth ashlar-fronted MANSE (No.

6) of 1839–40 by *Walter Newall*, the cornice over the door
supported on block-pendant brackets, the rounded chimneys
grouped in the centre of the piended roof. On the W corner
with Princes Street is a little municipal garden containing the
MARKET CROSS displaced from High Street by the Bruce
statue. The shaft and its finial, carved with floral decoration,
are probably late C16; on top, a ball-finialled sundial dated
1729. Opposite, THE CROWN, late Georgian, its pilastered
and corniced doorpiece decorated with Empire garlands. Heavy
pilastered doorpieces at the mid-C19 Georgian-survival Nos.
12 and 14. No. 16 is a classy curiosity. Its rendered street
elevation has an idiosyncratic mid-C19 Composite pilastrade,
the capitals decorated with thistles; only the lugged architraves
of the windows and door suggest the house's date of 1786.
Confirmation of this late C18 date is given by the (blocked)
pointed windows in the gables and by the garden front's ashlar
centrepiece, with a Venetian window framed by Corinthian
pilasters.

QUEEN STREET, the principal N continuation of High Street, is
much humbler, with long terraces, mostly of single-storey C19
cottages. At its N end, on the corner with Princes Street, the
polished granite EDWARD VII MEMORIAL FOUNTAIN, by
D. H. & J. Newall, 1910–11. Scrolled buttresses at the corners;
domed top surmounted by a crown on a cushion. On one face,
a bronze portrait relief of the King.

CORNCOCKLE, 3.7km. N. Innocently castellated single-storey-
and-attic cottage farmhouse of the earlier C19. Three-bay W
front, the advanced and battlemented ashlar centre gripped by
battlemented clasping buttresses. Tapered columns *in antis*
frame the entrance; cusped decoration over the openings. In
the outer bays, hoodmoulded three-light windows (the outer
lights blind). Pinnacles on the corners.

ELSHIESHIELDS TOWER. *See* p. 304.
HALLEATHS. *See* p. 336.

LOCHNAW CASTLE   *9060*
3km. W of Leswalt

Manor house developed from the C15 by addition and subtraction.
The offices of Constable of Lochnaw and Bailie of Leswalt,
together with the lands of Lochnaw, were granted to Andrew
Agnew by Margaret, Countess of Douglas, in 1426. Probably a
little later in the C15, a small tower house was built here.* In 1663
Sir Andrew Agnew of Lochnaw added an L-plan house S of the
tower, and in 1704 Sir James Agnew extended this with a W range,
producing a U-plan complex surrounding three sides of a deep
courtyard. A large Jacobean block designed by *Archibald Elliot*

---

* The tower is usually ascribed to the C16, but its simple rectangular form, machicolation and lack of gunloops (except for an obvious insertion) are all consistent with
a C15 date.

was built on the s side of the C17 range in 1820–1; this 1820s block, together with the w range of 1704, was demolished *c.* 1950, leaving the house a rather straggly appearance.

The C15 tower at the NE corner, 7m. square and of four storeys and an attic, is built of sneck-harled rubble. The w door is an insertion, perhaps of the C18, but on the E front is a smart C15 first-floor window of two roundheaded arches with a central pendant in place of a mullion. To its l., a panel; the worn inscription was recut and probably reworded in the early C19 to read 'DOM.ANDREAS.AGNEV 1426.NOMEN.DOMINI.FOR-TISSIMA.TURRIS' ('Lord Andrew Agnew 1426. The name of God [is] the strongest tower'). The panel is unlikely to be *in situ*; probably it was moved to impress a visitor passing this side of the house to reach the early C19 entrance on the E side of Elliot's addition. Below this panel, an inserted U-shaped gunloop, set on its side so it looks like an ear. High battlement pierced by cannon spouts and projected on a double row of continuous corbelling, its bowed NW, NE and SE corners timidly pretending to be angle rounds. The SW corner rises as a rectangular crowstep-gabled caphouse. On the battlement's w face beside the caphouse, a machicolation. On the N face, a canted projection carrying the wall-walk past the chimney of the crowstepped attic gable.

The interior of the tower is little altered. Turnpike stair in the wall thickness of the SW corner. Rubble tunnel-vault over the trapezoidal-shaped ground-floor room, apparently a store. In the first-floor hall, a N fireplace, its lintel renewed. Immediately to its w, an aumbry checked for a door, probably intended as a salt box. Another small aumbry, now without dressings, in the NE corner. The ceilings here and at the floors above are of wood; two of them have barely discernible fragments of tempera decoration, probably of the C16. Second-floor bedroom with stone window seats. Aumbries at each end of the N wall and in the SE corner. S fireplace. In the NW corner, a rounded wall recess with a lampstand; presumably it was a close garderobe. Another bedroom on the third floor. Narrow N fireplace. E and w windows, the w still with window seats. Aumbries in the S and E walls. Again a close garderobe but in the SE corner. In the attic room, a small S fireplace. At this level, steps off the stair lead to the parapet walk, but the main stair continues inconsequentially up for a few treads, probably the result of a builder's botch.

The ranges added on the E and s sides of the courtyard in 1663 are of three storeys, the top-floor windows rising through the eaves into gabled stone dormerheads. The main front faces N, with five evenly spaced windows at the first floor and three at the second. Two of the dormerheads are inscribed with the initials of Sir Andrew Agnew, eighth baronet, and his wife, Lady Louisa Noel, and the central one is carved with a coat of arms and topped by an eagle (the Agnew crest). These are all replacements of 1882, when Sir Andrew carried out restoration work, an event noted on this range's short NW return. On the S range's W gable, another eagle, probably also of 1882. Projecting from the E range's courtyard front, a round stair tower. To its N, a long first-floor window, the mid-C20 replacement of a C19 oriel. Above, two dormerheads, one bearing the initials of Sir Andrew Agnew, second baronet, and the date 1663, the other the initials of his wife, Dame Anne Stewart, and a coat of arms. The swept top to the window S of the tower probably replaces another dormerhead. On this range's E face, a pair of C19 stepped buttresses. More dormerheads, carved with the initials of Sir Andrew Agnew and Dame Anne Stewart, the inscription 'AGNUS MILES' (i.e. 'Agnew, knight') and a coat of arms and the date 1426; they may be C17 but were probably recut in 1882. At the NW corner of the C17 house, a conical-roofed tower, probably an addition of *c.* 1850. Little survives of the late C17 interior except a couple of vaulted ground-floor rooms in the S range. In the N first-floor room of the E range a large late C17 stone chimneypiece has been exposed. Its attached columns have simplified capitals carved with the initials of Sir Andrew Agnew and Lady Anne Stewart.

The W range of 1704 was of two storeys. In its place there is now only a dwarf wall, too low to give a sense of enclosure to the courtyard. On its N end, a birdcage bellcote with a stepped roof and ball finial; it used to stand on the range's gable. On the courtyard's N side, another dwarf wall, with a pair of C18 ball-finialled gatepiers towering above it.

Of the 1820s S addition all that remains is the basement, which has been infilled to form a terrace, its sides enclosed by open stone parapets taken from the balconies of the 1820s addition. C19 heraldic stones have been placed in some of the basement's blocked windows.

WALLED GARDEN, 0.4km. NW. The walls of whinstone with a little brickwork were built by *James McKie* in 1819. At the SE corner, a SUMMERHOUSE in the form of a circular tower with round-arched openings. It is probably of the earlier C19.

LOCHRUTTON see LOCHFOOT

LOCHRYAN HOUSE   *0060*
0.2km. N of Cairnryan

Small white-painted mansion house of great charm but deceptively unified appearance. The W-facing, H-plan main block was built for Colonel Andrew Agnew of Croach in 1701 (the eroded date on a weathered armorial panel over the front door, now enclosed in a late C19 flat-roofed porch). It was originally all of two storeys with a basement and attic; chamfered surrounds to the windows. The wings are now covered with half-piended lean-to roofs; but are these original, or did they replace piended double-pitch roofs, which would have given the wings

a tower-like appearance, as seen on the axial approach? The
wings' canted dormers are presumably late C19, as must be the
projecting triangular oriel inserted in the r. first-floor opening,
which allows an occupant to observe visitors coming to the
house from either the w or the s drive. The recessed three-bay
centre, perhaps originally balustraded, was heightened by a
floor in 1820–4; *Alan Dickie* provided specifications and perhaps
the design. Its front wall is carried up to screen the roof and
finished with a row of five tall merlons. At the back, the new
work is more obvious; the stonework of the surrounds to the
second-floor windows and the top of the heightened stair
window is redder than the rest. Extending laterally each side of
the main block are single-storey-and-basement wings, perhaps
dating from the improvements made by the mason *James Brown*
in 1826.

The front of the main block is joined by balustrades and
screen walls to single-storey service buildings, probably of the
early C18; the N is a byre, the s a stable. Across the w side of
this court, a dwarf wall topped by tall balusters. The court's
axial entrance is flanked by corniced gatepiers, again probably
early C18, decorated with skinny pilasters and each topped by
a white-painted stone eagle (the Agnew crest). On the N gatepier, a brass SUNDIAL dated 1780. Outer court with mid-C19
single-storey-and-attic ranges on the N and s, each with a stone
gablet on the front. To the s, a tall circular conical-roofed and
ball-finialled DOOCOT built by *William Ross* in 1846. From the
outer court the w drive runs between rubble walls to end at
very plain ball-finialled piers; from these balustered dwarf walls
stretch out to higher rubble walls ending in low battlemented
early C19 bastions.

Inside the house, early C18 work was extended and improved
in the same manner in the late C19. A large entrance hall fills
the main block's centre; two-panelled doors of *c.*1701 and a
contemporary bolection-moulded wooden mantelshelf over the
stone chimneypiece. The hall's back wall was removed in the
C20, opening the room to the stair behind, whose wooden
balusters are of early C18 silhouette type but probably date
from the late C19. On the first floor, the central dining room
contains a chimneypiece of veined white marble. This looks
early C18, but the panelling, with Corinthian pilasters framing
the broad door, looks more likely to be late C19. Panelling of
the same sort, with lugged door architraves, in the former
library to the N. Small NW room, again panelled; but is this
early C18 or late C19 work? On the s side of the main block, a
large drawing room and small morning room, both panelled;
the morning room has lugged architraves to the doors and
around the stone chimneypiece, which is flanked by Corinthian
pilasters. From the morning room a stair leads down to the
basement, so this may have been a bedchamber or closet in the
early C18.

The GARDEN behind the house retains the main elements of
its C18 layout, with a central avenue of neatly trimmed small

trees on the axis of the house leading to a transverse terraced bank. At the ends of this bank, square rubble-built PAVILIONS. The one at the S is simple. The one at the N has a truncated pyramid roof topped by a square glazed cupola; the base of its stone ball finial is pierced with holes, because it serves as chimney for a fireplace inside.

LOCHWOOD TOWER

_{5.2km. S of Beattock}

0090

Quite extensive remains of a stronghold commanding the upper part of Annandale, occupied by the Johnstones of that Ilk (later Earls of Annandale) from the late C12 to the early C18. Lands in Upper Annandale were granted to John, ancestor of the Johnstones, by Robert Bruce, lord of Annandale, *c.* 1180, and the motte immediately N of the present buildings must be of about that date. Probably in the late C13 or C14, the motte castle was superseded by a stone castle, apparently built in its bailey. In the late C15 this was remodelled as an adjunct to a new hall and tower house built immediately to the S. In 1547 it was captured and occupied by an English force under Sir Thomas Carleton, who described it as 'a fair large tower, able to lodge all our company safely, with a barmekin-hall, kitchen and stables all within the barmekin'. Lochwood was attacked and said to have been burned by Robert Maxwell of Cowhill in 1585, but damage must have been repaired by 1592, when James VI spent a night there. Alterations to the tower house's upper part seem to have been carried out in 1603. Probably at the same time a new range (now hardly visible) was built, running S from the barmkin's SW corner and a garden laid out to the W.

The MOTTE at the N is roughly oval, formed from a hillock rising *c.* 6.7m. above the sloping hillside on the W and 13.4m. on the E to a level summit of *c.* 3.7m. by 4.3m. Unusually it is terraced; but are the terraces C12 defences or C17 garden features?

The buildings S of the motte are now fairly fragmentary where they are visible, but excavation has allowed the general lines of the complex to be established. There were two adjoining rectangular courtyards; the tower house projects from the S courtyard's SE corner, the C17 range from its SW corner. The rubble-built walls of the courtyard are of different dates, those of the S courtyard butted against those of the earlier and broader N enclosure.

The remains in the N COURTYARD are very scanty, but there has been a N range of at least two storeys. There was also an E range, which contained three ground-floor rooms, with a passage along the W side. The N room was a kitchen or bakehouse with a rather small N fireplace, an oven projecting from the N gable and a second oven at the passage's N end. These ranges may have belonged to the C13 or C14 castle, but, if so, they were probably remodelled in the C15. On the W side of this courtyard was a third range, apparently of the C17.

More survives in the S COURTYARD, perhaps the outer ward of the C13 or C14 castle and originally defended by a palisade which was replaced by stone walls in the C15. The rubble ground-floor walls survive of the E range, whose upper floor probably contained the 'barmekin-hall' mentioned in 1547. At the ground floor, three rooms, all formerly tunnel-vaulted, entered from a W passage. The two S rooms have been stores. The N room, with two drains in its E wall and a large N fireplace, was the kitchen. To its W, built across the N end of the passage, a very small room with a N cupboard.

The late C15 TOWER HOUSE at the SE corner is rather better-preserved; its two lower floors are still mostly extant, the SE corner rising higher. It is L-plan, with its NE jamb abutting the S end of the courtyard's E range. Rubble-built with a splayed base. A ground-floor slit window in each of the N, W and E walls. Larger rectangular windows at the first floor, two having had their lintels renewed as part of a consolidation of the ruin. Roll-moulded door in the jamb's inner angle. It opens onto the foot of a comfortable turnpike stair. Off the E side of a short passage through the main block's N wall is the entrance to a low sloping passage running inside the wall thickness of the E gable and roofed with slabs re-used from a C13 or C14 parapet walk; ventilation shaft at the passage's N end. About two-thirds of the way along the passage is a doorway beyond which the passage narrows and then ends, with a tunnel-vaulted prison opening off its W side. The prison is windowless but has a ventilation flue in the SE corner. In the main part of the ground floor is a pair of stores, each covered with a tunnel-vault pierced by a hatch. Intruding into the E store's SE corner, a stone platform formed by the upper part of the prison's walls and its ceiling. The first floor has also contained two rooms, each with a fireplace. In the E room, under the S window sill, a slop sink. Two aumbries in the W room. A pair of garderobe chutes in the S wall suggests that there has been at least one floor above. When fallen debris was cleared from the first floor in the 1980s there were found small corbels carved with heads, pieces of chequer-corbelling, a dormer pediment displaying the initials of Sir James Johnstone †1608 and his wife, Dame Sarah Maxwell, and a stone bearing the date 1603, evidence of alterations to the top of the tower in that year.

LOCKERBIE

Town whose development began *c.*1730, when the Johnstones of Lockerbie granted feus and tacks for houses and gardens along the present Mains Street and High Street, soon followed by further buildings along Bridge Street E of the burn. From the C18, Lockerbie boasted the largest lamb fair in Scotland, about 20,000 beasts being sold there each August, mostly for export to England. The railway station on the main line from London to Glasgow, following closely the line of the existing turnpike road, was opened in 1847, and railway workshops were built later in the C19. Lockerbie became a burgh in 1863, and the appearance of its centre is mostly Victorian.

CHURCHES

ALL SAINTS (Episcopal), Ashgrove Terrace. Village-picturesque in red sandstone, by *John Douglas* of Chester, 1901–3. Simple Gothic detail. Low nave and taller chancel, both with broad-eaved red-tiled roofs. SW porch, its upper part of wood; SE vestry. Strongly battered W tower with flattened ogee tracery in the paired openings; slated broach spire studded with lead lucarnes.

Interior with exposed stone walls; collar-braced roof over the nave, a panelled wooden ceiling in the chancel. Stone chancel arch. Little W baptistery under the tower. – ALTARPIECE of 43 *c.*1920 by *J. Ninian Comper*, a rich but delicate expression of his ideal of Unity by Inclusion. Blue and gold painted wooden framework of Italian Renaissance inspiration. In the pilastered panels, gilded Gothic tabernacle work above carved and lightly gilded alabaster figures (a very youthful depiction of the Risen Lord flanked by types of the Eucharist). – STAINED GLASS. In the small high-set E window, one light (the Ascension) of *c.*1905. – In the S wall, a three-light window (Our Lord flanked by kneeling figures of St James and a soldier) by *Comper, c.*1920, clearly drawn but routine. – Beside it, another three-light window (the Annunciation) signed by *N. H. J. Westlake*, 1910. – In the N wall, a four-light window (Our Lord appearing to St Mary Magdalene, with St Peter and St John in the sidelights) by *William Morris & Co., c.*1925. – Baptistery window (Angels) of *c.*1905, a strongly coloured parody of the Burne-Jones manner.

DRYFESDALE PARISH CHURCH, Townhead Street. E.E., by *F. J. C. Carruthers*, 1896–8. Tall and boxy in coursed bullnosed red rubble. Nave and tall aisles, their two tiers of windows indicating the galleries inside, with flush transepts at their ends. Square wood and slate ventilator flèche over the centre. SE tower, its corner buttresses topped by crocketed pinnacles. Above the tall belfry stage, a battlement enclosing a short octagonal spire adorned with small lucarnes and plenty of crocketing.

Inside, the aisles are marked off by two tiers of elaborate neo-Jacobean classical piers. Panelled tunnel-vault over the nave, its transverse ribs enriched with foliage and rosettes. Tall round-headed arch into the semi-octagonal apse. At the back of the apse, the ORGAN of 1905 by *Forster & Andrews*; from it projects the tall bow-fronted marble PULPIT of 1898, carried on fat sandstone shafts. In the aisles and at the E end, deep GALLERIES, their fronts decorated with strapwork. – At the S aisle's W end, the 'SHRINE' CHAPEL formed and furnished as a War Memorial by *J. B. Gladstone*, 1922. In it, a Lorimerian REREDOS carved by *W. Macqueen*, surmounting a narrow stone

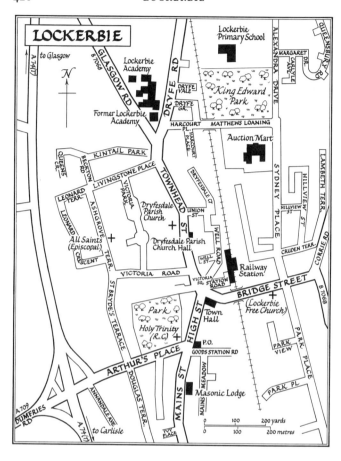

'ALTAR' by *Beattie & Co.* of Carlisle. – STAINED GLASS. S window of the chapel (a praying knight) by *Lilian Pococke*, 1922. – In the S aisle, one light (Acts of Mercy) of 1897, originally in the apse. – Still in the apse are two more dark-coloured lights (more Acts of Mercy) of 1897. – N aisle w end, the MONUMENT to Lieutenant-Colonel Cecil Francis Johnstone Douglas of the Royal Irish Lancers † 1894, a bronze relief of a mourning horse.

HOLY TRINITY (R.C.), Arthur's Place. Originally United Presbyterian. By *Ford Mackenzie* of Wigan and Manchester, 1874–5. E.E. of a sort ('pretty freely treated', said *The Builder*). Tall red Corncockle sandstone box, its buttresses looking rather insubstantial. In the front (S) gable, a pair of doors, their pointed arches carried on stumpy shafts of polished Dalbeattie granite; over the doors, corbelled gablets with voussoirs of alternating red and black stone. Higher up, a large rose window.

SE steeple, with a diagonally buttressed tower of two stages, and a belfry broached to support an octagonal spire decorated with stone lucarnes and an ornamental stone band. Inside, an open kingpost-truss roof; the organ provides the focal point.

LOCKERBIE FREE CHURCH, Bridge Street. Disused. Large but cheaply detailed lanceted Gothic box, by *John Honeyman*, 1866–7. Wheel window in the N gable front. NW steeple, with blind arcading on its second stage; large paired openings at the belfry. Broach spire with small lucarnes and a patterned band.

PUBLIC BUILDINGS

AUCTION MART, Sydney Place. Early C20 red brick octagon, the slate roof topped by a clearstorey under an onion-domed cupola. Carved bull's head above the door.

DRYFESDALE PARISH CHURCH HALL, Townhead Street. Designed by *Alexander Fraser* and built as a mechanics' institute in 1865–6. Plain except for the skinny tower, which has a lucarned spire squashed down on its corbelled eaves.

Former LOCKERBIE ACADEMY, Dryfe Road. By *F. J. C. Carruthers*, 1897. Stodgy despite the shaped gables and rounded corners corbelled out to the square.

LOCKERBIE ACADEMY, Dryfe Road. By *Dumfriesshire County Council*, 1963.

LOCKERBIE PRIMARY SCHOOL, off Alexandra Drive. By *Dumfries and Galloway Regional Council*, 1975–8. Low and sculptural in dark brick.

MASONIC LODGE, Mains Street. Late C19. Blocky plain Jacobean in red sandstone bullnosed ashlar. Artisan Mannerist doorpiece with fluted pilasters, the scrolled pediment broken by an heraldic cartouche.

RAILWAY STATION, Station Road. Built for the Caledonian Railway in 1848. Would-be picturesque, with chunky crowsteps and bracketed eaves; it now misses the canopy over the platform.

TOWN HALL, High Street and Bridge Street. A large red Corncockle sandstone presence, by *F. J. C. Carruthers*, 1887–91. Mixed Scottish Baronial and Jacobean, with crowstepped gables, not very martial bartizans and steeply pedimented dormerheads. Very tall but thriftily detailed corner tower. At its top, a corbelled balustrade and two-storey conical-roofed corner turrets. Behind the balustrade, a tall truncated slate spire carrying an ogee-roofed wooden cupola and fronted on each side by a big pedimented clockface. The clock was made by *J. W. Benson* of London. – Inside, a STAINED GLASS window commemorating those who died when a Pan Am airliner was blown up over Lockerbie by terrorists in 1988; by *John Clark*, 1991, a brightly coloured display of the national flags of the victims.

DESCRIPTION

MAINS STREET is the entry from the S. On the l., the single-
storey No. 75 of c. 1840 has broad eaves rising to form a little
gablet suggesting a pediment over the door. Deeply splayed
window sills. Then housing of the later C20 until THE OLD
MANSE on the r., late Georgian, with chunky cornices skied
above the ground-floor windows and an anta-pilastered doorpiece. On the W, the single-storey No. 27, dated 1783, originally
a symmetrical five-bay double house but with the r. door now
converted to a window; lugged architraves round the openings.
A little further along, on the E, the Masonic Lodge (*see* Public
Buildings, above). For Holy Trinity (R.C.) Church, *see* Churches, above.

ARTHUR'S PLACE provides a diversion. No. 12 is a mid-C19
cottage orné, broad-eaved with lacily fretted bargeboards. Consoles under the sills of the windows and supporting their
antefixae-topped block pediments. Round the corner, in ST
BRYDE'S TERRACE, FAIRFIELD is mid-Victorian with a
chunky Roman Doric portico and segmental-headed overarches framing the two-light ground-floor windows, the
Georgian-survival detail belied by bargeboarded dormers. To
its W, the large DRYFEMOUNT of c. 1870 is by *Ford Mackenzie*
of Wigan and Manchester. Bay windows at the ground floor,
Gothic lights above. Over the entrance, a Frenchy slate spire
with iron cresting.

HIGH STREET is low-key, an C18 and C19 medley with some
late C20 intrusions. Late Victorian BANK OF SCOTLAND (Nos.
81–83) on the W, gentle French Renaissance, with touches of
high-relief carving on its double-gabled front. The palazzo of
c. 1870 at No. 55 has an off-centre doorpiece with Roman Doric
columns and balustrades. No. 94 opposite, dated 1906, with
crowstepped gables and a conical-roofed corner turret, makes
a peaceful Baronial introduction to the Town Hall (*see* Public
Buildings, above). Here the street broadens out as a triangular
civic space. In its centre, the WAR MEMORIAL designed by
James B. Dunn, 1921–2. Big pedestal of polished Dalbeattie
granite carrying a skipping bronze figure of Victory (by *Henry
C. Fehr*). High Street continues N past the harled KING'S
ARMS, probably early C19 but dolled up in the late C19 with
half-timbering and bracketed balconies (their ironwork re-used
late Georgian); broad doorpiece carved with fruit and thistles.
Then TOWNHEAD STREET climbs past Dryfesdale Parish
Church and its Church Hall to the former Lockerbie Academy
(for these, *see* Churches and Public Buildings, above) at the
V-junction of the roads leading out towards Moffat and
Eskdalemuir.

LOCKERBIE MANOR
1.8km. N

Small rubble-built mansion house of *c.* 1800. Two storeys and a basement; three bays. Attached Roman Doric columns at the corniced tripartite doorpiece. The dormer windows were added *c.* 1900, when the piend-roofed ashlar-fronted end additions, each of two bays with pedimented ground-floor windows and rusticated quoins, were built. Back extension of 1950 for the house's present use as an hotel.

FARMS ETC.

BROOMHOUSES, Dryfe Road. Farmhouse of the earlier C19. Two storeys and three bays of white-painted rubble. Behind, a low courtyard steading built by *Robert Wilson* and *Homer Rodan*, 1827, with a big bullseye window in the N range's W gable.

HILLSIDE, 3.8km. N. Late C19 villa with bargeboarded dormerheads, a steep pitched roof and a bow projecting at the front. Offices behind; the single-storey W range of the earlier C19 enjoys a bowed Roman Doric portico.

SHILLAHILL, 2.5km. W. Early C19 two-storey three-bay farmhouse, built of painted rubble. On the W, an informal steading, some of it at least built by *Robert Williamson* in 1827. – SHILLAHILL BRIDGE, 0.3km. W, is by *George Cadell Bruce*, 1867. Five segmental ashlar arches with small rounded cutwaters.

ROMAN MARCHING CAMP, Torwood, 1.1km. W. Now only one visible rampart, through which there were two entrances, marked by the ditches of the traverses. A Roman fort covering an area of 2ha. was found nearby in 1989.

BALGRAY HOUSE. *See* p. 114.

LOGAN HOUSE
2.4km. N of Port Logan

0040

Tall pink harled mansion house built for Robert McDouall of Logan in 1702. An addition was constructed in 1848–51, followed by huge extensions (designed by *David Bryce*) in 1874–8. The house was sold in 1949 to R. Olaf Hambro, who three years later demolished most of the C19 additions in an attempt to restore the house's early C18 appearance. The interior decorator *David Style* advised on the work.

The appearance of the early C18 house is recorded by C19 photographs. It was of three storeys over a high basement, with a front of four bays, the centre two slightly advanced under a pediment. Rusticated quoins and bellcast piended roofs; small windows to the top floor. The 1950s restoration provided a centrepiece of the same width as the original but with only one window, instead of the original two, at each of the upper floors. The door to the *piano nobile* is framed by a segmental-pedimented Corinthian aedicule (copied from photographs of the original) and flanked by sidelights. In the central pediment, an armorial panel; the C18 house also had such a panel but it was placed between the first-floor windows. Projecting from each side of the C18 house was a full-height bow, probably added in the late C18. The s bow was removed in the 1870s and has not been replaced; the one on the N survives. At the w, a piend-roofed back wing, perhaps also a late C18 addition. Its ground-floor three-light window was made a French window in the 1950s.

The C18 house was linked by curved quadrants to low two-storey piend-roofed pavilions, perhaps early additions. These, together with a round doocot s of the s pavilion, were removed in the C19 and have not been replaced. N of the house, low service buildings of the 1870s, now mostly hidden by a harled screen wall. In front of the house, a terrace fronted with hammerdressed red sandstone marks the line of the 1870s extension.

Inside, a narrow entrance hall opening into a stair hall. Early C18 semicircular stair with twisted wooden balusters. The dining room N of the stair hall is a mixture. The panelling with Corinthian pilasters framing the s fireplace is probably early C18, but the pilasters which flank the panelled N bow are likely to be late C18 replicas. The smart marble chimneypiece itself could be late C18 but is more probably the 'Dining room Bardiglio chimney piece' supplied by *John Johnston* of Belfast in 1848.

To the s, a large GARDEN (now run by the Royal Botanic Gardens), the walls perhaps early C19, built partly of rubble and partly of brick. The N wall incorporates rubble masonry of the corner of a tall TOWER, now featureless except for the dressed stone of a window jamb. This seems to have been part of the castle or manor house of Logan, which was in existence by 1467 and is said to have been burned *c.*1500.

8060

LOTUS
0.6km. s of Beeswing

The harled two-storey-and-basement main block is early C19. Roman Doric aedicular doorpiece reached by a perron; rusticated quoins. Single-storey-and-basement lateral wings decorated with spiky finials; they are of *c.*1840.

9070

MABIE HOUSE
3.7km. s of Cargenbridge

Late C18 main block of three storeys and three bays, with bellcast eaves at the piended roof. The pedimented porch and bay-windowed wings were added *c.*1900. – To the w, an early C19 STABLES block, with a flat-topped obelisk over the battlemented centrepiece. – Single-storey LODGE, again early C19. It is octagonal, with Gothick windows.

MACHERMORE CASTLE

4060

1.4km. SE of Newton Stewart

Small mansion house of 1773–7 added to a plain C16 or early C17 tower (surviving at the SW corner). It was all remodelled and vastly extended in a fag-end Baronial manner by *Richard Park*, 1884–6. Big martial tower with a conical-roofed caphouse over the entrance.

MAXWELLTOWN *see* DUMFRIES

MAXWELTON HOUSE

8080

1.5km. SE of Kirkland

Much altered and 'restored' C17 house standing on or near the site of the medieval Glencairn Castle, which was acquired in 1611 by Stephen Laurie, a Dumfries merchant. The present U-plan building was probably begun by Laurie († 1637) and completed by his son, John, in 1641 (the date appearing on the E range). Remodelling, perhaps largely internal, seems to have been carried out *c.* 1685–9 by John's son, Sir Robert, first baronet. Further alterations were made *c.* 1800, when a bowed extension was added to the W range's S gable. It may well have been at the same time that the windows were Georgianized and a top floor was added to the W range's short SE wing. Yet more work took place in the mid-C19, probably in two stages, the first adding a second floor to the N and E ranges and extending the E range S, the second giving the W range a Baronial bay window on its outer side and another short wing projecting into the courtyard. The 'restoration' of 1968–72 by *Michael Laird & Partners* was far-reaching but made no attempt to return the appearance of the house to any of its several earlier states. Despite or perhaps because of the work being so confidently contrary to the principles of William Morris and the Society for the Protection of Ancient Buildings, it has been honoured with awards from the Saltire Society and to celebrate European Architectural Heritage Year.

The house is white-harled with red sandstone dressings, the earlier ones probably from the nearby Capenoch quarry, the late C20 ones of Locharbriggs stone. It forms a U-plan, although the courtyard's open S side was probably originally closed by a wall. The C17 arrangement seems to have comprised at least two dwellings, the laird's in the three-storey W range and one or two jointure houses in the two-storey N and E ranges.* All now have crowstepped gables; the N and E ranges' crowsteps

---

* The marriage contract of 1708 between Sir Walter Laurie and Jean Nisbet specified that if she were widowed she would enjoy, during the lifetime of her mother-in-law, a life rent of 'the third pairt of the said Mannor plaice of Maxweltoune' and, after her mother-in-law's death, a life rent 'in the equall halfe of the said mannor place'.

are C19 embellishments, those of the W range and its S E wing
are late C 20.

The courtyard is reached through a flat-ceilinged pend under
the N range. The entrances to the pend are roundheaded arches,
the outer one now provided with an iron yett. The courtyard
front of the N range is mostly of the mid-C19, with regularly
spaced windows at the upper floors, the three at the second
floor rising into crowstepped stone gablets. At the E end, a low
C17 door.

Like the N range, the E was heightened in the mid-C19, and
the second-floor windows were given crowstepped gablets. It
seems also to have been extended S at the same time. The two
lower floors have a mixture of Georgian windows and small,
almost square C17 windows exposed in 1968–72. Towards the
range's S end, a C17 door with rounded margins. Over it,
a hoodmoulded but weathered stone, inscribed 'NI COEPTA
DOMINUS IVVERIT FRUSTRA STRUIS MOLES SUPERBAS
AEDIUM' ('Except the Lord aid your undertakings, in vain you
construct proud heaps of houses'). Above, a panel carved with
the impaled arms and initials of John Laurie and his wife, Agnes
Grierson, together with the date 1641.

The W range seems always to have been of three storeys. In
the inner angle with the N range, a round stair tower, with a
late C 20 conical slated and ball-finialled roof. Over the door, a
panel which is probably now in its original position but was
moved here in 1968–72 from the range's C19 entrance further
S. It is carved with the impaled arms of Laurie and Riddell
above a cartouche inscribed

> Sir   Dame   ell
> Robert Lowrie   Jean Ridd

It must date from between 1685, when Robert Laurie was
created a baronet, and his death in 1698. The walling S of this
is partly late C 20 (rebuilt after the demolition of the Victorian
E wing abutting the stair tower) and partly C17, with some
of the windows perhaps dating from alterations of c. 1685–9.
Moulded door, much renewed and now surmounted by a panel
carved by *Hew Lorimer* with the date 1971 and the arms and
initials of Mr and Mrs Hugh Stenhouse, who had bought the
house in 1968. Short S E wing, originally C17 but remodelled
and heightened c. 1800. In 1968–72 the late Georgian piend-
roofed top floor was replaced by a lower crowstep-gabled attic;
new windows of simple Georgian type replaced Victorian openings. A C17 first-floor window in the N face was converted to a
door reached by a new forestair. The W range's bowed S
addition of c. 1800 was demolished at the same time, but, rather
than rebuild the main S gable in its likely C17 position, on a
line with the S E wing's outer wall, a new rectangular addition
was constructed with its gable on the outer point of its bowed
predecessor. In this crowstepped but chimneyless gable is a tier
of three-light windows which suggest a suburban roadhouse
sited to attract motorists driving in the valley below. There is

another late C20 crowstepped gable with roadhouse windows
on the range's w front, a shallow rectangular replacement for
the boldly projecting Victorian bay window which formerly
stood here. Low NW and NE extensions of 1968–72 in a crowstepped Scottish neo-vernacular manner.

The INTERIOR was largely gutted in 1968–72; some non-
structural features were put back and others replaced. In the E
range, a ground-floor room covered by a roughly semicircular
tunnel-vault, the windows cutting crudely into it. At the W
wall's s end, an aumbry. In the N wall, a simple C17 fireplace.
The w range's turnpike stair was rebuilt in 1968–72. At this
range's N end, the dining room, its doors and shutters plain
late Georgian. In the early C17 this was the kitchen, with a big
segmental-arched s fireplace. Probably c.1685–9, the room
changed its use and a smaller fireplace was constructed inside
the original, whose flue was narrowed in brickwork. Both these
fireplaces were later covered over, and a new one was provided
at the other end of the room. In 1968–72 this N fireplace was
removed and both the C17 fireplaces were exposed, making a
low inglenook. On top of the late C17 chimneypiece has been
placed a steep stone pediment, perhaps a dormerhead, formerly
in the courtyard. It displays the impaled arms and initials of Sir
Robert Laurie and Dame Jean (Riddell) and the date 168–. The
two bedrooms above the dining room have moulded stone
chimneypieces of the late C17.

s of the dining room, the entrance hall and principal stair,
remodelled in 1968–72 with muddled neo-Georgian detail. At
the s end of the w range, the ground-floor library and first-
floor drawing room, each keeping the shape, including the
bowed end, of the rooms provided here c.1800. The drawing
room has a veined grey marble chimneypiece of about that
date. In the SE wing is 'Annie Laurie's Boudoir', perhaps the
early C17 charter room. Quadripartite stone-vaulted ceiling,
with fat ribs springing from corbels (probably C19
replacements), carved with the Laurie coat of arms. At the w
wall, a gently rococo carved pine chimneypiece, perhaps late
C18, moved here from the room below.

N of the house, a small court of OFFICES, mostly Victorian,
but the s range, with a piend-roofed centrepiece, looks a little
earlier. To its w, an octagonal KENNEL (now lavatories),
perhaps early C19. – At the NE and s entrances to the policies,
early C19 GATEPIERS with square-jointed rustication, topped
by big vases. – Piend-roofed early C19 LODGES with Tudorish
centre chimneys, both rather altered.

CHAPEL, 0.3km. E of the house, built in 1868–9 as a memorial
to John Minet Laurie. Simple Gothic rectangle of bullnosed
purplish ashlar, with iron cresting on the steep slated roof.
Cusped windows set in pointed overarches. Three-light gable
windows, the w with a rose above, the E topped by three circles
containing quatrefoils. Gableted w bellcote with a pair of bells.
sw porch and lean-to NE vestry. Wooden lychgate of 1884 to
the w.

Inside the porch, stone seats and an open wooden roof. The interior of the chapel is a single space, again with an open roof. The E bay or sanctuary has STENCILLING. Broad band decorated with fleurs-de-lis and rosettes under a vine border. In the centre of this band, a stencilled gold cross on a red ground, flanked by corn and grapes on a gold ground. Either side of the E window, the stencilled Ten Commandments, Creed and Lord's Prayer. – The furnishings are almost all of 1869: Gothic oak PULPIT; brass LECTERN decorated with floral motifs; two CHANDELIERS, each a hanging circle, the E of brass, the W of brass and stencilled iron. – ORGAN by *Blacklock*, 1845, brought here in 1869 and restored by *Harrison & Harrison*. – STAINED GLASS. Complete scheme of 1868–73. Strongly coloured, with small religious scenes set in abstract borders.

MENNOCK

8000

Hamlet beside the Nith.

RAILWAY VIADUCT. By *John Miller* for the Glasgow, Dumfries and Carlisle Railway, 1850. Three roundheaded arches, the outer two treated as triumphal arches.

DESCRIPTION. At the W end, two short early C19 terraces of whinstone cottages, their windows enlarged. To their E, SMITHY HOUSE of *c.* 1840, a narrow two-storey front of buff-coloured sandstone. Tudor gablets over the first-floor windows; horizontal glazing. At the hamlet's E end, the former school, now a house (THE OLD SCHOOLHOUSE). Mid-C19 T-plan school and house, the school's windows enlarged, those of the house mostly two-light.

ARDOCK, 3.9km. SE. Rubble-built (partly whitewashed) farmhouse and steading of 1831. House of two storeys and three bays; the ground-floor windows have been enlarged and a gabled porch added. At the steading, a tall E range including a barn, its projecting wheel house containing an iron overshot millwheel; above the mill's tail race, a privy. The other ranges are low and plain.

ELIOCK HOUSE. *See* p. 303.

MERTON HALL

3060

3.3km. SW of Newton Stewart

Rubble-built laird's house described as 'new' in 1767, which gives an approximate date for the three-storey centre block, though its urn-finialled S front was remodelled in the early C19, when the outer bays acquired bows. Probably also early C19 are the recessed links and piend-roofed pavilions, with Venetian windows in their sides. Further remodelling of the front *c.* 1900 provided a baroquely aediculed doorpiece, aedicular window surrounds and probably the conical roofs of the bows.

MIDDLEBIE

2070

Little more than the church of a rural parish.

PARISH CHURCH. By *J. M. Bowie*, 1929. Blocky late Gothic cruciform kirk, built of snecked local rubble. Buttressed s gable with a bellcote on its E side. Inside, the arcades into the transepts have chamfered piers rising without capitals into pointed arches. Another pointed arch into the chancel. Collar-braced nave roof; wooden pointed tunnel roofs over the transepts and chancel. s gallery. – FURNISHINGS all of 1929.

In the GRAVEYARD, a fair number of C18 stones carved with heraldry and reminders of death.

MILNHEAD

9080

0.7km. SE of Kirkton

Small but well-finished piend-roofed country house of *c.*1760. Two storeys over a basement, built of squared red sandstone rubble. Entrance (E) front of three bays, with rusticated quoins at the advanced and pedimented centre, its door architrave simply moulded. The w front is of four bays, with the centre two advanced under a piended gable.

On the s side, a GARDEN, probably of the later C18. Its N wall is of brick, the others of brick and rubble, and the s wall is scooped up to join the higher E wall. – To the E, a pyramid-roofed square DOOCOT, probably also of the later C18; the lower storey is of red sandstone, the upper of brick.

MINNIGAFF *see* NEWTON STEWART

MOCHRUM

3040

Village with a curving main street, the houses mostly single-storey and terraced, several displaying club skewputts.

PARISH CHURCH. Rubble-built T-plan kirk of 1794. Round-headed windows. Ball-finialled birdcage bellcote on the w gable; more ball finials on the E gable and the N 'aisle', which was lengthened in 1878. Forestairs at the gables of the body and against the E side of the 'aisle'. Low w vestry, probably late C19. The corniced N porch looks earlier, perhaps an addition of 1832.

The interior was reseated in 1876. N, E and w galleries supported by wooden Tuscan columns. In the centre of the s wall, the PULPIT, probably of 1794, with attached Ionic columns on the back and a sounding board. – In the N gallery, ORGAN by *Walker*, originally in Penpont Free Church, Burnhead, and rebuilt here in 1973.

GRAVEYARD. Just SW of the church, the C18 HEADSTONE of William Hann, its front carved with an angel's head (the soul) above reminders of death. – N E of the church, a MONUMENT to Rose Anna Glen †1890, aged four, with the statue of a little girl holding a dove.

MANSE (now GREENMANTLE HOTEL) to the W. Harled two-storey T-plan. The E tail was probably the late C18 manse; the front block is an addition of 1822.

MOFFAT

oooo

Small town in upper Annandale, founded as a burgh of barony in 1643. It gained an early reputation as a spa; the medicinal properties of the sulphurous Moffat Well, 2km. N E, were recognized by 1657, when General Monk ordered a grant to be made towards the cost of enclosing it. A second (chalybeate) well, the Hartfell Spa, (q.v.), was discovered in 1748. From the 1760s major improvements were made to the town; most of the existing houses were rebuilt, and the High Street was widened in 1771–2. The Moffat Baths, served by water pumped from the Moffat Well, together with an assembly room (now the Town Hall), were built in the town centre in 1827; the burgh's popularity as a spa and resort was enhanced by the opening in 1847 of the nearby Beattock Railway Station on the line from Carlisle to Glasgow and Edinburgh. Victorian villas quickly appeared on the edges of the town. Now, with a population of *c.* 2,000, Moffat is still a resort (though not a spa) and a popular stopping place for sedate coach parties.

CHURCHES

OLD PARISH CHURCH, High Street. Of the medieval parish church, only the rubble-built S gable survives. Quite low down on its outer face, two corbels; above them, the upper fragment of a red sandstone MONUMENT, dated 1665, carved with the arms of Johnstone and Douglas and the initials AI and ND. – On the inner face of the gable, the top half of an heraldic MONUMENT with a scrolly broken pediment and the inscription 'arms of Gallaran'; it looks late C17. – Immediately W of the church, a MONUMENT, probably originally attached to a wall, commemorating John Johnstone †1597. Floriated border round the inscription tablet. Above it, a coat of arms; at the base, a skull and bones. – Some way to the E, the MONUMENT (now painted) to William Johnstone †1790, a big pedimented aedicule topped by an urn. – N E of the old church, the tall HEADSTONE erected in 1836 to the road engineer John Loudon McAdam, bearing a coat of arms and signed by *J. Walker* of Ayr. – Against the graveyard's N wall, a MONUMENT to John Pagan †1851, carpenter's Gothic in red sandstone.

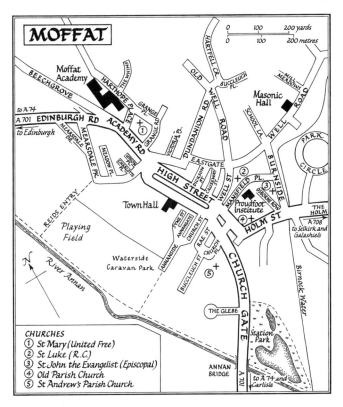

CHURCHES
1. St Mary (United Free)
2. St Luke (R.C.)
3. St John the Evangelist (Episcopal)
4. Old Parish Church
5. St Andrew's Parish Church

ST ANDREW'S PARISH CHURCH, Church Gate. Austere but ³⁴ powerful Gothic, by *John Starforth*, 1884–7. The body is a big two-storeyed buttressed box, built of squared and bullnosed red Corncockle snecked rubble, with minimally projecting transepts at the W end. Two-light lower windows set in pointed overarches, their heads containing circles pierced by quatrefoils. The upper-tier windows are each of three stepped lancet lights, with hoodmoulds springing from corbels carved with foliaged knots or human heads. In each alternate bay the centre light contains quatrefoil tracery. Door in the E bay of the N side, its surround decorated with beautifully executed but undemonstrative carved foliage, beasts and birds.

The architectural power is concentrated at the E front. At its outer corners, octagonal buttresses rise to sturdy pinnacles, panelled with blind Gothic arches and topped by crocket-finialled spires. Each buttress acts as a warder for a bowed and conical-roofed stair tower, also buttressed but circular and with cone-topped pinnacles; parapet panelled with quatrefoils set in circles. Tall nook-shafted lancet windows above cusped vesica lights. Breaking forward between the stair towers is the great four-stage bell tower just restrained by clasping buttresses. At its base, a gableted porch with praying angels at the outer corners. On the porch's splayed sides, nook-shafts, their tops carved with foliage and the heads of humans and animals. In the gablet's tympanum, blind stilted arches with well-foliaged capitals. At the back of the porch is the twin-doored entrance; its central pier and capital are carved with stylized foliage, the capitals of the attached side piers decorated with birds and dragons. More carved foliage on the lintel, the centre filled with an angel holding a crown of life. The tower's second stage has tall narrow arches (alternately glazed and blind) with slender attached columns. Blind-arcaded band course under the third stage. In each face of this stage, a big two-light nook-shafted and overarched window. At the belfry, tall three-light openings with nook-shafts, their capitals simply moulded. Corbelled and battlemented parapet, with a crocket-spired octagonal turret at the SE corner.

At the W end, a simple Gothic piend-roofed HALL, also by *Starforth* and contemporary with the church, but extended in 1898 by *MacGibbon & Ross*.

The interior is a huge space, its 15m. width spanned by a braced wagon roof. Two-bay arcades into the shallow transepts. Round the N and S sides and the E end, a gallery carried on quatrefoil-pierced iron brackets cantilevered from stone corbels, their support supplemented by thin cast-iron columns. The focus at the W end is on the pulpit. In the wall behind, a row of Gothic niches and, high up, a big rose window flanked by two smaller ones. – In a pointed niche at the back of the E gallery, the ORGAN by *Eustace Ingram*, 1894, with stencilled pipes.

STAINED GLASS. W rose window with decorative foliage and three small roundels containing figures of Faith, Hope and Charity, designed by *Starforth* and executed by *James Ballantine & Son*, 1887. – In the N transept, under the gallery, a window ('Be thou faithful unto death', a knight kneeling before a vision of Our Lady) of 1897 by *Ballantine & Son*. – Beside it, a gently expressionist window (David and Solomon) by *William Meikle & Sons*, 1924. – In the main N wall, a depiction of Moses and St Paul, by the *Abbey Studio*, 1961. – Under the S transept gallery, two windows, one (Our Lord's command to St Peter to feed his sheep, the sheep more convincingly portrayed than the humans) by *James Ballantine & Son*, 1887, the other (St Francis of Assisi and St Ninian) of 1923 by *William Meikle & Sons*, much like their window opposite. – In the main S wall below the gallery, four windows (Our Lord at the grave of Lazarus; Our Lord with the Samaritan woman; the Sermon on the Mount; Our Lord blessing children) of 1901–6, all by the *Ballantine* firm. – At the W end of the N and S galleries, two windows (saints; Moses and David) of *c.* 1900. – In the middle of the S gallery, three lights (Our Lord and the Disciples on the road to Emmaus) by *A. Ballantine & Gardiner*, 1898–9.

ST CUTHBERT'S CHAPEL, Chapel Farm, 1km. W. Only the rubble-built gables (formerly harled) stand of a chapel which probably dates from the C13. In the E gable (now with a cottage against it), a sizeable pointed window. The W window is of three acutely pointed lights grooved for glass.

St John the Evangelist (Episcopal), Burnside. By *Ian G. Lindsay*, 1951–3, replacing a church built of wood and corrugated iron in 1872. Studiedly simple, of harled brick with cement dressings. Roundheaded neo-Georgian window in the E (liturgical W) gable, now obscured by a porch added together with the NE hall *c.* 1984. – In the W gable, a three-light Victorian Gothic window.

Plain interior. – Neo-Georgian PULPIT and ALTAR RAILS of 1951–3. – Lumpy stone FONT by *Jones & Willis*, 1892. – ORGAN by *Henry Willis*, 1872. – STAINED GLASS. Three-light W window (the Crucifixion, St George and St Michael) by *C. E. Kempe*, 1903, re-used from the chapel of the former St Ninian's School in Well Road. – At the S wall E end, one late C19 light ('Feed my Lambs'). – In the porch, a window (the Good Shepherd), probably of 1872 by *James Ballantine & Son*.

St Luke (R.C.), Mansfield Place. Built as an Episcopal Church in 1866 but reclad and given a cross a century later. Wooden walls and a steep pitched slated roof. Angular Gothic detail.

St Mary (United Free), Academy Road and Harthope Place. Built as a Free church in 1890–2 to *David B. Burnie*'s design, of which *The Builder* remarked that 'there seems to be nothing particularly Scotch about it, and nothing Presbyterian'. Idiosyncratic E.E. on a huge scale, built of local whin from the Moffat Well quarry with a liberal admixture of red Corncockle sandstone dressings. Nave and double-pitch-roofed aisles halted against the E transepts. At the W, the nave's gable is dressed up with pinnacle buttresses and flanked by a slightly recessed steeple on the N; on the S, a semi-octagonal stair tower with a gabled porch. In the sides, two tiers of three-light windows, the lower with trefoil heads, the upper with untraceried lancet lights, the centre light of each squashed by a rose window. The transepts' upper windows are of the same type but taller. So too are those of the W gable, set in nook-shafted and hoodmoulded surrounds; below them, a row of fat lancets. In front of the gable's slightly recessed top, an uncrenellated parapet with dragon gargoyles. Four-stage tower, with a moulded door at its base; above, two tiers of lancets, the first tall, the second low. Belfry stage with canted corners filled by pinnacled octagonal buttresses. The tall belfry openings are set in nook-shafted overarches, their heads filled with quatrefoils.

The interior is divided by tall cast-iron columns into a nave and aisles. Galleries at the W end and in the aisles. Each bay of the aisle roofs is covered by a transverse wooden vault. Boarded nave roof. The pulpit has been pulled out from the E end to make room for a huge ORGAN of 1912, by *Norman & Beard*. – STAINED GLASS. Three-light E window with the centre panel displaying the Burning Bush emblem of the Free Church of Scotland, by *Guthrie & Wells*, 1893.

PUBLIC BUILDINGS

COLVIN FOUNTAIN. *See* Description, below.

MASONIC HALL, Well Road. Begun in 1837 as Morrison's School, a simple single-storey block with deeply splayed windows and a square pyramid-roofed wooden cupola. In 1892 it was converted to a masonic hall by *F. J. C. Carruthers* who added the projecting jamb, with a two-light window under a segmental pediment in its open-pedimented gable.

MOFFAT ACADEMY, Academy Road. Stripped neo-Georgian by the Dumfries County Architect, *John R. Hill*, 1932–3. Red sandstone walls with small whin panels. Undistinguished additions by Hill's successor, *George Bartholomew*, 1958.

MOFFAT HOSPITAL, Holm Road. By *Edward C. H. Maidman*, 1905–6. Determinedly cottagey. Additions of 1980–4 in an updated version of the same manner.

POST OFFICE. *See* Description, below.

PROUDFOOT INSTITUTE, Mansfield Place. Begun by *Campbell Douglas & Sellars* in 1885–6 as a working men's institute, but much enlarged and remodelled in 1893–4 by *Alan B. Crombie*, who added the back block. It is plain, with a faintly ecclesiastical look; round-arched windows in the E gable. The front block's present appearance also owes much to Crombie. Round-arched openings again but also rectangular windows under steep or curvy broken pediments. At the NW corner, an octagonal projection, with a swagged lead dome topped by an ogee-roofed cupola. Pompous Doric portico, its scroll-sided pediment broken by a triangular-pedimented aedicule containing a bronze BUST of William Proudfoot by *J. McLellan Arnott*, 1894.

STATION PARK, Dumfries Road. Laid out *c.* 1970. Chinesy PAVILION with a verandah all round and a pagoda roof of corrugated iron. – The MONUMENT to Air Chief Marshal Lord Dowding by *D. Bruce Walker*, 1972, has a wall of red sandstone ashlar bearing a bronze plaque with a relief portrait by *Scott Sutherland*. The wall is flanked and slightly overlapped by two freestanding and advanced upstanding quarter-circles, again of sandstone ashlar. On each quarter-circle, the bronze coat of arms of Fighter Command. Yew hedge behind.

TOWN HALL, High Street. Built as Moffat Baths in 1827. The baths themselves were placed at the back, and the tall single-storey front block contained an assembly room. The elevation was originally of five bays with a tall Greek Doric portico, its pediment a little too small. Moulded window architraves. In 1881 *James Barbour* added a further bay at each end, the S for a concert platform, the N for a vestibule; he also shifted the 1820s portico from the centre to the N end and erected a balancing Doric 'porch' at the S (its front blind except for a high-set window), with piers instead of columns. In the centre Barbour added the rectangular bay window with a Doric frieze under the steep pediment; in the pediment, strapwork framing the date of the baths' foundation.

DESCRIPTION

On the entry to the town from the S along the A701, a municipal garden, STATION PARK (*see* Public Buildings, above), on the S. It is overlooked from the N by prosperous villas, which end at the beginning of CHURCH GATE with the MANSE of 1885–7 by *John Starforth* and the huge presence of his St Andrew's Parish Church (*see* Churches, above). Opposite, a chunky little crow-stepped building (THE CORNER GALLERY), dated 1911, followed by the BLACK BULL HOTEL, probably C17 in origin but mostly late Georgian in appearance, crisp in black-trimmed white render; early C19 pilastered doorpiece. Then HARTHOPE HOUSE, perhaps late C18, the doorpiece early C19. On the E corner with High Street, the BANK OF SCOTLAND of 1874 by *Peddie & Kinnear*, tall and peaceful Baronial in whin with red sandstone dressings; crowstepped gables and a large conical-roofed corner turret. At High Street's SE corner, the graveyard containing the ruin of the Old Parish Church (*see* Churches, above).

HIGH STREET forms a broad market place, now with trees and cars planted down the middle. Near its S end, the WAR MEMORIAL, designed by *Reginald Fairlie* and executed by *Alexander Carrick* in 1919–20, looks like a tall mercat cross. The shaft's cushion capital is carved with the royal arms of Scotland and those of the three armed services. Bronze finial of a 'flying spur', the Annandale crest. The buildings at this end are grouped as short blocks divided by closes or streets, their architecture a medley of Georgian and Victorian with a few late C20 bits. On the W, the BUCCLEUCH ARMS of *c.* 1860 with a stumpy columned portico; two-light windows, corniced at the ground floor, segmental-headed at the first, and, at the second, topped by vase-finialled stone dormerheads carved with incised floral decoration. Dormerheads of the same type over the very tall first-floor windows of its S block. On the E side of the High Street, the whin and red sandstone CHAMBERS HOUSE of *c.* 1830 has tureens on top of its three gables and ground-floor windows with consoled cornices. Beside it, a simple two-storey block of *c.* 1840 with an anta-pilastered doorpiece. Across Mansfield Place, the red sandstone STAR HOTEL by *William Notman*, 1860, a three-storey bay window projecting from its narrow stepped gable. Across Star Street, a low late Georgian block with three-light windows in its piended gable front. – Diversion to the E into the narrow and winding WELL STREET. Most of its buildings are unassuming C19 of two storeys but the scale and unpretentious norm are broken by the tall late Victorian block of Nos. 15–17. It is resolutely Baronial, with cannon spouts projecting from the rope course of a corbelled round turret whose fishscale-slated roof is topped by the figure of a knight. Thistle finials on the crowstepped gables; neo-Jacobean aedicules framing the attic windows. Round the corner, No. 2 WELL ROAD, late Georgian with a heavy pilastered doorpiece and horizontal glazing.

N of Well Street, High Street continues with the two-storey OLD COURT HOUSE of 1772, a large bullseye window in the front pediment. Astride the pediment, a square pyramid-roofed cupola, given a clock (by *Wheatley* of Carlisle) in 1887. High Street's E side continues with the mid-C19 BONNINGTON HOTEL, large, piend-roofed and Georgian-survival, but with anthemion and palmettes incised in the pediments over the three-light first-floor windows. Beside it, the late C18 DICKSON HOUSE, its first-floor windows grouped 2/1/2 and set in moulded architraves; on the side elevation to Dickson Street, a doorway with a lugged architrave and pediment. The simple but elegant Georgian detail is bullied by a late C20 shopfront and 'olde worlde' shutters. Shutters of the same type on the harled brick BALMORAL HOTEL, its main part of *c.*1765, again with moulded architraves; rusticated quoins and club skewputts. Heavy early C19 porch. Beyond it, the POST OFFICE, a late Victorian commercial palazzo.

On High Street's W side, the ANNANDALE ARMS HOTEL, built *c.*1783, with moulded window architraves and scrolled skewputts; attached Doric columns and entablature at the broad doorpiece. Then the former Moffat Baths, now the Town Hall (*see* Public Buildings, above). In the centre of the street, just to its N, the COLVIN FOUNTAIN, a gift to the town from William Colvin of Craigielands, designed and executed by *William Brodie* in 1875. Tall craggy pedestal of red Corncockle sandstone surmounted by the bronze statue of a rather more than life-size and very determined ram. Aloof behind a forecourt at the N end of High Street's W side, Moffat House (*see* below). Opposite, ARDEN HOUSE, the former British Linen Bank of 1861, austere but suave in red sandstone ashlar. Three-light windows; the centre one on the first floor has Tower of the Winds columns *in antis*, a smaller version of the doorpiece below.

ACADEMY ROAD leaves High Street obliquely to the NE. Small-scale C19 vernacular both here and in the streets leading off. At STRATFORD HOUSE on the r., a mid-C19 pilastered doorpiece with a heavy pulvinated frieze. On the corner of Harthope Place, the huge bulk of St Mary's United Free Church (*see* Churches, above). At the end of the street, Moffat Academy (*see* Public Buildings, above). BEECHGROVE continues N, with recreation grounds on its W. On its E, houses, mostly C19, of one or two storeys. The mid-C19 No. 5 has a bracketed pediment over the door. Decorative iron verandah on the Victorian No. 13. At the rubble-built No. 20, a door lintel dated 1790. LAUREL BANK is of *c.*1850, single-storey-and-attic, with a pedimented porch and hoodmoulded two-light windows. The street-name now changes to OLD EDINBURGH ROAD and larger houses appear on both sides. On the r., BANKFOOT HOUSE, mid-Victorian with bracketed eaves and a slated Frenchy spire. Further on, WOODSIDE of *c.*1870, its broad eaves supported by heavy moulded wooden blocks; canted bay windows scooped up to the square at the attic.

MOFFAT HOUSE
High Street

Confident but understated mansion house designed by *John* 82 *Adam* for the second Earl of Hopetoun, curator of the extensive local estates of his insane cousin, the Earl of Annandale. It was begun in 1762 and completed by 1767. The house is built of local whin rubble with red sandstone dressings. Tall three-storey main block of five bays, the windows grouped 2/1/2, those of the first floor taller to denote a *piano nobile*, further emphasized by a band course. Tall chimneys at the ends of the platform of the piended bellcast roof. Simple detail, with moulded architraves at the openings. Broad doorpiece with attached Roman Doric columns and ball finials, containing an architrave with concave-splayed ingoes. The upper half of the door itself is glazed with square panes, a Georgian precedent for more recent neo-Georgian joinery derided by *cognoscenti*.

This centre block is linked by concave quadrants to low two-storey pavilions whose five-bay long sides face the court. In each gable towards the street, a pair of basket-arched coachhouse entrances (now blocked) below the small horizontal first-floor windows. The garden front has been badly overlaid by late C20 extensions built for the present hotel use. At each end, a full-height broad bow. The *piano nobile* is again distinguished by tall windows and a bandcourse. Inside, a tight geometric oval stair.

SUBURBAN VILLAS

BALLPLAY ROAD. HOLMVIEW. Small late C19 whinstone-walled and broad-eaved villa. At the front gable, a canted bay window of two diminishing stages. Carved bargeboards; bracketed segmental pediments over the dormer windows. – DUNMORE VILLA. Late Victorian, the idiom mostly Italianate. The first-floor windows enjoy roundheaded arches, some of them stilted, but the elaborately fretted bargeboards strike a different note.

OLD WELL ROAD. LARKHILL, on the E. Idiosyncratic classical of 1807, with a bowed portico and skied pediment at the centre. Angle pilasters topped by stone eagles. – PARK COTTAGE, on the W. Early C19, single-storey and of painted rubble. Octagonal chimneys at the ends of the piended roof; horizontal glazing.

SIDMOUNT AVENUE. SIDMOUNT COTTAGE. By *Walter* 122 *Newall*, 1832. Piend-roofed single-storey villa, built of whin with painted dressings. Three bays, the outer windows tripartite; anta-piered doorpiece at the boldly advanced and pedimented centre. Verandah towards the garden.

WELL ROAD. FLORAL and BRIARY COTTAGES. Pair of mid-C19 cottages, each with blocky consoles under the cornice of the doorway; carved decoration at the wooden dormers. – HUNTER'S CROFT. By *Walter Newall*, 1850. Single-storey and three bays, plentifully embellished, for the most part in a Scots Jacobean style. Parapeted canted bay windows at the end; shaped gablet at the centre. The pedimented door and attic window have buckle quoins of a sort. Upward scrolling skew-putts; lotus-leaf chimney pots.

FARMS ETC.

BRECONSIDE, 3.9km. SE. Rubble-built three-storey house, perhaps of the mid- or later C17. Projecting from the centre of the W front (now rendered), a semi-octagonal stair tower. The flanking windows were altered in the C19, those of the first floor each enlarged to two lights. Low C19 E wing. Inside the original house, two tunnel-vaulted rooms on the ground floor.

GRANTON HOUSE, 4.5km. N. Smart early C19 villa built of coursed whin with painted red sandstone dressings. On each of the W, S and N elevations, a pediment flanked by octagonal chimneys. Heavy pedimented W doorpiece. The *piano-nobile* windows have cornices; those of the S front are consoled and of three lights. Through the roof rises the pedimented top of the central hall, its corner chimneys carved with anthemion decoration.

Inside, Adamish plaster reliefs in the entrance hall and dining room. Full-height central hall, probably originally containing the stair. In the SW room, an imported pine and gesso chimneypiece of *c.* 1790; its frieze displays a classical harvest scene.

LANGSHAW HOUSE, 0.7km. SW. Villa of 1835, recast *c.* 1890, probably by *J. M. Dick Peddie*. Broad-eaved. Over the entrance, a battlemented tower with a round ogee-roofed angle turret.

CRAIGIEBURN. *See* p. 199.
DUMCRIEFF. *See* p. 231.
FRENCHLAND TOWER. *See* p. 308.
HARTFELL SPA. *See* p. 336.

7090   MONIAIVE

In appearance Moniaive is a large village, but it was founded in 1636 as a burgh of barony under the superiority of the Earl of Dumfries. In the later C18 the size of this baby town was increased by development on the lands of Dunreggan on the E side of the Cairn Water. Further growth followed in the early C19, but the population was still under 1,000 in 1831, and there has been little more development since.

CHURCHES AND PUBLIC BUILDINGS

GLENCAIRN FREE CHURCH, 0.4km. SE. Disused and partly demolished to form a garden feature. Opened in 1843, it has been a buttressed Gothic box. At the E end of the mostly missing S side, a gableted Gothic bellcote and a vestry. – Behind, the white-harled near-contemporary MANSE.

ST NINIAN, North Street. Built as a chapel of ease in 1887–8; *W. West Neve* was the architect. Long rectangle composed of a tall narrow nave and sturdily buttressed aisles. The w bellcote is now missing. Simple Gothic windows at the aisles and gables; continuous clearstorey glazing in the nave.

UNITED ASSOCIATE CHAPEL. *See* the Memorial Institute, below.

BRIDGES. *See* Description, below.

HALL, High Street. Built as a Free Church school, *c.* 1845. White-painted single-storey five-bay block with a gabled and trefoil-finialled porch.

MEMORIAL INSTITUTE, Chapel Street. Built as a United Associate chapel in 1834 and converted to an institute by *J. M. Bowie*, 1919. It is a big but plain white-painted box. The rectangular windows were probably enlarged to two-light in the conversion, which added the red sandstone doorpiece.

MONIAIVE SCHOOL, Chapel Street. School Board Gothic, by *James Barbour*, 1883–4.

DESCRIPTION

The village has one main street with a few branches off it. AYR STREET is the entry from the w. Set well back in a wooded garden, KILNEISS HOUSE by *J. J. Burnet*, 1884. English Arts and Crafts with black-painted half-timbering in crisp contrast to the white-harled walls. Then, on the N, terraced cottages, formerly thatched, of the late C18 or early C19, the whinstone walls of several now painted or harled. After a short stretch of undistinguished housing of the early and mid-C20, the street develops with buildings on both sides. On the l., single-storey early C19 cottages. On the r., mid-C19 two-storey houses with bracketed broad eaves and bargeboarded dormerheads; the bargeboards on HESTON are enriched with carving. More single-storey cottages beyond, ended on the r. by the garden of MILLBURN LODGE, a set-back two-storey mid-C19 villa. Opposite, but fronting the street, is the single-storey piend-roofed and whin-walled CARRADALE of 1865. Broad seg-mental-arched windows in the end bays; at the centre, a heavily corniced door flanked by narrow segmental-arched lights. Beside it, TOWER HOUSE of the later C19, a broad-eaved two-storey *cottage orné*, but the inner angle containing a tall clock tower, its top broached to carry a fishscale-slated octagonal spire which rises between stone gablets.

NORTH STREET to the NW mostly contains C19 cottages, one having to its r. a garden wall topped by urn-and-spike finials. It faces St Ninian's Church (*see* above). Near the end of the street, a pair of mid-C19 cottages (CRAIGIELEA) with hood-moulded doors and windows.

HIGH STREET begins at the corner of Chapel Street with a double cottage proclaiming its building history on a stone inscribed 'IW мG/1710/REBUILT/BY/JN° MURRAY/1822.' Beside it, the red sandstone MERCAT CROSS. Octagonal shaft

with a square base and cap topped by a heavy plain finial dated
1638.* It stands on a round pedestal (a replacement, probably
of the early C19).

In CHAPEL STREET to the SW, more cottages of the late
C18 and early C19. Near the street's beginning, on the l., OLD
BANK HOUSE and the BANK OF SCOTLAND, built as the
Union Bank c. 1850. Gentle neo-Jacobean but with an incongruous Roman Doric portico looking as if it had been re-
used from somewhere else. A little further out, the Memorial
Institute on the r. and Moniaive School on the l. (*see* above).
Just round the corner to the S, a pair of semi-detached two-
storey *cottages ornés* (KARNDALE and LARGMORE) dated 1840.
Now a bit altered but still with broad eaves, bargeboarded
dormerheads and one low mullioned first-floor window. At
this end of the village, a slightly humpbacked BRIDGE of one
segmental arch; rubble-built with ashlar parapets. It is probably
early C19.

On High Street's E corner with Chapel Street, the CRAIG-
DARROCH ARMS HOTEL of the later C19, its corner canted at
the ground floor and corbelled to the square above. At the
front, canted bay windows in recesses and a doorpiece with a
steep broken pediment and heavily decorated pilasters. High
Street continues with an unpretentious mixture of one-and
two-storey houses, mostly early C19. WESTFIELD of 1864 on
the l. is an enjoyable curiosity, single-storey-and-attic, with a
steep and large central pediment gable, its sides formed of
stepped blocks, its front pierced by a triangular window. This
is flanked by dentil cornices topped by tiny parapets decorated
with blind roundheaded arcading. Overlapping skews on the
end gables. Opposite, the white-rendered GEORGE HOTEL,
perhaps of the early or mid-C18. At one door, a simple lugged
architrave.

Then, a humpbacked BRIDGE over the Cairn Water, built
by *William Stewart* in 1796–1800. One arch, with ashlar voussoirs and rubble parapets. E of the bridge, more terraced cottages of the late C18 or early C19. Among them but set slightly
back on the l., a pair of c. 1900 (EUCHAN and MARNOCK).
Harled, with brick chimneys and mullioned windows. There
follows an L-plan quintet of cottages, dated 1906. Arts and
Crafts picturesque, with broad eaves, gabled porches and mullioned windows. They were built by Mrs Monteith of Glenluart
(*see* below) and may be by *W. West Neve*. A little further on,
INVEREE of c. 1840, its doorpiece dressed up with skinny pilasters and a battlemented cornice. Just E of the village, the
former Glencairn Free Church and manse (*see* above).

MONUMENT TO JAMES RENWICK, 0.5km. W. Built on a small
hilltop in 1828. It is of painted ashlar. Angle-buttressed base
with a hoodmoulded Tudor panel on each face; the front
bears an inscription to this Covenanting hero. On the shallowly

* It used to be surmounted by a sundial; this was replaced by a stone ball in the
late C19.

sloping top of the base stands a pillar composed of four stepped and gabled buttresses supporting a crocketed pinnacle.

CAITLOCH, 1.6km. NW. Plain rubble-built house, probably C18, dressed up *c*.1860 with a battlement and corner turrets and extended by one bay, which contains a Tudor-arched door, to link to a battlemented tower.

EWANSTON HOUSE, 0.6km. W. Harled and piend-roofed early C19 laird's house. Ionic columned doorpiece; end chimneys.

GLENLUART, 1.5km. W. Accomplished Arts and Crafts of a generally English character but with one crowstepped gable; by *W. West Neve* of London, 1899–1901, for his relation Mrs Monteith, widow of a minister of Glencairn parish. Rubble-built with dressings of red sandstone ashlar, the roofs slated but originally intended to be covered with red tiles. Asymmetrical, of two and three storeys over a high basement. The large windows are mullioned and transomed, the smaller mullioned only; all have leaded panes. Broad canted bay windows at the ground floor. Canopy over the door. – To the W, a contemporary LODGE, OUTBUILDINGS AND STABLES forming a courtyard. All in the same manner as the house. Red-tiled gambrel roofs over the stables and cartshed.

MOTTE, Lochrennie, 6.5 km. SW. Motte and bailey formed, probably in the late C12, by scarping a natural hillock which rises up to 7m. high between two burns. Roughly oblong motte at the W, its summit *c*.29m. by 14m. It is divided by a ditch, crossed by a causeway, from the lower and (unusually) smaller irregular oval of the bailey.

CRAIGDARROCH HOUSE. *See* p. 196.
CRAWFORDTON HOUSE. *See* p. 200.

MONREITH 3040

Row of C19 vernacular cottages, with the medieval Kirkmaiden Churchyard to the SE, Monreith House to the N.

KIRKMAIDEN CHURCHYARD, 1km. SE. Small graveyard beside the shore, probably an early ecclesiastical site and perhaps the original home of the C9 Monreith Cross, now in the Whithorn Museum. On its N side, remains of the CHURCH (dedicated to St Medan or Modwenna) of a parish which was united with Glasserton in 1618. The rubble-walled nave is still largely intact, although roofless. At the W end of the S wall, a round-arched chamfered door, probably late medieval rather than early. To its E, two quite large blocked windows, probably of the later C16. Inside, an off-centre roundheaded chancel arch (now built up). The chancel was rebuilt in the late C19 as the mausoleum of the Maxwells of Monreith. Large Romanesque S door, its red sandstone arch elaborately but mechanically carved, its face decorated with the Maxwell coat of arms and interlaced neo-Celtic work.

In the graveyard, the HEADSTONE of Elis[abeth] Dalrimple †1745, with panelled pilasters on its front framing reminders of death under an angel's head (the soul). – Another angel's head and a skull and crossbones are carved on a half-buried smaller headstone, almost certainly also mid-C18, to the W.

On the clifftop above, MONUMENT to the writer and naturalist Gavin Maxwell † 1969, by *Penny Wheatley*, 1978, a bronze otter standing on a rock; it recalls the subject of his best-known book, *Ring of Bright Water* (1960).

MONREITH HOUSE
1.8km. N

Stolid piend-roofed mansion house built for Sir William Maxwell of Monreith in 1790–4 by *Alexander Stevens Jun.*, who probably produced the design. Walls of rubble, formerly harled, with ashlar strips at the corners. Three storeys and a basement. Band course under the ground floor. Sill course below the small horizontally proportioned second-floor windows, giving this floor the status of an attic; cornices over the tall ground-floor windows denote the *piano nobile*. Overall parapet above a block-mutuled cornice.

The entrance (N) front is of five bays. Its broad centrepiece, slightly advanced, is tripartite, with the rubble walling of the outer sections framing a slightly recessed ashlar-clad centre. At the centre's top, plain mutule blocks under the parapet. First- and second-floor windows of three lights; the first-floor window has the relief of a stylized flower in the centre of its foliaged frieze and a consoled pediment over the centre light. The 1790s 'Venetian' door was replaced in 1820–1, when the masons *John* and *James Simpson* added the heavy portico, with paired Greek Doric columns supporting a heavy but plain entablature and parapet.*

At the garden (S) elevation, a full-height bow in the centre. In the flanking bays, a three-light window at each floor, the cornomiced ground-floor windows dignified with consoled sills and anta-pilastered mullions. A lower W wing was added in 1878 by *Richard Park*. This was curtailed to one piend-roofed bay by *Stewart & Paterson*, 1939; large corniced three-light window in each of the main fronts.

Inside, a large two-storey entrance hall, the principal stair climbing its W wall, a gallery round the other three sides. Big plaster ceiling rose. The E wall's chimney breast is of 1878. Across the E end of the ground floor, a double drawing room, remodelled by Park in 1878 in a late C18-revival manner but with Pre-Raphaelitish printed fabric on the walls. More work of the same sort, and a N fireplace placed in an alcove, in the ante-room to the library at the SW corner of the C18 house. The library, at the centre of the S side, originally oval, was remodelled in the C19 with a straight N wall. Its Gothick bookcases and doorpiece of *c.* 1800 were imported from Felix Hall (Essex) after that house was partially demolished in 1939.

---

* The design may owe something to *Robert Smirke*'s scheme of 1812 for refronting the house and adding wings.

Plain early C19 white and grey chimneypiece, thistles at the tops of the jambs. The upper floors have been converted to stylish holiday flats.

MYRTON CASTLE, 0.6km NE, was the predecessor of Monreith House. It has two distinct parts. The S occupies a steep-sided motte, probably constructed in the C12. On this, the rubble-built remains of the S end of a tower house erected *c.* 1500 by the McCullochs of Myrton.* Parapet on simply moulded individual corbels and drained by large semicircular spouts. At the SE corner, a timidly projecting angle round, supported on heavy moulded corbels. Ground-floor gunloops in the S, E and W walls. Their stepped sills are visible inside. Quite large corniced first-floor windows to the E and W, the E with a roll-and-hollow moulding, the W with a chamfered surround. Plain window high in the S gable. The interior was not vaulted. Two aumbries in the S wall of the ground floor. Remains of a first-floor S fireplace. The building was converted to a doocot *c.* 1870.

The other part of Myrton Castle, standing N of the motte, may be early C17. It has been a rubble-walled L-plan house, with a rounded stair tower in the inner angle. The ground floor of the main block survives. Near its N end, a roll-moulded doorpiece. Two S doors to the SE jamb, the one at the first floor approached by a forestair. They are probably insertions of *c.* 1800. Inside the jamb, E fireplaces; the one on the first floor is basket-arched and mid-C18. The ground floor of the main block had a vaulted passage along the E side giving access to three stores, also vaulted.

The ESTATE OFFICE just N of Myrton Castle is a *cottage orné* of *c.* 1860. To the E, some earlier buildings, including one with a bellcote, probably part of the farm offices built in 1813–14. Another has a S window whose surround incorporates re-used stonework which might be medieval.

FORT, Barsalloch Point, 1.2km. W. The site, a cliff-edged prom-ontory with a steeply sloping approach, has been defended by the construction in the late first millennium B.C. of two curved ramparts; between them, a ditch, *c.* 10m. wide and 3.5m. deep. D-plan enclosure behind, *c.* 0.1ha. in area. The entrance was in the NE sector.

FORT, Fell of Barhullion, 1.8km. NE. Hilltop fort, probably of the first millennium B.C. It has been an oval, *c.* 42m. by 20m., enclosed by a massive drystone wall.

STANDING STONES, Blairbuie, 1km. N. Large granite boulder poised on a low ridge; and, *c.* 15m. E, a pair of smaller standing stones. They were all erected in the later third or second millennium B.C.

OLD PLACE OF MONREITH. *See* p. 483.

---

* The estate was acquired, together with a McCulloch heiress, by the Maxwells in 1640.

MORTON

Former MORTON PARISH CHURCH. *See* Thornhill.
MORTON PARISH CHURCH. *See* Thornhill.

8090 ## MORTON CASTLE
2.4km. NE of Carronbridge

One of a chain of medieval castles which stretched up the valley
of the Nith, a main route from the Solway Firth to central Scotland. The site was almost certainly fortified before the C14 Wars
of Independence, but the present substantial remains are not easy
to date accurately. The position is naturally defensive, a triangular
promontory with steep NE and NW sides pointing into low and
boggy ground which was converted, although probably not before
the late C18, into a loch.

In the early C12 the honour of Morton formed part of the extensive possessions of Dunegal, lord of Strathnith, and a C12 date
seems likely for the cutting of the ditch across the promontory's
approach from the level and relatively high-lying ground to the S.
Almost certainly a castle existed by 1307, when the manor of
Morton was recorded as belonging to Sir Thomas Randolph, a
descendant of Dunegal and the nephew and supporter of Robert I.
Under the terms of the Treaty of Berwick of 1357 Morton was
named as one of thirteen Nithsdale castles whose defences were to
be dismantled. In 1440 the barony and castle (the term possibly
denoting a site rather than a building) were granted to James
Douglas of Dalkeith, father of the first Earl of Morton.

After the execution of the fourth Earl of Morton in 1580, the
lands of Morton were granted to John, eighth Lord Maxwell, but
in 1588, during James VI's punitive expedition against that peer,
Morton was taken and burned. Thereafter the castle reverted to
the Earls of Morton, but it was sold to Sir William Douglas of
Coshogle in 1608 and again, ten years later, to Sir William
Douglas of Drumlanrig (later the first Earl of Queensberry). It
continued to be occupied until 1714, after which the castle buildings seem to have been largely abandoned and used as a quarry
until the 1890s, when repair of the ruins was carried out; the
masonry patches (mostly at the main block's N wall) are delineated by tiling.

62 What survives is the main S range of an apparently triangular castle.
At its SE corner, a segment of a round tower; at the range's SW
corner, a D-plan tower, clearly part of a gatehouse. All this is
constructed of ashlar, and the principal elements seem to be of
one build. But what date is likely? The absence of any provision
for artillery defence makes it improbable that it can be later than
c. 1450. The removal of the W part of the gatehouse and most of
the SE tower, although just possibly the result of C18 quarrying,
would be consistent with a dismantling of the defences in
the late 1350s,* and, if the existing buildings pre-date that, the

---

* A masonry repair at the join of the main block to the SE tower is considerably

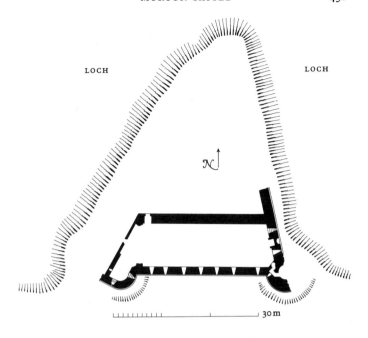

LOCH

LOCH

$\mathcal{N}$↑

30 m

Morton Castle. Plan

earlier C14 would be a probable time for their construction.

The MAIN BLOCK is a large but severe near-rectangle, c. 32.6m. by 13.1m., with the E gable canted to fit the triangular site. At the S front, quite small horizontally-proportioned ground-floor openings set high up above the battered base. Big first-floor windows, mostly transomed and with pointed heads. The entrances to this block are placed at the W end of the N elevation. Plain ground-floor door, its jambs C18 replacements. Above, a pointed and hoodmoulded first-floor door, presumably originally reached by a ladder. Its fat rounded mouldings are of a type more usually associated with the C15 than the C14; this is the main reason why a C14 date for the buildings has been questioned. To its r., a window with a shouldered straight lintel. Another window of the same type at the E end of this wall.

Of the round SE CORNER TOWER, only the SW segment survives. Square first-floor window under a triangular relieving arch. At the ground floor, the outlets of a sloping latrine drain which has been flushed from the SW to the NE.

The D-plan SW TOWER formed the E part of a twin-towered H-plan gatehouse. Plain rectangular windows. At the straight

earlier than the 1890s work and must have been carried out after this tower had been dismantled but before the main block was abandoned.

w wall, the r. jamb of the castle entrance's pointed arch. In it are checks which show that it could be defended by the raising of the drawbridge which spanned the pit extending from within the transe to *c*.4.9m. in front of the castle. Behind the raised drawbridge was first an outward-opening gate, then a portcullis, and, finally, an inward-opening gate. Above the entrance, the jamb of a pointed window to the portcullis room, whose wooden floor over the transe was supported on the now very weathered corbels on the sw tower's straight side.

There has been a building abutting the N side of the main block. Its w part, possibly contemporary with the main block, has been single-storey and covered by a lean-to roof, the ridge piece supported by corbels and protected by a stone water-table. The E part of the building is of two storeys and pre-sumably an addition, since one of the main block's first-floor windows has opened into it. Its E gable is formed by the castle's curtain wall, but the upper floor has been carried on two inward-projecting tiers of continuous corbelling, just as at the C15 drum tower of Sanquhar Castle (q.v.).

INSIDE the main block, the s and E ground-floor windows have shouldered lintels and bases which each consist of four steps up to a sloping sill. In the E gable's s window, a slop drain. More slop drains in two of the s windows, one provided with a basin. At the E end, a fireplace which has been topped by a canopy. Above it, the corbel and socket for a beam which presumably ran the length of the block, supported by posts, strengthening the centre of the 9.5m.-wide wooden floor above. At the side walls, this upper floor's beams and joists were carried on simply moulded corbels and a scarcement. Near the s wall's E end, a canopied fireplace. Pointed rear-arches to the large s windows, which have been provided with stone seats.

The fragmentary SE tower was entered from the main block. Its basement, perhaps a prison, has been covered with a domical vault. The floors above were carried on wall scarcements. Pointed rear-arch to the large first-floor window. At the second floor, a smaller window, its lintel shouldered.

The sw tower's ground floor must have been entered from the N and was probably a guardroom. Windows with stepped sills and shouldered lintels like those in the main block. In the w wall, a slit window looking into the gatehouse transe. Hatch in the floor giving access to a pit prison, windowless but with a ventilation flue in its s wall. The upper floors of the tower seem to have formed a virtually self-contained lodging. Smart first-floor room, probably originally reached by a wooden stair or ladder from the triangular close between the transe and the main block. Boldly projecting moulded stone cornice. Tall canopied fireplace, its moulded jambs with curved projections at top and bottom and chamfered at the sides, very like the fireplace of *c*.1300 in the gatehouse at Kildrummy Castle (Aberdeenshire). s window with a seat at its w ingo and the entrance to a garderobe at its E; pointed rear-arch. In the wall thickness, at the join with the main block, remains of a turnpike stair to the tower's three top floors. At the second floor, a window again with a pointed rear-arch and provided with stone seats.

MOSSKNOWE

0.9km. SE of Kirkpatrick-Fleming

Smart Palladian villa-country house built in 1767, probably to a design by *William Craik* of Arbigland, who produced a sketch elevation and plan three years earlier.* Narrow, pedimented three-bay centre block of two storeys, a basement and attic, joined by set-back links to two-storey two-bay piend-roofed pavilions. Bracketed sills under the architraved windows. Band course over the centre block's ground floor, becoming a sill course at the pavilions. Display is concentrated at the entrance (N) front, whose stugged ashlar is a superior finish to the squared rubble of the other elevations. Over the door, a pulvinated frieze and cornice. Balustraded aprons under the first-floor windows of the centre block. Roundheaded window in the tympanum of its acorn-finialled and weather-vaned pediment. Balustrades over the links. The s elevation is a plainer version of the front but acquired a canted bay window *c*. 1840 and a French window rather later. Low service court to the w.

GARDEN to the w, its N wall perhaps of *c*. 1770. This incorporates a rectangular moulded door, probably from the house's predecessor; its cornice is carved with dogtooth ornament. On the lintel, a thistle and fleur-de-lis flanking the inscription 'W^{M}G MI 1663. SOLI DEO HONOR & GLORIA', the initials those of Mr William Graham of Mossknowe and his wife, Margaret Irvine. – At the garden wall's w end, the STABLES court, its E and w ranges probably of *c*. 1770, the s C19; low quadrant walls on the N. In the w range's s end, a large carved crest. At the SE corner, a re-used lintel dated 1671.

MOUSWALD

Nondescript hamlet.

PARISH CHURCH. Simple kirk of white-painted rubble, built in 1816 and remodelled in 1929 by *J. M. Bowie,* who heightened the walls, introduced dull late Gothic windows and added the E chancel. At the w end, panelled buttresses topped by concave-sided gablets. w tower of red ashlar decorated with blind arcading under another concave-sided gablet enclosing a blind trefoil. The octagonal belfry was rebuilt in 1929 but probably repeats the Georgian design. Cusped pointed openings under a stringcourse which rises into more concave-sided gablets; dumpy crocketed spire. The interior is by Bowie, with a round-headed chancel arch. – STAINED GLASS E window (Our

* But a *Mr Irvine* also provided designs.

Lord with St Peter and St John) by *James Ballantine II*, 1929.

Against the s side of the church, a BURIAL ENCLOSURE; its battlement is late Georgian, but the chamfered doorway looks C17. Above it, a stone carved with the arms and initials of James Douglas of Mouswald and his wife, Agnes Rome, and the date 1655. – Immediately outside this enclosure, the weathered EFFIGY of a recumbent knight, his feet resting on a lion, his plate armour suggesting a date of *c.*1500. – To the s, a HEADSTONE to Katharine Bennie †1734, with an array of emblems of death under a grumpy angel (the soul). – To its s, the big pedimented MONUMENT of William Mundell †1796, its stonework with V-jointed rustication.

SCHOOL, 0.8km. NW. By *Alexander Crombie*, 1866, and extended in the same manner by *F. Adamson*, 1910. Broad eaves and Venetian windows, the effect hardly Palladian.

MOUSWALD PLACE
1.2km. NW

Mid-C19 country house, partly harled and partly of white-painted rubble. At the main (w) front, paired pediments over the l. three bays; to the r., two more bays, recessed and with aprons under the first-floor windows. The bay windows at the sides are late Victorian embellishments; the half-hearted NE tower is perhaps a little earlier.

To the SE, one wall and a few other fragments of the TOWER HOUSE, probably late C15, of the Carruthers family of Mouswald. It has been rectangular, of three storeys, and seemingly unvaulted.

FARMS ETC.

CLEUCHBRAE, 0.9km. N. Mid-C19 broad-eaved *cottage orné*, with carved bargeboards at the porch.

MOUNT KEDAR, 1.3km. SE. Built as Ruthwell Free Church Manse in 1844. Piend-roofed front block with a first-floor sill course. Its bay window and the broad-eaved back wing are additions of the later C19. – In the garden, a MONUMENT to the Rev. Dr Henry Duncan, founder of the savings bank movement, whose house this was. It is signed by *James Raeburn*, architect, and *Alexander Crombie*, builder, 1846. Battered base, each front pierced by a segmental arch with a boldly projecting keystone. Above, a pedestal, one face carved with a relief bust of Duncan, supporting a large broached ashlar obelisk.

MOUSWALD GRANGE, 1.4km. NW. Among the plain C19 farm buildings, a conical-roofed rubble-built circular WINDMILL tower of *c.*1700.

BROCKLEHIRST. *See* p. 134.
ROCKHALL. *See* p. 501.

MULL OF GALLOWAY   *1030*

The sw tip of Scotland, crowned with a lighthouse.

LIGHTHOUSE. By *Robert Stevenson*, 1828–30. Tapering tower of white-painted rubble. Walkway round the domed lantern projected on machicolation; a semicircle of stores clasping the base. – Contemporary flat-roofed KEEPERS' HOUSES, with pediments rising above the parapets at the advanced entrance bays.

MURRAY'S MONUMENT   *4070*
10km. NE of Newton Stewart

Prominently sited, blunt-topped granite obelisk on a corniced pedestal, the whole *c.*24m. high. It was erected in 1835 to commemorate the orientalist Dr Alexander Murray † 1813; the inscription recalls that he was 'Reared a Shepherd Boy on these Hillsides'.

MURRAYTHWAITE   *1070*
1.9km. SE of Dalton

C18 laird's house, enlarged and remodelled in the 1840s and again at the beginning of the C20. The piend-roofed main block was built for James Murray of Murraythwaite in 1767–9 by the mason *Robert Scott*. It was of two storeys and an attic, originally with five-bay frontages to the N and S. In 1844–5 James Dalrymple Murray of Murraythwaite added a low two-storey office range at the W, and made major changes to the N front: he recast its two W bays in a straightforward manner (their ashlar facing is probably part of this work) and remodelled its three E bays. The new front, slightly advanced from the line of the original, is in an ungainly Jacobean style, with steep gables at the outer bays, their tops decorated with large crosslet 'arrow-slits'. In each of these bays, four-light windows, their central mullions of stone, the other mullions and transoms of wood. Squashed centrepiece with an urn finial on its pediment. Above the simply moulded doorpiece, an armorial panel recording the alterations of 1845. Above that, a corniced first-floor window of two lights with a wooden mullion and transom. A single-storey E block and the U-plan stable court were probably added at the same time.

The house was further remodelled by *Reginald Blomfield*, 1902, after a fire. Blomfield made the main block a U-shape by adding S-projecting two-storey piend-roofed wings. The E wing (replacing the earlier single-storey addition) is recessed from the N front and stretches across the E side of the main block. The W wing overlays the W bay of the original S front. Projecting from each S gable, a two-storey canted bay window. At the same time, Blomfield altered the roofs, added three dormer windows (the outer two segmental-pedimented, the centre with a triangular pediment) on the S front, and placed a cupola (removed in the mid-C20) at the centre of the roof. Probably also of 1902 is the S elevation's off-centre French window; above it, a C19 or early C20 stone carved with the initials WM and IG (for William Murray and Jean Grierson, his wife) and the date 1660 and, above that, a dormer pediment, probably of the later C17, bearing the coats of arms of Murray and Grierson.

Inside, a large Jacobean entrance hall, probably of 1902 but looking a little earlier. At the house's SE corner, Blomfield's drawing room, entered through double doors with elaborate ormolu mounts. Large chimneypiece of late C18 type, with eagles' heads and a shell on the frieze; foliaged pendants on the jambs. At the SW corner, L-plan dining room, again by Blomfield. Tuscan-columned screen at the hinge. Restoration-revival chimneypiece, its frieze decorated with carved swags of fruit.

MYRTON CASTLE *see* MONREITH (Monreith House)

NEW ABBEY

Picturesque large village, its curving main street mostly contained within the precinct of Sweetheart (or New) Abbey, the now ruined monastery which has given this place its name.

SWEETHEART ABBEY

11 Extensive remains of the last of the major medieval monasteries founded in Scotland, its red sandstone masonry a warm counter-point to the white harling of most of the village buildings. In 1270 the Cistercian General Chapter commissioned the Abbots of Furness and Rievaulx to inspect the site where Devorgilla, lady of Galloway, the widow of John Balliol of Barnard Castle, intended to found a Cistercian abbey. The findings of this inspection apparently proved favourable, and preliminary work on the monastic buildings may have been begun before April 1273, when Devorgilla issued a charter granting property to endow 'the Church of St Mary of Sweetheart and the monks there . . . for the abbey to be built there in honour of God and the Blessed Virgin Mary' and on behalf of the souls of her ancestors, husband and deceased children. The next year the General Chapter ordered the Abbots of Holmcultran and Dundrennan to visit the abbey founded by Devorgilla and, if satisfied, to incorporate it into the Cistercian order as a daughter house of Dundrennan.

At her death in 1289 Devorgilla was buried in the choir of the abbey church, together, it was said, with a casket containing the embalmed heart of John Balliol, which she had kept close to hand since his death. By 1289 there had probably been built the choir, crossing and transepts of the abbey church, as well as the two E bays of the nave and the arcades of its four w bays. Work was almost certainly halted soon after; the unrest of the period *c.* 1290–1328 seems to have affected the monks of Sweetheart particularly badly, and they complained to Edward I in 1299 and 1308 of £5,400 worth of damage done to their property through war. In 1331 a charter of Simon, Bishop of Galloway, which gave the abbey leave to appropriate to its uses the tiends of the parish of Crossmichael, spoke of the 'outstanding and notorious poverty and manifest prostration of the said monastery', phrases repeated even more forcibly fifty years later when Thomas, Bishop of Galloway, confirmed a charter of 1369 granting the abbey the tiends of Buittle parish. Bishop Thomas mentioned also that the monastery had been 'totally' burned by lightning, doubtless an exaggeration, although there is evidence of scorching on the stonework of the s nave arcade.

The grant of 1369 had been made by Sir Archibald Douglas ('the Grim', later third Earl of Douglas), who in the same year had acquired the lordship of Galloway between the Nith and the Cree. He was described in Bishop Thomas's charter of 1381 as the 'founder and reformer of the said monastery', and it seems likely that work on the abbey church was resumed in the late c14 with his support. The church may have been substantially complete by 1397, when Douglas confirmed his gift to the abbey of the tiends of Buittle and obtained confirmation of this from the Antipope Benedict XIII, who granted the mitre to the Abbot of Sweetheart in 1398.

After the Reformation the abbey lands became a temporal barony and the abbey church was abandoned, a church for the parish of New Abbey being made in the monastic refectory. A new parish church was built against the s side of the abbey church nave in 1731, after which the cloister buildings seem to have been used as a quarry. In 1779 a consortium of local gentlemen bought the ruin of the abbey church itself with a view to its preservation, although in 1852 the government architect *Robert Matheson* reported that 'The Abbey appears to be entirely neglected, is very ruinous and delapidated [*sic*], and bears no evidence of any recent attempts having been made for the preservation of the interesting remains. Ivy and Trees have been allowed to overrun a large portion of the Ruins ...'

Repairs were carried out by *Alexander Crombie* in 1862–3, and the c18 parish church was removed in 1877. In 1928 the remains of the abbey were taken into the care of the Secretary of State for Scotland.

The general plan of the CHURCH is, unsurprisingly, close to that of the earlier Cistercian foundations of Dundrennan and Glenluce in Galloway (qq.v.). Aisled nave of six bays, the two w bays longer than the others; a crossing and transepts, each with E chapels; and an unaisled three-bay presbytery. The cloister buildings lie to the s. The surviving masonry is all built of red sandstone ashlar.

Of the WEST FRONT there survives the gable of the nave but

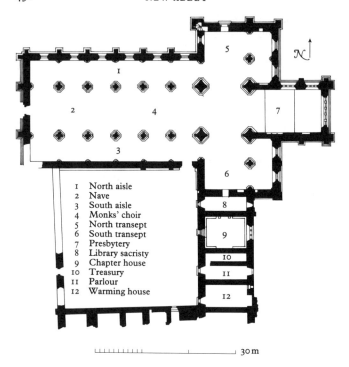

Sweetheart Abbey. Plan

1 North aisle
2 Nave
3 South aisle
4 Monks' choir
5 North transept
6 South transept
7 Presbytery
8 Library sacristy
9 Chapter house
10 Treasury
11 Parlour
12 Warming house

30 m

not the end walls of its aisles, of which no more can be said than that there were clasping buttresses at the outer corners. More buttresses mark off the nave gable. In it, a hoodmoulded and pointed door, its nook-shafts still with weathered foliage capitals. This is more probably late C14 than late C13. Above, a row of five sturdy corbels which have carried the ridge-beam of the roof of a lean-to porch; another corbel on the stub wall of the S aisle, so the porch presumably stretched across the full width of the front. Above the door and porch, a huge pointed arch, its label stops carved with human heads (which look like 1860s replacements). The head of the gable is filled by a rose window flanked by trefoiled triangles. Below this, an expanse of walling separates this traceried head from three pointed lights, the centre one taller and broader than the others and with stubs of cusping in its head. The mullions between these lights project as buttresses, presumably to support the masonry above. The effect is decidedly awkward. It looks as if the whole arch was designed, probably in the late C14, to be filled by one large window whose traceried head is in place but whose lower part was either executed to a different design or replaced later, perhaps c. 1500. In the apex of the gable, another trefoiled triangle, probably of the late C14.

The NORTH AISLE'S buttressed side wall has been demolished except for a fragment of the two E bays. The SOUTH AISLE'S windowless S wall is much more intact except at the W end. In its E bay is the processional door into the cloister. Pointed arch, much of its moulding replaced with plain stonework. It has been of three orders with nook-shafts (the central shaft slenderer than the other two), now represented only by weathered capitals. A stringcourse runs W from the base of the hoodmould (now weathered away) to stop against the adjoining buttress.

The CLEARSTOREY windows of the nave have risen from the ridges of the now missing aisle roofs. In the two E bays of each side, the windows (the E window on the N now fragmentary) are late C13, each composed of three lancet lights, their jambs deeply splayed. Linking the bases of the hoodmoulds, a stringcourse; sill course at the bottom. The windows of the four W bays belong to the late C14 work. Each is a semicircle containing five pointed lights divided by slender mullions. The end lights look very squashed. Hoodmoulds rise from the sill course to interrupt, inconsequentially, the higher stringcourse. On each side, at the nave's W end, remains of a moulded eaves course with a grotesque head projecting below.

The CROSSING TOWER is largely complete. Raggles on its faces show that the nave, transepts and presbytery have all been roofed at the same height. Above these roof raggles, narrow rectagular windows. At the top, a lot of smallish corbels carved as human heads. They support a shallowly projected but high battlement. All this is late C13, but the crowstep-gabled attic storey inside the parapet looks like a late C14 or C15 addition. In each of its gables, a rectangular two-light window.

The nave clearstorey's string and sill courses are carried round the largely surviving SOUTH TRANSEPT until halted against the now missing roof of the E cloister range. In the transept's W side, a large pointed window immediately above the ridge of the (missing) cloister roof. The gable of this transept has been exposed by the demolition of the E cloister range. At its ground floor, a segmental-arched door which looks like a late medieval insertion or replacement. At this gable's W end, a first-floor door which opened from the night stair into the monks' dormitory. In the top of the gable, remains of a thinly mullioned rose window, probably of the late C14. Its bottom segment consists of blank walling which was covered by the cloister roof, whose ridge ran into the window just above its centre. The window surround's inner and outer mouldings converge at the bottom. Over the E transept chapels have been lean-to roofs, their original pitch indicated by a raggle in the presbytery's S wall. At their E front, a buttress projects between the two chapels. Each chapel is lit by a broad pointed E window, its hoodmould springing from a stringcourse; narrower pointed window in the S chapel's side wall.

The NORTH TRANSEPT has been of the same size and height as the S and again has the string and sill courses of the nave

Sweetheart Abbey. North transept
(from R. W. Billings, *The Baronial and Ecclesiastical Antiquities
of Scotland*, Vol. iv, 1852)

carried across its W side and gable. At the NW corner, an
octagonal stair tower looking like a massive buttress. On top of
this stair tower, remains of a pinnacle, each of its faces panelled
with a blind pointed arch. In the W side of the transept, a tall
and narrow pointed window of the late C13 with a traceried
head. In the gable, a fat pointed and hoodmoulded door and,
above it, a large late C13 window. Only stubs of this window's
tracery survive, but it has been of four cusped lights with cusped
circlets in the head. In the top of the gable, an ineptly basket-
arched window containing three slimly mullioned lancet lights;
in appearance they are generally similar to the windows in the

W bays of the nave clearstorey and, like them, are of the late C14. This transept's chapels are generally like those of the S transept, but the presbytery's lower sill course jumps down to form a stringcourse across their front. At each, a sizeable E window, its head almost triangular. Small and narrow side window to the N chapel.

The PRESBYTERY's two buttressed E bays project clear of the transept chapels. In each of these, a late C13 hoodmoulded and pointed window, its jambs containing nook-shafts with simply moulded capitals; but the two N windows are considerably deeper than those of the S side, where the W opening is notably squat. In the SW window and each of the two N windows, three pointed lights under tracery composed of trefoiled circlets. In the SE window, tracery of the same sort but only two lights. The clearstorey, delineated by a stringcourse, survives only at the S wall's E bay. In it, a pair of lancets with the bases of their hoodmoulds linked by a stringcourse. In the E gable, a large Geometrical main window of five lights, the head filled with no fewer than five trefoiled circlets, the centre three grouped together within another circlet. The intention is ambitious, the result stodgy. Awkwardly juxtaposed above, a big round-arched window which has contained five lancet lights, a much larger version of the W windows of the nave clearstorey, and like them, late C14. Did it replace a rose window? In the apex of the gable, a semicircular window lighting the roof space. The presbytery walling is all tied together by stringcourses, the lowest forming a sill course under the main windows and carried across the buttresses, but with a break on the S side where it seems the designer could not cope with the different heights of the two windows. A second stringcourse, delineating the clearstorey, is returned across the gable to form the outer member of the main E window's hoodmould. A third stringcourse runs under the sill of the C14 window above.

Despite being roofless and missing sizeable parts of the outer walls, the INTERIOR appears, at least to first glance, relatively 12 complete. Hoodmould over the great W window, its label stops carved with human heads (probably C19 replacements). Nave arcades of pointed arches carried on piers of quatrefoil section, with moulded capitals and bases to their clustered shafts. These seem to be late C13. No triforium (a return to early Cistercian practice) but, at the clearstorey, a wall passage, with several of its openings (allowing light into the central vessel from the external windows) off-centre in relation to the arches below. Each of these clearstorey openings is of three lights, with cusped arches springing from shafts of quatrefoil section. The shafts in the E bays, probably completed in the late C13, have simply moulded capitals, those of the four bays to the W foliaged capitals, probably of the late C14. Stringcourses run under the sills of the openings and link their hoodmoulds, whose label stops at the centre light of each opening are carved with human heads. The aisles have been vaulted; some of the wallshafts and the springing at the W responds still survive. At the aisles' E ends, pointed arches into the transepts. Crossing arches of the same design as those of the nave arcades but much broader and taller. The tower above has contained several wooden floors supported on stone corbels. In each wall of the tower, a door for access to the roof spaces of the nave, transepts and presbytery.

The clearstorey passage has continued from the nave round the transepts and presbytery, crossing its E gable at a high level using the sill of the upper E window. The surviving openings have the same detail as those of the nave's E bays and are also late C13. The s transept's gable has much taller openings, presumably an attempt to provide decorative interest in what would otherwise be largely blank walling. The stair to the clearstorey is in the N transept's NW tower.

The transepts have no vaulting-shafts, so presumably were covered by wooden roofs. In the s transept's s wall, a segmental-arched TOMB RECESS. In each transept's E side, a two-bay arcade into the chapels. The hoodmould of the N transept's s arch has one label stop carved with a badly weathered head. All the chapels have been vaulted. In the N chapels, only the wallshafts survive, but the s chapels' sexpartite vaulting is intact, one boss carved with the coat of arms of an ecclesiastic. In the N chapels' s wall, remains of an arched recess, probably a piscina. In the s chapels' s wall, a round-arched recess, its back with cusped stone panelling, again probably a piscina.

On the N and s sides of the presbytery, linked hoodmoulds over the main windows, one label stop of the s side's W window carved with a human head. In the moulded ingoes of the windows, nook-shafts with simply moulded capitals. In the presbytery's s wall, remains of a triple-arched SEDILIA, with a weathered nook-shaft surviving on its E side. – To its E, a double-arched PISCINA, also much battered.

In the s transept's s chapel, a sarcophagus MONUMENT of 1931–3, its design by *J. Wilson Paterson* of *H.M. Office of Works* based on a sketch by *James S. Richardson*, then the Inspector of Ancient Monuments for Scotland. It incorporates four fragments of the inscribed top slab and six heraldic panels from a C16 monument commemorating Devorgilla, lady of Galloway, founder of the abbey. On top, the torso of a female effigy, the hands holding a heart-shaped casket. It was discovered in the presbytery in 1929 and probably belonged to the C16 monument. – GRAVESLABS. Among fragments of carved masonry in the s transept's chapels, the late medieval slab to Abbot Buiso–, displaying a stylized uprooted tree. – In the N transept, a broken slab, again probably late medieval, with a marginal inscription and incised with a sword and shield. – Also in this transept, the slab commemorating John Broun of Lands and his wife, Mariota, †1613. The Latin inscription has old-fashioned lettering; heraldry for decoration. – In the N transept's s chapel, the slab to – Brown †1683, carved with a coat of arms; a skull and crossbones at the bottom. – Probably also C17 is a weathered slab in the same chapel, a skull and bones at its bottom end. – Propped against this chapel's E wall, two panels, one displaying the Brown coat of arms, the other an inscription to Gavin Brown of Bishopton †1683. – Under the crossing, a slab to James Maxwell, younger of Kirkconnell, †1706, with a coat of arms at the top, a skull and crossbones at the bottom, both set in stylized foliage; more foliage forming a border. – In the presbytery, a slab on the supposed site of the tomb of Devorgilla, bearing her arms and those of John Balliol. It was designed by the *Ministry of Public Building and Works* and executed by *Dods* of Dumfries, 1966.

Very little remains of the CLOISTER BUILDINGS which enclosed the cloister walk and garth S of the nave and crossing. The lower part of the walls of the E range survives. It has been of two storeys, perhaps with an attic. On the ground floor, at the N end, there is a narrow library and sacristy with an entrance from the S transept as well as from the cloister walk; simple round-arched window to the E. To its S, the chapter house. The big E window, with remains of tracery in its pointed head, may be late C13. Originally in the refectory in the S range, it was moved in 1731 to the parish church built against the abbey church's S side, and was resited here after that church was demolished in 1877. Then the parlour, with a slit-like room, perhaps the treasury, opening off its N side. Finally the warming house, with the much restored jambs of a medieval fireplace in its E wall. Above this range was the monks' dormitory. Only foundations survive of the S (refectory) range. It is uncertain if the W (lay-brothers') range was built. On the line of its likely E front, a fragment of walling incorporating a round-arched DOORWAY enriched with dogtooth ornament. It looks like late C13 work. In the wall above have been placed an empty image niche, very weathered but perhaps with tabernacle work at the top, possibly of the late C13, and, flanking the niche, two worn heraldic shields, one said to have borne the arms of Douglas; both are perhaps of the C15. Above the N shield, an eroded stone carved with a human head, possibly of the late C13.

In the PARISH GRAVEYARD immediately E of the abbey, the mid-C19 BURIAL ENCLOSURE of the Stewarts of Shambellie, a coat of arms over the entrance.

The abbey and its cloister were set in a squarish precinct covering *c.* 12 ha., surrounded by stone walls on the N, W and E and with a ditch on the S. There are substantial remains of the PRECINCT WALL, constructed of granite boulders, probably cleared from the precinct area at the abbey's foundation.

CHURCHES

NEW ABBEY PARISH CHURCH. Mechanical Gothic, by *James Barbour*, 1875–7, built of grey granite with red sandstone dressings. Nave and chancel; lower transepts. At the N transept, a lean-to chapel, presumably intended to evoke the transept chapels of Sweetheart Abbey; its E wall is carried up to form a tall buttressed and gabled bellcote. NW porch. Inside, a rather

insubstantial hammerbeam roof constructed in 1963–4 after
a fire. – STAINED GLASS. Four-light E window (the Four
Evangelists) by *Morris & Co.* (using designs by *Edward Burne-
Jones*), 1914. Richly coloured but uninspired.

ST MARY (R.C.). Combined chapel and priest's house. Tudor,
by *Walter Newall*, 1824 (*see* the Introduction, p. 42). The house
is a harled villa with hoodmoulded windows. The chapel forms
a broad back (E) wing. Inside, at the W (liturgical E) end, a
REREDOS of 1890, its Gothic oak surround framing a copy
of Raphael's Sistine Madonna painted by *J. McLellan Arnott*,
1899. – STAINED GLASS. In the S wall, a two-light window
(the Crucifixion) of *c.* 1905. – In the N wall, a window (the
Ascension) signed by *Mayer & Co.* of Munich, *c.* 1890.

DESCRIPTION

At the entry from the N, first is the little WOMAN'S GUILD
HALL, broad-eaved Gothic of *c.* 1890. It stands beside the
humpbacked BRIDGE built over the New Abbey Pow in 1715.
Two unequally sized arches and small triangular cutwaters.
Immediately SW of the bridge, the monastic FISHPOND of
Sweetheart Abbey, its overflow channel passing under the road
to join the tail-race of the cornmill, which empties into the
burn. The CORNMILL itself, to the S of the bridge, is probably
late C18. Ball-finialled three-storey S block. Kiln vent with a
salmon weathervane on the longer three-storey N range, its N
end containing the mill house. Waterwheel (restored in the
1970s) on the W side.

A lane immediately to the N goes uphill. On its r. side, the
straightforward CHURCH HOUSE, built as a masonic lodge in
1806 (converted to a church hall in 1887 and later to a house).
Behind it, the small rubble-walled THE OLD HOUSE. One
window lintel is said* to have been inscribed 'IS 16–2 RB',
and a C17 date seems likely. It is of two storeys and has stepped
gables containing tiny attic windows; stone forestair to the first-
floor E door. S of this and Church House is the large MILL
POND, fed by a lade from the Sheep Burn. From its NW corner,
a channel to the fishpond and, from the NE, a channel to the
mill race, both constructed of drystone granite blocks. E of the
mill pond, the harled ABBEY HOUSE, a long two-storey block,
its first-floor windows grouped 4/3/2. It is clearly the product
of at least three phases of construction, the earliest probably
C17, although the detail is now mostly plain late Georgian.
Mid-C19 neo-classical doorpiece with attached piers. At the W
end, a lower ball-finialled store addition, perhaps early C19.
Large walled garden behind, with a small pavilion, possibly
mid-C18, projecting from its W side.

The road past Abbey House and the lower road S from the
bridge meet at a roughly triangular space (THE SQUARE)
where two inns confront each other. On the N, the harled

* By the RCAHMS.

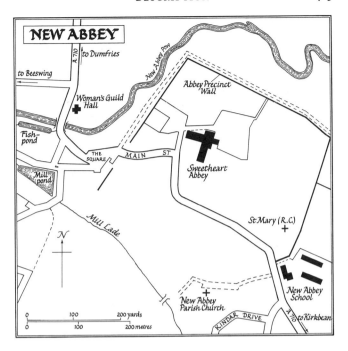

CRIFFEL INN of *c.* 1900, bargeboarded with touches of half-timbering; the grey granite ABBEY ARMS on the S is a little earlier. On the E side of the Square, a C19 cottage. In its front wall, a re-used painted stone carved with a hand holding a crowned hammer (the emblem of the smiths) and inscribed 'By hammer & hand All arts do stand R.M., 1775.'

Then the curving main street leads E, with a picture-postcard ¹ vernacular medley of painted and harled small houses and cottages, mostly of the C19. No. 14 may be C18. Its front displays folk art with two painted stones, one carved with a rose, the other with three men in a boat. Towards the E end of this mixture, the granite gable of the VILLAGE HALL, built as the Oddfellows Hall in 1892. Single-storey rear extension of 1990, with a big piended roof. Opposite, the broad-eaved gable of a two-storey block with a semicircular-pedimented stone inscribed 'J MᶜG 1847'; at its E side, a first-floor loft door.

On the street's N side, just by Sweetheart Abbey (*see* above), the gingerbread ABBEY COTTAGE of the later C19, granite-built with a picturesque bargeboarded porch. The road now becomes one-sided and turns S. On the E, No. 28, built as the Parish Manse by *Robert Callan* and *Jacob Murdoch*, masons in Dumfries, 1802, has a late Victorian granite porch contrasting with its painted rubble walling. The road turns E, with the Parish Church (*see* above) visible across a field to the S. Near the village's E end, St Mary's (R.C.) Church (*see* Churches, above) followed by the late C19 former SCHOOL AND SCHOOL-

HOUSE (No. 48), simple Jacobean in granite with sandstone dressings; small E addition of *c.*1900. Behind it, the present NEW ABBEY SCHOOL by the *Stewartry County Council,* 1975.

WATERLOO MONUMENT, 1.2km. SE. A 15m.-high tapering round tower of granite rubble, erected in 1815–16 to commemorate the valour of British, Belgian and Prussian troops at the Battle of Waterloo. Intake above the bottom stage, whose corbelled parapet is now missing. Stringcourse over the next stage. Corbels survive at the top but not the parapet.

GLENHARVIE, 2.4km. W. C18 snuffmill converted to a house early in the C19. Two-storey and five-bay main block built of painted rubble, with the N front's windows grouped 2/1/2. Linked by a screen wall to an outbuilding to the E. In the garden, a two-storey pyramid-roofed DOOCOT, perhaps early C19.

ABBOT'S TOWER. *See* p. 89.
KIRKCONNELL HOUSE. *See* p. 364.
SHAMBELLIE HOUSE. *See* p. 519.

ABBOT'S TOWER. *See* p. 89.
KIRKCONNELL HOUSE. *See* p. 364.
SHAMBELLIE HOUSE. *See* p. 519.

9070   NEWBRIDGE

Handful of C19 and C20 houses.

CLUDEN BRIDGE. Built by *Thomas Twaddell* and *Thomas Porteous,* masons in Dumfries, 1758–9. Slightly humpbacked, of red sandstone ashlar. Three segmental arches with boldly projecting keystones; low triangular cutwaters.

EMBASSY HOTEL. Rendered two-storey villa of the earlier C19. On the front, a pair of bows projecting from between panelled piers. Rather heavy Ionic portico at the centre. Chimneys grouped in the middle of the roof. Addition of 1966 for hotel use, extended in 1985. – Also of the early C19, the bow-fronted LODGE, built of broached ashlar.

DALAWOODIE. *See* p. 209.
FOURMERKLAND TOWER. *See* p. 307.
GRIBTON. *See* p. 335.

DALAWOODIE. *See* p. 209.
FOURMERKLAND TOWER. *See* p. 307.
GRIBTON. *See* p. 335.

6070   NEW GALLOWAY

Burgh of barony founded in 1630 which never became much more than a village.

CHURCHES

23 KELLS PARISH CHURCH, 0.5km. N. By *William McCandlish,* 1822. Rough granite cruciform kirk, the S limb formed by the tower. Hoodmoulded pointed windows; their intersecting stone tracery probably dates from *James Barbour & Bowie*'s alterations of 1910, which provided the stepped skews and the NW organ chamber. Battlemented tower, with diagonally set and

spikily pinnacled buttresses. The interior is all by *Barbour & Bowie*, with an elaborate open roof and galleries at the E, W and N. – ORGAN by *Harrison & Harrison*.

GRAVEYARD. s of the w end, an early C18 STONE bearing an inscription to the Covenanting martyr Adam MacQwhan; placed in its present classical surround in 1832. – E of the church, a tall foliage-finialled HEADSTONE to Anna Kennedy †1771, inscribed:

> Here youthful bloom fair as the Morning Rose
> Sleeps in the Silent Dust in soft Repose.
> Great was her Soul Integrity of Life
> Adorn'd the Maid and Dignified the wife.
>
> And now beyond where Stars and planets Shine
> She dwells in Love and Ioys divine
> Suns may decay & Stars may lose their Light
> And falling Worlds sink in Eternal Night
> Whilst thro Eternity She wafts her way
> And basks in Beams of Everlasting Day.

– Beside it, two TABLE STONES, one probably of the C18 to the Gordons of Largmore, with a coat of arms, the other to the Rev. Andrew Ewart †1739, again with a coat of arms but also a pie-crust border. – To their s, a truncated granite OBELISK on a tall pedestal; it commemorates John Macourtie †1814. – Propped against its small railed enclosure, some early C18 HEADSTONES, one carved with a skull and hourglass, another (of 1706) with Adam and Eve, and a coat of arms placed above the Tree of Knowledge. – A second early C18 HEADSTONE carved with figures of Adam and Eve is placed against the back of the heavy classical MONUMENT to Jannet (*sic*) Thomson †1847, presumably designed by her husband, the architect *William McCandlish*. It has a baroque urn on top of its consoled pediment. – Beside it, another small early C18 HEADSTONE, carved with a skull, crossbones and an hourglass. – To the SE, the HEADSTONE of the gamekeeper John Murray †1777, 'who for 46 years had been a faithfull servant to the family of Kenmore'. Its front is decorated with a grouse, a dog, gun, powder flask and fishing rod, the back with the verse inscription written by the parish minister, John Gillespie:

> Ah John, what changes since I saw thee last;
> Thy fishing and thy shooting days are past.
> Bagpipes and hautboys thou canst sound no more
> Thy nods, grimaces, winks and pranks are o'er.
> Thy harmless, queerish incoherent talk,
> Thy wild vivacity and trudging walk
> Will soon be quite forgot. Thy joys on earth,
> A snuff, a glass, riddles and noisy mirth,
> Are vanished all. Yet blest, I hope thou art,
> For in thy station weel thou playdst thy part.

MANSE in trees across the road. Main block of two storeys and three bays, built by *Robert Andrew* in 1804–6, its dormer windows a late Victorian addition; granite porch by *John McCulloch*, 1868. Back wing with hoodmoulded windows, by

William McCandlish, 1836. All of painted rubble. – To its W, the FORMER MANSE of 1742–3, converted to offices in 1806.

ST MARGARET OF SCOTLAND (Episcopal). Picturesque, with harled walls and broad-eaved red-tiled roofs, by *W. H. Harrison*, 1904; the chancel (again by Harrison) was added in 1908. Long and low, with sturdy buttresses and paired lancets in the side walls; three-light gable windows. Spire-roofed W belfry. Porch on the SW, low outshots to the N. Interior just as simple, with an open wooden roof. – STAINED GLASS. Clearly drawn E window (the Crucifixion), by *C. E. Kempe*, 1905. – In the side windows of the chancel's E bay, depictions of Our Lord as the Light of the World, the True Vine, the Good Shepherd, and the Way and the Life, by *Clayton & Bell*, 1906. – In the chancel's W bay, two lights (the Nativity; the Ascension) of 1909, by *James Powell & Sons*. – SE window of the nave (Pilgrim's Progress), *c.*1920. – NW nave window (the Annunciation) by *James Powell & Sons*, 1912. – Three-light W window (St David of Scotland, St Margaret of Scotland, and St Constantine) by *Kempe*, 1906.

LYCHGATE by *Harrison*, 1912.

PUBLIC BUILDINGS

KEN BRIDGE, 0.8km. NE. By *John Rennie*, 1820–1. Long elegant curve of granite ashlar. Five segmental arches; between them, shallowly projecting attached piers rising from the rounded cutwaters to the parapet. – At the E end, the KEN BRIDGE HOTEL of *c.*1830, with Tudor hoodmoulds over the windows but now bereft of chimneys.

OLD SCHOOL. Late C19. L-plan, with Gothic windows and broad eaves, the walls of granite.

TOWN HALL. Of 1875 in its present form. Rendered two-storey block with tall roundheaded first-floor windows. At the N end, a simple ball-finialled tower, with a steep pyramid roof broken by gableted belfry openings. Round-arched entrance under an heraldic panel.

DESCRIPTION

The approach from the E is overlooked by OVERTON HOUSE of *c.*1900, its first-floor windows topped by segmental and triangular pedimented dormerheads. In the garden, an octagonal early C19 DOOCOT, with an octagonal window to its upper floor. At the real beginning of the burgh, set back behind its garden wall and lychgate, the Church of St Margaret of Scotland (*see* Churches, above). Set further back but prominently sited on the S side of the road, the WAR MEMORIAL by *John W. Dods*, 1922, a rough grey granite version of a cenotaph. Beyond the church, HAMDON HOUSE of *c.*1840, rendered with rusticated quoins and a heavy doorpiece, is followed by the granite ashlar mid-C19 CLYDESDALE BANK, which looks like a Jacobean villa. Then the road turns S and, after the Old

School (*see* Public Buildings, above), starts the gentle rise of the terraced HIGH STREET, with one- and two-storey late Georgian and C19 vernacular houses built of granite, often painted or harled, quite plain but little altered. About halfway along, the Town Hall's tower (*see* Public Buildings, above) provides a needed gentle punch. Behind the street, on the W, the late Georgian GREENBANK HOUSE with a decorative fanlight. At the S end of the High Street, the white-harled MEADOWBANK of *c*. 1800 on the E, its stone portico a Victorian addition. It is set well back, the approach guarded by a pair of early C19 bow-ended cottages. The burgh ends with ARD-LAGGAN, a big relaxed Edwardian free-style villa; Venetian window in the gable, rectangular bay windows at the front.

CLATTERINGSHAWS. *See* p. 182.

KENMURE CASTLE. *See* p. 354.

NEWLANDS

1.8km. N of Duncow

9080

Large and dottily martial Baronial villa, completed in 1911. – At the S entrance to the drive, an early C19 LODGE with a Venetian window in its gable.

NEW LUCE

1060

Village with a single street of C18 and C19 houses and cottages, some now crushed by box dormers.

PARISH CHURCH. White-painted rubble rectangle of 1821, most of its windows roundheaded. Ball-finialled birdcage bellcote on the W gable. The S wall's sturdy buttress is presumably an addition, probably of the later C19. Low W vestry of 1957. The interior was refurnished in 1965.

S of the church, four C18 HEADSTONES, each carved with an angel's head (the soul) above reminders of death. Those commemorating members of the McKine family and John McMillan are segmental-pedimented aedicules dated 1762 and 1767.

PEDEN MEMORIAL FREE CHURCH. The church, by *Charles Withers*, 1871, has been demolished, but the bellcote survives in a public garden off Main Street.

BRIDGES. The CROSS WATER BRIDGE, carrying Main Street over the Water of Luce, and MAIN WATER BRIDGE, on the road to the W, are both probably early C19, rubble-built and humpbacked, each of one arch.

HALL. Built as a war memorial in 1924.

CAIRN, Cairn na Gath, 4.5km. NE. Long cairn of the third millennium B.C., built on ground which rises to the S. It is now a stony steep-sided trapezoid, *c*. 30.5m. long, 13.5m. broad at the high S end and 10.4m. at the N. It has been badly robbed at the S end and the N half of the W side.

CAIRN, Caves of Kilhern, 2.3km. E. Overgrown ruin of a much disturbed long cairn of the third millennium B.C., c.33.5m. long, its W end 12.2m. broad, its E 14.8m. It has developed to cover four randomly placed and roughly rectangular chambers.

STANDING STONES, Laggangarn, 8.5km. NE. A pair of rough sandstone slabs, the N 1.88m. high, the S 1.58m., probably erected in the second millennium B.C. On the W face of each has been incised, probably in the C7–C9, a cross with arms broadening outwards; in the corners of each cross are incised smaller crosses, each composed of two intersecting lines.

1090   NEWTON

Scattered handful of houses.

JOHNSTONE AND WAMPHRAY FREE CHURCH, 0.4km. W. Secularized. Rubble-built broad box of 1844, with round-headed windows. Small birdcage bellcote, its ball finial disproportionately large.

Beside the church, its MANSE, of 1846, with an off-centre two-storey bay window and pedimented porch.

WAMPHRAY UNITED PRESBYTERIAN CHURCH, 0.4km. E. Secularized. White-painted rubble kirk of 1849–50. Gothick glazing in the round-arched windows, their margins picked out in black.

4060   NEWTON STEWART

Founded as a burgh of barony under the superiority of the Stewarts of Castle Stewart in 1677, but the first feu contract for building here was not granted until 1701. Development was helped by the construction of a bridge over the Cree in 1745, and in 1760 Bishop Richard Pococke found Newton Stewart 'a neat little town'. In the 1770s the superiority was acquired by Sir William Douglas of Gelston, who changed the town's name to Newton Douglas, built a cotton factory and encouraged the establishment of carpet manufacture. The carpet factory failed almost immediately, the town soon reverted to its old name, and the cotton industry flourished for only a short time. A few small industries, among them the making of patent cartridge loaders, had some success in the C19, but the burgh's main source of prosperity, besides its being a market town for the surrounding area, was wool trading.

CHURCHES

MONIGAFF PARISH CHURCH, Old Minnigaff. Georgian Gothic, by *William Burn*, 1834–6. Broad five-bay box, with buttresses rising into gabled tops surmounted by pinnacles with flaming urn finials. Five-light E window under an ogee hoodmould. The side windows are of two lights with transoms

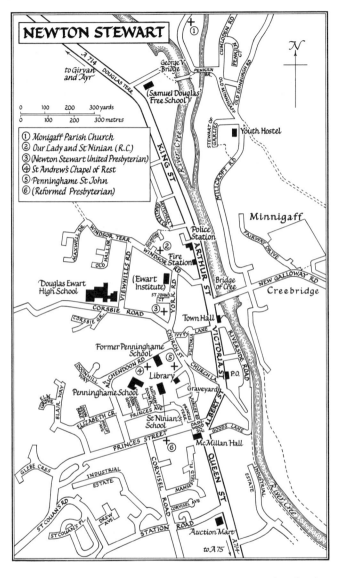

NEWTON STEWART

to Girvan
and Ayr

A 714 Douglas Terr.

George V
Bridge

PENKILN RD

CUMLODEN RD

OLD EDINBURGH RD

PENKILN
BR.

(Samuel Douglas
Free School)

KING ST

Cree

STEWART &
GARLIES

Youth Hostel

MILLCROFT RD

0   100   200   300 yards
0   100   200   300 metres

① Monigaff Parish Church
② Our Lady and St Ninian (R.C.)
③ (Newton Stewart United Presbyterian)
④ St Andrew's Chapel of Rest
⑤ Penninghame St John
⑥ (Reformed Presbyterian)

Minnigaff

MAXWELL DR

WINDSOR TERR.

OLD HALL DR.

WINDSOR RD

MITCHELL
HATTRICK

Police
Station

ARTHUR ST

FAIRWAY DRIVE

Fire
Station

②

VIEWHILLS RD

(Ewart
Institute)

ST JOHN'S
CT.

YORK RD

Bridge
of Cree

NEW GALLOWAY RD

Creebridge

Douglas Ewart
High School

③

CORSBIE ROAD

CORSBIE CRES.

Town Hall

RIVERSIDE ROAD

River Cree

IVY PL

VICTORIA LANE

VICTORIA ST

Former Penninghame
School

CHURCH ST

AUCHENDOON RD

⑤

CHURCH LA.

P.O.

Library

Graveyard

ALBERT ST

DONHILL WAY

BLAIR WAY

ELM
GROVE

Penninghame School

AUCHENDOON
RD

PRINCES AVE

ELIZABETH CR.

CHURCH
CRES

ALBERT
PL

PRINCES
TERR.

DARK
WOOD

GOODS LANE

St Ninian's
School

PRINCES STREET

⑥

McMillan Hall

GLEBE CRES.

INDUSTRIAL
ESTATE

CORVISEL ROAD

QUEEN ST

MANSFIELD PL

CORVISEL AVE

INDUSTRIAL
ESTATE

River Cree

ST COLLAN'S RD

ST COLLAN'S PL.

DREW
AVE

STATION ROAD

A 714

Auction Mart

to A 75

and simple Dec tracery. W tower of three stages, its clasping
buttresses becoming octagons above the first stage; three-light
openings at the top, their hoodmoulds joined by stringcourses
carried across the walls and buttresses. In the inner angles,
rectangular stair projections with blind 'Saxon' windows to the
front. Low semi-octagonal E vestry.

Inside, an almost flat ceiling with applied ribs forming sexpartite vaulting, the bosses foliaged. Gallery on squat cast-iron
columns round three sides. – At the E end, the PULPIT, a

replacement, probably of 1893. – Late Victorian ORGAN in the w gallery, by *Bryceson & Co.*

STAINED GLASS. Five-light E window (Scenes in the life of Our Lord) of 1868. – In the N wall, four windows with *grisaille* patterns and coloured borders (one border renewed), probably of the 1830s and perhaps by *William Cooper*, who supplied the original E window in 1836. – One window (Our Lord with Children; 'I was a Father to the Poor') of *c.* 1875. – At the s wall's E end, a modern-traditional window (Ruth and Boaz) of *c.* 1955. – Next to it, a window (the Good Samaritan; the Parable of the Talents) installed in 1868. – Then a lushly pictorial scene ('Her children rise up and call her blessed') signed by *A. Ballantine & Son*, 1910. – Beside it, a window ('Take I pray thee my blessing that is brought to thee') of *c.* 1920. – This wall's w window (the Madonna and Child; Our Lord in Glory) is of 1930.

In the graveyard to the s, the roofless OLD PARISH CHURCH. It is a rubble rectangle. In its E gable, a window of two pointed lights which could be late medieval. The rest seems mostly C17. E door with a moulded roundheaded arch. Rectangular w door; its margin is chamfered, as are those of the window above and the surviving s window. Crude ball-finialled birdcage bellcote. Inside, at the N wall's E end, a segmental-arched recess, robbed of its dressings, but its shape is that of a late medieval tomb. Above it, a reset C17 stone carved with a coat of arms and Latin inscription commemorating Patrick McKie of Cumloden.* The recess now shelters two worn Celtic STONES, each carved with a cross in relief, one with a bird above the cross, a creature on the back, and the crude figure of a man on one side.

s of the Old Parish Church, the HEADSTONE of Patrick McClurg †174–, its sides carved with foliage, the front with a coat of arms and symbols of death. – w of the Old Church, the BURIAL ENCLOSURE of the McKies of Bargaly. On its s wall, a MONUMENT to James McKie †1816, with a marble relief of a cherub weeping beside an urn, signed by *S. & F. Franceys* of Liverpool. – At the churchyard's w side, a balustraded C18 ENCLOSURE, its back formed by the huge scroll-flanked aedicular MONUMENT to Patrick Heron of Heron and Patrick Heron jun. of Heron, both †1761. Coupled Corinthian columns with pilasters behind; rinceau enrichment on the frieze. Elaborately carved urn finial. A lugged frame round the inscription panel, a coat of arms above.

NEWTON STEWART UNITED PRESBYTERIAN CHURCH, York Road. Now the Museum. By *Richard Park*, 1877–8. Buttressed and lancet-windowed preaching box. In the front (E) gable, a three-light trefoil-headed window above the hoodmoulded entrance. SE tower broached to an octagonal belfry under a slim spire of white and red sandstone bands. – In the front

49

* It was formerly at Kirroughtree House and was erected here early in the C20.

garden, red sandstone STATUES of a Covenanter and 'Old Mortality', by *John Currie, c.* 1840.

OUR LADY AND ST NINIAN (R.C.), Windsor Road. Plain Gothic of 1875–6, by *Goldie & Child* of London with *W. & R. Ingram* of Glasgow as executant architects. Nave and chancel under a continuous roof; a lower S transept. Picturesque wood and glass porch at the SE (liturgical SW), over which rears a heavy double bellcote of stone. – STAINED GLASS. W rose window (Our Lady Queen of Heaven) of 1876. – Late C19 NE window of two lights containing roundels of Our Lord and Our Lady.

The straightforward early C19 PRIEST'S HOUSE makes a SW wing to the church.

PENNINGHAME ST JOHN, Church Street. Big but thriftily detailed Gothic cruciform, by *William Burn*, 1838–40. It is built of coursed whin with buff sandstone dressings. Angle buttresses topped by leafily finialled pinnacles. Big hoodmoulded windows containing plain lancet lights. Simple neo-Norman transept doors. Bowed stair projections flanking the E steeple. At the bottom of its tower, a pointed door, the hoodmould springing from shafts with elided capitals. The tall belfry stage is broached to an octagonal clock-stage, the buttress tops in clined to follow the broaching. Inside the parapet, an octagonal stone spire with lucarnes. Hall at the back added in 1881–2.

Inside, an almost flat plaster ceiling with ribs to suggest sexpartite vaulting, the bosses foliaged. Tudor chancel arch. – In the short chancel, a tall PULPIT, best-quality Jacobean of the same type as Burn was to provide at Langholm Parish Church a few years later, with strapwork finials on the canopy. – U-plan gallery on cast-iron columns, the front simple neo-Jacobean. In the E gallery, an ORGAN with stencilled pipes, by *J. F. Harston*, 1878; rebuilt in 1962 by *Hill, Norman & Beard*. – STAINED GLASS. Floral design in the big W window, probably mid-C19.

REFORMED PRESBYTERIAN CHURCH, Princes Street. Secularized. Built in 1833, a rubble box with pointed windows. The E gable's porch and cross probably both date from alterations made in 1894.

Plain two-storey MANSE behind, its present appearance dating from a remodelling in 1843; back wing of 1895.

ST ANDREW'S CHAPEL OF REST, Auchendoon Road. Built as an Episcopal church in 1894 to a design by *James Caird Macfarlane*. Sturdy buttressed Gothic rectangle with a NW porch, the red of the sandstone dressings and tiled roof ridge an effective contrast to the whinstone walling and Welsh roof slates. – STAINED GLASS. Three-light E window (the Crucifixion) by *Heaton, Butler & Bayne*, 1910.

GRAVEYARD
Church Street

Opened in 1777 when the site of Penninghame Parish Church
was moved to Newton Stewart. Of the church built then there
is now no trace and the HEADSTONES are mostly C19. – At the
NW corner, a late C18 red sandstone MAUSOLEUM erected
by Samuel Douglas †1799, founder of Samuel Douglas' Free
School (later Douglas Academy). It is square, topped by a steep
pyramidal roof.

PUBLIC BUILDINGS

AUCTION MART, Queen Street. Designed by the auctioneer
William Agnew in 1894 and opened the next year. Rendered
octagon, a cupola on top of the slated roof.
BRIDGE OF CREE. By *John Rennie*, 1812–13. Strong-looking, in
hammerdressed granite ashlar, the parapet walling broached.
Four segmental arches; the stout, barely pointed cutwaters rise
to form small pedestrian refuges.
DOUGLAS EWART HIGH SCHOOL, Viewhills Road. By the
Wigtown County Architect, *R. M. Clive*, 1969, and extended
by his successor, *Raymond J. Hume*, 1975–7. Curtain-walled
main block of three storeys; octagonal brick hall added at the
N in 1977 by *Dumfries and Galloway Regional Council*.
EWART INSTITUTE, York Road. Originally a school and now
housing. By *Thomas Cook* of Liverpool, 1862–4. Picturesque
Gothic ends, each containing a schoolroom. The S end has a
gabled bellcote, the gabled N end has cusped lights in the
windows. Tall and dour centrepiece, originally the principal's
house and boarding accommodation. The octagonal NE tower
was added in 1869 by *Heath Wilson & Thomson* of Glasgow,
its Gothick appearance, with a battlement pierced by crosslet
arrowslits and quatrefoils, surprisingly frivolous for its mid-
Victorian date.
FIRE STATION, Arthur Street. By *Sutherland & Dickie*, 1965–6.
GEORGE V BRIDGE, Old Minnigaff. Suspension bridge built by
D. H. & F. Reid of the *Victoria Bridge Works*, Ayr, in 1911 to
commemorate the coronation of George V; it was repaired by
Crouch & Hogg, 1982. Latticed parapets and pylon towers on
which sit spike-finialled metal saucers.
LIBRARY, Church Street. By *Dumfries and Galloway Regional
Council*, 1991–2. Single-storey, of brick. Very mannered archi-
tecturally lightweight post-Modern.
MCMILLAN HALL, Dashwood Square. By *Richard Park*, 1884.
Big and plain, the sense of thrift barely relieved by the heavy
antefixae-topped pediment over the entrance. Steep pyramid
roofs of faintly French inspiration at the corners.
MUSEUM. *See* Newton Stewart United Presbyterian Church,
above.
PENNINGHAME SCHOOL, Auchendoon Road. By the Wigtown
County Architect, *R. M. Clive*, 1962–5.

Former PENNINGHAME SCHOOL, Auchendoon Road. The
building was begun in 1876 by *Richard Park,* who provided a
T-plan School Board Gothic school and schoolhouse. In 1890 it
became H-plan with the addition of a broad-eaved N classroom.
Further N addition of 1897.

POLICE STATION, Arthur Street. By *Sutherland, Dickie & Partners,* 1963–5.

ST NINIAN'S SCHOOL, Princes Avenue. Built as Penninghame
Parish School in 1849. Tudor, in grey granite; later alterations
and additions.

SAMUEL DOUGLAS' FREE SCHOOL, King Street. Now in other 113
use. Brute classical, by *John Henderson,* 1834. Single-storey, in
red sandstone ashlar, of seven bays by three. On the S front,
broad anta pilasters between the windows, which are dignified
with panelled aprons. The central entrance bay is emphasized
by a heavy parapet pierced by narrow roundheaded arches. On
the corners, panelled square blocks. Rising from the centre of
the roof is a square stone belfry. At its corners, panelled piers
surmounted by panelled block finials. Each face between the
piers is shallowly pedimented, the front intended for a clock,
the sides louvred. Plain late C19 additions at the back.

TOWN HALL, Victoria Street. Provincial classical of *c.*1800.
Two storeys of painted rubble. Three-bay front with round-
arched doors (two now converted to windows) at the ground
floor, Venetian windows above. S tower with roundheaded
windows and a weathercock on the short ogee-profile spire.

YOUTH HOSTEL, Millcroft Road. A former school, by *J. A.
Macgregor,* 1907. Plain with broad eaves.

DESCRIPTION

At the W end of the Bridge of Cree (*see* Public Buildings, above),
a MONUMENT to Randolph, ninth Earl of Galloway, erected
in 1874–5. *Richard Park* produced the design, *John Rhind* the
sculpture. Mechanical Gothic. Tall gableted base, its buttresses
topped by shield-bearing lions rampant. Above, an octagonal
nook-shafted pier with a gableted spire top crowned by a cross.
On the front of the base, a relief bust of Lord Galloway.

VICTORIA STREET is a not very distinguished architectural
mixture, mostly of two storeys and C19. At its N end, opposite
the Galloway Monument, No. 78 is a gently Italianate mid-
Victorian red sandstone villa with exceptionally broad eaves.
On the E side, the tall and severe mid-C19 CLYDESDALE
BANK, its three-light ground-floor windows Georgian-survival.
Beyond it, the Town Hall (*see* Public Buildings, above). On the
W, the GALLOWAY ARMS HOTEL. Its front has three-light
ground-floor windows, which look early C19, but at the side is
a mid-C18 moulded doorpiece with a broken segmental pediment. At No. 69 Victoria Street, an early C18 doorpiece with a
lugged architrave and segmental pediment. The ROYAL BANK
OF SCOTLAND, by *James M. Thomson,* 1873, is set back from
the building line, its red and white sandstone masonry breaking

the granite and render norm. Very tall three storeys with bare baronial detail. Beside it, Nos. 36–38, perhaps late C18, with cherry-cock pointing and club skewputts. Opposite, a pair of austere late Georgian buildings fronted with granite ashlar. There is a smarter version of Nos. 36–38 at Nos. 30–32, again probably late C18, with a columned doorpiece at the advanced and pedimented centre. Club skewputts and cherry-cock pointing, now covered in paint, at No. 28; cherry-cock pointing and a pilastered doorpiece at Nos. 22–26. At the s end of Victoria Street, on the l., No. 1 (MASONIC LODGE), sitting below pavement level, is late C18, with a columned and pedimented doorpiece. Across the street, the CENTRAL BAR, perhaps also late C18 in origin, but with an early C19 bowed addition, has three-light windows facing Church Lane.

ALBERT STREET continues the mixed character of Victoria Street. The prominently sited BANK OF SCOTLAND is early C19 but was remodelled in 1879 by *Wardrop & Reid,* who added a stone balcony above the Ionic columns and entablature which framed the twin doors (the l. now a window); corniced three-light windows at the outer bays. Also of 1879 are the overall urn-finialled balustrade and open-pedimented dormers. On No. 12, a heavy early C19 pilastered doorpiece.

DASHWOOD SQUARE is quite large but not very formal, despite the McMillan Hall (*see* Public Buildings, above) which fills its s side. In the square's centre, the WAR MEMORIAL by *R. W. Mackenzie,* 1921, a granite Celtic cross of routine character.

QUEEN STREET to the s begins well with the late Georgian No. 2, which has rusticated quoins, moulded skewputts and a pilastered doorpiece; chamfered NW corner at ground-floor level. For the Auction Mart, *see* Public Buildings, above. Then not very much. In PRINCES STREET, w of Dashwood Square, the old Reformed Presbyterian Church (*see* Churches, above).

JUBILEE ROAD leads N from Dashwood Square to CHURCH STREET and YORK ROAD, whose w sides are almost filled by the graveyard, two churches, the library and schools (*see* above). Among them, the BOWLING CLUB, its small Edwardian conservatory-like pavilion recently extended. In WINDSOR ROAD to the w, Our Lady and St Ninian (R.C.) Church (*see* above). Windsor Road's e stretch plunges downhill to ARTHUR STREET, running N beside the Cree. The Fire Station and Police Station (*see* above) are self-effacing. More assertive, though only of one storey and an attic, is the rubble-built No. 70, perhaps late C18, with large club skewputts and Victorian dormers. On KING STREET'S e side, No. 23 is a granite ashlar villa of *c.* 1800 with a Roman Doric aedicular doorpiece; club skewputts again. Still further N, Samuel Douglas' Free School (*see* above).

The Bridge of Cree (*see* above) joins the burgh of Newton Stewart to the parish of Minnigaff. Immediately e of the bridge is CREEBRIDGE, a little village laid out in the C18 with a short street running N from the main road. At its sw corner, an early C19 TOLLHOUSE, its semi-octagonal end disfigured by a C20 porch. On the opposite corner, the mid-C18 CREE INN, two storeys and three bays of painted rubble. On each side of the street, a terrace of housing. The W side is mostly single-storey and C19, but at its N end stands an earlier two-storey house of three bays, with widely spaced windows enlarged in the late C19 or early C20. It is built of rough granite ashlar with cherry-cock pointing; scrolled skewputts, one carved with a rosette. Over the door, a red sandstone panel bearing the initials JAMB and the figures 1769, a possible date for the house's erection; but is the stone *in situ*? On the street's other side, a corniced doorpiece, probably early C19, at No. 7. The late C20 Nos. 11–13 make only a half-hearted attempt to fit in. At the end of the street, the garden wall of CREEBRIDGE HOUSE, Tudorish of *c.*1840 with informal additions of 1908 by *Peddie & Washington Browne*.

MILLCROFT ROAD carries on N. In its straggly development, the mid-C19 FLOWERBANK, with a pedimented doorpiece and bay windows. To its N, a piend-roofed four-storey CORN MILL, built or reconstructed for John Black in 1823. Further on, the Youth Hostel (*see* above), converted from an Edwardian school. Then the tighter-knit OLD MINNIGAFF, still with a few much altered C18 houses but mostly C20. To its NW, Monigaff Parish Church (*see* Churches, above) prominently sited between the Penkiln Burn and the River Cree.

CORVISEL HOUSE, 1km. S. Smart early C19 house of two storeys over a sunk basement. Rusticated quoins, whin rubble walling, and a piended platform roof. Roman Doric aediculed door-piece.

STRATHMADDIE, 5.5km. SE. Crowstep-gabled two-storey three-bay farmhouse of the earlier C19, built of painted rubble. Advanced centre, with a quatrefoil panel in the top of the gable. Gableted dormerheads at the outer bays.

CAIRN, Boreland, 3.3km. N. Long cairn, probably of the second millennium B.C. It is a steep stony mound, *c.*20m. in length, the width tapering from E to W. At the E end, a concave façade formed of upright stones. The two small stones in its centre presumably flanked the entrance. The edges of the sides have been bounded by more upright stones, mostly pointed slabs.

CAIRN, Drannandow, 5.7km. N. Badly robbed long cairn of the third or second millennium B.C. It is a rough rectangle, *c.*24m. by 12.2m., containing five chambers. The one at the E is on an E–W axis, the four to its W are aligned N–S; each chamber is constructed of slabs and divided into two compartments.

CAIRN, Drumwhirn, 3.5km. NW. Constructed in the third or second millennium B.C., it is now a 3.65m.-high steep pile of stones, roughly circular, *c.*22m. in diameter. It may have been a long cairn which stretched S in a pear shape, but if so it has been robbed of its tail.

BARGALY HOUSE. *See* p. 117.
CUMLODEN. *See* p. 205.
GARLIES CASTLE. *See* p. 311.

KIRROUGHTREE HOUSE. *See* p. 396.
MACHERMORE CASTLE. *See* p. 431.
MERTON HALL. *See* p. 434.
MURRAY'S MONUMENT. *See* p. 455.

7060   OLD BRIDGE OF URR

Small group of rather randomly disposed C18 and C19 buildings.

BRIDGE. Probably late C16 in origin but widened to the N in
1772; the parapets were rebuilt in 1843. It is slightly humpbacked, rubble-built, of two roundheaded arches with triangular cutwaters. In the centre of the S side, two very
weathered red sandstone panels, the upper reputed to have
borne the royal arms of Scotland and the initials I R (for *Jacobus
Rex*), the lower a coat of arms and the date 1580.
MILL. Informal U-plan group, built of whitewashed rubble, probably mostly of the late C18. The S range beside the river contains
the waterwheel and grain mill. Single-storey cottage forming
an E range. On the N, a kiln and, at its W end, a cartshed,
perhaps late C19, with brick piers and a timber boarded loft.

OLD BUITTLE TOWER *see* BUITTLE CASTLE
AND OLD BUITTLE TOWER

3050   OLD PLACE OF MOCHRUM
                        7km. SW of Kirkcowan

97 House of almost magical appeal, created in the late C19 and early
C20 by the third and fourth Marquesses of Bute. The lands were
held by the Dunbars from the C14 until 1738, when Sir George
Dunbar sold them to Colonel William Dalrymple of Glenmure.
From him they descended to John, third Marquess of Bute, an
almost maniacal medievalizing restorer and remodeller of the
houses – Mount Stuart, Cardiff Castle, Castell Coch, Sanquhar
Castle and Rothesay Castle – on the hugely valuable Scottish and
Welsh estates he had inherited from his father in 1848, when he
was one year old.
    The buildings then standing at Old Place of Mochrum con-
sisted of two badly ruined tower houses, joined by one wall of
an otherwise demolished outbuilding which, together with the
foundations of other outbuildings, formed a roughly rectangular
courtyard. Between 1873 and *c.*1880 Lord Bute restored and
reroofed the two towers and joined them with a hall erected more
or less on old foundations; *Richard Park* acted as architect for
this work. In 1900, apparently commissioned by John, Earl of
Dumfries, almost as fervent an architectural enthusiast as his
father, whom he succeeded as fourth Marquess the next year,
Park prepared designs for new ranges on the courtyard's N and E

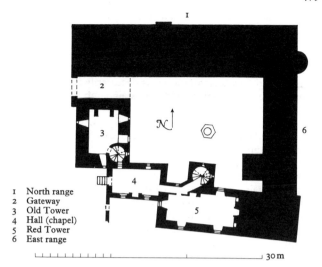

1 North range
2 Gateway
3 Old Tower
4 Hall (chapel)
5 Red Tower
6 East range

30 m

Old Place of Mochrum. Plan

sides.* These were completed externally in 1902, and the next
year Park was replaced by *R. W. Schultz,* who was responsible for
designing the Arts and Crafts interiors of the new ranges and of
the Red Tower, this work being finished in 1908.

The OLD TOWER on the courtyard's w side, which stood to
parapet level before its restoration in 1873–4, is probably C15.
Like the rest, it is built of whinstone rubble. Rectangular
(*c.* 8.99m. by 7.01m.), of three storeys and a crowstep-gabled
attic; the windows are almost all of the 1870s, but a couple of
first-floor slit windows in the E and W walls may be original.
At each corner, a round bartizan on heavy moulded corbels;
projecting from the bartizans, shelf-like drainage spouts. Crowstep-gabled SE caphouse, its form largely conjectural, giving
access to the battlement across the s gable. Another battlement
at the N gable but the side walls are now without parapets;
instead they enjoy late C19 crowstepped and rose-finialled stone
dormerheads. In the E front to the courtyard, a pointed door
of the 1870s.

Projecting from the Old Tower's SE corner is the HALL
added by Park in the 1870s. As first built, it presented crowstepped gables to the s and w, the w end containing a pointed
door reached by a forestair. But *c.* 1920 the Hall was converted
to an outwardly austere chapel; the door was built up, the
forestair removed, and the walls heightened and given moulded
rectangular windows. A new shallow-pitched roof was pro-

---

* Officially the client was the third Marquess of Bute, but his son is said to have
taken over the restoration of Old Place of Mochrum in 1898 or 1899, and the style
of the N and E ranges is quite unlike anything previously favoured by the third
Marquess in his long obsession with building works.

vided, hidden externally by a parapet broken by occasional crenelles and with a ball finial on its SW corner.

The RED TOWER, at the E end of the Hall, had probably been built early in the C17, the Old Tower perhaps being used afterwards as a jointure house. By the mid-C19 it was badly ruined and Park's restoration was necessarily based largely on conjecture. It is T-plan, with the stair jamb jutting into the courtyard from the centre of the N side. Main block of four storeys and an attic with crowstepped gables. This much seems to be based on fairly substantial evidence of what had originally existed. Apparently quite conjectural was Park's erection of a large crowstepped but chimneyless gable on each of the long N and S sides. Projecting from the N of these gables is the rectangular stair jamb. Its top, jettied out on continuous corbelling as a crowstep-gabled caphouse, is of the 1870s, although something similar is likely to have been there originally. In the caphouse's front, a round gunhole. In the W face of the stair jamb, a C19 pointed door. The panel frame above could well be C17; it encloses an uncarved block of C19 stone. Canted across the NW inner angle is a first-floor projection of the 1870s allowing passage from the stair to the Hall block without going through the Red Tower's first-floor drawing room. Hanging from this projection, a bell by *John C. Wilson & Co. Ltd*, 1903. The tower's roll-moulded windows are all by Park, their design possibly based on some fragments he found. On the S front they are arranged in a pattern which would be symmetrical were it not for the presence of a solitary rose-finialled dormer to the r. of the central gable. On the courtyard front, each side of the stair tower, Park placed a huge blind inverted keyhole 'gunloop', more Georgian castellated than C17 or late C19 Baronial in feeling.

N of the Old Tower is the COURTYARD'S gateway, provided by Park in 1900–2 on old foundations. It is a small two-storey crowstep-gabled block pierced by a roll-moulded segmental-headed pend arch. Of the same date are the N and E ranges. Both are of two storeys, with crowstepped gables and dormer-heads over the upper windows. To the courtyard they present an unaffectedly asymmetrical combination of pointed doors and rectangular windows, an evocation of a small and un-ostentatious medieval college. In the centre of the N range's N front, a projecting chimney is butted by a corbelled-out and crowstepped half-gable. Sticking out from this range's E gable, a half-domed semicircular stone oven, perhaps of the C17 but much restored. All this early C20 work is very simple but beautifully detailed: most of the windows are filled with leaded lights in an early C17 pattern, others with straightforward rectangular panes; the doors' iron hinges were executed by *Ernest Gimson* with abstract and foliage designs in his best Arts and Crafts manner. In the centre of the courtyard, a well, its octagonal stone base quite plain. Above is a wrought-iron wellhead designed by *Schultz* in 1902 and made by *Gimson*. Four ribs forming a thistle-finialled crown spire. On the ribs are scrolls, one on each rib topped by an iron bird. It succeeds in showing ingenuous charm without being twee.

The INTERIOR is disconnected, each part of the house being almost self-contained. On the ground floor of the Old Tower, the C15 kitchen, with a huge elliptically arched fireplace. The ceiling's wooden beams are supported on C19 stone corbels. Small first-floor hall with a pointed rubble-built tunnel-vault. The segmental-arched fireplace is of the 1870s. So too may be the pretty Gothic door, but it is more likely to belong to Schultz's work of 1903–8. On the second floor, a plainly finished sitting room (its stone window seats of the 1870s but perhaps following evidence that such seats originally existed here) and a bedroom. Top floor again very simple.

The chapel made out of the 1870s hall *c.* 1920 is austere. Plain panelling with a frieze of exposed rubble stonework at the top. Shallow-pitched wooden ceiling. Altar slab protruding from an off-centre niche in the E wall.

The Red Tower's interior is all of 1903–8 and designed by Schultz, with carved woodwork by *Joseph Armitage* and stonework by *H. W. Palliser*. The first floor is filled with the panelled drawing room (now a bedroom). Simple strapwork designs on the top panels under the frieze, which is carved with rinceau foliage and shields flanked by terms. Compartmented but light Jacobean ceiling. On the second floor, the W room is completely oak-panelled in an Arts and Crafts Jacobean manner, with carved thistles at the centre of the compartmented ceiling. Bed recess in the E wall. At the W, a small stone chimneypiece with a conical stone corbel lampstand projecting from its stone hood (the idea perhaps borrowed from Lethaby's hall at Melsetter House, Hoy). The E room is partly panelled. Carved roses form the centrepiece of the wooden ceiling. Again a bed recess, its arch springing from fluted pilasters. Another quite small stone chimneypiece but of Celtic inspiration, its frieze carved with flowers and fruits. Two more bedrooms on the third floor. The W has oak panelling, plain except for dwarf pilasters on the centre row of panels. The small stone chimneypiece has a frieze carved with prostrate thistles. In the E bedroom, slightly simpler panelling. At the sides of the chimneypiece, thin attached columns with thistle capitals. The lintel bears a stag's head and the date 1903; on the frieze, prostrate oak leaves and acorns.

The N range's interiors were also all designed by Schultz, with carved work again by Armitage and Palliser. Most of its ground floor is occupied by the dining hall (now drawing room), completed in 1903–7. Oak-panelled, with a trabeated ceiling. The beams are supported by corbels, those of the N wall decorated with the carved and painted coats of arms of successive owners of Old Place of Mochrum, those of the S with the arms of their wives. At the E end, a simple Arts and Crafts sideboard recess with vine leaves carved at the top. The W end has a huge stone chimneypiece; the overmantel bears the coats of arms of Crichton and Stuart (the family names of the Mar-

quesses of Bute) flanking the arms of McDowall, in honour of
John McDowall of Freuch, an ancestor of the third and fourth
Marquesses of Bute, from whom land in Wigtownshire,
although not Old Place of Mochrum itself, had been inherited.
An inscription records the restoration of the house by the Butes.
Frieze of large and rather blocky stylized thistles.

E of the dining hall is the kitchen, its wooden ceiling beams
carried on corbels. Segmental-arched fireplace filling the E wall.
W of the dining hall, but reached from the entrance pend, is
the former gunroom, probably intended to be used also as a
private sitting room. Stone fireplace looking like a late medieval
tomb recess. Elliptical-arched opening with a vine frieze. Above
are crocketed Gothic pinnacles, the central one carved with the
Bute coat of arms. Trabeated oak ceiling, the beams decorated
with little rosettes and resting on simple moulded corbels. In
the S wall, a stone aumbry, the spandrels of its cusped arch
carved with the relief of a spearman attacking a monstrous
beast. Pushing into the room's SE corner is the bowed projection of the wall of the turnpike stair behind, covered with
gunracks topped by slender balusters. To its N, a screen of
Jacobean-Celtic type.

The turnpike stair off the gunroom leads to the upper floor.
Its panelled and cove-ceilinged S passage is entered through a
wooden arch carved with the injunction 'Gang Warily' and the
date 1904. In the bedroom above the gunroom, the walls and
coved ceiling are panelled, and the ceiling is decorated with
thistles at the corners and a thistle pendant in the centre. Neo-
Jacobean chimneypiece, the wooden overmantel displaying the
impaled arms of Crichton-Stuart and Bellingham (for John,
fourth Marquess of Bute, and his wife, Augusta Bellingham).
The central bedroom was fitted up in 1905 for the fourth
Marquess's honeymoon. Again panelled and with a compartmented ceiling, but here decorated with seagulls. Fireplace
overmantel carved with a relief of the Old Place of Mochrum,
surrounded by trees, outsize birds and a gentleman in C17
dress; birds and rosettes on the frieze above. The E bedroom
of this range is also panelled. The coved ceiling has bosses
carved with flowers and foliage at the intersection of its ribs. In
the centre, a laurel wreath with swallows at the cardinal points.
On the fireplace overmantel, reliefs of monkeys, sheep, squir-
rels, birds, and a rose and a thistle. The E range contained
servants' bedrooms, well finished but without frills.

The rubble-walled GARDEN S of the house was laid out by
Schultz in 1903. Buttresses at the external face of the E wall; on
its top, boulders like rough ball finials. Semicircular slabs on
top of the other sides. At the SE corner, a quartet of angle
rounds provide a martial flourish. The stone-paved paths form
a star shape. At its centre, a sundial, the octagonal pedestal
inscribed 'JCS [for John Crichton-Stuart, fourth Marquess of
Bute] AD 1905'.

OLD PLACE OF MONREITH

3040

3km. NE of Monreith

Harled laird's house built for the Maxwells of Monreith, probably at the beginning of the C17. Two storeys and an attic. Irregular cruciform plan, with a wing projecting from the centre of the E side and, on the W, a conical-roofed rounded stair tower looking as if it had been pushed off-centre by the big wallhead chimney to its r. In the stair tower, two moulded round shotholes, one low down, the other high up. In its N segment, a moulded door, the lintel C17, the jambs reinstated by *Stewart Tod* in 1985. Some comfortably sized C17 windows with moulded surrounds at the first floor, but most have been Georgianized. Over the attic windows, stone dormerheads of 1985; something of the sort must have existed originally. In the E wing's gable, a small oval opening, probably a gunloop. Just above the S gable's first-floor window, a symmetrically arranged pair of stones crudely carved as human heads. They are unlikely to be *in situ* and were probably skewputts. Inside, big moulded stone fireplaces in the ground-floor kitchen (with an oven in the l. ingo) and the first-floor hall.

ORCHARDTON HOUSE

8050

2.2km. NE of Auchencairn

Austere and unmartial Baronial-manorial mansion house built in 1881 for William Douglas Robinson-Douglas, who had inherited the estate three years before. Three storeys, a basement and attic, all built of grey granite rubble, hammerdressed except for a patch at the NE corner which may be a remnant of the house's late C18 predecessor. The shape is basically an L, with a NE jamb, but projections sprout from it to give irregularity on every side. At the W end of the main (N) front, a projecting wing; in its crowstepped gable is the principal door, its Artisan Mannerist surround topped by panelled obelisks and strapwork framing a panel which bears Robinson-Douglas' coat of arms and initials and the dates of his birth and death. Higher up, a corniced frame containing a panel with the date 1881. At the jettied top floor, a canted oriel window; the base of its continuous corbelling is carved with the figure of a knight, the bottoms of the mullions with foliaged knots, their tops with human heads peering out from the frieze under the parapet. At the E end of this front, another crowstepped gable, but barely advanced and flanked by round turrets. The jamb's E end is again crowstepped. On its S side, Jacobean pedimented stone dormerheads. At the S end of the main block's E elevation, a shallow bay window, its corners rounded but corbelled to the square under the parapet. Crowstepped gables at the ends of the S front. Projecting from the more boldly advanced of these gables (the E), a canted bay window. Steeply pedimented Jacobean aedicule framing the attic window. The other gable's

canted sides are corbelled to the square under the attic. At the
main block's W corners, round towers, the one at the N a storey
taller than the one at the S. Both towers have jettied top floors
and fishscale-slated conical roofs. The rest of the detail is
restrained. Stone mullions and transoms at the larger windows,
cannon spouts projecting from the S front's parapet, rose and
thistle finials on the gables and stone dormerheads, bargeboarded wooden dormers to the N, W and S. Low service wing
to the W.

The interior is of generally Jacobean character, although the
entrance hall has a canopied stone fireplace which evokes an
earlier date. Set into the entrance hall's W wall, an elaborate
late medieval AUMBRY, probably of the C15. At the sides,
moulded corbels support pilaster-shafts, their fronts panelled
with two tiers of blind arches under circles. Above the gabled
tops of the pilasters, big but weathered crocketed pinnacles,
now truncated. In the centre, over the aumbry's roundheaded
opening, an ogee hoodmould rises to an exuberant fleur-de-lis.

On the principal floor, a broad passage, off which rises the
Jacobean great stair, heraldic stained glass in its four-light
window. Wooden chimneypieces with pedimented overmantels
(intended to contain paintings) in the passage and the dining
room at the house's SW corner. The SE drawing room was
redecorated in a sort of Georgian-revival manner c. 1920, when
it was given its high panelled dado, chimneypiece and curtain
pelmets, incongruous company for its 1880s ceiling.

W of the house, a mid-C19 rubble-built STABLES courtyard.
In the centre of the W range, a pyramid-roofed tower with a
pedimented door; its upper part has been a doocot. Pedimented
Doric portico at the W end of the S range, now framing a
window but probably not *in situ*. Did it come from the C18
house?

E of the house, a WALLED GARDEN, probably of the late
C18. On three sides, rubble walls faced internally with brick;
the fourth wall is all of brick. – In scrubby woodland to the NE,
a roofless seven-sided Gothic temple FOLLY of c. 1800. The
external render on its brick walls is lined out as ashlar to match
the dressings. Parapet decorated with blind quatrefoils and
rising into a merlon at each corner. Pointed openings (two
blind) in the faces.

ORCHARDTON TOWER

8050

1.7km. S of Palnackie

66 Roofless but well-preserved tower, probably built for John Cairns,
custumar of Linlithgow, who obtained sasine of the lands of
Irisbuitle or Orchardton in 1456. It stands on the N side of a
small courtyard which has been bounded on the S and W by
stone buildings, now much ruined but probably all originally
of two storeys; a ground-floor room at the SE corner is still
partly covered by a tunnel-vault. The tower, detached from

these ranges, must have contained the private apartments of the laird.

Uniquely for a freestanding medieval tower in Scotland, it is circular (c. 8.5m. in diameter). The tapered rubble walling rises unbroken by stringcourses to the simply moulded corbels under the uncrenellated parapet, which is carried up as a gabled caphouse over the internal SE stair. At the base of the SE segment, the opening of a drain which served the upper floors' garderobes; their presence, like that of the stair, is disclosed by small windows regarded as too unimportant to have dressed margins. Similarly small and crude openings light the ground floor. The main windows of the three upper floors are rectangular, with chamfered surrounds. Round-arched ground-floor door on the W. Pointed first-floor S door, the bottom of its stone forestair still surviving. This door was replaced, probably in the C17 or C18, when the first-floor E window was converted to a door and a new forestair was provided on that side.

Inside, the ground floor contains a rectangular tunnel-vaulted store room with no direct communication to the floors above. On each of these upper floors, a circular room. The wooden floors of the top two storeys are now missing, but a generous scarcement is provided in the wall for the second floor's joists. In the first-floor room, a W fireplace. Beside it, a gableted trefoil-headed piscina. Stone seats in the SW window embrasure. Narrow rectangular door at the SE; on its l. jamb, a flat-topped conical corbel carved with foliage, probably a lamp stand. This door opens into a tiny lobby at the foot of the turnpike stair which rises in the wall thickness to the upper floors. Off this lobby, a garderobe with a drain and lamp recess. At the second floor, another W fireplace. Plain aumbry at the N. N and S windows, both with seats. The stair door is pointed. Beside it, a rectangular door into the garderobe, which is again provided with a lamp recess. On the top floor, a small fireplace beside the rectangular door to the stair. Plain aumbry at the NW; N window. Stone-slabbed parapet walk reached through the caphouse; it is drained by weep-holes.

ORCHARDTON MAINS to the N. Simple painted rubble farmhouse of two storeys and three bays, probably late C18. Contemporary rubble-built farm offices adjoining.

ORROLAND

2.6km. SE of Dundrennan

In its present form, a neat harled laird's house of c. 1800. Two-storey main block of three bays by two, topped by a high piended roof. Bowed porch at the centre of the S front, probably an addition of c. 1900. The back is rather altered, with one ground-floor window enlarged to two lights. Beside this window is exposed a roll-moulded mullioned window of two round-headed lights (their heads blind). It may be C16, and it is likely that the present building has developed from an earlier house which has been completely remodelled and doubled in size to the S. Informal L-plan W wing, probably of the mid-C19, though there are two roll-moulded doors (one now a window) in the W wall which look like re-used work of the C16 or C17.

PALNACKIE

8050

Small village near the mouth of the River Urr. In the C18 and early C19 this was the port for Castle Douglas, but it declined after the opening of the railway to that town in 1861. C19 vernacular houses of painted rubble and some C20 incomers.

HARBOUR. Small rectangular basin constructed *c.* 1850; the walls are revetted with a variety of materials behind their timber facing.

BARLOCHAN HOUSE, 0.3km. NW. Hyperactively castellated small country house of the later C19, with a slender tower at the NW corner.

ORCHARDTON TOWER. *See* p. 484.

PARTON

6070

Edwardian hamlet of estate workers' housing, built by B. Rigby Murray, owner of Parton House,* with the Parish Church just to the SE.

PARISH CHURCH. By *Walter Newall*, 1832–3. Large but simple box, built of whin with red sandstone dressings; hoodmoulds over the depressed-arched windows. At the N gable, a battlemented tower of three stages, and a small porch in each inner angle. Inside, a coved plaster ceiling crossed by wooden beams, with one running along the centre. These spring from Tudor corbels; floriated paterae at the intersections. – FURNISHINGS mostly of the late C19 or early C20, but some box pews in the NE corner are probably of 1833. – At the W wall's E end, MONUMENT to Ebbie Gray or Murray †1892. Tiles painted with an angel and set in a brown tile frame.

Inside the NE porch, the fragment of a stone SLAB carved with the well-preserved relief of the lower part of the effigy of a priest, his chasuble richly embroidered, his stole unusually wide. It may be early C16.

To the E, now forming part of a C19 burial enclosure, is the surviving E gable of the OLD PARISH CHURCH (*see* the Introduction, p. 37), said to have been built in 1592.‡ In the gable, a segmental-arched window now filled with a pair of Victorian Gothic lights. On top, a sturdy bellcote incorporating a stone inscribed 'LAVS DEO/1635', a plausible date for the

---

* Demolished in 1964.
‡ According to *The New Statistical Account of Scotland* (1845). But the *Fasti Ecclesiae Scoticanae* states that the church was rebuilt in 1534.

bellcote. Built into the gable but apparently not *in situ* are two moulded corbels with badly weathered foliage decoration. – Just E of the Old Parish Church, the GRAVESLAB of the Rev. Samuel Spalding †1712, high-relief reminders of death carved at the bottom. – S of the Old Parish Church, a pair of pilastered C18 HEADSTONES, with angels' heads (souls) at their top. – On top of the graveyard wall's SE corner, ARCHITECTURAL FRAGMENTS. Two are heraldic lintels, one dated 1694; the third is a carved head. They could all be C17.

LOCH KEN VIADUCT, 1.1km. NW. Seven-span railway viaduct, by *B. & E. Blyth*, 1859–61. Roundheaded outer arches of bullnosed red sandstone. The three central bowed-truss spans over the loch are of iron carried on stone drums.

DESCRIPTION. Picturesque L-plan terrace of single-storey-and-attic cottages built in 1901. Gabled porches and bargeboarded dormers, all with pinnacled ball finials. Behind, a brick-built communal lavatory; octagonal, originally with a door in each face. It was converted to a summerhouse in 1992. At the W end of the terrace, the OLD LAUNDRY, also of 1901, with a wooden-sided tower, a weathervane on its slated pyramid roof. At the E end, a HALL of 1908, with half-timbering stuck onto its boarded walls; roof of red corrugated iron. Over the door, a metal sign bearing the motto 'FLOREAT PARTONA'.

MOTTE, S of the Parish Church. Presumably constructed in the C12 or C13. Truncated cone, *c.*8m. high, its summit *c.*16m. in diameter. It is circled by a 7m.-wide ditch.

BARWHILLANTY, 2.7km. E. Overgrown suburban villa, by *H. Thompson*, 1886, with a pyramid-roofed tower over the entrance. Service wings at the back have been demolished. (Elaborate interior.)

AIRDS HOUSE. *See* p. 90.

PENNINGHAME HOUSE

2.3km. N of Challoch

Baronial-Elizabethan mansion house, by *Brown & Wardrop*, 1869, built of whin with creamy sandstone dressings. Two storeys and an attic, the top windows gableted. Battlemented three-storey square tower at the SW corner. At its base, the roll-moulded door, under an heraldic panel. The rest is polite but unexciting.

PENPONT

Sizeable village which developed in the early C19 from the existing hamlets of Penpont, Townhead, Brierbush and Burnhead. Much of this new population had been displaced from the land by the amalgamation of farms.

PARISH CHURCH. By *Charles Howitt*, 1867; *see* the Introduction, p. 44. Big buttressed Gothic cruciform, built of hammerdressed red sandstone ashlar. Tall hoodmoulded lancet windows; at each gable they are placed in a stepped three-light arrangement. Eaves band of polished ashlar projected on moulded corbels. Angle-buttressed NE steeple. Three-light belfry opening in each face of the tower, whose eaves band is again projected on corbels, here with a Romanesque appearance. Broached stone spire with big gableted lucarnes.

Ashlar-clad interior, with hammerbeam roofs providing a display of intersecting carpentry over the crossing. – Early C20 PEWS. – The chancel was given simple pine PANELLING and an Art Nouveauish COMMUNION TABLE by *J. Jeffrey Waddell & Young* in 1923. – Also of 1923 are the FONT, an octagonal oak pillar with carved acanthus leaves at the top, and the routine late Gothic PULPIT. – ORGAN by *Forster & Andrews*, 1875.

CHURCHYARD. SW of the church, a cast-iron MONUMENT to Agnes Hay †1875, a scroll-sided pedestal carrying the figure of a boy lying down with a lamb. – E of the church, the HEADSTONE of the Rev. James Murray †1735, its front carved with caryatids at the sides and an angel's head (the soul) at the top; in the centre, a monogrammed cartouche surrounded by emblems of death. – Beside it, a big MONUMENT to the Rev. Samuel Austin †1669.* The base has projecting ends panelled and carved with ovals. This carries a basket-arched frame for the inscription, flanked by fluted pilasters. On top of the entablature, a steeply pedimented panel, the panel and pediment carved with grisly reminders of mortality. – To the E, two HEADSTONES (to William Hislop †1771 and James Hyslop †1778), both aedicular with fluted pilasters and open pediments containing angels' heads.

SCHOOL. Cottage-Tudor school and schoolhouse of 1844–5; the school was extended N in 1864, the schoolhouse enlarged by *Charles Howitt* five years later.

DESCRIPTION. The E end of MAIN STREET begins with mid-C19 cottages. Among them, ELMBANK has elaborately barge-boarded dormers and a gingerbread porch. In the centre of the village, the WAR MEMORIAL, a life-size bronze of a soldier by *Kellock Brown*, 1920. It stands beside the road leading S to the school and Parish Church (for these, *see* above). Main Street's scale now rises to two storeys. On the N side, a pair of late Georgian houses (Nos. 1–2 THE CROSS), both with corniced porches, No. 2 now rendered and with altered windows. No. 1 is of red sandstone ashlar, its corner to Marrburn Road chamfered at the ground floor and corbelled to the square above, a feature repeated at the roughly contemporary houses on the other corners of Marrburn Road and Keir Road. In MARRBURN ROAD to the N, ALBURY, a pair of cottages converted to a single house, is dated 1831. Further up, on the l., THE SMITHY, early C19, built of white-painted rubble, with an exceptionally wide door. On Main Street's E corner with Corse Brae, the plain Tudor MOOR HOUSE of 1888. On

* The present C20 inscription wrongly gives his date of death as 1694.

the W corner, the early C19 VOLUNTEER ARMS HOTEL, with a deep fluted frieze under the pediment of its doorpiece. Behind CORSE BRAE'S C19 cottages, a former GRAIN STORE of *c.* 1850 with a bullseye window in each gable. Further N, BURNBRAE HOUSE of *c.* 1840, its front of red sandstone ashlar with rusticated quoins. The entrance is recessed within a rusticated basket arch, infilled at the top above a lintel supported by fluted Doric columns. A little W of the village, SCAURBRIDGE HOUSE, built as a Reformed Presbyterian manse, *c.* 1840, with a pilastered doorpiece. Beside it, its plain and much altered former CHURCH of 1791.

CAPENOCH. *See* p. 154.
ECCLES. *See* p. 302.

PHYSGILL HOUSE   *4030*
1.6km. SE of Glasserton

The present form of the building is by *A. C. Wolffe,* 1958, but it incorporates earlier fabric. A late C17 house here was remodelled and greatly extended to the S *c.* 1790 to form a smart and gently classical E-facing villa. The work of 1958 removed almost all the late C18 addition and provided a conjectural new elevation for the re-exposed C17 S front. This is harled and of three storeys. Three bays, the W slightly recessed and gabled. To the N, a wing of two storeys, built on top of what had been a low NW service wing, which was infilled with material from the demolition. S of the main block, a piend-roofed single-storey pavilion formed from the NE corner of the late C18 addition, its upper floor removed. To the W this presents an overarched pedimented window, a reminder of the quality of the late C18 work. Below this window, a pair of doors to a garage made in the C18 basement. The main block's N front is much as it was before, the windows Georgian and regularly spaced. Here the basement, otherwise hidden, is partly exposed. The 1958 work was honoured with a Civic Trust commendation for 'reconstruction'.

PLUNTON CASTLE   *6050*
2.4km. N of Kirkandrews

Roofless tower house of granite rubble, probably built for the Lennoxes of Plunton in the later C16 to replace an earlier house on the triangular site, which is well defended by the Plunton Burn on the W, a ditch on the N and a second burn on the E. The present building is L-plan, with a SW stair jamb. Round turrets survive on the NE and SE corners; there has been a third turret at the NW. Plain gunloops on the ground floor of the main block. The windows above, where not robbed of their dressings, have simple rounded margins, and their glazing grooves show that they have contained fixed lights above shutters.

On the ground floor are two tunnel-vaulted store rooms, the N entered from the exterior, the S from the jamb containing the remains of the turnpike stair. In the first-floor hall, a W fireplace with a plain aumbry on its l. The two storeys above have had wooden floors. There are fireplaces in both gables on each floor, so they presumably each contained two rooms; those of the attic enjoyed the use of closets in the turrets.

PORT LOGAN

0040

Village and harbour, both begun on the estate of Colonel McDouall of Logan in the early C19. Short row of housing along the shore, more houses on the hill above.

FISH POND, o.8km. N. A natural, approximately circular pool in the rocks with a narrow inlet from the sea. It was artificially deepened in 1800, provided with a sluice-gate and enclosed by a crudely battlemented wall on the clifftop. Contemporary cottage, now rather altered, with crosslet 'arrowslits' and a battlemented round tower pierced by a Gothick window.

104 HARBOUR. Built in 1818–22 under the superintendence of *John Young*, its main features corresponding with proposals made by *John Rennie* in 1813. Curved boulder breakwater ending in a pier of rough ashlar. On the end of the pier, a round granite LIGHTHOUSE built in the 1830s, of three stages, its stone lantern crowned by an ogee-domed top. Inside, a fireplace in the ground-floor room. – Under the steps to the pier's parapet walk beside the lighthouse, a narrow room containing a two-seater LATRINE.

SCHOOL, o.8km. N. School and schoolhouse of *c*.1860, built of whitewashed rubble, the gables topped by ball finials.

KILLUMPHA. *See* p. 356.
LOGAN HOUSE. *See* p. 429.

PORTPATRICK

0050

Burgh of barony founded on the shore of a bay in 1620 but quite insignificant until after 1774, when a pier was built. Hopes that the harbour and town might develop as the main Scottish port for trade with Ireland continued until the 1830s, but the cost of the proposed harbour works and the naturally better-favoured position of Stranraer meant that they were not realized. Portpatrick's population rose only to about 1,200 in the mid-C19 and fell to half that by 1900; the decline was not arrested by the arrival in 1862 of the railway (closed in 1951). It is now a quiet resort, golf the main attraction.

CHURCHES

FREE CHURCH, School Brae. Now a hall. By *Richard Park*, 1886–7. Mechanical early Gothic, the gable front making little attempt to disguise the breadth of the box behind. NE tower broached to an octagonal clock-stage, its heavy corbelling intended to carry a spire.

OLD PARISH CHURCH (ST ANDREW'S KIRK), St Patrick Street. Roofless rubble cruciform kirk built in 1628–9; the date 1629 is incised on a skewputt of the chancel. Rectangular windows, their mullions removed in 1791. Doors in the W wall of the N transept, the S transept's gable, and (blocked) in the nave's S side. Round W tower, formerly harled, clearly earlier 19 than the church, whose construction has blocked its windows; the moulded margins of these windows suggest a C16 date for the tower. Four storeys, with a second-floor stringcourse. On top of the roof, a slated round cupola added by *Robert Montgomery*, mason, and *Alexander Robison*, wright, in 1791.

GRAVEYARD. Immediately W of the church, a crude MONUMENT erected by William Donaldson in 1751, according to the inscription on its top upright stone, which also bears the verse:

THANK MY GOD FOR POUERTY FOR RICHES & [FOR] GAIN FOR
GOD CAN MAKE A RICH MAN POOR A POOR MAN RICH AGAIN

PARISH CHURCH, Main Street. By *William Burn*, 1840–2. Big broad late Gothic rectangle, built of coursed whin with rough cherry-cock pointing. At the corners, angle buttresses, each jostled by a buttress at either end of the parapeted N and S walls. More buttresses against the E gable. Loop tracery in the windows. Tall W tower of three intaken stages under a corbelled battlement with cannon spouts; conical-roofed round turret at the tower's NE corner. NE porch.

Inside, the W GALLERY and E PULPIT are of 1932, when the Victorian PEWS were stripped of varnish. – STAINED GLASS. Darkly dramatic E window of three lights (Our Lord stilling the storm), by *J. & W. Guthrie & Andrew Wells Ltd*, 1918–19. – In the SE corner, a bronze BELL, dated 1748, from the Old Parish Church.

ST NINIAN'S CHURCH (Episcopal), Main Street. Harled hutchurch of 1937, now missing its W flèche.

PUBLIC BUILDINGS

HARBOUR. A weekly mail service between Portpatrick and Donaghadee in Ireland was established in 1662, and by 1677 there were two crossings a week; but Portpatrick's first pier (by *John Smeaton*) was not built until 1774. In 1790 a daily mail service to Ireland was introduced. After a survey in 1814–18, *John Rennie* recommended that the Portpatrick–Donaghadee route should be the principal Scotland–Ireland crossing, and in 1821 work was begun on a new harbour designed by him. His scheme was for a U-plan harbour with N and S piers, each with a

lighthouse, running out from the shore, the N pier's end being
joined by a breakwater to the rock of McCook's Craig. The S
pier was completed in 1836, but the need to deepen the harbour
for steam ships, which had by now replaced sailing vessels on
the Scotland–Ireland route, and to repair the S pier after a
storm in 1839, pushed the cost of the full scheme to such a
height that work on the incomplete N pier was abandoned. The
railway from Stranraer to Portpatrick, with a branch line to the
harbour, was opened in 1862, and in 1859–66 a rectangular
basin (designed by *Hannay*) was formed behind the stub of
Rennie's unfinished N pier. It is all of ashlar, the work of 1821–
36 built of Welsh limestone. On the S pier, a round brick
LIGHTHOUSE of 1896.*

SCHOOL, School Brae. By *Dumfries and Galloway Regional
Council*, 1979. Chunky but elegant, in brown brick with prominent thin buttresses.

DESCRIPTION

The burgh is roughly T-plan, the tail descending the hill to join
the cross-bar along the shore. HOLM STREET is the entry from
the NE. At its top, the Parish Church (*see* Churches, above).
Then housing begins; it is mostly C19, of one or two storeys,
harled or rendered. Just after the abutments of the demolished
RAILWAY BRIDGE (by *B. & F. Blyth*, 1859–62), the humble
St Ninian's Church (*see* above). On the r. side of the street, the
COMMERCIAL INN, early C19 with a chunky Roman Doric
columned and pedimented doorpiece, is followed by the bow-
ended IVY COTTAGE, also early C19 but dressed up with
bargeboarded Victorian dormers. On the corner of School Brae,
the old Free Church (*see* above).

The road now becomes MAIN STREET. On its l., the
DOWNSHIRE ARMS HOTEL, originally early C19 and of two
storeys, with a Roman Doric aedicular doorpiece, but made a
giant later in the C19 by the addition of two extra floors. ST
PATRICK STREET opposite leads to the Old Parish Church
(*see* Churches, above). Beside it, INGLENOOK (the former
Parish Manse); its two-storey front block is by *Archibald Paterson*, 1776, but it was altered in 1886–7 by *Richard Park*, who
probably provided the bargeboarded porch. Near the bottom
of Main Street, ROCKVILLE of *c*. 1800, with a bullseye window
and console-corniced doorpiece at the advanced centre. Below
it, HARBOUR HOUSE HOTEL, plain early C19 with a piend
roof. The end of Main Street bisects a curve of houses (NORTH
CRESCENT and SOUTH CRESCENT) overlooking the harbour
(*see* Public Buildings, above). They are predominantly small-
scale C19. On the hill above the S end of South Crescent, the
L-plan HOUSE O' HILL by *Ian Ballantine*, 1974–5, prominently
sited and tall, with steep monopitch roofs and chamfered
corners. Running back from North Crescent is BLAIR

* Rennie's stone lighthouse had been removed in 1869.

TERRACE of c.1900, a two-storey row, with harled walls and red-tiled roofs, enlivened by full-height bay windows.

A path from the end of North Crescent climbs up to the PORTPATRICK HOTEL by *James Kennedy Hunter*, 1905, much enlarged by *J. M. Dick Peddie* in 1906–7. This is a huge harled spread, its monotony alleviated by a few conical-roofed round towers. In HEUGH ROAD to its NE, the flat-roofed and rendered DRUMMUIE by *A. Maclean Goudie*, 1936. V-shaped but with a full-height bay window projecting from one arm to suggest a butterfly plan; balconies across the inner angle of the front.

DUNSKEY CASTLE. *See* p. 293.
DUNSKEY HOUSE. *See* p. 294.

PORTRACK HOUSE   9080
3.4km. N of Holywood

Picturesquely gableted and broad-eaved country house, mostly by *James Barbour*, 1879. Off-centre pyramid-roofed tower over the entrance, with a huge cross-shaped window lighting the hall to its l. This is an addition to an early C19 villa which survives behind, with hoodmoulded ground-floor windows and square upper windows with horizontal glazing. – In the garden, a single-storey octagonal LODGE (now a summerhouse) of *c.*1770, moved here from Mollance near Castle Douglas in 1970. (A remodelling of the garden to designs by *Maggie* and *Charles Jencks* is in progress (1996), the main elements provided by a wavy-headed drystone wall, large grassed mounds (the tallest a spiralling cone over 18m. high), and a diversion of the River Nith to make formally shaped inlets.)

PORT WILLIAM   3040

Sizeable village on the E shore of Luce Bay, founded *c.*1775 by Sir Willam Maxwell of Monreith.

FREE CHURCH, Church Street. Disused. Built in 1862–3 and remodelled in 1891 by *Richard Park*. Lancet-windowed whinstone box, with an awkward metal bellcote on the N gable.
HARBOUR. Begun in the 1790s with a harbour wall on the S and a quay on the W. In 1898 it was enlarged to the present kidney shape by *Henry H. Walker*, factor of the Monreith estate ('although he had not previously had any experience in such work'). He added the short pier and curved boulder breakwater at the NE. On the quay, a double-pile brick WAREHOUSE, perhaps of the mid-C19.
PRIMARY SCHOOL, High Street. Steep gabled school and schoolhouse by *Richard Park*, 1877, with a spired bellcast roof over the schoolhouse porch.
DESCRIPTION. The N end of MAIN STREET is unpromisingly bungaloid, but it soon settles down to mid-C19 single-storey-

and-attic housing on the E side; the W side has been left open
to the sea. Nos. 19–24 are two-storey, with fretted bargeboards
at the upper windows' dormerheads. Then a cottagey terrace,
in which WEST VIEW enjoys big club skewputts, Nos. 38–39
fretted bargeboards; cherry-cock pointing at Nos. 43–52. In
CHURCH STREET, climbing uphill to the E, the former Free
Church (*see* above) and its plain but substantial piend-roofed
MANSE (by *Richard Park*, 1891) behind. On reaching the shelter
of the harbour (*see* above), Main Street becomes two-sided and
the general scale rises to two storeys. Rusticated quoins and
club skewputts on the early C19 EAGLE HOTEL. No. 18,
opposite, with a twin-chimney gabled front, may be late C18.
More club skewputts on the mid-C19 BAYFIELD.

THE SQUARE is Port William's low-key Victorian commercial centre. On the N side, early C19 corniced GATEPIERS
to the harbour. Exiting from its SW corner, SOUTH STREET,
mostly single-storey-and-attic C19 vernacular. More promising
is HIGH STREET, climbing up to the E. Near its start, a rubble-
built MILL of *c.* 1800, with plenty of outshots projecting from
its two-storey main block. Further out, the villa-like BANK OF
SCOTLAND (originally City of Glasgow Bank), piend-roofed
Georgian-survival of 1858 with aproned windows and a pilastered doorpiece. High Street then bends. Off it to the r.,
MOUNT PLEASANT, a single-storey-and-attic terrace of the
later C19, leads to the garden of DOURIE BANK, a broad-
eaved villa of *c.* 1850 with a twin-gabled S front. High Street
ends with a cottagey mid-C19 terrace on the l. On the r., routine
housing ending with the Primary School (*see* above).

CUP-AND-RING MARKS, Balcraig, 3.7km. E. Rock face incised
in the second millennium B.C. with several complete cup-and-
ring marks, the largest with nine rings and an overall diameter
of 0.76m. To the S, another rock outcrop marked with ten
ringed cups, some with radial grooves; the largest also has nine
rings and is 0.75m. in diameter.

STANDING STONES, Drumtroddan, 2.7km. E. Line of three 3m.-
high standing stones erected in the second millennium B.C., the
centre stone now fallen. – To the NE, the faces of greywacke
outcrops have been carved with a variety of CUP-AND-RING
MARKS, some simple cups, others with rings, others with rings
and radial grooves often joining the cups.

1060   POWFOOT

Village begun *c.* 1800, beside the Solway.

HALL. By *W. Cox* of Liverpool, 1906. Red brick, with sparing
classical detail.

DESCRIPTION. Two main developments. At the W, single-storey
C19 cottages, mostly altered, and a gabled hotel of *c.* 1900 with
large later extensions. At the E, two-storey red-brick terraces
by *F. J. C. Carruthers*, 1900, redolent of suburban propriety
but not of seaside fun.

RAEHILLS HOUSE

0090

4.7km. NW of Johnstonebridge

Outsize and stylistically bizarre villa designed by *Alexander Stevens* 87 *Jun.* and built in 1782 for James, Earl of Hopetoun, tutor-in-law and heir of the mad third Marquess of Annandale. It was enlarged for John James Hope Johnstone of Annandale by *William Burn* in 1829–34. The 1780s house was L-plan, with the main block facing E over the valley of the Kinnel Water and a broad jamb projecting at the NW, all built of red Corsehill stone.

The E FRONT is of two and three storeys and eleven bays, the centre three forming a bow. This front is raised above a basement which projects in front of the ground floor as a terrace bounded by a parapet pierced with roundheaded arches. In the terrace front, paired windows framed by elliptical overarches. Before the drive was rerouted in the 1830s, the broad elliptically vaulted pend of the bowed centre allowed a carriage to be backed under shelter up to a door (now blocked) into the house. Across the whole length of the ground-floor *piano nobile*, a neo-Egyptian colonnade, an exceptionally early use of such a feature. It carries a pierced parapet along the straight end bays. Wrapped round the bowed centre at first-floor level are more neo-Egyptian columns, but these are thinner and support a latticed stone parapet. This centrepiece rises one storey above the rest and was originally intended to be topped by a dome. The decision to omit the dome does not explain why the wallhead above this neo-Egyptian work should be finished in the Adam castellated manner, with deeply crenellated battlements projected on delicate 'machicolation' and with small bartizans sticking up at the corners.

The same battlements and bartizans appear less incongruous on the N FRONT. Seven bays, the centre three slightly advanced and again carried one floor higher than the others. Round-arched ground-floor windows. At the centre bay, the two lower floors are framed by a rectangular overarch; from it projects a portico, again with neo-Egyptian columns and a pierced parapet. The use of battlements, bartizans and a higher centre-piece recurs at the jamb's W gable. It is built of rubble, not ashlar, but this suggestion of economy is belied by the three overarched Venetian windows on the ground floor and the three-light windows above, apparently oblivious of the castellation on top.

At the much narrower S GABLE of the main block, more castellation, but it is carried up at the centre in a ridiculous martial flourish. The dottiness must have been more endearing before Burn added an off-centre bay window to this gable and filled in the open court of the L. His addition is castellated but not at all light-hearted, its chief feature a squat square tower with an oriel window above its round-arched entrance door.

The plan of the INTERIOR is still largely by Stevens, the detail mostly Burn's. The 1830s principal entrance at the W end of the s front has a plain hall opening onto a corridor which Burn placed against the s side of Stevens' jamb to make a T with the existing corridor along the back of the 1780s main block. At the E end of Burn's addition is the dining room, austere with a black marble chimneypiece. At the s end of Stevens' main block, the drawing room. Its Frenchy chimneypiece of liver-coloured marble is a replacement of the 1830s. To its N, a sitting room with a bowed E end. Chimneypiece of brownish marble, also of the 1830s, its diagonally set jambs topped with consoles whose fronts are decorated with acanthus leaves, the sides with rosettes. Plain cornice and grained woodwork. Further N, a small and a large library, perhaps made from Stevens' dinner service room and dining room. The large library's frieze, decorated with big rosettes, looks like Burn's work, as does the brownish marble chimneypiece adorned with attached fluted columns. The stepped tops of the bookcases hint at pediments. w of the main C18 corridor, two stair halls: Stevens', in his NW jamb, contains a plain geometric stair; Burn's, immediately to the s, is grander. It is square, with a coffered plaster dome whose centre is cut out to allow light to enter from the windows of its crowning drum-cupola. Leafy cast-iron stair balusters. At the first floor, roundheaded arches open into the corridor on the E; cantilevered landing across the stair hall's s side. w of this stair hall, the Venetian-windowed breakfast room. Chimneypiece with fluted quarter columns; more fluting and lozenges on the frieze.

Just N of the house, but set obliquely to it, late C18 piend-roofed STABLES, built of droved ashlar. Segmental-arched coach entrances (now blocked), small first-floor windows, and a simple cavetto cornice.

At the s end of the drive, a pair of battlemented early C19 GATEPIERS. A screen wall, also battlemented, joins the E pier to ST ANN'S BRIDGE, built in 1795 and widened in 1817. Broad segmental arch over the Kinnel Water flanked by small hoodmoulded arches. Battlemented parapet with round turrets at its ends.

RAMMERSCALES
1.6km. sw of Hightae

0070

86 Well-dressed but restrained mansion house erected in 1768 by Dr James Mounsey, the former Chief Director of the Medical Chancery of Russia, who had bought the estate ten years before. Deep block of three by five bays and three storeys, built of red sandstone ashlar droved to a corduroy texture. Rusticated quoins at the ground floor rising to the first-floor band course. Overall mutuled cornice, the parapet broken by balustraded sections; heavy chimneystacks at the corners of the piended roof's platform. The detail is concentrated at the E front. Plain lugged architraves to the ground-floor windows flanking the entrance. The door itself, with a lugged architrave and side-

lights, is recessed behind a screen of Roman Doric columns *in antis*. In each side of the recess, a niche. Corniced first-floor openings, the centre window tripartite, with a consoled pediment over the middle light and rosettes carved on the bases of the mullions. Moulded lugged architraves to the second-floor windows.

Inside, the vestibule opens through a Roman Doric screen into the stair hall. Oval stair with cast-iron balusters. At the top, the bowed w end broadens into a rectangle whose corners contain a pair of concave-fronted pedestals bearing busts. Main rooms plain but well finished, some of the detail perhaps dating from an early C19 remodelling. Probably of *c.*1850 is the second-floor library occupying the full depth of the s side, its w end bowed. Grained bookcases and plain black marble chimneypieces.

E of the house, an octagonal WELLHEAD, its spired roof topped by an urn finial. It may be late C18. – s of the house, a simple STABLE COURT of whitewashed rubble, built in 1767. The N range, facing the house, has a two-storey pedimented and ball-finialled centrepiece; its first-floor window is roundheaded. The ground-floor coachhouse entrance has been converted to a window. Gothick windows in the E gables of the N and s ranges. Also in the s range's gable, a re-used stone inscribed

PC MD

16 87.

The initials are presumably those of members of the Carruthers family, owners of the estate in the late C17. – Plain WALLED GARDEN, perhaps late C18, to the SE.

RAVENSTONE CASTLE

3.7km. SW of Sorbie

4040

Substantial mansion house, now (1996) in the course of restoration after many years of dereliction. It has developed in four principal stages. The first, perhaps of *c.*1600, when the estate belonged to the Kennedys of Blairquhan, produced a four-storey L-plan tower house, its jamb projecting at the SE. Near the N wall's E end, a gunloop under a roll-moulded slit window to the ground floor. The other windows (several now blocked) are also roll-moulded, including an unexpectedly large one (possibly an insertion of the next phase) on the ground floor of the jamb's E gable.

In 1645 the estate was acquired by the first Earl of Galloway. His grandson, Robert Stewart of Ravenstone, extended the house about thirty years later, filling the sw inner angle with a new block and remodelling the existing building. The result was an M-roofed house. Would-be symmetrical w front of two chimney-topped gables, but the gable of the late C17 infill is narrower than that of the original main block. Three bays (the earlier w gable windows built up), the early C17 ground floor demoted to a basement, and the central entrance placed at the *piano nobile* above. Linking the upper windows of the centre, a panel carved with Robert Stewart's coat of arms. The side windows of the new block carefully repeat the roll-oulded detail of the original. Moulded stone cornice along the sides.

A third stage of development occurred in the late C18 – perhaps in 1773 (the date carved on the ingo of a window), although the work looks rather later – when the house was enlarged to the E, the new block having full-height bowed ends. Probably at the same time the W front's windows were given new unmoulded surrounds and the entrance a skinny pedimented doorpiece flanked by sidelights and approached by a perron (later removed but now reinstated).

In 1874 Ravenstone was sold to the twelfth Lord Borthwick, who contributed the undistinguished fourth stage, extending the house yet further E. Presumably he was also responsible for the short length of sandstone cornice on the W front at the join of the twin gables and for the crowsteps placed on those gables' skews.

Little has survived of the C17, C18 and C19 interior, except for tunnel-vaulted stores on the ground floor of the tower house, which, surprisingly for its likely date, had no integral kitchen.

On the approach from the S, a GATEHOUSE is in course of construction (1996), designed and executed, like the restoration work on the house, by *Frank Renwick*, the present holder of the feudal barony of Ravenstone. Very broad arch flanked by a stair tower on the W, and on the E, a two-storey block, its lower floor a garage equipped with a 'gunloop' covering the drive. A parapet with a working machicolation is contemplated. A BARMKIN WALL will join the gatehouse to the mansion house.

1030   REPENTANCE TOWER
                        3.3km. NW of Brydekirk

70 Mid-C16 landmark, a tower set in a hilltop graveyard, commanding extensive views of the Solway plain and up Annandale. Almost certainly this is the 'watchtower of great height' near Annan which John, Lord Herries, the owner of Hoddom Castle (q.v.), was reported as building in 1565. It is almost square (*c.* 7.3m. by 6.4m.), of three storeys, built of good-quality red sandstone rubble. The C16 windows are either slits or small and squarish. In the S wall, a big first-floor C18 window, now built up. In the N front, and reached by a stone forestair, the first-floor door, its lintel inscribed 'REPENTANCE', possibly an injunction to those visiting the graveyard. At the wallhead, a course of continuous moulded C16 corbelling. It supports a cornice and parapet, both mid-C18 replacements; the uncrenellated parapet is decorated with rusticated quoins. Inside the parapet rises a stone-slabbed pyramid roof topped

by a chimney-like stand for a beacon, built of square-jointed ashlar. SE caphouse over the stair. All this is again probably C18 work. (Inside, the second-floor room, reached by a ladder, has a fireplace in the NW corner and is covered by a tunnel-vault. It has been converted to a doocot, probably in the C18.)

GRAVEYARD. To the E of the tower, a BURIAL ENCLOS-URE, its walls built of rough ashlar. Above the corniced entrance, a stone with a worn inscription and, immediately on top of this, another which records that 'This burial place being in a ruinous state. was taken over rebuilt and considerably enlarged & heightened in the wall by John Murray of Murray-thwaite 1800'. Beside this stone, an heraldic panel, probably C17. – Immediately SW of this enclosure, a plain HEADSTONE commemorating Charles Murray †1776, 'A NATIVE OF AFRICA SERVANT TO M.R MURRAY OF MURRAYTHWAITE'. – Some way to the S, the HEAD-STONE of Wileam Ree †1740, decorated with an angel's head (the soul). – To its SE, the HEADSTONE of William Irving †1741, carved with a skull and crossbones in high relief.

RHONEHOUSE   7050

Village whose C19 and C20 vernacular houses are mostly unpretentious, though one, of the mid-C19, boasts a columned and pedimented doorpiece.

HALL. Built *c.* 1900. Of rubble with pointed windows.

OLD BRIDGE OF DEE, 0.8km. W. Four-span rubble-built early C18 bridge. Semicircular arches and triangular cutwaters.

THREAVE BRIDGE, 0.7km. NW. Three segmental arches of hammerdressed granite spanning the Dee; rounded cutwaters. It was built in 1825 and widened in 1986–7.

BILLIES, 3km. SW. Piend-roofed Gothick farmhouse of the earlier C19. Pinnacled buttresses at the gabled centrepiece, which has a Tudor-arched door flanked by pointed sidelights; Y-tracery in the pointed window above.

DILDAWN, 1.5km. SW. Straightforward rubble-walled and piend-roofed villa by *Walter Newall*, probably built in 1813 (the date on rainwater heads re-used at the porch). Two storeys and a basement. Entrance (E) front of four bays, the centre two slightly advanced under a blocking course. The porch probably dates from the alterations made for Dr James Cowan, head-master of a Sunderland school, by *John Dobson* of Newcastle in 1852, but the Roman Doric portico projecting in front may be re-used original work. Also probably of 1852, a full-height recessed N wing. At the back of the original block, a central bow. The bay window to the l. is an addition, perhaps of 1852, as is the full-height canted bay window on the S side.

THREAVE HOUSE. *See* p. 550.

RINGFORD

Small village of C19 and C20 houses.

TONGLAND AND TWYNHOLM FREE CHURCH, 1.6km. S.
Disused. Tall harled box of 1843–4. Gableted bellcote and
porch at the W end. Roundheaded windows rising into gablets
at the sides. – Immediately across the road to the N, the mid-
C18 OLD BRIDGE OF TARFF, a humpbacked rubble-built
segmental arch. – To its E, the HIGH BRIDGE OF TARFF,
built in 1832, again a segmental arch but with parapets of
broached ashlar.

HALL. Late C19 and plain.

SCHOOL, 0.7km. SW. Now in other use. Multi-gabled school of
the later C19, a plain painted schoolhouse adjoining.

MARTYRS MONUMENT, 3km. NW. Obelisk on a pedestal, all
of hammerdressed granite ashlar. It was erected in 1831 to
commemorate C17 Covenanters. – Beside it, a HEADSTONE,
probably early C18, to the Covenanter James Clemet †1685,
the top carved with a skull and crossbones.

NEILSON'S MONUMENT, 3km. N. Large and very prominent
granite pyramid erected in 1928, the centenary of the patenting
of the hot blast furnace method of iron production by James
Beaumont Neilson, who lived nearby.

FARMS

CHAPEL, 1.9km. SW. Spikily detailed mid-C19 Tudor farmhouse. Simple whitewashed low steading.

KIRKCONNELL, 2.9km. NW. Late C18 harled farmhouse of two
storeys and three bays. Over the W ground-floor window, a
small panel carved with the coat of arms and initials of William
Gordon of Kirkconnell. – C19 farm buildings behind.

MEIKLEWOOD, 0.5km. S. Farmhouse of two storeys and three
bays, the chimneys on the gables framing the piended roof. It
was built in 1815 by *McKinnell & Coltart*, masons, and *Andrew
Kirk*, joiner.

ARGRENNAN HOUSE. *See* p. 109.

ROBGILL TOWER
1.4km. SE of Kirtlebridge

Comfortable but unexciting small C19 mansion incorporating a
mid-C16 tower house, sited in a bend of the Kirtle Water. The
tower, probably built *c.* 1540 for Cuthbert Irving of Robgill, a
scion of the Irvings of Bonshaw, lies at the NE corner of the
house. A drawing of 1823, when it was derelict, shows it looking
very like Bonshaw Tower (q.v.). The red sandstone coursed
rubble masonry of its N side and E gable is still visible. Tall
projecting plinth. The windows and top are C19 and quite
plain; they may date from *c.* 1830, when an addition, straightforward late Georgian with a bowed E end, was built on the S

side. A further W extension came *c.* 1860; it is faintly Elizabethan, with a canted bay window at its S gable and a tower
over the NW entrance. The battlement of this tower was altered
to a straight parapet in the mid-C20, when a bowed oriel
window was added to the W elevation of this block and some
additions were made on the E side of the house.

The interior is mostly C19 (the chimneypieces replaced in
the C20), but the tower's ground floor is largely intact. It is
entered by a roll-and-hollow moulded door, now opening off
an internal passage, at the C16 S wall's E end. Inside the
entrance, a lobby from whose coved stone ceiling hangs an
octagonal stone pendant carved with the IHS monogram, just
as at Bonshaw Tower. Small aumbry in the W wall. E of the
lobby, the well which contained the turnpike stair. The lobby
and stairwell nudge into the SE corner of the tower's ground-
floor kitchen (now dining room). This is covered by an ashlar
tunnel-vault and was originally lit by small windows in the N
and E walls; the E window is now blocked, the W supplemented
by a C19 opening. Large segmental-arched C16 W fireplace.
The shape of the C16 first-floor hall has survived, but the
plasterwork and woodwork are of *c.* 1830 and the W chimneypiece is C20.

S and E of the house, a stone RETAINING WALL of *c.* 1830,
with a battlement to prevent the inhabitants' falling into the
river gorge, whose defensive quality presumably dictated the
siting of the C16 house.

To the W, U-plan STABLES of *c.* 1860. In the centre of the N
range, a round-arched pend under a battlemented caphouse. –
W of the stables, a GARDEN, its stone walls faced internally
with brickwork, probably in the early C20, when the S wall is
said to have been replaced with railings and a glasshouse was
built along the E side. – At the entrance to the drive, a LODGE
of *c.* 1860 with mullioned windows and carved bargeboards.

ROCKHALL *0070*
2.9km. NW of Mouswald

Rubble-built three-storey laird's house, the earliest part said in
1610 to have been 'laitlie constructit' by Sir William Grierson
of Lag. This forms the present W range, a simple rectangle with
a rounded stair jamb projecting from its E side. In the jamb, an
entrance door, now converted to a window. In the early C18
the house was enlarged to an L-plan by the addition of a broad
NE wing. It was remodelled by *Alexander Crombie* in 1854–5,
a possible date for the enlargement and insertion of several
windows. At the NE range's W end, a door of 1915 by *J. M.
Bowie*, with an armorial panel above.

Inside the W range, the early C17 turnpike stair survives in the
jamb. Along the E side of this range, a narrow ground-floor passage; a small recess in the original outer wall probably indicates
a blocked window. Kitchen (now a bar) at the S end its vault of

timber and an insertion. The rest of the interior largely dates from a remodelling of 1880 by *James Barbour*. In the NE range, a neo-Jacobean stair, its bottom part removed in 1967, when an hotel function room was added behind.

ROSS MAINS

0080

3km. SE of Garvald

Small but architecturally smart rectangular mansion house built in 1728 for the third Duke of Queensberry. Two storeys over a partly sunk basement. Symmetrically placed chimneys on the piended platform roof. Five-bay s front, the masonry of rubble (originally limewashed) with V-jointed rusticated pilaster strips at the corners, their bases provided by projections of the moulded ashlar plinth. Cornice under the eaves, its frieze linking the lintels of the upper windows. Central entrance, the door's moulded architrave with a depressed ogee head a little broader than the jambs. This is framed by a console-corniced surround, its frieze decorated with foliaged panels. Above, a pediment with sloping sides which rise from volutes to a horizontal top provided by the sill of the first-floor window. In the tympanum, the arms of the Dukes of Queensberry (a winged heart under a crown) and their motto ('Forward'), together with the date 1728. The other elevations are plain; the rear was rather altered in the C19, when a low NW wing was added. (Interior mostly of the C19, but some 1720s features survive: a couple of bead-moulded chimneypieces in the W ground-floor rooms, a bolection-moulded chimneypiece in the first-floor E room, and re-used urn-shaped silhouette balusters at the stair landing.)

RUSCO TOWER

5060

4.4km. N of Gatehouse of Fleet

67 Tower house of *c.*1500, extended N in the C17; in 1975–9, after being abandoned for three-quarters of a century, the tower was restored, and the ruin of the N extension was tidied up by *W. Murray Jack*, with the owner, *R. Graham Carson*, acting as clerk of works. In 1494 John Carson (or Acarsane) made over to his daughter Mariota and her husband, Robert Gordon, the lands of Glenskyreburn and Over Pulcree, which included the site of Rusco. The tower itself, a smaller and humbler version of Cardoness Castle, was probably begun almost immediately; a 'mansion' here was recorded in 1504, and eleven years later a charter was signed at 'Ruschen'.

The tower is a severe rubble-built rectangle. The walls rise to a rubble parapet projected on two tiers of chequer-set simply moulded corbels, the lower corbels smaller than those above. The parapet's stone spouts are of the 1970s, cannon-shaped (copied from Hills Tower) on the entrance (E) front, U-shaped on the other sides. This may well have been the original arrangement, since spouts of *c.*1500 of both types have been found here, although the original cannon spouts were more chunkily detailed than the C20 replacements. The merlons are also of the 1970s, their design based on a view of the tower made in 1805. At the SE corner, a crowstep-gabled caphouse over the stair. Inside the parapet, a wall-walk, many of its stone slabs re-used. This goes round the crowstepped attic (reroofed with Angus stone slabs in the 1970s), which may be a C16 addition, perhaps replacing a flat roof.* Chamfered windows, mostly renewed in the 1970s, those of the two main upper floors corniced.‡ In the W and E fronts, ground-floor gunloops of inverted keyhole type, again 1970s replacements, their design copied from those at Cardoness Castle. At the bottom of the W ends of the N and S gables, exposed garderobe chutes. The N gable's broad segmental-arched ground-floor door is a 1970s replacement for a door into the C17 N extension. In the centre of the E front, the original, very plain entrance to the tower. Above it, a moulded frame containing a worn stone panel carved with two shields, the upper with unicorn supporters and apparently bearing the royal arms of Scotland, the lower a quartered coat of arms, probably for Gordon and Carson. In the panel's bottom r. corner, the carved letter 'G' is still visible. The upper corners seem to have contained numerals; one on the r. looks like an '8'.

On the S inner jamb of the entrance door, an incised rosette, possibly a very elaborate mason's mark. The door opens onto a vestibule in the wall thickness; its shallow segmental plastered vault was renewed in the 1970s. Off its N end, a guardroom, with a gunloop in the E wall, a rectangular recess (probably for a lamp) in the N, and a tall segmental-arched recess in the W. In the main part of the tower, the two bottom floors (ground floor and entresol) are covered by a single stone vault. On the ground floor, two store rooms entered from the vestibule through a pair of rectangular doors (the N built up). In the S room, a crude rounded recess of uncertain purpose is hollowed out in the SW corner's walling. In the SE corner of the tower, and entered from the vestibule, a comfortable turnpike stair. Just below the level of the entresol floor, a door opens off the stair into a narrow room (perhaps a guardroom) in the thickness of the S gable. Small S window. At the room's W end, a garderobe with a stone pedestal; irregular small aumbry at the E end. In the floor, a trapdoor to a prison below, again with a garderobe but no window. The tunnel-vaulted entresol is occupied by a single room. In its N gable, a small aumbry. The E window has a sill sloping down through the thickness of the outer wall and the vault. High in the S gable (clear of the guardroom) is a window with splayed jambs. Opening off the stair just above the level of the entresol floor, a small room

* The garderobe chute at the N gable's W end now serves no purpose, suggesting that there was originally a garderobe at the level of the wall-walk.
‡ The N gable's first-floor window is a 1970s replacement of a door inserted here in the C17.

in the thickness of the E wall. Segmental tunnel-vault. Narrow
E window; a rectangular aumbry to the N.

The first floor is occupied by the hall, its beamed ceiling
supported on corbels (renewed in the 1970s). Segmental-
arched embrasures to the windows, their stone seats renewed.
At the W window, the N seat serves as a step to the door into a
wall chamber which is provided with a little window to the
outside and a round listening hole or 'laird's lug' into the hall.
The N window of the hall, lower than the others, replaces a
door into the C17 extension. There was a broad embrasure here
(restored to its original width in the 1970s), but it is more likely
to have been for a buffet recess than a window. In the hall's E
wall, but placed curiously far S (i.e. away from the dais end),
is a large fireplace with moulded late Gothic jambs and capitals
but a corniced straight lintel. The plastered wall above is
enriched with a coat of arms flanked by the initials of the owners
of Rusco in 1494 and 1979. At the hall's SW corner, the walling
contains a garderobe equipped with a small window and a lamp
recess.

The second floor was originally one room but has been
subdivided. Restored stone seats in the ingoes of the S window.
In the W wall, a garderobe. The chimneypiece from this floor
is now at Rusko (q.v.). Plain attic, now also subdivided. There
have been a window and small fireplace in the S gable. A
restored window in the N gable.

Of the three-storey C17 addition, only the lower parts of the
W and N walls and the foundations of the E now survive. It
seems to have been of two dates; the second phase of construction included the addition of a projecting stair jamb at the
W, apparently replacing an earlier internal stair to its S.

RUSKO

5050

2.5km. N of Gatehouse of Fleet

Harled laird's house of *c.*1800, much extended in the C19 and
C20 and given a small battlemented tower at the front of the
original building, which was a piend-roofed block of two storeys
and three bays with a bow at the back. Above the front door in
the tower, a stone carved with the quartered arms of Gordon
and Carson; it came from Rusco Tower (q.v.) and is probably
early C16. Inside, in the entrance hall, a tall stone chimneypiece
of *c.*1500, brought here from the second-floor room of Rusco
Tower. It is a narrow version of the hall chimneypiece in that
house, with Gothic jambs and capitals and a corniced straight
lintel.

RUTHWELL

1060

Village of single-storey cottages, mostly rather altered. One
housed Scotland's first savings bank, founded by the parish minister, Dr Henry Duncan, in 1810.

RUTHWELL AND MOUNT KEDAR CHURCH, 0.8km. N. Painted rubble kirk with a complex building history. It began as a very long and very narrow medieval church (*c.* 29.3m. by 4.3m.), and in the late C17 the Murrays of Cockpool added a s burial 'aisle'. In 1801–3 the main block was recast by *Sanderson* of Dalkeith, who cut *c.* 9.1m. off the E end and broadened it to the N by 3m. The N apse (housing the Ruthwell Cross) was added by *Campbell Douglas & Sellars* in 1886–7, and in 1906 *James Barbour & Bowie* again recast the building.

The general appearance is largely of 1906. Round-arched windows containing paired lancet lights under circular tops; rose windows and round-arched doors in the gables. At the roof, bracketed eaves and metal ventilators. In the apse, narrow roundheaded windows of 1886–7. Urn-finialled birdcage bellcote of 1801 on the gable of the s 'aisle'; on the other gables, small ball-finialled 'bellcotes' with quatrefoil openings but no bells. The blocked rectangular windows still visible at the s 'aisle' may be C17.

Inside, the ribbed tunnel-vaulted plaster ceiling and panelled elliptical arch into the s 'aisle' are probably of 1801. Half-dome over the 1880s apse. – Plain PEWS introduced by *Alexander Crombie* in 1863. – STAINED GLASS. In the apse, three lights (SS. Hilda, Cuthbert and Aidan) by *Percy Bacon Bros.*, 1910–14. – In the body's s wall, one window (Our Lord and Nicodemus) by *Gordon Webster*, 1958. – In the gable of the s 'aisle', an heraldic window of 1907. – Under this window, a segmental-arched TOMB RECESS, its keystone formed by a panel bearing the arms of Murray; above, a big carved heraldic achievement of the Murrays, Viscounts Stormont, and the date 1687.

The apse contains the RUTHWELL CROSS, the most important work in Scotland of the Anglo-Saxon Jarrow–Monkwearmouth school of sculpture. Its date, like that of the Bewcastle Cross (Cumbria), some of whose detail is almost identical, has been disputed, but the likeliest is the first half of the C8, when the Anglians were firmly in control of the former kingdom of Rheged and established a bishopric at Whithorn. The original site is also uncertain, but it is not inconceivable that the Cross was designed to stand inside an Anglian church on the present site. The long and narrow dimensions of the previous church here suggest it was of Saxon origin; and in 1642, when the Cross is first mentioned, it stood inside the church, as presumably it had since before the Reformation. In 1644, following a decree of the General Assembly of the Church of Scotland, the Cross was pulled down and smashed. The fragments were left on the clay floor of the church to serve as seating until 1771, when the larger bits at least were moved out into the graveyard.

In 1802 the minister of Ruthwell, Dr Henry Duncan, re-erected these pieces in the manse garden, and in 1823 he carried out further restoration with the 'aid of a country mason', who provided new arms decorated with masonic symbols (the N face carved with a sun flanked by a cock and cow, the S with a triangle flanked by a whale and dragon), and put the broken head on back to front. In 1887 the Cross was moved into the church's newly constructed apse, where it stands as if in a drained paddling pool, its base embedded in concrete.

Each of the main faces of the shaft bears a ladder-like grid of borders carved with Latin inscriptions (only partly decipherable), which framed sculptured panels. On the panels of the S face (the present front), are the following scenes, from the bottom to the transom: the Crucifixion (badly damaged); the Annunciation; Our Lord healing the blind man; the washing of Our Lord's feet by the penitent woman; Mary and Martha; an archer. The iconography of the intermediate panels apparently relates to the Christian life (obedience to God's call, conversion, penitence, and action and contemplation).

On the N face (probably intended as the more important since it contains the largest panel), the panels display: an obliterated scene, perhaps the Nativity of Our Lord; the Flight into or Return from Egypt through the desert; St Paul the Hermit and St Antony of Egypt sharing bread in the desert; Our Lord in Majesty, his feet resting on beasts; a representation of the Holy Trinity;* two men, probably St Matthew with his symbol, a man. The iconography shows Our Lord's presence, whether in person or sacrament in the desert, his reception of the homage of the desert beasts, all this pointing to the revelation of the Trinity. This face seems to have been intended to be surmounted by the four Evangelists: two would have been at the ends of the original arms; the figure of St Matthew is apparently in position; and the figure of St John was carved on the top stone of the cross, but because this stone was re-erected back to front, the evangelist with his attendant eagle now faces S, and there is a large eagle on the N front.

On the Cross's sides, carved birds and beasts set among spiralling foliage, very similar to the decoration of the back of the Bewcastle Cross. Also on the sides, runes which spell out a version of an Anglo-Saxon religious poem, *The Dream of the Rood*. They were probably incised a little after the Cross was first set up.

GRAVEYARD. Immediately E of the church's 'aisle', a large HEADSTONE to Gilbert Couper, factor to the Viscount of Stormont, †1709. It is a wonderful display of crude vigour. At the front's sides, what may have been intended as obelisks. Centre carved with a coat of arms in a foliaged border. Frieze decorated with a thistle, roses and fruiting branches. On top, a segmental pediment of a sort carved with an angel's head (the soul) and a skull and bones. – Much more conventionally correct is the E wall's MONUMENT of 1832 to the family of Dr

---

* Although the figure of a man holding the *Agnus Dei* has usually been taken as a representation of St John the Baptist, the likely reconstruction of the inscription seems to make it clear that this panel represents the Holy Trinity (i.e. the man represents God the Father; the *Agnus Dei* represents God the Son; and the Holy Spirit, probably in the form of a dove, has weathered away).

Henry Duncan, with a pedimented centre and obelisk finials at the ends. – NW of the church, a MONUMENT to David Dickson †1806, a tall two-stage pedestal topped by an urn-finialled obelisk carved with a coat of arms. – Just outside the churchyard, a piend-roofed rubble-built HEARSE HOUSE of 1875.

ST JOHN'S TOWN OF DALRY   6080

A village, despite its name; it apparently began as a medieval hamlet (St John's Clachan) but developed from the late C18, when the Earl of Galloway offered building leases here.

DALRY PARISH CHURCH, off Main Street. By *William McCandlish*, 1830–2, and a prototype for his Glencairn Parish Church at Kirkland, of a few years later. Cruciform, the s limb provided by the tower; built of whin with painted sandstone dressings. Tall spiky pinnacles at the corners and on top of the gables. Pointed and hoodmoulded doors and windows, whose intersecting glazing bars contribute to the innocent Gothick appearance. Blind quatrefoil in the N gable, whose huge arched recess was converted to a glazed porch in 1976. Tower of three stages, with another blind quatrefoil over the door; on the corners of the battlement, gableted finials with pinnacled tops.

Inside, basket arches over the deep-fronted N, E and W galleries. – CEILING ROUNDEL with radiating acanthus leaves. – Very grand PULPIT with clustered shafts supporting the ogee-domed and crown-finialled sounding board. – Boxy PEWS. – CHAMBER ORGAN by *The Positive Organ Co. Ltd.* – Chaste black and white marble MONUMENTS of the earlier C19 to the Gordons of Kenmure, each with a flaming urn.

GRAVEYARD. Immediately SE of the church, the crow-stepped GORDON AISLE, built in 1546 by Sir James Gordon of Lochinvar and his wife, Margaret Crichton; their arms and initials are carved on a panel over the roll-moulded s window. Now freestanding, the 'aisle' was built as a s jamb to the church's medieval predecessor. Walls of whinstone rubble. Rounded margin at the w door. In the N wall, a now blocked roundheaded arch which opened into the medieval church. The NW corner of the 'aisle' has been chamfered, presumably in the 1830s, to allow a space between it and the present church. – To the E, a SESSION HOUSE designed in 1880 by *Thomas Bell*, land steward of the Earlstoun estate, with endearingly old-fashioned Gothick openings and spiky pinnacles. – From the session house to the road, a lime avenue.

Between the Gordon Aisle and the session house, C18 HEADSTONES, three carved with angels' heads (souls). The one commemorating Alexander McMichael †1762 also displays hearts, a rose, a thistle and a crown. A fourth stone, to James Douglas †1747 and his wife, Mary Douglas, †1789, has, at the top, a skull and crossbones under a winged hourglass and the figure of an almost naked man; in the centre, mason's tools under a winged heart. – Between the church and the Gordon

Aisle, a small flat STONE decorated with a skull and crossbones; it may be early C18. – SW of the church and in a much lower part of the graveyard, a late Georgian BURIAL ENCLOSURE with a round-arched entrance. It contains MONUMENTS to the Newalls of Barskiach, the earliest (to John Newall †1658) apparently the slab of a table stone, bordered with stylized foliage. – Immediately W, the top fragment of an early C18 HEADSTONE carved with crude reliefs of two human figures inside a roundheaded arch. – At the graveyard's NW corner, an early C18 TABLE STONE, the slab incised with an inscription to two Covenanting martyrs, Robert Stewart and John Grierson, and with a eulogy beginning:

> Behold.Behold a stone HERE's forc'd to cry,
> COME SEE TWO MARTYRS UNDER ME THAT LY!
> AT WATER OF DEE WHO SLAIN WERE BY THE HAND,
> OF CRUEL CLAVERHOUSE AND'S BLOODIE BAND.
> NO SOONER HAD HE DON THIS HORRID THING,
> BUT'S FORC'D TO CRY STEWART'S SOUL IN HEAVEN DOTH SING.

DALRY UNITED PRESBYTERIAN CHURCH, Main Street. Disused and derelict. Plain Gothic box, by *Campbell Douglas & Morrison*, 1899. Four-centred arched entrance with crocketed finials.

DALRY SCHOOL, Kirkland Street. Single-storey block in brick and drydash, dated 1931. It now forms an appendage to the unexciting extensions of 1966 by the *Stewartry County Council*.

EARLSTOUN POWER STATION, 0.9km. NW. By *Sir Alexander Gibb & Partners*, 1936; built as part of the Galloway hydro-electric scheme. Tall cream-rendered box with vertical windows.

OLD SCHOOL, Kirkland Street. Built *c.*1878. Tall single-storey schoolroom; attached to it, a two-storey piend-roofed schoolhouse with bracketed eaves.

TOWN HALL, Main Street. Built in 1859 but enlarged and completely remodelled in 1895–7. Built of whin with red sandstone dressings and red-tiled roofs. Slightly advanced centre carried up as a tower, its tall truncated-pyramid roof broken by gabled belfry openings.

DESCRIPTION. Set back at the entry to the village from the S, DALRY MANSE of 1828–9, its roundheaded door in a surround of Roman Doric columns and a cornice. The village itself makes a triangle, the main road forming its W side with the large but cottagey late Victorian LOCHINVAR HOTEL facing a white-painted farm steading. The triangle's E side is KIRKLAND STREET, containing the past and present schools (*see* above). The N side is MAIN STREET, with the churchyard entrance at its W corner; its houses are mostly examples of C19 vernacular, several with C20 alterations whose own vernacular may perhaps win affection in time.

MOTTE, N of Dalry Parish Church. Apparently artificial, formed perhaps in the C12. Truncated cone, *c.* 9m. high, surrounded by a ditch; fairly level roughly circular summit of *c.* 34m. diameter.

FARMS ETC.

ALLANGIBBON COTTAGE, 0.9km. N. Picturesque estate workers' housing of *c.*1900 for Milton Park (*see* below). Harled,
with red-tiled roofs and small windows; the Arts and Crafts
appearance is belied by concrete window lintels and mullions.
On the E side, a broad rectangular pend arch under a tile-
roofed first-floor passage, with walls of wooden latticing. –
Immediately W, ALLANGIBBON BRIDGE, of 1926 replacing a
bridge of 1816. Ashlar-faced and slightly humpbacked; a single
segmental arch over the Water of Ken.
FORREST LODGE, 8.5km. NW. Scots Arts and Crafts, by
G. Ramsay Thomson, 1910. Asymmetrical, with round towers
to suggest a laird's house; built of harled whinstone with dressings of Creetown granite.
MILTON PARK, 1.2km. N. Jumble of a house. The earliest part
is on the W, a harled two-storey *cottage orné* of the earlier C19,
with gablets and hoodmoulded windows. At its E end, a small
tower dated 1895; E of that, a big two-storey early C20 addition
whose half-timbered upper floor is boldly jettied out over an
Ionic-columned verandah.
OLD GARROCH, 3.4km. NW. Two-storey laird's house with roll-
moulded door and windows, probably built in the late C17. C19
additions at each end.

EARLSTOUN CASTLE. *See* p. 300.
GLENLEE PARK. *See* p. 323.
KNOCKNALLING. *See* p. 398.

ST MUNGO

1070

Ruin of an isolated parish church.

OLD PARISH CHURCH. Only the E gable, part of the S wall and
a stub of the N wall survive of the church built in 1754 by the
masons *Walter Dryden* and *John Patton*,* incorporating some
of the fabric of its predecessor. In the S wall, a (blocked) door,
its lintel dated 1754, and bits of two windows. Rectangular
window with chamfered margins in the E gable; it looks C17.
The stringcourse below could be late medieval. These remains
were converted to a burial enclosure *c.*1880. On its N wall, two
heraldic stones, probably C18, one carved with a skull and
crossbones.
   In the surrounding graveyard, a few early C18 HEADSTONES
decorated with heraldry and emblems of death. – At the SW
corner, a large MONUMENT to John Johnstone †1825, with
three blunt obelisks on the top.

PARISH CHURCH. *See* Kettleholm.
SCHOOL. *See* Kettleholm.

* *James Jardine* and *Andrew Mundell* were the wrights.

ST NINIAN'S CAVE

4030

2km. s of Glasserton

On the shore of Luce Bay, a cleft in the rock cliff (the collapsed outer part of the cave) with a tapering cave behind. It has traditionally been regarded as a retreat of St Ninian and seems to have been a pilgrimage attraction. On the w side of the cleft and cave are incised seven small crosses; some have arms expanding outwards and bosses at their intersection, another has cross-bars at the ends. They are probably of the C8 or C9. Numerous later graffiti. Carved stones and slabs from the cave, all of the C11 or earlier, are now in Whithorn Museum.

SANDHEAD

0040

Village beside Luce Bay, a few of the buildings C19 but most C20.

CHURCH, Main Street. By *I. W. A. Macdonald*, 1962–3. Wooden hall church with a stone porch across the w front and a tapering slim bell-tower at the sw corner.

STONEYKIRK FREE CHURCH, 1.1km. s. Disused. Harled triple-gabled kirk of 1844, with roundheaded windows. – To the E, its plain MANSE, built in 1844–6 and extended in 1889 by *Richard Park*.

SANQUHAR

7000

Small industrial town with a population of *c.* 2,000. For the medieval parish church, *see* the Introduction, p. 35. The town was originally a burgh of barony under the superiority of the Crichtons, lords of the adjacent Sanquhar Castle; it became a royal burgh in 1598. Development of the town's industries began in the later C18 and continued in the C19, helped by the availability of local coal; mining, woollen and cotton manufacture, a brick works and iron works all provided employment. The coal mines have closed and industry declined since 1950.

CHURCHES

EVANGELICAL UNION CONGREGATIONAL CHURCH, St Mary's Street. Built as Sanquhar Free Church in 1844–5. Broad ashlar box with rectangular windows, quite plain except for the stumpy pinnacles on the corners and apex of the painted front gable.

NORTH UNITED PRESBYTERIAN CHURCH, St Mary's Street. Now a hall. Broad box of 1849, the architecture concentrated at the ashlar-faced front gable. This is innocent Gothic, with pinnacled corner buttresses. Octagonal pinnacles on the top and corners of the slightly advanced centre, its Y-traceried window surmounted by an ogee-arched hoodmould. Big flat-roofed extension across the façade, an absurdly unsympathetic

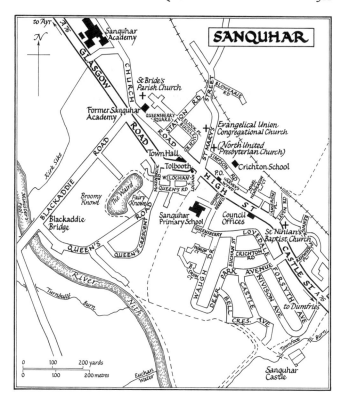

addition of 1954. – In front, a polished granite OBELISK commemorating the Rev. Robert Simpson †1867.

ST BRIDE'S PARISH CHURCH, Church Road. Georgian Gothic
by *James Thomson*, 1822–4. Three-bay buttressed ashlar box
and a W tower. Sill course along the long sides, under the Y-
traceried and hoodmoulded two-light windows. Moulded eaves
course which returns across the W gable to suggest a pediment,
broken by the tower, on which it forms a sill course for the
windows of the second stage. At the base of the tower, the main
entrance, with Y-tracery in its pointed fanlight. A single pointed
opening in each face of the belfry stage. On the corners of the
uncrenellated tower parapet, gableted spiky pinnacles, repeats
of those topping the buttresses of the main block. In 1930–1
J. Jeffrey Waddell & Young added a rectangular chancel, flanked
on the S by a two-storey flat-roofed vestry and on the N by an
organ chamber and short transept. Three-light late Gothic E
window at the chancel. Also of 1930–1 is the semi-octagonal
stair projection in the tower's S inner angle.

The interior, with exposed rubble walls and an open wooden
roof, is of 1930–1. Broad arch into the N transept springing
from corbelled wall-shafts. Deep W gallery. – Oak PEWS. –
The E end is arranged on High Presbyterian lines, the chancel

entrance flanked by the FONT and LECTERN on the l., the
PULPIT on the r.; the COMMUNION TABLE has pride of place.
All these sanctuary furnishings are by *J. W. Wilson*, who also
provided the chancel's oak PANELLING. – ORGAN, its pipes
placed either side of the chancel, by *H. Hilsdon*. – STAINED
GLASS. The chancel's three-light E window (the Crucifixion;
Our Lord in Glory), by *J. T. & C. E. Stewart*, 1930, is a crowded
composition in pre-Raphaelite colours. – Also of 1930 and by
J. T. & C. E. Stewart are the N and E transept windows (the
Calls of Isaiah and Elijah; St John the Baptist). – In the nave's
s wall, a two-light E window (Scenes from the life of St Bride)
by *C. E. Stewart*, 1949. – On the stair to the W gallery, two
lights ('Building the Wall'; 'Building the Temple') by *C. E.
Stewart*, 1950. – In a segmental-arched recess in the transept,
an EFFIGY of a priest, perhaps of *c.*1500, said to have been
taken from Sanquhar to Friars Carse and brought back in 1897
by the third Marquess of Bute, who provided its altar-tomb
base. – In the porch, a small STATUE of a bishop (perhaps St
Nicholas) accompanied by a boy, which was ploughed up at
Dunscore in 1923. It looks early C15.

GRAVEYARD. At the W entrance, corniced GATEPIERS of
the earlier C19, topped by stone pyramids. – Just SW of the
church, a GRAVESLAB in the shape of two adjoining coffins,
one large, the other small. It commemorates Rachel Hair and
her child, who died in 1657 when Rachel defended her husband
in a brawl with Cromwellian soldiers. It bears that date (recut),
her initials, and an incised sword. – Beside it, a GRAVESLAB,
probably C17, bearing the initials WAMP above a cross or
sword; symbols of mortality on the sloping sides. – Leaning
against the W end of the church's S wall, a couple of carved
STONES which have formed part of MONUMENTS, probably
of the C18. One has reminders of death and the inscription
MEMENTO MORI. The other has a scroll with the same inscription and a skull; flaming urns on the side panels. – Against the
graveyard's S wall, an ogee-pedimented aedicular HEAD-
STONE, with an angel's head (the soul) in the tympanum,
emblems of death at the base. It looks C18. – Near it, another
C18 HEADSTONE, with an angel's head at the top. – Further
to the E, and set into the graveyard's S wall, C17 or C18 STONES
carved with reminders of death and one with a coat of arms. –
Just NE of the church, the aedicular HEADSTONE of Nicholas
Hislop, erected in 1775 by his grandson James Heatson, the
curvy pediment broken by an acorn-finialled pedestal; lugged
inscription tablet. – A similar HEADSTONE, but with a segmental pediment containing an angel's head, commemorates
Janet Willson †1772 and her husband, Thomas Laurie,
†1809. – S of the church, a tall OBELISK to Robert Hamilton
†1827; at the pedestal's corners, Roman Doric columns with
rosettes on their necks. – To the W, a smaller urn-finialled
OBELISK of 1807 to Robert Lorimer; coat of arms on the front.
ST NINIAN'S BAPTIST CHURCH, High Street. Tall preaching
box built as a United Associate church in 1841–2. Ashlar-faced

gable front. Diagonal buttresses, now bereft of pinnacles, at
its outer corners; centre slightly advanced between octagonal
buttresses topped by foliage-finialled pinnacles. In the centre,
a Y-traceried window with an ogee-arched hoodmould; Tudor
door below. Narrow pointed windows, again hoodmoulded, in
the outer bays.

PUBLIC BUILDINGS

BLACKADDIE BRIDGE, Blackaddie Road. By *William McGowan*,
1855. Three segmental arches with rounded cutwaters, spanning the Nith.
COUNCIL OFFICES, High Street. Ashlar-fronted townhouse of
1814. Two storeys and five bays, the windows grouped 3/2. In
the channelled ground floor, an off-centre entrance with a
consoled cornice. Sill courses linking the architraved first-floor
windows. On the front wall, a bronze PLAQUE to Robert
Nivison, first Baron Glendyne of Sanquhar, with a portrait bust
by *J. H. Clark*, 1939. – EXTENSION of *c.*1930 in a not very
happy version of the original manner.
CRAWICK RAILWAY VIADUCT, 1.2km. NW. By *John Miller*,
1850. Six roundheaded arches of channelled hammerdressed
ashlar; brick parapets with iron railings.
CRICHTON SCHOOL (now QUEENSBERRY PRIVATE
NURSING HOME), Lawrie's Wynd. Founded under the will
of Dr James Crichton †1823, a native of the burgh who had
made a fortune in the Far East; built *c.*1833. Two buildings,
both of stugged ashlar. The W is a single-storey piend-roofed
block, with its absurdly skinny columns and a vestigial block pediment at its Roman Doric portico. To the E, a two-storey
house, again with a vestigially block-pedimented Roman Doric
portico. They are now linked by late C20 additions which try
unsuccessfully to be in keeping.
MONUMENT TO THE SANQUHAR DECLARATIONS, High
Street. Obelisk of Dalbeattie granite, by *D. H. & J. Newall*,
1864. It recalls the renunciations of allegiance to Charles II and
James VII made at the Cross of Sanquhar by the Presbyterian
extremist Richard Cameron and his followers.
POST OFFICE. *See* Description, below.
RAILWAY STATION, Leven Road. Built for the Glasgow, Dumfries & Carlisle Railway Co. in 1850. U-plan Tudor cottage.
Bracketed eaves, diagonally set chimneys, and hoodmoulded
windows, some still with horizontal glazing.
SANQUHAR ACADEMY, Glasgow Road. By *Dumfriesshire County
Council*, 1970. Lumpy assemblage of red brick and drydash.
Former SANQUHAR ACADEMY, Queensberry Square. Two
blocks. The s half of the N block is of the 1870s. Simple Tudor
with mullioned and transomed windows. It was doubled in size
to the front *c.*1890, in a quite smart Jacobean Renaissance
manner. Detached s block of *c.*1900 with bracketed eaves.
SANQUHAR PRIMARY SCHOOL, off Queensberry Court. By
Dumfries and Galloway Regional Council, 1981. Pyramid-roofed

square centre, with a wing extending from each corner like the arms of a swastika. Drydashed walls and tiled roofs. Ingenious, but it lacks the tautness necessary for excitement.

108 TOLBOOTH, High Street. Built by *Thomas* and *George Lawrie* and *James McCall*, 1735–7, 'in compliance with the plan proposed by his Grace the Duke of Queensberry'. *William Adam* was the architect. It is a chunkily detailed piend-roofed box of five bays by two, the sides and rear harled, the E front of ashlar. Two equal storeys, despite the upper being a *piano nobile*. The E front's three centre bays are slightly advanced under a pediment squashed under a tower. The tower's lower stage is a square pedestal bearing a clockface (a replacement of 1856–7); the upper stage is an octagonal belfry with narrow round-arched openings and a flattened dome whose weathercock was supplied by William Adam. In the pediment, a bullseye window above a stone bearing the date of erection, placed here *c.* 1920. Double forestair (rebuilt in 1856–7) to the door on the first-floor *piano nobile*; below it, a basket-arched ground-floor entrance. On the r. of the main door, a reset stone carved with a crest, the motto 'GOD SEND GRACE', and the date 1751, formerly on a building in St Mary's Street. At all the openings, lugged architraves and heavy keystones; consoled sills under the windows of the E and W fronts. A pair of prominent chimneystacks (rebuilt in 1991) on the roof's back slope.

The ground floor has contained tunnel-vaulted prison cells. On the first floor, an octagonal entrance hall with shell-headed niches in two walls. Behind, a tunnel-vaulted room. The flanking rooms are quite plain.

TOWN HALL, Church Road and High Street. By *J. Robart Pearson*, 1882. Peaceful Baronial in red sandstone, the thistle-finialled main gable containing an oriel window; flanking pepperpot turrets. Carved reliefs of thistles in the pediments above the paired entrance doors.

SANQUHAR CASTLE
off Castle Street

Badly ruined remains of the medieval castle of the Crichtons, lords of Sanquhar. Understanding of what survives has not been helped by a restoration of his ancestral home begun by John Crichton-Stuart, third Marquess of Bute, in 1895 and abandoned after his death in 1901. Lord Bute's architect was *R. W. Schultz*.

The position commanding the narrow upper valley of the Nith is of strategic importance, and the motte at Ryehill, 1.1km. SE, was probably erected by the Anglo-Norman family of de Ros, who held the manor of Sanquhar by the late C12. The *caput* of the manor had apparently shifted from Ryehill shortly before 1296, when there is mention of 'the New Place of Seneware', possibly at Newark, midway between Ryehill and the present castle. In the C14 the barony of Sanquhar passed by marriage to the Crichtons, who probably began the present complex a little before 1400.

The site is naturally strong, with almost sheer drops to the Nith and the Townfoot Burn on the W and N. A ditch has been cut through the more level ground on the E approach and was continued across the S side, although here it has been mostly infilled. Around the roughly rectangular summit enclosed by these drops and ditches was built a stone curtain wall with a keep at the SW corner, the enclosure probably divided then as later into an outer (N) and inner (S) court. In the early and mid-C15 the castle was remodelled, with the construction of a new curtain wall, whose W and S stretches at least were placed slightly outside the line of the original, and the erection of ranges of buildings along the N and E sides of the inner court. A W range was added later, probably in the C16, and there is or has been some evidence of C17 work of a relatively minor kind.

The approach leads across the E ditch. Part of a C17 gateway into the outer court was still standing in the 1930s but has since gone. This court's rubble-built curtain walls are now reduced to their lowest courses, in many places overgrown with grass.

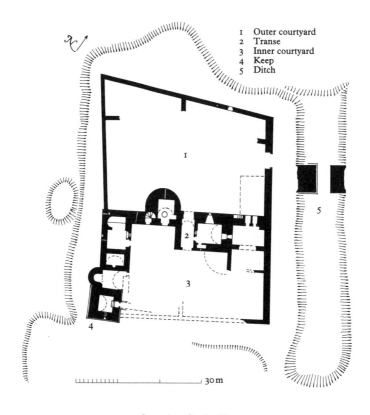

1 Outer courtyard
2 Transe
3 Inner courtyard
4 Keep
5 Ditch

Sanquhar Castle. Plan

In the centre of the N curtain, the stub of a wall, possibly part of an outbuilding, projects into the courtyard.

The boundary between the outer and inner courts is firmly defined by a range of buildings stretched across the site, its ends formed by the fragmentary gables of the E and W ranges; the W was refaced in the 1890s, the E has bits of a C17 door. Between these gables, the N RANGE, containing the much more substantial ruin of the mid-C15 lord's gatehouse lodging. This has an open-heeled L-plan consisting of a rectangular main block and a D-shaped drum tower projecting as a defence at its NW corner. The main block's N front stands quite high, its C15 masonry of light-coloured rough ashlar, the 1890s work in a more smoothly dressed purplish stone. At its W end, a barely pointed entrance gateway. Of the drum tower's bowed front there survives only the rubble core of the base, partly reclad in late C19 ashlar. The segmental-vaulted transe leading under this block to the inner courtyard is almost all of the 1890s, except for the N end of the W wall and the lowest courses of the E. Stone bench along the W wall, a restoration, but there is evidence that such a feature existed originally. Ground-floor room E of the transe, most of the lower part of its side walls C15 work. In the thickness of the S wall's W end, a garderobe. Heavy rounded corbels show that the room has been divided by an entresol floor, lit by small N and S windows, under the vault (restored in brickwork). The transe's segmental-arched entrance to the courtyard is of the 1890s. On this side, the main block's S wall rises only to first-floor level in a state of shaggy disrepair. The first-floor hall seems to have been vaulted at two different heights; the higher W third was perhaps for cooking, since there is a slop drain in the N wall. Near the centre of this wall, a heavily restored window provided with stone seats. The rubble-built straight S side of the DRUM TOWER stands to a fair height. At its ground floor, a round-arched door into a room containing a well, the vault renewed in brick. At the drum tower's SW corner, a gabled stair tower. This was still largely intact in the late C18 but was almost entirely rebuilt in the late C19, when it was given an entrance door of C16 type. Inside the drum tower, what survives of the ashlar-faced S wall's masonry is jettied inward on two tiers of continuous corbelling at the second and third floors.

The late C14 SW KEEP appears the most complete part of the castle, but that is because Lord Bute got a lot done here before his death. The W wall, much of the S wall, the S third of the E wall, and the W half of the N wall are C14, built of good-quality rubble with a splayed base; the rest is of the 1890s. It was clear from foundations and the medieval masonry of the N side that the original W and S curtains joined the keep in the centre of its N and E walls, and that there had been a third-floor door opening onto the W curtain's parapet walk. In the 1890s restoration, rough masonry was provided at the E wall's rebuilt centre to show how the curtain had originally run into it and had later been removed. New segmental-arched ground-

and first-floor entrances, presumably originally from lobbies in the curtain wall's thickness, were provided, as was a third-floor door onto the missing s curtain's parapet walk. Windows all of the 1890s, except in the W wall: the upper part of its moulded second-floor window, with two ogee-arched and transomed lights, is late C14. The interior is a late C19 reconstruction, with stone chimneypieces of late medieval type at the upper floors and a turnpike stair rising from the NE corner of the first-floor hall.

The W RANGE was built against the C15 curtain, probably in the C16. It is now very ruined, but there has been a kitchen fireplace at its N gable and, at the s end, an oven pushing through the curtain wall. Only fragments survive of the E range, which seems to have been built in the early C15 at the same time as the E curtain.

DESCRIPTION

GLASGOW ROAD is the main N entry. On its l., the unpromising mass of Sanquhar Academy (see Public Buildings, above). Then, on the corner of Blackaddie Road on the r., a picturesque double cottage of c.1840, built on an irregular U-plan. Sawtooth copes on the gables; big chimneystacks rising from the ground. CHURCH ROAD, running almost parallel to the E, passes St Bride's Parish Church and the former Sanquhar Academy (see Churches and Public Buildings, above). The two roads join at the Town Hall (see above). In front, a grey granite FOUNTAIN erected to commemorate Queen Victoria's Diamond Jubilee of 1897. On the corner, No. 2 Church Road, a late C18 tobacco factory, five bays of rough ashlar but now (1992) roofless.

HIGH STREET begins by squeezing past the back of the Tolbooth (see above), whose chimneys dominate this approach. Then the street establishes a plain norm of two-storey painted or rendered buildings, mostly of the C18 and C19. In ST MARY'S STREET to the N, the old North United Presbyterian and Evangelical Union Congregational Churches (see above). Beside the first, on the corner of SIMPSON ROAD, a mid-C19 house with stone gablets over the first-floor windows; on its front, a carved relief portrait of Robert Burns.

Further along High Street, on the r., the early C19 ROYAL BANK OF SCOTLAND, with a channelled ground floor and heavy Roman Doric portico. On the l., the humble mid-C18 POST OFFICE. At the top of LAWRIE'S WYND, the old Crichton School (see above), set well back in its own grounds. In High Street, opposite the Wynd's foot, THE CROWN, early C19 with a jolly Edwardian pub front. A little further, on the l., the BANK OF SCOTLAND of the earlier C19, guarded by spearhead railings. Two storeys and five bays of painted broached ashlar; a portico of coupled Ionic columns. On the r., Nos. 74–76, again of the earlier C19, have ground-floor windows surmounted by curved entablatures, rosettes on their fluted friezes. Pilastered shopfront on the mid-C19 Nos. 78–88.

For the Council Offices and the Monument to the Sanquhar Declarations, *see* above. At the end of High Street, St Ninian's Baptist Church (*see* above) and, beside it, its piend-roofed MANSE of 1849; the battlemented concrete porch is a C20 addition. On the garden wall, a couple of stone urns flanking a simply moulded stone, the finial from the MARKET CROSS of 1680. In CASTLE STREET, the burgh's exit to the E, C20 housing and C19 terraced cottages. A path leads across a field to the craggy ruins of Sanquhar Castle (*see* above).

FARMS ETC.

BLACKADDIE HOUSE, Blackaddie Road. Mid-C19 cottagey farmhouse. Sawtooth copes on the gables; horizontal glazing in the windows.

SANQUHAR HOUSE, off Glasgow Road. Built as the Parish Manse in 1822–4 to *James Thomson*'s design. Two storeys and three bays, of white-painted ashlar, the centre slightly advanced with skinny Roman Doric columns at the doorpiece. Tudorish chimneys on the piended platform roof. – Behind, single-storey L-plan offices.

SENWICK

6040

Graveyard of a medieval parish, on the edge of a wood beside Kirkcudbright Bay.

CHURCHYARD. The medieval PARISH CHURCH, abandoned in 1670, is now a heap of rubble. It was rectangular, *c.* 13.4m. by 4.9m. (*see* the Introduction, p. 35). – Built against its S side, probably in the mid-C18, is the rubble-walled BURIAL ENCLOSURE of the Blairs of Dunrod. In the enclosure's S wall, a basket-arched entrance under an armorial stone. – On the outside of the W wall, a large MONUMENT to Hugh Blair † 1771, with Ionic columns and a pediment; egg-and-dart border to the inscription panel. – On the inside of this wall, a SLAB with a floriated pie-crust border; it commemorates Mary Maxwell and was erected in 1762. – On the E wall, a sandstone pylon MONUMENT to Juliana J. Gallimore † 1824, the marble inscription panel carved with drapery.

LIGHTHOUSE, Little Ross, 2.8km. S. By *Thomas Stevenson*, 1843. Round tower, corbelling under the domed cupola light. Pedimented entrance. Flat-roofed keepers' houses.

BALMANGAN, 0.5km. SW. Plain white-painted C19 farmhouse. At its S end, the ground floor of a substantial rubble-built rectangular tower house, probably of the mid-C16. Door at the E wall's N end, opening onto the turnpike stair in the NE corner.

SENWICK HOUSE, 1.1km. NW. Rendered and piend-roofed main block of *c.* 1800. Two storeys and three bays, the quoins and lintels rusticated. The gabled porch and dormers were added in 1879 by *Kinnear & Peddie*. Large but plain early C20

N addition, its windows mostly of two lights. Broad-eaved
LODGE by *Kinnear & Peddie*, 1879.

SHAMBELLIE HOUSE

0.5km. NW of New Abbey

Low-key manor house of 1856 by *David Bryce*, his design a more
economical version of one he had produced two years before.
The flavour is generally Jacobethan but given a Scottish accent
by crowstepped gables, a turret at the NE corner, and a conical-
roofed round stair tower at the N. On the (E) garden front, a
pair of bay windows, the l. with a parapet, the r. wholeheartedly
Baronial, broached from the square to a semi-octagon at the
basement, then with the first floor projected on corbelling, and
the attic corbelled to the square. The interior has been very
little altered, but the chimneypieces are simple and the cornices
routine. Wooden main stair of Jacobean character.

SHAWHEAD

Small village, mostly of brightly painted C19 cottages.

DRUMCLYER, 2.2km. NE. White-painted mid-C19 *cottage orné*
curvaceously bargeboarded. Projecting central jamb with
a canted end. Gableted dormerheads over the first-floor
windows.

GLENKILN. *See* p. 323.

SHENNANTON HOUSE

3.5km. NE of Kirkcowan

Large and prominently sited villa by *H. E. Clifford*, 1908. The
manner is English Arts and Crafts Tudor but its handling cold-
blooded. One and two storeys; the main walling of crazy-paved
blocks of grey granite rubble, the dressings, bay windows and
porch of buff-coloured sandstone ashlar, the roof covered with
red tiles. Determinedly asymmetrical composition. The S
(entrance) front builds up from a single-storey W block through
a two-storey gable and a parapeted rectangular bay window to
a broad gable at the E end, its W corner gripped by a stepped
chimneystack and with a battered and battlemented semi-
octagonal porch projecting from it. On the S front, a canted
and parapeted bay window at the l. end is balanced by a
rectangular gabled bay window at the r., beyond which is a
lower oriel-windowed end bay. Low service wing at the N; two
of its windows were converted to doors *c.* 1990.

Internally, the ground floor divides into three zones; the S
range contains business rooms, with the billiard room at the W
end, the E range contains the reception rooms and the N range
the servants' quarters. Plenty of part-panelling in pale pine.

The drawing room is divided by an elliptical arch springing from Artisan Mannerist Ionic columns and with a second elliptical arch marking off the bay window, both these arches cutting awkwardly across the ceiling's border decorated with a relief of roses. Dark panelling and a Tudorish sideboard recess in the dining room. Inglenook in the billiard room.

SINNINESS CASTLE
2050
4.5km. s of Glenluce

Fragmentary ruin of a tower house said to have been built by Archibald Kennedy in the late C16. It seems to have been rectangular, of three storeys and an attic, with two vaulted cellars on the ground floor. Much of the N gable still stands. In it, a segmental-arched first-floor window. Stub of the E wall.

SORBIE
4040

L-plan village founded in the late C18 by John, seventh Earl of Galloway. The main street is mostly lined with terraced C19 cottages.

FREE CHURCH. Secularized. Rubble-built rectangle of 1843–4. Pointed windows; faintly Italianate birdcage bellcote on the E gable.

OLD PARISH CHURCH. Unroofed shell of the church completed in 1755. T-plan, the walls built of whinstone rubble with granite dressings. The main windows are roundheaded, with projecting keystones. Rectangular gallery windows above the gable doors; in the N wall, low rectangular windows. Above the door of the N 'aisle', a red sandstone panel frame enriched with egg-and-dart ornament; it looks mid-C18. On top of this gable, a scroll-sided chimney, perhaps of 1826, when the church was 'thoroughly repaired'. End galleries in the main block. The 'aisle' has contained a first-floor retiring room, with a basket-arched chimneypiece.

s of the church, a HEADSTONE to William McInim (?) † 1737, its front carved with reminders of death under an angel's head (the soul). – To the E, the corniced and parapeted MAUSO-LEUM of the Earls of Galloway, dated 1735. Rubble-built with rusticated ashlar quoins. Above the Gibbsian round-arched door, an heraldic panel.

SORBIE PARISH CHURCH. See Garlieston.

SCHOOL. Built in 1875–6. Small and plain.

SORBIE TOWER
1.3km. E

Big late C16 rubble-built tower house of the Hannays of Sorbie, now roofless. L-plan, the jamb projecting at the SE corner. Angle rounds at the NE, NW and SW corners of the main block;

their continuous corbelling is broken by the corners. In the inner angle, a stair turret projected from the first floor on continuous corbelling, the lowest member a grotesque head. Windows, large at the first floor, with chamfered surrounds where not robbed of dressings. In the N face of the jamb is the entrance, with its jambs mostly surviving and decorated with a roll-and-hollow moulding. Higher up on this face, the now empty frame for an armorial panel.

Inside, the main block has been vaulted, with a passage along its E side. Two store rooms in the S half. The not very large N room, with a huge segmental-arched fireplace (restored), has been the kitchen. In the jamb, a scale-and-platt stair to the first floor; in the inner angle's turret, turnpike stair to the floors above. At the first-floor hall, a large E fireplace. In its N gable, a wall chamber with a window each side of the kitchen flue. Small cupboards in the W and S walls.

LOW BLAIR, 0.3km. N. Mid-C19 rubble-fronted farmhouse of two storeys and three bays. Steep piended roof framed by the gables' chimneys.

RAVENSTONE CASTLE. *See* p. 497.

SOUTHERNESS

9050

Tiny village, laid out in the late C18 by Richard Oswald of Auchencruive in the mistaken expectation that coal would be found in the neighbourhood. It later became a bathing resort and is now an appendage to a caravan park.

LIGHTHOUSE. Battered rectangular tower of painted rubble, 103 built by Dumfries Town Council in 1748–9 as a landmark for shipping in the Solway; *see* the Introduction, p. 73. *Peter Milligan*, mason in Burran, was the contractor. It was heightened *c.*1785 and provided with an oil light and reflectors about ten years later. Further heightening by *Walter Newall* in 1842–3, when three of the corners were broached and moulded red sandstone corbels were added to carry an iron-railed walkway. Its circuit of the tower is interrupted at the fourth corner, which is carried up as a caphouse. Slate-roofed lantern. The effect is ungainly.

DESCRIPTION. The village is T-plan, the tail formed by a double-sided street, whose terraces return along the shore to form the cross-bar. Cottages, all single-storey, of harled or painted rubble, many now with altered windows and with a continuous line of sun-lounges overlooking the Solway. On the axis of the tail is the lighthouse (*see* above).

WEST PRESTON, 2.3km. NW. Early C19 farmhouse built of painted rubble. Piend roof framed by the gables' chimney-stacks.

SOUTHWICK CHURCHYARD *see* CAULKERBUSH

SOUTHWICK HOUSE

o.4km. NE of Caulkerbush

Trim piend-roofed rubble-built laird's house of *c.* 1750, remodelled in the mid-C19. Originally the house comprised a main block of two storeys over a high basement, with a front of five bays. Single-storey-and-basement one-bay links, each with a tripartite ground-floor front window, joined this centre block to piend-roofed pavilions, each again of a single storey over the basement. The C19 remodelling kept the generally Georgian character but gave it a staid pomposity; the parapeted porch, whose rusticated quoins quote those of the original work, was added, and the C18 flanking pairs of ground-floor windows were each replaced by a single three-light window. The first-floor outer windows were given cornices and consoled sills, the centre window a pediment. The links were heightened by a floor, and the new one-light first-floor windows and the existing ground-floor windows were provided with simplified consoles under the sills. The end pavilions seem to have been rebuilt on a larger scale. They are now of two storeys, with three-light windows to each floor, those of the ground floor tall and corniced. Bay windows at the sides.

STABLES to the S, by *Kinnear & Peddie*, 1888. Two-storey granite-walled U-plan. The E range has an advanced and gabled centre and ends, the centre containing a pend arch and topped by a flèche containing a clock. – Beside this, the mid-C19 WEST LODGE, with latticed glazing in the roundheaded windows. – At the end of the E drive, the EAST LODGE of the earlier C19, its windows roundheaded. – Across the road to the S, the HOME FARM. Nearest the road, a two-storey white-painted L-plan building of the earlier C19; its upper floor is a cheese loft. Behind it, the farmhouse, also of the earlier C19 but altered and extended E in 1914. To the SE, a rubble-built piend-roofed mill of *c.* 1870, its cast-iron wheel still in place. To its SW, a bow-ended rubble-walled barn, perhaps of *c.* 1800.

SOUTHWICK PARISH CHURCH *see* CAULKERBUSH

SPEDLINS CASTLE

3.4km. N of Applegarth

Substantial tower house of the Jardines of Applegarth. Its two lower floors are probably of *c.* 1500; the upper storeys were added in 1605. The building, long roofless, was restored in 1988–9. It is a rectangle, *c.* 11.6m. by 14m. Walling of red sandstone rubble with ashlar dressings at the openings and corners. This ashlar work is quite extensive at the bottom of the N E corner, possibly an early C17 strengthening for the insertion of the internal stair from the ground to the first floor, but more probably a C19 repair. At the N wall's E end, a roundheaded roll-moulded door, presumably made in 1605, when the original first-floor entrance, almost directly above, was converted to a window. In each gable, a ground-floor slit window. In the E gable, two narrow first-floor lights, the N placed much higher than the S. The long N and S walls' first-floor windows are comfortably sized. The early C17 floors above have a nearly symmetrical arrangement of openings. Round angle turrets, boldly projected on continuous corbelling, at the third floor; their roofs were restored in the 1980s. In the centre of this floor's N and S walls, a corniced window. Under the N window, a panel carved with the coats of arms of Sir Alexander Jardine of Applegarth and his first wife, Elizabeth Johnstone, together with the date 1605. M-roof, the ridges running N–S, the crowstepped gables' outer slopes cut into by the turrets.

Inside, a tunnel-vaulted ground floor. No fireplace, so this must have been for storage. Slop drain at the S wall's E end. In the wall thickness of the house's N E corner, a stair entered from the ingo of the entrance. It is narrow (only 0.71m. broad), suggesting that it was intended originally only as a service stair. The top flight is commanded by a squint piercing an ingo of the first-floor hall's E window. The hall itself is again tunnel-vaulted but is much higher than the ground floor. Windows in the N, S and E walls, one of the E windows at a high level. Rectangular embrasures with stone seats at the NW and SW windows. The main E window embrasure has splayed sides and only one seat. In the sill of the SW window, a slop drain. Cupboard in the NW window's E ingo. At the N wall's E end, a wall chamber, originally the lobby of the first-floor entrance to the house. In the centre of the W wall, a distinctly smart stone chimneypiece which must have been introduced in 1605. Jambs carved as fluted consoles with moulded bases and capitals. More fluted consoles along the frieze. It is almost identical to a chimneypiece of c.1600 at Newark Castle, Port Glasgow (Renfrewshire). At the SE corner of the hall, the door to a turnpike stair to the upper floors. At the foot of the stair, a hatch into a windowless pit prison. On each of the two floors above, which were added in 1605, a central passage running under the roof's valley gutter. On each side of the passage were originally two rooms, each provided with a fireplace, aumbry and close garderobe.

SPOTTES HALL
8060

0.2km. w of Haugh of Urr

Small late Georgian mansion house, altered in the late C19. The estate of Spottes was acquired by Michael Herries in 1784; the house was begun almost immediately and completed by 1789.

It comprised a main block with short recessed links to a pair of pavilion wings. The late C18 appearance of the piend-roofed main block survives best at the five-bay s front and in more obscured form at the N. Two storeys over a high basement, rubble-built with a band course under the ground floor, whose tall windows denote the *piano nobile*. Delicately moulded architraves of the same type as at Glenae (q.v.) to the ground- and first-floor windows. The N front has rusticated angle quoins. On the s elevation, the ground-floor windows and centre door are dignified by cornices; its basement openings are small and horizontal. It is possible that this was originally the entrance front, although the approach must always have been from the N.

Whatever the original arrangement, the entrance was firmly established on the N side in 1826–8, when *Walter Newall* added the broad full-height piend-roofed projection, with a low front parapet topped by a round chimney. In front of this, a parapeted porch, the entrance framed by coupled anta pilasters. In the porch's back wall, an off-centre door into the house.

The piend-roofed E wing was rebuilt in 1873. It has a corniced three-light ground-floor window and a segmental-headed stone dormer on each main front. Perhaps at the same time, a canted bay window was added to the s front of the main block, covering its two w bays. The w wing was rebuilt in 1887. It is generally of the same size as the E wing and has its eaves cornice at the same height; but the dormers are omitted, the roof rises higher into a glazed ridge (lighting the billiard room inside), and the s ground-floor window, again of three lights, is placed a little above the E wing's. On the N front there is a tall three-light window to the basement kitchen but no window above. A pedimented protrusion covers the recessed link to the main block. Perhaps also of 1887 is the plain piend-roofed service court to the w.

Inside, the 1820s N addition is divided into an entrance hall and a stairwell immediately to its w. They share a segmental arch, springing from leafily decorated early C19 consoles, which opens into an inner hall, probably the position of the 1780s stair. At its s end, a pilastered segmental-headed arch with a panelled soffit leads into a lobby, possibly the N end of the original entrance hall, with doors to the drawing room on the s side and the dining room on the E. The drawing room may have been enlarged to the E in the 1820s, the likely date of its deep frieze and cornice. Rather small marble chimneypiece (now painted), with a coat of arms on the keystone; it was supplied by *Thomas Lonsdale & Co.* of Dumfries in 1827. The dining room's cornice of upright acanthus leaves looks late C18. Black marble chimneypiece, quite plain except for a coat of arms at each end, also supplied by *Lonsdale & Co.*, 1827.

STABLE COURT to the NE, possibly the offices recorded as built in 1829. Rubble-walled and plain except for gablets over the N range's loft doors. The lean-to s range backs onto the

WALLED GARDEN, perhaps formed *c.* 1800. High rubble walls
to the N, E and S, a retaining wall on the W.

SPRINGFIELD *see* GRETNA GREEN
AND SPRINGFIELD

SPRINGHOLM   *8060*

Village begun *c.* 1800. Altered C19 cottages and some C20
development.

SCHOOL. By *Stewartry County Council*, 1969; a butterfly roof over
the hall.

NEWLANDS MILL, 0.5km. S. Rubble-built woollen mill of
c. 1804 accompanied by a plain whitewashed house.

SPRINGKELL   *2070*
1.7km. E of Eaglesfield

Smart early Georgian mansion house, provided with large wings
c. 1818, the interior entirely remodelled in the 1890s. The main
block was built in 1734 (the date at the door). Two storeys over
a band course marking off the high basement, whose small
windows are squashed down onto a plinth. Rusticated angle
quoins at the ground and first floors of the principal (S) front.
This is of seven ashlar-faced bays, the centre three slightly
advanced under a pediment, with semicircular lights flanking a
carved crest in its tympanum. Supporting the pediment are
four giant fluted Ionic pilasters, most unusually rising from the
plinth and not from the *piano nobile*. At the centrepiece's *piano
nobile*, pilastered and roundheaded overarches, their keystones
projecting. They enclose the door (its perron rebuilt, perhaps
c. 1840) and flanking windows. Carved monograms in the overarches' heads. Simple moulded architraves at the other ground-
and first-floor windows. Overall balustrade. Piended roof, originally platformed but altered in the 1890s. Plain N elevation,
its three-bay ashlar-fronted centrepiece advanced and with rusticated quoins at the ground and first floors. The outer bays
are of rubble, probably intended to be harled. Straightforward
parapet. A porch was added *c.* 1840 and a porte cochère in the
1890s.

The single-storey-and-basement wings, added *c.* 1818 and
each of four bays by four, are set back from the S front and
project boldly to the N. To the S, each has three closely spaced
inner bays and an advanced much broader fourth bay containing a tall overarched ground-floor window. Urns over the
corners. Regular N fronts, the windows larger than those to the
S. At the S end of the W wing's side, a full-height bow giving a
touch of asymmetry. The E wing acquired an attic in the 1890s.
E of this wing, a service court of *c.* 1818, altered in the 1890s.

On the edge of the wooded park, 0.5km. NW, is KIRK-CONNEL CHURCHYARD, serving a parish united to Kirkpatrick-Fleming in 1609. In it, the roofless W end of the old CHURCH. This surviving part is a rubble-built rectangle, c.6.8m. by 5.8m.; some of the walling is probably medieval, but the cornice (best-preserved on the S side) and the W gable's rusticated quoins look late C17. So too do the gable's empty frame for an heraldic panel, its large upper window, and the first-floor S door, approached by a forestair. This W end seems to have opened into the now missing E part of the church; the present E wall, containing a chamfered doorway, was clearly built after that was demolished, perhaps in the early C18.

Inside, the springing and line of a semicircular tunnel-vault over the ground floor survive. It looks as if this W end was converted after the Reformation to a mausoleum with a laird's loft above, presumably for the Maxwells of Springkell.

On the E wall's outer face, a big WALL MONUMENT to Mr Charles Catanach, Sir Patrick Maxwell and Mary Catanach †1725, with the cartouche-topped entablature breaking forward over the fluted Ionic piers which frame the inscription tablet. – Magnificent collection of C18 HEADSTONES, carved, often in high relief, with emblems of mortality, angels' heads and heraldry. Among them, S of the church, a stone, probably of the late C18, to John Mathison †1802 and his wife, Helen Bell, †1772. The front is decorated with a large roundel containing the high-relief portrait of a woman; at the bottom, a mantled helm over a shield which bears the relief of a mounted knight. – Some way E of the church, the headstone to William Beaty †1712 and his wife, Agnes Graham, †1742. The front displays the full-length figures of a man and woman in C18 dress, flanked by an angel's head (the soul) and a skull. – Nearer the church, two badly weathered thick slabs, perhaps of the C16. One is said* to have been carved with a sword and the inscription 'HI [sic] JACET A[D]AM FLEMENG'. Traditionally they are reputed to cover the graves of Helen Maxwell, the heroine of the ballad *Fair Helen of Kirkconnel*, and her lover, Adam Fleming.

₃₀₈₀   STAPLEGORDON

Graveyard of a parish whose church was transferred to Langholm in 1702.

CHURCHYARD. Most of the monuments are C19 but there is a line of C18 HEADSTONES, carved with emblems of death and angels' heads (souls). – To their SW, a grander version of the same type, commemorating Thomas Houd †1747 (?), with inept Ionic pilasters. – Nearby, a stone to the wife of James Cranstoun †1725, its front carved with a strapwork cartouche containing the half-length figure of a woman. At the top,

* By the RCAHMS.

drapery and an hourglass and skull. – In the SW corner, an C18 heraldic stone with vines at the sides and an angel's head at the top.

MILNHOLM, 0.6km. SE. Rendered farmhouse of *c.*1780, first occupied and probably designed by *William Keir*, the super-intendent of improvements on the Duke of Buccleuch's estates in the area. Two-storey main block of three bays, a projecting keystone at the roundheaded door. Lower wing to the W, probably an addition. – Rubble-built STEADING also of *c.*1780, with later additions.

POTHOLM, 0.2km. E. Broad-eaved and bay-windowed farm-house of *c.*1840.

CRAIGCLEUCH. *See* p. 196.

STAPLETON TOWER

2.7km. N of Dornock

2060

Tower house built in the mid- or later C16 for Edward Irving, a scion of the Irvings of Bonshaw. It has now been extricated from a C19 mansion house but is roofless. The tower is a four-storey rectangle, *c.*13.1m. by 8.4m., built of a mixture of whin and red sandstone, some of the blocks very large. Splay-topped plinth at the base of the walls. At the wallhead, a battlement supported on alternately recessed and projecting moulded corbels above continuous corbelling, breaking out at the corners into rather small and timidly projecting angle rounds. In the S face, a little W of centre, a broad-mouthed gunloop. Round shothole on the r. of the door placed towards the S front's E end. The door is elliptical-arched, the roll-and-hollow moulding decorated with low-relief foliage. Above it, at first-floor level, an empty panel frame carved with dogtooth ornament. More dogtooth at the surrounds of the large first-floor windows in the S, W and N sides and at the more modestly sized second-floor windows. Dogtooth also at the ground-floor N window, surprisingly large for an opening at this level and perhaps not *in situ*, possibly moved from the E side in the C19. Simply moulded S and E windows to the third floor and the stair. The E side was quite badly disturbed by the addition and subsequent removal of the C19 house; large hole at the first floor. The W gable's ground-floor window (now built up) was probably a C19 insertion.

Inside the entrance, a small lobby in the thickness of the wall. To its N, a vaulted kitchen with an E fireplace. Off the lobby's E side, a turnpike stair rises in the SE corner to the derelict upper floors.

At the drive's entrance from the W, an early C19 single-storey LODGE, built of polished red sandstone ashlar, with a pedimented tetrastyle Doric portico at its N front.

0050 # STONEYKIRK

Small and architecturally undistinguished village, mostly of the C19.

FREE CHURCH. *See* Sandhead.

PARISH CHURCH. Disused. Built in 1827. Tall buttressed box of whin rubble; Y-tracery in the pointed windows. Two-bay N gable with a central buttress, the doors blocked in *John B. Wilson*'s alterations of 1901–2. Three-stage S tower; obelisks with foliage-topped ball finials on the corners of its battlement.

(Inside, the ribbed plaster vault in the tower porch is of 1827. In the church itself, a D-plan gallery of 1901–2. – Contemporary PULPIT. – Behind it, the ORGAN of 1910.)

GRAVEYARD. W of the church, a scrolly pedimented HEADSTONE of the 1760s to Alexander McMurray, the front carved with the high-relief figure of a man holding a book. Foliage at the sides, an angel's head (the soul) on top. – To its S, an C18 HEADSTONE to Archibald Crackan, smith, again with foliage at the sides and an angel's head on top; but the main subjects carved on the front are a crowned hammer and a skull. – Lying on the ground immediately S of the church is another (but broken) C18 HEADSTONE, curly headed and with panelled pilasters which frame crudely executed reliefs of symbols of mortality flanked by foliage and topped by an angel's head.

GENOCH MAINS, 5.7km. NE. Plain mid-C19 farmhouse. – To its SW, a conical-roofed rubble-walled circular DOOCOT, perhaps of *c.* 1800.

0060 # STRANRAER

The principal town of Wigtownshire, and, with a population of almost 11,000, the second largest in Dumfries and Galloway; at the S end of the large and sheltered anchorage of Loch Ryan. It was founded in 1595 as a burgh of barony under the superiority of the Adairs of Kinhilt, the owners of the Castle of St John, and was created a royal burgh in 1617. However, in 1684 it was described as 'but a litle town', and the population in 1755 was still only 649. Major expansion of both population and industry took place in the later C18; the tonnage of ships belonging to the inhabitants rose from 65 tons in 1764 to 1,732 tons in 1801. In the C19 and C20, although still having small-scale industry and serving as a market town, it has been chiefly remarkable as the main port for ferries between Scotland and Ireland. The lack of a beach and the heavy traffic in its narrow streets discourage visitors from lingering.

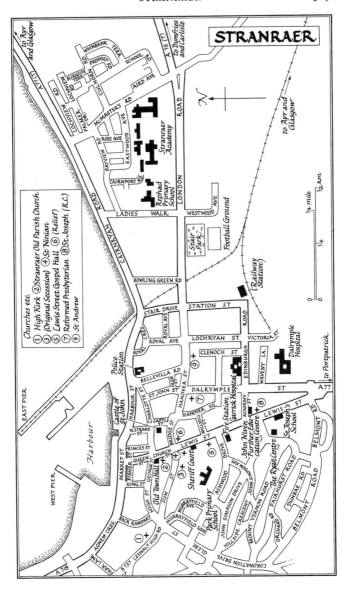

Churches etc.
① High Kirk ② Stranraer Old Parish Church
③ (Original Secession) ④ St Ninian
⑤ Lewis Street Gospel Hall ⑥ (Relief)
⑦ Reformed Presbyterian ⑧ St Joseph (R.C.)
⑨ St Andrew

CHURCHES

HIGH KIRK, Leswalt High Road. Weakly buttressed high box, built in 1841, of whin with sandstone dressings. Tall simply moulded round-arched 'Saxon' windows. Square w tower with a heavy battlement. E vestry of 1895, its porch added in 1912 by *P. MacGregor Chalmers*. Inside, a w gallery and PEWS of

1878–9. – At the E end, a High Presbyterian arrangement of furnishings by *P. MacGregor Chalmers*, 1912, with the COMMUNION TABLE placed in a recess flanked by the PULPIT and ORGAN (which is by *Norman & Beard*). – In the E recess, two STAINED GLASS windows (Jacob and his brothers; St Mary Magdalene anointing Our Lord) of 1922, by *James Ballantine II*.

HALL by *Robert Potter*, 1969–70.

LEWIS STREET GOSPEL HALL, Lewis Street. Originally Stranraer Free Church. By *Hugh McDowall*, 1843–4. The triple-gabled front was completed or remodelled in 1845–6 by *John Boyd* in a sort of Jacobean manner, and the outer gables were given an angular appearance; over the shaped centre gable, a pagoda-like birdcage bellcote. Round-arched and hood-moulded door and windows.

ORIGINAL SECESSION CHURCH, Sun Street. Now Masonic Hall. Built in 1843. Big preaching box, now drydashed, with rusticated quoins. Pointed windows, hoodmoulded at the front gable. On the corners, tall ball-topped foliaged finials; the finial of the gable's apex is missing.

REFORMED PRESBYTERIAN CHURCH, Dalrymple Street. Piend-roofed preaching box of 1824–5. In the rendered front gable, a pilastered and corniced door flanked by high-set console-corniced windows. – On the N, a HALL built in 1898, undecided whether it is Norman or Italianate.

RELIEF CHURCH, Bridge Street. Now a church hall. Piend-roofed two-storey box built in 1821. Three-bay rendered front, its door and ground-floor windows under consoled cornices of such deep projection that they look like lids.

ST ANDREW, London Road. Originally Ivy Place United Presbyterian Church. Late Gothic, by *John B. Wilson*, 1896–8. Built of whin with Prudham sandstone dressings, with a ridge of red tiles on the green slate roof. It is a broad box. At the front (N) end, a projecting centre whose gable contains the double door under an expensively traceried five-light window. In the NW inner angle, an octagonal tower, its tall ashlar belfry pierced by pairs of cusped lights; red-tiled spire rising within the parapet. At the sides, two tiers of windows, the lower ones of paired plain lights; at the upper tier, big four-light windows, those of the S bay rising into 'transept' gables. Short SW link to the contemporary HALL and VESTRY, whose semi-octagonal E bay is suggestive of a chapter house.

Inside, a nave and aisles, with elliptical-arched and columned stone arcades. Gallery across the N end shooting back over the narthex and carried along the aisles, its front breaking forward into the nave at each arch. Elaborate roof with queenpost trusses under the coved and boarded ceiling. – The focus is on the large oak PULPIT, its front carved with foliage, which projects from the pointed blind arch at the S end. – STAINED GLASS. Small but richly coloured three-light S window (the Presentation of Our Lord in the Temple) by *Stephen Adam & Son*, 1898. – Five-light N window (the Maries at the Tomb), also of 1898, by *Joseph Miller*, the colour much paler, the detail badly weathered. – Similar window (Our Lord and St Peter walking on the water), again by *Miller*, 1898, in the W gallery. – ORGAN by *J. J. Binns*, 1928–9, rebuilt by *David Daniell*, 1967.

ST JOSEPH (R.C.), Lewis Street. Simple buttressed Gothic box, now drydashed, built in 1852–3. In 1924 *Charles J. Menart* added the square E tower with a red-tiled roof and a round N turret; in the tower, three-light windows with traceried heads. Low W porch of 1961. Inside, a broad unaisled nave and narrower marble-clad chancel. – STAINED GLASS circular chancel window (the Crucifixion) by *Stalens* of Antwerp, 1924.

ST NINIAN, Lewis Street. Originally West United Presbyterian Church. Endearingly lumpy Gothic in whin and red sandstone, by *Alexander C. Pettigrew*, 1883–4. Nave and aisles, the nave projecting one bay E. In the S inner angle, a bowed stair tower topped by a corbelled-out semi-octagonal caphouse. On and beside this stair tower, large stone gargoyles. The nave's crow-stepped S gable is bodybuilder architecture, with a parapeted porch between ridiculously muscular stepped buttresses, those on the l. carrying an octagonal turret under a dumpy stone spire. Large plate-traceried rose window. Inside, three-bay stone arcades, the barely pointed arches springing from granite columns, whose big sandstone capitals are decorated with carved foliage. Gallery in the nave's S bay. The chancel is filled with an ORGAN by *Peter Conacher & Co.*; its pipes are stencilled. – More STENCILLING (gablets and stars) on the boarded ceiling. On the sides of the chancel arch, seven-light brass GASOLIERS.

STRANRAER OLD PARISH CHURCH, Church Street. Simple Perp, built in 1838–41 by *Hugh McDowall* and *Andrew McCrea*, masons, and *James Adair & Co.*, joiners, one or more of whom probably provided the design.* It is a tall box, the sides of whin, the front of sandstone ashlar badly eroded by cleaning. At the gable front, pinnacled octagonal corner buttresses; another pair marks off the centre to suggest a nave (*see* the Introduction, p. 41). From the top of the gable there projects an octagonal shaft, its pinnacled finial now missing. – In front, a pair of grand late Victorian cast-iron LAMP STANDARDS. Foliaged cresting round the top of the lights; cherubs engaged in physical training at the corners. These used to stand outside the house of whoever was Provost of the Burgh Council until that body was abolished in the local government reorganization of 1975. They were placed here in 1978.

Surprisingly large interior, with simple enrichment in three panels of the flat plaster ceiling. U-plan gallery on bell-capitaled cast-iron columns. – Simple PEWS, replacements of 1894. – At the W end, the PULPIT by *Mackenzie & Partners Ltd*, 1957. – ORGAN by *William Hill & Sons & Norman & Beard*, 1957, its stencilled pipes hidden by a screen. – STAINED GLASS. In the W end, two lights ('I am the Good Shepherd'; 'Suffer the Little

---

* *James Adair* had produced a design in 1834.

Children to Come unto Me'), sketchily realistic by *Alexander Kerr*, 1957–8. – In the N wall's W end, one window ('Behold I stand at the Door and knock') by *John Blyth*, 1991. In this wall's E bay, a window (the Risen Lord appearing to the Disciples) by *John Blyth*, 1979. – In the vestibule, a marble wall MONUMENT to Captain John Taylor †1863, with a high-relief bust. It is signed by *Irving*.

PUBLIC BUILDINGS

DALRYMPLE HOSPITAL, Dalrymple Street. By the Western Regional Hospital Board's architect, *Thomas Astorgan*, 1973–6. Long and low with aggregate-panelled walls.

FIRE STATION, Lewis Street. By *M. Purdon Smith & Partners*, 1960.

GARRICK HOSPITAL, Edinburgh Road. By *Richard Park*, 1897–8. Villa-like, of mildly Jacobean character, the front of hammer-dressed masonry, the gables of red brick. Small W addition, harled with a red-tile roof, by *A. Maclean Goudie*, 1933. On the E, low extensions of harl and brick: by the *Department of Health for Scotland* (chief architect *T. A. Jeffryes*; architect-in-charge *J. R. McKee*) in collaboration with *Forbes Murison*, chief architect of the Western Regional Hospital Board (Scotland), 1953–5; also by *Sutherland & Dickie*, 1967–8; and of 1985. In front of the original block, a pair of monkey-puzzles.

HARBOUR. Begun by *John Rennie* in 1803 but the principal features are much later. EAST PIER by *James Leslie*, 1861, extended by *Dundas & Melville*, 1893–6; at its seaward end, a RAILWAY STATION built in 1898 but completely remodelled in 1983–4. – WEST PIER by *British Rail*'s own engineers, 1978–9. Near its landward end, the small HARBOUR OFFICE of the 1930s, with an Art Deco clock tower.

JOHN NIVEN FURTHER EDUCATION CENTRE, Lewis Street and Academy Street. By *Dumfries and Galloway Regional Council*, 1988–90. Post-Modern, of reconstituted stone.

MASONIC HALL. *See* Churches, above: Original Secession Church.

OLD TOWN HALL (STRANRAER MUSEUM), George Street. Piend-roofed front block of 1777. Two storeys and three bays, the centre slightly advanced with a pediment over the ground floor; slightly intaken first floor. Another intake at the eaves to form a balustraded parapet surmounted by a square tower whose segmental-topped first stage frames a clockface. Above, an octagonal belfry and weathercock-finialled spire. A two-storey rear extension was added in 1854–5. On its front to Church Street, an arcaded ground floor; broad pedimented centrepiece at the first floor.

PARK PRIMARY SCHOOL, Ashwood Drive. By *R. G. Logan*, 1936. Two-storey and rendered, almost Art Deco.

POLICE STATION, Port Rodie. By *M. Purdon Smith*, 1955–8.

RAILWAY STATION, Station Street. Now in other use. By *B. & E. Blyth*, 1861. Single-storey with bracketed eaves. To the NE, contemporary WORKSHOPS, also by Blyth, the largest (now roofless) with bullseye windows in the gables.

REPHAD PRIMARY SCHOOL, Ladies Walk. By *R. M. Clive*, 1958. Low and brick-built, with a hall at the centre.

THE RYAN CENTRE, Fairhurst Road. By *Dumfries and Galloway Regional Council*, 1987–90. Big and blocky post-Modern, with walls of reconstituted stone. The adjoining SWIMMING POOL is by *Norwest Holst Construction Ltd*, 1992–3.

ST JOSEPH'S SCHOOL, Lewis Street. Built as Stranraer High School in 1936 but mostly recast in post-Modern dress by *Dumfries and Galloway Regional Council*, 1992.

SHERIFF COURT, Lewis Street. By *Brown & Wardrop*, 1871–4. Crowstepped Tudor, built of red Galashiels sandstone with dressings of buff-coloured Hexham stone. Tall two-storey front with crocketed pinnacles separating its three gables, the outer two topped by corbelled chimneys, the central one by a lion rampant. Balconied central porch. Dragon gargoyles on the front corners. Set-back NW tower, its upper part broached to carry a stone-spired octagonal belfry; dragon gargoyles at the corners of the eaves. Plain crowstep-gabled rear block, originally a prison but converted to other uses in 1882. – In front, WAR MEMORIAL of 1920, the bronze statue of a Royal Scots Fusilier on a pedestal of Creetown granite.

STAIR PARK. *See* Description, below.

STRANRAER ACADEMY, McMasters Road. Built in 1962–5 as two schools (Stranraer Academy and Stranraer High School) linked by a gymnasium and swimming pool. They were by the Wigtown County Architect, *R. M. Clive*, who was also responsible for their conversion to a single comprehensive school and the addition of a games hall in 1967. Long and lightweight. Two storeys, of brown and baby-blue panels. Large addition by *Dumfries and Galloway Regional Council*, 1995.

CASTLE OF ST JOHN

Charlotte Street

Now in the middle of the town which grew up round it, a big 75 rubble-walled tower house, said to have been built *c.* 1510 for Ninian Adair of Kinhilt but remodelled *c.* 1600 and again in 1821–2. It was restored and converted to a visitor centre in 1988–90. It is L-plan, with the rectangular stair jamb projecting at the NW. Originally it was of three storeys, probably with an attic, the parapet carried on continuous corbelling and drained by cannon spouts; barely projecting rounds at the NE, SE and SW corners, a caphouse over the jamb. Moulded margins at the rectangular windows, whose glazing grooves show that they have had fixed lights with shutters below. Moulded door in the centre of the main N front with an empty panel frame above and a wide-splayed gunloop to the l.

An additional main floor and attic were added *c.* 1600; the N and S walls were built on top of the original parapet, and the gables set back to allow the parapet walks across the ends to remain in use. In 1821–2 the second and third floors were remodelled as a prison, the rear (s) two-thirds of the top floor being heightened and given a flat roof surrounded by a battlement. Contemporary battlemented copings on the sloping front roof and caphouse. Segmental-arched windows were inserted at the two top floors to light the cells and their access passages. The birdcage bellcote on top of the C16 N chimney is slightly earlier.*

The N door opens into a short passage, behind which are two tunnel-vaulted rooms, each originally divided horizontally by an entresol floor. In the E room's s and E walls are gunloops, the s with a stepped sill. Recess in the w room's s wall which has contained a service stair from the entresol to the hall above. Comfortable turnpike stair in the jamb. Off it, at about the level of the main block's entresol, a narrow room in the thickness of the N wall. It has two aumbries and perhaps was a steward's or charter room. At its E end, a door (one of its moulded jambs surviving) into a narrow tunnel-vaulted room placed at a slightly lower level. Over the first-floor hall, a tunnel-vault; is it C16 or an insertion of 1821–2? N fireplace. Garderobes or closets in the thickness of the walls. On the second floor, another narrow room in the wall thickness, originally with a trap door to a pit prison behind the hall fireplace. In the 1820s this room became a passage serving two debtors' cells. A third debtor's cell with a small fireplace is entered directly from the stair. All these cells have tunnel-vaults and iron-plated doors. On the top floor, another passage giving access to two quite large and tunnel-vaulted criminals' cells. Just below the top of the main stair, a short secondary stair leads off to give access to the w parapet walk and the attic of c. 1600. The main stair now ends with a straight flight of steps constructed in the 1820s, leading to the flat roof.

DESCRIPTION

LONDON ROAD is the E entry. On its N side, playing fields in front of Stranraer Academy and Rephad Primary School (*see* Public Buildings, above). On the s, small C20 houses followed by the well-treed front garden of REPHAD HOUSE, a long two-storey whin-built *cottage orné* of c. 1850, with hoodmoulded windows and bracketed broad eaves. Then VIEWFIELD, dated 1876, with carved bargeboards. The adjoining monkey-puzzle belongs to STAIR PARK, which was laid out in 1905. In the park, an octagonal BANDSTAND supplied by *Walter Macfarlane & Co.* to commemorate George V's coronation in 1911. Opposite the park entrance, ROSLYN of 1907 displays the full range of Edwardian seaside villa accessories, a bay window, stained glass in the upper sashes, iron cresting on the roof, a small conservatory and a huge monkey-puzzle. After the BRIDGE over the railway (by *B. & E. Blyth*, 1861), the red-

* It is shown in a drawing of the castle made in 1812.

brick ALBERT TERRACE, mid-C19, with fretted canopies over the paired doors; scroll sides to the segmental-pedimented wooden dormers. London Road now becomes tighter-knit. On the l., the harled No. 25, probably late C18, the entrance containing a pilastered frame and linked by a panel to the window above. No. 29 is mid-C19, with a heavy stone canopy over the door at the Jacobean gabled centre; the large box dormer is an unfortunate addition. Also mid-C19 is No. 33, but with an Ionic-columned and block-pedimented doorpiece. Opposite, ALBANY PLACE, a mid-Victorian brick-built terrace. No. 37 London Road, set back in its garden, is of plain model farmhouse type of *c.* 1840. Of about the same date is the double house of MERSLAUGH and WENONA, the doorpieces pilastered. Another pilastered doorpiece on the detached BRUNSWICK HOUSE, again of *c.*1840. It is overpowered by St Andrew's Church (*see* Churches, above). w of the church, a short terrace of three houses of *c.*1860, all with channelled ground floors and rusticated quoins. The first-floor windows of the first two houses are basket-arched; those of the third have lugged architraves and aprons. Then IVY HOUSE (now L'APERITIF), a smart late C18 villa. Bullseye window in the ball-finialled central pediment; Venetian windows at the ground floor. Opposite, behind a large car park, is SAFEWAY, by the *McLean Gibson Partnership*, 1994, a long post-Modern shed trying to keep in with vernacular of a type not found in Scotland. A squat red-tiled tower is the main accent.

BELLEVILLA ROAD is a diversion to the N. Immediately below the site of the C19 Auction Mart (now demolished) is the piend-roofed ANNE HOUSE, a prosperous late Georgian villa with an aedicular Roman Doric doorpiece. On the NW corner, BELLEVILLA HOUSE, a mid-C19 *cottage orné*. Front of three broad-eaved gables; most of the console-corniced windows still contain horizontal glazing. In CHARLOTTE STREET to the w, No. 32 of 1841, set back from the building line, is an innocently gauche villa. Two storeys and three bays, the outer bays of brick, the advanced and battlemented centre of cherry-cock-pointed whin rubble. Tudor hoodmoulds over the outer windows of the ground floor and the first floor's centre window; under the latter, a panel carved with the date of erection and the Maxwell coat of arms. Pilastered and open-pedimented doorpiece. In PORT RODIE, E of Bellevilla Road and after the Police Station (*see* Public Buildings, above), the NORTH WEST CASTLE HOTEL, incorporating a tall villa of *c.*1820 with a balustraded double-bow front; large hotel extensions in various manners.

HANOVER STREET continues the line of London Road to the centre of the burgh. C19 and C20 small-town commercial medley, mostly on a modest scale. A pilastered doorpiece on the late Georgian No. 8. At the late Victorian No. 16, incised decoration above the windows and cresting on the eaves. Also late C19, but much larger and of red sandstone, is the Ruskinian Gothic block of Nos. 49–55, with carved beasts peering down from its end oriel. At the E corner with Hanover Square, No. 77, a block of 1902, the bowed corner topped by a square tower with a French pavilion roof. At the street's W end, the CLYDESDALE BANK of the later C19, Georgian-survival in spirit but with hammerdressed granite masonry.

BRIDGE STREET continues W. On its N side, THE GRAPES, plain C19 but with a ground-floor pilastrade (originally grained) added in 1922 by *R. & S. Sproule & Son*. On the S, the ROYAL (former Commercial) BANK OF SCOTLAND, a palazzo by *David Rhind*, 1874. Corniced and aproned ground-floor windows; at the windows above, lugged architraves and balustered aprons. Over the door, a heavily consoled pediment with antefixae.

CASTLE STREET leads N from the junction of Hanover Street and Bridge Street. At the NW corner, a cleared space beside the Castle of St John (*see* above), whose main front faces Charlotte Street and George Street across a lawn. At this lawn's NW corner, a cast-iron FOUNTAIN erected to commemorate Queen Victoria's Diamond Jubilee of 1897. On one front of the domed canopy, a relief bust of the Queen. Rising from the basin, a stalk of foliage topped by a bird. At the bottom of NORTH STRAND STREET, which runs down to the shore, one surviving late C18 warehouse (No. 28 HARBOUR STREET), with an elliptical-arched central pend.

GEORGE STREET W of the Castle of St John begins with C20 infill. Then the early C19 No. 30 on the N side; three storeys with aprons under the upper windows, those of the first floor also with consoled cornices. The two-storey Nos. 34–40 may be late C18; rope decoration on the club skewputts. No. 39 opposite is mid-C19 in its present form. Paired consoles at the ends of the mutuled cornice; elaborate architraves with small pediments at the first-floor windows. No. 47 introduces late C19 commercial-Renaissance. Thin coupled pilasters framing the first-floor windows; stalk-topped ball finials on the parapet. Beside it, the long GEORGE HOTEL, dated 1876 but probably incorporating a late Georgian building. Egg-and-dart cornice over the first-floor windows, their sills supported by scrolled pendants. Heavy neo-Jacobean doorpiece. The mansard roof has a Frenchy central dormer. On Church Street's opposite corner, the Old Town Hall (*see* Public Buildings, above). Facing it to the N is the GOLDEN CROSS, a jolly crowstep-gabled pub of the later C19, its windows hoodmoulded. On the front gable, a stone sundial, the top inscribed 'STRANRAER 1732'.

CHURCH STREET runs S from George Street. On the E side, after the flank of the George Hotel, the ARKHOUSE INN, probably of *c.* 1800, with columns at its doorpiece with clustered shafts and acanthus-leaf capitals, but now rather altered. At the late Georgian Nos. 21–25, a pilastraded ground floor with a Roman Doric aedicular doorpiece in its centre. For Stranraer Old Parish Church opposite, *see* Churches, above. To its N, a small GRAVEYARD. Set into its C20 brick wall facing the street, a stone carved with foliage which frames initials and the date 1727. S of the church, the early C19 No. 12 Church Street, with a broad Doric-columned doorpiece, the metopes of its frieze decorated with rosettes. Then the set-back DUNBAE HOUSE, a large villa of 1823, with a shaped chimney-gablet over the centre. The pediments above the front door and over the centre lights of the tripartite ground-floor windows look mid-C19 embellishments. In SUN STREET to the W, the Original Secession Church (now Masonic Hall), for which *see* Churches, above.

In LEWIS STREET, S of Church Street, St Ninian's Church is followed by the Sheriff Court (*see* Churches and Public Buildings, above). They face an early C19 terrace, the houses all rendered except for No. 19, whose brickwork is exposed. It has a pilastered doorpiece, the fluted frieze decorated with a swagged panel and rosettes. The oriel window and the neo-Jacobean gablet are mid-C19 adornments. At No. 21, a console-corniced door, with ovals decorating the centre panel of the frieze. Another consoled cornice at No. 23; its frieze has foliage decoration. No. 25 is more ambitious and perhaps a little later. Corinthian-pilastered doorpiece; over the ground-floor windows, cornices carved with egg-and-dart enrichment and supported on consoles decorated with jolly lions' heads. Overall dentil cornice with more egg-and-dart enrichment. Plain mid-C19 Georgian-survival at Nos. 27–31. No. 29 is of brick with a pilastered doorpiece; No. 31's door is also pilastered and has a block pediment. Across Millhill Street, No. 39, of the earlier C19, is a detached villa with rusticated quoins and an Ionic pilastered doorpiece. At the ground-floor windows, aprons and cornices carried on elaborately foliaged consoles. For the Lewis Street Gospel Hall opposite, *see* Churches, above. Further out, the John Niven Further Education Centre and St Joseph's (R.C.) Church (*see* Public Buildings and Churches, above). In ACADEMY STREET, No. 1 of *c.*1840 has an anta-pilastered doorpiece.

KING STREET goes N from George Street. On its W side, No. 14 with an Ionic pilastered doorpiece. Then HIGH STREET (whose name indicates topography rather than status) is an uphill curve of humble C18 and C19 housing with some C20 alteration and infill. In LESWALT HIGH ROAD at its W end, the High Kirk (*see* Churches, above). Set back in a garden opposite is the early C18 PARK HOUSE, of two storeys, a basement and attic. Three-bay front, the central door (now bereft of its forestair) with a lugged architrave under a pulvinated frieze and cornice. There used to be a moulded frame for an armorial panel above, but this was removed when the first-floor window was deepened in the later C20.

MOTTE, Innermessan, 3km. NE. Situated at the S end of a ridge, with Loch Ryan to the W and the Messan Burn on the S, a roughly circular motte hill, *c.*9m. high, with steeply scarped sides. It was probably made in the C12. Flat summit, *c.*29m. in diameter. Ditch round the base.

STROQUHAN

2.5km. SW of Dunscore

Unassuming laird's house which has developed into a not very coherent small mansion. It was begun in the later C18 as a plain two-storey rubble-built block. A rendered bowed projection was added at the E front's N end c.1800, and in 1845 the house was extended S. At the SE corner, a boldly advanced three-storey tower-like pavilion, pyramid-roofed and ashlar-fronted. The 1845 extension has corniced ground-floor windows and bracketed sills linking those above. Also of 1845 is the porch added to the C18 E front, its low pediment carried on large consoles. On the wall above, a panel, probably a blocked window, with a stone crest. – At the end of the drive, single-storey LODGE of c.1845, with hoodmoulded openings and a central chimney. Beside it, GATEPIERS with Gothic acanthus leaf finials; lighthearted Gothic iron gates.

SWEETHEART ABBEY see NEW ABBEY

TERRAUGHTIE

1.7km. NW of Cargenbridge

Small country house, by *Thomas Rickman*, 1825. Austere Tudor in red ashlar.

TERREGLES

Small L-plan village with the Parish Church and former school at the S end, the Maxwell Memorial Hall to the NW. Most of the housing is C20, but at the NW are two picturesque Tudor cottages of 1837, one bearing the Maxwell crest.

PARISH CHURCH. Early C19 kirk with a late C16 chancel projecting from its E end. The body of the church was built in 1814. Box of rough ashlar with round-arched windows; ball-finialled birdcage bellcote on the W gable, a ball finial on the E. The red-tiled roof cresting and the W and SE porches were added in 1900–2. The interior is almost all of 1900–2. Open wooden roof, a display of carpentry. W gallery. On the E wall, stencilled fleur-de-lis decoration. – STAINED GLASS. In the N wall, one window (Our Lord) of c.1950.

The CHANCEL or 'queir' was built, on the evidence of the initials on the armorial stone over the NE window and the date above the SW door and E window, by Agnes, Lady Herries, in 1588. The plan of a chancel ending in a semi-octagonal apse and its position at the church's E end make it appear a continuation of a medieval tradition, but its purpose seems to have been to provide a burial vault walled off from the body of the church, thus complying with the letter of the reformed Church of Scotland's ban of 1581 on burial within churches.* In 1875–9 it was heavily restored by *James Barbour* for Captain Alfred Constable-Maxwell of Terregles and converted to a Roman Catholic mortuary chapel.

The chancel is built largely of whin rubble with red sandstone dressings. Round-arched SW door with a bead-and-hollow moulding. Its hoodmould enriched with dogtooth ornament looks an 1870s replacement. The sill is formed by the fragment of a medieval graveslab incised with the base and lower part of the shaft of a cross. To its E, a round-arched window containing two depressed-arched lights, their mullion a replacement. To the E, a single light, again a depressed arch, just like the two windows in the N side. In each of the apse's NE and SE sides, a pointed two-light Y-traceried window, the mullion again renewed. Pointed E window of three lights, the mullions and intersecting tracery replacements of the 1870s. At each corner of the apse, a slender attached column topped, above the cornice, by a chunky finial, the SW probably original, the others replacements. The stepped buttresses all round were added in the 1870s.

The chancel interior is of 1875–9. The lightweight hammerbeam roof springs from stone shields, those of the chancel carved with coats of arms. Plaster blind arcading on the W wall; encaustic-tiled floor. The nave's centre is filled by a rectangular stairwell giving access to the burial vault. On three sides of the well, a low Gothic arcaded stone parapet; at its E end, directly under a rooflight, a white marble STATUE of the Angel of the Resurrection, by *J. B. Philip*. In the vault, compartmented stone ledges intended to hold coffins, the mouth of each occupied compartment closed by an inscribed white marble panel.

In the chancel, a stone COMMUNION RAIL pierced by arcading. – Stone ALTAR, the slab supported by columns, with shafts of polished granite, and foliaged capitals. – STAINED GLASS of *c.* 1875 in the chancel: three brightly coloured windows (the Resurrection; the Risen Lord's appearance to St Mary Magdalene; Our Lord's Commission to St Peter). – In the nave, contemporary heraldic glass.

MONUMENTS. Near the S wall's E end, a grey and white marble tablet to William, Earl of Nithsdale, †1776, the urn over the inscription panel now represented only by a shadow. It is signed by *Thomas Atkinson* of York. – Opposite, the tablet to William Haggerston Maxwell Constable †1797, of white marble with a border of veined grey marble round the inscription panel; at the sides, panelled pilasters with rosetted tops. – Near the S wall's W end, a monument of *c.* 1605 to Sir Robert Maxwell of Spottes †1615 and his first wife,

---

* Although the Maxwells of Herries had been supporters of Mary, Queen of Scots, and were later notable Roman Catholics, it seems that they adopted Protestantism at the Reformation of 1560 and did not return to active Catholicism until 1603; so it is unlikely that the 'queir' was designed as a liturgical chancel.

Elizabeth Gordon, †c.1606. Two step-topped panels separated and flanked by coupled baluster-like attached columns,
their capitals carved with crude stylized foliage. In each panel,
a high-relief kneeling figure, the l. a man, the r. a woman.
On the frieze, the coats of arms and initials of Maxwell and
his wife. On each end of the entablature, a ball-finialled
obelisk. Over the centre, a rectangular stone, its front carved
as a tabernacle niche containing the high-relief head, wings
and arms of an angel (the soul). On the roundheaded arch,
the inscription 'GLORIE BE TO GOD'. At the base of
the stone, a second inscription:

> COME .ZE.BLESSED.OF.YE.LORD
> RESAIF.ZOUR.INHERITANCE

– Set into the floor of the burial vault, N of the stair, a
GRAVESLAB commemorating Edward Maxwell of Lamington
†1568 and Margaret Bailie, his wife. It bears a vigorous folk-
art relief of a gentleman wearing a hat and sword and pointing
to a placard on his l. breast carved with the letters IHS (for
'Jesus'). Flanking his head, the coats of arms of Maxwell and
Bailie.

MAXWELL MEMORIAL HALL. Dated 1906. Of whin and sandstone. Quite simple, except for wavy bargeboards; the Maxwell
crest over the door.

SCHOOL. Now in other use. Picturesque Tudor of c.1860, with
broad eaves and hoodmoulded and mullioned windows.

KIRKLAND. White-painted rubble-built farmhouse and steading
of the earlier C19.

TERREGLES HOUSE

0.3km. N

The mansion house built in 1789 for William Constable-Maxwell
and enlarged in 1830–2 for his grandson William, tenth Lord
Herries, was demolished in 1964. The STABLES, almost certainly part of the 1830s work, survive. Large quadrangle, three
of the ranges utilitarian and rubble-built. The E range is taller,
faced with polished red sandstone ashlar, and evidently for
display. Open-pedimented gables. Front of seven bays, the
ends and centre slightly advanced, with coupled pilasters supporting the entablature, which runs the full length. Consoled
pediments over the end windows; cornices above the others.
Central pend arch with pilastered jambs and a lion's head
keystone.

8090   THORNHILL

Small town founded in 1664 as a burgh of barony (New Dalgarno)
under the superiority of the Earls (later Dukes) of Queensberry.
By 1714, when the town's cross was erected and an inn built,

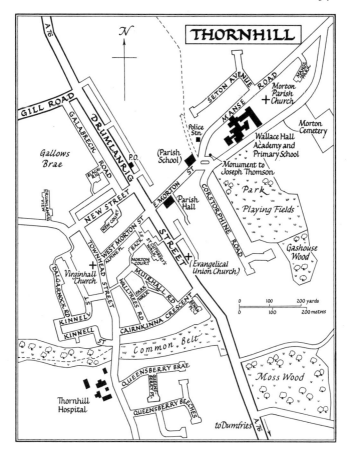

Thornhill was a staging post on the road from Dumfries to Kilmarnock and Glasgow, but it did not begin to grow into something more than an irregularly planned village until the later C18, when Morton Street and Drumlanrig Street were laid out and developed.

CHURCHES

EVANGELICAL UNION CHURCH, South Drumlanrig Street. Now a squash club. By *Charles Howitt*, 1873–4. Simple Gothic in red sandstone, with a large trefoil in the apex of the front gable.

Former MORTON PARISH CHURCH, Manse Road, 1.2km. NE. Only the gable survives of the church built by *Archibald Cleland* in 1781. Of coursed rubble, with a rectangular door and blind bullseye window. Simple birdcage bellcote. – To its SW, a smart HEADSTONE to George Kerr † 1830. Aedicular with acanthus-capitalled pilasters and a slim urn breaking the scrolly pediment. This frames the relief of an urn under a drapery swag. – To the SE, two more HEADSTONES of the same design, to Alexander Kellock †1813 and to Susan Twinnam †1828 (with the relief removed to make room for a later inscription), and a simpler version commemorating William Dargavel †1808. – S of this, a TABLE STONE to the Rev. John Howie †1734, the legs carved with emblems including a skull, bones, an angel's head (the soul), a hand holding a book, and a crowned hourglass. – Further S, the HEADSTONE of someone †1707, the front bearing a large moonfaced angel's head above reminders of death. – Near the gate, a small C18 HEADSTONE. Panelled pilasters at the sides. At the top, an angel's head, with outstretched wings shielding the heads of two children. Below this, a stack of grisly emblems of death. – Along the graveyard's SE side, more early C19 HEADSTONES resembling that of George Kerr but with shields instead of urns on the front. – Also here, a curly-headed C18 HEADSTONE decorated with an angel's head, skull and crossbones. – Near it, a TABLE STONE, probably also C18, with a foliaged border. One end support is carved with an angel's head, the other with a skull and crossbones. – Beside it, the HEADSTONE of William Kerr †1778 (?), with panelled pilasters framing an angel's head above a skull and crossbones. – On the graveyard's N edge, a smart MONUMENT to Gilbert McLachlan's wife and children †1815–30. Urn-finialled obelisk standing on a pedestal with columns at the corners.

MORTON PARISH CHURCH, East Morton Street. Simplified Romanesque, by *William Burn*, 1839–41. Big sturdily buttressed box of red sandstone ashlar. Square pinnacles at the corners. W tower of four stages; round clockfaces at the third stage, two-light belfry openings at the top. Arcaded corbelling carrying the trefoil-pierced parapet; conical pinnacles on top of the clasping buttresses. Low NE vestry added in 1904 by *James Barbour*. Inside, the huge single space is covered by a segmental-arched plaster ceiling decorated with applied ribs and bosses to suggest quadripartite vaulting. Horseshoe gallery on cast-iron columns, cutting across the windows. – At the E end, a PULPIT by *Gabriel Steel*, 1959, decorated with Lorimerian carving. – Lumpy Romanesque FONT by *John Hunter*, 1887. – ORGAN introduced in 1886. – STAINED GLASS. In the E window, three lights (mostly Scenes from the Life of Our Lord, Dorcas, and the Good Samaritan) by *J. A. Forrest & Son*, 1880–c.1886. – NE window (the Visitation; St John the Baptist) by *A. Ballantine & Gardiner*, c.1875. SE window (the Conversion of St Paul; St Peter and St John) of c.1905.

VIRGINHALL CHURCH, West Morton Street. Originally Thornhill United Presbyterian Church. Scots late Gothic, by *John B. Wilson*, 1897–8. Squat box of red Gatelawbridge sandstone. Its breadth is disguised because the front (E) gable has a notch taken out at each corner. The notch at the N is partly

filled by a transept, the one at the s by a steeple, with a red-
tiled spire rising inside the parapet and a porch projecting from
its front.

PUBLIC BUILDINGS

AUCTION MART. *See* Description, below.

MONUMENT TO JOSEPH THOMSON, East Morton Street.
Designed and executed by *Charles McBride*, 1896–7. Battered
red sandstone pedestal with lions' masks at the base, and, on
the front, a bronze relief of Mount Kilimanjaro behind a figure
of Fame holding a laurel wreath in one hand, a map of Africa
in the other. On top of the pedestal, a bronze bust of Thomson,
the African explorer, †1895.

PARISH HALL, East Morton Street. By *James Barbour*, 1893–4.
Ebullient red sandstone French Renaissance on a not very large
scale. Plenty of carving, with drapery over the door, swags of
fruit above the bullseye windows in the end bays of the upper
floor, and the burning bush emblem of the Church of Scotland
in the overall pediment.

PARISH SCHOOL, East Morton Street. Now a garage. Mid-C19
school and schoolhouse, in the Tudor manner of buildings on
the Buccleuch and Queensberry estates.

POLICE STATION, Manse Road. By *James Barbour & Bowie*,
1909. Crowstepped Jacobean, the steep dormerheads topped
by rose finials. On the l., a very martial squat tower rising from
a battered base. Inside its crudely corbelled parapet, a crowstep-
gabled caphouse.

POST OFFICE. *See* Description, below.

THORNHILL HOSPITAL, Townhead Street. Built in 1900.
Single-storey ward blocks with jerkin-head roofs; small two-
storey administrative building in the centre. HEALTH CARE
CENTRE by *Sutherland, Dickie & Copland*, 1978.

WALLACE HALL ACADEMY AND PRIMARY SCHOOL, East
Morton Street. The NW block is the school of 1864–5 by *Charles
Howitt*. Tudor, with heavy end chimneys and latticed glazing. –
To its s, a detached two-storey schoolhouse of 1867, also by
Howitt and again Tudor. – Behind, a single-storey Jacobean
Renaissance block (PRIMARY SCHOOL) of 1909, by *Edward
J. W. Dakers*. – To the e, the present ACADEMY, a lightweight
and rather random assemblage by *Dumfriesshire County Council*,
1959–78.

DESCRIPTION

The layout of the burgh is predominantly that of the C18, the
principal streets forming a cross.

NORTH DRUMLANRIG STREET, bringing the A76 in from the
N, begins with terraced vernacular cottages, their appearance
mostly C19, although the first on the r. (No. 161) has the
date 1795 on its door lintel, so perhaps some are earlier but
altered. On the l., Nos. 4–6, mid-C19 with carved bargeboards.

Next door and also mid-C19, the twin-gabled red sandstone front of Nos. 7–7A and the gableted No. 9. Then a gradual but not consistent rise in scale. Carved bargeboards again at No. 20. Smoother and more consciously architected is the symmetrical ashlar-fronted Tudor double house of Nos. 138–139 on the r., by *John Coltart*, *c.* 1875, with hoodmoulded openings and a pair of oriels. On the l., the POST OFFICE, dated 1912, again of red sandstone but asymmetrical and with an oriel window projecting from its crowstep-gabled s bay. Beyond, the mid-C19 No. 48, with a small French-looking roundheaded dormer window. In the middle of the road, at the intersection with East and West Morton Streets, is THE CROSS of 1714, moved here from South Drumlanrig Street *c.* 1775. Octagonal pedestal, its red sandstone ashlar sides panelled; it carries a fluted Ionic column, with volutes linked by swags. On top, a lead winged horse (one of the supporters of the coat of arms of the Duke of Queensberry).

WEST MORTON STREET is low-key mid-C19. The N side begins with No. 1 sporting a pilastered doorpiece, followed by the gableted Nos. 2–6. Large dormers with carved bargeboards on Nos. 12–14. Less prominent bargeboarded dormers at Nos. 35–36 opposite. The vista is closed by Virginhall Church (*see* Churches, above). To the N, in TOWNHEAD STREET, DALGARNOC, built as its manse *c.* 1855, is Georgian-survival, with an anta-pilastered doorpiece.

SOUTH DRUMLANRIG STREET continues the main road s. On its w corner with West Morton Street, the BUCCLEUCH AND QUEENSBERRY HOTEL by *Charles Howitt*, 1855. Row of stone dormerheads along the eaves. The hoodmoulded Tudor door is partly masked by a heavy C19 bracketed canopy, its fringed front reminiscent of a railway station awning. On the corner with East Morton Street opposite, a chunky late Victorian block, which has a semi-octagonal oriel window projected on scrolled stone brackets at its canted corner. Beside it, the early C19 No. 53, its doorpiece quite smart, with a consoled and mutuled cornice decorated with rosettes. The round-arched ground-floor shop windows on the l. must date from a late Victorian alteration. Further s, the mid-C19 BANK OF SCOTLAND (former BRITISH LINEN BANK) has a symmetrical front of two storeys and six bays, with canted two-storey bay windows at the gabled ends and Roman Doric porticoes next to them. Next door, the two-storey FREEMASONS' HALL of 1834. Three broad bays, the centre slightly advanced under a pediment. The ground-floor pilasters look a later embellishment. Blocky Jacobean double house of 1896 at Nos. 72–73. A little earlier is its neighbour (Nos. 74–75), again a double house but Tudor, with hoodmoulded windows and an oriel at the centre gable. Opposite, No. 95A, a big two-storey three-bay house built as the UNION BANK in 1852, has a Georgian-survival air, despite the Tudor hoodmoulds over the first-floor openings and the

canted bay windows which flank the thinly columned Roman
Doric portico. Just beyond, a little C19 MILL. Across the
street, at the burgh's s end, ASHOHA, mid-C19 Tudor, with
an oriel window on continuous corbelling that includes a
rope moulding.

EAST MORTON STREET leads E from The Cross. For its public
buildings, *see* above. E of the Parish Hall, a double house
(OAKBANK), mid-C19 Jacobean, with gableted stone dormers,
rustic porches and a shaped gable. In MANSE ROAD, Morton
Parish Church (*see* Churches, above). Set back N of the road,
the asymmetrical Tudor PARISH MANSE of 1847. 0.9km. NE,
just beyond the RAILWAY BRIDGE of 1850, the AUCTION
MART built in 1890, a wooden-walled slate-roofed octagon
topped by a cupola.

NEWTON, 1.7km. NE. Rubble-built two-storey farmhouse, begun
in the C17 but given a long N extension in the C18 and
remodelled in the later C19. The C17 openings were roll-
moulded. Inside the C17 part, a pair of vaulted ground-floor
rooms.

THREAVE CASTLE   7060
2.3km. W of Castle Douglas

Purposefully austere expression of baronial power, a roofless C14   64
tower standing on an island in the River Dee, the natural defences
supplemented by a later artillery fortification.

The island, approachable by a ford at its s end, was presumably
inhabited from an early date; its Old Welsh name ('tref' =
homestead) suggests that a settlement was well established here
before the C7 influx of Gaelic-speaking immigrants to Galloway,
but there is no evidence of its having been fortified before the
construction of the present tower. This is said,* almost certainly
correctly, to have been built by Archibald ('the Grim'), third Earl
of Douglas, probably soon after he was granted the lordship of
Galloway in 1369.

By the mid-C15 the Douglases were seen as overmighty subjects,
threats to the authority of the Crown. In 1440 the sixth Earl and
his younger brother were beheaded at Edinburgh Castle after
a rigged trial. Their cousin and brother-in-law, the eighth Earl,
who seems to have begun a strengthening of the fortifications of
Threave in 1447, was murdered at Stirling Castle in 1452, James
II being one of his assassins. In 1453 the ninth Earl, after an
uneasy three years in which he had alternately revolted against
and submitted to the Scottish Crown, fled to England, accused by
the Scottish Parliament of 'treacherous fortification' of Threave
Castle, an accusation given weight by Henry VI of England's
payment to him the same year of £100 on account of a grant of
400 merks (£266 13s. 4d.) for work at Threave. Threave itself
was besieged by a royal army armed with artillery, but it held out

* By a manuscript chronicle written at the beginning of the C16.

for more than three months; the garrison's eventual decision to surrender was apparently aided by bribery.

Thereafter the castle was held by the Crown, and a succession of keepers was appointed until 1523, when the post became hereditary in the Maxwell family. During this period some building work was carried out. In 1458 the keeper, William Edmondstone, was paid for repairing the 'artillery house', and two years later *John McLellane*, carpenter, received a fee of £5 6s. 8d. for repairs to the roof of the tower house and various other work. Robert Maxwell was ordered to make further repairs when appointed keeper in 1513.

In 1638, on the eve of the 'Bishops' Wars', the royalist Robert Maxwell, first Earl of Nithsdale, garrisoned Threave Castle with seventy men, a number which had increased to a hundred by 1640, when the castle surrendered to a Covenanting army after a thirteen-week siege. The defences were then dismantled and the tower house was abandoned until the early C19, when some work was carried out to fit it up as accommodation for French prisoners of war. It is now an Ancient Monument.

The castle is built on the w shore and near the s end of Threave Island, a sizeable but low-lying and, for the most part, easily flooded outcrop in the River Dee, whose waters were probably regarded as sufficient outer defence in the C14. The present E approach passes through the grassy remains of an outer enclosure defended by an earth rampart constructed in the early C17, probably in 1638.

Inside this outer enclosure, and close against the tower house's s and E walls, are the remains of a much more substantial fortification consisting of a broad L-plan moat filled from the Dee. On top of the moat's inner bank, a curtain wall, also L-plan, with round towers at the NE, SE and SW corners and a gatehouse in the centre of the E stretch. W of the tower house has been another stretch of wall beginning at the SW tower and curving along the line of the shore to a point a little beyond the N end of the tower house, from where it has returned to join its NW corner. This W wall has been broken by the entrance to a small rock-cut harbour, which could be closed by an oak gate. There used to be an earth rampart between the W wall's N end and the NE tower, the marshy land on this side an improbable stance for an artillery attack.

Large amounts of the E and W CURTAINS are still standing, rising to a maximum height of 3.5m. but now deprived of their parapets, which would have added another 2.5m. They are of rubble, built with a continuous external batter to provide greater resistance to the relatively flat trajectory of cannon balls. Tall slit openings with splayed ingoes, some of their embrasures segmental-arched, others with flat ceilings, perhaps a result of repairs made in 1910; they may have been intended for use by archers rather than gunners.

The GATEHOUSE is reached by a drawbridge (a replacement of 1976) which, when raised, fills a broad barely pointed arched

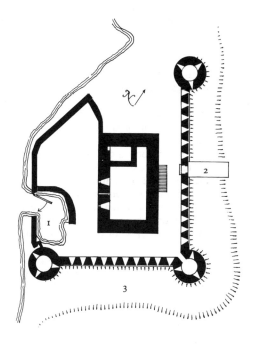

1 Harbour
2 Drawbridge
3 Ditch
4 Prison
5 Kitchen
6 Hall

SECOND FLOOR

THIRD FLOOR

GROUND FLOOR

ENTRESOL

FIRST FLOOR

30 m

Threave Castle.
Plans of tower house and fortifications

recess, its top pierced by a large vertical opening through which the bridge's single rope or chain was run. Below this opening, the entrance itself, a basket-arched gateway now missing its dressed jambs but which seems to have contained a wooden door backed by a yett. Above the first-floor room which housed the drawbridge pulley, a parapet-walled platform from which defenders could fire against an enemy.

Of the round CORNER TOWERS, the SW is now reduced to its lowest courses, the NE is slightly better preserved, and the SE still stands to a height of three storeys. They seem all to have been similar,* with battered bases, three dumb-bell gunloops at the ground floor and three gunloops of inverted keyhole type at the first; some of the gunloops have checks in their sills to house wooden mountings for small guns.‡ The towers were finished with tall crenellated parapets. The largely intact SE tower (the only one with a ground-floor entrance) has contained wooden floors, the beams of the first floor slotted into a groove in the wall, those of the second supported on a scarcement.

Only the base of the thinner W WALL survives and it is a late C20 rebuild; but the removal of quoins from the tower house's NW corner where the wall was tailed in shows that the NE stretch at least was c. 2.3m. high. Dendrochronological examination of two posts from the harbour gate found in a 1970s excavation has provided a provisional felling date for the trees of 1446; a coin found in the wall at the same time was minted c. 1400 and is unlikely to have been in circulation after c. 1465. This makes it highly probable that the W defence was built by the eighth Earl of Douglas in the 1440s. That would suggest that the fortification for which his younger brother was held responsible and which so protracted the siege in 1455 was the building of the E and S curtains, together with their corner towers and gatehouse. The designer of both phases of work may have been the artillery expert *John Dunbar*, who was present at Threave both in 1447 and during the siege of 1455.§

The late C15 TOWER HOUSE behind this fortification is an almost unadorned oblong, 18.6m. by 12.2m., rubble-built with quoins of good-quality ashlar. All the corners are perfect right-angles, except the NW, whose upper part is skewed, suggesting that the stair it contains, lit by a tier of narrow windows, may have been an afterthought. Five storeys, the two lower being a store and entresol; the store is lit by slit windows, the entresol by more comfortable openings. The three top floors have good-sized windows, those of the first-floor hall very large and for-merly mullioned and transomed. All have chamfered margins except for one in the hall's W side whose surround is moulded, perhaps a C16 alteration. On the hall's E side, a narrow door

---

* Masonry from the SW tower was excavated from the moat in the 1970s.
‡ The sills without checks may be replacements of 1910.
§ As suggested by Christopher J. Tabraham and George L. Good, 'The Artillery Fortification at Threave Castle', *Scottish Weapons and Fortifications*, ed. David H. Caldwell (Edinburgh, 1981), pp. 70–1.

(now converted to a window), again with a moulded surround, which has opened onto a projection supported on three corbels (now cut back flush with the wall-face). It is directly above the tower's main door and might have been for hoisting a removable wooden entrance stair; or perhaps it was a defence for the entrance. The entrance itself is at entresol level, through a tall obtusely pointed and simply moulded arch; but in the early C19 its lower part was narrowed, its threshold was raised, and it was given a straight lintel, leaving the arch head as a fanlight above. At the top floor over this entrance, one simply moulded corbel of a machicolation which was reached through a window. At the same level in the N, W and S walls, three chequer-set rows of joist holes to support a wooden hoarding, again reached through the third-floor windows. At the bottom of the W wall's S end, a very smart segmental-arched outlet for a garderobe chute. Near the same wall's N end, a much cruder garderobe outlet, probably an insertion of c. 1400, when the pit prison which it serves was formed.

Inside, the ground floor and entresol (its wooden floor now missing) are covered by a single segmental rubble vault. The GROUND FLOOR, probably reached originally by a ladder, seems to have been one large store, with a well cut through the rock in its SW corner. High in the W wall, a couple of slit windows, each with a stepped sill; between them, a roughly moulded recess containing a slop drain. In c. 1400 the store's NW corner was walled off as a vaulted pit prison entered by a trapdoor from the entresol. In the prison's W side, a small garderobe. Over the NW corner, continuous corbelling carries the stair from the entresol to the upper floors.

The ENTRESOL was probably divided by a wooden screen or partition (perhaps doglegged) into a N vestibule leading from the entrance to the stair and a S kitchen. Window and door embrasures cut into the vault. In the r. jamb of the NW window, a slop drain. Near the E wall's S end, an aumbry checked for a door. In the S gable, a large and heavily restored elliptical-arched fireplace, flanked on the E by an aumbry and on the W by the entrance to a garderobe. Cutting across the entresol's NW corner, as it does at the floors above, is the corner of the stair rising in the wall thickness. It is a tight turnpike, the treads up to the first floor renewed in concrete.

The FIRST FLOOR is filled by the hall. Two large windows in the W wall and one in the N, all formerly with seats in their arched embrasures. In the E wall, the narrow door (now a window) above the tower house entrance. To its S, a large fireplace, robbed of its dressings. In the S gable, an aumbry and the door to a garderobe. The now missing SECOND FLOOR's joists were supported on a groove cut in the walls. Quite large windows to the N, S and W, all with stone seats. At each end of the E wall, a small window. Also in this wall, two fireplaces (the one at the S still with a heavy corniced lintel), so presumably this floor contained two bedrooms. Garderobe at the SW corner; an aumbry in the N gable. The

THIRD FLOOR's joists were supported on a scarcement. The windows, set in segmental-arched embrasures, are smaller than those of the floor below but still of a decent size and allowing access to the now missing hoarding and bretasche outside. No fireplace, so presumably this was intended only to house a garrison during a siege.

7060

THREAVE HOUSE
1.2km. NE of Rhonehouse

94 Large red sandstone villa by *C. G. H. Kinnear* of *Peddie & Kinnear*, 1871–3, for William Gordon, a Liverpool businessman. Well sited to enjoy the W view. Asymmetrical and, for the most part, unaggressive Baronial, with the full panoply of mullioned and transomed windows, conical-roofed round turrets, neo-Jacobean dormerheads, and corbelled stone balconies. A more martial touch is provided by the large round tower containing the NE entrance, whose general appearance was taken from the early C17 tower at Castle Fraser (Grampian). Its top floor, projected on a crenellated corbel-course, has massive corbelling under the overall balustrade; ogee-roofed caphouse on the S.

Inside the tower, a round entrance hall from which a stair rises to the main floor. Here the three principal rooms are ranged along the W front, all fairly plain, two with rather small, faintly Adam-revival chimneypieces, probably replacements of *c.*1900. The dining room's chimneypiece is of grey marble and more solidly Victorian. Heavy turned wooden balusters at the stair.

To the N, single-storey U-plan STABLES AND COACHHOUSE of 1872, again by *Kinnear*. On the l. of its gabled centrepiece, a small tower, its bellcast-eaved conical roof covered with fish-scale slating. – W of this, the contemporary GARDEN, its rubble walls faced internally with brickwork. – E of the stables, the VISITOR CENTRE by *Bill Murphie*, 1975, a wooden boarded and slate-roofed octagonal pavilion the principal feature. – At the N entry to the policies, a broad-eaved LODGE with a wooden porch, again of 1872 and by *Kinnear*.

0080

TINWALD

Hamlet beside the church.

PARISH CHURCH. Coursed rubble rectangle of 1763–5. Ball-finialled birdcage bellcote on the W gable, a ball finial on the E. The windows of paired pointed lights were provided by *James Barbour* in 1898–9, replacing rectangular openings. Also of 1898–9, the E vestry-cum-porch and the NW porch. The hammerbeam-roofed interior is mostly of 1898–9. – STAINED GLASS. All by *Gordon Webster* and strongly coloured. W window (Our Lord carrying the Cross) of 1938. – In the N wall, a two-light window (a knight and an angel) of

1940. – In the s wall, another two-light window (Mr Valiant for Truth before the Mountains of the Valley of the Shadow) of 1955.

GRAVEYARD. On the church's w gable, a plain Roman Doric aedicule MONUMENT to the Rev. Alexander Robison † 1761. – More enjoyable is the s wall's MONUMENT to Thomas Mundal † 1799, its pediment carved with a coat of arms; at the sides, two heads in high relief. – On the E gable, another aedicular MONUMENT, commemorating the Rev. John Marshall † 1776, with clustered shafts and a pediment carved with flowers. – Against the church's N side, the BURIAL ENCLOSURE of the Charterises of Amisfield; set into its N wall, a worn armorial stone with the date 1618 and the initials I^S C M^D F (for Sir John Charteris of Amisfield and Dame Margaret Fleming, his wife). – s of the church, an urn-finialled OBELISK to Joseph Mundal † 1787, with a foliaged frieze on its pedestal. – E of the church, the HEADSTONE of John Houston, probably early C18, carved with crude reminders of death and an angel's head with down-cast wings (the soul). – N of the church, a TABLE STONE to John Corbet † 1706, a Covenanter who had suffered trans-portation. The inscription begins:

T—IS.STON.LET.SPEAKE.WHEN.SPEECH.IS.FRO
HOW.GOD.ME.LEDD.WHEN.I.WAS.FAR.FROM.HOM
BANISHT.I.WAS.FOR.COVENANTED.CAUSE
AND.NONE.COMPLYANCE.WITH.T—EIR.WICKED.LAWES
GOD.WHOM.I.SERVD.MADE.ME.T—ERE.FIRME.TO.STAND
BROUGHT.BACK.AGAIN.UNTO.MY.NATIVE.LAND
MY.SOBER.WALKE.IN.EACH.PLACE.OF.ABOAD
MADE.ME.BELOVD:OF.ALL.THAT.LOVED.GOD

TINWALD HOUSE
1.9km. SE

Modestly sized but quite ambitiously classical mansion house 81 built in 1738–40 for Charles Erskine of Tinwald, the Lord Advocate. The architect was *William Adam* and the design, an example of his not very faithful Palladian manner, is a slightly richer version of his Haddo House (Aberdeenshire), built a few years before; it would have been closer still had the intended quadrants and pavilions been executed.

The house is a straightforward rectangle covered by a piended platform roof and is built of brick faced with red sandstone ashlar. Two storeys over an exposed basement which projects slightly to form a plinth. w front of seven bays, the centre three advanced under an urn-finialled pediment. Rusticated quoins at the corners. Overall balustrade topped by urns (the outer two replaced by *Ian Ketchin* in 1990). Channelled masonry at the basement, almost hidden by the large balustraded imperial stair.* The basement windows are horizontally proportioned. Tall aproned windows at the ground floor (*piano nobile*) with

---

* William Adam's design illustrated in *Vitruvius Scoticus* shows a perron, but 'the form of the Stair' was under discussion in 1739.

lugged architraves and projecting keystones. Another lugged architrave at the entrance (the partly glazed door a replacement by *Simpson & Brown*, 1990) surmounted by a pulvinated frieze and segmental pediment. More lugged architraves with projecting keystones to the first-floor windows, their sills supported by consoles.

Projecting from the centre of each gable is a full-height semi-octagon, its corners dignified with giant pilaster strips, whose capitals are formed by forward breaks of the main cornice. Here the detail is simplified, the first-floor windows' consoles, the ground-floor windows' aprons and the channelling of the basement masonry omitted. At the w bay of each side, a small basement porch, probably mid-c19.

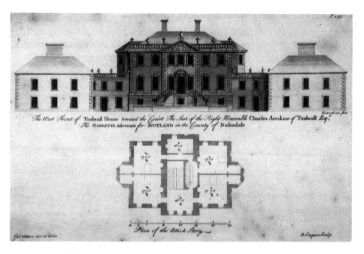

Tinwald House. Plan and elevation of the west front.
Engraving of *c.* 1738

The E front is a plainer version of the w. Six bays, the centre two advanced, their pediment containing a blind bullseye window. No balustrade, urns or channelling. Window detail generally like that of the gables, but the architraves of four of the first-floor windows have been replaced in plainer form, probably in 1948.

The interior was largely destroyed by a fire in 1946 and reconstructed by *J. G. L. Poulson* two years later; this 1940s work was replaced in 1990 by *Simpson & Brown* in would-be William Adam manner. In the entrance hall, a pedimented c18 doorpiece each side. The basket-arched opening to the stairwell and the stair itself are of 1990. The drawing room (originally dining room) fills the *piano nobile*'s N side. Basket arch of 1990 to the bay window. The chimneypiece, which was found crated in the house, is c18, but more likely to be of *c.* 1760 than *c.* 1740. Frieze decorated with a head in the centre of a sunburst, grapes, and *paterae* at the ends. The dining room (originally state bedchamber) at the house's SE corner still has its C18 panelling with swags over the corniced doorcases. Basket-arched marble chimneypiece of 1990. In the morning room occupying the E side's semi-octagonal projection, an imported C18 chimneypiece.

Outbuildings very close to the positions of *William Adam*'s proposed pavilions. White-painted STABLES AND STEADING to the N. One range, containing a large (blocked) basket arch, may be mid-C18; the rest is probably early C19. – S of the house, a two-storey ashlar L-plan of OFFICES, with a bowed and parapeted projection in the inner angle. Blocked basket arch in the SE wings. They look mid-C18.

FARMS ETC.

MANSE, 0.3km. W. By *Walter Newall*, 1837. T-plan, with a pedimented canopy over the door; three-light ground-floor windows in the front block's S gable and the jamb's S elevation. – To the N, the roofless shell of the rubble-built two-storey five-bay OLD MANSE of 1720.

TINWALD SHAWS, 1.4km. SE. Long piend-roofed farmhouse, possibly late C18. In the added porch, a datestone of 1761. – Set into a wall of the late C20 breeze-block STEADING, an heraldic stone bearing the initials IM and MS and the date 1603.

TONDERGHIE
3.7km. SW of Isle of Whithorn

4030

Harled laird's house of the late C18 overlooking the Irish Sea. Main block of two storeys, a basement and attic. Three-bay entrance (N) front, its gabled wooden dormers late C19 additions. Curved low quadrants link this to single-storey gabled pavilions. The garden front has been altered in the C20, with a full-height piend-roofed extension added to the centre of the main block and the E pavilion made into a garage. – To the S, a courtyard STEADING of the earlier C19. Single-storey-and-attic rubble-built ranges (the S and W roofless). The main front is to the E, with the pend arch contained in the advanced centrepiece topped by a pyramid-roofed doocot. The N range contained the barn. Projecting from its back, a conical-roofed circular horsemill; much of the machinery is still in place.

TONGLAND

6050

Scattered grouping of church, power station, bridge and a few houses.

PARISH CHURCH. Disused. Built in 1813. Broad box of red sandstone rubble, the side walls buttressed. Diagonally set buttresses at the corners; hoodmoulded Tudor windows. In the centre of the S gable, a battlemented tower, with diagonal buttresses topped by crocketed pinnacles, and pointed window and door openings.

To the W, the W gable and part of the N wall of the OLD PARISH CHURCH of 1723. At the gable, rectangular windows and a sturdy birdcage bellcote. In the N wall, a re-used door (restored in 1851) from Tongland Abbey, a Premonstratensian house, founded probably in 1218, which stood on the site. Round-arched, with a roll-and-hollow moulding and some dogtooth enrichment. Is it C13 or a late medieval replacement?

W of both churches, the neo-classical mid-C19 MAUSOLEUM of the Neilsons of Queenshill, its battered walls built of bullnosed granite ashlar and containing large openings on three sides. Pedimented ends. Inside, three Victorian BUSTS.

TONGLAND AND TWYNHOLM FREE CHURCH. *See* Ringford.

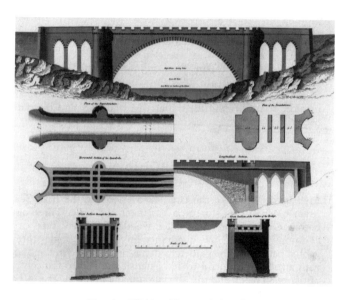

Tongland Bridge. Plans and elevations
(*The Scots Magazine*, 1807)

TONGLAND BRIDGE, 0.7km. SW. 1804–8, by *Thomas Telford*, apparently with advice from *Alexander Nasmyth*, who may have been responsible for the choice of rock-faced ashlar ('a bold rustic stile of masonry, which accords well with the surrounding scenery [a gorge of the River Dee]', claimed *The Scots Magazine*) and for the battlemented parapet. Large segmental arch over the river, flanked by rounded cutwaters carried up as pedestrian refuges. On each side of this centrepiece there is a trio of narrow pointed arches to cope with floodwater.

126 TONGLAND POWER STATION, 0.5km. SW. By *Sir Alexander Gibb & Partners*, 1934; built as part of the Galloway hydro-

electric scheme. Cream-rendered main block with tall windows between pier-like vertical strips of walling. An Art Deco version of a lugged architrave at the entrance. – To the N, a huge metal TANK supported by roundheaded concrete arches.

TORTHORWALD 0070

Small village watched over by the stark ruin of a tower house.

PARISH CHURCH. White painted T-plan kirk built in 1782, incorporating work of 1730; enlarged in 1791 and 1809. Piend-roofed body. On the E jamb's straight gable, a ball-finialled birdcage bellcote. Round-arched windows with projecting imposts and keystones. In each gable, a bullseye window over the door. Flat-roofed N porch of 1967. On the W, a red sandstone vestry added in 1898. In its W gable, a GRAVESLAB carved with a floriated cross, its shaft sprouting foliage, and a sword partly covered by a shield; on the l., the date 1450. – In the vestry's N wall, a stone inscribed w^{M}H and the date 1644. The interior has been refurnished and is now very plain.

SE of the church, set in the back of the big and boring monument to James Potter †1846, a pair of MONUMENTS to the Rev. John McMurdo †1720 and his wife Mary Muir †1714, each with an inscription framed by fluted pilasters and with emblems of death below. – To the E, the MONUMENT to James Craik †1852, a tall pedestal topped by an urn. – On the graveyard's gatepiers, two bronze PLAQUES commemorating Dr John G. Paton †1907, a native of Torthorwald and missionary to the New Hebrides; one has a relief bust, the other a map of Australasia.

HALL. Built as the Nicolson Bequest Female Industrial School in 1868. Plain school, extended to the N c.1935. In front, the two-storey schoolhouse, with stone dormerheads; a heavy moulded stone finial on the gabled porch.

SCHOOL. Built in 1911. Mullioned windows and a central gablet.

DESCRIPTION. On the road from Longrigg to the N, CRUCK COTTAGE, probably of the later C18; its rubble walls and thatched roof look unnaturally spick and span since their restoration in 1991–2. It is of cruck-framed construction (see the Introduction, p. 85). The few other older houses are along the A709 main road. The white-painted early C19 two-storey CROSSWAY HOUSE is of three broad bays with a gableted centre. To its E and set back, TORR HOUSE, the former Parish Manse, begun in 1738 but much changed by a succession of alterations and additions from the late C18 to the C20. C20 housing to the SW along the road to the Parish Church, hall and school (for which, see above).

TORTHORWALD CASTLE

Craggy remains of the large but austere tower house of the Kirk-patricks of Torthorwald and their successors, the Carlyles. The surviving walls still stand as high as *c.*18m., but about half of the W wall and N gable have fallen. The rubble-built S two-thirds may have been constructed in the mid-C14, perhaps soon after 1321, when Humphrey de Kirkpatrick was granted the lands and barony of Torthorwald. In the E wall, a first-floor door. Probably in the C15, the house was remodelled, heightened and extended N, the new work executed in ashlar. In the E and W walls, small windows lighting an entresol; the E wall's S window was made by largely blocking the earlier door. Large first-floor windows. Small stair window at the N gable's E end. No door now visible, so it was presumably in the missing NW part.

The interior is mostly C15. On the ground floor, two rooms, the S occupying the original two-thirds, the N the extension. Over the S room there is now an ashlar tunnel-vault spanning from E to W. It is clearly an insertion, since the springing blocks not only the upper part of the original E entrance to the house but also a door into a wall chamber at the E end of the S gable. The upper part of this room has formed an entresol, lit by the small side windows and with a straight stair in the S gable to the first-floor hall. The N room's vault spanned from N to S. Probably it was also divided by an entresol floor, since the E window is at the same level as those lighting the S entresol. In the thickness of the NE corner, a turnpike stair from the ground to the first floor. The whole of this floor was probably occupied by the hall, covered by a high tunnel-vault whose S end survives. Big windows with segmental-arched embrasures facing each other across the S end, whose gable contained a fireplace.

The tower stands on the summit of a small hill which has been steeply scarped to the N and E and surrounded by an artificial ditch and rampart, still clearly visible except on the W and NW. The summit itself has been enclosed by a curtain wall (now apparent as grassy mounds), which once ran S from the tower's SW corner to what may have been a small round tower; from here it returned round the summit to rejoin the tower near its W wall's S end, where tusking is still in place. These outworks all seem to be C14.

0080   ## TRAILFLAT

Remains of the church of a parish which was united with Tinwald in 1650.

PARISH CHURCH. Ruin of a rubble-built rectangular church, *c.*12.8m. by 4.9m. Much of the W gable still stands, containing a rectangular window, perhaps of *c.*1600. It looks as if there may have been a door almost in the centre of the S wall, suggesting a post-Reformation rather than a medieval date.

The church stands in a small GRAVEYARD, its WALL built in 1905. – SE of the church, the HEADSTONE of Mary Bryden †1812, whose inscription includes the verse:

> Stop Passenger When this you vew [*sic*]
> Remember I was once like you.
> A feeble worm, a clod of earth,
> Man's life is death e'en from his birth.

– SW of the church, the GRAVESLAB of John Wells †1705. It is dated 1701, so presumably was made in advance of his death. Near the bottom, a carved skull and bones.

TUNDERGARTH

1080

Rural parish with an isolated church.

PARISH CHURCH. Scots late Gothic, by *James Barbour*, 1899–1900. Broad-eaved box, with walls of crazy-paved rubble and a red-tile ridge on the slated roof. Bracketed wooden canopy over the NW door. Small SE vestry with a rose window. SW tower, presumably less stark before it was harled in 1912. Its battlement has exceptionally broad crenelles; chunky Gothic version of a birdcage bellcote on the NE corner. Open-roofed interior, the furnishings almost all of 1900. – Gothic PULPIT with a spikily pinnacled back rising above the sounding board. – STAINED GLASS. S window (Our Lord in the house at Bethany) by *Swaine, Bourne & Son*, 1900. It commemorates the Rev. Robert Sanders, whose portrait is placed at the bottom. – In the long E wall, a three-light window (the Nativity and Ascension of Our Lord) of 1909, again by *Swaine, Bourne & Son*. – The same artists were responsible for the four-light N window (Our Lord with Children; the Four Evangelists; Christ the King) of 1908.

To the SW, the roofless and ivy-clad ruin of the OLD PARISH CHURCH built by *James Barton*, joiner in Lockerbie, in 1771–2. – Outside its S wall, the HEADSTONE of George McLean, mason, †1760, carved with his full-length portrait. – To its S, other C18 HEADSTONES decorated with heraldry and reminders of death.

TWYNHOLM

6050

Substantial village, the houses mostly C19 vernacular but with some C20 intruders.

PARISH CHURCH. Built in 1818 (the date inscribed on a skew-putt of the S vestry). T-plan, of rubble, with moulded skewputts and hoodmoulded Tudor windows. Ball-finialled N bellcote, a replacement of 1913. Porch added in 1955. The interior is mostly of 1913–14 with a boarded ceiling, its queenpost trusses intersecting at the crossing. – The two big BOX PEWS look rather earlier, perhaps dating from the alterations of 1865. – PULPIT of 1963. – COMMUNION TABLE of 1930, formerly in Tongland Parish Church. – CHAMBER ORGAN by *Hill, Norman & Beard*, *c.*1963. – STAINED GLASS. Two richly coloured windows in the s wall. The l. ('The Dawn of Heaven Breaks') is signed by *Stephen Adam*, 1906; the r. (Our Lord blessing a knight) is of 1921.

s of the church, a HEADSTONE, probably C19, to Andrew McRobert:

WHO WAS SURPRISED AND SHOT TO DEATH IN THE PAROCH OF
TONGLAND BY GRIER [*sic*] OF LAGG FOR HIS ADHEREENCE [*sic*] TO
SCOTLANDS REFORMATION COVENANTS NATIONALL AND SOLEMN
LEAGUE 1685

Former SCHOOL. Perhaps C18 in origin but extended by *Robert Hume*, 1844–5, and heightened 1862–3. Ball finial on one gable.
SCHOOL. By *J. A. Macgregor*, 1911. Broad eaves, carved bargeboards, and a ventilator flèche. Addition of 1954.

BARWHINNOCK. *See* p. 124.
CUMSTOUN. *See* p. 206.

8090   TYNRON

L-plan hamlet of early C19 housing beside the Parish Church.

PARISH CHURCH. Lancet Gothic, by *William Burn*, 1835–7. Angle-buttressed and cruciform, built of stugged pinkish ashlar, with the s arm formed by a low vestry. In each gable, a stepped three-light window; skewputts carved as dragon gargoyles. On the N limb, a Gothic birdcage bellcote with a stone pyramid roof and more dragon gargoyles at the corners. Pair of large Tudor chimneys at the join of the church and vestry. Inside, plaster tunnel-vaults with applied ribs. – PULPIT in the centre of the s wall, tall and light Jacobean with an octagonal sounding board. – STAINED GLASS. Lushly pre-Raphaelite three-light w window (Truth, Justice and Mercy) by *Cottier & Co.*, 1893. – N window also of three lights (the Parable of the Talents), a brightly coloured narrative scene of *c.*1880. – One rather anaemic light in the s wall (Love) of 1913.

Propped against the outside of the s wall, C18 HEADSTONES, one carved with an angel's head (the soul) above a hammer and dividers. – Also the GRAVESLAB of Thomas Hunter †1727. – Beside the churchyard's s wall, a TABLE STONE, probably early C18, to the Covenanting martyr William Smith, its recut inscription recording that:

I WILLIAM SMITH NOW HERE DO LY
ONCE MARTYR,D FOR CHRIST'S VERITY.
DOUGLAS OF STENHOUSE, LAURIE OF MAXWELTON,
CAUSED CORNET BAILIE GIVE ME MARTYRDOM,
WHAT CRUELTY THEY TO MY CORPS THEN US'D
LIVING MAY JUDGE; ME BURIAL THEY REFUS'D.

– Up the hill to the w, a mid-C18 HEADSTONE commemorating the three wives and five children of James McCall, smith, the front's panelled pilasters framing a hand holding a hammer; inscription:

BY.HAMBER [*sic*] AND.HAND
AL.ARTES DO.STAND

– Beside the N wall, a very similar HEADSTONE to another
smith, James McGhie (?), †1748. – E of the church, a weathered
crude TABLE STONE to someone †1683; it is decorated with a
skull and crossbones.

BRIDGE over the Shinnel Water. Built by *William Stewart*, 1785–6.
Slightly humpbacked, of ashlar.

AUCHENHESSNANE, 3.8km. N. Piend-roofed farmhouse of
c.1830. Two storeys and three bays, built of cherry-cock-
pointed whin with red sandstone dressings. Roman Doric columned doorpiece. Low office wing with a forestair at its E
gable.

KIRKLAND, 0.2km. E. Late C18 laird's house of two storeys and
three bays, with a central chimneyed pediment and Roman
Doric columned doorpiece. In *c*.1840 it acquired full-height
canted bay windows and additions to the sides and back.

FORT, Tynron Doon, 1.7km. NE. Conspicuously sited hilltop fort
of the first millennium B.C., occupying the summit of a steep-
sided spur of Auchengibbert Hill. On the spur's relatively
accessible W side have been made ditches and curved earth and
stone ramparts. Round the summit, a wall of boulders. In its
enclosure, the sites of several round houses.

LANN HALL. *See* p. 405.

URR *see* HAUGH OF URR

WAMPHRAY   *1090*

Rural parish, the church sitting in an isolated graveyard.

PARISH CHURCH. Neat rubble-built rectangle, by *William
McGowan*, 1834. Round-arched windows with intersecting
tracery in their top sashes. At the W gable, a slender tower
carrying a birdcage bellcote, its stepped roof finished with a
ball finial (*see* the Introduction, p. 40). Above the tower door
is a re-used weathered stone, perhaps of the C11, divided by a
rope moulding into two unequal panels, the l. carved with a
circular pattern of foliage, the r. with a spiralling dragon (*see*
the Introduction, p. 32). At the ball-finialled E gable, a vestry
added in 1859, designed in the same style as the church but
given a steep-pitched attic in 1928.

HEADSTONES in the graveyard. S of the church, John Burges
†1742, the aedicular front carved with a man standing on a
skull; an angel's head (the soul) in the pediment. – SW of the
church, James McLean †1774, aedicular again, with an angel's
head at the top, a coat of arms in the middle, and a skull and
bone at the bottom. – To its N, Margaret Holladay †1740,
carved with the full-length figure of a woman holding bones.

UNITED PRESBYTERIAN CHURCH. *See* Newton.

SCHOOL, 1.3km. SW. By *Alexander Morison*, 1862–3. Single-storey school, the gabled ends slightly advanced and ball-finialled. It forms an L with the contemporary two-storey schoolhouse, which has a blocky pediment over its door.

WANLOCKHEAD

8010

High-lying village in the Lowther Hills. It was begun as a permanent settlement in 1675, when commercial exploitation of the adjoining lead mines began. Much rebuilding of the houses took place in the 1840s and 1850s, and further development occurred after 1906, when a new lease on the mines was taken by the Lead Mining Company. Mining stopped in 1934 and, although the mines were again worked on a small scale in the 1950s, the village's principal industry is now tourism.

CHURCH. By *John Douglas*, the clerk of works at Drumlanrig Castle, 1847–8. A buttressed box of harled rubble, with hood-moulded pointed windows. The interior has been subdivided, but the E end still has church furnishings, including a heavy PULPIT. – STENCILLING on the walls. – STAINED GLASS. Three-light E window (the Ascension) by *William Meikle & Sons*, 1911.

GRAVEYARD, Meadow Foot, 1km. NW. At the E end, the HEAD-STONE of William Philip †1751, with the incised inscription 'MEMNTO [*sic*] MORI' above a skull flanked by bones. – Otherwise, a good number of large HEADSTONES, each with the low relief of an urn at the top; the earliest is of the 1790s, the latest of the 1880s.

COMMUNITY AND OUTDOOR CENTRE. Tudorish L-plan school by *John Douglas*, 1846. Long low schoolroom block with stone dormerheads rising through the eaves. Tall bellcote beside the E gable at its join with the two-storey schoolhouse jamb. Interwar brick addition in the inner angle.

LIBRARY. By *Charles Howitt*, 1850. Single-storey, of painted rubble, and quite plain. On the front wall, a bronze plaque to the poet Robert Reid, a native of Wanlockhead, with a high-relief bust by *Kellock Brown*, 1931.

WAR MEMORIAL. Erected *c.*1920. Small stone statue of a soldier.

DESCRIPTION. Collection of harled or rendered miners' cottages, mostly of the C19 or early C20. Among them, towards the E end, some grander houses, including the piend-roofed two-storey former MANSE of 1850. On the road leading out to the NW, just after the church (*see* above), a late C19 water-powered BEAM ENGINE, used to pump water from the Strait-steps lead seam. Further out, roofless stone-built SMELTING SHEDS, perhaps early C19, with pits and two hearths. To their S, standing in front of an Alp-like slagheap, roofless early C20 MINE BUILDINGS constructed of harled concrete and quite utilitarian.

WARMANBIE   *1060*

2.3km. N of Annan

Smart little two-storey mansion house of *c.* 1820, built of polished red sandstone ashlar. It is almost square on plan (three bays by three), each front treated differently. Austere S (entrance) elevation with deeper ground-floor windows denoting the *piano nobile*. Heavy portico (now converted to a porch) with unfluted Greek Doric columns. The W front has a bowed centrepiece; the l. ground-floor opening is now a French window, perhaps a later C19 alteration. Plain N elevation, the windows grouped 2/2. At the E front, the centre bay is slightly advanced under a pediment containing a semicircular light. Projecting from this side are mid-C19 single-storey ranges enclosing a small service court. Heavy chimneys rising from the platform of the main block's piended roof.

Inside, the ground floor is bisected by the entrance hall, which opens into the stairwell. In the entrance hall, a segmental-vaulted plaster ceiling, its cornice decorated with paired acanthus leaves. Cast-iron balustrades at the scale-and-platt stair. Over it, a high coved ceiling pierced by a big oval cupola. The three principal rooms are ranged along the house's W side. All have rather small ceiling roses. At the S end, the library, with a pair of bookcases flanking the S window and a simple but smart chimneypiece of veined black marble, a design which reappears in bedrooms above. In the centre of the W side, the bow-ended drawing room, its chimneypiece of grey marble. Dining room to the N, with a fluted architrave round its shallow buffet's roundheaded arch. At the S wall, a black marble chimneypiece, the mantelshelf supported by thin fluted Doric columns; the lack of an entablature contributes to its nervous elegance.

At the entrance to the drive and halfway along it are a couple of harled early C19 LODGES, each with a pointed door and windows.

WATERBECK   *2070*

Small village with some mid-C19 cottages; villas of the late C19 and early C20. Church, manse and hall at the E end.

CHURCH. Built for the United Presbyterians in 1868–9. The architect was *James Barbour*. Big and confident Gothic cruciform, of hammerdressed ashlar. Tall lancets in the main gables, those of the S gable under a hoodmould-stringcourse. SW tower rising sheer to the belfry, whose gableted openings break through the corbelled cornice; broached octagonal stone spire. Gloriously spacious interior. Braced roofs, the transepts' collars springing from wooden clustered columns. – N PULPIT with a Gothic gabled back. – Strongly coloured STAINED GLASS. In the W transept, one light (Our Lord healing the sick) of *c.* 1920. – The S gable's three lights (each showing Our Lord

blessing a knight) are of *c.*1917–20, the centre light signed by
William Meikle & Sons, 1917.

Contemporary MANSE to the S, with a Gothic porch and
stair window.

HALL. Built as a school *c.*1900. Sturdy gableted bellcote.

FULTON. Farmhouse of two storeys and three bays, built
*c.*1800.

WESTERHALL
1.2km. SE of Bentpath

Laird's house which has developed into an informal U-shape.
Evidence of the building history has been obscured by repairs
and alterations after fire damage in 1873 and 1955 (the second
repair by *Stanley P. Ross-Smith*). The earliest part may be at
the NE corner, where there seems to have been an L-plan C17
house, with a conical-roofed round tower in the SW inner angle.
Perhaps early in the C18, the N range was extended W; a bowed
stair tower (given a conical roof in the 1950s) projects from the
N side of the addition. *Thomas Telford* produced designs for
alterations in 1783, a likely date for remodelling of the N range
and the addition of a broad shallow bow to its S front. Perhaps
at the same time or a little later, the SE wing was remodelled
and enlarged on plan as a not very regular two-storey double
pile. Possibly of 1783, but more likely to be of *c.*1800, is the
shallow porch near the E end of the N elevation. Two storeys
with broad corner pilasters supporting a cornice and blocking
course. Sidelit door under a Diocletian window. Single-storey
SW wing, probably of the earlier C19. At the main block's E
end, a C19 N wing (its height reduced in the 1950s).

WHITHORN

Small town, whose site was a centre of population by the early
C5, when St Ninian established it as the seat of a bishopric.
Evidence of the early history, discovered by excavation since 1986,
shows successive developments from the C8 to the C11, their
character apparently changing from British to Anglian to Irish;
see the Introduction, p. 30. The church, housing the relics of St
Ninian and a place of pilgrimage, was rebuilt as a cathedral and
priory church in the C12, the date of the earliest parts of the
present ruin. A burgh was erected under the feudal superiority
of the priory in 1325, and Whithorn became a royal burgh in
1511, but it was never of more than minor local importance.
There is one main street, its middle stretch appearing very
broad since 1814, when the Town House which had projected
into it was replaced; the houses were mostly rebuilt from the
early C19.

WHITHORN PRIORY
Bruce Street

Disappointing remains of the cathedral and priory church which housed the relics of St Ninian, one of the most important pilgrimage attractions of medieval Scotland. A Christian community almost certainly already existed at Whithorn by the early C5,[*] when St Ninian came here after his consecration at Rome and built a stone church ('*Candida Casa*'). The community serving this church, regarded as a shrine after St Ninian's canonization, seems to have become monastic, perhaps through Irish influence, by the C8.

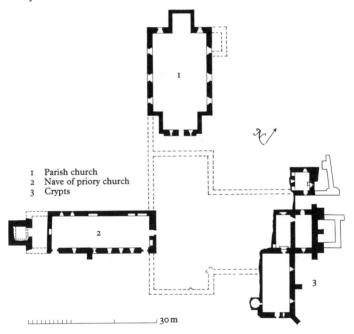

1   Parish church
2   Nave of priory church
3   Crypts

30 m

Whithorn Priory. Plan

The bishopric of Whithorn or Galloway, after three centuries of abeyance, was revived *c.* 1128, probably at the instigation of Fergus, lord of Galloway, who is also credited in numerous medieval sources with the endowment here of a priory of canons regular. The first canons, perhaps Augustinians, erected a new priory and cathedral church in the mid-C12. It was cruciform, with a nave of *c.* 11m. by 7.3m. and small transepts. Probably in the 1170s, the priory became Premonstratensian, and in the C13 the church was virtually rebuilt on a much larger scale to produce a nine-bay nave (with some of the four E bays' masonry retained

---

[*] A C5 pillar stone commemorating a man called Latinius and his daughter was found here in 1880.

from the C12 church); two-bay transepts, each with an E chapel; and an E limb (partly over a crypt) of six bays, the W five probably aisled, the sixth (containing the shrine of St Ninian) projecting clear.

Names of the prior and twenty canons were recorded in 1238, but by 1408 their number had fallen to twelve canons besides the prior and it was reported that '. . . the structure of the church of Whithorn, in which the body of the blessed Ninian is enshrined, and to which the people are wont to resort in great multitudes, because of the miracles which God . . . frequently performs there, is unsound, mean and old, more than is fitting for such a church . . .'

Whether or not as a result of this report, which asked for a papal order that half of the priory's income for ten years be devoted to repairs, the church was enlarged in the early C15; the Princess Margaret, Countess of Douglas, paid for the construction of a chapel in 1424, and Prior Thomas McGilliachnisy built a new Lady Chapel, probably at the SE, c. 1430. Further construction or repair at the priory buildings was in progress in 1491 and 1502, when the King gave drinksilver to the masons; more work took place in 1560, on the eve of the Reformation, when Bishop Alexander Gordon acknowledged the receipt of 500 merks for the 'reparation and bigging of his kirk'.

The church was still in use in 1573, but the Act of Parliament of 1581 formally prohibiting pilgrimages ended any need for maintenance of the priory church as a shrine. By the end of the C16 the nave was derelict, but c. 1600 it was decided to bring it back into use as a parish church, lowering the wallhead and adding a W tower,* but abandoning the crossing and choir, which were subsequently almost entirely demolished, together with the cloister buildings. The nave was further remodelled, probably c. 1635, in accordance with the High Church teachings of the Caroline divines, the E end being raised as the platform for an altar. Later in the C17 this rearrangement was obliterated by a raising of the floor level of the whole nave. At the end of the C17 the W tower collapsed, destroying the adjoining gable and W end. Following this, a new W gable was built c. 1700, a little E of the original, and galleries were erected at the ends and N side. The church was finally abandoned and unroofed after a new parish church was built in 1822, incorporating part of the dormitory (see St Ninian's Priory Church, below). Consolidation of the nave walls and the crypts under the priory church's E end was begun by *William Galloway* (working for the third Marquess of Bute) in the late C19 and has been continued by the government.

The roofless NAVE stands to the height of its wallhead of c. 1600. The S wall's E corner is of thin whinstone slabs, probably a repair of damage caused by the removal of the adjoining transept. In the E bay, a round-arched door, now missing its nookshafts. The hoodmould has a keystone decorated with a shield

* A bell by *Evert Burgerhuys* of 1610, now in the Whithorn Museum, probably came from the tower and provides a likely date for its completion.

bearing a lion rampant under a crown (probably for Galloway). Label stops (the E very badly weathered) carved with angels bearing shields, one displaying the arms of Vaus. Presumably the door was either provided by Alexander Vaus, Bishop of Galloway from 1422 to 1450, by George Vaus, who was Bishop from 1482 to 1508, or by Patrick Vaus, Prior of Whithorn from 1478 to 1514; but it is not *in situ* and was probably moved here from the demolished choir or Lady Chapel *c.* 1635.* Over the door, the top of an acutely pointed window, perhaps of *c.* 1600. The three bays W of this door and the lower part of the E half of the next bay are built of rough sandstone ashlar with a sloping basecourse. Below the windows, a moulded stringcourse, partly renewed. Heavily restored buttresses up to the level of the stringcourse. In its essentials this work is of the mid-C12. The three E windows, likely from their width to have been originally of three lights, are very plain and may date from C15 repairs, but their barely pointed heads are probably work of *c.* 1600, when the windows were shortened to fit under the lowered wallhead. The much more elaborate moulded and pointed window to their W is probably a replacement of *c.* 1600, when it is likely to have stood above the pulpit. It is squeezed by a big stepped buttress, probably of the late C19. Beside the buttress, a built-up late C17 or C18 door. The masonry from here to the W corner is C13 rubble. In it, a narrow pointed window of the C13, its sill higher than those to the E.

In the W bay, an elaborate Romanesque DOORWAY; the 9 work is almost all C12, but has been made up, probably either *c.* 1600 or *c.* 1635,‡ from two different features. The three nook-shafted inner orders clearly belong together, since they have a continuous abacus. The arches of the first and third order are carved with chevron; the weathered second order has stylized decoration including balls. One voussoir of the second order has been replaced by a smaller stone. The hoodmoulded outer order has come from a larger and higher opening (its bases now missing), probably an arch inside the E part of the church; but it is contemporary with the doorway and has capitals and nook-shafts of the same type and chevron carving on the voussoirs. It is built into a slight projection, necessary because otherwise the doorway would have been too thick for the wall. Set in the masonry of this projection are the voussoir missing from the second order, a stone, probably also of the C12, carved with three animals, and another, perhaps of *c.* 1000, bearing two small standing figures. Cutting across the door is the raggle of a porch roof, perhaps of the C18 (though it had been removed by 1811). Above, a small pointed window (now blocked), probably C13.

In the rubble-built W gable of *c.* 1700, a blocked door and a

* The door is placed 1.06m. above the medieval floor level but had three steps down to the altar platform of *c.* 1635.

‡ The door's threshold was raised when the internal floor level was altered in the late C17, so it must have been inserted before then; it is unlikely to pre-date the abandonment of the church's E end.

narrow gallery door with chamfered jambs and a pointed head
(much restored), apparently a fanlight. This head may be a re-
use of the dressings of an early C17 window. The N wall's W
end was rebuilt with the gable. In it, rectangular windows, now
built up, The rest of this side was lowered c. 1600. Towards its
E end there survive a couple of moulded C13 corbels which
supported the roof of the cloister walk. Also towards this end,
a blocked door which served the C18 N and E galleries. E gable
of c. 1600, built of mixed whin and red sandstone rubble. Large
pointed window, perhaps contemporary with the gable but
more likely to date from the remodelling of c. 1635. Under it,
an C18 door. W of the church, rubbly remains of the bottom
courses of its C13 W gable and the tower added c. 1600.

The late C17 floor level of the interior is c. 0.91m. above the
medieval level, cutting across TOMB RECESSES in the N wall.
Just W of this wall's centre, a simple round-arched recess,
perhaps of the early C16. – Near the wall's E end, a pair of tomb
recesses sharing a central column. They look C14. Each has a
broad four-centred arch containing a cinquefoiled sub-arch, all
enriched with dogtooth* (heavily restored) and with rosettes
on the cusps. – Near the S wall's E end, part of the arch of a
tomb recess, perhaps of c. 1200, which has been cut through in
the late C17 when the SW door was inserted. – Outside, placed
against the S wall's heavy C19 buttress, a GRAVESLAB carved
with a circle which encloses a weathered shield bearing a stag
sejant and surmounted by the letters I^{M}D.

Of the E end of the medieval church, there remain only
CRYPTS necessitated by the fall in the ground; their walling
was much restored in the late C19. The crypt under the presbytery's E end has been divided, perhaps in the C15, into a pair
of tunnel-vaulted chambers. The earlier arrangement, probably
of c. 1200, comprised a single space with a central pier; from
this and from wall corbels sprang a four-bay vault. One of these
corbels and the springing of its vaulting rib have been exposed
in the W chamber's S wall. Projecting outside this crypt are
dwarf walls built to mark the shape of an earlier rectangular
building whose E end was discovered by excavation in the late
C19; it may have been the C5 church ('*Candida Casa*') built by
St Ninian. The buttress-like projection at its NE corner recalls
some later structure built after the first building had been
demolished and covered over. The crypt under the putative
early C15 Lady Chapel at the SE contains a long tunnel-vaulted
room with small windows to the E and S. Off its SW corner,
a small chamber covered with a semi-domical vault. At the
presbytery's NE corner there was probably a sacristy. Its surviving crypt, now covered by a monopitch roof, once extended
further E but was curtailed when the boundary wall of the
graveyard was built, probably c. 1600. Much-restored pointed
windows, perhaps of the C14, in the N and W walls. Along these

---

* Some stones carved with foliage have been inserted in a repair to the W recess's
arch.

walls is a ledge, possibly a seat but placed rather high. In the W wall, rectangular recesses flanking the pointed arch of a central recess.

Of the cloister buildings which stood to the N, almost nothing is now visible.

CHURCHES

SS. NINIAN, MARTIN AND JOHN (R.C.), George Street. By *Goodhart-Rendel, Broadbent & Curtis*, 1959–60. Rendered with cement dressings. On plan it comprises a nave, transepts, choir and sanctuary, all covered by pitched slated roofs, and flat-roofed chapels flanking the choir. Lighting from clearstorey windows, the S (liturgical W) in a broad angular arch, the triangular transept windows diamond-paned. Broad gableted double bellcote on the S gable; a wooden 'belfry' at the S end.

ST NINIAN'S PRIORY PARISH CHURCH OF WHITHORN, Bruce Street. Harled three-bay box with pointed windows, built by *James Laurie, James McQueen* and *Authy McMillan* in 1822, the E wall incorporating masonry of the dormitory of the medieval Whithorn Priory. At the S gable, a rubble-walled three-stage tower added in the mid-C19. Hoodmoulds over the pointed windows; plain low parapet. It is flanked by lean-to porches, one at least added in 1914 by *P. MacGregor Chalmers*.

Inside, a gallery round three sides. – CEILING ROSE in a swagged husk surround. – The neo-C17 PULPIT and COMMUNION TABLE are by *Chalmers*, 1915. – STAINED GLASS. N windows flanking the pulpit (the Good Shepherd; St Ninian) by *Alexander Kerr*, 1956–7. Brightly coloured modernistic. – On the W wall, a MONUMENT to the Rev. Christopher Nicholson †1867, with a high-relief portrait bust. – CHAMBER ORGAN by *J. W. Walker & Sons Ltd*, 1974.

WHITHORN FREE CHURCH, King's Road. Disused and derelict. Built in 1844. Very broad box with pointed windows, the front gable of whinstone, the sides harled. Rather small birdcage bellcote topped by a spiky obelisk; club skewputts.

WHITHORN UNITED PRESBYTERIAN CHURCH, St John Street. Now St John's Garage and altered. By *Thomson & Sandilands*, 1892. Boxy Scots late Gothic, built of grey whin with red sandstone dressings. Dumpy battlemented tower.

PUBLIC BUILDINGS

LIBRARY, St John Street. By *Alexander Young*, 1911. Diminutive, its drydash set off by dressings of red and blue brick.

NEW TOWN HALL, St John Street. By *David Henry* of St Andrews, 1885–6. Mullioned and transomed windows; stump of a ventilator flèche on the roof. Henry was also responsible for the lower S hall added in 1898 to commemorate Queen Victoria's Diamond Jubilee.

TOWN HOUSE, George Street. Two-storey three-bay main block 107 of 1814, with rusticated quoins and a rusticated segmental-arched doorpiece. Behind and rising well above, a plain square tower (the town steeple), some of its windows roundheaded. Slightly intaken top (the clock-stage) under a balustrade within which rises a conical stone spire with a ship weathervane. It was built to replace the tower of Whithorn Priory (which had collapsed) and was probably completed in 1708, the date of its bell (cast by *Peter van der Ghein*). Behind, a short rubble-built block, perhaps also early C18.

WHITHORN SCHOOL, Castlehill. Begun in 1862 and extended in 1895, 1899, 1907, 1910 (by *J. A. Macgregor*), 1934, 1938 (by *R. G. Logan*), and 1957 (by *R. M. Clive*). The earlier parts are of whin, the later harled.

DESCRIPTION

ST JOHN STREET, the entry from the N, begins with THE BLACK HART INN on the l., a solid broad-eaved whinstone villa of the later C19. On the r., No. 3 of *c.* 1900, another broad-eaved villa but more cheerful, with white harling and a red-tiled roof and tile-hung bay window. Then C19 vernacular terraced housing of one and two storeys. Opposite the former Whithorn United Presbyterian Church, now a garage (*see* Churches, above), the whin-built Nos. 7–11 of the earlier C19, the rusticated quoins of the windows and corners with exaggeratedly long work. Then the New Town Hall facing the Library (*see* Public Buildings, above).

The road curves slightly to become GEORGE STREET. On the l., the early C19 No. 4, with a fluted door architrave. Basket-arched doorpiece at the mid-C18 No. 14. On the r., the plain ROYAL BANK OF SCOTLAND, dated 1885, of two tall storeys with a centre gablet. The early C19 No. 29 is quite smart, with a round-arched and keyblocked doorpiece and mutuled cornice. After No. 53, the PEND ARCH or priory gatehouse spans the entry to Bruce Street leading to Whithorn Priory and St Ninian's Priory Parish Church (for which, *see* above). The arch itself is semicircular and chamfered, springing from columns whose foliaged capitals bear shields, one displaying the arms of Vaus quartered with Shaw under a mitre, the other the arms of Vaus backed by crossed croziers. Presumably they indicate that the arch was built during the episcopate of either Alexander Vaus (1422–50) or, perhaps more probably, George Vaus (1482–1508). On the harled front of the dwelling house above the pend, the carved and painted royal arms of Scotland.

Beside the pend, the Town House with the town steeple rising behind (*see* Public Buildings, above). Opposite, the late Georgian No. 62 with rusticated quoins. At No. 66, also late Georgian, a basket-arched pend. On the r., the late C19 CLYDESDALE BANK, a tall two-storey granite-built villa. Segmental-arched ground-floor openings and consoled eaves. No. 79 is early C19, with Ionic columns at the paired doors (one now built up). The R.C. Church of SS. Ninian, Martin and John (*see* Churches, above) is set back on the l. Then, on both

114

sides of the street, well-built but unpretentious late Georgian or Georgian-survival houses, rusticated quoins or pilaster strips their only embellishments.

George Street's top end narrows, and a gable-ended house on the l. makes a gateway into the humbler HIGH STREET, whose Victorian terraced cottages face straightforward C20 council housing.

RISPAIN CAMP, 1.5km. W. On the N slope of a small hill, a nearly rectangular enclosure of *c*.0.35ha., constructed as a defensible native homestead *c*.60 B.C. (the date established by radiocarbon testing). It is surrounded by two broad earth banks separated by a ditch, originally 5.8m. deep. In the ditch's SE corner, excavation uncovered a square pit, perhaps a cistern. Across the centre of the ditch's NE side, a solid 6.1m.-wide bridge to the enclosure's entrance, which may have been timber-framed. On the enclosure's NW side there has been at least one round house, *c*.13.5m. in diameter.

CASTLEWIGG. *See* p. 178.

WIGTOWN

4050

Small town (its population only *c*.1,000), first mentioned as a royal burgh in 1292 but probably founded before the 1260s, when the sheriffdom of Wigtown was already in existence and a Dominican convent was founded here. Its castle beside the Blad-noch was of sufficient importance in 1291 to be one of those specified for delivery to Edward I preparatory to his adjudication on the rival claims to the Scottish crown. In 1341 Wigtown became a burgh of barony; the superiority was granted to Sir Malcolm Fleming, from whose family it later passed to the Earls of Douglas. After the forfeiture of the Douglas earldom in 1455, Wigtown again received the status of a royal burgh but never developed into more than a town serving the needs of the immediate neighbourhood, although it was also the administrative capital of Wigtownshire.

CHURCHES

CHURCH OF THE SACRED HEART (R.C.), South Main Street. Simple brick-built Gothic, by *J. Garden Brown*, 1879. Cruciform, with a bellcote on the S (liturgical E) gable.

WIGTOWN PARISH CHURCH, Bank Street. By the London architect *Henry Roberts*, 1851; *see* the Introduction, p. 44. Big and bare Gothic, built of granite. Broad box of a nave and E transept, both with angle buttresses. Three-stage E tower, its French pavilion roof now deprived of cresting. The organ chamber on the transept's N was added, together with an extension to the W vestry, by *P. MacGregor Chalmers* in 1913–14.

Open wooden roof over the interior. The pulpit stood originally in the centre of the W wall facing the transept, which opens into the body through a three-bay Gothic arcade. In 1913–14 Chalmers rearranged the seating to face N, the new focus being provided by his communion table and font. – ORGAN by *Ingram & Co.*, 1924. – STAINED GLASS. In the N window, three lights of abstract patterning with some heraldry, probably of the 1850s. – E transept window also of three lights (Moses, Solomon, and St Paul), by *James Ballantine & Son*, 1866–7, brightly coloured and rather two-dimensional. – In the transept, three GRAVESLABS moved here from the churchyard. One is a Celtic cross shaft decorated on both faces with bands of interlaced rings. The other two are early C17, one dated 1620.

GRAVEYARD. W of the church, the ivy-clad remains of the OLD PARISH CHURCH, which was repaired *c.*1560 and 'mostly rebuilt' in 1730. Much of the E gable and S wall still stand. In the S wall, two large pointed windows. Round-arched gable window with a small rectangular opening to its S. There has been a S 'aisle', perhaps late C16 or early C17; its S gable survives, with a large window. Inside the 'aisle', a round-arched tomb recess, its keystone carved with the coat of arms of Vans of Barnbarroch. On the church's S wall within the 'aisle', a TABLET commemorating Roger Gordon †1737, its top carved with a coat of arms. Inscription ending:

> His pious Soul taught to aspire
> by genrous deeds hath winged its way
> to happier climes death only here
> detains a mouldiring frame of clay

– N of the Old Parish Church, three stones of *c.*1720 to Covenanting martyrs executed in 1685. One, a TABLE STONE, records the death of the eighteen-year-old Margaret Willson who was tied to a stake in Wigtown Bay and drowned by the incoming tide. Inscription on the slab:

> LET EARTH AND STONE STIL WITNES BEARE
> THEIR LYES A VIRGINE MARTYRE HERE
> MURTHER'D FOR OWNING CHRIST SUPREAME,
> HEAD OF HIS CHURCH AND NO MORE CRIME
> BUT NOT ABJURING PRESBYTRY,
> AND HER NOT OWNING PRELACY,
> THEY HER CONDEM'D, BY UNJUST LAW,
> OF HEAVEN NOR HELL THEY STOOD NO AW
> WITHIN THE SEA TYD TO A STAKE
> SHE SUFFERED FOR CHRIST JESUS SAKE;
> THE ACTORS OF THIS CRUEL CRIME
> WAS LAGG.STRACHAN.WINRAM.AND GRHAME.
> NEITHER YOUNG YEARES NOR YET OLD AGE
> COULD STOP THE FURY OF THERE RAGE.

PUBLIC BUILDINGS

ALL SOULS R.C. SCHOOL, New Road. Late C19, single-storey, with broad eaves and a big centre gablet. Addition of the later C20 on the N.

III COUNTY BUILDINGS AND TOWN HALL, The Square. By

Brown & Wardrop, 1862–3, a big piend-roofed rectangle of red and yellow Cumbrian sandstone, the general impression French early medieval, the detailing of the two-light first floor windows Flemish Gothic. On the centre of the N side, a tower of three stages; the lower two were built *c.* 1756 as the tower of the Court House which formerly stood on the site, but they were refaced in 1862–3, when Brown & Wardrop added the tall belfry, with a large three-light opening in each face. Below the N belfry opening, a stone balcony. Above the belfry, deep arcaded corbelling with dragon gargoyles at the corners, supporting the swept eaves of the tall French pavilion roof, its metal cresting still intact. On the porch beside the tower, a 1750s panel from the old Court House, carved with the royal arms; contemporary panel bearing the burgh arms on the tower itself. At the main (W) front, the door is flanked by gabled buttresses flanking the door, and the tympanum of its arch is carved with the royal arms and flanked by carved seals of Wigtownshire's two other royal burghs, Whithorn and Stranraer. Over the door, a long stone balcony with heraldic lions perched on the ends.

COVENANTERS MONUMENT, Windyhill, off High Vennel. By *James Maclaren*, 1858. Of grey sandstone ashlar. Square, gently Ægypto-Greek battered plinth. On this, a tapered octagonal shaft surmounted by a stone cinerary urn.

HARBOUR, off Harbour Road. Begun in 1822. Wood and rubble quay beside the River Bladnoch; small rectangular basin.

JAIL, Harbour Road. Now housing. By *Thomas Brown Jun.*, 1846–8. Like a large Tudor villa, with hoodmoulded windows and a terrific display of chimneys.

WIGTOWN SCHOOL, New Road. Dated 1910. Long and single-storey, with sparing Jacobean detail, the windows now much altered. S extension by *Wigtownshire County Council*, 1957.

DESCRIPTION

BANK STREET, the entry from the E, curves uphill past Wigtown Parish Church (*see* Churches, above) and the WAR MEMORIAL of 1921–2, a big tower-like granite monument, its front carved with a laurel-wreathed sword. Then, on the l., the back of the WIGTOWN HOUSE HOTEL, the former British Linen Company Bank of *c.* 1840; at its red sandstone ashlar S front, corniced windows and a portico with piers and a block pediment. Chimneys grouped like a belvedere on the centre of the M-roof. It stands in an C18 walled garden. Granite ashlar gatepiers on the S side. At its E corners, square pavilions (the S roofless) with keyblocked round-arched windows and rusticated quoins. The street proper now starts with an informal C19 cottagey mixture, Nos. 13–15 with a club skewputt, No. 11 dated 1840. Rather larger but plain late Georgian, the two-storey Nos. 2–10 at the top.

THE SQUARE, Wigtown's central space, is a big rectangle, its centre filled with a bowling green and public garden first laid out (replacing a dunghill) in 1809 and remodelled in 1887. At the garden's W end, two MARKET CROSSES. One, dated 1738, has a fat round shaft which carries a square sundial, its pineapple finial now truncated. The other, put up in 1816, is much suaver. Three progressively narrowing stages of granite ashlar, the first with corner buttresses and Gothic cusp-panelled sides, the second with corner shafts and simple pointed panels, the third simpler again. Cross on the top.

SOUTH MAIN STREET runs along The Square's S side but begins to its E, the outward vista closed by the late Georgian APPLEGARTH. No. 4 on the N side of this stretch is also late Georgian, with a heavy entablature on its Roman Doric portico. The OLD BANK on the S is double-pile, the front block mid-C19 with two-light windows and a broad-eaved piend roof. Doorpiece of Ionic columns *in antis*; another Ionic columned doorpiece on the E gable. The back block is probably late C18 but quite plain. Just to the NE, a battle-mented single-storey late Georgian outbuilding. South Main Street bordering The Square is largely plain two-storey late Georgian, with some fairly discreet infill of the later C20 and the brick R.C. Church of the Sacred Heart (*see* Churches, above) modestly set back behind a front garden. Early C19 Roman Doric columned doorpiece with a heavy entablature at No. 18. No. 22, with an advanced and pedimented centre, looks late C18; an early C19 Roman Doric columned doorpiece on its l. bay. The GALLOWAY INN beside it may also be C18 but is much humbler. The late Georgian No. 29 is smart, with three-light windows in the outer bays and a consoled cornice over the door; the main cornice's metal cresting is a late Victorian embellishment. Club skews on No. 31, probably of the mid-C19.

NORTH MAIN STREET on The Square's other side is a similar mixture. The very simple RED LION looks C18. On the late C20 Nos. 7–9, a re-used long marriage stone of 1819. The rendered No. 11 on the corner of New Road, probably mid-C18, has a prosperous Ionic portico on its side. At the early C19 No. 17, a ground floor of hammerdressed granite ashlar; V-jointed ashlar above. The bargeboarded dormers are Victorian additions. A late C18 aedicular doorpiece at No. 18, whose l. skewputt, perhaps re-used, is carved with a head.

After the Market Crosses, the two Main Streets converge and, from the junction with Agnew Crescent, become HIGH STREET, mostly C19 vernacular with C20 infill, providing the town's W exit.

AGNEW CRESCENT to the S, towards the harbour (for which *see* Public Buildings, above), provides more C19 vernacular. At the single-storey Nos. 8–10 on the l., big club skewputts and concave-sided door surrounds. On the r., No. 11 and ROWAN HOUSE both have early C19 pilastered doorpieces, No. 11's now bereft of its cornice. Set back on the l., ORCHARDTON HOUSE, a straightforward early C19 farmhouse-villa of two

storeys and three bays. At Agnew Crescent's s end, WOODSIDE
is mid-C19 Georgian-survival, with an aedicular doorpiece and
bracketed piend roof. 0.1km. s, an early C19 bow-ended TOLL-
HOUSE.

HARBOUR ROAD runs e from Agnew Crescent. On its N,
DUNURE, an ambitious brute classical two-storey villa of 1833.
Three bays, the centre advanced with a Roman Doric portico
under a three-light first-floor window. Channelled masonry at
the outer bays of the ground floor. Corner pilasters at the centre
and ends, each surmounted by a corniced plinth on the heavy
parapet. It is set well back in a garden whose pedestrian gate-
ways are topped by antefixae. In Harbour Road's NE stretch
running uphill to South Main Street, the former Jail on the l.
(*see* Public Buildings, above). On the r., the MANSE (the former
Free Church Manse) of *c.*1845, two storeys and three bays
without frills.

STONE CIRCLE, Torhousekie, 5km. w. Formed in the second
millennium B.C., a remarkably intact circle (its diameter
*c.*18.6m.–20.1m.) of nineteen squat granite boulders, smaller
and more closely spaced in the NW segment, largest (up to
1.4m. high) at the SE. In the centre, placed across this NW–SE
axis, a line of three more stones, the centre one smaller than
the others. Facing towards the circle, but *c.*24m. to the s, a
standing stone *c.*1.47m. high.
    c. 119m. E of the circle and across the road, a line of three
more upended boulders.

WOODHOUSE TOWER   *2070*
1.7km. SE of Kirtlebridge

Remains of a tower house, probably of the mid-C16; the ruin was
consolidated and 'restored' in 1877. The house has been a
simple four-storey rubble-walled rectangle, *c.*9.7m. by 7.5m.
The N gable and stubs of the E and W sides stand to the
wallhead. At the top, a fat stringcourse runs immediately below
the individual moulded corbels, which support a cavetto cornice
under the missing parapet. This work seems to be of the 1870s,
re-using old stones; angle turrets might have been expected
originally. At the base of each of the N and W walls, a rectangular
gunloop containing a round shothole. In the N wall, roll-
moulded windows. Slit windows to the stair contained in the
wall thickness of the NE corner. This is a tight turnpike; its
lower steps still survive, but the doors to the upper floors are
built up. Springers for a (now missing) ground-floor vault. At
the first-floor level, the N window has an aumbry in its w ingo
and the remains of stone seats. Roll-moulded jamb of a w
fireplace, now projecting boldly from the wall. Large aumbry
to its r. Another aumbry in the same position at the second
floor, whose joists, like those of the top floor, were probably
carried on moulded stone corbels, of which a few appear in the

N gable but not necessarily *in situ*. At the third floor, dressed stones, perhaps of a fireplace jamb, in the W wall.

WREATHS TOWER

2.5km. SE of Caulkerbush

Only the rubble-built SE corner still stands of a house of at least three storeys, probably put up early in the C16 for the Douglas Earls of Morton. The corner has contained a turnpike stair. In the E wall, next the stair, one chamfered jamb and part of the lintel of a first-floor window.

GLOSSARY

Numbers and letters refer to the illustrations by John Sambrook
on pp. 586–93.

ABACUS: flat slab forming the top of
a capital (3a).

ACANTHUS: classical formalized leaf
ornament (3b).

ACCUMULATOR TOWER: *see* Hydraulic power.

ACHIEVEMENT: a complete display
of armorial bearings (i.e. coat of
arms, crest, supporters and
motto).

ACROTERION: plinth for a statue or
ornament on the apex or ends of a
pediment; more usually, both the
plinth and what stands on it (4a).

ADDORSED: descriptive of two
figures placed back to back.

AEDICULE (*lit.* little building):
architectural surround, consisting
usually of two columns or pilasters
supporting a pediment.

AFFRONTED: descriptive of two
figures placed face to face.

AGGREGATE: *see* Concrete, Harling.

AISLE: subsidiary space alongside
the body of a building, separated
from it by columns, piers or posts.
Also (Scots) projecting wing of a
church, often for special use, e.g.
by a guild or by a landed family
whose burial place it may contain.

AMBULATORY (*lit.* walkway): aisle
around the sanctuary (q.v.).

ANGLE ROLL: roll moulding in the
angle between two planes (1a).

ANSE DE PANIER: *see* Arch.

ANTAE: simplified pilasters (4a),
usually applied to the ends of the
enclosing walls of a portico (q.v.)
in antis.

ANTEFIXAE: ornaments projecting
at regular intervals above a Greek
cornice, originally to conceal the
ends of roof tiles (4a).

ANTHEMION: classical ornament
like a honeysuckle flower (4b).

APRON: panel below a window or
wall monument or tablet.

APSE: semicircular or polygonal end
of an apartment, especially of a
chancel or chapel. In classical
architecture sometimes called an
exedra.

ARABESQUE: non-figurative surface
decoration consisting of flowing
lines, foliage scrolls etc., based
on geometrical patterns. Cf. Grotesque.

ARCADE: series of arches supported by piers or columns. *Blind
arcade* or *arcading*: the same
applied to the wall surface. *Wall
arcade*: in medieval churches, a
blind arcade forming a dado
below windows. Also a covered
shopping street.

ARCH: Shapes *see* 5c. *Basket arch* or
anse de panier (basket handle):
three-centred and depressed, or
with a flat centre. *Nodding*: ogee
arch curving forward from the wall
face. *Parabolic*: shaped like a chain
suspended from two level points,
but inverted.
Special purposes. *Chancel*: dividing chancel from nave or crossing.
Crossing: spanning piers at a crossing (q.v.). *Relieving* or *discharging*:
incorporated in a wall to relieve
superimposed weight (5c). *Skew*:
spanning responds not diametrically opposed. *Strainer*:
inserted in an opening to resist
inward pressure. *Transverse*: spanning a main axis (e.g. of a vaulted
space). *See also* Jack arch, Overarch, Triumphal arch.

ARCHITRAVE: formalized lintel, the
lowest member of the classical entablature (3a). Also the moulded
frame of a door or window (often
borrowing the profile of a classical architrave). For *lugged* and
shouldered architraves *see* 4b.

ARCUATED: dependent structurally

on the arch principle. Cf. Trabeated.

ARK: chest or cupboard housing the tables of Jewish law in a synagogue.

ARRIS: sharp edge where two surfaces meet at an angle (3a).

ASHLAR: masonry of large blocks wrought to even faces and square edges (6d). *Broached ashlar* (Scots): scored with parallel lines made by a narrow-pointed chisel (broach). *Droved ashlar*: similar but with lines made by a broad chisel.

ASTRAGAL: classical moulding of semicircular section (3f). Also (Scots) glazing-bar between window panes.

ASTYLAR: with no columns or similar vertical features.

ATLANTES: *see* Caryatids.

ATRIUM (plural: atria): inner court of a Roman or C20 house; in a multi-storey building, a toplit covered court rising through all storeys. Also an open court in front of a church.

ATTACHED COLUMN: *see* Engaged column.

ATTIC: small top storey within a roof. Also the storey above the main entablature of a classical façade.

AUMBRY: recess or cupboard, especially one in a church, to hold sacred vessels used for the Mass.

BAILEY: *see* Motte-and-bailey.

BALANCE BEAM: *see* Canals.

BALDACCHINO: freestanding canopy, originally fabric, over an altar. Cf. Ciborium.

BALLFLOWER: globular flower of three petals enclosing a ball (1a). Typical of the Decorated style.

BALUSTER: pillar or pedestal of bellied form. *Balusters*: vertical supports of this or any other form, for a handrail or coping, the whole being called a *balustrade* (6c). *Blind balustrade*: the same applied to the wall surface.

BARBICAN: outwork defending the entrance to a castle.

BARGEBOARDS (corruption of 'vergeboards'): boards, often carved or fretted, fixed beneath the eaves of a gable to cover and protect the rafters.

BARMKIN (Scots): wall enclosing

courtyard attached to a tower house.

BARONY: *see* Burgh.

BAROQUE: style originating in Rome *c*.1600 and current in England *c*.1680–1720, characterized by dramatic massing and silhouette and the use of the giant order.

BARROW: burial mound.

BARTIZAN: corbelled turret, square or round, frequently at an angle (8a).

BASCULE: hinged part of a lifting (or bascule) bridge.

BASE: moulded foot of a column or pilaster. For *Attic* base *see* 3b. For *Elided* base *see* Elided.

BASEMENT: lowest, subordinate storey; hence the lowest part of a classical elevation, below the piano nobile (q.v.).

BASILICA: a Roman public hall; hence an aisled building with a clerestory.

BASTION: one of a series of defensive semicircular or polygonal projections from the main wall of a fortress or city.

BATTER: intentional inward inclination of a wall face.

BATTLEMENT: defensive parapet, composed of *merlons* (solid) and *crenelles* (embrasures) through which archers could shoot (8a); sometimes called *crenellation*. Also used decoratively.

BAY: division of an elevation or interior space as defined by regular vertical features such as arches, columns, windows etc.

BAY LEAF: classical ornament of overlapping bay leaves (3f).

BAY-WINDOW: window of one or more storeys projecting from the face of a building. *Canted*: with a straight front and angled sides. *Bow window*: curved. *Oriel*: rests on corbels or brackets and starts above ground level; also the bay window at the dais end of a medieval great hall.

BEAD-AND-REEL: *see* Enrichments.

BEAKHEAD: Norman ornament with a row of beaked bird or beast heads usually biting into a roll moulding (1a).

BEE-BOLL: wall recess to contain a beehive.

BELFRY: chamber or stage in a tower where bells are hung. Also belltower in a general sense.

BELL CAPITAL: *see* 1b.

BELLCAST: *see* Roof.

BELLCOTE: bell-turret set on a roof or gable. *Birdcage bellcote*: framed structure, usually of stone.

BERM: level area separating a ditch from a bank on a hillfort or barrow.

BILLET: Norman ornament of small half-cylindrical or rectangular blocks (1a).

BIVALLATE: of a hillfort: defended by two concentric banks and ditches.

BLIND: *see* Arcade, Baluster, Portico.

BLOCK CAPITAL: *see* 1a.

BLOCKED: columns etc. interrupted by regular projecting blocks (*blocking*), as on a Gibbs surround (4b).

BLOCKING COURSE: course of stones, or equivalent, on top of a cornice and crowning the wall.

BÖD: *see* Bü.

BOLECTION MOULDING: covering the joint between two different planes (6b).

BOND: the pattern of long sides (*stretchers*) and short ends (*headers*) produced on the face of a wall by laying bricks in a particular way (6e).

BOSS: knob or projection, e.g. at the intersection of ribs in a vault (2c).

BOW WINDOW: *see* Bay-window.

BOX FRAME: timber-framed construction in which vertical and horizontal wall members support the roof. Also concrete construction where the loads are taken on cross walls; also called *cross-wall construction*.

BRACE: subsidiary member of a structural frame, curved or straight. *Bracing* is often arranged decoratively, e.g. quatrefoil, herringbone. *See also* Roofs.

BRATTISHING: ornamental crest, usually formed of leaves, Tudor flowers or miniature battlements.

BRESSUMER (*lit.* breast-beam): big horizontal beam supporting the wall above, especially in a jettied building.

BRETASCHE (*lit.* battlement): defensive wooden gallery on a wall.

BRICK: *see* Bond, Cogging, Engineering, Gauged, Tumbling.

BRIDGE: *Bowstring*: with arches rising above the roadway which is suspended from them. *Clapper*: one long stone forms the roadway. *Roving*: *see* Canal. *Suspension*: roadway suspended from cables or chains slung between towers or pylons. *Stay-suspension* or *stay-cantilever*: supported by diagonal stays from towers or pylons. *See also* Bascule.

BRISES-SOLEIL: projecting fins or canopies which deflect direct sunlight from windows.

BROACH: *see* Spire and 1c.

BROCH (Scots): circular tower-like structure, open in the middle, the double wall of dry-stone masonry linked by slabs forming internal galleries at varying levels; found in W and N Scotland and mostly dating from between 100 B.C. and A.D. 100.

BÜ or BÖD (Scots, esp. Shetland; *lit.* booth): combined house and store.

BUCRANIUM: ox skull used decoratively in classical friezes.

BULLSEYE WINDOW: small oval window, set horizontally (cf. Oculus). Also called *oeil de boeuf*.

BURGH: formally constituted town with trading privileges. *Royal Burghs*: monopolized foreign trade till the C17 and paid duty to the Crown. *Burghs of Barony*: founded by secular or ecclesiastical barons to whom they paid duty on their local trade. *Police Burghs*: instituted after 1850 for the administration of new centres of population and abolished in 1975. They controlled planning, building etc.

BUT-AND-BEN (Scots, *lit.* outer and inner rooms): two-room cottage.

BUTTRESS: vertical member projecting from a wall to stabilize it or to resist the lateral thrust of an arch, roof or vault (1c, 2c). A *flying buttress* transmits the thrust to a heavy abutment by means of an arch or half-arch (1c).

CABLE or ROPE MOULDING: originally Norman, like twisted strands of a rope.

CAMES: *see* Quarries.

CAMPANILE: freestanding belltower.

CANALS: *Flash lock*: removable weir or similar device through which boats pass on a flush of water. Predecessor of the *pound lock*: chamber with gates at each end allowing boats to float from one level to another. *Tidal gates*: single pair of lock gates allowing vessels to pass when the tide makes a level. *Balance beam*: beam projecting horizontally for opening and closing lock gates. *Roving bridge*: carrying a towing path from one bank to the other.

CANDLE-SNUFFER ROOF: conical roof of a turret (8a).

CANNON SPOUT: *see* 8a.

CANTILEVER: horizontal projection (e.g. step, canopy) supported by a downward force behind the fulcrum.

CAPHOUSE (Scots): small chamber at the head of a turnpike stair, opening onto the parapet walk (8a). Also a chamber rising from within the parapet walk.

CAPITAL: head or crowning feature of a column or pilaster; for classical types *see* 3a; for medieval types *see* 1b.

CARREL: compartment designed for individual work or study, e.g. in a library.

CARTOUCHE: classical tablet with ornate frame (4b).

CARYATIDS: female figures supporting an entablature; their male counterparts are *Atlantes* (*lit.* Atlas figures).

CASEMATE: vaulted chamber, with embrasures for defence, within a castle wall or projecting from it.

CASEMENT: side-hinged window. Also a concave Gothic moulding framing a window.

CASTELLATED: with battlements (q.v.).

CAST IRON: iron containing at least 2.2 per cent of carbon, strong in compression but brittle in tension; cast in a mould to required shape, e.g. for columns or repetitive ornaments. *Wrought iron* is a purer form of iron, with no more than 0.3 per cent of carbon, ductile and strong in tension, forged and rolled into e.g. bars, joists, boiler plates; *mild steel* is its modern equivalent, similar but stronger.

CATSLIDE: *See* 7.

CAVETTO: concave classical moulding of quarter-round section (3f).

CELURE or CEILURE: enriched area of roof above rood or altar.

CEMENT: *see* Concrete.

CENOTAPH (*lit.* empty tomb): funerary monument which is not a burying place.

CENTRING: wooden support for the building of an arch or vault, removed after completion.

CHAMBERED TOMB: Neolithic burial mound with a stone-built chamber and entrance passage covered by an earthen barrow or stone cairn.

CHAMFER (*lit.* corner-break): surface formed by cutting off a square edge or corner. For types of chamfers and *chamfer stops see* 6a. See *also* Double chamfer.

CHANCEL: E end of the church containing the sanctuary; often used to include the choir.

CHANTRY CHAPEL: often attached to or within a church, endowed for the celebration of Masses principally for the soul of the founder.

CHECK (Scots): rebate.

CHERRY-CAULKING or CHERRY-COCKING (Scots): decorative masonry technique using lines of tiny stones (*pins* or *pinning*) in the mortar joints.

CHEVET (*lit.* head): French term for chancel with ambulatory and radiating chapels.

CHEVRON: V-shape used in series or double series (later) on a Norman moulding (1a). Also (especially when on a single plane) called *zigzag*.

CHOIR: the part of a church E of the nave, intended for the stalls of choir monks, choristers and clergy.

CIBORIUM: a fixed canopy over an altar, usually vaulted and supported on four columns; cf. Baldacchino.

CINQUEFOIL: *see* Foil.

CIST: stone-lined or slab-built grave.

CLADDING: external covering or skin applied to a structure, especially a framed one.

CLEARSTOREY: uppermost storey of the nave of a church, pierced by windows. Also high-level windows in secular buildings.

CLOSE (Scots): courtyard or passage giving access to a number of buildings.

CLOSER: a brick cut to complete a bond (6e).

CLUSTER BLOCK: *see* Multi-storey.

COADE STONE: ceramic artificial stone made in Lambeth 1769–c.1840 by Eleanor Coade (†1821) and her associates.

COB: walling material of clay mixed with straw.

COFFERING: arrangement of sunken panels (coffers), square or polygonal, decorating a ceiling, vault or arch.

COGGING: a decorative course of bricks laid diagonally (6e). Cf. Dentilation.

COLLAR: see Roofs and 7.

COLLEGIATE CHURCH: endowed for the support of a college of priests, especially for the saying of masses for the soul(s) of the founder(s).

COLONNADE: range of columns supporting an entablature. Cf. Arcade.

COLONNETTE: small column or shaft.

COLOSSAL ORDER: see Giant order.

COLUMBARIUM: shelved, niched structure to house multiple burials.

COLUMN: a classical, upright structural member of round section with a shaft, a capital and usually a base (3a, 4a).

COLUMN FIGURE: carved figure attached to a medieval column or shaft, usually flanking a doorway.

COMMENDATOR: receives the revenues of an abbey *in commendam* ('in trust') when the position of abbot is vacant.

COMMUNION TABLE: table used in Protestant churches for the celebration of Holy Communion.

COMPOSITE: see Orders.

COMPOUND PIER: grouped shafts (q.v.), or a solid core surrounded by shafts.

CONCRETE: composition of *cement* (calcined lime and clay), *aggregate* (small stones or rock chippings), sand and water. It can be poured into *formwork* or *shuttering* (temporary frame of timber or metal) on site (*in-situ* concrete), or *pre-cast* as components before construction. *Reinforced*: incorporating steel rods to take the tensile force. *Prestressed*: with tensioned steel rods. Finishes include the impression of boards left by formwork (*board-marked* or *shuttered*), and texturing with steel brushes (*brushed*) or hammers (*hammer-dressed*). *See also* Shell.

CONDUCTOR (Scots): down-pipe for rainwater; *see also* Rhone.

CONSOLE: bracket of curved outline (4b).

COPING: protective course of masonry or brickwork capping a wall (6d).

COOMB or COMB CEILING (Scots): with sloping sides corresponding to the roof pitch up to a flat centre.

CORBEL: projecting block supporting something above. *Corbel course*: continuous course of projecting stones or bricks fulfilling the same function. *Corbel table*: series of corbels to carry a parapet or a wall-plate or wall-post (7). *Corbelling*: brick or masonry courses built out beyond one another to support a chimney-stack, window etc. For *continuous* and *chequer-set* corbelling see 8a.

CORINTHIAN: see Orders and 3d.

CORNICE: flat-topped ledge with moulded underside, projecting along the top of a building or feature, especially as the highest member of the classical entablature (3a). Also the decorative moulding in the angle between wall and ceiling.

CORPS-DE-LOGIS: the main building(s) as distinct from the wings or pavilions.

COTTAGE ORNÉ: an artfully rustic small house associated with the Picturesque movement.

COUNTERSCARP BANK: low bank on the downhill or outer side of a hillfort ditch.

COUR D'HONNEUR: formal entrance court before a house in the French manner, usually with flanking wings and a screen wall or gates.

COURSE: continuous layer of stones etc. in a wall (6e).

COVE: a broad concave moulding, e.g. to mask the eaves of a roof. *Coved ceiling*: with a pronounced cove joining the walls to a flat central panel smaller than the whole area of the ceiling.

CRADLE ROOF: see Wagon roof.

CREDENCE: shelved niche or table, usually beside a piscina (q.v.), for the sacramental elements and vessels.

CRENELLATION: parapet with cren-elles (*see* Battlement).

CRINKLE-CRANKLE WALL: garden wall undulating in a series of serpentine curves.

CROCKETS: leafy hooks. *Crocketing* decorates the edges of Gothic features, such as pinnacles, canopies etc. *Crocket capital: see* 1b.

CROSSING: central space at the junction of the nave, chancel and transepts. *Crossing tower*: above a crossing.

CROSS-WINDOW: with one mullion and one transom (qq.v.).

CROWN-POST: *see* Roofs and 7.

CROWSTEPS: squared stones set like steps, especially on a crowstepped gable (7, 8a).

CRUCKS (*lit.* crooked): pairs of inclined timbers (*blades*), usually curved, set at bay-lengths; they support the roof timbers and, in timber buildings, also support the walls. *Base*: blades rise from ground level to a tie-or collar-beam which supports the roof timbers. *Full*: blades rise from ground level to the apex of the roof, serving as the main members of a roof truss. *Jointed*: blades formed from more than one timber; the lower member may act as a wall-post; it is usually elbowed at wall-plate level and jointed just above. *Middle*: blades rise from halfway up the walls to a tie-or collar-beam. *Raised*: blades rise from halfway up the walls to the apex. *Upper*: blades supported on a tie-beam and rising to the apex.

CRYPT: underground or half-underground area, usually below the E end of a church. *Ring crypt*: corridor crypt surrounding the apse of an early medieval church, often associated with chambers for relics. Cf. Undercroft.

CUPOLA (*lit.* dome): especially a small dome on a circular or polygonal base crowning a larger dome, roof or turret. Also (Scots) small dome or skylight as an internal feature, especially over a stairwell.

CURSUS: a long avenue defined by two parallel earthen banks with ditches outside.

CURTAIN WALL: a connecting wall between the towers of a castle. Also a non-load-bearing external wall applied to a C20 framed structure.

CUSP: *see* Tracery and 2b.

CYCLOPEAN MASONRY: large irregular polygonal stones, smooth and finely jointed.

CYMA RECTA and CYMA REVERSA: classical mouldings with double curves (3f). Cf. Ogee.

DADO: the finishing (often with panelling) of the lower part of a wall in a classical interior; in origin a formalized continuous pedestal. *Dado rail*: the moulding along the top of the dado.

DAGGER: *see* Tracery and 2b.

DEC (DECORATED): English Gothic architecture *c.* 1290 to *c.* 1350. The name is derived from the type of window tracery (q.v.) used during the period.

DEMI- or HALF-COLUMNS: engaged columns (q.v.) half of whose circumference projects from the wall.

DENTIL: small square block used in series in classical cornices (3c). *Dentilation* is produced by the projection of alternating headers along cornices or string-courses.

DIAPER: repetitive surface decoration of lozenges or squares flat or in relief. Achieved in brickwork with bricks of two colours.

DIOCLETIAN or THERMAL WINDOW: semicircular with two mullions, as used in the Baths of Diocletian, Rome (4b).

DISTYLE: having two columns (4a).

DOGTOOTH: E.E. ornament, consisting of a series of small pyramids formed by four stylized canine teeth meeting at a point (1a).

DOOCOT (Scots): dovecot. When freestanding, usually *Lectern* (rectangular with single-pitch roof) or *Beehive* (circular, diminishing towards the top).

DORIC: *see* Orders and 3a, 3b.

DORMER: window projecting from the slope of a roof (7). *Dormer head*: gable above a dormer, often formed as a pediment (8a).

DOUBLE CHAMFER: a chamfer applied to each of two recessed arches (1a).

DOUBLE PILE: *see* Pile.

DRAGON BEAM: *see* Jetty.

DRESSINGS: the stone or brickwork worked to a finished face about an angle, opening or other feature.

DRIPSTONE: moulded stone projecting from a wall to protect the lower parts from water. Cf. Hoodmould, Weathering.

DRUM: circular or polygonal stage supporting a dome or cupola. Also one of the stones forming the shaft of a column (3a).

DRY-STONE: stone construction without mortar.

DUN (Scots): small stone-walled fort.

DUTCH or FLEMISH GABLE: *see* 7.

EASTER SEPULCHRE: tomb-chest, usually within or against the N wall of a chancel, used in Holy Week ceremonies for reservation (entombment) of the sacrament after the mass of Maundy Thursday.

EAVES: overhanging edge of a roof; hence *eaves cornice* in this position.

ECHINUS: ovolo moulding (q.v.) below the abacus of a Greek Doric capital (3a).

EDGE RAIL: *see* Railways.

EDGE-ROLL: moulding of semicircular section or more at the edge of an opening.

E.E. (EARLY ENGLISH): English Gothic architecture *c.* 1190–1250.

EGG-AND-DART: *see* Enrichments and 3f.

ELEVATION: any face of a building or side of a room. In a drawing, the same or any part of it, represented in two dimensions.

ELIDED: used to describe a compound feature, e.g. an entablature, with some parts omitted. Also, parts of, e.g., a base or capital, combined to form a larger one.

EMBATTLED: with battlements.

EMBRASURE: splayed opening in a wall or battlement (q.v.).

ENCAUSTIC TILES: earthenware tiles fired with a pattern and glaze.

EN DELIT: stone laid against the bed.

ENFILADE: reception rooms in a formal series, usually with all doorways on axis.

ENGAGED or ATTACHED COLUMN: one that partly merges into a wall or pier.

ENGINEERING BRICKS: dense bricks, originally used mostly for railway viaducts etc.

ENRICHMENTS: the carved decoration of certain classical mouldings, e.g. the ovolo with *egg-and-dart*, the cyma reversa with *waterleaf*, the astragal with *bead-and-reel* (3f).

ENTABLATURE: in classical architecture, collective name for the three horizontal members (architrave, frieze and cornice) carried by a wall or a column (3a).

ENTASIS: very slight convex deviation from a straight line, used to prevent an optical illusion of concavity.

ENTRESOL: mezzanine floor subdividing what is constructionally a single storey, e.g. a vault.

EPITAPH: inscription on a tomb or monument.

EXEDRA: *see* Apse.

EXTRADOS: outer curved face of an arch or vault.

EYECATCHER: decorative building terminating a vista.

FASCIA: plain horizontal band, e.g. in an architrave (3c, 3d) or on a shopfront.

FENESTRATION: the arrangement of windows in a façade.

FERETORY: site of the chief shrine of a church, behind the high altar.

FESTOON: ornamental garland, suspended from both ends. Cf. Swag.

FEU (Scots): land granted, e.g. by sale, by the *feudal superior* to the *vassal* or *feuar*, on conditions that usually include the annual payment of a fixed sum of *feu duty*. Any subsequent proprietor of the land becomes the feuar and is subject to the same obligations.

FIBREGLASS (or glass-reinforced polyester (GRP)): synthetic resin reinforced with glass fibre. GRC: glass-reinforced concrete.

FIELD: *see* Panelling and 6b.

FILLET: a narrow flat band running down a medieval shaft or along a roll moulding (1a). It separates larger curved mouldings in classical cornices, fluting or bases (3c).

FLAMBOYANT: the latest phase of French Gothic architecture, with flowing tracery.

FLASH LOCK: *see* Canals.

FLATTED: divided into apartments. Also with a colloquial (Scots) meaning: 'He stays on the first flat' means that he lives on the first floor.

FLÈCHE or SPIRELET (*lit.* arrow): slender spire on the centre of a roof.

FLEURON: medieval carved flower or leaf, often rectilinear (1a).

FLUSHWORK: knapped flint used with dressed stone to form patterns.

FLUTING: series of concave grooves (flutes), their common edges sharp (arris) or blunt (fillet) (3).

FOIL (*lit.* leaf): lobe formed by the cusping of a circular or other shape in tracery (2b). *Trefoil* (three), *quatrefoil* (four), *cinquefoil* (five) and *multifoil* express the number of lobes in a shape.

FOLIATE: decorated with leaves.

FORE-BUILDING: structure protecting an entrance.

FORESTAIR: external stair, usually unenclosed.

FORMWORK: *see* Concrete.

FRAMED BUILDING: where the structure is carried by a framework – e.g. of steel, reinforced concrete, timber – instead of by load-bearing walls.

FREESTONE: stone that is cut, or can be cut, in all directions.

FRESCO: *al fresco*: painting on wet plaster. *Fresco secco*: painting on dry plaster.

FRIEZE: the middle member of the classical entablature, sometimes ornamented (3a). *Pulvinated frieze* (*lit.* cushioned): of bold convex profile (3c). Also a horizontal band of ornament.

FRONTISPIECE: in C16 and C17 buildings the central feature of doorway and windows above linked in one composition.

GABLE: peaked external wall at end of double-pitch roof. For types *see* 7. Also (Scots): whole end wall of whatever shape. *Pedimental gable*: treated like a pediment.

GADROONING: classical ribbed ornament like inverted fluting that flows into a lobed edge.

GAIT or GATE (Scots): street, usually with a prefix indicating use, direction or destination.

GALILEE: chapel or vestibule usually at the W end of a church enclosing the main portal(s).

GALLERY: a long room or passage; an upper storey above the aisle of a church, looking through arches to the nave; a balcony or mezzanine overlooking the main interior space of a building; or an external walkway.

GALLETING: small stones set in a mortar course.

GAMBREL ROOF: *see* 7.

GARDEROBE: medieval privy.

GARGOYLE: projecting water spout, often carved into human or animal shape. For cannon spout *see* 8.

GAUGED or RUBBED BRICKWORK: soft brick sawn roughly, then rubbed to a precise (gauged) surface. Mostly used for door or window openings (5c).

GAZEBO (jocular Latin, 'I shall gaze'): ornamental lookout tower or raised summer house.

GEOMETRIC: English Gothic architecture *c.* 1250–1310. *See also* Tracery. For another meaning, *see* Stairs.

GIANT or COLOSSAL ORDER: classical order (q.v.) whose height is that of two or more storeys of the building to which it is applied.

GIBBS SURROUND: C18 treatment of an opening (4b), seen particularly in the work of James Gibbs (1682–1754).

GIRDER: a large beam. *Box*: of hollow-box section. *Bowed*: with its top rising in a curve. *Plate*: of I-section, made from iron or steel plates. *Lattice*: with braced framework.

GLACIS: artificial slope extending out and downwards from the parapet of a fort.

GLAZING-BARS: wooden or sometimes metal bars separating and supporting window panes.

GLAZING GROOVE: groove in a window surround into which the glass is fitted.

GNOMON: vane or indicator casting a shadow onto a sundial.

GRAFFITI: *see* Sgraffito.

GRANGE: farm owned and run by a religious order.

GRC: *see* Fibreglass.

GRISAILLE: monochrome painting on walls or glass.

GROIN: sharp edge at the meeting of two cells of a cross-vault; *see* Vault and 2b.

GROTESQUE (*lit.* grotto-esque): wall decoration adopted from Roman

GLOSSARY 583

examples in the Renaissance. Its foliage scrolls incorporate figurative elements. Cf. Arabesque.

GROTTO: artificial cavern.

GRP: *see* Fibreglass.

GUILLOCHE: classical ornament of interlaced bands (4b).

GUNLOOP: opening for a firearm (8a).

GUTTAE: stylized drops (3b).

HALF-TIMBERING: archaic term for timber-framing (q.v.). Sometimes used for non-structural decorative timberwork.

HALL CHURCH: medieval church with nave and aisles of approximately equal height. Also (Scots C20) building for use as both hall and church, the double function usually intended to be temporary until a separate church is built.

HAMMERBEAM: *see* Roofs and 7.

HARLING (Scots, *lit.* hurling): wet dash, i.e. a form of roughcasting in which the mixture of aggregate and binding material (e.g. lime) is dashed onto a wall.

HEADER: *see* Bond and 6e.

HEADSTOP: stop (q.v.) carved with a head (5b).

HELM ROOF: *see* IC.

HENGE: ritual earthwork with a surrounding ditch and outer bank.

HERM (*lit.* the god Hermes): male head or bust on a pedestal.

HERRINGBONE WORK: *see* 6e (for brick bond). Cf. Pitched masonry.

HEXASTYLE: *see* Portico.

HILLFORT: Iron Age earthwork enclosed by a ditch and bank system.

HIPPED ROOF: *see* 7.

HOODMOULD: projecting moulding above an arch or lintel to throw off water (2b, 5b). When horizontal often called a *label*. For label stop *see* Stop.

HORIZONTAL GLAZING: with panes of horizontal proportions.

HORSEMILL: circular or polygonal farm building with a central shaft turned by a horse to drive agricultural machinery.

HUNGRY-JOINTED: *see* Pointing.

HUSK GARLAND: festoon of stylized nutshells (4b).

HYDRAULIC POWER: use of water under high pressure to work machinery. *Accumulator tower*: houses a hydraulic accumulator

which accommodates fluctuations in the flow through hydraulic mains.

HYPOCAUST (*lit.* underburning): Roman underfloor heating system.

IMPOST: horizontal moulding at the springing of an arch (5c).

IMPOST BLOCK: block between abacus and capital (1b).

IN ANTIS: *see* Antae, Portico and 4a.

INDENT: shape chiselled out of a stone to receive a brass. Also, in restoration, new stone inserted as a patch.

INDUSTRIALIZED or SYSTEM BUILDING: system of manufactured units assembled on site.

INGLENOOK (*lit.* fire-corner): recess for a hearth with provision for seating.

INTERCOLUMNATION: interval between columns.

INTERLACE: decoration in relief simulating woven or entwined stems or bands.

INTRADOS: *see* Soffit.

IONIC: *see* Orders and 3c.

JACK ARCH: shallow segmental vault springing from beams, used for fireproof floors, bridge decks etc.

JAMB (*lit.* leg): one of the vertical sides of an opening. Also (Scots) wing or extension adjoining one side of a rectangular plan making it into an L-, T- or Z-plan.

JETTY: the projection of an upper storey beyond the storey below. In a stone building this is achieved by corbelling. In a timber-framed building it is made by the beams and joists of the lower storey oversailing the wall; on their outer ends is placed the sill of the walling for the storey above.

JOGGLE: the joining of two stones to prevent them slipping by a notch in one and a projection in the other.

KEEL MOULDING: moulding used from the late C12, in section like the keel of a ship (1a).

KEEP: principal tower of a castle.

KENTISH CUSP: *see* Tracery.

KEY PATTERN: *see* 4b.

KEYSTONE: central stone in an arch or vault (4b, 5c).

KINGPOST: see Roofs and 7.

KNEELER: horizontal projecting stone at the base of each side of a gable to support the inclined coping stones (7).

LABEL: see Hoodmould and 5b.

LABEL STOP: see Stop and 5b.

LACED BRICKWORK: vertical strips of brickwork, often in a contrasting colour, linking openings on different floors.

LACING COURSE: horizontal reinforcement in timber or brick to walls of flint, cobble etc.

LADY CHAPEL: dedicated to the Virgin Mary (Our Lady).

LAIGH or LAICH (Scots): low.

LAIRD (Scots): landowner.

LANCET: slender single-light, pointed-arched window (2a).

LANTERN: circular or polygonal windowed turret crowning a roof or a dome. Also the windowed stage of a crossing tower lighting the church interior.

LANTERN CROSS: churchyard cross with lantern-shaped top.

LAVATORIUM: in a religious house, a washing place adjacent to the refectory.

LEAN-TO: see Roofs.

LESENE (lit. a mean thing): pilaster without base or capital. Also called pilaster strip.

LIERNE: see Vault and 2c.

LIGHT: compartment of a window defined by the mullions.

LINENFOLD: Tudor panelling carved with simulations of folded linen.

LINTEL: horizontal beam or stone bridging an opening.

LOFT: gallery in a church. Organ loft: in which the organ, or sometimes only the console (keyboard), is placed. Laird's loft, Trades loft etc. (Scots): reserved for an individual or special group. See also Rood (loft).

LOGGIA: gallery, usually arcaded or colonnaded along one side; sometimes freestanding.

LONG-AND-SHORT WORK: quoins consisting of stones placed with the long side alternately upright and horizontal, especially in Saxon building.

LOUVRE: roof opening, often protected by a raised timber structure, to allow the smoke from a central hearth to escape. Louvres: overlapping boards to allow ventilation but keep the rain out.

LOWSIDE WINDOW: set lower than the others in a chancel side wall, usually towards its W end.

L-PLAN: see Tower house and 8b.

LUCARNE (lit. dormer): small gabled opening in a roof or spire.

LUCKENBOOTH (Scots): lock-up booth or shop.

LUGGED ARCHITRAVE: see 4b.

LUNETTE: semicircular window or blind panel.

LYCHGATE (lit. corpse-gate): roofed gateway entrance to a churchyard for the reception of a coffin.

LYNCHET: long terraced strip of soil on the downward side of prehistoric and medieval fields, accumulated because of continual ploughing along the contours.

MACHICOLATIONS (lit. mashing devices): series of openings between the corbels that support a projecting parapet through which missiles can be dropped (8a). Used decoratively in post-medieval buildings.

MAINS (Scots): home farm on an estate.

MANOMETER or STANDPIPE TOWER: containing a column of water to regulate pressure in water mains.

MANSARD: see 7.

MANSE: house of a minister of religion, especially in Scotland.

MARGINS (Scots): dressed stones at the edges of an opening. 'Back-set margins' (RCAHMS) are actually set forward from a rubble wall to act as a stop for harling (q.v.). Also called rybats.

MARRIAGE LINTEL (Scots): door or window lintel carved with the initials of the owner and his wife and the date of building work, only coincidentally of their marriage.

MATHEMATICAL TILES: facing tiles with the appearance of brick, most often applied to timber-framed walls.

MAUSOLEUM: monumental building or chamber usually intended for the burial of members of one family.

MEGALITHIC: the use of large stones, singly or together.

MEGALITHIC TOMB: massive stonebuilt Neolithic burial chamber covered by an earth or stone mound.

MERCAT (Scots): market. The *Mercat Cross* of a Scottish burgh was the focus of market activity and local ceremonial. Most examples are post-Reformation with heraldic or other finials (not crosses).

MERLON: *see* Battlement.

MESOLITHIC: Middle Stone Age, in Britain *c.* 5000 to *c.* 3500 B.C.

METOPES: spaces between the triglyphs in a Doric frieze (3b).

MEZZANINE: low storey between two higher ones or within the height of a high one, not extending over its whole area.

MILD STEEL: *see* Cast iron.

MISERICORD (*lit.* mercy): shelf on a carved bracket placed on the underside of a hinged choir stall seat to support an occupant when standing.

MIXER-COURTS: forecourts to groups of houses shared by vehicles and pedestrians.

MODILLIONS: small consoles (q.v.) along the underside of a Corinthian or Composite cornice (3d). Often used along an eaves cornice.

MODULE: a predetermined standard size for co-ordinating the dimensions of components of a building.

MORT-SAFE (Scots): device to secure corpse(s): either an iron frame over a grave or a building where bodies were kept during decomposition.

MOTTE-AND-BAILEY: CII and CI2 type of castle consisting of an earthen mound (motte) topped by a wooden tower within or adjoining a bailey, an enclosure defended by a ditch and palisade, and also, sometimes, by an inner bank.

MOUCHETTE: *see* Tracery and 2b.

MOULDING: shaped ornamental strip of continuous section; *see* Cavetto, Cyma, Ovolo, Roll.

MULLION: vertical member between window lights (2b).

MULTI-STOREY: five or more storeys. Multi-storey flats may form a *cluster block*, with individual blocks of flats grouped round a service core; a *point block*, with flats fanning out from a service core; or a *slab block*, with flats approached by corridors or galleries from service cores at intervals or towers at the ends (plan also used for offices, hotels etc.). *Tower block* is a generic term for a high multi-storey building.

MULTIVALLATE: of a hillfort: defended by three or more concentric banks and ditches.

MUNTIN: *see* Panelling and 6b.

MUTULE: square block under the corona of a Doric cornice.

NAILHEAD: E.E. ornament consisting of small pyramids regularly repeated (1a).

NARTHEX: enclosed vestibule or covered porch at the main entrance to a church.

NAVE: the body of a church w of the crossing or chancel, often flanked by aisles (q.v.).

NEOLITHIC: New Stone Age in Britain, *c.* 3500 B.C. until the Bronze Age.

NEWEL: central or corner post of a staircase (6c). For Newel stair *see* Stairs.

NIGHT STAIR: stair by which religious entered the transept of their church from their dormitory to celebrate night offices.

NOGGING: *see* Timber-framing.

NOOK-SHAFT: shaft set in the angle of a wall or opening (1a).

NORMAN: *see* Romanesque.

NOSING: projection of the tread of a step (6c). *Bottle nosing*: half round in section.

NUTMEG: medieval ornament with a chain of tiny triangles placed obliquely.

OCULUS: circular opening.

OEIL DE BOEUF: *see* Bullseye window.

OGEE: double curve, bending first one way and then the other, as in an *ogee* or *ogival arch* (5c). Cf. Cyma recta and Cyma reversa.

OPUS SECTILE: decorative mosaic-like facing.

OPUS SIGNINUM: composition flooring of Roman origin.

ORATORY: a private chapel in a church or a house. Also a church of the Oratorian Order.

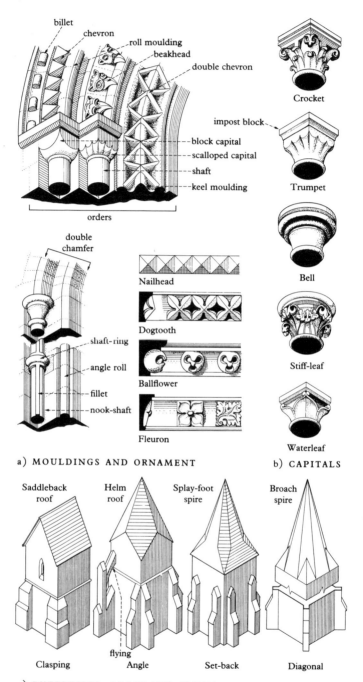

a) MOULDINGS AND ORNAMENT   b) CAPITALS

c) BUTTRESSES, ROOFS AND SPIRES

FIGURE 1: MEDIEVAL

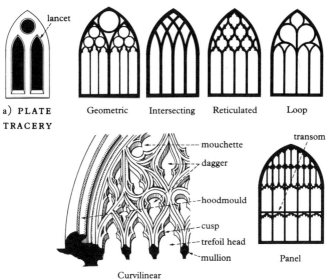

a) **PLATE TRACERY**

lancet

Geometric   Intersecting   Reticulated   Loop

mouchette

dagger

hoodmould

cusp

trefoil head

mullion

transom

Curvilinear   Panel

b) **BAR TRACERY**

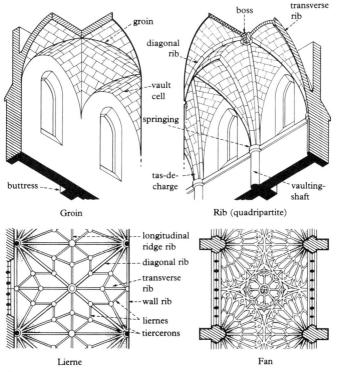

groin

diagonal rib

vault cell

springing

buttress

tas-de-charge

boss

transverse rib

vaulting-shaft

Groin   Rib (quadripartite)

longitudinal ridge rib

diagonal rib

transverse rib

wall rib

liernes

tiercerons

Lierne   Fan

c) **VAULTS**

FIGURE 2: MEDIEVAL

ORDERS

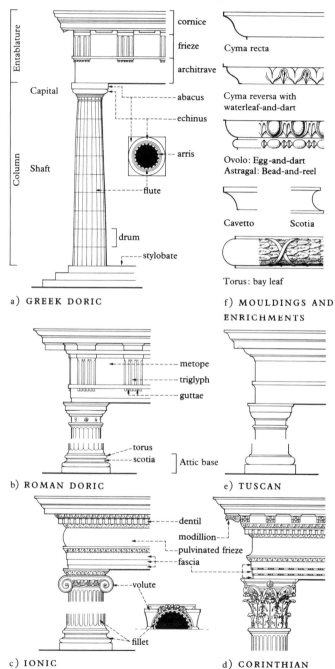

a) GREEK DORIC

cornice
frieze
architrave
abacus
echinus
arris
flute
drum
stylobate

Entablature
Capital
Column
Shaft

Cyma recta

Cyma reversa with
waterleaf-and-dart

Ovolo: Egg-and-dart
Astragal: Bead-and-reel

Cavetto   Scotia

Torus: bay leaf

f) MOULDINGS AND
ENRICHMENTS

b) ROMAN DORIC

metope
triglyph
guttae
torus
scotia
Attic base

e) TUSCAN

c) IONIC

dentil
modillion
pulvinated frieze
fascia
volute
fillet

d) CORINTHIAN

FIGURE 3: CLASSICAL

a) PORTICO

Anthemion & Palmette

Guilloche

Key pattern

Rinceau

Husk garland

Vitruvian scroll

Console

Diocletian window

Acanthus

Broken pediment

Segmental pediment

Venetian window

Lugged architrave

Shouldered architrave

Open pediment

Swan-neck pediment

Gibbs surround

b) ORNAMENTS AND FEATURES

FIGURE 4: CLASSICAL

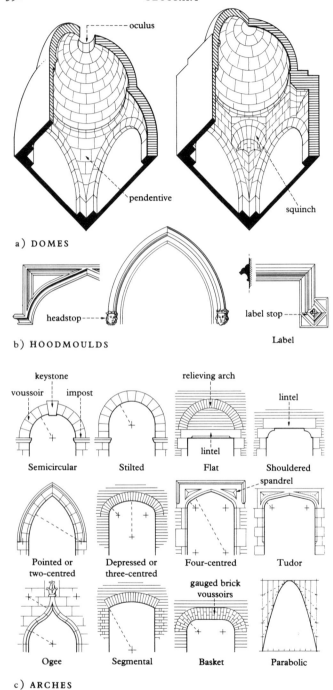

a) DOMES

b) HOODMOULDS

Label

c) ARCHES

FIGURE 5: CONSTRUCTION

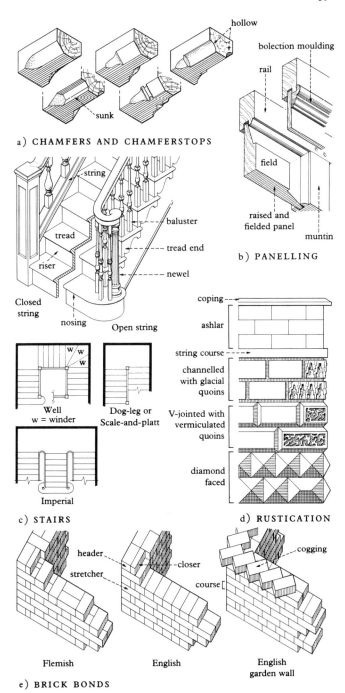

a) CHAMFERS AND CHAMFERSTOPS

hollow

bolection moulding

rail

field

raised and
fielded panel

muntin

b) PANELLING

string

baluster

tread

tread end

riser

newel

Closed
string

nosing

Open string

w w
w

Well
w = winder

Dog-leg or
Scale-and-platt

Imperial

c) STAIRS

coping

ashlar

string course

channelled
with glacial
quoins

V-jointed with
vermiculated
quoins

diamond
faced

d) RUSTICATION

header

closer

stretcher

course

cogging

Flemish

English

English
garden wall

e) BRICK BONDS

FIGURE 6: CONSTRUCTION

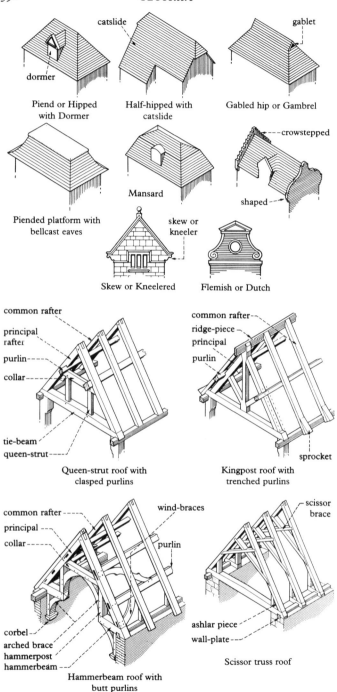

Piend or Hipped with Dormer — catslide, dormer

Half-hipped with catslide — catslide

Gabled hip or Gambrel — gablet

Piended platform with bellcast eaves

Mansard

crowstepped — shaped

Skew or Kneelered — skew or kneeler

Flemish or Dutch

Queen-strut roof with clasped purlins — common rafter, principal rafter, purlin, collar, tie-beam, queen-strut

Kingpost roof with trenched purlins — common rafter, ridge-piece, principal, purlin, sprocket

Hammerbeam roof with butt purlins — common rafter, principal, collar, wind-braces, purlin, corbel, arched brace, hammerpost, hammerbeam

Scissor truss roof — scissor brace, ashlar piece, wall-plate

FIGURE 7: ROOFS AND GABLES

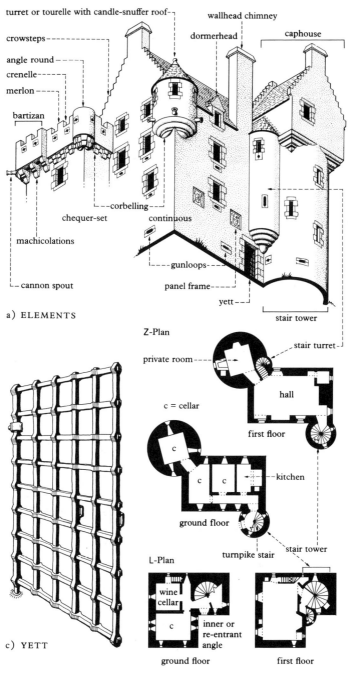

turret or tourelle with candle-snuffer roof
crowsteps
angle round
crenelle
merlon
bartizan
machicolations
cannon spout
chequer-set
corbelling
continuous
gunloops
panel frame
yett

wallhead chimney
dormerhead
caphouse
stair tower

a) ELEMENTS

Z-Plan
stair turret
private room
hall
first floor

c = cellar
c
c
c
kitchen
ground floor
turnpike stair
stair tower

c) YETT

L-Plan
wine cellar
c
inner or re-entrant angle
ground floor
first floor

b) FORMS

FIGURE 8: THE TOWER HOUSE

ORDER: one of a series of recessed arches and jambs forming a splayed medieval opening, e.g. a doorway or arcade arch (1a).

ORDERS: the formalized versions of the post-and-lintel system in classical architecture. The main orders are *Doric, Ionic* and *Corinthian*. They are Greek in origin but occur in Roman versions. *Tuscan* is a simple version of Roman Doric. Though each order has its own conventions (3), there are many minor variations. The *Composite* capital combines Ionic volutes with Corinthian foliage. *Superimposed orders*: orders on successive levels, usually in the upward sequence of Tuscan, Doric, Ionic, Corinthian, Composite.

ORIEL: *see* Bay-window.

OVERARCH: framing a wall which has an opening, e.g. a window or door.

OVERDOOR: painting or relief above an internal door. Also called a *sopraporta*.

OVERTHROW: decorative fixed arch between two gatepiers or above a wrought-iron gate.

OVOLO: wide convex moulding (3f).

PALIMPSEST: of a brass: where a metal plate has been reused by engraving on the back; of a wall painting: where one overlaps and partly obscures an earlier one.

PALLADIAN: following the examples and principles of Andrea Palladio (1508–80).

PALMETTE: classical ornament like a palm shoot (4b).

PANEL FRAME: moulded stone frame round an armorial panel, often placed over the entrance to a tower house (8a).

PANELLING: wooden lining to interior walls, made up of vertical members (*muntins*) and horizontals (*rails*) framing panels: also called *wainscot*. *Raised-and-fielded*: with the central area of the panel (*field*) raised up (6b).

PANTILE: roof tile of S section.

PARAPET: wall for protection at any sudden drop, e.g. at the wallhead of a castle where it protects the *parapet walk* or wall-walk. Also used to conceal a roof.

PARCLOSE: *see* Screen.

PARGETING (*lit.* plastering): ex-terior plaster decoration, either in relief or incised.

PARLOUR: in a religious house, a room where the religious could talk to visitors; in a medieval house, the semi-private living room below the solar (q.v.).

PARTERRE: level space in a garden laid out with low, formal beds.

PATERA (*lit.* plate): round or oval ornament in shallow relief.

PAVILION: ornamental building for occasional use; or projecting sub-division of a larger building, often at an angle or terminating a wing.

PEBBLEDASHING: *see* Rendering.

PEDESTAL: a tall block carrying a classical order, statue, vase etc.

PEDIMENT: a formalized gable derived from that of a classical temple; also used over doors, windows etc. For variations *see* 4b.

PEEL (*lit.* palisade): stone tower, e.g. near the Scottish-English border.

PEND (Scots): open-ended ground-level passage through a building.

PENDENTIVE: spandrel between adjacent arches, supporting a drum, dome or vault and consequently formed as part of a hemi-sphere (5a).

PENTHOUSE: subsidiary structure with a lean-to roof. Also a separately roofed structure on top of a C20 multi-storey block.

PEPPERPOT TURRET: bartizan with conical or pyramidal roof.

PERIPTERAL: *see* Peristyle.

PERISTYLE: a colonnade all round the exterior of a classical building, as in a temple which is then said to be *peripteral*.

PERP (PERPENDICULAR): English Gothic architecture *c.* 1335–50 to *c.* 1530. The name is derived from the upright tracery panels then used (*see* Tracery and 2a).

PERRON: external stair to a doorway, usually of double-curved plan.

PEW: loosely, seating for the laity outside the chancel; strictly, an enclosed seat. *Box pew*: with equal high sides and a door.

PIANO NOBILE: principal floor of a classical building above a ground floor or basement and with a lesser storey overhead.

PIAZZA: formal urban open space surrounded by buildings.

PIEND and PIENDED PLATFORM ROOF: *see* 7.

PIER: large masonry or brick support, often for an arch. *See also* Compound pier.

PILASTER: flat representation of a classical column in shallow relief. *Pilastrade*: series of pilasters, equivalent to a colonnade.

PILE: row of rooms. *Double pile*: two rows thick.

PILLAR: freestanding upright member of any section, not conforming to one of the orders (q.v.).

PILLAR PISCINA: *see* Piscina.

PILOTIS: C20 French term for pillars or stilts that support a building above an open ground floor.

PINS or PINNINGS (Scots): *see* Cherry-caulking.

PISCINA: basin for washing Mass vessels, provided with a drain; set in or against wall to S of an altar or freestanding (*pillar piscina*).

PITCHED MASONRY: laid on the diagonal, often alternately with opposing courses (*pitched and counterpitched* or herringbone).

PIT PRISON: sunk chamber with access from above through a hatch.

PLATE RAIL: *see* Railways.

PLATEWAY: *see* Railways.

PLATT (Scots): platform, doorstep or landing. *Scale-and-platt stair*: *see* Stairs and 6c.

PLEASANCE (Scots): close or walled garden.

PLINTH: projecting courses at the foot of a wall or column, generally chamfered or moulded at the top.

PODIUM: a continuous raised platform supporting a building; or a large block of two or three storeys beneath a multi-storey block of smaller area.

POINT BLOCK: *see* Multi-storey.

POINTING: exposed mortar jointing of masonry or brickwork. Types include *flush*, *recessed* and *tuck* (with a narrow channel filled with finer, whiter mortar). *Bag-rubbed*: flush at the edges and gently recessed in the middle. *Ribbon*: joints formed with a trowel so that they stand out. *Hungry-jointed*: either with no pointing or deeply recessed to show the outline of each stone.

POPPYHEAD: carved ornament of leaves and flowers as a finial for a bench end or stall.

PORTAL FRAME: C20 frame comprising two uprights rigidly connected to a beam or pair of rafters.

PORTCULLIS: gate constructed to rise and fall in vertical gooves at the entry to a castle.

PORTE COCHÈRE: porch large enough to admit wheeled vehicles.

PORTICO: a porch with the roof and frequently a pediment supported by a row of columns (4a). A portico *in antis* has columns on the same plane as the front of the building. A *prostyle* porch has columns standing free. Porticoes are described by the number of front columns, e.g. tetrastyle (four), hexastyle (six). The space within the temple is the *naos*, that within the portico the *pronaos*. *Blind portico*: the front features of a portico applied to a wall.

PORTICUS (plural: porticūs): subsidiary cell opening from the main body of a pre-Conquest church.

POST: upright support in a structure.

POSTERN: small gateway at the back of a building or to the side of a larger entrance door or gate.

POTENCE (Scots): rotating ladder for access to doocot nesting boxes.

POUND LOCK: *see* Canals.

PREDELLA: in an altarpiece, the horizontal strip below the main representation, often used for subsidiary representations.

PRESBYTERY: the part of a church lying E of the choir where the main altar is placed. Also a priest's residence.

PRESS (Scots): cupboard.

PRINCIPAL: *see* Roofs and 7.

PRONAOS: *see* Portico and 4a.

PROSTYLE: *see* Portico and 4a.

PULPIT: raised and enclosed platform for the preaching of sermons. *Three-decker*: with reading desk below and clerk's desk below that. *Two-decker*: as above, minus the clerk's desk.

PULPITUM: stone screen in a major church dividing choir from nave.

PULVINATED: *see* Frieze and 3c.

PURLIN: *see* Roofs and 7.

PUTHOLES or PUTLOG HOLES: in wall to receive putlogs, the horizontal timbers which support scaffolding boards; not always filled after construction is complete.

PUTTO (plural: putti): small naked boy.

QUARRIES: square (or diamond) panes of glass supported by lead strips (*cames*); square floor-slabs or tiles.

QUATREFOIL: *see* Foil.

QUEEN-STRUT: *see* Roofs and 7.

QUIRK: sharp groove to one side of a convex medieval moulding.

QUOINS: dressed stones at the angles of a building (6d).

RADBURN SYSTEM: pedestrian and vehicle segregation in residential developments, based on that used at Radburn, New Jersey, U.S.A., by Wright and Stein, 1928–30.

RADIATING CHAPELS: projecting radially from an ambulatory or an apse (*see* Chevet).

RAFTER: *see* Roofs and 7.

RAGGLE: groove cut in masonry, especially to receive the edge of a roof-covering.

RAIL: *see* Panelling and 6b.

RAILWAYS: *Edge rail*: on which flanged wheels can run. *Plate rail*: L-section rail for plain unflanged wheels. *Plateway*: early railway using plate rails.

RAISED AND FIELDED: *see* Panelling and 6b.

RAKE: slope or pitch.

RAMPART: defensive outer wall of stone or earth. *Rampart walk*: path along the inner face.

RATCOURSE: projecting string-course on a doocot to deter rats from climbing to the flight holes.

REBATE: rectangular section cut out of a masonry edge to receive a shutter, door, window etc.

REBUS: a heraldic pun, e.g. a fiery cock for Cockburn.

REEDING: series of convex mouldings, the reverse of fluting (q.v.). Cf. Gadrooning.

RENDERING: the covering of outside walls with a uniform surface or skin for protection from the weather. *Lime-washing*: thin layer of lime plaster. *Pebble-dashing*: where aggregate is thrown at the wet plastered wall for a textured effect. *Roughcast*: plaster mixed with a coarse aggregate such as gravel. *Stucco*: fine lime plaster worked to a smooth surface. *Cement rendering*: a cheaper substitute for stucco, usually with a grainy texture.

REPOUSSÉ: relief designs in metalwork, formed by beating it from the back.

REREDORTER (*lit.* behind the dormitory): latrines in a medieval religious house.

REREDOS: painted and/or sculptured screen behind and above an altar. Cf. Retable.

RESPOND: half-pier or half-column bonded into a wall and carrying one end of an arch. It usually terminates an arcade.

RETABLE: painted or carved panel standing on or at the back of an altar, usually attached to it.

RETROCHOIR: in a major church, the area between the high altar and E chapel.

REVEAL: the plane of a jamb, between the wall and the frame of a door or window.

RHONE (Scots): gutter along the eaves for rainwater: *see also* Conductor.

RIB-VAULT: *see* Vault and 2c.

RINCEAU: classical ornament of leafy scrolls (4b).

RISER: vertical face of a step (6c).

ROCK-FACED: masonry cleft to produce a rugged appearance.

ROCOCO: style current between *c.* 1720 and *c.* 1760, characterized by a serpentine line and playful, scrolled decoration.

ROLL MOULDING: medieval moulding of part-circular section (1a).

ROMANESQUE: style current in the C11 and C12. In England often called Norman. *See also* Saxo-Norman.

ROOD: crucifix flanked by representations of the Virgin and St John, usually over the entry into the chancel, painted on the wall, on a beam (*rood beam*) or on top of a *rood screen* or pulpitum (q.v.) which often had a walkway (*rood loft*) along the top, reached by a *rood stair* in the side wall. *Hanging rood*: cross or crucifix suspended from roof.

ROOFS: For the main external shapes (hipped, gambrel etc.) *see* 7. *Helm* and *Saddleback*: *see* 1C. *Lean-to*: single sloping roof built against a vertical wall; also applied to the part of the building beneath. *Bellcast*: sloping roof slightly swept out over the eaves.
Construction. *See* 7.
Single-framed roof: with no main trusses. The rafters may be fixed to the wall-plate or ridge, or longitudinal timbers may be absent altogether.

Double-framed roof: with longitudinal members, such as purlins, and usually divided into bays by principals and principal rafters. Other types are named after their main structural components, e.g. *hammerbeam*, *crown-post* (*see* Elements below and 7).

Elements. *See* 7.

Ashlar piece: a short vertical timber connecting an inner wall-plate or timber pad to a rafter.

Braces: subsidiary timbers set diagonally to strengthen the frame. *Arched braces*: curved pair forming an arch, connecting wall or post below with a tie- or collarbeam above. *Passing braces*: long straight braces passing across other members of the truss. *Scissor braces*: pair crossing diagonally between pairs of rafters or principals. *Wind-braces*: short, usually curved braces connecting side purlins with principals; sometimes decorated with cusping.

Collar or *collar-beam*: horizontal transverse timber connecting a pair of rafter or cruck blades (q.v.), set between apex and the wall-plate.

Crown-post: a vertical timber set centrally on a tie-beam and supporting a collar purlin braced to it longitudinally. In an open truss lateral braces may rise to the collar-beam; in a closed truss they may descend to the tie-beam.

Hammerbeams: horizontal brackets projecting at wall-plate level like an interrupted tie-beam; the inner ends carry *hammerposts*, vertical timbers which support a purlin and are braced to a collarbeam above.

Kingpost: vertical timber set centrally on a tie-or collar-beam, rising to the apex of the roof to support a ridge piece (cf. Strut).

Plate: longitudinal timber set square to the ground. *Wall-plate*: along the top of a wall to receive the ends of rafters; cf. Purlin.

Principals: pair of inclined lateral timbers of a truss. Usually they support side purlins and mark the main bay divisions.

Purlin: horizontal longitudinal timber. *Collar purlin* or *crown plate*: central timber which carries collar-beams and is supported by crown-posts. *Side purlins*: pairs of timbers placed some way up the slope of the roof, which carry common rafters. *Butt* or *tenoned purlins* are tenoned into either side of the principals. *Through purlins* pass through or past the principal; they include *clasped purlins*, which rest on queenposts or are carried in the angle between principals and collar, and *trenched purlins* trenched into the backs of principals.

Queen-strut: paired vertical, or near-vertical, timbers placed symmetrically on a tie-beam to support side purlins.

Rafters: inclined lateral timbers supporting the roof covering. *Common rafters*: regularly spaced uniform rafters placed along the length of a roof or between principals. *Principal rafters*: rafters which also act as principals.

Ridge, ridge piece: horizontal longitudinal timber at the apex supporting the ends of the rafters.

Sprocket: short timber placed on the back and at the foot of a rafter to form projecting eaves.

Strut: vertical or oblique timber between two members of a truss, not directly supporting longitudinal timbers.

Tie-beam: main horizontal transverse timber which carries the feet of the principals at wall level.

Truss: rigid framework of timbers at bay intervals, carrying the longitudinal roof timbers which support the common rafters. *Closed truss*: with the spaces between the timbers filled, to form an internal partition.

See also Cruck, Wagon roof.

ROPE MOULDING: *see* Cable moulding.

ROSE WINDOW: circular window with tracery radiating from the centre. Cf. Wheel window.

ROTUNDA: building or room circular in plan.

ROUGHCAST: *see* Rendering.

ROUND (Scots): bartizan, usually roofless.

ROVING BRIDGE: *see* Canals.

RUBBED BRICKWORK: *see* Gauged brickwork.

RUBBLE: masonry whose stones are wholly or partly in a rough state. *Coursed*: coursed stones with rough faces. *Random*: uncoursed stones in a random pattern.

Snecked: with courses broken by smaller stones (snecks).

RUSTICATION: *see* 6d. Exaggerated treatment of masonry to give an effect of strength. The joints are usually recessed by V-section chamfering or square-section channelling (*channelled rustication*). *Banded rustication* has only the horizontal joints emphasized. The faces may be flat, but can be *diamond-faced*, like shallow pyramids, *vermiculated*, with a stylized texture like worm-casts, and *glacial* (frost-work), like icicles or stalactites.

RYBATS (Scots): *see* Margins.

SACRAMENT HOUSE: safe cupboard in a side wall of the chancel of a church and not directly associated with an altar, for reservation of the sacrament.

SACRISTY: room in a church for sacred vessels and vestments.

SADDLEBACK ROOF: *see* 1c.

SALTIRE CROSS: with diagonal limbs.

SANCTUARY: part of church at E end containing high altar. Cf. Presbytery.

SANGHA: residence of Buddhist monks or nuns.

SARCOPHAGUS: coffin of stone or other durable material.

SARKING (Scots): boards laid on the rafters to support the roof covering.

SAXO-NORMAN: transitional Romanesque style combining Anglo-Saxon and Norman features, current *c.* 1060–1100.

SCAGLIOLA: composition imitating marble.

SCALE-AND-PLATT (*lit.* stair and landing): *see* Stair and 6c.

SCALLOPED CAPITAL: *see* 1a.

SCARCEMENT: extra thickness of the lower part of a wall, e.g. to carry a floor.

SCARP: artificial cutting away of the ground to form a steep slope.

SCOTIA: a hollow classical moulding, especially between tori (q.v.) on a column base (3b, 3f).

SCREEN: in a medieval church, usually at the entry to the chancel; *see* Rood (screen) and Pulpitum. A *parclose screen* separates a chapel from the rest of the church.

SCREENS or SCREENS PASSAGE:

screened-off entrance passage between great hall and service rooms or between the hall of a tower house and the stair.

SCUNTION (Scots): reveal.

SECTION: two-dimensional representation of a building, moulding etc., revealed by cutting across it.

SEDILIA (singular: sedile): seats for clergy (usually for a priest, deacon and sub-deacon) on the S side of the chancel.

SEPTUM: dwarf wall between the nave and choir.

SESSION HOUSE (Scots): a room or separate building for meetings of the minister and elders who form a kirk session. Also a shelter by the church or churchyard entrance for an elder collecting for poor relief, built at expense of kirk session.

SET-OFF: *see* Weathering.

SGRAFFITO: decoration scratched, often in plaster, to reveal a pattern in another colour beneath. *Graffiti*: scratched drawing or writing.

SHAFT: vertical member of round or polygonal section (1a, 3a). *Shaftring*: at the junction of shafts set *en délit* (q.v.) or attached to a pier or wall (1a).

SHEILA-NA-GIG: female fertility figure, usually with legs apart.

SHELL: thin, self-supporting roofing membrane of timber or concrete.

SHOULDERED ARCH: *see* 5a.

SHOULDERED ARCHITRAVE: *see* 4b.

SHUTTERING: *see* Concrete.

SILL: horizontal member at the bottom of a window-or doorframe; or at the base of a timber-framed wall into which posts and studs are tenoned.

SKEW (Scots): sloping or shaped stones finishing a gable upstanding from the roof. *Skewputt*: bracket at the bottom end of a skew. *See* 7.

SLAB BLOCK: *see* Multi-storey.

SLATE-HANGING: covering of overlapping slates on a wall. *Tilehanging* is similar.

SLYPE: covered way or passage leading E from the cloisters between transept and chapter house.

SNECKED: *see* Rubble.

SOFFIT (*lit.* ceiling): underside of an arch (also called *intrados*), lintel etc. *Soffit roll*: medieval roll moulding on a soffit.

SOLAR: private upper chamber in a medieval house, accessible from the high end of the great hall.

SOPRAPORTA: *see* Overdoor.

SOUNDING-BOARD: *see* Tester.

SOUTERRAIN: underground stone-lined passage and chamber.

SPANDRELS: roughly triangular spaces between an arch and its containing rectangle, or between adjacent arches (5c). Also non-structural panels under the windows in a curtain-walled building.

SPERE: a fixed structure screening the lower end of the great hall from the screens passage. *Spere-truss*: roof truss incorporated in the spere.

SPIRE: tall pyramidal or conical feature crowning a tower or turret. *Broach*: starting from a square base, then carried into an octagonal section by means of triangular faces; *splayed-foot*: a variation of the broach form, found principally in the south-east of England, in which the four cardinal faces are splayed out near their base, to cover the corners, while oblique (or intermediate) faces taper away to a point (1c). *Needle spire*: thin spire rising from the centre of a tower roof, well inside the parapet: when of timber and lead often called a *spike*.

SPIRELET: *see* Flèche.

SPLAY: of an opening when it is wider on one face of a wall than the other.

SPRING OR SPRINGING: level at which an arch or vault rises from its supports. *Springers*: the first stones of an arch or vaulting-rib above the spring (2c).

SQUINCH: arch or series of arches thrown across an interior angle of a square or rectangular structure to support a circular or polygonal superstructure, especially a dome or spire (5a).

SQUINT: an aperture in a wall or through a pier, usually to allow a view of an altar.

STAIRS: *see* 6c. *Dog-leg stair* or (Scots) *Scale-and-platt stair*: parallel flights rising alternately in opposite directions, without an open well. *Flying stair*: cantilevered from the walls of a stairwell, without newels; sometimes called a *geometric* stair when

the inner edge describes a curve. *Turnpike* or *newel stair*: ascending round a central supporting newel (8b); also called a *spiral stair* or *vice* when in a circular shaft, a *winder* when in a rectangular compartment. (Winder also applies to the steps on the turn.) *Well stair*: with flights round a square open well framed by newel posts. *See also* Perron.

STAIR TOWER: full-height projection from a main block (especially of a tower house) containing the principal stair from the ground floor (8a).

STAIR TURRET: turret corbelled out from above ground level and containing a stair from one of the upper floors of a building, especially a tower house (8a).

STALL: fixed seat in the choir or chancel for the clergy or choir (cf. Pew). Usually with arm rests, and often framed together.

STANCHION: upright structural member, of iron, steel or reinforced concrete.

STANDPIPE TOWER: *see* Manometer.

STEADING (Scots): farm building or buildings; generally used for the principal group of buildings on a farm.

STEAM ENGINES: *Atmospheric*: worked by the vacuum created when low-pressure steam is condensed in the cylinder, as developed by Thomas Newcomen. *Beam engine*: with a large pivoted beam moved in an oscillating fashion by the piston. It may drive a flywheel or be *non-rotative*. *Watt* and *Cornish*: single-cylinder; *compound*: two cylinders; *triple expansion*: three cylinders.

STEEPLE: tower together with a spire, lantern or belfry.

STIFFLEAF: type of E.E. foliage decoration. *Stiffleaf capital*: *see* 1b.

STOP: plain or decorated terminal to mouldings or chamfers, or at the end of hoodmoulds and labels (*label stop*), or stringcourses (5b, 6a); *see also* Headstop.

STOUP: vessel for holy water, usually near a door.

STRAINER: *see* Arch.

STRAPWORK: decoration like interlaced leather straps, late C16 and C17 in origin.

STRETCHER: *see* Bond and 6e.

STRING: *see* 6c. Sloping member holding the ends of the treads and risers of a staircase. *Closed string*: a broad string covering the ends of the treads and risers. *Open string*: cut into the shape of the treads and risers.

STRINGCOURSE: horizontal course or moulding projecting from the surface of a wall (6d).

STUCCO: decorative plasterwork. *See also* Rendering.

STUDS: subsidiary vertical timbers of a timber-framed wall or partition.

STUGGED (Scots): of masonry hacked or picked as a key for rendering; used as a surface finish in the C19.

STUPA: Buddhist shrine, circular in plan.

STYLOBATE: top of the solid platform on which a colonnade stands (3a).

SUSPENSION BRIDGE: *see* Bridge.

SWAG: like a festoon (q.v.), but representing cloth.

SYSTEM BUILDING: *see* Industrialized building.

TABERNACLE: safe cupboard above an altar to contain the reserved sacrament or a relic; or architectural frame for an image or statue.

TABLE STONE or TABLE TOMB: memorial slab raised on freestanding legs.

TAS-DE-CHARGE: the lower courses of a vault or arch which are laid horizontally (2c).

TENEMENT: holding of land, but also applied to a purpose-built flatted block.

TERM: pedestal or pilaster tapering downward, usually with the upper part of a human figure growing out of it.

TERRACOTTA: moulded and fired clay ornament or cladding.

TERREPLEIN: in a fort the level surface of a rampart behind a parapet for mounting guns.

TESSELLATED PAVEMENT: mosaic flooring, particularly Roman, made of *tesserae*, i.e. cubes of glass, stone or brick.

TESTER: flat canopy over a tomb or pulpit, where it is also called a *sounding-board*.

TESTER TOMB: tomb-chest with effigies beneath a tester, either freestanding (tester with four or more columns), or attached to a wall (*half-tester*) with columns on one side only.

TETRASTYLE: *see* Portico.

THERMAL WINDOW: *see* Diocletian window.

THREE-DECKER PULPIT: *see* Pulpit.

TIDAL GATES: *see* Canals.

TIE-BEAM: *see* Roofs and 7.

TIERCERON: *see* Vault and 2c.

TILE-HANGING: *see* Slate-hanging.

TIMBER-FRAMING: method of construction where the structural frame is built of interlocking timbers. The spaces are filled with non-structural material, e.g. *infill* of wattle and daub, lath and plaster, brickwork (known as *nogging*) etc., and may be covered by plaster, weatherboarding (q.v.) or tiles.

TOLBOOTH (Scots; *lit.* tax booth): burgh council building containing council chamber and prison.

TOMB-CHEST: chest-shaped tomb, usually of stone. Cf. Table tomb, Tester tomb.

TORUS (plural: tori): large convex moulding, usually used on a column base (3b, 3f).

TOUCH: soft black marble quarried near Tournai.

TOURELLE: turret corbelled out from the wall (8a).

TOWER BLOCK: *see* Multi-storey.

TOWER HOUSE (Scots): for elements and forms *see* 8a, 8b. Compact fortified house with the main hall raised above the ground and at least one more storey above it. A medieval Scots type continuing well into the C17 in its modified forms: *L-plan* with a jamb at one corner; *Z-plan* with a jamb at each diagonally opposite corner.

TRABEATED: dependent structurally on the use of the post and lintel. Cf. Arcuated.

TRACERY: openwork pattern of masonry or timber in the upper part of an opening. *Blind tracery* is tracery applied to a solid wall.
Plate tracery, introduced *c.* 1200, is the earliest form, in which shapes are cut through solid masonry (2a).

Bar tracery was introduced into England *c.* 1250. The pattern is formed by intersecting moulded ribwork continued from the mullions. It was especially elaborate during the Decorated period (q.v.). Tracery shapes can include circles, *daggers* (elongated ogee-ended lozenges), *mouchettes* (like daggers but with curved sides) and upright rectangular *panels*. They often have *cusps*, projecting points defining lobes or *foils* (q.v.) within the main shape: *Kentish* or *split-cusps* are forked.

Types of bar tracery (*see* 2b) include *geometric(al)*: *c.* 1250–1310, chiefly circles, often foiled; *Y-tracery*: *c.* 1300, with mullions branching into a Y-shape; *intersecting*: *c.* 1300, formed by interlocking mullions; *reticulated*: early C14, net-like pattern of ogee-ended lozenges; *curvilinear*: C14, with uninterrupted flowing curves; *loop*: *c.* 1500–45, with large uncusped loop-like forms; *panel*: Perp, with straight-sided panels, often cusped at the top and bottom.

TRANSE (Scots): passage.

TRANSEPT: transverse portion of a cruciform church.

TRANSITIONAL: generally used for the phase between Romanesque and Early English (*c.* 1175–*c.* 1200).

TRANSOM: horizontal member separating window lights (2b).

TREAD: horizontal part of a step. The *tread end* may be carved on a staircase (6c).

TREFOIL: *see* Foil.

TRIFORIUM: middle storey of a church treated as an arcaded wall passage or blind arcade, its height corresponding to that of the aisle roof.

TRIGLYPHS (*lit.* three-grooved tablets): stylized beam-ends in the Doric frieze, with metopes between (3b).

TRIUMPHAL ARCH: influential type of Imperial Roman monument.

TROPHY: sculptured or painted group of arms or armour.

TRUMEAU: central stone mullion supporting the tympanum of a wide doorway. *Trumeau figure*: carved figure attached to it (cf. Column figure).

TRUMPET CAPITAL: *see* 1b.

TRUSS: braced framework, spanning between supports. *See also* Roofs.

TUMBLING or TUMBLING-IN: courses of brickwork laid at right angles to a slope, e.g. of a gable, forming triangles by tapering into horizontal courses.

TURNPIKE: *see* Stairs.

TUSCAN: *see* Orders and 3e.

TWO-DECKER PULPIT: *see* Pulpit.

TYMPANUM: the surface between a lintel and the arch above it or within a pediment (4a).

UNDERCROFT: usually describes the vaulted room(s) beneath the main room(s) of a medieval house. Cf. Crypt.

UNIVALLATE: of a hillfort: defended by a single bank and ditch.

VAULT: arched stone roof (sometimes imitated in timber or plaster). For types *see* 2c.
Tunnel or *barrel vault*: continuous semicircular or pointed arch, often of rubble masonry.
Groin vault: tunnel vaults intersecting at right angles. *Groins* are the curved lines of the intersections.
Rib vault: masonry framework of intersecting arches (ribs) supporting *vault cells*, used in Gothic architecture. *Wall rib* or *wall arch*: between wall and vault cell. *Transverse rib*: spans between two walls to divide a vault into bays. *Quadripartite* rib vault: each bay has two pairs of diagonal ribs dividing the vault into four triangular cells. *Sexpartite* rib vault: most often used over paired bays, has an extra pair of ribs springing from between the bays. More elaborate vaults may include *ridge-ribs* along the crown of a vault or bisecting the bays; *tiercerons*: extra decorative ribs springing from the corners of a bay; and *liernes*: short decorative ribs in the crown of a vault, not linked to any springing point. A *stellar* or *star* vault has liernes in star formation.
Fan vault: form of barrel vault used in the Perp period, made up of halved concave masonry cones decorated with blind tracery.

VAULTING-SHAFT: shaft leading

up to the spring or springing (q.v.) of a vault (2c).

VENETIAN or SERLIAN WINDOW: derived from Serlio (4b). The motif is used for other openings.

VERMICULATION: *see* Rustication and 6d.

VESICA: oval with pointed ends.

VICE: *see* Stair.

VILLA: originally a Roman country house or farm. The term was revived in England in the C18 under the influence of Palladio and used especially for smaller, compact country houses. In the later C19 it was debased to describe any suburban house.

VITRIFIED: bricks or tiles fired to a darkened glassy surface. *Vitrified fort*: built of timber-laced masonry, the timber having later been set on fire with consequent vitrification of the stonework.

VITRUVIAN SCROLL: classical running ornament of curly waves (4b).

VOLUTES: spiral scrolls. They occur on Ionic capitals (3c). *Angle volute*: pair of volutes, turned outwards to meet at the corner of a capital.

VOUSSOIRS: wedge-shaped stones forming an arch (5c).

WAGON ROOF: with the appearance of the inside of a wagon tilt; often ceiled. Also called *cradle roof*.

WAINSCOT: *see* Panelling.

WALLED GARDEN: in C18 and C19 Scotland, combined vegetable and flower garden, sometimes well away from the house.

WALLHEAD: straight top of a wall. *Wallhead chimney*: chimney rising from a wallhead (8a). *Wallhead gable*: gable rising from a wallhead.

WALL MONUMENT: attached to the wall and often standing on the floor. *Wall tablets* are smaller with the inscription as the major element.

WALL-PLATE: *see* Roofs and 7.

WALL-WALK: *see* Parapet.

WARMING ROOM: room in a religious house where a fire burned for comfort.

WATERHOLDING BASE: early Gothic base with upper and lower mouldings separated by a deep hollow.

WATERLEAF: *see* Enrichments and 3f.

WATERLEAF CAPITAL: Late Romanesque and Transitional type of capital (1b).

WATER WHEELS: described by the way water is fed on to the wheel. *Breastshot*: mid-height, falling and passing beneath. *Overshot*: over the top. *Pitchback*: on the top but falling backwards. *Undershot*: turned by the momentum of the water passing beneath. In a *water turbine*, water is fed under pressure through a vaned wheel within a casing.

WEALDEN HOUSE: type of medieval timber-framed house with a central open hall flanked by bays of two storeys, roofed in line; the end bays are jettied to the front, but the eaves are continuous.

WEATHERBOARDING: wall cladding of overlapping horizontal boards.

WEATHERING: or SET-OFF: inclined, projecting surface to keep water away from the wall below.

WEEPERS: figures in niches along the sides of some medieval tombs. Also called *mourners*.

WHEEL HOUSE: Late Iron Age circular stone dwelling; inside, partition walls radiating from the central hearth like wheel spokes.

WHEEL WINDOW: circular, with radiating shafts like spokes. Cf. Rose window.

WROUGHT IRON: *see* Cast iron.

WYND (Scots): subsidiary street or lane, often running into a main street or gait (q.v.).

YETT (Scots, *lit.* gate): hinged openwork gate at a main doorway, made of iron bars alternately penetrating and penetrated (8c).

Z-PLAN: *see* Tower house and 8b.

INDEX OF ARTISTS

Logan, Robert George (*c.* 1879–1961) 532, 568

Lonsdale, Horatio Walter (artist, 1844–1919) 50, 394

Lonsdale (Thomas) & Co. (marble-cutters) 524

Lorimer, Hew (sculptor, b. 1907) 432

Lorimer, Sir Robert Stodart (1864–1929) 189, 190, 245, 310, Pl. 98

Loudon, John Claudius (1783–1843) 123, 409

Lucas, Thomas Geoffrey (1872–1947) 46, 49, 331, 333

Lugar, Robert (*c.* 1773–1855) 67, 68, 323, 338

Lukup, William (mason, b. *c.* 1642) 55, 77, 183, 223, 230, 248, 299

Lyon, Walter Fitzgerald Knox (1844–94) 68, 192, 193, 395

McAlla, Thomas (gardener) 409

McBride, Charles (sculptor) 543

McCaig, William (builder, 1789–1879) 353

McCall, James (builder) 514

McCandlish, William (*c.* 1779–1855) 39–40, 43, 114, 191, 354, 384, 466, 467, 468, 507, Pls. 23–4

McClure, John (builder) 290

McConnel, John (mason) 356

McCracken, John (mason and architect) 39, 42, 125, 243, 389

McCrea, Andrew (mason) 531

McCulloch, John (*c.* 1809–80) 467

McDonald & Creswick Ltd (founders) 301

Macdonald, I. W. A. 510

MacDonald, John (mason and architect) 352

McDowall, Hugh (mason and architect) 530, 531

McEwen, William 376

Macfarlane, James Caird 46, 473

Macfarlane (Walter) & Co. Ltd (founders) 534

McGaw, Peter (builder) 107

MacGibbon & Ross (David MacGibbon, 1832–1902; Thomas Ross, 1839–1930; Alfred Lightly MacGibbon, 1874–1915) 362, 438

McGill, Alexander (d. 1734) 38

McGowan, William (*c.* 1794–1858) 39, 40, 250, 255, 258, 260, 322, 356, 380, 393, 513, 559

Macgregor, John Alexander (*c.* 1867–1919) 169, 191, 213, 475, 558, 568

Macintyre, Alastair Duncan 79, 163, 264; *see also* Dumfriesshire County Council Architect's Department

Mack, John (mason) 290

McKee, J. R. 532

Mackenzie, Ford 44, 426, 428

Mackenzie & Partners Ltd (cabinet-makers) 531

Mackenzie, R. W. (sculptor) 476

McKie, James (builder) 421

McKie, Peter (joiner and architect, *c.* 1791–1872) 202

McKinnell & Coltart (masons) 500

MacKinnell, William A. (1871–1940) 373

Maclaren, James 55, 571

MacLauchlan, Messrs (masons) 138

McLean Gibson Partnership 535

McLellan, David (mason and architect) 203

McLelland, Alexander (mason) 327

McLellane, John (carpenter) 546

McLundie, R. Douglas (glass-stainer) 165, 362; *see also* Abbey Studio

Maclure, Hugh Hough (d. 1892) 355

McMillan, Authy (builder) 567

McPhie, James (glass-stainer) 362

McQueen, I. (glass-stainer) 211

McQueen, James (builder) 567

Macqueen, W. (carver) 425

McSkimming, J. (clockmaker) 373

McTaldroch, James (joiner) 356

Maidman, Edward Charles Henry 440

Mair, Alexander 380

Marston & Son (organ builders) 180

Martin, John (builder) 103

Marwick, Thomas Purves (1854–1927) 328

Matheson, Robert (1808–77) 457

Maxwell, Frederick (joiner) 393

Maxwell, Robert (bell founder) 165

May, Edward John (1853–1941) 351

Mayer & Co. (glass-stainers) 97, 464

Meikle, Andrew (millwright, 1719–1811) 86, 282

Meikle (William) & Sons (glass-stainers) 51, 328, 371, 438, 560, 562

Mein, Andrew (builder) 153

Menart, Charles J. 47, 271, 531

Merz & McLellan 181, Pl. 127

Meteyard, H. S. (glass-stainer) 263

Miller, J. C. 242

Miller, John (1805–83) 73, 434, 513

Miller, John, Jun. 72, 330

Miller, Joseph (glass-stainer) 531

Miller, Walter 305

Milligan, John 351

Milligan, Peter (mason) 521

Milwain 81, 278

INDEX OF PLACES

Principal references are in **bold** type; demolished buildings are shown in *italic*.